YBM
실전토익
LC 1000

1

YBM 실전토익 ① LC 1000

발행인	허문호
발행처	YBM
문항 개발	Marilyn Hook
편집	윤경림, 이진열, 정유상
디자인	김현경, 이현숙
마케팅	정연철, 박천산, 고영노, 김동진, 박찬경, 김윤하
초판인쇄	2024년 12월 10일
2쇄발행	2025년 4월 1일
신고일자	1964년 3월 28일
신고번호	제1964-000003호
주소	서울시 종로구 종로 104
전화	(02) 2000-0515 [구입문의] / (02) 2000-0305 [내용문의]
팩스	(02) 2285-1523
홈페이지	www.ybmbooks.com
ISBN	978-89-17-23962-1

최신 토익 경향 완벽 반영!
100% 전면 개정!

○ **최신 토익 경향 반영**

토익 시험 최신 출제 경향 및 난이도 완벽 반영!
새로운 문제들로 구성한 최신 개정판!

○ **고품질, 고난도 문제로 실전 대비**

고품질, 고난도 문제로 엄선된 모의고사 10세트 수록!
OMR 답안지 마킹까지 실전처럼 연습!

○ **상세하고 명쾌한 해설**

모든 문제 정답 및 오답 이유 + 핵심 출제 포인트 상세히 설명!
문제 유형 표시, 패러프레이징 및 핵심 어휘 선별 정리!

○ **맞춤 학습 가이드**

테스트 맞은 개수에 따라 앞으로의 공부 방향을 제시!
현재 실력에 따라 점수를 더 빠르게 올릴 수 있는 가이드 제공!

○ **부가 학습자료 무료 제공**

YBM 1등 강사 동영상 강의 + 단어장 + 단어 암기용 MP3 모두 무료 제공!
단어장 및 MP3: www.ybmbooks.com ▶ MP3·학습자료

토익의 구성 & 수험 정보

TOEIC 소개 Test of English for International Communication(국제적 의사소통을 위한 영어 시험)의 약자로서, 영어가 모국어가 아닌 사람들을 대상으로 커뮤니케이션 능력에 중점을 두고 일상생활 또는 국제업무 등에 필요한 실용영어 능력을 평가하는 글로벌 평가 시험이다.

시험 구성

구성	Part	내용		문항수	시간	배점
듣기 (L/C)	1	사진 묘사		6문항	45분	495점
	2	질의 & 응답		25문항		
	3	짧은 대화		39문항		
	4	짧은 담화		30문항		
읽기 (R/C)	5	단문 빈칸 채우기(문법/어휘)		30문항	75분	495점
	6	장문 빈칸 채우기		16문항		
	7	독해	단일 지문	29문항		
			이중 지문	10문항		
			삼중 지문	15문항		
Total		7 Parts		200문항	120분	990점

TOEIC 접수 TOEIC 접수는 한국 토익 위원회 사이트(www.toeic.co.kr)에서 온라인 상으로만 가능하다. 사이트에서 매월 자세한 접수 일정과 시험 일정 등의 구체적 정보 확인이 가능하니, 미리 일정을 확인하여 접수하도록 한다.

TOEIC 성적 확인 성적 확인은 TOEIC 홈페이지에 안내된 성적발표일에 인터넷 홈페이지, 어플리케이션을 통해 확인이 가능하다. 최초 성적표 발급은 우편 또는 온라인을 통해 수령이 가능하며 재발급은 성적 유효기간(2년) 내에만 가능하다. 단, 공공기관에 한하여 2023년 4월부터 5년으로 유효기간이 연장되었다.

시험장 준비물

신분증	규정 신분증만 가능 (주민등록증, 운전면허증, 기간 만료 전의 여권, 공무원증 등)
필기구	연필, 지우개 (볼펜이나 사인펜은 사용 금지)

시험 진행 시간

09:20	입실 (09:50 이후는 입실 불가)
09:30 - 09:45	답안지 작성에 관한 오리엔테이션
09:45 - 09:50	휴식
09:50 - 10:05	신분증 확인
10:05 - 10:10	문제지 배부 및 파본 확인
10:10 - 10:55	듣기 평가 (Listening Test)
10:55 - 12:10	독해 평가 (Reading Test)

TOEIC 점수

TOEIC 점수는 듣기 영역(LC) 점수, 읽기 영역(RC) 점수, 그리고 이 두 영역을 합계한 전체 점수 세 부분으로 구성된다. 각 부분의 점수는 5점 단위이며, 5점에서 495점에 걸쳐 주어지고, 전체 점수는 10점에서 990점까지이며, 만점은 990점이다. TOEIC 성적은 각 문제 유형의 난이도에 따른 점수 환산표에 의해 결정된다.

토익 경향 분석 & 고득점 전략

PART 1 사진 묘사
Photographs

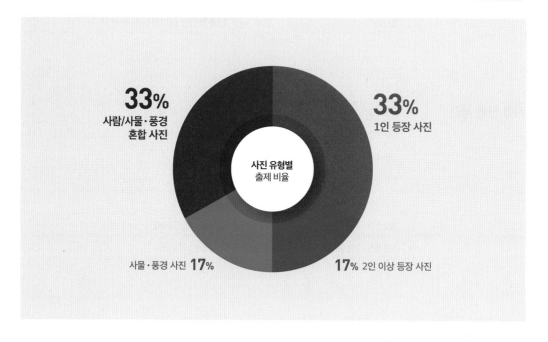

사진 유형별 출제 비율

- **33%** 사람/사물·풍경 혼합 사진
- **33%** 1인 등장 사진
- 사물·풍경 사진 **17%**
- **17%** 2인 이상 등장 사진

고득점 전략

1인 등장 사진	사람의 동작을 설명하는 수식어구가 늘어나는 추세이다. 동사 하나만으로는 섣불리 판단 금지!
2인 이상 등장 사진	사람들의 공통 동작과 개별 동작에 주의한다.
사물·풍경 사진	\<be + p.p.\>, \<have + been + p.p.\> 구문이 주로 나오며, 위치를 표현할 때는 \<There is/are\> 구문도 등장한다. 사물의 위치를 표현하는 전치사구를 유의해서 듣도록 한다.
사람/사물·풍경 혼합 사진	사람 묘사 보기와 사물·풍경 묘사 보기가 함께 제시되는 경우가 많기 때문에 주어를 듣는 순간 사진에서 해당 주어에 초점을 맞추어 묘사의 진위 여부를 재빨리 파악한다.

PART 2 질의 & 응답
Question-Response

(총 25문제)

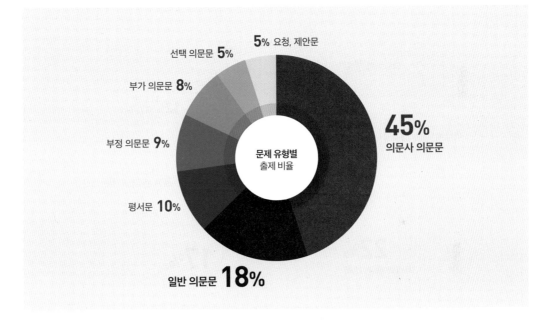

문제 유형별
출제 비율

45%
의문사 의문문

5% 요청, 제안문

선택 의문문 5%

부가 의문문 8%

부정 의문문 9%

평서문 10%

일반 의문문 18%

고득점 전략

의문사 의문문에 Yes/No/Sure/Okay로 답하면 오답이다	단, 제안문으로 쓰이는 의문사 의문문은 Yes/No/Sure/Okay로 답할 수 있다. → Why don't you[we] ~ ? / What[How] about ~ ? 　~하는 것이 어때요?
발음이 유사한 오답 보기가 가장 많이 출제된다	질문 속 단어가 선택지에 반복 사용되면 정답일 때도, 혹은 오답일 때도 있으므로 주의한다. 하지만, 유사한 발음의 어휘가 사용되면 오답일 가능성이 높다.
만능 정답 답변	→ 모르겠어요/확실하지 않아요/~가 알아요 → 확인/찾아/알아 볼게요 → (아직) 결정/논의되지 않았어요

토익 경향 분석 & 고득점 전략

PART 3 짧은 대화
Short Conversations

총 13대화문 39문제(지문당 3문제)

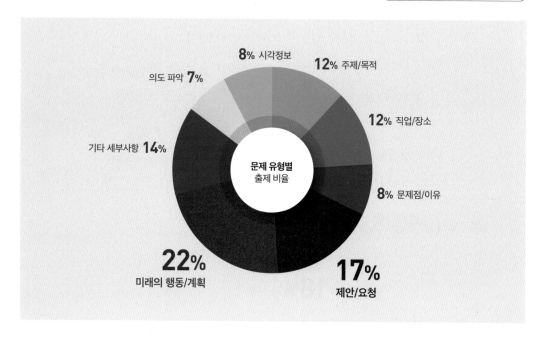

문제 유형별 출제 비율

- 8% 시각정보
- 12% 주제/목적
- 의도 파악 7%
- 12% 직업/장소
- 기타 세부사항 14%
- 8% 문제점/이유
- 22% 미래의 행동/계획
- 17% 제안/요청

고득점 전략

주제/목적

정답 단서의 80%가 첫 대사에서 제시되므로 시작 부분을 최대한 집중해서 들어야 한다.
두 번째 대사까지 들어야 정답을 알 수 있는 경우가 약 20%이며,
아주 가끔은 세 번째 대사까지 들어야 파악할 수 있다.

제안/요청

주로 대화 후반부에 정답의 단서가 등장한다. 요청 또는 제안하는 사람과
받는 사람의 성별을 정확히 구분해야 하며, 제안/요청 관련 표현도 미리 알아두면 유용하다.

문제점/이유

not/never/unfortunately 등 부정적인 뉘앙스의 표현이나 but/however 같은 반전을
나타내는 어휘가 등장하는 곳에서 문제점이 언급되므로 이 부분에 집중해서 듣는다.

미래의 행동/계획

대화가 끝난 다음 있을 일에 대해 묻는 질문이 나오면 마지막 화자나 바로 그 앞의 화자,
즉 마지막 두 사람의 대사에서 단서가 제시되는 경우가 많다.

PART 4 짧은 담화
Short Talks

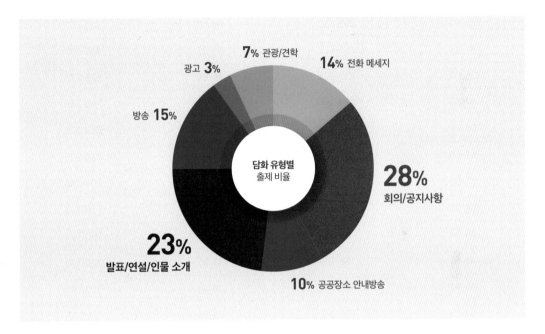

7% 관광/견학
광고 3%
14% 전화 메세지
방송 15%

담화 유형별
출제 비율

28%
회의/공지사항

23%
발표/연설/인물 소개

10% 공공장소 안내방송

고득점 전략

전화 메세지

전화 건 용건 • 목적은 대부분 지문의 초반에 거론되지만 요즘에는 점점 담화문의 중반까지 들어야 파악할 수 있는 경우도 늘어나고 있다.

회의/공지사항

회의를 소집한 이유를 언급한 후 관련 세부사항들을 설명하고 이어서 제안사항, 요청사항으로 담화가 마무리되는 큰 흐름으로 담화가 전개된다.

공공장소 안내방송

요청/조언(ask/advise/encourage) 질문에는 Please/so/remember/ need to ask 등이 정답 단서가 된다.

방송

일반 방송 담화문에서 host 등의 정답 단서를 통해 화자의 신분을 알 수 있다. 진행자가 혼자 방송을 진행할 경우 관련 세부사항들을 언급한 후, 다음 프로그램에 대한 소개로 마무리하는 흐름이 많다.

점수 환산표

LISTENING Raw Score (맞은 개수)	LISTENING Scaled Score (환산 점수)	READING Raw Score (맞은 개수)	READING Scaled Score (환산 점수)
96-100	480-495	96-100	460-495
91-95	435-490	91-95	410-475
86-90	395-450	86-90	380-430
81-85	355-415	81-85	355-400
76-80	325-375	76-80	325-375
71-75	295-340	71-75	295-345
66-70	265-315	66-70	265-315
61-65	240-285	61-65	235-285
56-60	215-260	56-60	205-255
51-55	190-235	51-55	175-225
46-50	160-210	46-50	150-195
41-45	135-180	41-45	120-170
36-40	110-155	36-40	100-140
31-35	85-130	31-35	75-120
26-30	70-105	26-30	55-100
21-25	50-90	21-25	40-80
16-20	35-70	16-20	30-65
11-15	20-55	11-15	20-50
6-10	15-40	6-10	15-35
1-5	5-20	1-5	5-20
0	5	0	5

이 환산표는 본 교재에 수록된 Test용으로 개발된 것이다. 이 표를 사용하여 자신의 실제 점수를 환산 점수로 전환하도록 한다. 즉, 예를 들어 Listening Test의 실제 정답 수가 61~65개이면 환산 점수는 240점에서 285점 사이가 된다. 여기서 실제 정답 수가 61개이면 환산 점수가 240점이고, 65개이면 환산 점수가 285점임을 의미하는 것은 아니다. 본 책의 Test를 위해 작성된 이 점수 환산표가 자신의 영어 실력이 어느 정도인지 대략적으로 파악하는 데 도움이 되긴 하지만, 이 표가 실제 TOEIC 성적 산출에 그대로 사용된 적은 없다는 사실을 밝혀 둔다.

LC 학습 기록표

테스트별로 맞은 개수를 기록하세요. 학습 성취도와 취약한 PART가 어디인지 알 수 있습니다.

	맞은 개수					환산 점수
	PART 1 (총 6문제)	PART 2 (총 25문제)	PART 3 (총 39문제)	PART 4 (총 30문제)	맞은 개수 합계	총점
TEST 1						
TEST 2						
TEST 3						
TEST 4						
TEST 5						
TEST 6						
TEST 7						
TEST 8						
TEST 9						
TEST 10						

TEST의 환산 점수를 점(•)으로 표시해서 점수 변화를 확인해보세요.

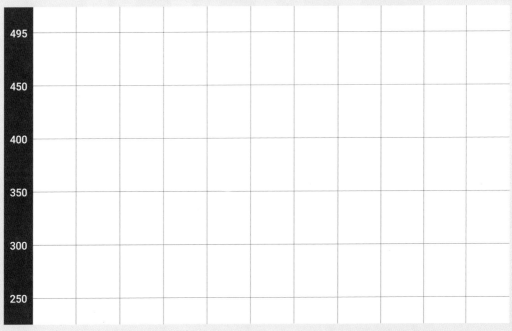

점수대별 학습 가이드

토익 초급 LEVEL
맞은 개수 50개 미만

성적 진단 실전 문제를 풀이하기엔 기본기가 부족합니다. 입문서를 통해 필수단어와 빈출표현을 암기하면서 기초를 다지는 것이 좋습니다.

학습 POINT 어휘 / 빈출표현 / part별 문제 유형 학습

연계 교재

토익 중급 LEVEL
맞은 개수 50~70개

성적 진단 기본기는 갖췄지만 기복이 큰 점수대입니다. 전략서를 병행하면서 자주 틀리는 유형에 대한 풀이 전략을 익혀 보세요. 자주 등장하는 오답의 유형도 함께 기억해두면 정답을 찾을 때 고민하는 시간을 크게 줄일 수 있습니다.

학습 POINT 풀이 전략 학습 / 오답 유형 확인 / 다양한 문제 풀이

연계 교재

토익 고급 LEVEL
맞은 개수 70개 이상

성적 진단 중간 휴식 없이 실제 시험처럼 풀이하면서 집중력을 유지하는 훈련을 하는 것이 좋습니다. 틀린 문제 위주로 검토하면서 약점을 보완해 나간다면 고득점은 문제없을 겁니다.

학습 POINT 연습은 실전처럼 / 집중력 유지 / 오답 피드백

연계 교재

CONTENTS

YBM
실전토익
LC 1000

테스트 전 체크리스트

- 중간 휴식 없이 제한 시간을 지켜서 풀이하세요.
- 제한 시간은 답안지에 마킹하는 시간도 포함시켜야 합니다.
- 찍은 문제는 번호 옆에 꼭 체크해 주세요.
- 시간 안에 풀지 못한 문제는 틀린 것으로 채점해 주세요.

LC

TEST 1

LISTENING TEST

In the Listening test, you will be asked to demonstrate how well you understand spoken English. The entire Listening test will last approximately 45 minutes. There are four parts, and directions are given for each part. You must mark your answers on the separate answer sheet. Do not write your answers in your test book.

PART 1

Directions: For each question in this part, you will hear four statements about a picture in your test book. When you hear the statements, you must select the one statement that best describes what you see in the picture. Then find the number of the question on your answer sheet and mark your answer. The statements will not be printed in your test book and will be spoken only one time.

Statement (C), "They're sitting at a table," is the best description of the picture, so you should select answer (C) and mark it on your answer sheet.

1.

2.

GO ON TO THE NEXT PAGE

3.

4.

5.

6.

GO ON TO THE NEXT PAGE ➤

PART 2

Directions: You will hear a question or statement and three responses spoken in English. They will not be printed in your test book and will be spoken only one time. Select the best response to the question or statement and mark the letter (A), (B), or (C) on your answer sheet.

7. Mark your answer on your answer sheet.

8. Mark your answer on your answer sheet.

9. Mark your answer on your answer sheet.

10. Mark your answer on your answer sheet.

11. Mark your answer on your answer sheet.

12. Mark your answer on your answer sheet.

13. Mark your answer on your answer sheet.

14. Mark your answer on your answer sheet.

15. Mark your answer on your answer sheet.

16. Mark your answer on your answer sheet.

17. Mark your answer on your answer sheet.

18. Mark your answer on your answer sheet.

19. Mark your answer on your answer sheet.

20. Mark your answer on your answer sheet.

21. Mark your answer on your answer sheet.

22. Mark your answer on your answer sheet.

23. Mark your answer on your answer sheet.

24. Mark your answer on your answer sheet.

25. Mark your answer on your answer sheet.

26. Mark your answer on your answer sheet.

27. Mark your answer on your answer sheet.

28. Mark your answer on your answer sheet.

29. Mark your answer on your answer sheet.

30. Mark your answer on your answer sheet.

31. Mark your answer on your answer sheet.

PART 3

Directions: You will hear some conversations between two or more people. You will be asked to answer three questions about what the speakers say in each conversation. Select the best response to each question and mark the letter (A), (B), (C), or (D) on your answer sheet. The conversations will not be printed in your test book and will be spoken only one time.

32. Why did the woman go to Rodney's office?
    (A) To repair a computer
    (B) To drop off a package
    (C) To negotiate a deadline
    (D) To present some data

33. Why is Rodney unavailable?
    (A) He is out for lunch.
    (B) He is seeing a doctor.
    (C) He is at a trade show.
    (D) He is leading a facility tour.

34. What will the woman most likely do tomorrow?
    (A) Hold some job interviews
    (B) Work from a different location
    (C) Install some electronics
    (D) Finalize a sales report

35. Why is the man calling?
    (A) To confirm a requirement
    (B) To exchange some tickets
    (C) To purchase a membership
    (D) To inquire about volunteering

36. What does the woman explain to the man?
    (A) A performance is sold out.
    (B) A computer service is down.
    (C) A neighborhood is usually busy.
    (D) A policy does not apply to everyone.

37. What does the man decide to do?
    (A) Pay some additional fees
    (B) Arrive early at a location
    (C) Have his name put on a list
    (D) Gather opinions from others

38. What is the man trying to do?
    (A) Buy a guidebook
    (B) Store some luggage
    (C) Have his picture taken
    (D) Pick up an application

39. What did the man forget to bring?
    (A) A travel itinerary
    (B) A carrier bag
    (C) Some clothing
    (D) Some size information

40. What does the woman offer to do?
    (A) Search the Internet
    (B) Wait for the man to return
    (C) Consult with a manager
    (D) Lend an item

41. What is the conversation about?
    (A) An advertising campaign
    (B) A product design
    (C) A hiring committee
    (D) A business relocation

42. What does the woman imply when she says, "that was the president's decision"?
    (A) It is not possible to change a plan.
    (B) Some contract terms are acceptable.
    (C) An executive has returned from a trip.
    (D) An announcement gave incorrect information.

43. What does the man say he will do?
    (A) Visit a building site
    (B) Save some paperwork
    (C) Provide a price estimate
    (D) Speak with some employees

GO ON TO THE NEXT PAGE

44. Where do the speakers most likely work?

(A) At a supermarket
(B) At a restaurant
(C) At a vegetable farm
(D) At a catering company

45. According to the men, what is causing a problem?

(A) An appliance is not working.
(B) An event was canceled.
(C) Some food has gone bad.
(D) A shipment has not arrived.

46. What does the woman suggest doing?

(A) Revising a menu
(B) Driving to a store
(C) Putting up a sign
(D) Postponing a task

47. Where does the conversation most likely take place?

(A) At an outdoor market
(B) At an auto repair shop
(C) At a subway station
(D) At a parking garage

48. Why is the man unsure about the woman's idea?

(A) Bad weather is predicted.
(B) A destination is far away.
(C) A process is complicated.
(D) A warranty is strict.

49. Why does the woman say, "I've never been to this area before"?

(A) To express enthusiasm
(B) To ask for a recommendation
(C) To refuse an assignment
(D) To explain a mistake

50. What did the man win a prize for?

(A) Improving the workflow for a service
(B) Receiving high ratings from customers
(C) Reaching a special work anniversary
(D) Finding a use for some waste

51. What did the man do earlier in the year?

(A) He read an advice book.
(B) He distributed a survey.
(C) He attended a workshop.
(D) He started a new hobby.

52. What does the man say he will do with the prize money?

(A) Take a short vacation
(B) Contribute to his savings
(C) Treat coworkers to a meal
(D) Make a donation to a charity

53. What are the speakers discussing?

(A) Office furniture
(B) Budget allocations
(C) An internship program
(D) A departmental reorganization

54. According to the woman, what is the main problem?

(A) Her team is unhappy with a seating arrangement.
(B) Some applicants are not qualified for a position.
(C) A cost estimate was calculated incorrectly.
(D) A project has been very time-consuming.

55. What will the speakers most likely do?

(A) Distribute a questionnaire
(B) Spend some extra money
(C) Add an item to a meeting agenda
(D) Clear out an unused room

56. Why is the man at Browder Holdings?

(A) To hold a client consultation
(B) To conduct research for an article
(C) To tour an available property
(D) To discuss a business deal

57. What does the man mention about Browder Holdings?

(A) It has a large customer base.
(B) It was founded a long time ago.
(C) It is involved in the local community.
(D) It has an experienced management team.

58. What does the man say his company puts effort into?

(A) Designing efficient work spaces
(B) Improving businesses' public images
(C) Producing creative ideas for products
(D) Following industry regulations strictly

---

59. Which industry do the speakers most likely work in?

(A) Manufacturing
(B) Tourism
(C) Health care
(D) Information technology

60. What does the woman suggest?

(A) Ordering extra materials
(B) Closing a business early
(C) Issuing some safety reminders
(D) Double-checking some specifications

61. What will the man do next?

(A) Print a set of handouts
(B) Submit a budget document
(C) Cancel some appointments
(D) Use a public address system

CAST	
Nadia	Purva Shah
Rick	Hugh Macdonald
Jasmine	Lily Heath
Shane	Lorenzo Bertolazzi

62. What does the woman say about the production?

(A) It is hard to get tickets for.
(B) It is about to begin a tour.
(C) It has been running for a month.
(D) It has new cast members.

63. Look at the graphic. Which role was played by a different performer this evening?

(A) Nadia
(B) Rick
(C) Jasmine
(D) Shane

64. Where will the speakers most likely go next?

(A) To a parking structure
(B) To the theater office
(C) To a restaurant
(D) To a conference center

GO ON TO THE NEXT PAGE

INVOICE

Item	Quantity	Price
Pens	3 boxes	$10
Sticky notes	5 boxes	$75
Paperclips	7 boxes	$11
Binders	4 boxes	$120

Destination	Departure Time	Status
Montreal	15:00	Delayed – 40 minutes
Winnipeg	15:30	On time
Toronto	16:00	On time
Calgary	16:30	Delayed – one hour

65. Where does the conversation most likely take place?

(A) At a government office
(B) At a print shop
(C) At a law firm
(D) At a marketing agency

66. Look at the graphic. Which quantity does the woman say is incorrect?

(A) 3 boxes
(B) 5 boxes
(C) 7 boxes
(D) 4 boxes

67. What does the man ask about?

(A) Placing another order
(B) Informing some coworkers
(C) Testing some of the products
(D) Moving some of the boxes

68. What problem does the man mention?

(A) There is a mistake on a schedule.
(B) A facility is unusually busy.
(C) An airport's layout is confusing.
(D) He forgot to bring a travel document.

69. Look at the graphic. Where are the speakers flying to?

(A) Montreal
(B) Winnipeg
(C) Toronto
(D) Calgary

70. What does the man ask the woman to do?

(A) Check a weather forecast
(B) Notify an event organizer
(C) Research transportation options
(D) Ask about an airline policy

PART 4

Directions: You will hear some talks given by a single speaker. You will be asked to answer three questions about what the speaker says in each talk. Select the best response to each question and mark the letter (A), (B), (C), or (D) on your answer sheet. The talks will not be printed in your test book and will be spoken only one time.

71. What is the main purpose of the message?
(A) To congratulate the listener on some exam results
(B) To describe a career opportunity
(C) To inform the listener of an attendance issue
(D) To suggest a classroom activity

72. What does the speaker say she did this morning?
(A) She watched a demonstration.
(B) She reviewed some school records.
(C) She ordered some supplies.
(D) She received a call from a student.

73. What is the listener asked to do?
(A) Postpone a class session
(B) Send some teaching materials
(C) Visit a business's Web site
(D) Meet with a supervisor

74. What is the main topic of the broadcast?
(A) A famous resident of a city
(B) The renovation of a building
(C) The creation of some public art
(D) A new educational program

75. According to the speaker, who is Victor Hook?
(A) A painter
(B) An architect
(C) A museum director
(D) A local historian

76. What is the Eddix Foundation planning to do?
(A) Fund an exhibition
(B) Hire more personnel
(C) Purchase a piece of land
(D) Host an outdoor celebration

77. What kind of equipment has been purchased?
(A) Display screens
(B) Microphones
(C) Lighting
(D) Video cameras

78. What does the speaker emphasize about the products?
(A) They have many features.
(B) They are lightweight.
(C) They are inexpensive.
(D) They will last a long time.

79. Why does the speaker say, "but he'll be out in the field when they arrive"?
(A) To indicate that training will not be available
(B) To question a staffing decision
(C) To request help unloading the equipment
(D) To explain an expected delay

80. What type of business does the speaker work for?
(A) At a car dealership
(B) At a utility company
(C) At a recruiting agency
(D) At a newspaper office

81. What does the speaker say about himself?
(A) He has moved offices.
(B) He is on a business trip.
(C) He is preparing some documents.
(D) His job duties have changed.

82. What is the listener instructed to do?
(A) Call another person
(B) Review a list of suggestions
(C) Leave a voice message
(D) Complete an online form

GO ON TO THE NEXT PAGE

83. What industry does the speaker most likely work in?

(A) Finance
(B) Marketing
(C) Hospitality
(D) Publishing

84. What is the speaker mainly discussing?

(A) A job opening
(B) A company celebration
(C) Technology upgrades
(D) Survey results

85. What does the speaker ask the listeners to do?

(A) Share an announcement
(B) Collaborate on a report
(C) Revise a budget
(D) Indicate a preference

86. Who most likely are the listeners?

(A) Technical support agents
(B) Personal trainers
(C) Factory workers
(D) Construction supervisors

87. What does the speaker imply when he says, "many people are not familiar with this equipment"?

(A) An achievement is surprising.
(B) It is difficult to find qualified staff.
(C) A clear explanation should be given.
(D) It is not necessary to keep the equipment.

88. According to the speaker, what is the listeners' main goal?

(A) To retain customers
(B) To finish a project on schedule
(C) To resolve a safety issue
(D) To simplify a process

89. Where does the speaker most likely work?

(A) At a footwear company
(B) At a video game developer
(C) At a beverage manufacturer
(D) At a sports team organization

90. What does the business want people to do?

(A) Join a loyalty program
(B) Sign up for a mailing list
(C) Write a product review
(D) Follow a social media account

91. What incentive is being offered?

(A) A discount code
(B) Entry in a prize drawing
(C) Tickets to a virtual event
(D) A promotional poster

92. Where do the listeners most likely work?

(A) At a real estate firm
(B) At a community center
(C) At a medical laboratory
(D) At a business school

93. What does the speaker imply when he says, "Now, there's a single file on our shared network"?

(A) A task has not been finished.
(B) There is space to save more data.
(C) Some complaints have been addressed.
(D) A security rule is not being followed.

94. What does the speaker say he will do quickly?

(A) Draft a timeline
(B) Respond to inquiries
(C) Update some software
(D) Issue log-in credentials

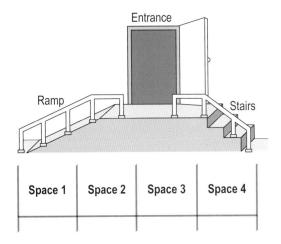

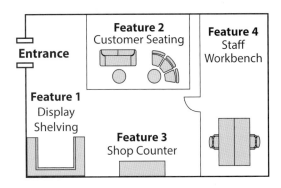

95. What type of business do the listeners most likely work for?

(A) A flooring contractor
(B) A plumbing service
(C) A delivery company
(D) An Internet service provider

96. Look at the graphic. Which parking space will be reserved for the listeners?

(A) Space 1
(B) Space 2
(C) Space 3
(D) Space 4

97. What should the listeners do after a job is completed?

(A) Return to their current location
(B) Send a message to a supervisor
(C) Check an electronic schedule
(D) Take a required meal break

98. Who most likely is the listener?

(A) An interior designer
(B) An event coordinator
(C) A delivery person
(D) A cleaner

99. What does the speaker say about flower arrangements?

(A) They were just delivered.
(B) They are difficult to care for.
(C) There will be a variety of them.
(D) They can be moved out of the way.

100. Look at the graphic. Which feature will have to be changed?

(A) Feature 1
(B) Feature 2
(C) Feature 3
(D) Feature 4

This is the end of the Listening test.

YBM
실전토익
LC 1000

LC

TEST 2

LISTENING TEST

In the Listening test, you will be asked to demonstrate how well you understand spoken English. The entire Listening test will last approximately 45 minutes. There are four parts, and directions are given for each part. You must mark your answers on the separate answer sheet. Do not write your answers in your test book.

PART 1

Directions: For each question in this part, you will hear four statements about a picture in your test book. When you hear the statements, you must select the one statement that best describes what you see in the picture. Then find the number of the question on your answer sheet and mark your answer. The statements will not be printed in your test book and will be spoken only one time.

Statement (C), "They're sitting at a table," is the best description of the picture, so you should select answer (C) and mark it on your answer sheet.

1.

2.

GO ON TO THE NEXT PAGE

3.

4.

5.

6.

GO ON TO THE NEXT PAGE ➤

Directions: You will hear a question or statement and three responses spoken in English. They will not be printed in your test book and will be spoken only one time. Select the best response to the question or statement and mark the letter (A), (B), or (C) on your answer sheet.

7. Mark your answer on your answer sheet.

8. Mark your answer on your answer sheet.

9. Mark your answer on your answer sheet.

10. Mark your answer on your answer sheet.

11. Mark your answer on your answer sheet.

12. Mark your answer on your answer sheet.

13. Mark your answer on your answer sheet.

14. Mark your answer on your answer sheet.

15. Mark your answer on your answer sheet.

16. Mark your answer on your answer sheet.

17. Mark your answer on your answer sheet.

18. Mark your answer on your answer sheet.

19. Mark your answer on your answer sheet.

20. Mark your answer on your answer sheet.

21. Mark your answer on your answer sheet.

22. Mark your answer on your answer sheet.

23. Mark your answer on your answer sheet.

24. Mark your answer on your answer sheet.

25. Mark your answer on your answer sheet.

26. Mark your answer on your answer sheet.

27. Mark your answer on your answer sheet.

28. Mark your answer on your answer sheet.

29. Mark your answer on your answer sheet.

30. Mark your answer on your answer sheet.

31. Mark your answer on your answer sheet.

PART 3

Directions: You will hear some conversations between two or more people. You will be asked to answer three questions about what the speakers say in each conversation. Select the best response to each question and mark the letter (A), (B), (C), or (D) on your answer sheet. The conversations will not be printed in your test book and will be spoken only one time.

32. What is the woman getting ready for?

(A) A seasonal sale
(B) A business's reopening
(C) A book's publication
(D) A local festival

33. What new feature of the bookstore does the woman point out?

(A) Its search kiosks
(B) Its gift certificates
(C) Its author readings
(D) Its in-store café

34. What will the woman most likely do next?

(A) Purchase some supplies
(B) Start a cleaning process
(C) Hang up some signs
(D) Write a job posting

35. Where most likely does the woman work?

(A) At a bank
(B) At a medical clinic
(C) At a real estate agency
(D) At a fitness center

36. What was the man unable to do yesterday?

(A) Locate a building
(B) Keep an appointment
(C) Transfer a payment
(D) Arrange transportation

37. What does the man like about the woman's suggestion?

(A) It suits his schedule.
(B) It is good for his health.
(C) It will be more enjoyable.
(D) It will reduce a fee.

38. Why does the man say, "That wasn't free"?

(A) To show surprise
(B) To explain a refusal
(C) To request reimbursement
(D) To emphasize an item's value

39. What problem does the man report?

(A) An appliance has broken down.
(B) Some paperwork is missing.
(C) Some technicians are unavailable.
(D) A budget has been exceeded.

40. What does the woman say she will do?

(A) Look for a manual
(B) Cancel an order
(C) Make some copies
(D) Speak with a manager

41. Why is the woman calling?

(A) To check on an order
(B) To receive a cost estimate
(C) To reserve an event venue
(D) To ask for a change to a route

42. What kind of business does the woman own?

(A) A tour company
(B) A ski resort
(C) An insurance agency
(D) A pharmacy

43. Why was the woman unable to use the online service?

(A) A form is confusing.
(B) She was not aware of it.
(C) A Web site was down.
(D) Her computer is outdated.

GO ON TO THE NEXT PAGE

44. What does the man ask the woman about?

    (A) Who will lead a meeting
    (B) Why a report is not finished
    (C) What topics a newsletter covers
    (D) When an executive will visit

45. What will happen next month?

    (A) A new logo will be chosen.
    (B) A parking area will be expanded.
    (C) A department will be restructured.
    (D) A review will be published.

46. What does the woman say the man should look at?

    (A) A revised list of names
    (B) Guidelines for a competition
    (C) Blueprints for a building
    (D) A budget proposal

47. What does the man want to do?

    (A) Clear a drain
    (B) Remove a stain
    (C) Protect some flooring
    (D) Improve a room's odor

48. Why does the woman recommend a product?

    (A) It is environmentally friendly.
    (B) It has a variety of uses.
    (C) It is powerful.
    (D) It is inexpensive.

49. What does the woman tell the man to do?

    (A) Leave some windows open
    (B) Watch some videos
    (C) Wear a pair of gloves
    (D) Read a product label

50. Where is the conversation taking place?

    (A) At an appliance store
    (B) At a movie theater
    (C) At an airport
    (D) At a school

51. Where will the speakers go later in the morning?

    (A) To a staff break area
    (B) To a cafeteria
    (C) To a loading zone
    (D) To a conference room

52. What does the man ask about?

    (A) Who is part of a team
    (B) How long a certain shift is
    (C) Where to submit a document
    (D) How to obtain a uniform

53. What is the conversation about?

    (A) A company policy
    (B) A production delay
    (C) A damaged machine
    (D) An upcoming interview

54. What department does the woman most likely work for?

    (A) Security
    (B) Accounting
    (C) Public Relations
    (D) Human Resources

55. What does the man imply when he says, "I spoke with him after lunch"?

    (A) He missed a group outing.
    (B) He already received some instructions.
    (C) A plan changed a short time ago.
    (D) A task has been completed.

56. What did the speakers' company recently do?

(A) It launched a Web site.
(B) It renovated its office.
(C) It hired a spokesperson.
(D) It introduced a new policy.

57. What do the men say is a benefit of the change?

(A) It will attract new customers.
(B) It will lower maintenance costs.
(C) It will improve staff collaboration.
(D) It will make some travel unnecessary.

58. What do the men ask the woman about?

(A) The reaction to an announcement
(B) The quality of a service
(C) The origin of an idea
(D) The status of a project

---

59. Where do the speakers work?

(A) At a fashion magazine
(B) At a restaurant
(C) At a Web development firm
(D) At a tailor shop

60. What has the man been assigned to do?

(A) Mentor some colleagues
(B) Oversee social media accounts
(C) Organize a storage space
(D) Research a competitor

61. What does the man ask the woman to do?

(A) Review a presentation
(B) Make some suggestions
(C) Take some pictures
(D) Pick up some food

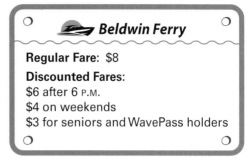

Beldwin Ferry

Regular Fare: $8
Discounted Fares:
$6 after 6 P.M.
$4 on weekends
$3 for seniors and WavePass holders

62. What is the purpose of the man's trip?

(A) To get exercise outdoors
(B) To create artworks
(C) To collect samples of plants
(D) To repair electronics

63. Look at the graphic. Why does the man receive a discount?

(A) It is after 6 P.M.
(B) It is a weekend day.
(C) He is a senior.
(D) He has a pass.

64. What will the man most likely do next?

(A) Have a small meal
(B) Board a passenger ferry
(C) Shop for souvenirs
(D) Retrieve his bicycle

GO ON TO THE NEXT PAGE

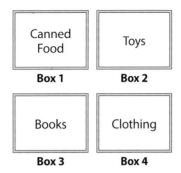

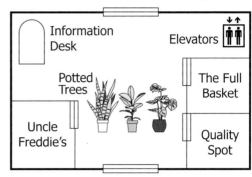

Randholm Building

65. Where most likely are the speakers?

(A) At a travel agency
(B) At a school
(C) At a hospital
(D) At a bank

66. Look at the graphic. Which box will the man use?

(A) Box 1
(B) Box 2
(C) Box 3
(D) Box 4

67. What does the woman suggest doing?

(A) Assessing the value of the contents
(B) Printing some new labels for the boxes
(C) Placing some items in individual bags
(D) Checking to see if there are missing pieces

68. What does the man plan to do?

(A) Make a purchase
(B) Meet a friend
(C) Deliver a package
(D) Attend a job interview

69. Look at the graphic. Where will the man most likely go?

(A) To the Information Desk
(B) To The Full Basket
(C) To Quality Spot
(D) To Uncle Freddie's

70. What does the woman inform the man about?

(A) An elevator skips some floors.
(B) A parking space has a time limit.
(C) A sales event is happening.
(D) An entrance is closed.

PART 4

Directions: You will hear some talks given by a single speaker. You will be asked to answer three questions about what the speaker says in each talk. Select the best response to each question and mark the letter (A), (B), (C), or (D) on your answer sheet. The talks will not be printed in your test book and will be spoken only one time.

71. Where most likely are the listeners?

(A) At a university
(B) At a sports arena
(C) At a national park
(D) At a science museum

72. What does the speaker emphasize about an institution?

(A) It has won awards.
(B) It has a large facility.
(C) It runs many programs.
(D) It uses new technology.

73. What will the listeners do next?

(A) Take a tour
(B) Fill out forms
(C) Introduce themselves
(D) Put on special clothing

74. Who most likely is the speaker?

(A) A technical support provider
(B) A marketing manager
(C) A legal advisor
(D) A product development specialist

75. What does the speaker say will take place tomorrow?

(A) A welcome reception
(B) An equipment installation
(C) A photography session
(D) An online seminar

76. According to the speaker, why will the listeners need a number code?

(A) To receive a discount
(B) To operate a machine
(C) To log in to a Web site
(D) To enter a building

77. What is the main topic of the report?

(A) A music concert
(B) A sports tournament
(C) A transportation project
(D) An approaching storm

78. According to the speaker, what has been posted online?

(A) A list of road closures
(B) Contact information
(C) Video footage
(D) A technical drawing

79. What does the speaker mean when he says, "the subways run until midnight"?

(A) Subway schedules have changed recently.
(B) Attendees of an event should use the subway.
(C) Some work must take place after midnight.
(D) A city's transit services are well-funded.

80. What job has the listener applied for?

(A) Film critic
(B) Radio producer
(C) Event coordinator
(D) Book editor

81. What does the speaker say she wants to discuss?

(A) A writing style
(B) A training process
(C) A company's goals
(D) A podcast's creation

82. What does the speaker say she will do next?

(A) Forward some documents
(B) Leave for a business trip
(C) Confirm a pay rate
(D) Update a job advertisement

GO ON TO THE NEXT PAGE

83. Who is the message intended for?

 (A) A hotel manager
 (B) A café owner
 (C) A city official
 (D) A gallery curator

84. What does the speaker mean when he says, "do you show works by local artists"?

 (A) He wants to buy art that was made nearby.
 (B) He hopes to learn about regional trends.
 (C) He thinks a museum exhibit is incomplete.
 (D) He wants the listener to display his work.

85. What does the speaker offer to do?

 (A) Send some electronic files
 (B) Answer the listener's questions
 (C) Pay to use some images
 (D) Give some driving directions

86. What is the focus of the seminar?

 (A) Meeting management
 (B) Cost-reduction ideas
 (C) Staff recruitment
 (D) Data organization

87. According to the speaker, what can be found on a Web site?

 (A) A trial version of some software
 (B) A calendar of events
 (C) Sample contracts
 (D) Client testimonials

88. What will the listeners most likely do next?

 (A) Talk with a partner
 (B) Watch a short film
 (C) Listen to some rules
 (D) Get some refreshments

89. What is the speaker mainly discussing?

 (A) A facility tour
 (B) A security upgrade
 (C) An employee orientation
 (D) A cleaning requirement

90. What will the listeners receive?

 (A) An identification badge
 (B) A safety helmet
 (C) A floor plan
 (D) A computer program

91. Why does the speaker say, "the process only takes a few minutes"?

 (A) To express concern
 (B) To correct a scheduling mistake
 (C) To reassure the listeners
 (D) To ask for assistance

92. Where do the listeners most likely work?

 (A) At a commercial laundry facility
 (B) At an auto repair shop
 (C) At a warehouse
 (D) At a moving company

93. What should the listeners use a certain technique for?

 (A) Storing chemicals
 (B) Lifting loads
 (C) Packing boxes
 (D) Folding fabric items

94. What benefit of the technique does the speaker mention?

 (A) Less wasting of supplies
 (B) Fewer complaints from customers
 (C) Increased productivity
 (D) Lower risk of injury

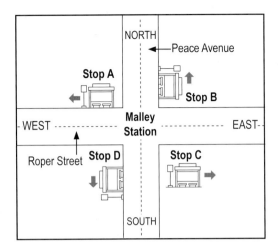

95. Look at the graphic. Where is the speaker?

(A) At Stop A
(B) At Stop B
(C) At Stop C
(D) At Stop D

96. According to the speaker, what is the main reason for building the shelters?

(A) To give people a place to sit while waiting
(B) To keep people comfortable despite bad weather
(C) To protect people from air pollution
(D) To prevent traffic accidents

97. What is available online?

(A) A virtual tour
(B) Some statistics
(C) A feedback form
(D) A project schedule

98. Where does the announcement most likely take place?

(A) At a coffee shop
(B) At a fruit orchard
(C) At a grocery store
(D) At a cooking school

99. Look at the graphic. What is today's special?

(A) Cheesecake
(B) Pie
(C) Pudding
(D) Tarts

100. What is offered with a purchase?

(A) A coupon
(B) Eating utensils
(C) Gift wrapping
(D) Storage instructions

This is the end of the Listening test.

YBM
실전토익
LC 1000

테스트 전 체크리스트

- 중간 휴식 없이 제한 시간을 지켜서 풀이하세요.
- 제한 시간은 답안지에 마킹하는 시간도 포함시켜야 합니다.
- 찍은 문제는 번호 옆에 꼭 체크해 주세요.
- 시간 안에 풀지 못한 문제는 틀린 것으로 채점해 주세요.

LC

TEST 3

LISTENING TEST

In the Listening test, you will be asked to demonstrate how well you understand spoken English. The entire Listening test will last approximately 45 minutes. There are four parts, and directions are given for each part. You must mark your answers on the separate answer sheet. Do not write your answers in your test book.

PART 1

Directions: For each question in this part, you will hear four statements about a picture in your test book. When you hear the statements, you must select the one statement that best describes what you see in the picture. Then find the number of the question on your answer sheet and mark your answer. The statements will not be printed in your test book and will be spoken only one time.

Statement (C), "They're sitting at a table," is the best description of the picture, so you should select answer (C) and mark it on your answer sheet.

1.

2.

GO ON TO THE NEXT PAGE

3.

4.

5.

6.

GO ON TO THE NEXT PAGE ➤

PART 2

Directions: You will hear a question or statement and three responses spoken in English. They will not be printed in your test book and will be spoken only one time. Select the best response to the question or statement and mark the letter (A), (B), or (C) on your answer sheet.

7. Mark your answer on your answer sheet.

8. Mark your answer on your answer sheet.

9. Mark your answer on your answer sheet.

10. Mark your answer on your answer sheet.

11. Mark your answer on your answer sheet.

12. Mark your answer on your answer sheet.

13. Mark your answer on your answer sheet.

14. Mark your answer on your answer sheet.

15. Mark your answer on your answer sheet.

16. Mark your answer on your answer sheet.

17. Mark your answer on your answer sheet.

18. Mark your answer on your answer sheet.

19. Mark your answer on your answer sheet.

20. Mark your answer on your answer sheet.

21. Mark your answer on your answer sheet.

22. Mark your answer on your answer sheet.

23. Mark your answer on your answer sheet.

24. Mark your answer on your answer sheet.

25. Mark your answer on your answer sheet.

26. Mark your answer on your answer sheet.

27. Mark your answer on your answer sheet.

28. Mark your answer on your answer sheet.

29. Mark your answer on your answer sheet.

30. Mark your answer on your answer sheet.

31. Mark your answer on your answer sheet.

PART 3

Directions: You will hear some conversations between two or more people. You will be asked to answer three questions about what the speakers say in each conversation. Select the best response to each question and mark the letter (A), (B), (C), or (D) on your answer sheet. The conversations will not be printed in your test book and will be spoken only one time.

32. Where do the speakers most likely work?

    (A) At a manufacturing plant
    (B) At a department store
    (C) At a restaurant
    (D) At a dry cleaner

33. What does the man say he forgot?

    (A) A handout
    (B) Some safety equipment
    (C) Some identification
    (D) A key card

34. According to the woman, why is an order important?

    (A) It could result in long-term business.
    (B) It is for a local charity event.
    (C) It is for a renowned company.
    (D) It will be featured in a magazine.

35. What is the conversation mainly about?

    (A) A training session
    (B) An event registration
    (C) Some promotional materials
    (D) Some festival booths

36. What does the woman offer to do?

    (A) Check a Web site
    (B) Request a price reduction
    (C) Proofread a document
    (D) Research other businesses

37. What will the man send this afternoon?

    (A) Schedules for upcoming shows
    (B) Images of a recent event
    (C) A sample contract
    (D) A mailing address

38. What kind of business does the woman most likely work for?

    (A) A construction firm
    (B) A dental clinic
    (C) An appliance store
    (D) A post office

39. What does the man say he wants to do?

    (A) Add a service request
    (B) Reschedule a visit
    (C) Receive an invoice
    (D) Make a complaint

40. What does the man offer advice about?

    (A) Whom to contact
    (B) When to arrive
    (C) What samples to bring
    (D) Which road to take

41. What is mainly being discussed?

    (A) A fund-raising campaign
    (B) A company policy
    (C) A workshop
    (D) An advertisement

42. What good news does the man share?

    (A) Some customers were impressed.
    (B) A task was completed early.
    (C) Product sales have increased.
    (D) The company received a grant.

43. What will happen next Tuesday?

    (A) Some investors will visit.
    (B) Some managers will meet.
    (C) A winner will be announced.
    (D) A business trip will begin.

GO ON TO THE NEXT PAGE

44. What does the woman offer to do?

   (A) Wait for Pamela
   (B) Contact a coworker
   (C) Check a schedule
   (D) Proofread a document

45. What does Pamela usually do?

   (A) Write media announcements
   (B) Conduct performance evaluations
   (C) Make travel arrangements
   (D) Introduce new clients to the business

46. According to the woman, why should Shawn help with a task?

   (A) He used to perform it regularly.
   (B) He wants to learn new skills.
   (C) He has a relevant degree.
   (D) He has the lightest workload.

47. Where most likely does the woman work?

   (A) At a factory
   (B) At a department store
   (C) At a repair shop
   (D) At a consulting firm

48. What does the man inquire about?

   (A) A contract period
   (B) A color option
   (C) A discount offer
   (D) A shipping fee

49. What does the woman recommend doing?

   (A) Making an in-person visit
   (B) Speaking to a supervisor
   (C) Changing a design
   (D) Placing a large order

50. Where most likely are the speakers?

   (A) At a bookstore
   (B) At a warehouse
   (C) At a medical clinic
   (D) At a library

51. According to the man, what will the women do in the morning?

   (A) Take a building tour
   (B) Complete some paperwork
   (C) Observe other colleagues
   (D) Read a user manual

52. What does Clara ask Bethany about?

   (A) The usefulness of some training
   (B) The number of participants in a program
   (C) The duration of her previous job
   (D) The reason she transferred branches

53. What is the purpose of the call?

   (A) To change a phone number
   (B) To report a potential error
   (C) To pay an outstanding bill
   (D) To update an address

54. What did the man do in September?

   (A) He took a trip overseas.
   (B) He extended a warranty.
   (C) He upgraded his phone.
   (D) He downloaded a lot of files.

55. According to the woman, what was the man advised to do?

   (A) Make a copy of a receipt
   (B) Keep a product's packaging
   (C) Speak to a manager
   (D) Read an agreement carefully

56. What did the woman do last week?

(A) She started her own business.
(B) She got a book published.
(C) She relocated to a new city.
(D) She was featured in an article.

57. What does the woman say she hopes to receive?

(A) Some price estimates
(B) Some favorable reviews
(C) A local award
(D) A bank loan

58. Why does the woman say, "I have a stack of business cards"?

(A) To ask for a favor
(B) To cancel an order
(C) To express concern
(D) To correct an error

59. What are the speakers discussing?

(A) Submitting an annual report
(B) Recruiting staff for a project
(C) Taking an overseas business trip
(D) Registering for an industry event

60. What does the man imply when he says, "I did it last year"?

(A) He knows some personnel well.
(B) An experience was valuable for his career.
(C) He can provide advice on a process.
(D) A responsibility should be given to someone else.

61. What information will the woman ask a manager for?

(A) A sales goal
(B) A final budget
(C) A preferred size
(D) A departure time

▭▢▣
✉ Inbox	Subject
Tony Parsons	Volunteers needed
Roy Martino	Approved catering companies
Beth Landrum	New extension number
Anna Cordero	Vacation request reminder

62. What are the speakers planning?

(A) A recruitment event
(B) A product launch
(C) A food festival
(D) A board meeting

63. Look at the graphic. Whose e-mail does the woman refer to?

(A) Mr. Parsons's
(B) Mr. Martino's
(C) Ms. Landrum's
(D) Ms. Cordero's

64. What does the man suggest doing?

(A) Contacting technical support
(B) Practicing a presentation
(C) Checking a budget
(D) Reserving a room

GO ON TO THE NEXT PAGE

WORTHINGTON EXITS

Oakridge Lane	Exit 11	→
Ashford Street	Exit 13	↗
Powell Street	Exit 14	↘
Yorkie Road	Exit 16	↑

STOCK UP AND SAVE!

Hazel Fertilizer

1 bag $22.00 ⇨ **$20.00**
2 bags $40.00 ⇨ **$36.00**
3 bags $59.50 ⇨ **$49.50**
4 bags $75.00 ⇨ **$60.00**

65. What does the woman remind the man about?

(A) She has attended the event before.
(B) She currently lives near the man.
(C) She is borrowing a company car.
(D) She has an office in the event center.

66. Look at the graphic. Which exit will the speakers use?

(A) Oakridge Lane
(B) Ashford Street
(C) Powell Street
(D) Yorkie Road

67. What will the man ask Benjamin to do?

(A) Meet the speakers at a different entrance
(B) Pick up some informational pamphlets
(C) Save the speakers' seats in the auditorium
(D) Approve funds for a parking fee

68. What will the woman do next month?

(A) Start a different job
(B) Have some guests
(C) Move to a new home
(D) Teach a workshop

69. What does the woman say about Hazel fertilizer?

(A) It is often sold out.
(B) It has a good reputation.
(C) It has the cheapest price.
(D) It is environmentally friendly.

70. Look at the graphic. How much will the woman pay?

(A) $20.00
(B) $36.00
(C) $49.50
(D) $60.00

PART 4

Directions: You will hear some talks given by a single speaker. You will be asked to answer three questions about what the speaker says in each talk. Select the best response to each question and mark the letter (A), (B), (C), or (D) on your answer sheet. The talks will not be printed in your test book and will be spoken only one time.

71. What is the advertisement about?

(A) A pharmacy
(B) A dental clinic
(C) A fitness center
(D) A hotel

72. What has the business recently changed?

(A) Its staff responsibilities
(B) Its standard fees
(C) Its cancelation policy
(D) Its hours of operation

73. What will happen on November 3 ?

(A) A construction project will begin.
(B) A prize drawing will be held.
(C) A newsletter will be sent.
(D) A new branch will open.

74. What is the speaker mainly discussing?

(A) Launching a product
(B) Relocating the office
(C) Attracting new clients
(D) Reorganizing some teams

75. Why does the speaker say, "I've had several unexpected visits from clients this week"?

(A) To issue an invitation
(B) To offer an excuse
(C) To express encouragement
(D) To request assistance

76. According to the speaker, what will become easier for employees?

(A) Communicating with colleagues
(B) Accessing a database
(C) Completing work assignments
(D) Receiving performance bonuses

77. Where do the speakers most likely work?

(A) At a department store
(B) At a moving service
(C) At a tour company
(D) At a commercial airline

78. What will be the topic of the video?

(A) The history of the company
(B) Current sales territories
(C) Mandatory safety procedures
(D) Tips for new employees

79. What will the listeners probably do next?

(A) Watch a demonstration
(B) Pick up some equipment
(C) Read a script
(D) Set up some tables

80. Why does the speaker say, "the print shop used the wrong address"?

(A) To ask for some suggestions
(B) To apologize for a delay
(C) To recommend canceling a contract
(D) To explain some missing items

81. What does the speaker say about the seating plan?

(A) It does not need to be followed.
(B) It was carefully considered.
(C) It is the same every year.
(D) It had guests added to it.

82. Who does the speaker give a special thanks to?

(A) A singer
(B) A designer
(C) A researcher
(D) A building manager

GO ON TO THE NEXT PAGE

83. What does the speaker congratulate the listener for?

(A) She was given an award.
(B) She opened her own gallery.
(C) Her paintings are selling quickly.
(D) Her exhibition has been popular.

84. According to the speaker, what will happen in July?

(A) A museum will shut down.
(B) Copies of some artwork will go on sale.
(C) Some art will be featured in a magazine.
(D) A television interview will take place.

85. Why should the listener visit a Web site?

(A) To register for an event
(B) To read some comments
(C) To upload some photographs
(D) To join a mailing list

86. Where does the speaker most likely work?

(A) At a research institute
(B) At a radio station
(C) At a manufacturing plant
(D) At a grocery store

87. What does Dr. Ramirez specialize in?

(A) Hospital management
(B) Audio production
(C) Mechanical engineering
(D) Food science

88. What benefit of an item is mentioned?

(A) It enables people to concentrate better.
(B) It helps with weight loss efforts.
(C) It can be stored for a long time.
(D) It improves the quality of people's sleep.

89. What does the speaker mean when he says, "We've never done this before"?

(A) He can explain an error.
(B) He wants to adjust a schedule.
(C) He is nervous about a plan.
(D) He is praising an accomplishment.

90. What will happen at the company next Monday?

(A) Some investors will visit.
(B) A new executive will be hired.
(C) Some training sessions will take place.
(D) A promotion will be announced.

91. What does the speaker remind the listeners to do?

(A) Stay within a budget
(B) Review some job duties
(C) Clean up a workspace
(D) Use a sign-up sheet

92. Why is the company holding an event?

(A) To celebrate an anniversary
(B) To promote a new product
(C) To welcome new employees
(D) To congratulate a department

93. What does the speaker say about Mr. Diaz?

(A) He designed a training program.
(B) He oversaw a company expansion.
(C) He improved some security measures.
(D) He negotiated an important contract.

94. According to the speaker, what will happen after a meal is served?

(A) A group photo will be taken.
(B) A series of videos will be shown.
(C) Other workers will be recognized.
(D) Messages from clients will be read.

Diagram (Museum Map)

```
                    ┌─────────────────┐
                    │ North Wing:     │
                    │ Early Flights   │
        ┌───────────┼─────────────────┼──────────────┐
        │ West Wing:│ Main Hall:      │ East Wing:    │
        │ Pilot     │ Model           │ The Jet Age   │
        │ Accessories│ Airplanes      │               │
┌───────┼───────┬───┼─────────────────┴──────────────┘
│ Event │ Gift  │ Entrance           │
│ Room  │ Shop  │                    │
└───────┴───────┴────────────────────┘
```

OCTOBER Calendar

4	5	6
Magazine Photo Shoot		Preview Screening

7	8	9
	Awards Banquet	

95. Look at the graphic. Which area is temporarily closed?

(A) The East Wing
(B) The West Wing
(C) The North Wing
(D) The Main Hall

96. What does the speaker suggest doing?

(A) Keeping a receipt
(B) Visiting a gift shop
(C) Attending a talk
(D) Taking a brochure

97. Who is Celia Watson?

(A) A professional photographer
(B) A history professor
(C) A film director
(D) A commercial pilot

98. Look at the graphic. For which day has the speaker scheduled a television appearance?

(A) October 4
(B) October 5
(C) October 6
(D) October 7

99. What does the speaker say she will send?

(A) Suggestions for revisions
(B) Some driving directions
(C) A confirmation number
(D) A guest list

100. What problem does the speaker mention?

(A) A hotel was fully booked.
(B) No direct flights were available.
(C) A fee has recently increased.
(D) A building is difficult to find.

This is the end of the Listening test.

YBM
실전토익
LC 1000

테스트 전 체크리스트

- 중간 휴식 없이 제한 시간을 지켜서 풀이하세요.
- 제한 시간은 답안지에 마킹하는 시간도 포함시켜야 합니다.
- 찍은 문제는 번호 옆에 꼭 체크해 주세요.
- 시간 안에 풀지 못한 문제는 틀린 것으로 채점해 주세요.

LC

TEST 4

LISTENING TEST

In the Listening test, you will be asked to demonstrate how well you understand spoken English. The entire Listening test will last approximately 45 minutes. There are four parts, and directions are given for each part. You must mark your answers on the separate answer sheet. Do not write your answers in your test book.

PART 1

Directions: For each question in this part, you will hear four statements about a picture in your test book. When you hear the statements, you must select the one statement that best describes what you see in the picture. Then find the number of the question on your answer sheet and mark your answer. The statements will not be printed in your test book and will be spoken only one time.

Statement (C), "They're sitting at a table," is the best description of the picture, so you should select answer (C) and mark it on your answer sheet.

1.

2.

GO ON TO THE NEXT PAGE ➤

3.

4.

5.

6.

GO ON TO THE NEXT PAGE

Directions: You will hear a question or statement and three responses spoken in English. They will not be printed in your test book and will be spoken only one time. Select the best response to the question or statement and mark the letter (A), (B), or (C) on your answer sheet.

7. Mark your answer on your answer sheet.

8. Mark your answer on your answer sheet.

9. Mark your answer on your answer sheet.

10. Mark your answer on your answer sheet.

11. Mark your answer on your answer sheet.

12. Mark your answer on your answer sheet.

13. Mark your answer on your answer sheet.

14. Mark your answer on your answer sheet.

15. Mark your answer on your answer sheet.

16. Mark your answer on your answer sheet.

17. Mark your answer on your answer sheet.

18. Mark your answer on your answer sheet.

19. Mark your answer on your answer sheet.

20. Mark your answer on your answer sheet.

21. Mark your answer on your answer sheet.

22. Mark your answer on your answer sheet.

23. Mark your answer on your answer sheet.

24. Mark your answer on your answer sheet.

25. Mark your answer on your answer sheet.

26. Mark your answer on your answer sheet.

27. Mark your answer on your answer sheet.

28. Mark your answer on your answer sheet.

29. Mark your answer on your answer sheet.

30. Mark your answer on your answer sheet.

31. Mark your answer on your answer sheet.

PART 3

Directions: You will hear some conversations between two or more people. You will be asked to answer three questions about what the speakers say in each conversation. Select the best response to each question and mark the letter (A), (B), (C), or (D) on your answer sheet. The conversations will not be printed in your test book and will be spoken only one time.

32. Who most likely are the speakers?
    (A) Architects
    (B) Real estate agents
    (C) Property managers
    (D) City officials

33. What does the woman give the man?
    (A) Some safety gear
    (B) Some blueprints
    (C) A report
    (D) A tool

34. Why has a project been postponed?
    (A) The weather is unfavorable for it.
    (B) The client has not provided some information.
    (C) An inspection must be carried out first.
    (D) Some financing is no longer available.

35. What product are the speakers discussing?
    (A) Refrigerators
    (B) Display cases
    (C) Coffee makers
    (D) Light fixtures

36. What department does the man most likely work in?
    (A) Sales
    (B) Accounting
    (C) Customer Support
    (D) Product Development

37. What will the man do next?
    (A) Schedule a site visit
    (B) Correct an invoice
    (C) Test some equipment himself
    (D) Add a note to a file

38. Who most likely is the woman?
    (A) A florist
    (B) A caterer
    (C) A musician
    (D) A photographer

39. Where does the woman want to go first?
    (A) To an outdoor patio
    (B) To a dining space
    (C) To a loading area
    (D) To a commercial kitchen

40. According to the man, what should the woman do?
    (A) Bring extra supplies
    (B) Use lightweight equipment
    (C) Place tables in separate locations
    (D) Revise a set-up timeline

41. What is the conversation mostly about?
    (A) Expanding a workforce
    (B) Repairing some machinery
    (C) Participating in a trade show
    (D) Arranging a business loan

42. What do the men say is important?
    (A) Keeping up with a competitor
    (B) Addressing employee feedback
    (C) Increasing brand recognition
    (D) Avoiding legal issues

43. What problem does the woman mention?
    (A) A decision-making process is slow.
    (B) A cost estimate may be incorrect.
    (C) An application might be rejected.
    (D) A new technology is difficult to use.

GO ON TO THE NEXT PAGE

44. Why does the man talk to the woman?

    (A) To question a baggage policy
    (B) To share a passenger complaint
    (C) To explain a new boarding procedure
    (D) To discuss a seating shortage

45. What does the woman say she will do?

    (A) Search in an employee handbook
    (B) Give upgrades to some passengers
    (C) Inform flight attendants of a problem
    (D) Change the text on a digital sign

46. What does the man plan to do?

    (A) Offer compensation for an inconvenience
    (B) Continue monitoring an entrance
    (C) Instruct some travelers to form a line
    (D) Ask for assistance with moving an object

47. Why has the woman come to Australia?

    (A) For a business trip
    (B) For a study program
    (C) For a visit with family
    (D) For some sightseeing

48. What problem does the woman have?

    (A) She does not remember an address.
    (B) She forgot to bring some identification.
    (C) She cannot log in to an e-mail account.
    (D) She does not have a local phone
        number.

49. What does the man offer the woman?

    (A) A map of the area
    (B) An Internet connection
    (C) A trial membership
    (D) A facility tour

50. Where most likely do the speakers work?

    (A) At a hospital
    (B) At a university
    (C) At a restaurant
    (D) At a factory

51. What does the man mean when he says, "That pizza was very good"?

    (A) The taste of a dish has changed.
    (B) A dish should be ordered again.
    (C) A business deserves a positive review.
    (D) He is disappointed to miss a party.

52. What is the woman concerned about?

    (A) Staying under a budget
    (B) Starting her shift on time
    (C) Providing food to everyone
    (D) Following a complicated recipe

53. Who most likely are the speakers?

    (A) Security guards
    (B) Plumbers
    (C) Office cleaners
    (D) Mailroom staff

54. What does the woman say she did?

    (A) Consulted a manual
    (B) Reported a safety problem
    (C) Turned on an air conditioner
    (D) Disposed of some waste

55. What does the man say may cause a delay?

    (A) The nearest parking area is closed.
    (B) A special telephone line is down.
    (C) A product warranty cannot be located.
    (D) A worker in another department is
        absent.

56. Where does the conversation take place?

(A) At a history exhibition
(B) At a private residence
(C) At a storage facility
(D) At a local park

57. Who are the women?

(A) Museum curators
(B) Tour guides
(C) Restoration experts
(D) Archaeological surveyors

58. What does the man say he hopes to do?

(A) Sell some artifacts
(B) Write a fiction book
(C) Plan an outdoor event
(D) Build a new road

59. Who most likely is the man?

(A) An advertising executive
(B) A fashion photographer
(C) A professional athlete
(D) An event organizer

60. What does the woman say she will request?

(A) Sales projections
(B) A venue recommendation
(C) A long-term contract
(D) Clothing samples

61. Why does the woman say, "they're still in the design stage"?

(A) To indicate that the man's input is not needed yet
(B) To encourage the man to suggest some changes
(C) To show frustration about a lack of progress
(D) To explain why some accessories are not being used

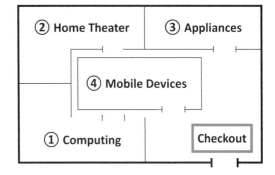

62. What did the man do recently?

(A) He accepted a job offer.
(B) He moved to a new city.
(C) He started writing a book.
(D) He attended a presentation.

63. Look at the graphic. Where will the speakers go next?

(A) To Section 1
(B) To Section 2
(C) To Section 3
(D) To Section 4

64. What does the woman mention about the products?

(A) They come with a warranty.
(B) They are part of a sales promotion.
(C) They are compatible with an app.
(D) They were released recently.

GO ON TO THE NEXT PAGE

Readings	
Author	**Book**
Eun-Young Cho	*Silver Flame*
Conrad Morris	*My Father's Hands*
Break	
Igor Bartosz	*Nights on the Oder*
Arletta DeWitt	*Let Us Run*

The Best Energy Bars Following Dietary Restrictions	
Category	**Winner**
Vegan	YouFuel
Dairy-free	Savorette
Nut-free	Power Crunch
Gluten-free	The Go Bar

65. What are the speakers organizing?

(A) A birthday celebration for an author
(B) An anniversary party for a library
(C) A special event for a book festival
(D) The grand opening of a bookstore

66. Look at the graphic. Which book title will be replaced?

(A) *Silver Flame*
(B) *My Father's Hands*
(C) *Nights on the Oder*
(D) *Let Us Run*

67. What does the man remind the woman to do?

(A) Update a Web page
(B) Buy refreshments
(C) Change a window display
(D) Contact a newspaper company

68. Why is the woman calling?

(A) To check on the status of an article
(B) To cancel an editorial meeting
(C) To suggest some relevant products
(D) To discuss the theme of an upcoming issue

69. Look at the graphic. Which energy bar is the man currently writing about?

(A) YouFuel
(B) Savorette
(C) Power Crunch
(D) The Go Bar

70. What does the man ask about?

(A) A request from a reader
(B) A reimbursement process
(C) The word limit for a review
(D) The previous work of a journalist

PART 4

Directions: You will hear some talks given by a single speaker. You will be asked to answer three questions about what the speaker says in each talk. Select the best response to each question and mark the letter (A), (B), (C), or (D) on your answer sheet. The talks will not be printed in your test book and will be spoken only one time.

71. Where does the speaker work?
    (A) At a moving company
    (B) At an apartment complex
    (C) At a landscaping firm
    (D) At a hardware store

72. According to the speaker, what has the business received?
    (A) An advance deposit
    (B) A signed agreement
    (C) A product shipment
    (D) A repair request

73. What does the speaker say about the business's vehicles?
    (A) They are easy to recognize.
    (B) They make a lot of noise.
    (C) They are large in size.
    (D) They have tracking devices.

74. According to the speaker, why is a hiring process behind schedule?
    (A) A manager was out of the office.
    (B) A job description was outdated.
    (C) A posting received too few responses.
    (D) Some funding had to be secured.

75. What does the speaker say will happen tomorrow?
    (A) Some interviews will take place.
    (B) An office tour will be given.
    (C) An orientation will begin.
    (D) A job offer will be extended.

76. What will some of the listeners most likely do next?
    (A) Read a handout
    (B) Greet a new colleague
    (C) Go to a conference room
    (D) Clean up a work space

77. What event is being planned?
    (A) A festival
    (B) A fund-raiser
    (C) An awards ceremony
    (D) A job fair

78. What task is the speaker having difficulty with?
    (A) Obtaining a permit
    (B) Recruiting volunteers
    (C) Creating advertisements
    (D) Renting furniture

79. What does the speaker propose doing?
    (A) Changing the event date
    (B) Hiring an outside specialist
    (C) Confirming some attendees
    (D) Reviewing records from last year

80. What is the topic of the broadcast?
    (A) Holiday travel
    (B) A sports tournament
    (C) The opening of a movie
    (D) A sales promotion at a store

81. What does the speaker imply when he says, "the number of visitors overloaded its Web site"?
    (A) A service is currently unavailable.
    (B) It is better to make a purchase in person.
    (C) There is high demand for some tickets.
    (D) Many people received a special discount.

82. According to the speaker, how did a company make an announcement?
    (A) By issuing text messages
    (B) By posting on social media
    (C) By holding a press conference
    (D) By sending a mass e-mail

GO ON TO THE NEXT PAGE

83. What does the speaker mean when she says, "my family has lived here for generations"?

(A) She recommends moving to the city.
(B) She has a useful background for her job.
(C) She prefers to vacation in other places.
(D) She is unhappy about a redevelopment plan.

84. What were listeners instructed to do?

(A) Bring a bottle of water
(B) Arrive a few minutes early
(C) Wear comfortable shoes
(D) Place a lunch order

85. What will the listeners see first?

(A) Some public art
(B) A government building
(C) An outdoor market
(D) A waterway

86. What is the company preparing to do?

(A) Relocate its headquarters
(B) Negotiate a merger
(C) Undergo an audit
(D) Launch a product line

87. What department does the listener most likely work for?

(A) Human Resources
(B) Finance
(C) Public Relations
(D) Security

88. What does the speaker ask the listener to do?

(A) Revise a proposal
(B) Organize a meeting
(C) Gather some documents
(D) Postpone an announcement

89. What is the meeting mainly about?

(A) Finding uses for some waste
(B) Improving manufacturing practices
(C) Increasing staff retention rates
(D) Replacing a supplies vendor

90. What has recently changed?

(A) A storage method
(B) A training period
(C) A uniform policy
(D) A safety regulation

91. What will the listeners do next?

(A) Watch a slide presentation
(B) Report on their activities
(C) Handle some materials
(D) Establish a project team

92. Who most likely are the listeners?

(A) Research team members
(B) Grocery store workers
(C) Theater actors
(D) Publishing staff

93. What does the speaker imply when she says, "he has the hardest role in the project"?

(A) An employee needs more assistance.
(B) An initial deadline may be missed.
(C) A personnel decision was easy to make.
(D) An accomplishment is especially impressive.

94. What did the speaker make copies of?

(A) A list of incomplete tasks
(B) Images of similar products
(C) The floor plan of a building
(D) A recent journal article

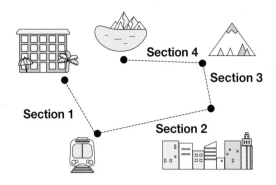

Video	Length
▶ Choosing the Right Guitar	11:25
▶ Improve your Strumming Technique	6:10
▶ Practice Exercises for Beginners	14:35
▶ How to Hold the Pick	4:50
⋮	

95. What does the speaker say will happen today?

(A) Snow will fall periodically.
(B) A road will be resurfaced.
(C) A public facility will reopen.
(D) A competition will begin.

96. Look at the graphic. Which section of the route does the speaker warn the listeners about?

(A) Section 1
(B) Section 2
(C) Section 3
(D) Section 4

97. What are the listeners asked to do?

(A) Hold on to their belongings
(B) Silence their mobile phones
(C) Press a button before their stop
(D) Move to the back of the vehicle

98. Look at the graphic. What is the length of the video that the speaker recommends?

(A) 11:25
(B) 6:10
(C) 14:35
(D) 4:50

99. Who most likely is Natalie Newman?

(A) The composer of a song
(B) A recording studio owner
(C) A professional videographer
(D) A fan of the speaker's videos

100. What does the speaker encourage the listeners to give him?

(A) Positive ratings
(B) Topic suggestions
(C) Monetary donations
(D) Used musical instruments

This is the end of the Listening test.

YBM
실전토익
LC 1000

테스트 전 체크리스트

- 중간 휴식 없이 제한 시간을 지켜서 풀이하세요.
- 제한 시간은 답안지에 마킹하는 시간도 포함시켜야 합니다.
- 찍은 문제는 번호 옆에 꼭 체크해 주세요.
- 시간 안에 풀지 못한 문제는 틀린 것으로 채점해 주세요.

LC

TEST 5

LISTENING TEST

In the Listening test, you will be asked to demonstrate how well you understand spoken English. The entire Listening test will last approximately 45 minutes. There are four parts, and directions are given for each part. You must mark your answers on the separate answer sheet. Do not write your answers in your test book.

PART 1

Directions: For each question in this part, you will hear four statements about a picture in your test book. When you hear the statements, you must select the one statement that best describes what you see in the picture. Then find the number of the question on your answer sheet and mark your answer. The statements will not be printed in your test book and will be spoken only one time.

Statement (C), "They're sitting at a table," is the best description of the picture, so you should select answer (C) and mark it on your answer sheet.

1.

2.

GO ON TO THE NEXT PAGE

TEST 5

3.

4.

5.

6.

GO ON TO THE NEXT PAGE

TEST 5

PART 2

Directions: You will hear a question or statement and three responses spoken in English. They will not be printed in your test book and will be spoken only one time. Select the best response to the question or statement and mark the letter (A), (B), or (C) on your answer sheet.

7. Mark your answer on your answer sheet.

8. Mark your answer on your answer sheet.

9. Mark your answer on your answer sheet.

10. Mark your answer on your answer sheet.

11. Mark your answer on your answer sheet.

12. Mark your answer on your answer sheet.

13. Mark your answer on your answer sheet.

14. Mark your answer on your answer sheet.

15. Mark your answer on your answer sheet.

16. Mark your answer on your answer sheet.

17. Mark your answer on your answer sheet.

18. Mark your answer on your answer sheet.

19. Mark your answer on your answer sheet.

20. Mark your answer on your answer sheet.

21. Mark your answer on your answer sheet.

22. Mark your answer on your answer sheet.

23. Mark your answer on your answer sheet.

24. Mark your answer on your answer sheet.

25. Mark your answer on your answer sheet.

26. Mark your answer on your answer sheet.

27. Mark your answer on your answer sheet.

28. Mark your answer on your answer sheet.

29. Mark your answer on your answer sheet.

30. Mark your answer on your answer sheet.

31. Mark your answer on your answer sheet.

32. What did the man just do?
    (A) He selected a rental car.
    (B) He changed a travel itinerary.
    (C) He upgraded a hotel reservation.
    (D) He approved some vacation time.

33. What does the man remind the woman about?
    (A) Weighing her luggage carefully
    (B) Purchasing some travel insurance
    (C) Saving receipts for purchases
    (D) Bringing a company credit card

34. What does the woman inquire about?
    (A) A job requirement
    (B) A dining establishment
    (C) A business center
    (D) A shuttle service

35. What industry do the speakers most likely work in?
    (A) Finance
    (B) Publishing
    (C) Technology
    (D) Pharmaceutical

36. What does the man suggest doing?
    (A) Consulting employees from other branches
    (B) Giving demonstrations in the store
    (C) Creating a smartphone application for customers
    (D) Featuring an item in a magazine advertisement

37. What is the woman worried about?
    (A) The business will relocate soon.
    (B) The suggested plan will cost too much.
    (C) An activity requires too much space.
    (D) A room needs to be redecorated.

38. Why does the man want to order a cake for Ms. Wilkins?
    (A) She has received an award.
    (B) She will celebrate her birthday.
    (C) She has recently been promoted.
    (D) She will leave the company soon.

39. According to the woman, where is Maxwell Bakery?
    (A) Across from a pharmacy
    (B) Next to the office
    (C) In a shopping mall
    (D) Behind a bank

40. What does the man plan to do before taking a lunch break?
    (A) Ask Ms. Wilkins for a preference
    (B) Check a department's budget
    (C) Set up a job interview
    (D) Review some documents

41. Where do the speakers most likely work?
    (A) At a real estate agency
    (B) At a cleaning service
    (C) At a moving company
    (D) At an architecture firm

42. What problem do the women mention?
    (A) Some employees do not have enough experience.
    (B) The area has been experiencing bad weather.
    (C) A requested item is not currently available.
    (D) Potential clients are considering other options.

43. What does the man suggest doing?
    (A) Canceling a business contract
    (B) Offering a free service
    (C) Updating a software package
    (D) Extending a proposed deadline

GO ON TO THE NEXT PAGE

44. Where most likely are the speakers?

(A) At a shipping company
(B) At a clothing shop
(C) At a fitness club
(D) At a dry cleaner's

45. Why does the woman say, "there are not many apartment buildings around here"?

(A) To explain why a closing time is earlier
(B) To suggest searching for a new home
(C) To complain about a long commute
(D) To apologize for a lack of available parking

46. What will happen tomorrow?

(A) Staff evaluations will be carried out.
(B) Some employees will attend a meeting.
(C) A new company policy will go into effect.
(D) A staff member will transfer from another branch.

47. Where does the woman work?

(A) At a department store
(B) At a law office
(C) At a recruitment firm
(D) At an art institute

48. Why is the man unable to use a service on June 5 ?

(A) Some employees will be trained.
(B) Some tiles will be repaired.
(C) An entrance will be blocked.
(D) A schedule is already full.

49. What will the man most likely do next?

(A) Select a payment method
(B) Provide a list of attendees
(C) Confirm a mailing address
(D) Wait for some information

50. What problem are the speakers discussing?

(A) An order for supplies is not being processed.
(B) An employee handbook is missing information.
(C) Some equipment has broken components.
(D) Some team members were not assigned tasks.

51. Who most likely is the man?

(A) A product designer
(B) A sales manager
(C) A company accountant
(D) A delivery person

52. What will the women most likely do next?

(A) Update their computer passwords
(B) Read some work-related messages
(C) Depart for a business trip
(D) Print a budget report

53. Who is the man?

(A) A caterer
(B) A driver
(C) A journalist
(D) A florist

54. Why does the woman say, "We signed a contract with Newton Services"?

(A) To reject an offer
(B) To apologize for a delay
(C) To recommend a company
(D) To reassure the man

55. What does the woman ask the man to do?

(A) Plan an orientation session
(B) Fulfill a last-minute request
(C) Suggest a day to meet
(D) Provide a bulk discount

56. Which industry do the speakers most likely work in?

(A) Interior design
(B) Construction
(C) Film production
(D) Tourism

57. What is the man concerned about?

(A) Saving space
(B) Maintaining authenticity
(C) Reducing expenses
(D) Following regulations

58. What does the woman ask the man to do?

(A) Look into hiring some temporary workers
(B) Perform photo editing on some images
(C) Research architecture in the area
(D) Find some colors to match a logo

---

59. Why did the woman visit the man's business?

(A) To repair some cooking equipment
(B) To share her opinions about products
(C) To meet with some investors
(D) To lead a business strategy seminar

60. What does the man ask the woman to put on?

(A) A staff uniform
(B) An ID badge
(C) A safety vest
(D) A hard hat

61. What will the woman probably do next?

(A) Take a building tour
(B) Enjoy a meal
(C) Sign some paperwork
(D) Provide her contact information

Development Process

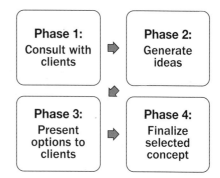

62. What is the conversation mainly about?

(A) Hiring methods
(B) Vehicle designs
(C) Safety regulations
(D) Marketing plans

63. Look at the graphic. What phase is the project currently in?

(A) Phase 1
(B) Phase 2
(C) Phase 3
(D) Phase 4

64. What does the man say he has to do today?

(A) Arrange a quality inspection
(B) Approve some legal agreements
(C) Draft a financial report
(D) Check the business's inventory

GO ON TO THE NEXT PAGE

Invitation: First draft

Date: Saturday, December 7
Location: Hillhaven Banquet Hall

✳ ✳ ✳

- 6:30 P.M. Dinner
- 7:30 P.M. Main Program
- 8:30 P.M. Live Music
- 9:30 P.M. Photo Slideshow

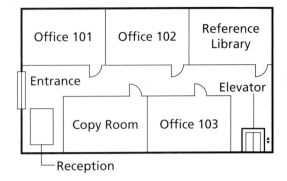

65. What kind of event is being planned?

    (A) A coworker's birthday celebration
    (B) A company awards ceremony
    (C) A new employee training session
    (D) A colleague's retirement dinner

66. Look at the graphic. What time does the man think the photo slideshow should begin?

    (A) At 6:30 P.M.
    (B) At 7:30 P.M.
    (C) At 8:30 P.M.
    (D) At 9:30 P.M.

67. What does the man suggest adding to the invitation?

    (A) A list of menu options
    (B) The venue's phone number
    (C) Some driving directions
    (D) Some employees' job titles

68. Why is the man visiting the business?

    (A) To pick up some brochures
    (B) To give a sales pitch
    (C) To sign a contract
    (D) To make a repair

69. Look at the graphic. Where does the woman direct the man to go?

    (A) Office 101
    (B) Office 102
    (C) Office 103
    (D) Copy room

70. What does the woman ask the man to do?

    (A) Avoid using an elevator
    (B) Return a badge later
    (C) Leave his business card
    (D) Remove his outerwear

Directions: You will hear some talks given by a single speaker. You will be asked to answer three questions about what the speaker says in each talk. Select the best response to each question and mark the letter (A), (B), (C), or (D) on your answer sheet. The talks will not be printed in your test book and will be spoken only one time.

71. What does the speaker's company produce?
   (A) Exercise equipment
   (B) Light fixtures
   (C) Automobiles
   (D) Beverages

72. What does the speaker remind the listeners to do?
   (A) Check some expiration dates
   (B) Update their contact information
   (C) Review a purchasing agreement
   (D) Record their working hours

73. What can be found in the main corridor?
   (A) A collection container
   (B) A box of tools
   (C) An order form
   (D) An employee directory

74. What will the speaker do at the community center?
   (A) Serve some food samples
   (B) Give a public speech
   (C) Take people's photographs
   (D) Advertise a family vacation

75. Why does the speaker say, "I can see several power outlets"?
   (A) To reject an offer of assistance
   (B) To provide reassurance to the listener
   (C) To complain about an unfinished task
   (D) To ask for some clarification

76. What does the speaker remind the listener to do?
   (A) Proofread some brochures
   (B) Post some information online
   (C) Fill out a reimbursement request
   (D) Renew a business license

77. What did Rinehart Manufacturing recently do?
   (A) It passed an annual factory safety inspection.
   (B) It changed the location of its headquarters.
   (C) It hired a new CEO to lead the company.
   (D) It introduced a popular new line of products.

78. What kind of product does Rinehart Manufacturing make?
   (A) Tools
   (B) Automobiles
   (C) Clothing
   (D) Appliances

79. What can the listeners find online?
   (A) Some job descriptions
   (B) Some driving directions
   (C) An updated staff directory
   (D) A collection of images

80. What event is taking place?
   (A) A retirement party
   (B) A company picnic
   (C) A grand opening
   (D) A writing competition

81. What kind of business does Mr. Rowley most likely own?
   (A) An electronics store
   (B) A clothing shop
   (C) A car dealership
   (D) An insurance company

82. What has the speaker prepared for attendees?
   (A) Some tote bags
   (B) Some pens
   (C) Some business cards
   (D) Some printed calendars

TEST 5

GO ON TO THE NEXT PAGE

83. Where do the listeners work?

  (A) At a fitness facility
  (B) At a clothing store
  (C) At a dental clinic
  (D) At a financial institution

84. What does the speaker imply when she says, "Five or six would be better"?

  (A) The length of an event is too short.
  (B) A task requires more people.
  (C) More tables need to be set up.
  (D) Pages should be added to a tour brochure.

85. What will the listeners probably do next?

  (A) Watch a sales presentation
  (B) Enjoy some free refreshments
  (C) Sign a membership contract
  (D) Share some of their suggestions

86. What is scheduled for next Monday?

  (A) A group interview session
  (B) A corporate board meeting
  (C) An annual factory inspection
  (D) An industry trade fair

87. Why does the speaker say, "this device will be the first of its kind"?

  (A) To express confidence in a proposal
  (B) To request more time for a project
  (C) To show concern about an investment
  (D) To correct an error in a business report

88. What does the speaker say about Carl?

  (A) He was involved in recruiting members.
  (B) He has given a demonstration for a device.
  (C) He will be the director of a project.
  (D) He can provide some helpful advice.

89. What kind of business does the speaker most likely work for?

  (A) A home improvement store
  (B) A flower shop
  (C) A jewelry store
  (D) A hair salon

90. What is the speaker concerned about?

  (A) Several nearby roads will be closed.
  (B) Some merchandise was damaged in transit.
  (C) An advertising campaign was expensive.
  (D) Competition in the market has increased.

91. What does the speaker say he will do?

  (A) Purchase more attractive display cases
  (B) Hire an experienced marketing consultant
  (C) Offer a discount to new customers
  (D) Provide free shipping on all orders

92. Where is the announcement taking place?

  (A) At a repair shop
  (B) At a construction site
  (C) At an airport
  (D) At a warehouse

93. Where should some listeners go after completing their shifts?

  (A) To the security desk
  (B) To the loading dock
  (C) To the speaker's office
  (D) To the conference room

94. What will happen on Wednesday?

  (A) A training session will be held.
  (B) A new policy will be implemented.
  (C) Some electronic equipment will be purchased.
  (D) Some promotions will be announced.

Date	Event
Saturday, September 9	Company picnic
Wednesday, September 27	Board meeting
Friday, October 6	Retirement party
Thursday, October 19	Awards dinner

95. Why does the speaker praise the listeners?

(A) Some invitations are attractive.
(B) Some tasks were done in a short time.
(C) The company saved some money.
(D) An executive enjoyed an event.

96. Look at the graphic. Which date is no longer correct?

(A) September 9
(B) September 27
(C) October 6
(D) October 19

97. What does the speaker ask Damien to do with a coworker?

(A) Choose a venue
(B) Work on a presentation
(C) Search for some decorations
(D) Draft a guest list

Summary of Fees		Due
Deposit:	$350	June 8
Site assessment:	$90	June 15
Filing:	$35	June 15
Phase 1:	$1,200	June 21

98. Who most likely is the speaker?

(A) A real estate agent
(B) A building contractor
(C) A vehicle repair person
(D) A corporate attorney

99. Look at the graphic. Which fee must be paid online?

(A) Deposit
(B) Site assessment
(C) Filing
(D) Phase 1

100. What service does the speaker tell the listener about?

(A) A free color consultation
(B) An extended warranty
(C) An annual membership
(D) An overnight delivery

This is the end of the Listening test.

YBM
실전토익
LC 1000

테스트 전 체크리스트

- 중간 휴식 없이 제한 시간을 지켜서 풀이하세요.
- 제한 시간은 답안지에 마킹하는 시간도 포함시켜야 합니다.
- 찍은 문제는 번호 옆에 꼭 체크해 주세요.
- 시간 안에 풀지 못한 문제는 틀린 것으로 채점해 주세요.

LC

TEST 6

LISTENING TEST

In the Listening test, you will be asked to demonstrate how well you understand spoken English. The entire Listening test will last approximately 45 minutes. There are four parts, and directions are given for each part. You must mark your answers on the separate answer sheet. Do not write your answers in your test book.

PART 1

Directions: For each question in this part, you will hear four statements about a picture in your test book. When you hear the statements, you must select the one statement that best describes what you see in the picture. Then find the number of the question on your answer sheet and mark your answer. The statements will not be printed in your test book and will be spoken only one time.

Statement (C), "They're sitting at a table," is the best description of the picture, so you should select answer (C) and mark it on your answer sheet.

1.

2.

GO ON TO THE NEXT PAGE

TEST 6

3.

4.

5.

6.

GO ON TO THE NEXT PAGE

PART 2

Directions: You will hear a question or statement and three responses spoken in English. They will not be printed in your test book and will be spoken only one time. Select the best response to the question or statement and mark the letter (A), (B), or (C) on your answer sheet.

7. Mark your answer on your answer sheet.

8. Mark your answer on your answer sheet.

9. Mark your answer on your answer sheet.

10. Mark your answer on your answer sheet.

11. Mark your answer on your answer sheet.

12. Mark your answer on your answer sheet.

13. Mark your answer on your answer sheet.

14. Mark your answer on your answer sheet.

15. Mark your answer on your answer sheet.

16. Mark your answer on your answer sheet.

17. Mark your answer on your answer sheet.

18. Mark your answer on your answer sheet.

19. Mark your answer on your answer sheet.

20. Mark your answer on your answer sheet.

21. Mark your answer on your answer sheet.

22. Mark your answer on your answer sheet.

23. Mark your answer on your answer sheet.

24. Mark your answer on your answer sheet.

25. Mark your answer on your answer sheet.

26. Mark your answer on your answer sheet.

27. Mark your answer on your answer sheet.

28. Mark your answer on your answer sheet.

29. Mark your answer on your answer sheet.

30. Mark your answer on your answer sheet.

31. Mark your answer on your answer sheet.

PART 3

Directions: You will hear some conversations between two or more people. You will be asked to answer three questions about what the speakers say in each conversation. Select the best response to each question and mark the letter (A), (B), (C), or (D) on your answer sheet. The conversations will not be printed in your test book and will be spoken only one time.

32. Why is the man calling the woman?
    (A) To receive help with a technical issue
    (B) To ask her to make an announcement
    (C) To explain why he missed a meeting
    (D) To confirm that he read a message

33. What does the woman inform the man about?
    (A) A sales catalog has not been updated.
    (B) A computer system is currently down.
    (C) A request must be approved by a supervisor.
    (D) A new version of some software is available.

34. What does the woman say she will have to do?
    (A) Wait until tomorrow to start a task
    (B) Look through a product manual
    (C) Visit the man's workstation
    (D) Dispose of some equipment

35. What does the woman want to do?
    (A) Rent some bicycles
    (B) Purchase some parts
    (C) Check on a repair
    (D) Join a riding club

36. Why does the man apologize?
    (A) A message was not sent.
    (B) A shelf was not restocked.
    (C) The business is closed.
    (D) A sign is wrong.

37. What will the man most likely do next?
    (A) Go to the front entrance
    (B) Search a stockroom
    (C) Consult with a mechanic
    (D) Wait at a checkout counter

38. What is the man doing this month?
    (A) Taking a group vacation
    (B) Celebrating an anniversary
    (C) Putting up holiday decorations
    (D) Organizing an athletic event

39. What concern does the man express?
    (A) His order arrived later than scheduled.
    (B) A product is the wrong size.
    (C) Some purchased items are missing.
    (D) Some boxes broke open.

40. What does Sheila explain to the man?
    (A) How to repair some damage
    (B) How shipments are packed
    (C) How to request a refund
    (D) How long a process took

41. What industry do the speakers work in?
    (A) Electronics
    (B) Cosmetics
    (C) Clothing
    (D) Pharmaceutical

42. Why did the company change its product packaging?
    (A) To make the packaging easier to remove
    (B) To prevent damage to some goods
    (C) To reduce production expenses
    (D) To become more environmentally friendly

43. What will the woman most likely do in her replies to some reviews?
    (A) Offer a one-time discount
    (B) Post a link to a Web page
    (C) Direct customers to a help line
    (D) Express gratitude for feedback

GO ON TO THE NEXT PAGE

44. What type of business do the speakers most likely work at?

(A) An advertising agency
(B) An accounting firm
(C) An insurance company
(D) A career coaching service

45. What does the man most likely mean when he says, "A lot of employees are remote now"?

(A) Some office space could be used in a different way.
(B) A company event might not be well-attended.
(C) Fewer supplies will be needed for a break room.
(D) It will be difficult to train some new staff members.

46. What does the woman decide to do?

(A) Send out a survey
(B) Plan a virtual celebration
(C) Make revisions to a food order
(D) Ask a question to an executive

47. What do the men like about the exposition?

(A) It lasts for several days.
(B) Its organizers are responsive.
(C) Its layout is convenient.
(D) It has many vendors.

48. What does the woman sell?

(A) Heavy machinery
(B) Building materials
(C) Safety gear
(D) Hand tools

49. What does the woman ask the men about?

(A) The brand of products they currently use
(B) Their desired product specifications
(C) The number of products they need
(D) Their interest in a product demonstration

50. What are the speakers mainly discussing?

(A) Choosing a venue for a talk
(B) Arranging renovations to a building
(C) Becoming investors in a business
(D) Finding a tenant for a property

51. According to the man, what might cause a problem?

(A) A lack of access to public transportation
(B) A scheduling conflict
(C) A disruptive noise
(D) Confusion about some regulations

52. What does the woman warn the man about?

(A) Some earnings may be low.
(B) A manager may reject a proposal.
(C) It will take time to collect some data.
(D) A location may need to be changed.

53. Why is the woman calling the man?

(A) To discuss a potential deal
(B) To inquire about a job applicant
(C) To announce a price change
(D) To extend an event invitation

54. What does the man's company do?

(A) International travel planning
(B) Audio content creation
(C) Foreign language education
(D) Recording equipment manufacturing

55. What does the woman say about Sonore Group?

(A) It has a large customer base.
(B) It has offices throughout the area.
(C) It has a lot of relevant experience.
(D) It has a prestigious certification.

56. Who most likely is the man?

    (A) A university employee
    (B) A television reporter
    (C) A public librarian
    (D) A newspaper editor

57. What does the woman mention about her industry?

    (A) It is not related to her degree.
    (B) It is difficult to enter.
    (C) It is predicted to grow.
    (D) It has not existed for long.

58. What does the woman agree to do?

    (A) Sign a consent form
    (B) Pose for a photograph
    (C) Write an opinion column
    (D) Provide some contact information

---

59. What problem does the man describe?

    (A) A colleague has gone on leave.
    (B) A member of his family has been injured.
    (C) A medication is not working.
    (D) A speaker has canceled.

60. Why most likely does the woman say, "Dr. Diaz is the best-rated surgeon in the area"?

    (A) To show surprise
    (B) To refuse an offer
    (C) To make a suggestion
    (D) To complain about a decision

61. What does the man say he will do next?

    (A) Update a Web site
    (B) Reschedule an appointment
    (C) Send a message to Dr. Diaz
    (D) Research a surgical procedure

#2061

• short, square
• 2 shelves
• swinging door

#2077

• short, wide
• 2 shelves
• 2 sliding doors

#2084

• tall, thin
• 3 shelves
• swinging door

#2095

• tall, thin
• 3 shelves
• swinging door
• display part on top

62. According to the woman, what happened recently?

    (A) A refrigerator broke down.
    (B) The business's sales decreased.
    (C) New countertops were installed.
    (D) The weather changed.

63. Look at the graphic. Which refrigerator will the man order?

    (A) #2061
    (B) #2077
    (C) #2084
    (D) #2095

64. What does the woman suggest about some drinks?

    (A) They should be inexpensive.
    (B) They should promote health.
    (C) They should have a variety of flavors.
    (D) They should come in small containers.

GO ON TO THE NEXT PAGE

Orientation Packet

Item 1 – Welcome Message
Item 2 – Organization Chart
Item 3 – Employee Handbook
Item 4 – Human Resources Paperwork
Item 5 – Workstation Setup
        Instructions

RECEIPT

Item	Quantity	Price
Bananas	1	$3.00
Spinach	1	$4.50
Avocados	3	$6.30
Watermelon	2	$10.10
		Total: $23.90

65. What kind of business do the speakers work for?

(A) An accounting firm
(B) A graphic design company
(C) A translation service
(D) A travel agency

66. What does the woman say she learned in a previous job?

(A) How to set work performance goals
(B) How to recruit talented job candidates
(C) How to ensure an orientation is thorough
(D) How to keep employee information confidential

67. Look at the graphic. Which item in the orientation packet does the man express concern about?

(A) Item 2
(B) Item 3
(C) Item 4
(D) Item 5

68. What problem does the woman describe?

(A) A checkout machine is malfunctioning.
(B) An item's quantity was entered incorrectly.
(C) An available discount was not applied.
(D) Some fruit is in poor condition.

69. Look at the graphic. Which amount will be partially refunded?

(A) $3.00
(B) $4.50
(C) $6.30
(D) $10.10

70. What does the man ask the woman for?

(A) A coupon code
(B) A container of produce
(C) A rewards card
(D) A payment method

PART 4

Directions: You will hear some talks given by a single speaker. You will be asked to answer three questions about what the speaker says in each talk. Select the best response to each question and mark the letter (A), (B), (C), or (D) on your answer sheet. The talks will not be printed in your test book and will be spoken only one time.

71. Who is the speaker calling?
    (A) A publicist
    (B) A graphic designer
    (C) A property manager
    (D) A corporate attorney

72. What is the speaker concerned about?
    (A) The terms of a contract
    (B) A building directory
    (C) A logo design
    (D) A shipping method

73. What does the speaker say about Rinford Services?
    (A) It is in a different field.
    (B) It was recently founded.
    (C) It is based overseas.
    (D) It is well-known.

74. What most likely is being advertised?
    (A) A construction company
    (B) A real estate Web site
    (C) A hardware store
    (D) An interior design firm

75. What is the business known for?
    (A) Its pricing
    (B) Its speed
    (C) Its creativity
    (D) Its customer service

76. What does the speaker say is on a Web site?
    (A) Hours of operation
    (B) Details about a sale
    (C) Pictures of houses
    (D) Positive reviews

77. Where most likely does the speaker work?
    (A) At a hair salon
    (B) At a dentist's office
    (C) At an auto repair shop
    (D) At a dry cleaning business

78. What is the speaker calling about?
    (A) An appliance delivery
    (B) A customer appointment
    (C) A safety inspection
    (D) A job interview

79. Why does the speaker say, "It can be hard to find parking around here"?
    (A) To explain a recommendation
    (B) To justify an expense
    (C) To express doubt about a plan
    (D) To request patience with a delay

80. What is the focus of the episode?
    (A) Developing a mobile application
    (B) Taking advantage of a new technology
    (C) Selecting a training program
    (D) Evaluating job candidates

81. What does the speaker say is important?
    (A) Conducting thorough research
    (B) Specifying a set of goals
    (C) Joining an industry association
    (D) Asking others for recommendations

82. Who most likely is Hinata Kondo?
    (A) A professional recruiter
    (B) An online journalist
    (C) A business consultant
    (D) A computer programmer

GO ON TO THE NEXT PAGE

83. Where is the tour taking place?

(A) At a city zoo
(B) At a national park
(C) At a vegetable farm
(D) At a historical site

84. What does the speaker tell the listeners to do during a drive?

(A) Refrain from speaking
(B) Handle some electronics carefully
(C) Watch out for some animals
(D) Leave their seat belts on

85. According to a speaker, what is shown on a handout?

(A) A route map
(B) Meal options
(C) Operating instructions
(D) Images of plants

---

86. What does the speaker imply when she says, "you can't get that online"?

(A) It is becoming difficult to obtain some merchandise.
(B) She is proud of the high-quality service provided at the store.
(C) Some news has not been communicated to the public yet.
(D) The company will differentiate itself from some competitors.

87. What is the main topic of the announcement?

(A) A revision to a corporate policy
(B) The relocation of a store branch
(C) A search for a new supplier
(D) The launch of a marketing campaign

88. What are some of the listeners asked to do?

(A) Check some inventory
(B) Visit some retail spaces
(C) Join a committee
(D) Set up a display

---

89. What event is taking place?

(A) A community fund-raiser
(B) A going-away party
(C) An awards dinner
(D) A press conference

90. What does the speaker praise Angela Thorne for?

(A) Improving a workplace's culture
(B) Increasing awareness of a local issue
(C) Forming an effective project team
(D) Managing a budget wisely

91. What does the speaker say he has done?

(A) Prepared a visual presentation
(B) Invited another person to speak
(C) Made a charitable donation
(D) Purchased a personal gift

---

92. What did the speaker recently do?

(A) She took a factory tour.
(B) She read a journal article.
(C) She spoke with some workers.
(D) She hosted some visitors.

93. What does the speaker's company make?

(A) Musical instruments
(B) Sporting goods
(C) Snack foods
(D) Wooden furniture

94. What does the speaker mean when she says, "I'm not an architect"?

(A) She does not know if a proposal is reasonable.
(B) She will need assistance with an assignment.
(C) She is not interested in the details of a building plan.
(D) She is concerned that the listeners have been misled.

Venegas Fashion Store

Staff Development Day

Introduction to Upcoming Products   1:00 P.M.

Good Customer Service   2:00 P.M.

How to Arrange Displays   3:00 P.M.

Career Paths at Venegas Fashion   4:00 P.M.

Main Reason for Cancellation

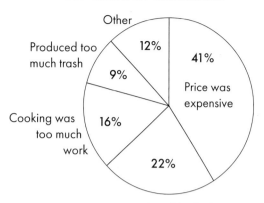

Did not like the food

95. What are the listeners asked to do?

(A) Put on name tags
(B) Silence their mobile phones
(C) Sign an attendance sheet
(D) Take their seats

96. Look at the graphic. Which workshop will be shorter than the others?

(A) Introduction to Upcoming Products
(B) Good Customer Service
(C) How to Arrange Displays
(D) Career Paths at Venegas Fashion

97. According to the speaker, what will Ms. Ikeda do?

(A) Make an audio recording
(B) Give a short speech
(C) Lead one of the workshops
(D) Distribute an employee survey

98. What does the speaker mention about the survey?

(A) It has been simplified.
(B) It does not receive many responses.
(C) A question has been added to it.
(D) It is delivered by e-mail.

99. Look at the graphic. Which figure does the speaker call attention to?

(A) 41%
(B) 22%
(C) 16%
(D) 9%

100. What will the listeners most likely do next?

(A) Divide into groups
(B) Look at more data
(C) Sample some food
(D) Give their opinions

This is the end of the Listening test.

YBM
실전토익
LC 1000

테스트 전 체크리스트

- 중간 휴식 없이 제한 시간을 지켜서 풀이하세요.
- 제한 시간은 답안지에 마킹하는 시간도 포함시켜야 합니다.
- 찍은 문제는 번호 옆에 꼭 체크해 주세요.
- 시간 안에 풀지 못한 문제는 틀린 것으로 채점해 주세요.

LC

TEST 7

LISTENING TEST

In the Listening test, you will be asked to demonstrate how well you understand spoken English. The entire Listening test will last approximately 45 minutes. There are four parts, and directions are given for each part. You must mark your answers on the separate answer sheet. Do not write your answers in your test book.

PART 1

Directions: For each question in this part, you will hear four statements about a picture in your test book. When you hear the statements, you must select the one statement that best describes what you see in the picture. Then find the number of the question on your answer sheet and mark your answer. The statements will not be printed in your test book and will be spoken only one time.

Statement (C), "They're sitting at a table," is the best description of the picture, so you should select answer (C) and mark it on your answer sheet.

1.

2.

GO ON TO THE NEXT PAGE

3.

4.

5.

6.

GO ON TO THE NEXT PAGE

PART 2

Directions: You will hear a question or statement and three responses spoken in English. They will not be printed in your test book and will be spoken only one time. Select the best response to the question or statement and mark the letter (A), (B), or (C) on your answer sheet.

7. Mark your answer on your answer sheet.

8. Mark your answer on your answer sheet.

9. Mark your answer on your answer sheet.

10. Mark your answer on your answer sheet.

11. Mark your answer on your answer sheet.

12. Mark your answer on your answer sheet.

13. Mark your answer on your answer sheet.

14. Mark your answer on your answer sheet.

15. Mark your answer on your answer sheet.

16. Mark your answer on your answer sheet.

17. Mark your answer on your answer sheet.

18. Mark your answer on your answer sheet.

19. Mark your answer on your answer sheet.

20. Mark your answer on your answer sheet.

21. Mark your answer on your answer sheet.

22. Mark your answer on your answer sheet.

23. Mark your answer on your answer sheet.

24. Mark your answer on your answer sheet.

25. Mark your answer on your answer sheet.

26. Mark your answer on your answer sheet.

27. Mark your answer on your answer sheet.

28. Mark your answer on your answer sheet.

29. Mark your answer on your answer sheet.

30. Mark your answer on your answer sheet.

31. Mark your answer on your answer sheet.

PART 3

Directions: You will hear some conversations between two or more people. You will be asked to answer three questions about what the speakers say in each conversation. Select the best response to each question and mark the letter (A), (B), (C), or (D) on your answer sheet. The conversations will not be printed in your test book and will be spoken only one time.

32. Where does the man most likely work?

(A) At a real estate company
(B) At an art auction house
(C) At a non-profit organization
(D) At a financial institution

33. What does the woman express concern about?

(A) The lack of after-hours staff
(B) The risk of damage to items
(C) The cost of hosting an event
(D) The timeline for getting approval

34. What does the woman suggest that the man do?

(A) Decorate a room
(B) Review the museum's policies
(C) Submit a proposal
(D) Attend a board meeting

35. What does the woman need a suitcase for?

(A) A family trip
(B) A friend's birthday
(C) A business trip
(D) A house move

36. What does the woman dislike about the display suitcase?

(A) Its size
(B) Its pattern
(C) Its price
(D) Its fabric

37. According to the man, what is included in the price?

(A) Spare wheels
(B) A tracking device
(C) Free shipping
(D) A warranty

38. What task is the man in charge of?

(A) Organizing a trade fair schedule
(B) Planning a staff retreat
(C) Analyzing customer feedback
(D) Recruiting new company employees

39. What does the woman want to do on August 4 ?

(A) Give out achievement awards
(B) Introduce some new products
(C) Lead a team-building activity
(D) Answer questions from the staff

40. What is the woman asked to do?

(A) Review employee performance
(B) Check a list of attendees
(C) Give a welcome address
(D) Provide a time estimate

41. What does the woman have to prepare for?

(A) A session to test new products
(B) An inspection by a government official
(C) A visit from potential investors
(D) A training workshop for employees

42. Who most likely is the man?

(A) A company owner
(B) A computer technician
(C) A financial advisor
(D) A sales director

43. What does the woman plan to give the man on Thursday morning?

(A) A hard drive
(B) A meeting agenda
(C) A lunch menu
(D) A cost estimate

GO ON TO THE NEXT PAGE

44. What kind of product does the speakers'
    company most likely sell?
    (A) Gardening equipment
    (B) Casual clothing
    (C) Kitchen appliances
    (D) Light fixtures

45. Why is the woman surprised?
    (A) The man could not access a database.
    (B) The man requested a deadline
        extension.
    (C) The price of some items has changed.
    (D) Some devices use a lot of energy.

46. Why does the woman say, "I just saw her go
    into her office"?
    (A) To suggest discussing an issue with a
        supervisor
    (B) To indicate that a meeting has finished
        early
    (C) To express disagreement about an
        absence
    (D) To confirm that a task has been
        completed

47. What does the woman imply when she says,
    "These reports are not urgent"?
    (A) She wants to rearrange a schedule.
    (B) She does not need the man's
        assistance.
    (C) She can respond to a question.
    (D) She plans to take a day off.

48. What did the man notice about some
    shampoo?
    (A) Its bottles have cracked.
    (B) Its labels are faded.
    (C) Its appearance has changed.
    (D) Its ingredients are harmful.

49. What does the man suggest that the
    business do in the future?
    (A) Move items to a different place
    (B) Offer discounts to customers
    (C) Hire a full-time receptionist
    (D) Use a more reliable supplier

50. Who most likely is Amy Ogren?
    (A) An author
    (B) A librarian
    (C) A painter
    (D) A reporter

51. What does the woman mention about a
    committee?
    (A) It is recruiting new members.
    (B) It has rejected an order.
    (C) It must finalize a budget.
    (D) It meets every quarter.

52. What does the woman suggest doing?
    (A) Joining a waiting list
    (B) Signing up for a newsletter
    (C) Attending a monthly talk
    (D) Participating in a book club

53. Who is the man?
    (A) A politician
    (B) A banker
    (C) A lawyer
    (D) A journalist

54. Why does the man apologize?
    (A) A cost will be higher than expected.
    (B) A timeline was not explained well.
    (C) Some staff members are absent.
    (D) Some services are no longer available.

55. Why should Ms. Harper complete some
    paperwork?
    (A) To apply for a temporary position
    (B) To update her mailing address
    (C) To use an express service
    (D) To open a new account

56. According to the woman, what will happen in June?

(A) A product will go on the market.
(B) A new office will open overseas.
(C) A branch will undergo renovations.
(D) A staff member will be transferred.

57. What does the man want to know about?

(A) When an assignment must be submitted
(B) Where he should upload a file
(C) Who will be leading a project
(D) What is required for a position

58. What does the woman say the company will provide?

(A) Paid vacation days
(B) On-site meals
(C) A work vehicle
(D) A credit card

---

59. What industry do the speakers most likely work in?

(A) Architecture
(B) Tourism
(C) Agriculture
(D) Electronics

60. What does the woman say a project will do in the area?

(A) Protect historic buildings
(B) Promote local businesses
(C) Reduce travel times
(D) Increase tax revenue

61. What does Eric say needs to happen?

(A) Equipment needs to be rented.
(B) Materials need to be delivered.
(C) A team leader needs to be selected.
(D) Measurements need to be taken.

Section 1: Labels	Section 2: Markers	Section 3: Scissors	Section 4: Tape

62. Where does the conversation take place?

(A) At a gift shop
(B) At a warehouse
(C) At an office-supply store
(D) At a post office

63. Look at the graphic. Where will the tape be moved to?

(A) To section 1
(B) To section 2
(C) To section 3
(D) To section 4

64. What does the woman say her supervisor did for her?

(A) Let her borrow an item
(B) Showed her a storage area
(C) Approved a special request
(D) Packed some large boxes

GO ON TO THE NEXT PAGE

TEST 7

Provost Anniversary Dinner

Service	Cost
Food and servers	$8,175
Flowers	$1,750
Photography	$1,200
Live Music	$680
Total	$11,805

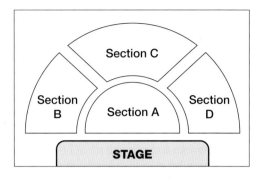

65. Look at the graphic. What was the fee for the services provided by the man?

(A) $8,175
(B) $1,750
(C) $1,200
(D) $680

66. Why does the man apologize to the woman?

(A) He did not answer a phone call.
(B) Some items were forgotten.
(C) A start time was delayed.
(D) An invoice contained an error.

67. What does the woman like about the hotel?

(A) It has affordable rental rates.
(B) It has a beautiful interior.
(C) It is near a major roadway.
(D) It has several meeting spaces.

68. What is the man surprised about?

(A) The woman has joined a jazz band.
(B) A group is offering a second performance.
(C) The price of some tickets has changed.
(D) A new venue for an event was announced.

69. Look at the graphic. For which section does the woman have tickets?

(A) Section A
(B) Section B
(C) Section C
(D) Section D

70. What will the woman do this Friday?

(A) Help her friend move
(B) Attend an art exhibition
(C) Host a holiday party
(D) Do some home repair tasks

PART 4

Directions: You will hear some talks given by a single speaker. You will be asked to answer three questions about what the speaker says in each talk. Select the best response to each question and mark the letter (A), (B), (C), or (D) on your answer sheet. The talks will not be printed in your test book and will be spoken only one time.

71. Where is the announcement taking place?

(A) At a public library
(B) At a history museum
(C) At a concert hall
(D) At a sports stadium

72. Why does the speaker apologize to the listeners?

(A) Some lights were malfunctioning.
(B) The building is hotter than usual.
(C) An event began later than scheduled.
(D) Some tickets had a misprint.

73. What is offered to the listeners?

(A) A discount coupon
(B) A partial refund
(C) A complimentary beverage
(D) A gift shop voucher

74. What type of business is the speaker most likely calling?

(A) An employment agency
(B) A vehicle repair shop
(C) A dental office
(D) A hair salon

75. What does the speaker mention about her appointment?

(A) It was booked with the wrong person.
(B) It has to be postponed.
(C) It must be at another branch.
(D) It includes a new customer discount.

76. What does the speaker want to find out about?

(A) Taking public transportation
(B) Updating insurance information
(C) Receiving an employee discount
(D) Handling unexpected charges

77. What is the advertisement about?

(A) An art festival
(B) A museum tour
(C) A boat ride
(D) A holiday parade

78. What will participants be given?

(A) A tote bag
(B) A prepared meal
(C) A group photograph
(D) An area map

79. What does the speaker say can be done on a Web site?

(A) Accessing a group discount
(B) Viewing videos of the area
(C) Making a dinner reservation
(D) Watching a safety video

80. Which department does the speaker work in?

(A) Human resources
(B) Building maintenance
(C) Research and development
(D) Information technology

81. Why does the speaker say, "we know that you're highly experienced"?

(A) To explain the reason for a promotion
(B) To accept a request for a pay raise
(C) To show understanding of a busy schedule
(D) To approve working remotely for a task

82. What does the speaker want to discuss with the listener?

(A) A start date
(B) A payment method
(C) Some necessary tools
(D) Some coworkers' skills

GO ON TO THE NEXT PAGE

TEST 7

83. What kind of event is taking place?

(A) A product launch
(B) A group interview session
(C) A medical conference
(D) A film festival

84. Why does the speaker say, "we've added an online option"?

(A) To encourage listeners to make a purchase
(B) To apologize for some technical difficulties
(C) To demonstrate that listeners' ideas are being used
(D) To explain why a group is smaller in size

85. What are the listeners asked to do?

(A) Turn off their phones temporarily
(B) Check the locations of some activities
(C) Complete a form to provide feedback
(D) Wear a name tag during the event

86. What kind of business does the speaker work for?

(A) A package delivery service
(B) A computer software distributor
(C) A fashion design company
(D) A flooring manufacturer

87. What advantage of the new material does the speaker mention?

(A) It is very durable.
(B) It is inexpensive.
(C) It is available in many sizes.
(D) It is good for the environment.

88. What will the speaker do next?

(A) Respond to listeners' questions
(B) Distribute a product catalog
(C) Show the listeners a chart
(D) Introduce one of her colleagues

89. What event does the speaker mention?

(A) A comedy show
(B) A graduation ceremony
(C) A theater performance
(D) A cooking competition

90. Why does the speaker say, "There will be plenty to go around"?

(A) To ask people to be patient when receiving items
(B) To confirm that the selected venue is large enough
(C) To explain that tickets will probably not sell out
(D) To encourage the listeners to attend an event

91. What will happen tomorrow?

(A) An enrollment period will begin.
(B) A discount on tickets will be offered.
(C) A Web site will be launched.
(D) A list of prizes will be announced.

92. According to the speaker, what is the purpose of the project?

(A) To cut public spending
(B) To promote a healthy habit
(C) To reduce road accidents
(D) To attract more businesses

93. Who will be targeted in an ad campaign?

(A) Students
(B) Business owners
(C) Tourists
(D) Prospective investors

94. What will happen next year?

(A) A communication network will be upgraded.
(B) An assessment will be carried out.
(C) Voters will elect a new mayor.
(D) The city will host a bicycle race.

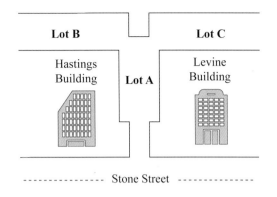

Lot B   Lot C

Hastings Building   Lot A   Levine Building

---------- Stone Street ----------

Interviews This Week	
Monday:	Ravi Dayal
Tuesday:	Maya Mendoza
Wednesday:	Kami Foster
Thursday:	Yun Bai – Part 1
Friday:	Yun Bai – Part 2

95. Who most likely is the listener?

(A) A potential customer
(B) A corporate trainer
(C) A truck driver
(D) A repair technician

96. What should the listener inform the speaker of?

(A) Her technology needs
(B) Her meal preference
(C) Her vehicle information
(D) Her expected arrival time

97. Look at the graphic. According to the speaker, where can visitors with parking permits park?

(A) In Lot A
(B) In Lot B
(C) In Lot C
(D) Along Stone Street

98. Why are guests included on the radio show?

(A) To offer financial advice
(B) To talk about business opportunities
(C) To provide health tips
(D) To discuss a hospital expansion

99. According to the speaker, what can listeners do on a Web site?

(A) Read product reviews from the host
(B) Enter an upcoming prize drawing
(C) Download full episodes of the show
(D) Get guests' contact details

100. Look at the graphic. When is this episode being broadcast?

(A) On Monday
(B) On Tuesday
(C) On Wednesday
(D) On Thursday

TEST 7

This is the end of the Listening test.

YBM
실전토익
LC 1000

테스트 전 체크리스트

- 중간 휴식 없이 제한 시간을 지켜서 풀이하세요.
- 제한 시간은 답안지에 마킹하는 시간도 포함시켜야 합니다.
- 찍은 문제는 번호 옆에 꼭 체크해 주세요.
- 시간 안에 풀지 못한 문제는 틀린 것으로 채점해 주세요.

LC

TEST 8

LISTENING TEST

In the Listening test, you will be asked to demonstrate how well you understand spoken English. The entire Listening test will last approximately 45 minutes. There are four parts, and directions are given for each part. You must mark your answers on the separate answer sheet. Do not write your answers in your test book.

PART 1

Directions: For each question in this part, you will hear four statements about a picture in your test book. When you hear the statements, you must select the one statement that best describes what you see in the picture. Then find the number of the question on your answer sheet and mark your answer. The statements will not be printed in your test book and will be spoken only one time.

Statement (C), "They're sitting at a table," is the best description of the picture, so you should select answer (C) and mark it on your answer sheet.

1.

2.

GO ON TO THE NEXT PAGE

3.

4.

5.

6.

GO ON TO THE NEXT PAGE ➡

TEST 8

PART 2

Directions: You will hear a question or statement and three responses spoken in English. They will not be printed in your test book and will be spoken only one time. Select the best response to the question or statement and mark the letter (A), (B), or (C) on your answer sheet.

7. Mark your answer on your answer sheet.

8. Mark your answer on your answer sheet.

9. Mark your answer on your answer sheet.

10. Mark your answer on your answer sheet.

11. Mark your answer on your answer sheet.

12. Mark your answer on your answer sheet.

13. Mark your answer on your answer sheet.

14. Mark your answer on your answer sheet.

15. Mark your answer on your answer sheet.

16. Mark your answer on your answer sheet.

17. Mark your answer on your answer sheet.

18. Mark your answer on your answer sheet.

19. Mark your answer on your answer sheet.

20. Mark your answer on your answer sheet.

21. Mark your answer on your answer sheet.

22. Mark your answer on your answer sheet.

23. Mark your answer on your answer sheet.

24. Mark your answer on your answer sheet.

25. Mark your answer on your answer sheet.

26. Mark your answer on your answer sheet.

27. Mark your answer on your answer sheet.

28. Mark your answer on your answer sheet.

29. Mark your answer on your answer sheet.

30. Mark your answer on your answer sheet.

31. Mark your answer on your answer sheet.

PART 3

Directions: You will hear some conversations between two or more people. You will be asked to answer three questions about what the speakers say in each conversation. Select the best response to each question and mark the letter (A), (B), (C), or (D) on your answer sheet. The conversations will not be printed in your test book and will be spoken only one time.

32. What are the speakers discussing?

(A) Appointing a spokesperson
(B) Relocating a storefront
(C) Postponing some repairs
(D) Meeting customer demand

33. What is the man concerned about?

(A) Paying for some expenses
(B) Unpredictable market trends
(C) Inconvenience to employees
(D) A decrease in product quality

34. What does the man suggest doing?

(A) Listing the steps of a process
(B) Determining a budget limit
(C) Involving staff in a decision
(D) Attending an upcoming event

35. What problem does the man report?

(A) He has run out of some meals.
(B) He is unfamiliar with some software.
(C) An Internet connection is slow.
(D) Some utensils are missing.

36. Who most likely are the speakers?

(A) Caterers
(B) Tour guides
(C) Flight attendants
(D) Conference organizers

37. What does the woman say she will try to do?

(A) Inform some coworkers
(B) Remember some seat locations
(C) Find an extra box of supplies
(D) Reset an electronic device

38. Who most likely is the man?

(A) A market researcher
(B) A cleaning professional
(C) A sales associate
(D) A business journalist

39. What does the woman say she likes about a briefcase?

(A) Its durable material
(B) Its large capacity
(C) Its attractive color
(D) Its reasonable price

40. What does the man recommend doing?

(A) Purchasing an extra item
(B) Visiting a special Web site
(C) Speaking with his colleague
(D) Trying out several briefcases

41. Where does the conversation most likely take place?

(A) On a train
(B) At a bus stop
(C) At a taxi stand
(D) In an elevator

42. What does the woman offer to do?

(A) Drive to a destination
(B) Check a mobile app
(C) Make a phone call
(D) Draw a map

43. What will Min-Jae ask his friend to do?

(A) Stand outside a venue
(B) Buy tickets for a show
(C) Choose dishes for a meal
(D) Confirm a street's name

GO ON TO THE NEXT PAGE

44. What did the woman do yesterday?
    (A) She drafted a project proposal.
    (B) She applied for a mentorship program.
    (C) She finished conducting some research.
    (D) She took a professional development seminar.

45. What kind of business do the speakers most likely work for?
    (A) An employment agency
    (B) A publishing company
    (C) An engineering firm
    (D) A financial institution

46. Why does the woman say, "this is my first time writing one"?
    (A) To express excitement
    (B) To request some assistance
    (C) To complain about an assignment
    (D) To explain some mistakes

47. What industry do the speakers most likely work in?
    (A) Agriculture
    (B) Hospitality
    (C) Electronics
    (D) Construction

48. According to the woman, what happened at a business recently?
    (A) An executive retired.
    (B) A Web site was upgraded.
    (C) A new sign was put on display.
    (D) A famous product was discontinued.

49. What does the man offer the woman?
    (A) Some printouts
    (B) Some samples
    (C) A special discount
    (D) A business referral

50. What does the man mean when he says, "I was late to work today"?
    (A) He has not met a new colleague yet.
    (B) He was negatively affected by a change.
    (C) He was not present for an announcement.
    (D) He is behind schedule on an assignment.

51. Where do the speakers most likely work?
    (A) At a driving school
    (B) At a recording studio
    (C) At a translation firm
    (D) At a medical clinic

52. What does the man say he is worried about?
    (A) Hiring too many workers
    (B) Obtaining enough supplies
    (C) Offering poor customer service
    (D) Revising some materials quickly

53. What industry are the women training to work in?
    (A) Fashion retail
    (B) Laundry services
    (C) Clothing alteration
    (D) Textile manufacturing

54. What are the speakers mainly discussing?
    (A) Customer complaints
    (B) Equipment maintenance
    (C) Workspace layouts
    (D) Shift scheduling

55. What will the women do next?
    (A) Practice a procedure
    (B) Watch a demonstration
    (C) Read some instructions
    (D) Look at some photographs

56. Why is the woman calling the man?

(A) To discuss a payment
(B) To arrange a consultation
(C) To provide an order update
(D) To follow up on some feedback

57. What information does the woman ask the man to send her?

(A) A home address
(B) A credit card number
(C) Design preferences
(D) Space measurements

58. What does the woman remind the man to do?

(A) Move any parked vehicles
(B) Prepare some paperwork
(C) Complete a transaction
(D) Check his mail frequently

59. Why is the woman calling?

(A) She is disappointed with a virtual tour.
(B) She found inaccurate information on a Web site.
(C) She cannot make a reservation online.
(D) She did not receive a confirmation e-mail.

60. What does the man tell the woman about?

(A) An improvement project
(B) A computer program setting
(C) A membership requirement
(D) A cancellation policy

61. What most likely is the woman's job?

(A) Historian
(B) Landscaper
(C) Interior decorator
(D) Event planner

Digital Photo Packages	
One image 30-minute shoot $100	Two images 45-minute shoot $190
Three images 60-minute shoot $270	Four images 75-minute shoot $340

62. What field does the woman work in?

(A) Photography
(B) Entertainment
(C) Real estate
(D) Law

63. Look at the graphic. How much will the woman pay for her photo package?

(A) $100
(B) $190
(C) $270
(D) $340

64. What does the woman ask the man about?

(A) Additional services
(B) Payment methods
(C) A wait time
(D) A clothing choice

GO ON TO THE NEXT PAGE

TEST 8

Tasks

1. Clear out designated shelves and stands
2. Unpack new merchandise
3. Put new merchandise out
4. Make a new window display
5. Dispose of old merchandise

UPSHAW HOTEL	
Floor 4	Suites
Floor 3	Rooms
Floor 2	Restaurant
Floor 1	Lobby

65. Why did the man ask the woman to work today?

(A) A lot of customers are expected today.
(B) He wants to teach her how to do a task.
(C) Another worker had to take a day off.
(D) They need to prepare the store for a holiday.

66. Look at the graphic. Which task will the man do first?

(A) Task 1
(B) Task 2
(C) Task 3
(D) Task 4

67. What does the woman suggest doing before they start?

(A) Buying some refreshments
(B) Opening the windows
(C) Turning on some music
(D) Putting on gloves

68. Why has the woman come to the hotel?

(A) For a job interview
(B) For a business dinner
(C) For an equipment repair
(D) For an overnight stay

69. Who does the man agree to contact?

(A) A current guest
(B) A maintenance supervisor
(C) A parking attendant
(D) A hotel manager

70. Look at the graphic. Which floor will the woman most likely go to next?

(A) Floor 1
(B) Floor 2
(C) Floor 3
(D) Floor 4

Directions: You will hear some talks given by a single speaker. You will be asked to answer three questions about what the speaker says in each talk. Select the best response to each question and mark the letter (A), (B), (C), or (D) on your answer sheet. The talks will not be printed in your test book and will be spoken only one time.

71. Who most likely is the speaker?

(A) An author
(B) A bookstore clerk
(C) A university professor
(D) A museum guide

72. What does the speaker mention about the book?

(A) It is unusually old.
(B) It is in good condition.
(C) It contains useful advice.
(D) It is very popular.

73. What will the listeners do next?

(A) Look at some shelves
(B) Ask some questions
(C) Introduce themselves
(D) Listen to a reading

74. Where does the speaker most likely work?

(A) A chemical factory
(B) A vegetable farm
(C) An auto-mechanic shop
(D) A waste disposal company

75. What problem does the speaker mention?

(A) A cost has increased.
(B) A regulation has changed.
(C) A contract has been canceled.
(D) A vehicle has broken down.

76. What does the speaker reassure the listeners about?

(A) A difficult task will be temporary.
(B) Extra compensation will be offered.
(C) There will still be work available.
(D) They will be able to vote on a proposal.

77. What kind of building is being planned?

(A) A hospital
(B) A train station
(C) A manufacturing plant
(D) An apartment complex

78. According to the speaker, what is near the proposed building site?

(A) A retail district
(B) A nature area
(C) A primary school
(D) A major highway

79. What does the speaker say some citizens are concerned about?

(A) Effects on wildlife
(B) An increase in noise
(C) A decline in property values
(D) Worsening of road traffic

80. What type of event will take place next month?

(A) A board meeting
(B) An office renovation
(C) An industry conference
(D) A branch opening

81. What does the speaker tell the listeners to do?

(A) Practice giving a presentation
(B) Distribute surveys to their staff
(C) Submit some budget figures
(D) Arrange their own transportation

82. What will the speaker send the listeners?

(A) A catalog
(B) A template
(C) An agenda
(D) A floor plan

GO ON TO THE NEXT PAGE

83. What kind of business is recruiting employees?

(A) An amusement park
(B) A shopping mall
(C) A sports stadium
(D) A convention center

84. What does the speaker imply when she says, "the Reef will be open year-round"?

(A) Many workers will be needed.
(B) The jobs are not suitable for students.
(C) Applications will be accepted at any time.
(D) The positions are relatively stable.

85. What should interested listeners do?

(A) Fill out a form online
(B) Attend a recruiting event
(C) E-mail some documents
(D) Call an information line

86. What problem does the speaker's company have?

(A) Declining sales
(B) A staffing shortage
(C) Limited office space
(D) Outdated equipment

87. Why does the speaker thank the IT department?

(A) It provided technology for remote work.
(B) It agreed to move to another location.
(C) It recovered some employees' lost data.
(D) It discovered an issue with some software.

88. Why does the speaker say, "we don't have a lot of meetings"?

(A) To encourage the listeners to speak now
(B) To announce a change in business practices
(C) To express concern about a company's culture
(D) To support an expert's recommendation

89. Who is the speaker?

(A) A town official
(B) A television host
(C) A company spokesperson
(D) A radio producer

90. What does the business do for its customers?

(A) It provides short-term care for their cats.
(B) It shares reviews of local veterinary clinics.
(C) It builds custom play structures for their pets.
(D) It gives them an opportunity to interact with animals.

91. What can the listeners do on a Web site?

(A) Suggest interview questions
(B) Post videos of themselves
(C) Request a service consultation
(D) Submit a job application

92. What is being announced?

(A) A trade show
(B) A park cleanup
(C) A charity dinner
(D) An outdoor festival

93. What does the speaker imply when she says, "Last year we actually had to refuse a few businesses"?

(A) Many organizations want to participate.
(B) A submission deadline must be followed.
(C) Some registration materials were not complete.
(D) The same recruitment strategy should be used again.

94. What are the listeners asked to do?

(A) Keep some messages short
(B) Keep their records organized
(C) Keep some information confidential
(D) Keep their schedules clear

REGISTRATION FORM

Name: _____

Category:
Youth ($16) ____
Adult ($25) ____
Senior ($20) ____

Early Registration Discount (-$10)

____

Payment Method:
Cash ____   Debit/Credit Card ____

Italian Cooking Classes

5 P.M. on Tuesdays

Date	Dish
October 2	Pesto Spaghetti
October 9	Classic Meatballs
October 16	Eggplant Parmesan
October 23	Cheese Ravioli

95. What is the speaker organizing?
   (A) An art class
   (B) A nature hike
   (C) A bicycle race
   (D) A baking contest

96. What does the speaker thank the listeners for?
   (A) Being patient during a delay
   (B) Volunteering to support the event
   (C) Completing registration in advance
   (D) Giving feedback on a past event

97. Look at the graphic. Which amount has been newly added?
   (A) $10
   (B) $16
   (C) $20
   (D) $25

98. Look at the graphic. On which date will the speaker skip a class?
   (A) October 2
   (B) October 9
   (C) October 16
   (D) October 23

99. What is the speaker unsure about?
   (A) Whether some classes are already full
   (B) What time the classes will end
   (C) Who will teach each class
   (D) How the class fees are charged

100. What will the speaker most likely do next?
   (A) Complete a registration form
   (B) Wait for a call from the listener
   (C) Contact the community center
   (D) Read some lists of ingredients

This is the end of the Listening test.

YBM
실전토익
LC 1000

테스트 전 체크리스트

- 중간 휴식 없이 제한 시간을 지켜서 풀이하세요.
- 제한 시간은 답안지에 마킹하는 시간도 포함시켜야 합니다.
- 찍은 문제는 번호 옆에 꼭 체크해 주세요.
- 시간 안에 풀지 못한 문제는 틀린 것으로 채점해 주세요.

LC

TEST 9

LISTENING TEST

In the Listening test, you will be asked to demonstrate how well you understand spoken English. The entire Listening test will last approximately 45 minutes. There are four parts, and directions are given for each part. You must mark your answers on the separate answer sheet. Do not write your answers in your test book.

PART 1

Directions: For each question in this part, you will hear four statements about a picture in your test book. When you hear the statements, you must select the one statement that best describes what you see in the picture. Then find the number of the question on your answer sheet and mark your answer. The statements will not be printed in your test book and will be spoken only one time.

Statement (C), "They're sitting at a table," is the best description of the picture, so you should select answer (C) and mark it on your answer sheet.

1.

2.

GO ON TO THE NEXT PAGE ➡

TEST 9

3.

4.

5.

6.

GO ON TO THE NEXT PAGE

TEST 9

PART 2

Directions: You will hear a question or statement and three responses spoken in English. They will not be printed in your test book and will be spoken only one time. Select the best response to the question or statement and mark the letter (A), (B), or (C) on your answer sheet.

7. Mark your answer on your answer sheet.

8. Mark your answer on your answer sheet.

9. Mark your answer on your answer sheet.

10. Mark your answer on your answer sheet.

11. Mark your answer on your answer sheet.

12. Mark your answer on your answer sheet.

13. Mark your answer on your answer sheet.

14. Mark your answer on your answer sheet.

15. Mark your answer on your answer sheet.

16. Mark your answer on your answer sheet.

17. Mark your answer on your answer sheet.

18. Mark your answer on your answer sheet.

19. Mark your answer on your answer sheet.

20. Mark your answer on your answer sheet.

21. Mark your answer on your answer sheet.

22. Mark your answer on your answer sheet.

23. Mark your answer on your answer sheet.

24. Mark your answer on your answer sheet.

25. Mark your answer on your answer sheet.

26. Mark your answer on your answer sheet.

27. Mark your answer on your answer sheet.

28. Mark your answer on your answer sheet.

29. Mark your answer on your answer sheet.

30. Mark your answer on your answer sheet.

31. Mark your answer on your answer sheet.

PART 3

Directions: You will hear some conversations between two or more people. You will be asked to answer three questions about what the speakers say in each conversation. Select the best response to each question and mark the letter (A), (B), (C), or (D) on your answer sheet. The conversations will not be printed in your test book and will be spoken only one time.

32. Where does the man most likely work?

(A) At a bakery
(B) At a florist shop
(C) At a jewelry store
(D) At a tailor shop

33. What does the woman like about the business?

(A) Its fast service
(B) Its friendly staff
(C) Its high-quality work
(D) Its reasonable pricing

34. What does the woman accept from the man?

(A) A receipt
(B) Some samples
(C) A discount coupon
(D) Some instructions

35. Where does the conversation most likely take place?

(A) At a print shop
(B) At a repair shop
(C) At an electronics store
(D) At a sporting goods store

36. Why does the woman apologize?

(A) A product is out of stock.
(B) A computer is not working.
(C) An employee is absent.
(D) A sales promotion has ended.

37. What does the woman offer to do for the man?

(A) Take a message
(B) Restart a device
(C) Check a storage room
(D) Ship an item to him

38. What does the woman show the man?

(A) A city map
(B) A business card
(C) A Web page
(D) A brochure

39. Why does the man say, "that's pretty far outside of town"?

(A) To ask for help with a move
(B) To reject a suggested property
(C) To point out misinformation in a listing
(D) To express concern about an appointment time

40. What does the man ask about?

(A) An area's affordability
(B) A parking facility
(C) A building's condition
(D) A person's availability

41. Who most likely is the man?

(A) A city official
(B) A café owner
(C) A language teacher
(D) A newspaper reporter

42. What does the woman say about a proposal?

(A) It will go into effect next year.
(B) It is misunderstood by the public.
(C) It will be expensive to implement.
(D) It was inspired by laws in other cities.

43. What does the man decide to do?

(A) Join a volunteer group
(B) Revise a timeline
(C) Post on social media
(D) Conduct some research

GO ON TO THE NEXT PAGE

44. Where do the speakers most likely work?

(A) In a laundry facility
(B) In an appliance store
(C) In a medical center
(D) In a hotel kitchen

45. According to the man, what probably caused a problem?

(A) A setting was not adjusted.
(B) A material is not water-resistant.
(C) A part was not connected properly.
(D) A power outage occurred last night.

46. What does the woman offer to do?

(A) Clean up a hazard
(B) Schedule a training
(C) Locate a warranty
(D) Call a repair person

47. What do members of the speakers' club do together?

(A) Discuss books
(B) Play a sport
(C) Take photographs
(D) Make handicrafts

48. What is the conversation mainly about?

(A) A learning opportunity
(B) A change in leadership
(C) A promotional campaign
(D) A requirement for members

49. What are the men concerned about?

(A) Covering an additional expense
(B) Having too few participants
(C) Transporting some supplies
(D) Giving incorrect time estimates

50. What type of business does the woman work for?

(A) A department store
(B) An insurance company
(C) An employment agency
(D) A landscaping firm

51. Why is the woman calling the man?

(A) To advertise a business
(B) To arrange a workshop
(C) To offer him a job
(D) To inquire about a loan

52. What document does the woman mention?

(A) An agreement
(B) A résumé
(C) A rates sheet
(D) A client testimonial

53. What problem does the woman describe?

(A) A receipt is missing some information.
(B) A reimbursement has not been issued.
(C) Some travel plans have not been completed.
(D) The budget for a trip is very limited.

54. Why does the man say, "the employee handbook is very detailed"?

(A) To give a recommendation
(B) To decline an offer
(C) To indicate frustration
(D) To praise an accomplishment

55. Why does the man apologize?

(A) He forgot to process a request.
(B) He did not read an e-mail carefully.
(C) He is not allowed to discuss an issue.
(D) He has misplaced a report.

56. Who visited the speakers' workplace this morning?

(A) A property appraiser
(B) A safety inspector
(C) A building contractor
(D) A moving company agent

57. What problem does Julie mention?

(A) A window was installed incorrectly.
(B) A permit has not been approved.
(C) Some machinery has been disassembled.
(D) A space is not wide enough for some equipment.

58. What does the man suggest doing?

(A) Reviewing a contract
(B) Postponing a start date
(C) Taking some measurements
(D) Seeking another opinion

59. What is the purpose of the man's visit?

(A) To complete a process
(B) To thank a colleague
(C) To announce a visitor
(D) To ask about a decision

60. What department does the woman most likely work in?

(A) Human Resources
(B) Purchasing
(C) Marketing
(D) Technical Support

61. What does the woman say she will do?

(A) Share some Web site links
(B) Cancel a supply order
(C) Practice a presentation
(D) Dispose of some documents

•	Sanford Tower	•
101	Tabor Sales	
102	Ace Publishing	
201	Norris Inc.	
202	EG Interior Designs	

62. Who most likely is the man?

(A) A construction worker
(B) A safety inspector
(C) A facilities manager
(D) A computer technician

63. Look at the graphic. Which business name will be changed?

(A) Tabor Sales
(B) Ace Publishing
(C) Norris Inc.
(D) EG Interior Designs

64. What does the woman say she will do this afternoon?

(A) Wait to greet a visitor
(B) Move in some furniture
(C) Pick up some parking passes
(D) Order some business cards

GO ON TO THE NEXT PAGE

TEST 9

Service Prices	
Haircut and styling	$60
Facial treatment	$50
Pedicure	$40
Manicure	$30

65. Look at the graphic. How much will the woman pay for her service?

(A) $60
(B) $50
(C) $40
(D) $30

66. What event is the woman going to participate in later?

(A) A photo shoot
(B) An award ceremony
(C) A press conference
(D) A job interview

67. What will the man most likely do next?

(A) Look for a colleague
(B) Put out some magazines
(C) Prepare a beverage
(D) Accept a payment

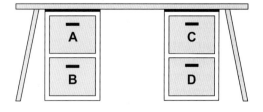

68. Why is the woman away from the office?

(A) For an industry conference
(B) For a client meeting
(C) For a property inspection
(D) For a doctor's appointment

69. What does the man say to reassure the woman?

(A) He is not very busy today.
(B) He knows a project is important.
(C) He has made similar mistakes.
(D) He is familiar with a location.

70. Look at the graphic. Where should the man look for an item?

(A) In drawer A
(B) In drawer B
(C) In drawer C
(D) In drawer D

Directions: You will hear some talks given by a single speaker. You will be asked to answer three questions about what the speaker says in each talk. Select the best response to each question and mark the letter (A), (B), (C), or (D) on your answer sheet. The talks will not be printed in your test book and will be spoken only one time.

71. What is the main purpose of the call?

(A) To suggest applying for a promotion
(B) To confirm a biographical detail for an article
(C) To tell the listener that she is an award candidate
(D) To thank the listener for joining a committee

72. What field does the listener work in?

(A) Shipping
(B) Education
(C) Advertising
(D) Finance

73. What is the listener invited to do?

(A) Attend a meeting
(B) Browse a Web site
(C) Submit a work sample
(D) Refer a coworker

74. What is being advertised?

(A) A store opening
(B) A park cleanup
(C) A sports competition
(D) A community fund-raiser

75. What will happen during the event?

(A) A street will be closed to vehicles.
(B) A government official will give a speech.
(C) Some of the attendees will win prizes.
(D) Musical performances will take place.

76. What does the speaker say the listeners can do on a Web site?

(A) Make a donation
(B) Complete a registration
(C) View some images
(D) Cast some votes

77. Where do the listeners work?

(A) At a theater
(B) At a television studio
(C) At a university library
(D) At a bank

78. What does the speaker imply when she says, "this building was built over 70 years ago"?

(A) The facility lacks some amenities.
(B) The building is a local landmark.
(C) A renovation project was difficult.
(D) An organization should relocate soon.

79. What does the speaker ask the listeners to do?

(A) Rearrange some furniture
(B) Put down their belongings
(C) Take copies of a handout
(D) Silence their mobile phones

80. What is the speaker reviewing?

(A) A video script
(B) A research paper
(C) A slide presentation
(D) An audio file

81. According to the speaker, what caused a problem?

(A) Some names
(B) Some visual aids
(C) A password requirement
(D) A formatting choice

82. What does the speaker recommend doing in the future?

(A) Reading a manual
(B) Hiring a specialist
(C) Marking any changes
(D) Upgrading some equipment

GO ON TO THE NEXT PAGE

83. Why is the cycling class canceled?

(A) A staffing issue
(B) A lack of participants
(C) A scheduling conflict
(D) A maintenance problem

84. Why does the speaker say, "there is an aerobics class at 8:15"?

(A) To explain a refusal
(B) To propose an alternative
(C) To complain about a timetable
(D) To request some assistance

85. What are the listeners asked to check?

(A) A list of rules
(B) A membership card
(C) An electronic device
(D) A floor plan

86. Where is the speech most likely being given?

(A) At a trade show
(B) At a press conference
(C) At a shareholder meeting
(D) At a welcome reception

87. What industry does the speaker most likely work in?

(A) Law
(B) Energy
(C) Health care
(D) Technology

88. What will the speaker's business do next year?

(A) Begin offering new services
(B) Acquire one of its competitors
(C) Conduct some market research
(D) Discontinue an employee program

89. What is the announcement about?

(A) The arrival of new workers
(B) A change in a company practice
(C) The customer reviews for a product
(D) A decision about the yearly budget

90. What does the speaker encourage the listeners to do?

(A) Take detailed notes
(B) Volunteer for an event
(C) Speak to their managers
(D) Give honest feedback

91. What does the company plan to do soon?

(A) Reorganize a space
(B) Conduct some testing
(C) Send out some guidelines
(D) Finalize a schedule

92. Where do the listeners most likely work?

(A) At a garden center
(B) At a real estate firm
(C) At a car-rental company
(D) At a grocery store

93. What has the business received complaints about?

(A) The availability of its inventory
(B) The design of its signage
(C) The length of its operating hours
(D) The restrictions of its loyalty program

94. What does the speaker mean when she says, "the new location is supposed to open next month"?

(A) A business is doing well.
(B) Some staff members will be busy.
(C) An announcement should be made later.
(D) Some work should be completed quickly.

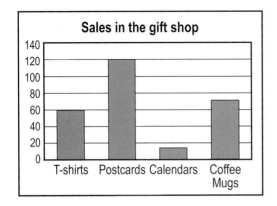

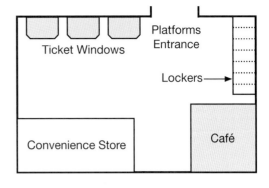

95. Who most likely is the speaker?

(A) An interior designer
(B) A coffee shop owner
(C) A graphic artist
(D) A theater manager

96. What will take place in October?

(A) An annual community festival
(B) A building renovation project
(C) An official press conference
(D) An employee sales contest

97. Look at the graphic. Which type of item does the speaker want to discuss further?

(A) T-shirts
(B) Postcards
(C) Calendars
(D) Coffee mugs

98. Who most likely is the speaker?

(A) A ticket agent
(B) A tour guide
(C) A train conductor
(D) A maintenance supervisor

99. Look at the graphic. What will the listeners meet in front of?

(A) The ticket windows
(B) The lockers
(C) The convenience store
(D) The café

100. What will the speaker do next?

(A) Post a written notice
(B) Check a weather forecast
(C) Distribute an itinerary
(D) Make a phone call

This is the end of the Listening test.

YBM
실전토익
LC 1000

테스트 전 체크리스트

- 중간 휴식 없이 제한 시간을 지켜서 풀이하세요.
- 제한 시간은 답안지에 마킹하는 시간도 포함시켜야 합니다.
- 찍은 문제는 번호 옆에 꼭 체크해 주세요.
- 시간 안에 풀지 못한 문제는 틀린 것으로 채점해 주세요.

LC

TEST 10

LISTENING TEST

In the Listening test, you will be asked to demonstrate how well you understand spoken English. The entire Listening test will last approximately 45 minutes. There are four parts, and directions are given for each part. You must mark your answers on the separate answer sheet. Do not write your answers in your test book.

PART 1

Directions: For each question in this part, you will hear four statements about a picture in your test book. When you hear the statements, you must select the one statement that best describes what you see in the picture. Then find the number of the question on your answer sheet and mark your answer. The statements will not be printed in your test book and will be spoken only one time.

Statement (C), "They're sitting at a table," is the best description of the picture, so you should select answer (C) and mark it on your answer sheet.

1.

2.

GO ON TO THE NEXT PAGE ➡

TEST 10

3.

4.

5.

6.

GO ON TO THE NEXT PAGE ➤

TEST 10

PART 2

Directions: You will hear a question or statement and three responses spoken in English. They will not be printed in your test book and will be spoken only one time. Select the best response to the question or statement and mark the letter (A), (B), or (C) on your answer sheet.

7. Mark your answer on your answer sheet.

8. Mark your answer on your answer sheet.

9. Mark your answer on your answer sheet.

10. Mark your answer on your answer sheet.

11. Mark your answer on your answer sheet.

12. Mark your answer on your answer sheet.

13. Mark your answer on your answer sheet.

14. Mark your answer on your answer sheet.

15. Mark your answer on your answer sheet.

16. Mark your answer on your answer sheet.

17. Mark your answer on your answer sheet.

18. Mark your answer on your answer sheet.

19. Mark your answer on your answer sheet.

20. Mark your answer on your answer sheet.

21. Mark your answer on your answer sheet.

22. Mark your answer on your answer sheet.

23. Mark your answer on your answer sheet.

24. Mark your answer on your answer sheet.

25. Mark your answer on your answer sheet.

26. Mark your answer on your answer sheet.

27. Mark your answer on your answer sheet.

28. Mark your answer on your answer sheet.

29. Mark your answer on your answer sheet.

30. Mark your answer on your answer sheet.

31. Mark your answer on your answer sheet.

Directions: You will hear some conversations between two or more people. You will be asked to answer three questions about what the speakers say in each conversation. Select the best response to each question and mark the letter (A), (B), (C), or (D) on your answer sheet. The conversations will not be printed in your test book and will be spoken only one time.

32. What most likely is the man's job?

(A) House painter
(B) Interior designer
(C) Real estate agent
(D) Hardware store employee

33. What does the man say about a type of paint?

(A) It is easy to apply evenly.
(B) It can be used to hide flaws.
(C) It is suitable for busy spaces.
(D) It dries relatively quickly.

34. What does the man ask the woman to do?

(A) Select a color theme
(B) Estimate some dimensions
(C) Remove furniture from a room
(D) Sign an agreement

35. Where are the speakers?

(A) At a radio station
(B) At an art museum
(C) At a movie theater
(D) At a community center

36. What did the woman do yesterday?

(A) She won a contest.
(B) She read a news article.
(C) She made a reservation.
(D) She requested time off.

37. What does the man tell the woman about?

(A) A membership program
(B) A job opening
(C) A building renovation
(D) An anniversary celebration

38. What problem does the woman have?

(A) She is unable to contact a friend.
(B) She left an item on a train.
(C) She cannot catch a taxi.
(D) She got off at the wrong station.

39. Why does the man say, "You just have to download an app"?

(A) To request some feedback
(B) To express surprise
(C) To support a suggestion
(D) To disagree with an opinion

40. What will the woman most likely do soon?

(A) Wait near an entrance
(B) Complete some paperwork
(C) Talk to an official
(D) Check a departure board

41. Who most likely is the woman?

(A) An office manager
(B) A hotel receptionist
(C) A laboratory assistant
(D) A construction supervisor

42. What problem is the man reporting?

(A) A room is inaccessible.
(B) He will arrive late.
(C) Some work is very noisy.
(D) He cannot find some supplies.

43. What does the woman say she will do next?

(A) Research some alternatives
(B) Authorize a discount
(C) Arrange a delivery
(D) Update a schedule

GO ON TO THE NEXT PAGE

44. What are the speakers mainly discussing?

   (A) Investing in some new machinery
   (B) Reorganizing a work space
   (C) Conducting regular safety inspections
   (D) Starting a performance review program

45. What do the men suggest doing?

   (A) Determining a timeline
   (B) Assembling a team
   (C) Consulting an expert
   (D) Looking for some studies

46. What does the woman decide to do?

   (A) Draft an announcement
   (B) Reevaluate a budget
   (C) Reassign some tasks
   (D) Attend an industry event

47. What problem does the woman report?

   (A) She has not received a bill.
   (B) A utility is not working properly.
   (C) She needs to update her address.
   (D) A charge is higher than usual.

48. What did the man's department recently do?

   (A) It hired additional employees.
   (B) It transferred tasks to a new department.
   (C) It increased the rates for a service.
   (D) It upgraded some equipment.

49. What will take place tomorrow?

   (A) A city council meeting
   (B) An office closure
   (C) Some repair work
   (D) An information session

50. Where most likely are the speakers?

   (A) At a pet supply store
   (B) At a community park
   (C) At a veterinary clinic
   (D) At an apartment building

51. How does the woman suggest addressing a problem?

   (A) By changing an animal's feed
   (B) By spending more time outdoors
   (C) By filling out a complaint form
   (D) By taking a training course

52. What will the man do next?

   (A) Photograph an item
   (B) Pick up a flyer
   (C) Go for a walk
   (D) Check a calendar

53. What does the man want to discuss?

   (A) Some customer reviews
   (B) Some travel arrangements
   (C) A manufacturing procedure
   (D) A proposed sales event

54. What problem is mentioned?

   (A) A delivery has been delayed.
   (B) An entranceway may be too narrow.
   (C) A material has become more expensive.
   (D) An item can be uncomfortable to wear.

55. What does the man ask the women to do?

   (A) Make some drawings
   (B) Purchase some luggage
   (C) Revise an advertisement
   (D) Contact a business partner

56. What does the woman ask the man about?

(A) Workshop participants
(B) A hiring process
(C) A project deadline
(D) Remote work policies

57. What idea does the woman have?

(A) Adjusting a requirement
(B) Advertising on a special Web site
(C) Offering reimbursement for an expense
(D) Gathering opinions from others

58. What does the man tell the woman to do?

(A) Calculate a cost
(B) Forward some résumés
(C) Postpone the release of a report
(D) Organize a meeting

---

59. Where do the speakers most likely work?

(A) At a publishing company
(B) At a catering service
(C) At a landscaping firm
(D) At a television network

60. What does the man imply when he says, "most of the company is planning to go"?

(A) An event should be moved to a different date.
(B) Staff members are excited about an award.
(C) They will need to prepare additional food.
(D) It will be difficult to find workers for a shift.

61. What does the woman say she will do?

(A) Send out an e-mail
(B) Speak to an executive
(C) Make changes to a menu
(D) Rent some transportation

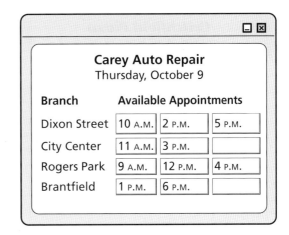

Carey Auto Repair
Thursday, October 9

Branch	Available Appointments		
Dixon Street	10 A.M.	2 P.M.	5 P.M.
City Center	11 A.M.	3 P.M.	
Rogers Park	9 A.M.	12 P.M.	4 P.M.
Brantfield	1 P.M.	6 P.M.	

62. Look at the graphic. Which branch does the woman work at?

(A) Dixon Street
(B) City Center
(C) Rogers Park
(D) Brantfield

63. Why does the woman apologize?

(A) Some instructions are confusing.
(B) A time slot is no longer available.
(C) Appointments cannot be made by phone.
(D) A business is understaffed today.

64. What service does the man require for his car?

(A) A tire rotation
(B) A window repair
(C) An oil change
(D) A brake replacement

GO ON TO THE NEXT PAGE

TEST 10

Critchfield Plaza
Coupon Pack

1 **20% off any service**
   at Vayla Salon

2 **Free cookie**
   at Sugaree Bakery

3 **Free drink with ticket purchase**
   at Thacker Cinema

4 **10% off any item**
   at Ochoa Shoes

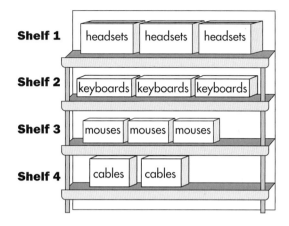

65. Look at the graphic. Which coupon will the man use?

(A) Coupon 1
(B) Coupon 2
(C) Coupon 3
(D) Coupon 4

66. What does the woman check?

(A) Her coworkers' schedules
(B) A purchase receipt
(C) A price list
(D) Some stock levels

67. What will the man most likely do next?

(A) Look at a menu board
(B) Sit in a waiting area
(C) Provide his phone number
(D) Speak with a manager

68. What problem does the man report?

(A) A device no longer works.
(B) A storage space is becoming too full.
(C) Some boxes are unorganized.
(D) Employees do not have necessary items.

69. Look at the graphic. Which shelf's boxes will the woman work on first?

(A) Shelf 1
(B) Shelf 2
(C) Shelf 3
(D) Shelf 4

70. What is the woman asked to do?

(A) Keep an inventory list updated
(B) Clean some of the accessories
(C) Call a specialty recycling service
(D) Implement a new labeling system

Directions: You will hear some talks given by a single speaker. You will be asked to answer three questions about what the speaker says in each talk. Select the best response to each question and mark the letter (A), (B), (C), or (D) on your answer sheet. The talks will not be printed in your test book and will be spoken only one time.

71. What does the speaker like about an event?

(A) It is held in a special location.
(B) It has a long history.
(C) It features various activities.
(D) Its proceeds go toward a good cause.

72. According to the speaker, what should the event have?

(A) More food options
(B) A dedicated Web site
(C) Official merchandise
(D) A prize raffle

73. What does the speaker offer to do?

(A) Perform volunteer work
(B) Inquire about a regulation
(C) Recommend potential sponsors
(D) Lend the listener some equipment

74. What is the topic of today's program?

(A) Trends in online shopping
(B) The opening of a retail complex
(C) A custom clothing maker
(D) Pop-up stores

75. According to the speaker, why is a type of business popular with consumers?

(A) It is convenient to use.
(B) It has unique products.
(C) Its prices are reasonable.
(D) It offers an enjoyable experience.

76. Who is Patty Tyner?

(A) A tailor
(B) An entrepreneur
(C) A property manager
(D) An economic researcher

77. What is the topic of the conference?

(A) Increasing agricultural productivity
(B) Promoting trade between countries
(C) Using an educational technology
(D) Improving access to the Internet

78. What does the speaker say happened in the last year?

(A) A law was enacted.
(B) A study was conducted.
(C) A fund-raising campaign took place.
(D) A product was released.

79. What will the speaker's organization provide funding for?

(A) Filming a documentary
(B) Building some facilities
(C) Training some workers
(D) Publicizing a service

80. Where does the speaker work?

(A) At a law school
(B) At a construction firm
(C) At a software company
(D) At an advertising agency

81. Why does the speaker say, "none of us is a lawyer"?

(A) To offer an apology for a mistake
(B) To turn down the listener's request
(C) To complain about a legal requirement
(D) To explain why he needs the listener's help

82. What does the speaker offer to do for the listener?

(A) Pay for a service
(B) Provide a referral
(C) Review a contract
(D) Contribute to a blog

GO ON TO THE NEXT PAGE

TEST 10

83. What is the talk mainly about?

(A) Designs for brand logos
(B) Promotional contests for customers
(C) Company policies on staff attire
(D) Online profiles of executives

84. According to the speaker, what is the benefit of a practice?

(A) It can improve employee satisfaction.
(B) It makes a manager's job easier.
(C) It reduces operating costs.
(D) It is good for a business's image.

85. How did the speaker develop content for a handout?

(A) By drawing on her work experience
(B) By visiting several Web pages
(C) By studying some reference books
(D) By surveying the listeners beforehand

86. What does the speaker point out to the listeners?

(A) Some seating
(B) Cooling fans
(C) A venue map
(D) A drinking fountain

87. According to the speaker, what is Watkins Stadium known for?

(A) Hosting major competitions
(B) Having an unusual architectural style
(C) Being the home field of a popular team
(D) Providing a view of a city skyline

88. What does the speaker imply when he says, "there are no matches today"?

(A) Most on-site businesses are closed.
(B) There is not much traffic around the stadium.
(C) The listeners should not expect to see athletes.
(D) The listeners will be able to visit special areas.

89. Who most likely are the listeners?

(A) Restaurant staff
(B) Security guards
(C) Factory workers
(D) Laboratory technicians

90. What is the purpose of a machine?

(A) To process orders
(B) To transmit speech
(C) To track working hours
(D) To package some goods

91. How will the listeners learn more about the machine?

(A) By trying it themselves
(B) By reading an explanation
(C) By examining some diagrams
(D) By watching a demonstration

92. Who is the speaker?

(A) A board member
(B) A financial analyst
(C) A graphic designer
(D) A team leader

93. What project does the speaker mention?

(A) A video game
(B) A Web site redesign
(C) A theme park attraction
(D) A television commercial

94. Why does the speaker say, "the company earned more revenue than expected this year"?

(A) To encourage the listeners to make suggestions
(B) To give a reason for a spending decision
(C) To recommend raising some estimates
(D) To congratulate the listeners on an achievement

1. _____ The shipping box is sealed.

2. _____ The packing slip is correct.

3. _____ All products' packaging is intact.

4. _____ No products are expired.

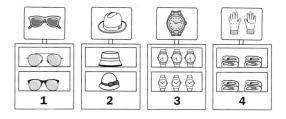

95. What job are the listeners being trained for?

(A) Safety inspector
(B) Pharmacy assistant
(C) Grocery store stocker
(D) Warehouse shipping clerk

96. Look at the graphic. Which item does the speaker highlight?

(A) Item 1
(B) Item 2
(C) Item 3
(D) Item 4

97. What does the speaker recommend?

(A) Wearing protective gloves
(B) Writing down some figures
(C) Removing some trash
(D) Learning some special terms

98. Look at the graphic. Where will the discounted necklaces be displayed?

(A) In Display Case 1
(B) In Display Case 2
(C) In Display Case 3
(D) In Display Case 4

99. What should be placed near the fitting room?

(A) Chairs
(B) Handbags
(C) Gift certificates
(D) Rings

100. What should the listener expect to receive by courier?

(A) Some printer cartridges
(B) Some promotional posters
(C) Some display stands
(D) Some product samples

This is the end of the Listening test.

ANSWERS

TEST 1

1 (A)	2 (D)	3 (B)	4 (D)	5 (C)
6 (D)	7 (A)	8 (C)	9 (B)	10 (B)
11 (B)	12 (A)	13 (A)	14 (C)	15 (C)
16 (B)	17 (C)	18 (A)	19 (A)	20 (B)
21 (B)	22 (B)	23 (C)	24 (A)	25 (B)
26 (A)	27 (C)	28 (C)	29 (C)	30 (A)
31 (B)	32 (D)	33 (B)	34 (A)	35 (B)
36 (D)	37 (A)	38 (C)	39 (D)	40 (A)
41 (D)	42 (A)	43 (D)	44 (C)	45 (D)
46 (B)	47 (B)	48 (C)	49 (B)	50 (A)
51 (C)	52 (B)	53 (C)	54 (D)	55 (C)
56 (D)	57 (A)	58 (C)	59 (A)	60 (B)
61 (D)	62 (B)	63 (A)	64 (C)	65 (A)
66 (B)	67 (D)	68 (B)	69 (A)	70 (C)
71 (C)	72 (D)	73 (B)	74 (B)	75 (C)
76 (A)	77 (D)	78 (B)	79 (A)	80 (B)
81 (D)	82 (C)	83 (D)	84 (A)	85 (A)
86 (B)	87 (C)	88 (A)	89 (A)	90 (B)
91 (D)	92 (C)	93 (C)	94 (B)	95 (C)
96 (A)	97 (A)	98 (A)	99 (C)	100 (D)

TEST 2

1 (B)	2 (C)	3 (A)	4 (B)	5 (D)
6 (A)	7 (B)	8 (B)	9 (B)	10 (C)
11 (C)	12 (A)	13 (C)	14 (C)	15 (A)
16 (B)	17 (A)	18 (C)	19 (A)	20 (C)
21 (A)	22 (B)	23 (B)	24 (A)	25 (C)
26 (B)	27 (A)	28 (C)	29 (B)	30 (A)
31 (C)	32 (B)	33 (D)	34 (A)	35 (D)
36 (B)	37 (A)	38 (A)	39 (D)	40 (D)
41 (B)	42 (D)	43 (A)	44 (C)	45 (A)
46 (B)	47 (A)	48 (C)	49 (D)	50 (C)
51 (A)	52 (D)	53 (D)	54 (C)	55 (C)
56 (A)	57 (C)	58 (C)	59 (D)	60 (B)
61 (B)	62 (B)	63 (B)	64 (A)	65 (C)
66 (B)	67 (C)	68 (D)	69 (C)	70 (D)
71 (D)	72 (B)	73 (A)	74 (A)	75 (B)
76 (B)	77 (A)	78 (C)	79 (B)	80 (B)
81 (D)	82 (A)	83 (A)	84 (D)	85 (A)
86 (A)	87 (D)	88 (C)	89 (B)	90 (A)
91 (C)	92 (C)	93 (B)	94 (D)	95 (C)
96 (C)	97 (D)	98 (C)	99 (C)	100 (B)

TEST 3

1 (C)	2 (A)	3 (B)	4 (D)	5 (A)
6 (D)	7 (A)	8 (C)	9 (B)	10 (B)
11 (B)	12 (C)	13 (A)	14 (B)	15 (C)
16 (A)	17 (C)	18 (B)	19 (B)	20 (C)
21 (C)	22 (B)	23 (A)	24 (A)	25 (C)
26 (A)	27 (A)	28 (B)	29 (C)	30 (B)
31 (A)	32 (D)	33 (C)	34 (A)	35 (C)
36 (B)	37 (B)	38 (C)	39 (A)	40 (D)
41 (D)	42 (A)	43 (B)	44 (C)	45 (A)
46 (C)	47 (A)	48 (D)	49 (D)	50 (D)
51 (B)	52 (C)	53 (B)	54 (C)	55 (D)
56 (A)	57 (B)	58 (A)	59 (D)	60 (C)
61 (C)	62 (A)	63 (B)	64 (B)	65 (B)
66 (D)	67 (A)	68 (B)	69 (B)	70 (B)
71 (C)	72 (D)	73 (A)	74 (D)	75 (B)
76 (C)	77 (C)	78 (D)	79 (B)	80 (D)
81 (B)	82 (C)	83 (D)	84 (C)	85 (B)
86 (B)	87 (D)	88 (D)	89 (D)	90 (A)
91 (C)	92 (A)	93 (C)	94 (C)	95 (B)
96 (C)	97 (A)	98 (B)	99 (A)	100 (A)

TEST 4

1 (B)	2 (D)	3 (C)	4 (D)	5 (A)
6 (B)	7 (C)	8 (A)	9 (C)	10 (B)
11 (A)	12 (C)	13 (A)	14 (B)	15 (C)
16 (B)	17 (A)	18 (C)	19 (B)	20 (A)
21 (B)	22 (B)	23 (B)	24 (B)	25 (A)
26 (A)	27 (B)	28 (C)	29 (A)	30 (C)
31 (C)	32 (A)	33 (C)	34 (D)	35 (D)
36 (C)	37 (A)	38 (B)	39 (B)	40 (C)
41 (D)	42 (A)	43 (C)	44 (D)	45 (B)
46 (A)	47 (B)	48 (A)	49 (B)	50 (A)
51 (B)	52 (C)	53 (A)	54 (B)	55 (D)
56 (B)	57 (D)	58 (D)	59 (C)	60 (D)
61 (A)	62 (A)	63 (D)	64 (C)	65 (B)
66 (D)	67 (A)	68 (A)	69 (C)	70 (B)
71 (C)	72 (A)	73 (C)	74 (B)	75 (D)
76 (D)	77 (D)	78 (D)	79 (C)	80 (C)
81 (C)	82 (B)	83 (B)	84 (C)	85 (A)
86 (C)	87 (A)	88 (C)	89 (B)	90 (A)
91 (C)	92 (A)	93 (D)	94 (D)	95 (D)
96 (C)	97 (A)	98 (B)	99 (C)	100 (B)

TEST 5

1 (C)	2 (C)	3 (D)	4 (D)	5 (B)
6 (B)	7 (C)	8 (B)	9 (A)	10 (B)
11 (C)	12 (A)	13 (B)	14 (A)	15 (A)
16 (C)	17 (C)	18 (C)	19 (B)	20 (B)
21 (A)	22 (C)	23 (C)	24 (A)	25 (C)
26 (B)	27 (C)	28 (C)	29 (C)	30 (B)
31 (B)	32 (B)	33 (D)	34 (D)	35 (C)
36 (B)	37 (C)	38 (C)	39 (A)	40 (D)
41 (C)	42 (D)	43 (B)	44 (D)	45 (A)
46 (B)	47 (D)	48 (B)	49 (D)	50 (A)
51 (C)	52 (B)	53 (A)	54 (A)	55 (B)
56 (C)	57 (B)	58 (C)	59 (B)	60 (B)
61 (C)	62 (D)	63 (C)	64 (B)	65 (B)
66 (C)	67 (C)	68 (D)	69 (C)	70 (B)
71 (D)	72 (A)	73 (A)	74 (C)	75 (B)
76 (B)	77 (B)	78 (D)	79 (D)	80 (C)
81 (A)	82 (B)	83 (A)	84 (B)	85 (D)
86 (B)	87 (A)	88 (D)	89 (C)	90 (D)
91 (C)	92 (D)	93 (C)	94 (A)	95 (D)
96 (C)	97 (A)	98 (B)	99 (C)	100 (A)

TEST 6

1 (B)	2 (D)	3 (B)	4 (A)	5 (C)
6 (C)	7 (C)	8 (B)	9 (C)	10 (C)
11 (A)	12 (A)	13 (A)	14 (A)	15 (B)
16 (C)	17 (C)	18 (A)	19 (C)	20 (A)
21 (A)	22 (A)	23 (C)	24 (B)	25 (B)
26 (B)	27 (C)	28 (B)	29 (A)	30 (B)
31 (B)	32 (A)	33 (D)	34 (C)	35 (B)
36 (D)	37 (A)	38 (D)	39 (C)	40 (B)
41 (C)	42 (D)	43 (B)	44 (A)	45 (B)
46 (D)	47 (C)	48 (A)	49 (B)	50 (D)
51 (C)	52 (A)	53 (A)	54 (B)	55 (C)
56 (A)	57 (C)	58 (D)	59 (A)	60 (B)
61 (B)	62 (D)	63 (C)	64 (B)	65 (A)
66 (C)	67 (D)	68 (B)	69 (C)	70 (D)
71 (D)	72 (C)	73 (A)	74 (C)	75 (D)
76 (B)	77 (B)	78 (D)	79 (A)	80 (C)
81 (A)	82 (B)	83 (B)	84 (D)	85 (D)
86 (D)	87 (A)	88 (C)	89 (B)	90 (A)
91 (C)	92 (A)	93 (B)	94 (A)	95 (C)
96 (D)	97 (B)	98 (A)	99 (B)	100 (D)

TEST 7

1 (C)	2 (A)	3 (C)	4 (D)	5 (A)
6 (B)	7 (C)	8 (A)	9 (A)	10 (C)
11 (A)	12 (B)	13 (B)	14 (C)	15 (A)
16 (A)	17 (C)	18 (B)	19 (B)	20 (A)
21 (C)	22 (B)	23 (A)	24 (A)	25 (C)
26 (B)	27 (C)	28 (C)	29 (C)	30 (A)
31 (C)	32 (C)	33 (B)	34 (C)	35 (C)
36 (B)	37 (D)	38 (B)	39 (C)	40 (D)
41 (C)	42 (B)	43 (A)	44 (C)	45 (B)
46 (A)	47 (C)	48 (C)	49 (A)	50 (A)
51 (C)	52 (B)	53 (B)	54 (B)	55 (B)
56 (D)	57 (D)	58 (C)	59 (A)	60 (C)
61 (D)	62 (B)	63 (A)	64 (B)	65 (C)
66 (B)	67 (B)	68 (B)	69 (C)	70 (B)
71 (C)	72 (A)	73 (A)	74 (C)	75 (B)
76 (B)	77 (C)	78 (B)	79 (A)	80 (C)
81 (D)	82 (A)	83 (C)	84 (D)	85 (B)
86 (D)	87 (A)	88 (B)	89 (D)	90 (D)
91 (D)	92 (B)	93 (C)	94 (B)	95 (B)
96 (C)	97 (A)	98 (C)	99 (B)	100 (B)

TEST 8

1 (B)	2 (D)	3 (A)	4 (C)	5 (A)
6 (C)	7 (A)	8 (A)	9 (B)	10 (C)
11 (A)	12 (B)	13 (A)	14 (A)	15 (A)
16 (C)	17 (B)	18 (C)	19 (A)	20 (C)
21 (B)	22 (C)	23 (B)	24 (B)	25 (B)
26 (A)	27 (C)	28 (C)	29 (A)	30 (B)
31 (C)	32 (D)	33 (D)	34 (A)	35 (A)
36 (C)	37 (B)	38 (C)	39 (B)	40 (A)
41 (B)	42 (B)	43 (C)	44 (D)	45 (C)
46 (B)	47 (A)	48 (C)	49 (D)	50 (C)
51 (A)	52 (C)	53 (D)	54 (B)	55 (D)
56 (B)	57 (A)	58 (B)	59 (C)	60 (B)
61 (C)	62 (B)	63 (D)	64 (A)	65 (D)
66 (B)	67 (C)	68 (B)	69 (A)	70 (B)
71 (A)	72 (C)	73 (D)	74 (D)	75 (B)
76 (A)	77 (D)	78 (B)	79 (C)	80 (A)
81 (C)	82 (B)	83 (A)	84 (D)	85 (B)
86 (C)	87 (A)	88 (D)	89 (B)	90 (D)
91 (A)	92 (C)	93 (A)	94 (D)	95 (D)
96 (B)	97 (C)	98 (B)	99 (D)	100 (C)

TEST 9

1 (D)	2 (D)	3 (B)	4 (B)	5 (C)
6 (A)	7 (A)	8 (B)	9 (A)	10 (A)
11 (C)	12 (C)	13 (B)	14 (C)	15 (A)
16 (B)	17 (A)	18 (C)	19 (B)	20 (C)
21 (A)	22 (B)	23 (A)	24 (C)	25 (B)
26 (C)	27 (C)	28 (B)	29 (B)	30 (A)
31 (A)	32 (A)	33 (C)	34 (D)	35 (C)
36 (A)	37 (D)	38 (C)	39 (B)	40 (A)
41 (C)	42 (B)	43 (D)	44 (A)	45 (C)
46 (A)	47 (A)	48 (D)	49 (B)	50 (C)
51 (A)	52 (C)	53 (B)	54 (A)	55 (D)
56 (D)	57 (D)	58 (A)	59 (D)	60 (B)
61 (A)	62 (C)	63 (B)	64 (C)	65 (D)
66 (D)	67 (C)	68 (B)	69 (C)	70 (C)
71 (C)	72 (D)	73 (A)	74 (D)	75 (D)
76 (C)	77 (A)	78 (C)	79 (B)	80 (D)
81 (A)	82 (B)	83 (D)	84 (B)	85 (C)
86 (B)	87 (C)	88 (A)	89 (B)	90 (D)
91 (C)	92 (A)	93 (B)	94 (D)	95 (D)
96 (B)	97 (C)	98 (B)	99 (B)	100 (B)

TEST 10

1 (C)	2 (D)	3 (B)	4 (A)	5 (C)
6 (A)	7 (A)	8 (C)	9 (B)	10 (C)
11 (A)	12 (A)	13 (B)	14 (A)	15 (C)
16 (B)	17 (A)	18 (B)	19 (A)	20 (B)
21 (C)	22 (C)	23 (B)	24 (A)	25 (C)
26 (B)	27 (B)	28 (C)	29 (B)	30 (A)
31 (C)	32 (D)	33 (C)	34 (B)	35 (C)
36 (B)	37 (A)	38 (C)	39 (C)	40 (A)
41 (B)	42 (D)	43 (C)	44 (C)	45 (B)
46 (A)	47 (A)	48 (D)	49 (D)	50 (C)
51 (A)	52 (B)	53 (A)	54 (D)	55 (A)
56 (B)	57 (A)	58 (D)	59 (C)	60 (A)
61 (B)	62 (D)	63 (B)	64 (B)	65 (A)
66 (A)	67 (B)	68 (A)	69 (C)	70 (B)
71 (C)	72 (B)	73 (A)	74 (D)	75 (B)
76 (C)	77 (D)	78 (B)	79 (C)	80 (C)
81 (D)	82 (A)	83 (C)	84 (D)	85 (A)
86 (D)	87 (C)	88 (D)	89 (A)	90 (A)
91 (D)	92 (D)	93 (A)	94 (B)	95 (B)
96 (B)	97 (C)	98 (C)	99 (B)	100 (B)

ANSWER SHEET

YBM 실전토익 LC 1000

수험번호

응시일자 : 20   년   월   일

성명
- 한글
- 한자
- 영자

Test 01 (Part 1~4)

Test 02 (Part 1~4)

ANSWER SHEET

YBM 실전토익 LC 1000

성명
한글
한자
영자

Test 03 (Part 1~4)

	1	2	3	4
1				
2				
3				
4				
5				
6				
7				
8				
9				
10				
11				
12				
13				
14				
15				
16				
17				
18				
19				
20				

Test 04 (Part 1~4)

	1	2	3	4
1				
2				
3				
4				
5				
6				
7				
8				
9				
10				
11				
12				
13				
14				
15				
16				
17				
18				
19				
20				

ANSWER SHEET

YBM 실전토익 LC 1000

성명: 한글 / 한자 / 영자
평: 한글 / 한자 / 영자

수험번호

응시일자 : 20   년   월   일

Test 05 (Part 1~4)

(Answer bubbles for questions 1–100, Parts 1–4)

Test 06 (Part 1~4)

(Answer bubbles for questions 1–100, Parts 1–4)

ANSWER SHEET

YBM 실전토익 LC 1000

수험번호

응시일자 : 20   년   월   일

성명

	한글
성	한자
명	영자

Test 07 (Part 1~4)

1	2	3	...	20
21	...	40
41	...	60
61	...	80
81	...	100

Test 08 (Part 1~4)

1	2	3	...	20
21	...	40
41	...	60
61	...	80
81	...	100

ANSWER SHEET

YBM 실전토익 LC 1000

수험번호

응시일자 : 20   년   월   일

성명	한글
	한자
	영자

Test 09 (Part 1~4)

Test 10 (Part 1~4)

ANSWER SHEET

YBM 실전토익 LC 1000

수험번호

응시일자 : 20　　　년　　　월　　　일

성명
| 한글 |
| 한자 |
| 영자 |

Test (Part 1~4)

Test (Part 1~4)

ANSWER SHEET

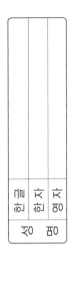

YBM 실전토익 LC 1000

수험번호

응시일자 : 20   년   월   일

성명 | 한글 |
| 한자 |
| 영자 |

Test (Part 1~4)

YBM

YBM 실전토익 LC 1000

전면 개정판

1

정답 및 해설

YBM
실전토익
LC 1000

1

정답 및 해설

TEST 1

1 (A)	**2** (D)	**3** (B)	**4** (D)	**5** (C)
6 (D)	**7** (A)	**8** (C)	**9** (B)	**10** (B)
11 (B)	**12** (A)	**13** (A)	**14** (C)	**15** (C)
16 (B)	**17** (C)	**18** (A)	**19** (A)	**20** (B)
21 (B)	**22** (B)	**23** (C)	**24** (A)	**25** (B)
26 (A)	**27** (C)	**28** (C)	**29** (C)	**30** (A)
31 (B)	**32** (D)	**33** (B)	**34** (A)	**35** (B)
36 (D)	**37** (A)	**38** (C)	**39** (D)	**40** (A)
41 (D)	**42** (A)	**43** (D)	**44** (C)	**45** (D)
46 (B)	**47** (B)	**48** (C)	**49** (B)	**50** (A)
51 (C)	**52** (B)	**53** (C)	**54** (D)	**55** (C)
56 (D)	**57** (A)	**58** (C)	**59** (A)	**60** (B)
61 (D)	**62** (B)	**63** (A)	**64** (C)	**65** (A)
66 (B)	**67** (D)	**68** (B)	**69** (A)	**70** (C)
71 (C)	**72** (D)	**73** (B)	**74** (B)	**75** (C)
76 (A)	**77** (D)	**78** (B)	**79** (A)	**80** (B)
81 (D)	**82** (C)	**83** (D)	**84** (A)	**85** (A)
86 (B)	**87** (C)	**88** (A)	**89** (A)	**90** (B)
91 (D)	**92** (C)	**93** (C)	**94** (B)	**95** (C)
96 (A)	**97** (A)	**98** (A)	**99** (C)	**100** (D)

PART 1

1

W-Am

(A) He's looking at a mobile phone.
(B) He's boarding a train.
(C) He's putting on his glasses.
(D) He's placing his bag under a seat.

번역 **(A) 남자가 휴대폰을 보고 있다.**
(B) 남자가 열차에 탑승하고 있다.
(C) 남자가 안경을 끼고 있다.
(D) 남자가 의자 아래에 가방을 놓고 있다.

해설 **1인 등장 사진**
(A) 정답. 남자가 휴대폰을 보고 있는 모습이므로 정답이다.
(B) 동사 오답. 남자가 열차에 탑승하고 있는 모습이 아니다.
(C) 동사 오답. 남자가 안경을 착용한(wearing) 상태이지 안경을 끼고 있는(putting on) 동작의 모습은 아니다.
(D) 동사 오답. 남자가 의자 아래에 가방을 놓고 있는 모습이 아니다.

어휘 board 탑승하다

2

M-Au

(A) She's kneeling to check an oven.
(B) She's washing some baking pans.
(C) She's cutting a piece of bread.
(D) She's sliding a tray into a rack.

번역 (A) 여자가 오븐을 확인하려고 무릎을 꿇고 있다.
(B) 여자가 빵 굽는 팬을 씻고 있다.
(C) 여자가 빵 한 조각을 자르고 있다.
(D) 여자가 쟁반을 선반에 밀어 넣고 있다.

해설 **1인 등장 사진**
(A) 사진에 없는 명사. 사진에 오븐이 보이지 않는다.
(B) 동사 오답. 여자가 빵 굽는 팬을 씻고 있는 모습이 아니다.
(C) 동사 오답. 여자가 빵 한 조각을 자르고 있는 모습이 아니다.
(D) 정답. 여자가 쟁반을 선반에 밀어 넣는 모습이므로 정답이다.

어휘 kneel 무릎을 꿇다   slide 밀어 넣다, 미끄러지다   tray 쟁반
rack 선반

3

W-Br

(A) Bricks are piled in the back of a truck.
(B) A man is emptying a wheelbarrow.
(C) Poles are being taken out of the ground.
(D) A man is holding a power tool.

번역 (A) 벽돌이 트럭 뒤에 쌓여 있다.
(B) 남자가 손수레를 비우고 있다.
(C) 기둥들이 땅에서 뽑히고 있다.
(D) 남자가 전동 공구를 손에 들고 있다.

해설 **사람/사물·풍경 혼합 사진**
(A) 사진에 없는 명사. 사진에 트럭이 보이지 않는다.
(B) 정답. 남자가 손수레를 비우고 있는 모습이므로 정답이다.
(C) 동사 오답. 기둥들이 땅에서 뽑히고 있는 모습이 아니다.
(D) 사진에 없는 명사. 사진에 전동 공구가 보이지 않는다.

어휘 brick 벽돌   pile 쌓다, 포개다   empty 비우다; 텅 빈
wheelbarrow 외바퀴 손수레   power tool 전동 공구

4

M-Cn

(A) The woman is hanging up an apron.
(B) The man is pushing a shopping cart.
(C) The man is entering a grocery store.
(D) The woman is helping a customer.

번역 (A) 여자가 앞치마를 걸고 있다.
(B) 남자가 쇼핑 카트를 밀고 있다.
(C) 남자가 식료품점 안으로 들어가고 있다.
(D) 여자가 손님을 돕고 있다.

해설 **2인 이상 등장 사진**
(A) 동사 오답. 여자가 앞치마를 걸고 있는 모습이 아니다.
(B) 동사 오답. 남자가 쇼핑 카트를 밀고 있는 모습이 아니다.
(C) 동사 오답. 남자가 식료품점 안으로 들어가고 있는 모습이 아니다.
(D) 정답. 여자가 손님을 돕고 있는 모습이므로 정답이다.

어휘 hang up 걸다, 매달다 apron 앞치마 grocery store 식료품점

5

W-Am

(A) A woman is strolling along the pier.
(B) Tourists are posing for a photograph.
(C) Some boats are docked in a harbor.
(D) Some awnings extend over a canal.

번역 (A) 여자가 부두를 따라 산책하고 있다.
(B) 관광객들이 사진을 찍기 위해 포즈를 취하고 있다.
(C) 배들이 항구에 정박해 있다.
(D) 차양들이 운하 위까지 뻗어 있다.

해설 **사람/사물·풍경 혼합 사진**
(A) 동사 오답. 여자가 부두를 따라 산책하고 있는 모습이 아니다.
(B) 동사 오답. 관광객들이 사진을 찍고 있는 모습이 아니다.
(C) 정답. 배들이 항구에 정박해 있는 모습이므로 정답이다.
(D) 동사 오답. 차양들이 운하 위까지 뻗어 있는 모습이 아니다.

어휘 stroll 산책하다 pier 부두 dock (배를) 부두에 대다 harbor 항구 awning 차양 extend over ~에 이르다 canal 운하, 수로

6

M-Cn

(A) A fan is hanging from the ceiling.
(B) Two chairs are positioned side by side.
(C) A table has been moved next to a window.
(D) A rug has been unrolled on the floor.

번역 (A) 선풍기가 천장에 매달려 있다.
(B) 의자 두 개가 나란히 놓여 있다.
(C) 탁자가 창가로 옮겨져 있다.
(D) 양탄자가 바닥에 깔려 있다.

해설 **사물·풍경 사진**
(A) 사진에 없는 명사. 사진에 선풍기가 보이지 않는다.
(B) 위치 오답. 의자 두 개가 나란히 놓여 있는 모습이 아니다.
(C) 사진에 없는 명사. 사진에 창문이 보이지 않는다.
(D) 정답. 양탄자가 바닥에 깔려 있는 모습이므로 정답이다.

어휘 fan 선풍기 hang 매달리다, 걸리다 ceiling 천장 side by side 나란히 rug 양탄자 unroll 펼치다, 펼쳐지다

PART 2

7

W-Am Where are the recycling bins located?
M-Au (A) In the hallway.
(B) Every weekday.
(C) Just paper and glass.

번역 재활용 분리수거함은 어디에 있나요?
(A) 복도예요.
(B) 평일마다요.
(C) 종이와 유리만요.

해설 **Where 의문문**
(A) 정답. 분리수거함의 위치를 묻는 질문에 복도라고 응답하고 있으므로 정답이다.
(B) 질문과 상관없는 오답. When 의문문에 대한 응답이므로 오답이다.
(C) 연상 오답. 질문의 recycling bins에서 연상 가능한 paper와 glass를 이용한 오답이다.

어휘 recycling bin 재활용 분리수거함 be located 위치하다 hallway 복도

8

W-Br　Why are you returning this sweater?
M-Cn　(A) The returns and exchanges counter.
　　　(B) It's my sister's birthday.
　　　(C) Because there's a stain on it.

번역　왜 이 스웨터를 반품하시나요?
　　　(A) 반품 교환 창구요.
　　　(B) 여동생의 생일이에요.
　　　(C) 얼룩이 있어서요.

해설　**Why 의문문**
　　　(A) 단어 반복 오답. 질문의 return을 반복 사용한 오답이다.
　　　(B) 연상 오답. 질문의 Why와 sweater에서 연상 가능한 my sister's birthday를 이용한 오답이다.
　　　(C) 정답. 스웨터를 반품하는 이유를 묻는 질문에 얼룩이 있기 때문이라고 이유를 적절히 설명한 정답이다.

어휘　return 반품하다; 반품　exchange 교환하다; 교환　stain 얼룩

9

M-Cn　Do you want me to call a taxi for you?
M-Au　(A) I'm sure some of them do.
　　　(B) That would be great, thanks.
　　　(C) A more important phone call.

번역　제가 택시를 불러드릴까요?
　　　(A) 분명히 그들 중 일부는 그럴 거예요.
　　　(B) 그래 주시면 감사하죠.
　　　(C) 더 중요한 전화요.

해설　**조동사(Do) 의문문**
　　　(A) 질문과 상관없는 오답. 질문에 3인칭 대명사 them으로 지칭할 인물이 언급된 적이 없으므로 오답이다.
　　　(B) 정답. 택시 호출 도움이 필요한지 묻는 질문에 긍정적인 답변을 하고 있으므로 정답이다.
　　　(C) 단어 반복 오답. 질문의 call을 반복 사용한 오답이다.

10

W-Am　When will the Dubai trade show take place?
M-Cn　(A) At a large hotel.
　　　(B) In November.
　　　(C) The marketing team.

번역　두바이 무역 박람회가 언제 열리나요?
　　　(A) 큰 호텔에서요.
　　　(B) 11월에요.
　　　(C) 마케팅팀이요.

해설　**When 의문문**
　　　(A) 질문과 상관없는 오답. Where 의문문에 대한 응답이므로 오답이다.
　　　(B) 정답. 무역 박람회 개최 시점을 묻는 질문에 11월이라고 응답하고 있으므로 정답이다.
　　　(C) 질문과 상관없는 오답. Who 의문문에 대한 응답이므로 오답이다.

어휘　trade show 무역 박람회　take place 열리다

11

W-Br　Who's going to cover Emiko's shift this weekend?
M-Cn　(A) They're hardcover books.
　　　(B) A part-time worker volunteered.
　　　(C) At the service desk.

번역　이번 주말에 누가 에미코 대신 근무할 건가요?
　　　(A) 그것들은 양장본 책입니다.
　　　(B) 시간제 근무직원이 자원했어요.
　　　(C) 서비스 창구에서요.

해설　**Who 의문문**
　　　(A) 유사 발음 오답. 질문의 cover와 부분적으로 발음이 비슷한 hardcover를 이용한 오답이다.
　　　(B) 정답. 에미코 대신 근무할 사람을 묻는 질문에 이름을 답하지는 않았지만 한 시간제 근무직원이 자원했다고 응답하고 있으므로 정답이다.
　　　(C) 질문과 상관없는 오답. Where 의문문에 대한 응답이므로 오답이다.

어휘　cover (다른 사람의 일을) 대신하다　shift 교대 근무 시간　hardcover book 양장본 책　volunteer 자원하다

12

M-Cn　Which kind of sandwich do you want?
W-Am　(A) I'd like ham-and-cheese, please.
　　　(B) Yes, at lunchtime.
　　　(C) The customer over there.

번역　어떤 샌드위치를 원하시나요?
　　　(A) 햄 치즈로 부탁드려요.
　　　(B) 네, 점심 시간에요.
　　　(C) 저기 있는 손님이요.

해설　**Which+명사 의문문**
　　　(A) 정답. 어떤 샌드위치를 원하는지 묻는 질문에 햄 치즈라는 정확한 종류로 응답하고 있으므로 정답이다.
　　　(B) Yes/No 불가 오답. Which 의문문에는 Yes/No 응답이 불가능하므로 오답이다.
　　　(C) 질문과 상관없는 오답. Who 의문문에 대한 응답이므로 오답이다.

13

M-Au　You don't offer boat tours at this time of year, do you?
W-Am　(A) No, not during the winter.
　　　(B) An experienced guide.
　　　(C) What an incredible view!

번역　연중 이맘때는 보트 투어를 운영하지 않으시죠, 그렇죠?
　　　(A) 네, 겨울 동안에는 안 해요.
　　　(B) 경험이 풍부한 가이드예요.
　　　(C) 굉장히 멋진 풍경이네요!

해설　**부가 의문문**
　　　(A) 정답. 보트 투어 운영 여부를 묻는 질문에 안 한다(No)고 대답한 뒤, 겨울 동안에는 하지 않는다며 일관된 내용을 덧붙이고 있으므로 정답이다.
　　　(B) 연상 오답. 질문의 tour에서 연상 가능한 guide를 이용한 오답이다.

(C) 연상 오답. 질문의 tour에서 연상 가능한 view를 이용한 오답
이다.

어휘   experienced 경험이 풍부한   incredible (믿기 어려울 만큼) 굉장한

14

M-Au   Where's the new warehouse?

W-Br   (A) I wear this outfit all the time.
     (B) The low housing prices.
     (C) A few miles outside of town.

번역   새 창고는 어디에 있나요?
     (A) 난 이 옷을 항상 입어요.
     (B) 낮은 주택 가격이요.
     (C) 도시 밖으로 몇 마일 떨어져 있어요.

해설   **Where 의문문**
     (A) 유사 발음 오답. 질문의 warehouse와 부분적으로 발음이 유사
     한 wear를 이용한 오답이다.
     (B) 유사 발음 오답. 질문의 warehouse와 부분적으로 발음이 유사
     한 housing을 이용한 오답이다.
     (C) 정답. 새 창고의 위치를 묻는 질문에 도시 밖으로 몇 마일 떨어져
     있다고 적절히 응답하고 있으므로 정답이다.

어휘   warehouse 창고   outfit 옷   housing 주택, 주택 공급

15

M-Cn   Who got the promotion to vice president?

W-Br   (A) The card was very kind of you.
     (B) For increasing sales last year.
     (C) It should be announced today.

번역   누가 부사장으로 승진했나요?
     (A) 카드 너무 감사드립니다.
     (B) 작년에 매출을 늘렸기 때문에요.
     (C) 오늘 발표될 거예요.

해설   **Who 의문문**
     (A) 질문과 상관없는 오답.
     (B) 연상 오답. 질문의 promotion을 듣고 '승진'한 이유로 연상할 수
     있는 increasing sales를 이용한 오답.
     (C) 정답. 부사장으로 승진한 사람이 누구인지 묻는 질문에 아직 발표
     되지 않아서 지금은 모른다고 우회적으로 응답하고 있으므로 정답
     이다.

어휘   promotion 승진   vice president 부사장

16

M-Cn   There's a fitness center in this hotel, right?

W-Am   (A) No, I help guests check in.
     (B) Yes, it's next to the swimming pool.
     (C) He's a certified trainer.

번역   이 호텔에는 피트니스 센터가 있죠, 맞죠?
     (A) 아니요, 저는 손님의 체크인을 도와요.
     (B) 네, 수영장 바로 옆에 있어요.
     (C) 그 남자는 공인 트레이너예요.

해설   **부가 의문문**
     (A) 연상 오답. 질문의 hotel에서 연상 가능한 check in을 이용한 오
     답이다.
     (B) 정답. 피트니스 센터의 유무를 묻는 질문에 네(Yes)라고 대답한
     뒤, 수영장 바로 옆에 있다며 세부 위치를 덧붙이고 있으므로 정답
     이다.
     (C) 연상 오답. 질문의 fitness center에서 연상 가능한 trainer를
     이용한 오답이다.

어휘   certified 공인된

17

W-Br   How did you like the seminar?

M-Au   (A) She took it home.
     (B) Some special software.
     (C) I learned a lot.

번역   세미나는 어땠어요?
     (A) 그 여자가 그걸 집으로 가져갔어요.
     (B) 특별한 소프트웨어요.
     (C) 많은 것을 배웠어요.

해설   **How 의문문**
     (A) 질문과 상관없는 오답. 질문에 3인칭 대명사 She로 지칭할 인물
     이 언급된 적이 없으므로 오답이다.
     (B) 질문과 상관없는 오답.
     (C) 정답. 세미나 참석 소감을 묻는 질문에 많은 것을 배웠다고 긍정적
     으로 응답하고 있으므로 정답이다.

18

W-Am   Does your company let office staff wear
     headphones?

M-Au   (A) Oh, I work from home.
     (B) The open floor plan.
     (C) Did you listen to music or podcasts?

번역   당신의 회사는 사무실 직원들이 헤드폰을 쓰는 것을 허용하나요?
     (A) 아, 저는 재택 근무해요.
     (B) 개방형 평면도요.
     (C) 음악을 들으셨나요, 아니면 팟캐스트를 들으셨나요?

해설   **조동사(Does) 의문문**
     (A) 정답. 사무실 직원들의 헤드폰 사용 허용 여부를 묻는 질문에 자신
     은 집에서 일한다며 모른다는 사실을 우회적으로 전달하고 있으므
     로 정답이다.
     (B) 연상 오답. 질문의 office에서 연상 가능한 floor plan을 이용한
     오답이다.
     (C) 연상 오답. 질문의 headphone에서 연상 가능한 music과
     podcasts를 이용한 오답이다.

어휘   work from home 재택 근무하다   open floor plan 개방형
     평면도

19

M-Au   What's the name of this dish?

W-Br   (A) Let me check the menu card.
     (B) Robert Wilson, I believe.
     (C) It comes with a piece of bread.

번역   이 요리 이름이 뭐예요?
(A) 메뉴판을 확인해 볼게요.
(B) 로버트 윌슨일 거예요.
(C) 빵 한 조각이 곁들여져 나와요.

해설   **What 의문문**
(A) 정답. 요리 이름을 묻는 질문에 메뉴판을 확인해 보겠다며 모른다는 사실을 우회적으로 전달하고 있으므로 정답이다.
(B) 연상 오답. 질문의 name에서 연상 가능한 Robert Wilson을 이용한 오답이다.
(C) 연상 오답. 질문의 dish에서 연상 가능한 bread를 이용한 오답이다.

20

M-Cn This road leads to the highway, doesn't it?
W-Am (A) Yes, the pay is quite high.
(B) I think we should have turned left earlier.
(C) A reliable online map.

번역   이 길은 고속도로로 이어지죠, 그렇지 않아요?
(A) 네, 보수가 꽤 높아요.
(B) 아까 좌회전을 했어야 하나 봐요.
(C) 신뢰할 만한 온라인 지도예요.

해설   **부가 의문문**
(A) 유사 발음 오답. 질문의 highway와 부분적으로 발음이 유사한 high를 이용한 오답이다.
(B) 정답. 길이 고속도로로 이어지는지 묻는 질문에 고속도로로 이어지는 길을 이미 지나쳐 왔다는 말로 이 길이 고속도로로 이어지지 않는다는 부정의 답변을 우회적으로 전달하고 있으므로 정답이다.
(C) 연상 오답. 질문의 road와 highway에서 연상 가능한 map을 이용한 오답이다.

어휘   reliable 신뢰할 만한

21

M-Cn Could you show me how to use the packaging machine?
W-Br (A) Sure, I'll take it to the post office.
(B) Have you finished reading the manual?
(C) That show received poor reviews.

번역   포장 기계 사용하는 법을 보여주실 수 있나요?
(A) 그럼요, 제가 그걸 우체국으로 가져갈게요.
(B) 사용 설명서를 다 읽으셨나요?
(C) 그 공연은 형편없는 평가를 받았어요.

해설   **요청·제안문**
(A) 연상 오답. 질문의 packaging에서 연상 가능한 post office를 이용한 오답이다.
(B) 정답. 포장 기계 사용하는 법을 보여달라는 질문에 그 내용이 나와 있는 사용 설명서를 읽었는지 되묻고 있으므로 정답이다.
(C) 단어 반복 오답. 질문의 show를 반복 사용한 오답이다.

어휘   packaging 포장   review 평가, 후기

22

M-Au Which notebook do you like better, the gray one or the brown one?
W-Am (A) It's several pages long.
(B) The gray one is on sale.
(C) I have to notify the attendees.

번역   회색 공책과 갈색 공책 중에 어느 것이 더 마음에 드세요?
(A) 몇 페이지 분량이에요.
(B) 회색 공책이 할인 중이에요.
(C) 참석자들에게 알려야 해요.

해설   **선택 의문문**
(A) 연상 오답. 질문의 notebook에서 연상 가능한 pages를 이용한 오답이다.
(B) 정답. 회색 공책과 갈색 공책 중 마음에 드는 것을 묻는 질문에 둘 중 하나를 골라 응답하고 있으므로 정답이다.
(C) 질문과 상관없는 오답.

어휘   notify 알리다   attendee 참석자

23

W-Am Would printing these handouts in color cost much more?
M-Cn (A) No, the training budget.
(B) I enjoyed the presentation.
(C) The price list is on the wall.

번역   이 인쇄물을 컬러로 출력하려면 비용이 훨씬 많이 들까요?
(A) 아니요, 교육비 예산이에요.
(B) 발표 내용이 좋았어요.
(C) 가격표는 벽에 붙어 있습니다.

해설   **조동사(Would) 의문문**
(A) 연상 오답. 질문의 cost에서 연상 가능한 budget을 이용한 오답이다.
(B) 연상 오답. 질문의 handout에서 연상 가능한 presentation을 이용한 오답이다.
(C) 정답. 인쇄물의 컬러 출력 비용을 묻는 질문에 비용이 나와 있는 가격표를 보라고 안내하고 있으므로 정답이다.

어휘   handout 인쇄물   budget 예산

24

W-Br The air conditioner in the waiting room isn't working.
M-Au (A) There's a fan in the supply closet.
(B) Here're your patient records.
(C) Right, he's on his break.

번역   대기실에 있는 에어컨이 작동이 안 돼요.
(A) 비품 수납장에 선풍기가 있어요.
(B) 당신의 환자 기록입니다.
(C) 맞아요, 그는 지금 휴가 중이에요.

해설   **사실·정보 전달의 평서문**
(A) 정답. 에어컨이 작동이 안 된다는 평서문에 비품 수납장에 선풍기가 있다며 적절한 대안을 제시하고 있으므로 정답이다.

(B) 연상 오답. 평서문의 waiting room(병원의 대기실)에서 연상 가능한 patient를 이용한 오답이다.

(C) 평서문과 상관없는 오답. 평서문에 3인칭 대명사 he로 지칭할 인물이 언급된 적이 없으므로 오답이다.

어휘 supply closet 비품 수납장 patient 환자 on one's break 휴가 중인

25

W-Am These focus group results are promising.
M-Cn (A) The design options are in this file.
(B) The feedback was very positive.
(C) No, the inspector's still here.

번역 이 포커스 그룹 결과가 매우 고무적입니다.
(A) 디자인 시안들은 이 파일에 들어 있어요.
(B) 피드백이 매우 긍정적이었어요.
(C) 아니요, 그 조사관은 아직 이곳에 있어요.

해설 사실·정보 전달의 평서문
(A) 평서문과 상관없는 오답.
(B) 정답. 포커스 그룹 결과가 고무적이라는 평서문에 피드백이 긍정적이었다며 적절히 호응하고 있으므로 정답이다.
(C) 연상 오답. 평서문의 result에서 연상 가능한 inspector를 이용한 오답이다.

어휘 promising 유망한, 촉망되는 inspector 조사관

26

W-Br Let's get coffee before we go back to the office.
W-Am (A) I have a deadline this afternoon.
(B) No, I haven't been there.
(C) The machine in the breakroom.

번역 사무실로 복귀하기 전에 커피를 마시러 갑시다.
(A) 오후까지 마감해야 하는 일이 있어요.
(B) 아니요, 거기에는 가본 적이 없어요.
(C) 휴게실에 있는 기계요.

해설 요청·제안문
(A) 정답. 사무실로 복귀하기 전에 커피를 마시러 가자는 제안에 오후까지 마감해야 하는 일이 있다며 우회적으로 거절 의사를 전달하고 있으므로 정답이다.
(B) 제안문과 상관없는 오답.
(C) 연상 오답. 제안문의 coffee와 office에서 연상 가능한 machine과 breakroom을 이용한 오답이다.

어휘 deadline 마감 기한 breakroom 휴게실

27

M-Cn Where should I park when I arrive at the venue?
W-Br (A) In a couple of minutes.
(B) The catering van.
(C) At the loading dock.

번역 그 장소에 도착하면 어디에 주차해야 하나요?
(A) 몇 분 후에요.
(B) 푸드 트럭이요.
(C) 하역장에요.

해설 Where 의문문
(A) 질문과 상관없는 오답. When 의문문에 대한 응답이므로 오답이다.
(B) 연상 오답. 질문의 park에서 연상 가능한 catering van을 이용한 오답이다.
(C) 정답. 주차할 수 있는 장소를 묻는 질문에 하역장이라고 응답하고 있으므로 정답이다.

어휘 venue 장소 catering van 푸드 트럭 loading dock 하역장

28

M-Au When will you begin advertising the conference?
W-Br (A) The newspaper runs job advertisements.
(B) Yes, it was interesting.
(C) We don't have a keynote speaker yet.

번역 그 회의에 대한 홍보를 언제 시작할 건가요?
(A) 그 신문은 구인 광고를 게시해요.
(B) 네, 흥미로웠어요.
(C) 아직 기조 연설자를 못 구했어요.

해설 When 의문문
(A) 파생어 오답. 질문의 advertising과 파생어 관계인 advertisement를 이용한 오답이다.
(B) Yes/No 불가 오답. When 의문문에는 Yes/No 응답이 불가능하므로 오답이다.
(C) 정답. 회의 홍보 시작 시점을 묻는 질문에 기조 연설자를 아직 못 구했다며 홍보를 시작하지 못하는 이유를 우회적으로 전달하고 있으므로 정답이다.

어휘 conference 회의, 학회 keynote speaker 기조 연설자

29

W-Am Does anyone have extra tickets for tonight's charity concert?
M-Cn (A) I only have a one-way ticket.
(B) Do you know your seat number?
(C) The concert is tomorrow evening.

번역 오늘 밤 자선 콘서트의 남는 티켓을 갖고 계신 분 있나요?
(A) 저는 편도 티켓만 있어요.
(B) 좌석 번호를 알고 계세요?
(C) 그 콘서트는 내일 밤이에요.

해설 조동사(Does) 의문문
(A) 단어 반복 오답. 질문의 ticket을 반복 사용한 오답이다.
(B) 연상 오답. 질문의 ticket과 concert에서 연상 가능한 seat number를 이용한 오답이다.
(C) 정답. 오늘 밤 자선 콘서트의 남는 티켓이 있는지 묻는 질문에 자선 콘서트가 열리는 날은 오늘이 아닌 내일이라고 정정해 주고 있으므로 정답이다.

어휘 extra 여분의, 추가의 charity 자선 one-way 편도의

30

M-Au How much training is required to become a nurse?
W-Am (A) Are you thinking about changing careers?
(B) She was hired last month.
(C) An annual medical checkup.

번역　간호사가 되기 위해서는 얼마나 많은 교육이 필요한가요?
(A) 직업을 바꾸려고 생각 중이세요?
(B) 그녀는 시난달에 고용됐어요.
(C) 연례 건강 검진이요.

해설　How+형용사/부사 의문문
(A) 정답. 간호사가 되는 데 필요한 교육 기간을 묻는 질문에 직접적으로 답하지는 않았지만 직업을 바꾸려고 생각 중인지 관련 있는 내용을 되묻고 있으므로 정답이다.
(B) 연상 오답. 질문의 nurse에서 연상 가능한 She was hired를 이용한 오답이다.
(C) 연상 오답. 질문의 nurse에서 연상 가능한 medical checkup을 이용한 오답이다.

어휘　require 요구하다　career 경력　annual 연례의
medical checkup 건강 검진

31

W-Br　Doesn't the big conference room have a better projector?

M-Au　(A) Yes, this gear will protect her.
(B) Some managers are meeting in there.
(C) Eric is bringing more chairs.

번역　대회의실에 더 좋은 프로젝터가 있지 않나요?
(A) 네, 이 장비가 그녀를 보호해 줄 거예요.
(B) 관리자들이 거기에서 회의 중이에요.
(C) 에릭이 의자를 더 가져오고 있어요.

해설　부정 의문문
(A) 유사 발음 오답. 질문의 projector와 부분적으로 발음이 유사한 protect her를 이용한 오답이다.
(B) 정답. 프로젝터 비치 여부를 묻는 질문에 관리자들이 거기에서 회의 중이기 때문에 대회의실에 있는 프로젝터를 이용할 수 없다는 사실을 우회적으로 전달하고 있으므로 정답이다.
(C) 연상 오답. 질문의 conference room에서 연상 가능한 chairs를 이용한 오답이다.

PART 3

32-34

W-Am　Sorry to bother you, Carl, but do you know where Rodney is? **32 I was supposed to show him these sales figures for our new tablet computer as soon as they came in, but he's not in his office.**

M-Cn　**33 He's at a doctor's appointment,** and he won't be back today. But if you give that paper to me, I'll pass it on to him tomorrow.

W-Am　Thank you, I'd appreciate that. **34 I'll be conducting job interviews all day tomorrow.**

번역　여: 방해해서 미안해요, 칼, 하지만 로드니가 어디에 있는지 아시나요? 새로 출시한 태블릿 컴퓨터 매출액 자료를 입수하는 대로 그에게 보여주기로 했는데 그가 사무실에 없네요.
남: 그는 진료를 받으러 갔어요. 오늘은 안 돌아올 거예요. 그 자료를 저에게 주시면 내일 전달해 드릴게요.
여: 그렇게 해주신다니 정말 감사합니다. 제가 내일 하루 종일 면접을 진행해야 하거든요.

어휘　bother 귀찮게 하다　sales figures 매출액
appointment (진료 등의) 예약　appreciate 고맙게 여기다
conduct 실시하다

---

32 Why did the woman go to Rodney's office?
(A) To repair a computer
(B) To drop off a package
(C) To negotiate a deadline
(D) To present some data

번역　여자는 왜 로드니의 사무실에 갔는가?
(A) 컴퓨터를 수리하려고
(B) 소포를 갖다주려고
(C) 마감 기한을 협의하려고
(D) 자료를 보여주려고

해설　**세부 사항 관련 - 여자가 로드니의 사무실에 간 이유**
여자가 첫 번째 대사에서 새로 출시한 태블릿 컴퓨터 매출액 자료를 입수하는 대로 그에게 보여주기로 했는데 그가 사무실에 없다(I was supposed to show him these sales figures for our new tablet computer ~, but he's not in his office)고 말하고 있으므로 정답은 (D)이다.

어휘　repair 수리하다　drop off ~을 갖다주다　negotiate 협상하다
deadline 마감 기한　present 제시하다, 발표하다

> **Paraphrasing**
> 대화의 show him these sales figures
> → 정답의 present some data

---

33 Why is Rodney unavailable?
(A) He is out for lunch.
(B) He is seeing a doctor.
(C) He is at a trade show.
(D) He is leading a facility tour.

번역　로드니는 왜 자리에 없는가?
(A) 점심을 먹으러 나가서
(B) 진료를 받는 중이어서
(C) 무역 박람회에 가서
(D) 시설 견학을 진행 중이어서

해설　**세부 사항 관련 - 로드니가 자리에 없는 이유**
남자가 첫 번째 대사에서 그는 진료를 받으러 갔다(He's at a doctor's appointment)고 말하고 있으므로 정답은 (B)이다.

어휘　trade show 무역 박람회　lead 이끌다　facility 시설

Paraphrasing
대화의 He's at a doctor's appointment
→ 정답의 He is seeing a doctor.

여: 네, 그러시면 **변경 수수료는 1매당 8달러입니다.** 하지만 오늘 회원권을 구매하시면 이 수수료를 면제해 드릴 수 있습니다.

남: 감사하지만, **그냥 변경만 하겠습니다.** 제가 이 도시에 살지 않아서 이 극장에 정기적으로 오기 힘들거든요.

어휘   assist 돕다   performance 공연   exchange 교환:
교환하다   policy 정책   apply to ~에 적용되다   waive
면제하다   charge 수수료, 요금

34   What will the woman most likely do tomorrow?
(A) Hold some job interviews
(B) Work from a different location
(C) Install some electronics
(D) Finalize a sales report

번역   여자는 내일 무엇을 하겠는가?
(A) 채용 면접을 진행한다.
(B) 다른 장소에서 일한다.
(C) 전자 제품을 설치한다.
(D) 매출 보고서를 완성한다.

해설   **세부 사항 관련 - 여자가 할 일**
여자가 두 번째 대사에서 자신은 내일 하루 종일 면접을 진행해야 한다
(I'll be conducting job interviews all day tomorrow)고 말
하고 있으므로 정답은 (A)이다.

어휘   install 설치하다   electronics 전자 제품   finalize 완성하다

Paraphrasing
대화의 conducting job interviews
→ 정답의 Hold some job interviews

35   Why is the man calling?
(A) To confirm a requirement
(B) To exchange some tickets
(C) To purchase a membership
(D) To inquire about volunteering

번역   남자는 왜 전화를 걸고 있는가?
(A) 요구조건을 확인하려고
(B) 티켓을 변경하려고
(C) 회원권을 구매하려고
(D) 자원봉사에 대해 문의하려고

해설   **전체 내용 관련 - 남자가 전화를 건 이유**
남자가 첫 번째 대사에서 8월 8일 <두 마을> 공연 티켓을 예매했는
데, 날짜를 미루고 싶다(I have tickets for the August eighth
performance of Two Villages, but I'd like to go on a later
date)며 무료로 변경을 해주는 게 맞는지(I understand that you
allow free exchanges?) 묻고 있으므로 정답은 (B)이다.

어휘   confirm 확인하다   requirement 요구조건   inquire 문의하다

35-37

W-Am   Wilmoth Theater box office. How can I assist you today?

M-Au   Hi, **35 I have tickets for the August eighth performance of _Two Villages_, but I'd like to go on a later date. I understand that you allow free exchanges?**

W-Am   Actually, **36 that policy only applies to theater members.** Are you a member of our theater?

M-Au   Oh... no, I'm not.

W-Am   OK, **37 then the exchanges will cost you eight dollars per ticket. However, if you buy a membership today, I could waive those charges.**

M-Au   Thanks, but **37 I'll just take the exchanges.** I don't live in the city, so it would be hard for me to come to your theater regularly.

여: 윌모스 극장 매표소입니다. 무엇을 도와드릴까요?

남: 안녕하세요. 8월 8일 <두 마을> 공연 티켓을 예매했는데, 날짜를 미루고 싶어서요. 무료로 변경을 해주시는 걸로 알고 있는데요?

여: 사실 그 방침은 극장 회원에게만 적용이 돼요. 저희 극장 회원이신가요?

남: 아… 아니요, 회원이 아닙니다.

36   What does the woman explain to the man?
(A) A performance is sold out.
(B) A computer service is down.
(C) A neighborhood is usually busy.
(D) A policy does not apply to everyone.

번역   여자는 남자에게 무엇을 설명하는가?
(A) 공연이 매진되었다.
(B) 컴퓨터 서비스가 다운되었다.
(C) 동네는 보통 혼잡하다.
(D) 방침이 모두에게 적용되는 것은 아니다.

해설   **세부 사항 관련 - 여자가 설명하는 것**
여자가 두 번째 대사에서 무료로 변경을 해주는 그 방침은 극장 회
원에게만 적용이 된다(that policy only applies to theater
members)고 말하고 있으므로 정답은 (D)이다.

어휘   sold out 매진된

Paraphrasing
대화의 only applies to theater members
→ 정답의 does not apply to everyone

37 What does the man decide to do?
(A) Pay some additional fees
(B) Arrive early at a location
(C) Have his name put on a list
(D) Gather opinions from others

번역 남자는 무엇을 하기로 했는가?
(A) 추가 수수료 내기
(B) 장소에 일찍 도착하기
(C) 명단에 이름 올리기
(D) 다른 사람들의 의견 취합하기

해설 **세부 사항 관련 - 남자가 하기로 한 일**
앞에서 여자가 변경 수수료가 1매당 8달러(then the exchanges will cost you eight dollars per ticket)라고 말하고 극장 회원으로 가입하면 이를 면제해 주겠다(~ if you buy a membership today, I could waive those charges)고 하자, 남자가 그냥 변경만 하겠다(I'll just take the exchanges)고 답변했으므로 정답은 (A)이다.

어휘 additional 추가의 gather 모으다 opinion 의견

> **Paraphrasing**
> 대화의 cost you eight dollars
> → 정답의 Pay some additional fees

38-40

> M-Au Hi. ³⁸**I need a photograph of myself for a travel visa application.** Does your studio do that kind of thing?
>
> W-Br Absolutely. I can take that for you right away. Did the application instructions mention any special requirements for the photo?
>
> M-Au Oh, yes, actually. ³⁹**It's supposed to be a certain size… I forgot to bring that information, though.**
>
> W-Br Don't worry. ⁴⁰**I can look it up online for you on this computer.** What country are you trying to go to?
>
> 남: 안녕하세요. **여행 비자 신청을 위해 증명 사진이 필요한데요.** 당신의 스튜디오에서 그런 일도 하시나요?
>
> 여: 그럼요. 바로 찍어드릴 수 있습니다. 신청 안내에 증명 사진에 대한 특별한 요구조건이 언급되어 있었나요?
>
> 남: 아, 네, 있었습니다. **특정 크기여야 하는데… 그 정보를 깜빡 잊고 놓고 왔네요.**
>
> 여: 걱정 마세요. **컴퓨터에서 온라인으로 찾아봐 드릴 수 있습니다.** 어느 나라로 가려고 하세요?
>
> 어휘 application 신청, 신청서 instruction 설명, 지시 requirement 필요조건 look up (컴퓨터 등에서) 찾아보다

38 What is the man trying to do?
(A) Buy a guidebook
(B) Store some luggage
(C) Have his picture taken
(D) Pick up an application

번역 남자는 무엇을 하려고 하는가?
(A) 여행 안내서 사기
(B) 짐 보관하기
(C) 사진 찍기
(D) 신청서 받아가기

해설 **세부 사항 관련 - 남자가 하려는 일**
남자가 첫 번째 대사에서 여행 비자 신청을 위해 증명 사진이 필요하다(I need a photograph of myself for a travel visa application)고 말하고 있으므로 정답은 (C)이다.

어휘 store 보관하다, 저장하다 luggage 짐 pick up (어떤 장소로) 와서 가져가다

> **Paraphrasing**
> 대화의 need a photograph of myself
> → 정답의 Have his picture taken

39 What did the man forget to bring?
(A) A travel itinerary
(B) A carrier bag
(C) Some clothing
(D) Some size information

번역 남자가 깜빡 잊고 놓고 온 것은?
(A) 여행 일정표
(B) 쇼핑백
(C) 옷
(D) 크기 정보

해설 **세부 사항 관련 - 남자가 놓고 온 것**
남자가 두 번째 대사에서 증명 사진이 특정 크기여야 하는데 그 정보를 깜빡 잊고 놓고 왔다(It's supposed to be a certain size… I forgot to bring that information)고 말하고 있으므로 정답은 (D)이다.

어휘 itinerary 일정표

40 What does the woman offer to do?
(A) Search the Internet
(B) Wait for the man to return
(C) Consult with a manager
(D) Lend an item

번역 여자는 무엇을 하겠다고 제안하는가?
(A) 인터넷 검색하기
(B) 남자가 돌아올 때까지 기다리기
(C) 관리자와 상의하기
(D) 물건 빌려주기

해설　세부 사항 관련 - 여자가 제안하는 것

여자가 두 번째 대사에서 컴퓨터에서 온라인으로 찾아봐 줄 수 있다(I can look it up online for you on this computer)고 말하고 있으므로 정답은 (A)이다.

어휘　consult 상의하다　lend 빌려주다

> **Paraphrasing**
> 대화의 look it up online → 정답의 Search the Internet

41-43

M-Au　Tina, **⁴¹I just saw your announcement about the company moving offices**—how exciting! It looks like the new space has more square footage, so we'll finally have room to expand our workforce.

W-Am　Yes, and the transportation situation in that neighborhood is also better. We'll have access to a bigger parking area.

M-Au　That's great. Umm… **⁴²I'm concerned about the timing of the move, though. Couldn't you postpone it by a few weeks?** The end of this month will be a busy time for my team.

W-Am　I mean, that was the president's decision.

M-Au　Oh, I see. Then I guess **⁴³I'll discuss the problem with the team** and figure out how we can rearrange our work schedule.

W-Am　Good idea. Let me know if I can help.

남:　티나, 회사 사무실 이전에 관해 당신이 공지한 내용을 방금 봤어요. 정말 신나네요! 새로운 곳은 더 넓은 것 같아서 마침내 직원을 늘릴 수 있는 여지가 생기겠네요.

여:　네, 그 동네 교통 환경도 더 좋아요. 더 넓은 주차장도 이용할 수 있어요.

남:　좋네요. 음… 이사 시기가 좀 우려가 되긴 해요. 몇 주 정도만 미룰 수 없나요? 이달 말은 저희 팀이 바쁜 시기예요.

여:　근데, 그건 회장님 결정이에요.

남:　아, 그렇군요. 그러면 그 문제를 팀원들과 상의해서 업무 일정을 어떻게 조정할지 알아봐야겠네요.

여:　좋은 생각이에요. 제가 도울 수 있는 일이 있다면 알려주세요.

어휘　announcement 공지, 발표　square footage 평방 피트
expand 확장하다　workforce 노동자, 직원
transportation 교통, 운송　postpone 연기하다
president 회장　decision 결정　figure out 이해하다,
알아내다　rearrange 재조정하다

41 What is the conversation about?
(A) An advertising campaign
(B) A product design
(C) A hiring committee
(D) A business relocation

번역　무엇에 대한 대화인가?
(A) 광고 캠페인
(B) 제품 디자인
(C) 고용 위원회
(D) 사업장 이전

해설　전체 내용 관련 - 대화의 주제

남자가 첫 번째 대사에서 회사 사무실 이전에 관해 여자가 공지한 내용을 방금 봤다(I just saw your announcement about the company moving offices)고 말하고 있으므로 정답은 (D)이다.

어휘　relocation 이전

> **Paraphrasing**
> 대화의 moving offices → 정답의 A business relocation

42 What does the woman imply when she says, "that was the president's decision"?
(A) It is not possible to change a plan.
(B) Some contract terms are acceptable.
(C) An executive has returned from a trip.
(D) An announcement gave incorrect information.

번역　여자가 "그건 회장님 결정이에요"라고 말할 때, 그 의도는 무엇인가?
(A) 계획을 바꾸는 것은 불가능하다.
(B) 몇몇 계약 조건들은 수용할 만하다.
(C) 임원이 여행에서 돌아왔다.
(D) 공지에 부정확한 정보가 들어갔다.

해설　화자의 의도 파악 - 회장님 결정이라는 말의 의도

앞에서 남자가 이사 시기가 좀 우려가 된다며 몇 주 정도만 미룰 수 없는지(I'm concerned about the timing of the move, though. Couldn't you postpone it by a few weeks?) 묻자, 그 질문에 대한 답변으로 여자가 인용문을 언급한 것으로 보아 이사 시기를 몇 주 정도 미루는 일이 불가능하다는 의도로 한 말임을 알 수 있다. 따라서 정답은 (A)이다.

어휘　contract 계약　terms 조건　acceptable 수용할 만한
executive 임원, 중역　incorrect 부정확한

43 What does the man say he will do?
(A) Visit a building site
(B) Save some paperwork
(C) Provide a price estimate
(D) Speak with some employees

번역　남자는 무엇을 하겠다고 말하는가?
(A) 건축 현장 방문하기
(B) 서류 작업 생략하기
(C) 견적서 제공하기
(D) 직원들과 이야기하기

해설 **세부 사항 관련 - 남자가 할 일**
남자가 마지막 대사에서 그 문제를 팀원들과 상의하겠다(I'll discuss the problem with the team)고 말하고 있으므로 정답은 (D)이다.

어휘 building site 건축 현장   save 절약하다   estimate 견적서

> **Paraphrasing**
> 대화의 discuss the problem with the team
> → 정답의 Speak with some employees

44-46 3인 대화

> W-Br Hi, Tim and Rafael. I heard that **⁴⁴we've been unable to prepare the soil in the carrot field for planting.** What's going on?
>
> M-Au **⁴⁵The special fertilizer we ordered hasn't arrived.** Rafael just called the supplier, but they couldn't help.
>
> M-Cn Right—their records show the shipment was completed, even though it wasn't. It might take a while to figure out what went wrong.
>
> W-Br Well, we need to get the carrots planted. **⁴⁶Why don't you take the truck over to pick up fertilizer from the local farm supply store?**
>
> ---
>
> 여: 안녕하세요, 팀, 라파엘. 당근 밭에 있는 흙이 아직 당근을 심을 준비가 되지 않았다고 들었어요. 어떻게 되고 있는 거예요?
>
> 남1: 우리가 주문한 특수 비료가 아직 도착하지 않았어요. 방금 라파엘이 공급업자에게 전화했지만 해줄 수 있는 게 없대요.
>
> 남2: 맞아요. 그쪽 기록에는 배송이 완료되지 않았는데도 배송이 완료되었다고 나온대요. 뭐가 잘못된 건지 알아내려면 시간이 좀 걸릴 것 같아요.
>
> 여: 음, 당근을 심어야 하는데요. 트럭을 타고 가까운 동네 농업 용품 판매점에 가서 비료를 사오는 건 어때요?
>
> ---
>
> 어휘 planting (나무 등을) 심기   fertilizer 비료   supplier 공급업자   shipment 배송, 배송품   complete 완료하다   figure out 알아내다   go wrong 일이 잘못되다   farm supply store 농업 용품 판매점

44 Where do the speakers most likely work?
(A) At a supermarket
(B) At a restaurant
(C) At a vegetable farm
(D) At a catering company

번역 화자들은 어디서 일하겠는가?
(A) 슈퍼마켓
(B) 식당
(C) 채소 농장
(D) 출장 요리 업체

해설 **전체 내용 관련 - 화자들의 근무지**
여자가 첫 번째 대사에서 당근 밭에 있는 흙이 아직 당근을 심을 준비가 되지 않았다고 들었다(we've been unable to prepare the soil in the carrot field for planting)며 밭에 당근을 심는 일을 언급하고 있는 것으로 보아 화자들이 채소 농장에서 근무한다는 것을 알 수 있다. 따라서 정답은 (C)이다.

45 According to the men, what is causing a problem?
(A) An appliance is not working.
(B) An event was canceled.
(C) Some food has gone bad.
(D) A shipment has not arrived.

번역 남자들에 따르면 문제의 원인은 무엇인가?
(A) 기기가 작동하지 않는다.
(B) 행사가 취소되었다.
(C) 일부 음식이 상했다.
(D) 배송품이 도착하지 않았다.

해설 **세부 사항 관련 - 문제의 원인**
앞에서 여자가 흙이 준비되지 않은 이유를 묻자, 첫 번째 남자가 첫 번째 대사에서 주문한 특수 비료가 아직 도착하지 않았다(The special fertilizer we ordered hasn't arrived)고 말하고 있으므로 정답은 (D)이다.

어휘 appliance 기구, 장치   go bad (음식이) 상하다

> **Paraphrasing**
> 대화의 The special fertilizer we ordered
> → 정답의 A shipment

46 What does the woman suggest doing?
(A) Revising a menu
(B) Driving to a store
(C) Putting up a sign
(D) Postponing a task

번역 여자는 무엇을 제안하는가?
(A) 메뉴 수정하기
(B) 차를 타고 상점으로 가기
(C) 간판 내걸기
(D) 할 일을 미루기

해설 **세부 사항 관련 - 여자가 제안하는 것**
여자가 마지막 대사에서 트럭을 타고 가까운 동네 농업 용품 판매점에 가서 비료를 사오는 건 어떤지(Why don't you take the truck over to pick up fertilizer from the local farm supply store?) 묻고 있으므로 정답은 (B)이다.

어휘 revise 수정하다   put up a sign 간판을 내걸다   postpone 연기하다   task 일, 과제

> **Paraphrasing**
> 대화의 take the truck over to pick up
> → 정답의 Driving to a store

47-49

M-Cn OK, ma'am, **⁴⁷ we've figured out what's wrong with your car.** The fuel filter needs to be replaced. We can do that for you right away for two hundred dollars.

W-Br Oh, that's a lot. I've done some basic repairs in the past. Could I buy the part from you, and handle the replacement myself?

M-Cn Hmm… **⁴⁸ with the way your car is designed, it wouldn't be an easy job. There are a lot of steps.** It would take us over an hour.

W-Br OK, then I guess you should do it. **⁴⁹ I'll go out and get something to eat while I wait.** Uh, I've never been to this area before…

M-Cn There's a great diner over that way.

남: 됐습니다, 고객님, **차에 무슨 문제가 있는지 알아냈습니다.** 연료 필터를 교체해야 합니다. 200달러의 비용으로 바로 해드릴 수 있습니다.

여: 아, 비싸네요. 예전에 기본 수리를 직접 해본 적이 있어요. 여기서 부품을 사서 제가 직접 교체해도 될까요?

남: 음… **고객님의 차가 설계된 방식을 감안할 때 쉬운 일이 아닐 거예요. 많은 단계를 거쳐야 해요.** 저희가 해도 한 시간 이상 걸립니다.

여: 그렇군요, 그러면 해주시는 게 좋겠네요. **기다리는 동안 나가서 뭐 좀 먹고 오겠습니다.** 근데, 제가 이 동네는 처음 와봐서요…

남: 저쪽으로 가시면 괜찮은 식당이 있어요.

어휘 figure out 알아내다 fuel 연료 replace 교체하다 handle 다루다, 처리하다 replacement 교체품, 대용품 step 단계

47 Where does the conversation most likely take place?
(A) At an outdoor market
(B) At an auto repair shop
(C) At a subway station
(D) At a parking garage

번역 대화는 어디서 이루어지겠는가?
(A) 야외 시장
(B) 자동차 정비소
(C) 지하철역
(D) 주차 빌딩

해설 **전체 내용 관련 - 대화의 장소**
남자가 첫 번째 대사에서 여자의 차에 무슨 문제가 있는지 알아냈다(we've figured out what's wrong with your car)고 말하는 것으로 보아 대화 장소가 자동차 정비소임을 알 수 있다. 따라서 정답은 (B)이다.

48 Why is the man unsure about the woman's idea?
(A) Bad weather is predicted.
(B) A destination is far away.
(C) A process is complicated.
(D) A warranty is strict.

번역 남자는 왜 여자의 아이디어에 확신이 없는가?
(A) 기상 악화가 예상되어서
(B) 목적지가 멀어서
(C) 과정이 복잡해서
(D) 보증이 엄격해서

해설 **세부 사항 관련 - 남자가 확신이 없는 이유**
남자가 두 번째 대사에서 차가 설계된 방식을 감안할 때 (부품을 직접 교체하는 일이) 쉬운 일이 아닐 것(with the way your car is designed, it wouldn't be an easy job)이라며 많은 단계를 거쳐야 한다(There are a lot of steps)고 말하는 것으로 보아 정답은 (C)이다.

어휘 predict 예측하다 destination 목적지 complicated 복잡한 warranty 보증(서) strict 엄격한

> **Paraphrasing**
> 대화의 There are a lot of steps.
> → 정답의 A process is complicated.

49 Why does the woman say, "I've never been to this area before"?
(A) To express enthusiasm
(B) To ask for a recommendation
(C) To refuse an assignment
(D) To explain a mistake

번역 여자가 "제가 이 동네는 처음 와봐서요"라고 말한 이유는?
(A) 열정을 표현하려고
(B) 추천을 부탁하려고
(C) 할당된 일을 거절하려고
(D) 실수를 설명하려고

해설 **화자의 의도 파악 - 이 동네를 처음 와본다는 말의 의도**
앞에서 여자가 기다리는 동안 나가서 뭐 좀 먹고 오겠다(I'll go out and get something to eat while I wait)고 말한 뒤에 인용문을 언급한 것으로 보아, 남자에게 근처에 먹을 만한 곳을 추천해 달라는 의도로 한 말임을 알 수 있다. 따라서 정답은 (B)이다.

어휘 express 표현하다 enthusiasm 열정 recommendation 추천 refuse 거절하다 assignment 할당된 일

50-52

W-Am Sung-ho, didn't I see your name on the list of this year's employee award winners?

M-Cn Yes, **⁵⁰ I won a prize for streamlining our customer support processes.**

W-Am Ah, I heard about the improvements to our workflow in that area. So those were your ideas?

M-Cn Actually, ⁵¹ **I got most of them from a workshop I went to earlier this year.**

W-Am Well, you still deserve credit for bringing them to the company. So, do you know what the prize will be?

M-Cn It's three hundred dollars.

W-Am Wow! What are you going to do with it?

M-Cn ⁵² **I'm going to set it aside for now.** I'd like to make a down payment on a house someday.

여: 성호, 올해 우수사원 수상자 명단에 당신 이름이 안 보이네요?

남: 제 이름 있어요. **고객 지원 프로세스를 간소화한 공로로 상을 받았어요.**

여: 아, 그 분야에서 업무 흐름을 개선했다는 이야기 들었어요. 그럼 그게 당신 아이디어였어요?

남: 사실, **아이디어 대부분은 올해 초반에 갔던 워크숍에서 배운 거였어요.**

여: 그래도 그 아이디어를 회사로 가져온 공로가 있잖아요. 그럼 어떤 상품을 받게 되는지 알아요?

남: 300달러예요.

여: 우와! 그걸로 뭘 할 건가요?

남: **지금은 저축해 두려고요.** 나중에 집 계약금으로 쓰고 싶어요.

어휘 winner 수상자 streamline 간소화하다 improvement 개선 workflow 업무 흐름 deserve ~을 받을 만하다 credit 공로, 인정 set aside (돈, 비상금 등을) 남겨두다 down payment 계약금

50 What did the man win a prize for?
(A) Improving the workflow for a service
(B) Receiving high ratings from customers
(C) Reaching a special work anniversary
(D) Finding a use for some waste

번역 남자는 무엇 때문에 상을 받았는가?
(A) 서비스를 위한 업무 흐름을 개선해서
(B) 고객에게 높은 평가를 받아서
(C) 특별한 근속 기념일이 다가와서
(D) 폐기물 활용 방안을 찾아내서

해설 **세부 사항 관련 - 남자가 상을 받은 이유**
남자가 첫 번째 대사에서 고객 지원 프로세스를 간소화한 공로로 상을 받았다(I won a prize for streamlining our customer support processes)고 말하고 있으므로 정답은 (A)이다.

어휘 work anniversary 근속 기념일

Paraphrasing
대화의 streamlining → 정답의 Improving the workflow

51 What did the man do earlier in the year?
(A) He read an advice book.
(B) He distributed a survey.
(C) He attended a workshop.
(D) He started a new hobby.

번역 남자는 올해 초반에 무엇을 했는가?
(A) 조언서를 읽었다.
(B) 설문지를 배포했다.
(C) 워크숍에 참석했다.
(D) 새로운 취미 활동을 시작했다.

해설 **세부 사항 관련 - 남자가 한 일**
남자가 두 번째 대사에서 아이디어 대부분은 올해 초반에 갔던 워크숍에서 배웠다(I got most of them from a workshop I went to earlier this year)고 말하고 있으므로 정답은 (C)이다.

어휘 advice book 조언서 distribute 배포하다 survey 설문지, 설문 조사 attend 참석하다

52 What does the man say he will do with the prize money?
(A) Take a short vacation
(B) Contribute to his savings
(C) Treat coworkers to a meal
(D) Make a donation to a charity

번역 남자는 상금으로 무엇을 하겠다고 말하는가?
(A) 짧은 휴가 가기
(B) 저축하기
(C) 직장 동료들에게 밥 사주기
(D) 자선 단체에 기부하기

해설 **세부 사항 관련 - 남자가 하려는 일**
남자가 마지막 대사에서 지금은 저축해 두려고 한다(I'm going to set it aside for now)고 말하고 있으므로 정답은 (B)이다.

어휘 contribute 기여하다 savings 저금, 예금 treat a meal 식사 대접을 하다 donation 기부금 charity 자선 단체

Paraphrasing
대화의 set it aside → 정답의 Contribute to his savings

53-55

W-Br Mr. Ramsay, ⁵³ **can we talk for a minute about the summer internships? The program has been going differently from what we'd hoped...**

M-Cn Oh, really? I've been checking in with the interns regularly, and their feedback has been positive so far. They say the experience has been very educational.

W-Br Well, ⁵⁴ **the main problem is that the project of managing the two of them is interfering**

with our team's regular duties. We've been spending hours each day on it.

M-Cn I see. Then ⁵⁵ **let's include this issue on the agenda for tomorrow's staff meeting so that we can brainstorm possible solutions together.**

W-Br That would be great.

여: 램지 씨, **여름 인턴십에 대해 잠깐 이야기하실 수 있나요?** 그 프로그램이 저희가 바랐던 것과는 다르게 진행되고 있는데요…

남: 아, 정말요? 인턴들과 정기적으로 확인을 해왔는데, 지금까지 그들의 피드백은 긍정적이었어요. 그들은 인턴 경험이 매우 유익하다고 하던데요.

여: 음, **가장 큰 문제는 인턴들 중 두 명을 관리하는 일이 우리 팀의 정규 업무에 방해가 된다는 점이에요. 그 일에 매일 몇 시간씩 할애하고 있어요.**

남: 그렇군요. 그럼 **가능한 해결책을 함께 모색해볼 수 있도록 내일 직원 회의 안건에 이 문제를 넣읍시다.**

여: 좋습니다.

어휘   educational 교육적인, 유익한   interfere with ~을 방해하다   agenda 안건   brainstorm 아이디어를 자유롭게 제시하다   solution 해결책

---

53 What are the speakers discussing?
(A) Office furniture
(B) Budget allocations
(C) An internship program
(D) A departmental reorganization

번역   화자들은 무엇을 논의하는가?
(A) 사무용 가구
(B) 예산 할당
(C) 인턴십 프로그램
(D) 부서 개편

해설   **전체 내용 관련 - 대화의 주제**
여자가 첫 번째 대사에서 여름 인턴십에 대해 잠깐 이야기할 수 있는지(can we talk for a minute about the summer internships?) 묻고 나서 그 프로그램이 바랐던 것과는 다르게 진행되고 있다(The program has been going differently from what we'd hoped)고 말하고 있으므로 정답은 (C)이다.

어휘   furniture 가구   allocation 할당

---

54 According to the woman, what is the main problem?
(A) Her team is unhappy with a seating arrangement.
(B) Some applicants are not qualified for a position.
(C) A cost estimate was calculated incorrectly.
(D) A project has been very time-consuming.

번역   여자에 따르면 가장 큰 문제는 무엇인가?
(A) 그녀의 팀이 좌석 배치에 대해 불만족하고 있다.
(B) 일부 지원자들은 직책에 적합하지 않다.
(C) 비용 견적서가 부정확하게 계산되었다.
(D) 프로젝트가 시간 소모가 매우 크다.

해설   **세부 사항 관련 - 여자가 생각하는 가장 큰 문제**
여자가 두 번째 대사에서 가장 큰 문제는 인턴들 중 두 명을 관리하는 일이 팀의 정규 업무에 방해가 된다는 점(the main problem is that the project of managing the two of them is interfering with our team's regular duties)이라며 그 일에 매일 몇 시간씩 할애하고 있다(We've been spending hours each day on it)고 말하고 있으므로 정답은 (D)이다.

어휘   seating arrangement 좌석 배치   applicant 지원자   qualify 자격을 갖추다   cost estimate 비용 견적서   calculate 계산하다   incorrectly 부정확하게   time-consuming 시간 소모가 큰

> **Paraphrasing**
> 대화의 spending hours → 정답의 time-consuming

---

55 What will the speakers most likely do?
(A) Distribute a questionnaire
(B) Spend some extra money
(C) Add an item to a meeting agenda
(D) Clear out an unused room

번역   화자들은 무엇을 하겠는가?
(A) 설문지 배포하기
(B) 비용 더 쓰기
(C) 회의 안건에 항목 추가하기
(D) 사용하지 않은 방 청소하기

해설   **세부 사항 관련 - 화자들이 하려는 일**
남자가 마지막 대사에서 가능한 해결책을 함께 모색해볼 수 있도록 내일 직원 회의 안건에 이 문제를 넣자(let's include this issue on the agenda for tomorrow's staff meeting so that we can brainstorm possible solutions together)고 말하고 있으므로 정답은 (C)이다.

어휘   distribute 배포하다   questionnaire 설문지   clear out 청소하다   unused 사용하지 않은

> **Paraphrasing**
> 대화의 include this issue → 정답의 Add an item

56-58 3인 대화

W-Br Welcome, Mr. Alvarado. I'm Ellen Browder, the CEO of Browder Holdings. This is our director of business development, Kayoko Tokachi.

W-Am Hello, Mr. Alvarado. ⁵⁶ **Thank you for coming in to talk about our proposal to acquire your game studio.**

M-Au It's a very exciting possibility. ⁵⁷ **Browder's**

customer base is so large. I would love for our video games to reach a wider audience.

W-Br That's what we want as well.

M-Au Wonderful. But... I am concerned about how becoming part of Browder might affect our game development process.

W-Am Tell us more about that.

M-Au Well, I know that companies like yours value efficiency. But for us, [58] **the more important goal is coming up with unique ideas for games. We spend a lot of time and effort on that.**

여1: 어서 오세요, 알바라도 씨. 저는 브라우더 홀딩스의 CEO 엘런 브라우더라고 합니다. 이쪽은 우리 회사의 사업개발부장인 가요코 토카치입니다.

여2: 안녕하세요, 알바라도 씨. **귀하의 게임 제작사를 인수하려는 저희쪽 제안에 대해 이야기하기 위해 방문해 주셔서 감사합니다.**

남: 매우 흥미진진한 가능성입니다. **브라우더의 고객층은 매우 넓잖아요.** 저희가 만든 비디오게임이 더 많은 사람들에게 다가가기를 고대합니다.

여1: 그게 저희도 바라는 바예요.

남: 너무 좋습니다. 하지만… 브라우더의 회사 일부로 편입되는 것이 저희 게임 개발 과정에 어떤 영향을 미칠지 좀 우려됩니다.

여2: 좀 더 자세히 얘기해 주세요.

남: 귀사와 같은 회사들은 능률을 중요시한다고 알고 있습니다. 하지만 저희에게 더 중요한 목표는 게임을 위해 독창적인 아이디어를 발굴하는 것입니다. 이를 위해 엄청난 시간과 노력을 들이고 있어요.

어휘 proposal 제안 acquire 획득하다, 매입하다 customer base 고객층 audience 청중 affect 영향을 미치다 value 소중하게 생각하다 efficiency 능률 come up with ~을 제시하다 unique 독창적인 effort 수고, 노력, 활동

56 Why is the man at Browder Holdings?
(A) To hold a client consultation
(B) To conduct research for an article
(C) To tour an available property
(D) To discuss a business deal

번역 남자는 왜 브라우더 홀딩스에 갔는가?
(A) 고객 상담을 해주려고
(B) 기사 작성에 필요한 조사를 하려고
(C) 부동산 매물을 둘러보려고
(D) 사업 거래를 논의하려고

해설 세부 사항 관련 - 남자가 찾아간 이유
두 번째 여자가 첫 번째 대사에서 남자의 게임 제작사를 인수하려는 제안에 대해 이야기하기 위해 방문해 주셔서 감사하다(Thank you for coming in to talk about our proposal to acquire your game studio)고 말하고 있으므로 정답은 (D)이다.

어휘 consultation 상담 conduct 실시하다 article 글, 기사 available 이용 가능한 property 재산, 부동산

> **Paraphrasing**
> 대화의 talk about our proposal to acquire your game studio → 정답의 discuss a business deal

57 What does the man mention about Browder Holdings?
(A) It has a large customer base.
(B) It was founded a long time ago.
(C) It is involved in the local community.
(D) It has an experienced management team.

번역 남자는 브라우더 홀딩스에 대해 무엇을 언급하는가?
(A) 넓은 고객층을 보유하고 있다.
(B) 오래전에 설립되었다.
(C) 지역 사회에 참여하고 있다.
(D) 경험이 풍부한 경영진을 보유하고 있다.

해설 세부 사항 관련 - 남자가 브라우더 홀딩스에 대해 언급하는 것
남자가 첫 번째 대사에서 브라우더의 고객층은 매우 넓다(Browder's customer base is so large)고 말하고 있으므로 정답은 (A)이다.

어휘 found 설립하다 be involved in ~에 개입되다 local community 지역 사회 experienced 경험이 풍부한

58 What does the man say his company puts effort into?
(A) Designing efficient work spaces
(B) Improving businesses' public images
(C) Producing creative ideas for products
(D) Following industry regulations strictly

번역 남자는 자신의 회사가 무엇에 노력을 쏟는다고 말하는가?
(A) 능률적인 작업 공간 설계
(B) 회사의 대외적 이미지 개선
(C) 제품을 위한 창의적인 아이디어 생산
(D) 산업 규제를 엄격하게 준수하는 것

해설 세부 사항 관련 - 남자가 노력을 쏟는다고 말하는 대상
남자가 마지막 대사에서 더 중요한 목표는 게임을 위해 독창적인 아이디어를 발굴하는 것(the more important goal is coming up with unique ideas for games)이며 이를 위해 엄청난 시간과 노력을 들이고 있다(We spend a lot of time and effort on that)고 말하고 있으므로 정답은 (C)이다.

어휘 efficient 능률적인 work space 작업 공간 improve 개선하다 public image 대외적 이미지 creative 창의적인 regulation 규제 strictly 엄격하게

> **Paraphrasing**
> 대화의 coming up with unique ideas for games → 정답의 Producing creative ideas for products

59-61

W-Am Greg—good news! **⁵⁹ The assembly line is about to finish making the mountain bikes for Kellum Sporting Goods.** We'll be able to ship the order out as scheduled after all.

M-Au Excellent. The next order to fulfill is another set of mountain bikes for a different dealer, right?

W-Am Yes, but… that one isn't urgent, and the workers are tired from the overtime they've done for the Kellum order. **⁶⁰ What do you think about shutting down early and giving them the afternoon off?**

M-Au Hmm… OK. **⁶¹ I'll make an announcement over the loudspeakers now.** Thanks for the idea, Marisa.

여: 그렉, 좋은 소식이 있어요! 생산 라인이 켈럼 스포팅 굿즈 사를 위한 산악용 자전거 생산을 곧 끝낼 거예요. 결국 발주 물량을 예정대로 배송할 수 있을 거예요.

남: 잘됐네요. 다음으로 완수해야 하는 주문은 다른 거래처를 위한 산악용 자전거 맞죠?

여: 네, 하지만… 그 주문은 급하지 않아요. 그리고 작업자들은 켈럼 주문을 맞추기 위해 초과근무를 한 탓에 피로가 쌓였어요. 공장 문을 일찍 닫고 오후에 쉬게 하는 게 어떻겠어요?

남: 음… 알겠어요. 지금 사내 방송으로 공지사항을 전달할게요. 의견 고마워요, 마리사.

어휘 assembly line 생산 라인 ship out 배송하다 fulfill 이행하다, 달성하다 urgent 긴급한 shut down 문을 닫다, 기계가 멈추다 announcement 공지, 발표 loudspeaker 확성기, 스피커

59 Which industry do the speakers most likely work in?
(A) Manufacturing
(B) Tourism
(C) Health care
(D) Information technology

번역 화자들은 어떤 업계에 종사하겠는가?
(A) 제조업
(B) 관광업
(C) 의료
(D) 정보기술

해설 전체 내용 관련 - 화자들이 종사하는 업계
여자가 첫 번째 대사에서 생산 라인이 켈럼 스포팅 굿즈 사를 위한 산악용 자전거 생산을 곧 끝낼 것(The assembly line is about to finish making the mountain bikes for Kellum Sporting Goods)이라고 말하고 있으므로 정답은 (A)이다.

60 What does the woman suggest?
(A) Ordering extra materials
(B) Closing a business early
(C) Issuing some safety reminders
(D) Double-checking some specifications

번역 여자는 무엇을 제안하는가?
(A) 추가 자재 주문하기
(B) 사업장을 일찍 닫기
(C) 안전 수칙 전달하기
(D) 일부 사양 재확인하기

해설 세부 사항 관련 - 여자가 제안하는 것
여자가 두 번째 대사에서 공장 문을 일찍 닫고 오후에 쉬게 하는 게 어떻겠는지(What do you think about shutting down early and giving them the afternoon off?) 남자에게 묻고 있으므로 정답은 (B)이다.

어휘 material 자재 safety 안전 reminder 상기시키는 것 double-check 재확인하다 specification 사양

> **Paraphrasing**
> 대화의 shutting down → 정답의 Closing

61 What will the man do next?
(A) Print a set of handouts
(B) Submit a budget document
(C) Cancel some appointments
(D) Use a public address system

번역 남자는 다음으로 무엇을 하겠는가?
(A) 인쇄물 출력하기
(B) 예산 문서 제출하기
(C) 약속 취소하기
(D) 방송 설비 사용하기

해설 세부 사항 관련 - 남자가 할 일
남자가 마지막 대사에서 지금 사내 방송으로 공지사항을 전달하겠다(I'll make an announcement over the loudspeakers now)고 말하고 있으므로 정답은 (D)이다.

어휘 handout 인쇄물 submit 제출하다 appointment 약속, 예약 public address system 건물 내 방송 설비

> **Paraphrasing**
> 대화의 make an announcement over the loudspeakers → 정답의 Use a public address system

62-64 대화 + 극장 프로그램

M-Cn Oh hi, Sachiko! I didn't know you were seeing this play this evening, too.

W-Br Yes, I'm here with Ian. **⁶² We wanted to catch the production one more time before it goes on tour next month.** Had you seen it before as well?

TEST 1 **17**

M-Cn No, and I loved it! Hugh Macdonald was wonderful. **63 It's too bad that Purva Shah was sick, though. Her replacement gave a good performance**, but I've heard that Shah's really great in the role.

W-Br That's true. Hey, **64 Ian and I are planning to grab dinner nearby. Do you want to join us?**

M-Cn **64 Sure!** I just have to keep an eye on the time. The parking garage where I left my car closes at ten.

남: 아, 안녕하세요, 사치코! 당신도 오늘 밤에 이 연극을 보고 있었는지 몰랐어요.

여: 맞아요, 이언이랑 같이 왔어요. **이 작품이 다음 달에 순회공연을 가기 전에 한 번 더 보고 싶었어요.** 당신도 전에 이 작품을 본 적이 있었나요?

남: 아니요, 근데 너무 좋았어요! 휴 맥도널드는 정말 훌륭했어요. **푸르바 샤가 아파서 아쉬웠지만요. 그녀의 대체 배우가 훌륭한 연기를 선보였지만,** 샤가 그 역할을 정말 잘한다고 들었거든요.

여: 맞아요. 저기, **이언과 저는 이 근처에서 간단히 저녁을 먹으려고 하는데요. 함께 가실래요?**

남: **그럼요!** 시간만 잘 지켜보면 돼요. 제가 차를 주차한 주차 빌딩이 10시에 문을 닫거든요.

어휘 play 연극   catch ~을 보다   production 제작, 작품
go on tour 순회공연을 가다   replacement 교체, 대신할 사람   performance 공연, 연기   role 역할
grab 급히 ~을 하다   keep an eye on ~을 지켜보다
parking garage 주차 빌딩

CAST
63 Nadia .... Purva Shah
Rick .... Hugh Macdonald
Jasmine........................... Lily Heath
Shane .... Lorenzo Bertolazzi

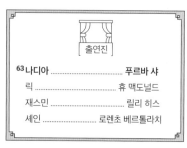

출연진
63 나디아 .... 푸르바 샤
릭 .... 휴 맥도널드
재스민 .... 릴리 히스
셰인 .... 로렌초 베르톨라치

---

62 What does the woman say about the production?
(A) It is hard to get tickets for.
(B) It is about to begin a tour.
(C) It has been running for a month.
(D) It has new cast members.

번역 여자는 작품에 대해 뭐라고 말하는가?
(A) 표를 구하기가 어렵다.
(B) 곧 순회 공연을 시작할 예정이다.
(C) 한 달째 상연되고 있다.
(D) 새 배우들이 들어왔다.

해설 세부 사항 관련 - 여자가 작품에 대해 하는 말
여자가 첫 대사에서 이 작품이 다음 달에 순회공연을 가기 전에 한 번 더 보고 싶었다(We wanted to catch the production one more time before it goes on tour next month)고 하므로 정답은 (B)이다.

어휘 be about to ~하려는 참이다   cast member 출연자, 배우

---

63 Look at the graphic. Which role was played by a different performer this evening?
(A) Nadia
(B) Rick
(C) Jasmine
(D) Shane

번역 시각 정보에 의하면, 오늘 밤 다른 출연자가 맡은 역할은 무엇인가?
(A) 나디아
(B) 릭
(C) 재스민
(D) 셰인

해설 시각 정보 연계 - 오늘 밤 다른 출연자가 맡은 역할
남자가 두 번째 대사에서 푸르바 샤가 아파서 아쉬웠지만 그녀의 대체 배우가 훌륭한 연기를 선보였다(It's too bad that Purva Shah was sick, though. Her replacement gave a good performance)고 했고, 극장 프로그램에 따르면 푸르바 사의 원래 역할이 나디아이므로 정답은 (A)이다.

어휘 performer 연기자

---

64 Where will the speakers most likely go next?
(A) To a parking structure
(B) To the theater office
(C) To a restaurant
(D) To a conference center

번역 화자들은 다음으로 어디로 가겠는가?
(A) 주차 빌딩
(B) 극장 매표소
(C) 식당
(D) 회의장

해설 세부 사항 관련 - 화자들이 다음에 갈 곳
여자가 두 번째 대사에서 이언과 이 근처에서 간단히 저녁을 먹으려고 하는데(Ian and I are planning to grab dinner nearby) 함께 갈 것(Do you want to join us?)을 제안하자, 남자가 그럼요(Sure!)라고 수락하고 있으므로 정답은 (C)이다.

M-Au Camila, the shipment from Gillespie Office Supplies arrived.

W-Am Oh good! We need those binders. **⁶⁵Ms. Chen is going to use them when she presents the housing department's budget to the city administrators.**

M-Au Let's get everything unpacked.

W-Am I'll check the invoice... Wait, this isn't right. **⁶⁶I'm sure I ordered more sticky notes than this.**

M-Au Can I take a look at the invoice? Ah, there's a note here at the bottom. It says the manufacturer is behind on production, so this is all that Gillespie had in stock. They'll send the rest to us by the end of the month.

W-Am OK. That should be fine.

M-Au Good. So, **⁶⁷should we take these boxes of binders to Ms. Chen's office?**

남: 카밀라, 길레스피 사무용품에서 온 배송품이 도착했어요.

여: 아 잘됐네요! 바인더가 필요해요. 첸 씨가 주택부 예산을 시 행정관들에게 제출할 때 사용할 거예요.

남: 그럼 포장을 풀어봅시다.

여: 저는 송장을 확인할게요··· 잠깐만요, 이거 안 맞아요. 저는 분명히 이것보다 더 많은 접착식 메모지를 주문했어요.

남: 제가 송장을 봐도 될까요? 아, 여기 하단에 메모가 있네요. 제조업체에 생산이 밀리고 있어서 이만큼이 길레스피에서 보유한 재고 전부라고 적혀 있어요. 이달 말까지 나머지를 보내주겠대요.

여: 알겠습니다. 문제는 없겠네요.

남: 좋습니다. 그럼, 이 바인더 상자들을 첸 씨 사무실로 옮겨야 할까요?

어휘 shipment 배송품 present 제출하다 housing 주택 공급 budget 예산 city administrator 시 행정관 unpack (짐 등을) 꺼내다, 풀다 invoice 송장 sticky note 접착식 메모지 manufacturer 제조업체 behind 뒤떨어져 production 생산 in stock 재고가 있는 rest 나머지

INVOICE

Item	Quantity	Price
Pens	3 boxes	$10
⁶⁶Sticky notes	5 boxes	$75
Paperclips	7 boxes	$11
Binders	4 boxes	$120

송장

품목	수량	가격
펜	3박스	10달러
⁶⁶접착식 메모지	5박스	75달러
종이 클립	7박스	11달러
바인더	4박스	120달러

65 Where does the conversation most likely take place?
(A) At a government office
(B) At a print shop
(C) At a law firm
(D) At a marketing agency

번역 대화는 어디서 이루어지겠는가?
(A) 관공서
(B) 인쇄소
(C) 법률 사무소
(D) 마케팅 대행사

해설 **전체 내용 관련 - 대화의 장소**
여자가 첫 대사에서 첸 씨가 주택 예산을 시 행정관들에게 제출할 때 사용할 것(Ms. Chen is going to use them when she presents the housing department's budget to the city administrators)이라고 말하는 것으로 보아 관공서에서 이루어지는 대화임을 알 수 있다. 따라서 정답은 (A)이다.

66 Look at the graphic. Which quantity does the woman say is incorrect?
(A) 3 boxes
(B) 5 boxes
(C) 7 boxes
(D) 4 boxes

번역 시각 정보에 의하면, 여자는 어떤 수량이 부정확하다고 말하는가?
(A) 3박스
(B) 5박스
(C) 7박스
(D) 4박스

해설 **시각 정보 연계 - 여자가 수량이 부정확하다고 말하는 것**
여자가 두 번째 대사에서 자신은 분명히 이것보다 더 많은 접착식 메모지를 주문했다(I'm sure I ordered more sticky notes than this)고 말하고 있고, 송장에 따르면 접착식 메모지는 5박스이므로 정답은 (B)이다.

67 What does the man ask about?
(A) Placing another order
(B) Informing some coworkers
(C) Testing some of the products
(D) Moving some of the boxes

번역　남자는 무엇에 대해 문의하는가?
(A) 또 다른 주문하기
(B) 동료들에게 알리기
(C) 제품들 중 일부 시험해 보기
(D) 상자들 중 일부 옮기기

해설　**세부 사항 관련 - 남자의 문의 사항**
남자가 마지막 대사에서 바인더 상자들을 첸 씨 사무실로 옮겨야 할지(should we take these boxes of binders to Ms. Chen's office?) 묻고 있으므로 정답은 (D)이다.

어휘　place an order 주문하다　inform 알리다　coworker 동료

> **Paraphrasing**
> 대화의 take these boxes of binders to Ms. Chen's office → 정답의 Moving some of the boxes

---

68-70 대화+출발 안내 전광판

M-Cn　Hi, Ivy. It's Craig. Are you at the gate already? **68 I'm still waiting to get through the security screening. I've never seen lines this long at this terminal before.**

W-Br　Yeah, I was surprised by that too. I just arrived at our gate. But—**69 the departure board now says our flight is delayed by forty minutes.** So you have time.

M-Cn　I'm glad to hear that. That does mean that **70 we'll land too late to catch the last shuttle bus, though. Could you look into other options for getting to the convention center?**

남: 안녕하세요, 아이비. 크레이그예요. 이미 탑승구에 도착하셨나요? 저는 아직 보안 검색대 앞에서 기다리는 중이에요. 여태껏 이 터미널에서 이렇게 긴 줄은 처음 봐요.

어: 맞아요, 저도 깜짝 놀랐어요. 저는 방금 탑승구에 도착했어요. 하지만, 출발 안내 전광판을 보니 우리 비행기가 40분 지연된다고 써 있네요. 그러니 당신은 시간이 있어요.

남: 다행이네요. 그 말인즉 우리가 너무 늦게 착륙해서 마지막 셔틀버스를 놓칠 거라는 뜻이지만요. 컨벤션 센터까지 갈 수 있는 다른 방법을 찾아봐 줄 수 있어요?

어휘　get through ~을 통과하다　security screening 보안 검색
delay 지연시키다　look into ~을 조사하다

Destination	Departure Time	Status
69 Montreal	15:00	Delayed – 40 minutes
Winnipeg	15:30	On time
Toronto	16:00	On time
Calgary	16:30	Delayed – one hour

목적지	출발 시각	상태
69 몬트리올	15시	40분 지연
위니펙	15시 30분	정시
토론토	16시	정시
캘거리	16시 30분	1시간 지연

68 What problem does the man mention?
(A) There is a mistake on a schedule.
(B) A facility is unusually busy.
(C) An airport's layout is confusing.
(D) He forgot to bring a travel document.

번역　남자는 어떤 문제를 언급하는가?
(A) 일정표에 오류가 있다.
(B) 시설이 유난히 붐빈다.
(C) 공항 내부 구조가 헷갈리게 되어 있다.
(D) 여행 서류를 깜빡 잊고 놓고 왔다.

해설　**세부 사항 관련 - 남자가 언급하는 문제**
남자가 첫 번째 대사에서 아직 보안 검색대 앞에서 기다리는 중(I'm still waiting to get through the security screening)이며 여태껏 이 터미널에서 이렇게 긴 줄은 처음 본다(I've never seen lines this long at this terminal before)고 말하고 있으므로 정답은 (B)이다.

어휘　facility 시설　unusually 평소와 달리　layout 배치

69 Look at the graphic. Where are the speakers flying to?
(A) Montreal
(B) Winnipeg
(C) Toronto
(D) Calgary

번역　시각 정보에 의하면, 화자들은 비행기를 타고 어디로 가는가?
(A) 몬트리올
(B) 위니펙
(C) 토론토
(D) 캘거리

해설　**시각 정보 연계 - 화자들의 목적지**
여자가 첫 번째 대사에서 출발 안내 전광판을 보니 우리 비행기가 40분 지연된다고 써 있다(the departure board now says our flight is delayed by forty minutes)고 말했고, 출발 안내 전광판에 따르면 40분 지연된 비행기는 몬트리올행이므로 정답은 (A)이다.

70 What does the man ask the woman to do?
(A) Check a weather forecast
(B) Notify an event organizer
(C) Research transportation options
(D) Ask about an airline policy

번역 남자는 여자에게 무엇을 요청하는가?
(A) 일기 예보 확인하기
(B) 행사 주최자에게 알리기
(C) 교통 수단 조사하기
(D) 항공사 정책에 대해 문의하기

해설 세부 사항 관련 - 남자가 여자에게 요청하는 것
남자가 마지막 대사에서 우리가 너무 늦게 착륙해서 마지막 셔틀 버스를 놓칠 것(we'll land too late to catch the last shuttle bus, though)이라며 컨벤션 센터까지 갈 수 있는 다른 방법을 찾아봐 줄 수 있느냐(Could you look into other options for getting to the convention center?)고 여자에게 요청하고 있으므로 정답은 (C)이다.

어휘 weather forecast 일기 예보   notify 알리다   organizer 주최자   airline 항공사   policy 정책

> **Paraphrasing**
> 대화의 look into other options for getting ~
> → 정답의 Research transportation options

PART 4

71-73 전화 메시지

> W-Br Hello, this is Na-Rim from the culinary school's administration. **71, 72 I'm calling to let you know that Terrence Hill, who's enrolled in your food history course, won't be able to attend the next two sessions.** **72 He phoned this morning and notified me that he has an urgent family matter to deal with.** We'll excuse these absences, and we don't want him to fall behind in the course. **73 Could you e-mail him any slides or handouts you'll be using in those sessions?** Thank you.
>
> ---
>
> 안녕하세요, 요리 학교 행정실의 나림입니다. 당신의 음식 역사 수업에 등록한 테런스 힐이 다음 두 번의 수업에 참석할 수 없음을 알려드리려고 전화했습니다. 그가 오늘 아침에 전화해서 집안에 급한 일이 생겼다고 제게 알려주었어요. 이 결석은 출석으로 인정해 줄 거예요. 그가 수업에 뒤처지지 않았으면 좋겠는데요. 다음 두 번의 수업 시간에 사용할 슬라이드나 인쇄물을 그에게 이메일로 보내주실 수 있을까요? 감사합니다.
>
> 어휘 culinary 요리의   administration 행정실   enroll in ~에 등록하다   attend 참석하다   notify 알리다   urgent 긴급한   excuse an absence 결석을 출석으로 인정해 주다   fall behind 뒤처지다

71 What is the main purpose of the message?
(A) To congratulate the listener on some exam results
(B) To describe a career opportunity
(C) To inform the listener of an attendance issue
(D) To suggest a classroom activity

번역 메시지의 주된 목적은 무엇인가?
(A) 시험 결과에 대해 청자를 축하하려고
(B) 일자리 기회를 알려주려고
(C) 출석 관련 문제를 청자에게 설명해 주려고
(D) 교실 활동을 제안하려고

해설 전체 내용 관련 - 메시지의 목적
화자가 초반부에 청자의 음식 역사 수업에 등록한 테런스 힐이 다음 두 번의 수업에 참석할 수 없음을 알려주려고 전화했다(I'm calling to let you know that Terrence Hill, who's enrolled in your food history course, won't be able to attend the next two sessions)고 말하고 있으므로 정답은 (C)이다.

어휘 congratulate 축하하다   opportunity 기회   attendance 출석   activity 활동

> **Paraphrasing**
> 담화의 let you know → 정답의 inform
> 담화의 won't be able to attend
> → 정답의 attendance issue

72 What does the speaker say she did this morning?
(A) She watched a demonstration.
(B) She reviewed some school records.
(C) She ordered some supplies.
(D) She received a call from a student.

번역 화자는 자신이 오늘 아침에 무엇을 했다고 말하는가?
(A) 시연을 감상했다.
(B) 성적표를 검토했다.
(C) 비품을 주문했다.
(D) 한 학생에게 전화를 받았다.

해설 세부 사항 관련 - 화자가 한 일
화자가 초반부에 청자의 음식 역사 수업에 등록한 테런스 힐이 다음 두 번의 수업에 참석할 수 없음을 알려주려고 전화했다(I'm calling to let you know that Terrence Hill, who's enrolled in your food history course, won't be able to attend the next two sessions)고 말한 뒤에 그가 오늘 아침에 전화해서 집안에 급한 일이 생겼다고 자신에게 알려주었다(He phoned this morning and notified me that he has an urgent family matter to deal with)고 말하고 있으므로 정답은 (D)이다.

어휘 demonstration 시연, 시범 설명   school record 학업 성적

> **Paraphrasing**
> 담화의 He phoned
> → 정답의 She received a call from a student.

73 What is the listener asked to do?
(A) Postpone a class session
(B) Send some teaching materials
(C) Visit a business's Web site
(D) Meet with a supervisor

번역 청자는 무엇을 요청받는가?
(A) 수업 미루기
(B) 수업 자료 보내기
(C) 사업체의 웹사이트 방문하기
(D) 관리자 만나기

해설 **세부 사항 관련 - 청자가 요청받은 일**
화자가 후반부에 다음 두 번의 수업 시간에 사용할 슬라이드나 인쇄물을 그에게 이메일로 보내줄 수 있느냐(Could you e-mail him any slides or handouts you'll be using in those sessions?)고 부탁하고 있으므로 정답은 (B)이다.

어휘 postpone 미루다　teaching material 수업 자료　supervisor 감독관, 관리자

> **Paraphrasing**
> 담화의 e-mail him any slides or handouts
> → 정답의 Send some teaching materials

번역 방송의 주된 주제는 무엇인가?
(A) 도시의 유명한 거주민
(B) 건물의 보수 공사
(C) 공공 예술 창작
(D) 새로운 교육 프로그램

해설 **전체 내용 관련 - 방송의 주제**
화자가 초반부에 메이휴 미술관이 도심의 본관을 새단장하고 확장한다는 계획을 발표했다(the Mayhew Museum of Art has announced plans to update and expand its downtown home)고 말하고 있으므로 정답은 (B)이다.

어휘 resident 거주민　creation 창조, 창작　public art 공공 예술　educational 교육의

> **Paraphrasing**
> 담화의 update and expand its downtown home
> → 정답의 The renovation of a building

74-76 방송

> M-Au In local cultural news, **74 the Mayhew Museum of Art has announced plans to update and expand its downtown home.** The renovation will be the first major initiative undertaken by **75 Victor Hook since his appointment as the Mayhew's director earlier this year.** The work will mainly involve making the museum more accessible and adding a five-thousand-square-foot gallery to be used for short-term exhibitions. **76 The Eddix Foundation has already agreed to sponsor the first show in the new space**—an overview of contemporary Haitian art. If construction is completed on schedule, it will begin in March.
>
> 지역 문화 뉴스에서 **메이휴 미술관이 도심의 본관을 새단장하고 확장한다는 계획을 발표했습니다** 보수 공사는 **빅터 훅이 올해 초 메이휴 미술관장으로 임명된 후** 빅터 훅에 의해 착수되는 첫 번째 주요 계획이 될 것입니다. 이 공사의 주 목적은 미술관의 접근성을 높이고 단기 전시회에 사용될 5,000평방 피트 규모의 화랑을 추가하는 것입니다. **에딕스 재단은 이미 새 공간에서 개최할 첫 번째 전시회를 후원하기로 했습니다.** 그 전시회는 현대 아이티 미술 개관이 될 것입니다. 공사가 예정대로 완료되면 3월에 시작될 것입니다.
>
> 어휘　expand 확장하다　renovation 보수 공사　initiative 계획, 주도권　undertake 착수하다　appointment 임명　accessible 접근 가능한　short-term 단기의　exhibition 전시회　overview 개관　construction 공사, 건설

74　What is the main topic of the broadcast?
(A) A famous resident of a city
(B) The renovation of a building
(C) The creation of some public art
(D) A new educational program

75　According to the speaker, who is Victor Hook?
(A) A painter
(B) An architect
(C) A museum director
(D) A local historian

번역 화자에 따르면, 빅터 훅은 누구인가?
(A) 화가
(B) 건축가
(C) 미술관장
(D) 지역 역사가

해설 **세부 사항 관련 - 빅터 훅의 신분**
화자가 중반부에 빅터 훅이 올해 초 메이휴 미술관장으로 임명된 인물(Victor Hook since his appointment as the Mayhew's director earlier this year)이라고 밝히고 있으므로 정답은 (C)이다.

어휘 historian 역사가

76　What is the Eddix Foundation planning to do?
(A) Fund an exhibition
(B) Hire more personnel
(C) Purchase a piece of land
(D) Host an outdoor celebration

번역 에딕스 재단은 무엇을 할 예정인가?
(A) 전시회 후원하기
(B) 더 많은 직원 고용하기
(C) 토지 매입하기
(D) 야외 기념행사 주최하기

해설 **세부 사항 관련 - 에딕스 재단이 할 일**
화자가 후반부에 에딕스 재단이 이미 새 공간에서 개최할 첫 번째 전시회를 후원하기로 했다(The Eddix Foundation has already agreed to sponsor the first show in the new space)고 말하고 있으므로 정답은 (A)이다.

어휘 personnel 직원, 인사과　celebration 기념행사

> **Paraphrasing**
> 담화의 sponsor the first show
> → 정답의 Fund an exhibition

77-79 공지

> **W-Am** Hi, everyone. I'm excited to announce that **77 our station has bought new portable news cameras.** We looked into the display screens for the studio that some of you suggested, but they were over our budget. Now, **78 the great thing about the new cameras is that they aren't heavy like our current ones.** Our news teams are going to be able to move around more easily when reporting on live events. Uh, for our camera operators—**79 Omar is familiar with this model,** but he'll be out in the field when they arrive. **79 I'll make sure you each get a user manual along with the camera, though.**
>
> 안녕하세요, 여러분. 우리 방송국에서 새로운 휴대용 뉴스 카메라를 구매했다는 사실을 알려드리게 되어 기쁩니다. 여러분 중 몇몇이 제안한 스튜디오용 디스플레이 스크린도 알아봤지만 예산 범위를 초과했어요. 자, 새로운 카메라의 가장 좋은 점은 현재 쓰는 카메라처럼 무겁지 않다는 점이죠. 우리 뉴스팀은 현장 취재를 나갈 때 훨씬 쉽게 이동할 수 있을 거예요. 아, 촬영 기사 여러분은… 오마르가 이 모델을 잘 알아요. 하지만 카메라가 도착할 때 그는 현장에 나가 있을 거예요. 어쨌든 모두 카메라와 함께 사용자 매뉴얼을 받게 해드릴게요.
>
> **어휘** portable 휴대가 쉬운 camera operator 촬영 기사 be familiar with ~에 대해 잘 알다 be out in the field 현장에 나가다

77 What kind of equipment has been purchased?
(A) Display screens
(B) Microphones
(C) Lighting
(D) Video cameras

번역 어떤 장비가 구매되었는가?
(A) 디스플레이 스크린
(B) 마이크
(C) 조명
(D) 비디오카메라

해설 세부 사항 관련 - 장비의 종류
화자가 초반부에 새로운 휴대용 뉴스 카메라를 구매했다(our station has bought new portable news cameras)고 밝히고 있으므로 정답은 (D)이다.

78 What does the speaker emphasize about the products?
(A) They have many features.
(B) They are lightweight.
(C) They are inexpensive.
(D) They will last a long time.

번역 화자는 제품에 대해 무엇을 강조하는가?
(A) 많은 기능이 있다.
(B) 가볍다.
(C) 저렴하다.
(D) 오래 사용할 수 있다.

해설 세부 사항 관련 - 제품에 대해 강조하는 것
화자가 중반부에 새로운 카메라의 가장 좋은 점은 현재 쓰는 카메라처럼 무겁지 않다는 점이다(the great thing about the new cameras is that they aren't heavy like our current ones)라고 말하고 있으므로 정답은 (B)이다.

어휘 feature 특색. 기능 lightweight 가벼운 inexpensive 저렴한 last 지속되다

> **Paraphrasing**
> 담화의 aren't heavy → 정답의 are lightweight

79 Why does the speaker say, "but he'll be out in the field when they arrive"?
(A) To indicate that training will not be available
(B) To question a staffing decision
(C) To request help unloading the equipment
(D) To explain an expected delay

번역 화자가 "하지만 카메라가 도착할 때 그는 현장에 나가 있을 거예요"라고 말한 이유는?
(A) 교육이 진행될 수 없다는 사실을 알리려고
(B) 직원 채용 결정에 대해 문의하려고
(C) 장비를 내릴 때 도움을 요청하려고
(D) 예상된 지연을 설명하려고

해설 화자의 의도 파악 - 카메라가 도착할 때 그는 현장에 나가 있을 거라고 한 말의 의도
앞에서 오마르가 이 모델을 잘 안다(Omar is familiar with this model)고 말한 뒤 인용문을 언급하고 있으며, 어쨌든 모두 카메라와 함께 사용자 매뉴얼을 받게 해주겠다(I'll make sure you each get a user manual along with the camera, though)고 대안을 제시하는 것으로 보아 해당 카메라를 잘 아는 오마르가 부재 중이라 교육을 할 수 없다는 사실을 전하려는 의도로 한 말임을 알 수 있다. 따라서 정답은 (A)이다.

어휘 available 이용 가능한 staffing 직원 채용 decision 결정 unload 짐을 내리다

80-82 자동 응답 메시지

> **M-Cn** Hello, **80 you have reached the desk of Kevin Greco, senior business analyst at Dorsey Electric Company.** I am currently unable to take your call. Also, **81 please note that due to a shift in my duties toward our renewable energy projects, I no longer manage our vendor invoices.** However, **82 if you need to speak with me regarding another matter, please leave a message after the tone that includes your name and contact information.** I will

get back to you within two business days. Thank you.

안녕하세요. 돌시 전력의 선임 경영 분석가 케빈 그레코입니다. 저는 지금 귀하의 전화를 받을 수 없습니다. 또한, **재생 에너지 프로젝트 관련 업무로 담당 업무가 변동되었기 때문에 더 이상 공급업체 송장 관리를 하지 않는다는 사실을 양지해 주십시오.** 하지만, 다른 사안에 대해 저와 이야기를 하셔야 한다면 삐 소리 후에 성함과 연락처와 함께 메시지를 남겨주십시오. 영업일 기준 이틀 내로 다시 연락드리겠습니다. 감사합니다.

어휘   analyst 분석가   shift 변동   duty 업무, 임무   renewable 재생 가능한   vendor 공급업체, 상인

---

80   What type of business does the speaker work for?
(A) At a car dealership
(B) At a utility company
(C) At a recruiting agency
(D) At a newspaper office

번역   화자는 어떤 종류의 회사에서 일하는가?
(A) 자동차 대리점
(B) 공익 기업
(C) 채용 대행사
(D) 신문사

해설   **전체 내용 관련 - 화자의 근무지**
화자가 초반부에 돌시 전력의 선임 경영 분석가 케빈 그레코(you have reached the desk of Kevin Greco, senior business analyst at Dorsey Electric Company)라고 밝히고 있으므로 정답은 (B)이다.

어휘   dealership 대리점   utility company (전기·가스 등을 공급하는) 공익 기업   recruiting 채용

> **Paraphrasing**
> 담화의 Electric Company → 정답의 utility company

---

81   What does the speaker say about himself?
(A) He has moved offices.
(B) He is on a business trip.
(C) He is preparing some documents.
(D) His job duties have changed.

번역   화자가 자신에 대해 무엇을 말하는가?
(A) 사무실을 옮겼다.
(B) 출장 중이다.
(C) 문서 작업을 하는 중이다.
(D) 담당 업무가 바뀌었다.

해설   **세부 사항 관련 - 화자가 자신에 대해 한 말**
화자가 중반부에 재생 에너지 프로젝트 관련 업무로 담당 업무가 변동되었기 때문에 더 이상 공급업체 송장 관리를 하지 않는다는 사실을 양지해 달라(please note that due to a shift in my duties toward our renewable energy projects, I no longer manage

---

our vendor invoices)고 말하고 있으므로 정답은 (D)이다.

어휘   prepare 준비하다

> **Paraphrasing**
> 담화의 a shift in my duties
> → 정답의 His job duties have changed

---

82   What is the listener instructed to do?
(A) Call another person
(B) Review a list of suggestions
(C) Leave a voice message
(D) Complete an online form

번역   청자는 무엇을 하도록 지시받는가?
(A) 다른 사람에게 전화하기
(B) 제안 목록 검토하기
(C) 음성 메시지 남기기
(D) 온라인 양식 작성하기

해설   **세부 사항 관련 - 청자가 지시받은 일**
화자가 후반부에 다른 사안에 대해 자신과 이야기를 해야 한다면 삐 소리 후에 메시지를 남겨달라(if you need to speak with me regarding another matter, please leave a message after the tone ~)고 말하고 있으므로 정답은 (C)이다.

어휘   suggestion 제안

83-85 회의 발췌

W-Am Thank you all for coming to this meeting. As you know, [83] **the volume of books that we publish has grown rapidly over the past year.** We've always outsourced our design tasks to freelancers, but I believe there's now enough work that it makes more sense financially to have a book designer on staff. So, [84] **we're now seeking to hire someone for a full-time position.** I posted a listing online this morning, and notified our freelancers about it. [85] **I'm going to e-mail the job ad to you all as well. Please send it around to anyone you think might be interested.**

오늘 회의에 참석해 주셔서 감사드립니다. 아시다시피, **우리가 출판하는 도서의 양이 지난 1년간 급격히 증가했습니다.** 우리는 그동안 항상 디자인 업무를 프리랜서에게 외주를 주었지만, 지금은 북디자이너를 직원으로 채용하는 것이 재정적으로 유리할 정도로 일감이 늘어났다고 생각합니다. 따라서, **정규직으로 일할 사람을 고용하려고 합니다.** 오늘 아침에 온라인에 채용 공고를 게시했고 우리 프리랜서들에게도 알렸습니다. **여러분에게도 채용 공고를 이메일로 보내드리겠습니다. 여러분이 생각하기에 관심 있을 만한 사람에게 보내주시기 바랍니다.**

어휘   publish 출판하다   outsource 외주를 주다   financially 재정적으로   seek 찾다   listing 목록, 공고

83
What industry does the speaker most likely work in?
(A) Finance
(B) Marketing
(C) Hospitality
(D) Publishing

번역 화자는 어떤 산업에 종사하겠는가?
(A) 금융업
(B) 마케팅
(C) 서비스업
(D) 출판업

해설 **전체 내용 관련 - 화자가 종사하는 산업 분야**
화자가 초반부에 우리가 출판하는 도서의 양이 지난 1년간 급격히 증가했다(the volume of books that we publish has grown rapidly over the past year)고 말하고 있으므로 정답은 (D)이다.

84
What is the speaker mainly discussing?
(A) A job opening
(B) A company celebration
(C) Technology upgrades
(D) Survey results

번역 화자는 주로 무엇에 대해 이야기하는가?
(A) 일자리 공석
(B) 회사 기념행사
(C) 기술 업그레이드
(D) 설문조사 결과

해설 **전체 내용 관련 - 담화의 주제**
화자가 중반부에 정규직으로 일할 사람을 고용하려고 한다(we're now seeking to hire someone for a full-time position)고 말하고 있으므로 정답은 (A)이다.

어휘 celebration 기념행사

85
What does the speaker ask the listeners to do?
(A) Share an announcement
(B) Collaborate on a report
(C) Revise a budget
(D) Indicate a preference

번역 화자는 청자들에게 무엇을 하라고 요청하는가?
(A) 공지 내용 공유하기
(B) 보고서를 공동으로 작업하기
(C) 예산 수정하기
(D) 선호도 표시하기

해설 **세부 사항 관련 - 청자들이 요청받은 일**
화자가 후반부에 채용 공고를 이메일로 보내겠다(I'm going to e-mail the job ad to you all as well)며 관심 있을 만한 사람에게 보내줄 것(Please send it around to anyone you think might be interested)을 요청하고 있으므로 정답은 (A)이다.

어휘 announcement 공지, 발표   collaborate 협력하다   revise 수정하다   preference 선호도

Paraphrasing
담화의 send it around → 정답의 Share an announcement

86-88 담화

M-Cn   OK, **86 now that I've shown you how our gym expects you to format your client workout plans,** let's talk about actually implementing them. **87 We believe your first task is to make sure that the client understands what they're supposed to do. For example, when you ask them to use something like the leg press machine,** be aware that many people are not familiar with this equipment. You may even want to demonstrate how to use it yourself. **88 It's important that the client feel confident about what they're doing. It will make them want to keep scheduling sessions with you— which is your main goal.**

좋습니다. 이제 우리 체육관이 여러분에게 고객 운동 계획을 짜는 방법을 보여드렸으니 이를 실제로 시행하는 방법에 대해 이야기해 봅시다. 여러분이 첫 번째로 할 일은 고객이 무엇을 해야 하는지 이해하도록 돕는 것입니다. 예를 들어, 여러분이 고객에게 레그 프레스 기구 따위를 사용하라고 했을 때 많은 사람들이 이 장비에 대해 잘 모른다는 사실을 유념하세요. 이것을 어떻게 사용하는지 직접 시범을 보이셔야 할 거예요. 고객이 하고 있는 것에 자신감을 가지게 하는 것이 중요합니다. 그래야 여러분과 수업 일정을 계속 잡고 싶을 거예요. 그게 여러분의 주 목표이죠.

어휘 format 포맷을 만들다   workout 운동   implement 시행하다   be familiar with ~에 대해 잘 알다   equipment 장비   demonstrate 시연하다   confident 자신감 있는

86
Who most likely are the listeners?
(A) Technical support agents
(B) Personal trainers
(C) Factory workers
(D) Construction supervisors

번역 청자들은 누구이겠는가?
(A) 기술 지원 담당자
(B) 개인 트레이너
(C) 공장 근로자
(D) 공사 감독관

해설 **전체 내용 관련 - 청자들의 신분**
화자가 초반부에 지금까지 우리 체육관이 여러분에게 요구하는 고객 운동 계획을 작성하는 방법을 보여주었다(now that I've shown you how our gym expects you to format your client workout plans)고 말하는 것으로 보아 청자들은 운동을 하려는 고객을 관리하는 사람임을 알 수 있다. 따라서 정답은 (B)이다.

어휘 technical support 기술 지원   construction 공사, 건설   supervisor 감독관, 관리자

87 What does the speaker imply when he says, "many people are not familiar with this equipment"?
(A) An achievement is surprising.
(B) It is difficult to find qualified staff.
(C) A clear explanation should be given.
(D) It is not necessary to keep the equipment.

번역 화자가 "많은 사람들이 이 장비에 대해 잘 모른다"고 말할 때, 그 의도는 무엇인가?
(A) 업적이 놀랍다.
(B) 자격을 갖춘 직원을 찾기가 어렵다.
(C) 명확한 설명이 제공되어야 한다.
(D) 장비를 가지고 있을 필요가 없다.

해설 **화자의 의도 파악 - 많은 사람들이 이 장비에 대해 잘 모른다는 말의 의도**
앞에서 화자가 청자가 첫 번째로 할 일은 고객이 무엇을 해야 하는지 이해하도록 돕는 것(We believe your first task is to make sure that the client understands what they're supposed to do)이라며 청자가 고객에게 레그 프레스 기구 따위를 사용하라고 했을 때(For example, when you ask them to use something like the leg press machine)를 예로 든 뒤 인용문을 언급한 것으로 보아 고객이 레그 프레스 기구의 사용법을 이해하도록 돕는 역할을 해야 한다는 의도로 한 말임을 알 수 있다. 따라서 정답은 (C)이다.

어휘 achievement 업적, 성취 qualified 자격이 있는 clear 명확한 explanation 설명

---

88 According to the speaker, what is the listeners' main goal?
(A) To retain customers
(B) To finish a project on schedule
(C) To resolve a safety issue
(D) To simplify a process

번역 화자에 따르면, 청자들의 주 목표는 무엇인가?
(A) 고객을 유지하는 것
(B) 예정대로 프로젝트를 끝내는 것
(C) 안전 문제를 해결하는 것
(D) 절차를 간소화하는 것

해설 **세부 사항 관련 - 청자들의 주 목표**
화자가 후반부에 고객이 하고 있는 일에 자신감을 가지게 하는 것이 중요하다(It's important that the client feel confident about what they're doing)며 그래야 청자들과 수업 일정을 계속 잡고 싶을 것(It will make them want to keep scheduling sessions with you)이라고 말한 뒤에 그게 청자들의 주 목표(which is your main goal)라고 밝히고 있으므로 정답은 (A)이다.

어휘 retain 유지하다 resolve 해결하다 safety 안전 simplify 간소화하다

> **Paraphrasing**
> 담화의 keep scheduling sessions with you
> → 정답의 retain customers

89-91 회의 발췌

> W-Br Next, **89 I have an update on the project to increase customer engagement with our athletic shoe line.** As you may remember, **90 we added a pop-up advertisement to our Web site in order to encourage visitors to subscribe to our mailing list.** Well, after one week, we have over ten thousand new subscribers—well over the goal we set! **91 It seems that a lot of people want the giveaway poster of our spokesperson playing basketball in our shoes.** I know there was some concern about the cost of offering this incentive, but I think these results show that it's worth it. We now have a direct channel of communication with many more potential customers.

> 다음으로는, 운동화 제품군에 고객 참여를 증진하는 프로젝트에 대한 추가 소식이 있습니다. 기억하시겠지만, 우리는 웹사이트 방문자들이 메일링 리스트에 가입하도록 독려하기 위해 웹사이트에 팝업 광고를 추가했습니다. 일주일 후에 우리는 1만 명이 넘는 신규 구독자가 생겼습니다. 우리가 설정한 목표를 훨씬 초과했죠! 많은 사람들이 우리 광고 모델이 우리 운동화를 신고 농구 경기를 하는 증정용 포스터를 갖고 싶어 하는 것 같습니다. 이러한 혜택을 제공하는 비용에 대해 우려가 있었다는 것을 알지만 이러한 결과는 그만한 가치가 있다는 것을 보여준다고 생각합니다. 이제 우리는 더 많은 잠재 고객들과 직접 소통하는 채널이 생겼습니다.

> 어휘 customer engagement 고객 참여 athletic shoe 운동화 advertisement 광고 encourage 장려하다 subscribe 구독하다 subscriber 구독자 giveaway 증정품 spokesperson 대변인, 광고 모델 potential 잠재적인

---

89 Where does the speaker most likely work?
(A) At a footwear company
(B) At a video game developer
(C) At a beverage manufacturer
(D) At a sports team organization

번역 화자는 어디서 근무하겠는가?
(A) 신발 회사
(B) 비디오게임 개발 회사
(C) 음료 제조 회사
(D) 스포츠팀 단체

해설 **전체 내용 관련 - 화자의 근무지**
화자가 초반부에 운동화 제품군에 고객 참여를 증진하는 프로젝트에 대한 추가 소식이 있다(I have an update on the project to increase customer engagement with our athletic shoe line)고 밝히고 있으므로 정답은 (A)이다.

어휘 footwear 신발류 developer 개발자, 개발 회사 manufacturer 제조 회사 organization 조직

> **Paraphrasing**
> 담화의 athletic shoe → 정답의 footwear

90 What does the business want people to do?
(A) Join a loyalty program
(B) Sign up for a mailing list
(C) Write a product review
(D) Follow a social media account

번역 회사는 사람들이 무엇을 하기를 원하는가?
(A) 충성 고객 프로그램 가입하기
(B) 메일링 리스트에 가입하기
(C) 제품 사용 후기 작성하기
(D) 소셜 미디어 계정 팔로우하기

해설 **세부 사항 관련 - 회사가 사람들에게 원하는 것**
화자가 중반부에 웹사이트 방문자들이 메일링 리스트에 가입하도록 독려하기 위해 웹사이트에 팝업 광고를 추가했다(we added a pop-up advertisement to our Web site in order to encourage visitors to subscribe to our mailing list)고 말하고 있으므로 정답은 (B)이다.

어휘 loyalty program 충성 고객 프로그램   sign up for ~에 가입하다   account 계정

> **Paraphrasing**
> 담화의 subscribe to → 정답의 Sign up for

91 What incentive is being offered?
(A) A discount code
(B) Entry in a prize drawing
(C) Tickets to a virtual event
(D) A promotional poster

번역 어떤 혜택이 제공되고 있는가?
(A) 할인 코드
(B) 경품 응모권
(C) 온라인 이벤트 티켓
(D) 홍보용 포스터

해설 **세부 사항 관련 - 혜택의 종류**
화자가 후반부에 많은 사람들이 우리 광고 모델이 우리 운동화를 신고 농구 경기를 하는 증정용 포스터를 갖고 싶어 하는 것 같다(It seems that a lot of people want the giveaway poster of our spokesperson playing basketball in our shoes)고 말하고 있으므로 정답은 (D)이다.

어휘 entry 가입할 수 있는 권리[기회]   prize drawing 경품 추첨   virtual event 온라인 이벤트   promotional 홍보의

> **Paraphrasing**
> 담화의 giveaway poster → 정답의 promotional poster

92-94 공지

> M-Au Can I have everyone's attention, please? **92 I know you have a lot of patient samples to perform tests on today,** but this will just take a moment. I have an announcement about our benefits for employees. **93 Several of you have expressed**

frustration that there hasn't been a clear overview of the retirement savings plans, insurance coverage, and everything else that the lab offers its workers. Until now, the information was scattered throughout different documents or was only made available to human resources staff. Now, there's a single file on our shared network. In addition, **94 I promise to provide a prompt response to any questions you have about this information.**

> 모두 주목해 주시겠습니까? 오늘 검사해야 할 환자 샘플이 매우 많다는 사실을 알고 있습니다. 하지만 잠시만 시간을 내어주세요. 직원을 위한 복지 혜택에 대한 공지 내용이 있습니다. 몇몇 분들이 은퇴 저축 상품, 보험 보장 범위 및 기타 연구소에서 근로자들에게 제공하는 내용에 대해 명확한 설명이 없었던 것에 대해 불만을 표명하셨습니다. 지금까지 그 정보는 여러 문서에 걸쳐 흩어져 있거나 인사부 직원들만 열람이 가능했습니다. 이제 공유 네트워크에는 단 하나의 파일이 있습니다. 더불어 이 정보에 대해 궁금한 점이 있으시다면 즉각적으로 응답해 드리겠다고 약속합니다.

어휘 perform 수행하다   benefit 혜택   frustration 불만   retirement savings plan 은퇴 저축 상품   insurance 보험   coverage 범위   scatter 흩어지다   prompt 즉각적인

92 Where do the listeners most likely work?
(A) At a real estate firm
(B) At a community center
(C) At a medical laboratory
(D) At a business school

번역 청자들은 어디서 근무하겠는가?
(A) 부동산 회사
(B) 지역 문화 센터
(C) 의학 연구소
(D) 경영 대학원

해설 **전체 내용 관련 - 청자들의 근무지**
화자가 초반부에 오늘 검사해야 할 환자 샘플이 매우 많다는 사실을 알고 있다(I know you have a lot of patient samples to perform tests on today)고 말하고 있고, 중반부에 연구소(the lab)라고 언급하는 부분이 있는 것으로 보아 정답은 (C)이다.

어휘 real estate 부동산   laboratory 연구소

93 What does the speaker imply when he says, "Now, there's a single file on our shared network"?
(A) A task has not been finished.
(B) There is space to save more data.
(C) Some complaints have been addressed.
(D) A security rule is not being followed.

번역 화자가 "이제 공유 네트워크에는 단 하나의 파일이 있습니다"라고 말할 때, 그 의도는 무엇인가?
(A) 일이 아직 끝나지 않았다.
(B) 더 많은 데이터를 저장할 공간이 있다.
(C) 불만들이 시정되었다.
(D) 보안 규칙이 준수되고 있지 않다.

해설 **화자의 의도 파악 - 공유 네트워크에 단 하나의 파일이 있다는 말의 의도**

앞에서 몇몇 사람이 은퇴 저축 상품, 보험 보장 범위 및 기타 연구소에서 근로자들에게 제공하는 내용에 대해 명확한 설명이 없었던 것에 대해 불만을 표명했다(Several of you have expressed frustration ~ the lab offers its workers)며 지금까지 그 정보는 여러 문서에 걸쳐 흩어져 있거나 인사부 직원들만 열람이 가능했다(Until now, the information was scattered throughout different documents or was only made available to human resources staff)고 덧붙인 뒤 인용문을 언급한 것으로 보아, 과거에 불만이었던 부분을 개선했다는 의도로 한 말임을 알 수 있다. 따라서 정답은 (C)이다.

어휘 complaint 불평, 불만 address (문제 등을) 다루다 follow (규칙 등을) 준수하다

> **Paraphrasing**
> 담화의 frustration → 정답의 Some complaints

94 What does the speaker say he will do quickly?
(A) Draft a timeline
(B) Respond to inquiries
(C) Update some software
(D) Issue log-in credentials

번역 화자는 무엇을 빨리 하겠다고 말하는가?
(A) 일정 초안 잡기
(B) 문의에 응답하기
(C) 소프트웨어 업데이트하기
(D) 로그인 자격 증명 발급하기

해설 **세부 사항 관련 - 화자가 할 일**

화자가 후반부에 이 정보에 대해 궁금한 점이 있다면 즉각적으로 응답해 주겠다고 약속한다(I promise to provide a prompt response to any questions you have about this information)고 말하고 있으므로 정답은 (B)이다.

어휘 draft 초안을 작성하다 timeline 일정표 inquiry 문의 credential 자격 증명

> **Paraphrasing**
> 담화의 a prompt response to any questions
> → 정답의 Respond to inquiries

95-97 안내＋지도

> W-Am OK, team. ⁹⁵**Your first job today is taking a shipment of desks to Augustine Industries.** Make sure to put the protective mats down before you move them in—the company's very worried about damage to their floors. Uh... ⁹⁶**the office manager's going to keep a parking space open for you near the entrance—specifically, the spot at the bottom of the ramp**, so you won't have to navigate the stairs. And ⁹⁷**you have another job scheduled for**

eleven A.M., so come straight back here when you're done.

> 좋습니다, 팀원 여러분. **오늘 여러분이 첫 번째로 할 일은 책상들을 오거스틴 산업으로 배송하는 겁니다.** 책상들을 안으로 들여놓기 전에 보호 매트를 까는 것을 잊지 마세요. 그 회사는 바닥에 손상이 갈까 봐 매우 우려하고 있습니다. 어… **사무장이 출입구 근처에 여러분을 위한 주차 공간을 비워놓을 겁니다. 구체적으로 말하자면 경사로 하단에 있는 자리요.** 그래야 여러분이 계단을 걸어 올라가지 않아도 되니까요. 그리고 **오전 11시에 예정된 일이 하나 더 있으니, 일을 마치는 대로 곧장 복귀해 주십시오.**

어휘 shipment 배송, 배송품 protective 보호용의 damage 손상 floor 바닥 office manager 사무장 entrance 입구 specifically 구체적으로 말하자면 spot 자리 ramp 경사로 navigate 걸어서 가다 straight 곧장

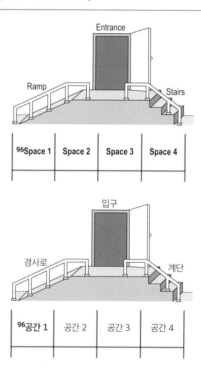

95 What type of business do the listeners most likely work for?
(A) A flooring contractor
(B) A plumbing service
(C) A delivery company
(D) An Internet service provider

번역 청자들은 어떤 종류의 사업체에서 일하겠는가?
(A) 바닥 시공업체
(B) 배관 공사업체
(C) 택배 회사
(D) 인터넷 서비스 공급업체

해설 **전체 내용 관련 - 청자들의 근무지**

화자가 도입부에 오늘 여러분이 첫 번째로 할 일은 책상들을 오거스틴 산업으로 배송하는 것(Your first job today is taking a

shipment of desks to Augustine Industries)이라고 한 것으로 보아, 청자들은 택배 회사에서 근무하고 있다는 것을 알 수 있다. 따라서 정답은 (C)이다.

어휘 flooring 바닥재 contractor 도급업체 plumbing 배관 공사

---

96 Look at the graphic. Which parking space will be reserved for the listeners?
(A) Space 1
(B) Space 2
(C) Space 3
(D) Space 4

번역 시각 정보에 의하면, 청자들을 위해 어떤 주차 공간이 확보되겠는가?
(A) 공간 1
(B) 공간 2
(C) 공간 3
(D) 공간 4

해설 **시각 정보 연계 - 청자들을 위한 주차 공간**
화자가 중반부에 사무장이 출입구 근처에 청자들을 위한 주차 공간을 비워놓을 건데 구체적으로 말하자면 경사로 하단에 있는 자리(the office manager's going to keep a parking space open for you near the entrance—specifically, the spot at the bottom of the ramp)라고 말하고 있고, 지도에 따르면 경사로 하단에 있는 자리는 공간 1이므로 정답은 (A)이다.

---

97 What should the listeners do after a job is completed?
(A) Return to their current location
(B) Send a message to a supervisor
(C) Check an electronic schedule
(D) Take a required meal break

번역 청자들은 일이 끝난 후에 무엇을 해야 하는가?
(A) 현재 위치로 복귀하기
(B) 관리자에게 메시지 보내기
(C) 전자 일정표 확인하기
(D) 보장된 식사 휴게 시간 갖기

해설 **세부 사항 관련 - 청자들이 일이 끝난 후에 할 일**
화자가 마지막에 오전 11시에 예정된 일이 하나 더 있으니, 일을 마치는 대로 곧장 복귀해 줄 것(you have another job scheduled for eleven A.M., so come straight back here when you're done)을 요청하고 있으므로 정답은 (A)이다.

어휘 current 현재의 supervisor 감독관, 관리자 electronic 전자의

> **Paraphrasing**
> 담화의 come straight back here
> → 정답의 Return to their current location

98-100 전화 메시지+평면도

M-Au Hi, it's Cory Watkins. **98 I just looked over the initial floor plan you designed for my flower shop.** Overall, I'm quite happy with it. I like that you included so much display shelving. **99 That will let us feature a wide assortment of our floral arrangements at one time.** However, I'll need you to make one change to the plan. **100 The staff workbench in the back room will have to be shortened to make space for a storage cooler.** I forgot to include that piece of equipment in my list of required features—sorry.

안녕하세요, 코리 왓킨스입니다. **제 꽃가게를 위해 당신이 설계한 평면도 초안을 방금 살펴봤는데요.** 전체적으로 매우 만족합니다. 진열 선반을 많이 넣어주신 점이 마음에 들어요. **다양한 꽃꽂이 작품을 한꺼번에 보여줄 수 있을 거예요.** 하지만 평면도에서 한 가지만 수정해 주시면 좋겠습니다. **뒷방에 있는 직원용 작업대는 보관 냉장고를 놓을 공간을 위해 길이를 줄여야 합니다.** 필요 공간 리스트에 그 장비를 깜빡 잊고 빠뜨렸네요. 죄송합니다.

어휘 initial 처음의 floor plan 평면도 shelving 선반 assortment 모음, 종합 floral arrangement 꽃꽂이 작품 workbench 작업대 shorten 단축하다

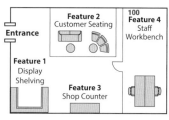

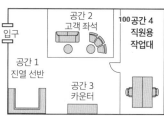

98 Who most likely is the listener?
(A) An interior designer
(B) An event coordinator
(C) A delivery person
(D) A cleaner

번역 청자는 누구이겠는가?
(A) 인테리어 디자이너
(B) 행사 기획자
(C) 배송 기사
(D) 청소부

해설 **전체 내용 관련 - 청자의 신분**
화자가 초반부에 내 꽃가게를 위해 당신이 디자인한 평면도 초안을 방금 살펴봤다(I just looked over the initial floor plan you designed for my flower shop)고 했으므로 청자는 꽃가게 평면도를 디자인한 사람임을 알 수 있다. 따라서 정답은 (A)이다.

어휘 coordinator 기획자, 조정자

99 What does the speaker say about flower arrangements?
(A) They were just delivered.
(B) They are difficult to care for.
(C) There will be a variety of them.
(D) They can be moved out of the way.

번역　화자는 꽃꽂이 작품들에 대해 무엇을 말하는가?
(A) 방금 배송되었다.
(B) 관리하기가 어렵다.
(C) 종류가 매우 다양할 것이다.
(D) 치워질 수 있다.

해설　**세부 사항 관련 - 화자가 꽃꽂이 작품들에 대해 한 말**
화자가 중반부에 다양한 꽃꽂이 작품을 한꺼번에 보여줄 수 있을 것 (That will let us feature a wide assortment of our floral arrangements at one time)이라고 말하고 있으므로 정답은 (C) 이다.

어휘　care for ~을 보살피다　move out of the way 치우다

> **Paraphrasing**
> 담화의 a wide assortment of → 정답의 a variety of

100 Look at the graphic. Which feature will have to be changed?
(A) Feature 1
(B) Feature 2
(C) Feature 3
(D) Feature 4

번역　시각 정보에 의하면, 어느 공간이 변경되어야 하겠는가?
(A) 공간 1
(B) 공간 2
(C) 공간 3
(D) 공간 4

해설　**시각 정보 연계 - 변경되어야 할 공간**
화자가 후반부에 뒷방에 있는 직원용 작업대는 보관 냉장고를 놓을 공간을 위해 길이를 줄여야 한다(The staff workbench in the back room will have to be shortened to make space for a storage cooler)고 했고, 평면도에 따르면 직원용 작업대가 있는 곳은 공간 4이므로 정답은 (D)이다.

TEST 2

1 (B)	**2** (C)	**3** (A)	**4** (B)	**5** (D)
6 (A)	**7** (B)	**8** (B)	**9** (B)	**10** (C)
11 (C)	**12** (A)	**13** (C)	**14** (C)	**15** (A)
16 (B)	**17** (A)	**18** (C)	**19** (A)	**20** (C)
21 (A)	**22** (B)	**23** (B)	**24** (A)	**25** (C)
26 (B)	**27** (A)	**28** (C)	**29** (B)	**30** (A)
31 (C)	**32** (B)	**33** (D)	**34** (A)	**35** (D)
36 (B)	**37** (A)	**38** (A)	**39** (D)	**40** (D)
41 (B)	**42** (D)	**43** (A)	**44** (C)	**45** (A)
46 (B)	**47** (A)	**48** (C)	**49** (D)	**50** (C)
51 (A)	**52** (D)	**53** (D)	**54** (C)	**55** (C)
56 (A)	**57** (C)	**58** (C)	**59** (D)	**60** (B)
61 (B)	**62** (B)	**63** (B)	**64** (A)	**65** (C)
66 (B)	**67** (C)	**68** (D)	**69** (C)	**70** (D)
71 (D)	**72** (B)	**73** (A)	**74** (A)	**75** (B)
76 (B)	**77** (A)	**78** (C)	**79** (B)	**80** (B)
81 (D)	**82** (A)	**83** (A)	**84** (D)	**85** (A)
86 (A)	**87** (D)	**88** (C)	**89** (B)	**90** (A)
91 (C)	**92** (C)	**93** (B)	**94** (D)	**95** (C)
96 (C)	**97** (D)	**98** (C)	**99** (C)	**100** (B)

PART 1

1

M-Au

(A) They're wiping off a desk.
(B) They're examining a camera.
(C) They're lifting a computer monitor.
(D) They're holding some files.

번역 (A) 사람들이 책상을 닦고 있다.
(B) 사람들이 카메라를 살펴보고 있다.
(C) 사람들이 컴퓨터 모니터를 들어 올리고 있다.
(D) 사람들이 서류철을 들고 있다.

해설 2인 이상 등장 사진
(A) 동사 오답. 사람들이 책상을 닦고 있는 모습이 아니다.
(B) 정답. 사람들이 카메라를 살펴보고 있으므로 정답이다.
(C) 동사 오답. 사람들이 컴퓨터 모니터를 들어 올리고 있는 모습이 아니다.
(D) 사진에 없는 명사. 사진에 서류철이 보이지 않는다.

어휘 wipe off ~을 닦다   examine 조사하다   lift 들어 올리다
file 파일, 서류철

2

M-Cn

(A) She's writing notes on a clipboard.
(B) She's sliding open a glass door.
(C) There are products stacked on shelves.
(D) There are binders on a counter.

번역 (A) 여자가 클립보드에 메모를 적고 있다.
(B) 여자가 유리문을 밀어서 열고 있다.
(C) 선반에 제품들이 쌓여 있다.
(D) 카운터에 바인더들이 놓여 있다.

해설 1인 등장 사진
(A) 동사 오답. 여자가 클립보드에 메모를 적고 있는 모습이 아니다.
(B) 동사 오답. 여자가 유리문을 밀어서 열고 있는 모습이 아니다.
(C) 정답. 선반에 제품들이 쌓여 있으므로 정답이다.
(D) 사진에 없는 명사. 사진에 카운터가 보이지 않는다.

어휘 slide open 밀어서 열다   stack 쌓다, 포개다

3

W-Br

(A) The men are on opposite sides of a table.
(B) One of the men is wrapping a box in plastic.
(C) The men are moving some shelving.
(D) One of the men is unpacking some stationery
   supplies.

번역 **(A) 남자들이 탁자의 맞은편에 있다.**
(B) 남자들 중 한 명이 상자를 비닐로 싸고 있다.
(C) 남자들이 선반을 옮기고 있다.
(D) 남자들 중 한 명이 사무용품의 포장을 풀고 있다.

해설 2인 이상 등장 사진
(A) 정답. 남자들이 탁자의 맞은편에 있으므로 정답이다.
(B) 동사 오답. 상자를 비닐로 싸고 있는 남자의 모습이 보이지 않는다.
(C) 동사 오답. 남자들이 선반을 옮기고 있는 모습이 아니다.
(D) 동사 오답. 문구용품의 포장을 풀고 있는 남자의 모습이 보이지 않
   는다.

어휘 wrap 싸다, 포장하다   plastic 비닐   shelving 선반
unpack (짐 등을) 풀다   stationery supply 문구용품

4

M-Cn

(A) Some people are gathered around a display.
(B) Some people are standing behind a vehicle.
(C) One of the people is searching through a suitcase.
(D) One of the people is picking up a piece of furniture.

번역 (A) 사람들이 전시품 주변에 모여 있다.
(B) 사람들이 자동차 뒤에 서 있다.
(C) 사람들 중 한 명이 여행 가방을 뒤지고 있다.
(D) 사람들 중 한 명이 가구 한 점을 들어 올리고 있다.

해설 **2인 이상 등장 사진**
(A) 사진에 없는 명사. 사진에 전시품이 보이지 않는다.
(B) 정답. 사람들이 자동차 뒤에 서 있으므로 정답이다.
(C) 동사 오답. 여행 가방을 뒤지고 있는 사람이 보이지 않는다.
(D) 사진에 없는 명사. 사진에 가구가 보이지 않는다.

어휘 gather 모으다, 모이다   display 전시, 진열   search through ~을 샅샅이 뒤지다   suitcase 여행 가방   pick up 들어 올리다

5

M-Au

(A) Some windows overlook a busy street.
(B) Some cars are stopped at an intersection.
(C) Some lines are being painted in a parking lot.
(D) Some trees are growing by a building.

번역 (A) 창문들이 붐비는 거리를 내려다보고 있다.
(B) 차들이 교차로에 정차해 있다.
(C) 주차장에 선들이 그려지고 있다.
(D) 건물 옆에 나무들이 자라고 있다.

해설 **사물·풍경 사진**
(A) 사진에 없는 명사. 사진에 붐비는 거리가 보이지 않는다.
(B) 사진에 없는 명사. 사진에 교차로가 보이지 않는다.
(C) 동사 오답. 주차장에 선들이 그려지고 있는 모습이 아니다.
(D) 정답. 건물 옆에 나무들이 자라고 있으므로 정답이다.

어휘 overlook 내려다보다   intersection 교차로   grow 자라다

6

W-Am

(A) A framed picture is mounted on the wall.
(B) Some books are scattered on a rug.
(C) A bench is being placed on the floor.
(D) Some light fixtures are being installed.

번역 **(A) 벽에 액자가 걸려 있다.**
(B) 깔개 위에 책들이 흩어져 있다.
(C) 벤치가 바닥에 놓이고 있다.
(D) 조명 기구들이 설치되고 있다.

해설 **사물·풍경 사진**
(A) 정답. 벽에 액자가 걸려 있으므로 정답이다.
(B) 사진에 없는 명사. 사진에 깔개가 보이지 않는다.
(C) 동사 오답. 벤치가 바닥에 놓이고 있는 모습이 아니다.
(D) 동사 오답. 조명 기구들이 설치되고 있는 모습이 아니다.

어휘 framed picture 액자에 넣은 사진이나 그림   mount 고정시키다   scatter 흩뿌리다   rug 깔개   light fixture 조명 기구

PART 2

7

W-Am Why is the doctor running late?
M-Cn (A) OK, but I don't feel sick.
(B) She had car trouble.
(C) No, that's not too early.

번역 의사가 왜 늦나요?
(A) 알겠습니다, 하지만 저는 아프지 않아요.
(B) 자동차에 문제가 있었대요.
(C) 아니요, 너무 일찍은 아니에요.

해설 **Why 의문문**
(A) 연상 오답. 질문의 doctor에서 연상 가능한 sick을 이용한 오답이다.
(B) 정답. 의사가 늦는 이유를 묻는 질문에 자동차에 문제가 있었다고 구체적인 이유를 제시하고 있으므로 정답이다.
(C) Yes/No 불가 오답. Why 의문문에는 Yes/No 응답이 불가능하므로 오답이다.

어휘 run late 예정보다 늦다

8

W-Br Where can I find art supplies?

M-Cn (A) Three types of paint.
     (B) In aisle seven.
     (C) To pass the time.

번역 미술용품은 어디에서 찾을 수 있나요?
     (A) 세 종류의 페인트요.
     (B) 7번 통로에요.
     (C) 시간을 때우려고요.

해설 **Where 의문문**
     (A) 연상 오답. 질문의 art에서 연상 가능한 paint를 이용한 오답이다.
     (B) 정답. 미술용품의 위치를 묻는 질문에 7번 통로라고 구체적인 위치로 응답하고 있으므로 정답이다.
     (C) 질문과 상관없는 오답. Why 의문문에 대한 응답이므로 오답이다.

어휘 aisle 통로   pass the time 시간을 때우다

9

M-Au Who waters the plants in the lobby?

W-Br (A) We can take the elevator.
     (B) Gerald does.
     (C) I'm not thirsty right now.

번역 누가 로비에 있는 화분에 물을 주나요?
     (A) 우리는 엘리베이터를 타면 돼요.
     (B) 제럴드가 해요.
     (C) 저는 지금 목이 마르지 않아요.

해설 **Who 의문문**
     (A) 연상 오답. 질문의 lobby에서 연상 가능한 elevator를 이용한 오답이다.
     (B) 정답. 로비에 있는 화분에 누가 물을 주는지 묻는 질문에 제럴드가 한다고 알려 주고 있으므로 정답이다.
     (C) 연상 오답. 질문의 water에서 연상 가능한 thirsty를 이용한 오답이다.

어휘 water 물을 주다   plant 식물   thirsty 목이 마른

10

M-Cn Do you have a phone I could use?

W-Br (A) Who was it?
     (B) Try this coupon.
     (C) I'm expecting a call.

번역 제가 사용할 수 있는 전화기가 있나요?
     (A) 누구였어요?
     (B) 이 쿠폰을 사용해 보세요.
     (C) 제가 기다리는 전화가 있어서요.

해설 **조동사(Do) 의문문**
     (A) 질문과 상관없는 오답.
     (B) 연상 오답. 질문의 use에서 연상 가능한 Try를 이용한 오답이다.
     (C) 정답. 사용할 수 있는 전화기가 있는지 묻는 질문에 기다리는 전화가 있다며 전화기를 빌려줄 수 없음을 간접적으로 표현하고 있으므로 정답이다.

어휘 expect a call 전화를 기다리다

11

M-Au How can we welcome our summer interns?

W-Am (A) We have air conditioning.
     (B) She's graduating in spring.
     (C) The team could go out to lunch together.

번역 여름 인턴사원들을 어떻게 환영할 수 있을까요?
     (A) 우리는 에어컨이 있어요.
     (B) 그녀는 봄에 졸업할 거예요.
     (C) 팀이 다 같이 밖에 나가서 점심을 먹을 수 있어요.

해설 **How 의문문**
     (A) 연상 오답. 질문의 summer에서 연상 가능한 air conditioning을 이용한 오답이다.
     (B) 질문과 상관없는 오답. 질문에 3인칭 대명사 She로 지칭할 인물이 언급된 적이 없으므로 오답이다.
     (C) 정답. 여름 인턴사원들을 환영할 수 있는 방법을 묻는 질문에 팀이 다 같이 밖에 나가서 점심을 먹을 수 있다고 알려 주고 있으므로 정답이다.

어휘 graduate 졸업하다

12

M-Cn When will the product testing start?

W-Am (A) My coworker Flora would know.
     (B) The third page of our report.
     (C) From a special laboratory.

번역 제품 검사는 언제 시작할 건가요?
     (A) 제 동료 플로라가 알 거예요.
     (B) 우리 보고서의 세 번째 페이지요.
     (C) 특수 실험실에서요.

해설 **When 의문문**
     (A) 정답. 제품 검사 시작 시기를 묻는 질문에 동료 플로라가 알 거라며 알 만한 사람을 알려 주고 있으므로 정답이다.
     (B) 연상 오답. 질문의 product testing에서 연상 가능한 report를 이용한 오답이다.
     (C) 질문과 상관없는 오답. Where 의문문에 대한 응답이므로 오답이다.

어휘 product testing 제품 검사   coworker 동료   laboratory 실험실, 연구소

13

W-Am Do you know the deadline for that project?

M-Au (A) I met him at a workshop.
     (B) A new projector.
     (C) It's not urgent.

번역 그 프로젝트의 기한을 알고 있어요?
     (A) 저는 그를 워크숍에서 만났어요.
     (B) 새 프로젝터요.
     (C) 급하지 않아요.

해설 **조동사(Do) 의문문**
     (A) 질문과 상관없는 오답. 질문에 3인칭 대명사 him으로 지칭할 인물이 언급된 적이 없으므로 오답이다.
     (B) 파생어 오답. 질문의 project와 파생어 관계인 projector를 이용한 오답이다.

(C) 정답. 프로젝트의 기한을 묻는 질문에 급하지 않다며 기한이 남아 있음을 간접적으로 표현하고 있으므로 정답이다.

어휘 deadline 기한 urgent 긴급한

14

W-Br What did you think of the job candidate?
M-Au (A) At a recent job fair.
　　　(B) It tastes delicious.
　　　(C) I thought he was impressive.

번역 그 입사 지원자에 대해 어떻게 생각했나요?
　　　(A) 최근 취업 박람회에서요.
　　　(B) 맛있네요.
　　　(C) 그가 인상적이라고 생각했어요.

해설 What 의문문
　　　(A) 단어 반복 오답. 질문의 job을 반복 이용한 오답이다.
　　　(B) 질문과 상관없는 오답.
　　　(C) 정답. 입사 지원자에 대한 의견을 묻는 질문에 인상적이라고 말하고 있으므로 정답이다.

어휘 job candidate 입사 지원자 job fair 취업 박람회 taste 맛이 나다 delicious 맛있는 impressive 인상적인

15

M-Au Did you find a buyer for the Maple Street house?
M-Cn (A) No, it's still on the market.
　　　(B) Yes, a sign in the front yard.
　　　(C) Twelve hundred square feet.

번역 메이플 가 주택의 매수자를 찾으셨나요?
　　　(A) 아니요, 아직 매물로 나와 있어요.
　　　(B) 네, 앞마당에 있는 표지판이요.
　　　(C) 1,200 평방 피트요.

해설 조동사(Did) 의문문
　　　(A) 정답. 메이플 가 주택의 매수자를 찾았는지 묻는 질문에 아니요(No)라고 대답한 뒤, 아직 매물로 나와 있다며 부정 답변과 일관된 내용을 덧붙였으므로 정답이다.
　　　(B) 연상 오답. 질문의 house에서 연상 가능한 front yard를 이용한 오답이다.
　　　(C) 연상 오답. 질문의 house에서 연상 가능한 면적 단위인 square feet를 이용한 오답이다.

어휘 on the market 시장에 나와 있는 yard 마당, 뜰 square feet 평방 피트

16

W-Am What do we have to wear for the company photo shoot?
M-Cn (A) I'm aware of them.
　　　(B) Didn't you read the memo?
　　　(C) Yes, he's popular on social media.

번역 회사 사진 촬영 때 무엇을 입어야 하나요?
　　　(A) 저는 그들을 알아요.
　　　(B) 회람 안 읽으셨어요?
　　　(C) 네, 그는 소셜 미디어에서 인기가 많아요.

해설 What 의문문
　　　(A) 유사 발음 오답. 질문의 wear와 부분적으로 발음이 유사한 aware를 이용한 오답이다.
　　　(B) 정답. 회사 사진 촬영 때 입어야 할 복장을 묻는 질문에 회람을 안 읽었는지 물으며 회람을 보면 알 수 있음을 간접적으로 알려 주고 있으므로 정답이다.
　　　(C) Yes/No 불가 오답. What 의문문에는 Yes/No 응답이 불가능하므로 오답이다.

어휘 photo shoot 사진 촬영 be aware of ~을 알다 popular 인기 있는

17

M-Au That gallery's been closed for months.
W-Br (A) I hope the renovations end soon.
　　　(B) Yes, the drawer is open.
　　　(C) We'll probably visit one.

번역 저 화랑은 몇 달째 닫혀 있어요.
　　　(A) 보수 공사가 빨리 끝났으면 좋겠네요.
　　　(B) 네, 그 서랍은 열려 있어요.
　　　(C) 우리는 아마도 한 곳을 방문할 거예요.

해설 사실·정보 전달의 평서문
　　　(A) 정답. 화랑이 몇 달째 닫혀 있다는 평서문에 공사가 빨리 끝났으면 좋겠다며 호응하고 있으므로 정답이다.
　　　(B) 연상 오답. 평서문의 closed에서 연상 가능한 open을 이용한 오답이다.
　　　(C) 연상 오답. 평서문의 gallery에서 연상 가능한 visit을 이용한 오답이다.

어휘 gallery 화랑 renovation 보수 공사 drawer 서랍 probably 아마도

18

M-Au Could you design the event invitations?
W-Am (A) A soft color scheme.
　　　(B) They're excited to attend.
　　　(C) My vacation starts tomorrow.

번역 행사 초대장을 디자인해 줄 수 있나요?
　　　(A) 부드러운 배색이요.
　　　(B) 그들은 참석할 생각에 들떠 있어요.
　　　(C) 제가 내일부터 휴가예요.

해설 요청·제안문
　　　(A) 연상 오답. 질문의 design에서 연상 가능한 color scheme을 이용한 오답이다.
　　　(B) 연상 오답. 질문의 event에서 연상 가능한 attend를 이용한 오답이다.
　　　(C) 정답. 행사 초대장을 디자인해달라는 요청에 내일부터 휴가라 해 줄 수 없음을 간접적으로 표현하고 있으므로 정답이다.

어휘 invitation 초대, 초대장 color scheme 색채의 배합 attend 참석하다 vacation 휴가

19

W-Br This author's last book was nominated for a Voss Award, right?

M-Cn (A) No, for some other award.
(B) The top shelf.
(C) A few films.

번역 이 저자의 최근작이 보스 상에 후보로 올랐었죠, 맞죠?
(A) 아니요, 다른 상이에요.
(B) 맨 위 선반이요.
(C) 몇몇 영화요.

해설 **부가 의문문**
(A) 정답. 저자의 최근작이 보스 상에 후보로 올랐었는지 여부를 확인하는 질문에 아니요(No)라고 대답한 뒤, 다른 상이라며 부정 답변과 일관된 내용을 덧붙였으므로 정답이다.
(B) 연상 오답. 질문의 nominated에서 연상 가능한 top을 이용한 오답이다.
(C) 연상 오답. 질문의 nominated에서 연상 가능한 films를 이용한 오답이다.

어휘 nominate 임명하다, 지명하다   award 상

20

W-Am When will the roadwork end?

M-Au (A) Oh, did he?
(B) More than 60 workers.
(C) They're making good progress.

번역 도로 공사는 언제 끝날까요?
(A) 아, 그가 했대요?
(B) 60명 이상의 근로자요.
(C) 많이 진척되고 있어요.

해설 **When 의문문**
(A) 질문과 상관없는 오답. 질문에 3인칭 대명사 he로 지칭할 인물이 언급된 적이 없으므로 오답이다.
(B) 유사 발음 오답. 질문의 roadwork과 부분적으로 발음이 유사한 workers를 이용한 오답이다.
(C) 정답. 도로 공사의 완료 시기를 묻는 질문에 많이 진척되고 있다며 완료 시기가 가까워지고 있음을 우회적으로 알려 주고 있으므로 정답이다.

어휘 roadwork 도로 공사   make progress 진척을 이루다

21

W-Am Would you like that shirt in a larger size?

M-Cn (A) Thanks, it is a bit tight.
(B) That's good to know.
(C) I'll print out the sales data.

번역 그 셔츠를 더 큰 치수로 드릴까요?
(A) 고맙습니다, 이건 약간 끼네요.
(B) 좋은 정보네요.
(C) 제가 매출 자료를 출력할게요.

해설 **요청·제안문**
(A) 정답. 더 큰 치수의 셔츠가 필요한지 묻는 제안에 고맙다는 답변과 함께 약간 낀다며 더 큰 치수가 필요한 이유를 덧붙이고 있으므로

정답이다.
(B) 연상 오답. 질문의 like에서 연상 가능한 good을 이용한 오답이다.
(C) 연상 오답. 질문의 shirt에서 연상 가능한 sales를 이용한 오답이다.

어휘 tight (옷이 몸에) 꽉 조이는

22

W-Br There are a lot of empty seats in the theater today, aren't there?

M-Au (A) Just some soft drinks.
(B) Weekdays are always quiet.
(C) Here's my ticket.

번역 오늘 극장에 빈자리가 정말 많네요, 그렇지 않나요?
(A) 그냥 탄산음료만이요.
(B) 평일은 언제나 한산해요.
(C) 여기 제 티켓입니다.

해설 **부가 의문문**
(A) 연상 오답. 질문의 theater에서 연상 가능한 soft drinks를 이용한 오답이다.
(B) 정답. 극장에 빈자리가 많다며 동의를 구하는 말에 평일은 언제나 한산하다며 관련된 내용으로 응답하고 있으므로 정답이다.
(C) 연상 오답. 질문의 theater에서 연상 가능한 ticket을 이용한 오답이다.

어휘 soft drink 탄산음료   quiet 조용한, 한산한

23

M-Cn When can I visit the factory to see the production samples?

W-Am (A) Make sure you purchase apples at the store.
(B) Come by anytime next week.
(C) No, that's not the only factor.

번역 생산 샘플을 보러 제가 언제 공장에 방문하면 될까요?
(A) 그 상점에서 사과를 꼭 구매하세요.
(B) 다음 주에 아무 때나 들르세요.
(C) 아니요, 그게 유일한 요인은 아니에요.

해설 **When 의문문**
(A) 유사 발음 오답. 질문의 samples와 부분적으로 발음이 유사한 apples를 이용한 오답이다.
(B) 정답. 공장 방문 시점을 묻는 질문에 다음 주에 아무 때나 들르라고 알려 주고 있으므로 정답이다.
(C) Yes/No 불가 오답. When 의문문에는 Yes/No 응답이 불가능하므로 오답이다.

어휘 factory 공장   production 생산, 제작   purchase 구매하다
come by 잠깐 들르다   factor 요인

24

M-Au Didn't Ms. Oba tell us to call her when the printer was repaired?

W-Br (A) Yes—we'd better call her now.
(B) We sell office equipment.
(C) No, that belongs to the technician.

번역　오바 씨가 프린터가 수리되면 전화해 달라고 하지 않았나요?
(A) 네, 지금 그녀에게 전화해야겠어요.
(B) 우리는 사무용 장비를 팔아요.
(C) 아니요, 그건 수리 기사 거예요.

해설　부정 의문문
(A) 정답. 오바 씨가 프린터가 수리되면 전화해 달라고 했는지 묻는 질문에 네(Yes)라고 대답한 뒤, 지금 그녀에게 전화해야겠다며 긍정 답변과 일관된 내용을 덧붙였으므로 정답이다.
(B) 연상 오답. 질문의 printer에서 연상 가능한 office equipment를 이용한 오답이다.
(C) 연상 오답. 질문의 repaired에서 연상 가능한 technician을 이용한 오답이다.

어휘　repair 수리하다　office equipment 사무용 장비　belong to ~에 속하다. ~의 소유이다　technician 기술자. 기사

25

M-Cn　Will the keynote speaker arrive today, or is she flying in tomorrow?
W-Br　(A) They're first-time attendees.
(B) Possible speech topics.
(C) She'll get here this evening.

번역　기조 연설자가 오늘 도착하나요, 아니면 내일 비행기로 오나요?
(A) 그들은 처음 참석하는 사람들이에요.
(B) 연설 주제 후보들이요.
(C) 그녀는 오늘 밤에 도착할 거예요.

해설　선택 의문문
(A) 질문과 상관없는 오답. 질문에 3인칭 복수 대명사 They로 지칭할 대상이 언급된 적이 없으므로 오답이다.
(B) 파생어 오답. 질문의 speaker와 파생어 관계인 speech를 이용한 오답이다.
(C) 정답. 기조 연설자의 도착 시간이 오늘과 내일 중 언제인지 묻는 질문에 오늘 밤이라며 둘 중 하나를 선택해 응답하고 있으므로 정답이다.

어휘　keynote speaker 기조 연설자　fly in 비행기로 도착하다 attendee 참석자

26

W-Am　What kinds of articles do you write for the magazine?
M-Au　(A) Through a news magazine.
(B) I mostly do editing.
(C) Thanks, we're proud of it.

번역　잡지에 어떤 종류의 기사를 쓰시나요?
(A) 뉴스 잡지를 통해서요.
(B) 저는 주로 편집을 해요.
(C) 감사합니다. 저희는 그것에 자부심을 갖고 있어요.

해설　What+명사 의문문
(A) 단어 반복 오답. 질문의 magazine을 반복 이용한 오답이다.
(B) 정답. 쓰고 있는 기사의 종류를 묻는 질문에 주로 편집을 한다며 기사를 쓰지 않음을 간접적으로 표현하고 있으므로 정답이다.
(C) 질문과 상관없는 오답.

어휘　article 글. 기사　editing 편집　be proud of ~에 자부심을 갖다

27

W-Br　How did you like Monday's class?
W-Am　(A) I was traveling for work.
(B) Yes, definitely.
(C) A different instructor.

번역　월요일 수업은 어땠어요?
(A) 저는 출장 갔어요.
(B) 네, 물론이죠.
(C) 다른 강사요.

해설　How 의문문
(A) 정답. 월요일 수업이 어땠는지 묻는 질문에 자신은 출장 갔다며 모른다는 사실을 우회적으로 표현하고 있으므로 정답이다.
(B) Yes/No 불가 오답. How 의문문에는 Yes/No 응답이 불가능하므로 오답이다.
(C) 연상 오답. 질문의 class에서 연상 가능한 instructor를 이용한 오답이다.

어휘　travel for work 출장을 가다　definitely 물론. 확실히 instructor 강사

28

W-Br　Do you want to have dinner at the restaurant in our hotel?
M-Au　(A) No, eight P.M. at the latest.
(B) Some members of the tour group.
(C) Does it have vegetarian options?

번역　저희 호텔에 있는 식당에서 저녁 식사하기를 원하시나요?
(A) 아니요, 아무리 늦어도 저녁 8시요.
(B) 단체 관광 그룹의 일부 사람들이요.
(C) 채식 메뉴가 있나요?

해설　조동사(Do) 의문문
(A) 연상 오답. 질문의 dinner에서 연상 가능한 저녁 시간 eight P.M.을 이용한 오답이다.
(B) 연상 오답. 질문의 hotel에서 연상 가능한 tour group을 이용한 오답이다.
(C) 정답. 호텔에 있는 식당에서 저녁 식사를 하기를 원하는지 묻는 질문에 채식 메뉴가 있는지 식당과 관련된 내용을 묻고 있으므로 정답이다.

어휘　at the latest 아무리 늦어도　vegetarian 채식주의자　option 선택. 선택권

29

M-Cn　If the conference room's taken, where can we hold a meeting?
W-Br　(A) Half an hour ago.
(B) My new office is pretty big.
(C) The rescheduled directors' meeting.

번역　회의실이 사용 중이면 어디에서 회의를 할 수 있을까요?
(A) 30분 전에요.
(B) 저의 새 사무실이 꽤 넓어요.
(C) 일정이 변경된 이사 회의요.

해설 **Where 의문문**
(A) 질문과 상관없는 오답. When 의문문에 대한 응답이므로 오답이다.
(B) 정답. 회의 가능 장소를 묻는 질문에 새 사무실이 꽤 넓다며 자신의 사무실을 추천하고 있으므로 정답이다.
(C) 단어 반복 오답. 질문의 meeting을 반복 이용한 오답이다.

어휘 hold a meeting 회의를 열다　pretty 꽤, 상당히　reschedule 일정을 변경하다

30

M-Cn I'm not sure we're ready to play this song at the concert.
W-Am (A) Let's rehearse it some more.
(B) No, the venue's on the right.
(C) The lead guitarist.

번역 우리가 콘서트에서 이 노래를 연주할 준비가 되었는지 잘 모르겠어요.
(A) 리허설을 좀 더 해봅시다.
(B) 아니요, 그 장소는 오른쪽에 있어요.
(C) 리드 기타리스트요.

해설 **의견·희망 사항의 평서문**
(A) 정답. 콘서트에서 이 노래를 연주할 준비가 되었는지 모르겠다는 평서문에 리허설을 좀 더 해볼 것을 제안하고 있으므로 정답이다.
(B) 연상 오답. 평서문의 concert에서 연상 가능한 venue를 이용한 오답이다.
(C) 연상 오답. 평서문의 concert에서 연상 가능한 lead guitarist를 이용한 오답이다.

어휘 rehearse 리허설을 하다　venue 장소

31

W-Am Why don't you load up the packages so we can deliver them?
M-Cn (A) There was plenty of space before.
(B) Most of us enjoyed it.
(C) They're already in the truck.

번역 우리가 배송할 수 있도록 그 소포들을 좀 실어주시겠어요?
(A) 예전에는 충분한 공간이 있었어요.
(B) 우리 중 대부분이 즐거워했어요.
(C) 그것들은 이미 트럭에 실려 있어요.

해설 **요청·제안문**
(A) 연상 오답. 질문의 packages에서 연상 가능한 space를 이용한 오답이다.
(B) 질문과 상관없는 오답. How 의문문에 대한 응답이므로 오답이다.
(C) 정답. 배송할 소포들을 실어줄 것을 요청하는 질문에 그것들은 이미 트럭에 실려 있다며 관련된 내용으로 답하고 있으므로 정답이다.

어휘 load up 짐을 싣다　package 소포　plenty of 충분한

PART 3

32-34

M-Au Hi, Nancy. I just saw you through the window, so I thought I'd stop in. As a fellow Main Street business owner, **[32] I'm glad to see you're getting the bookstore ready for reopening.**

W-Am Yes, we'll finally reopen this weekend. What do you think of the changes to the layout? **[33] We'll have staff selling coffee and tea from that counter,** and customers will be able to relax at the tables with their drinks and books.

M-Au Sounds nice. Will you serve snacks too, or just drinks?

W-Am We'll sell a few baked goods. Oh, that reminds me—**[34] I need to head out now to buy the plates and silverware we'll need.**

남: 안녕하세요, 낸시. 창문으로 당신이 보여서 잠깐 들러봤어요. 같은 메인 가 상인으로서 **서점의 재개점을 준비하시는 모습을 보니 기뻐요.**

여: 네, 마침내 이번 주말에 재개점해요. 배치가 바뀐 부분은 어떻게 생각해요? **저쪽 카운터에 커피와 차를 파는 직원을 둘 거예요.** 손님들은 음료와 책을 들고 테이블에서 쉴 수 있을 거구요.

남: 좋네요. 간식도 팔 건가요? 아니면 음료만 팔 건가요?

여: 제빵류도 몇 가지 팔 거예요. 아, 그러고 보니, **필요한 접시와 식기류를 사러 지금 나갔다 와야겠네요.**

어휘 stop in 잠시 들르다　reopen 다시 문을 열다　layout 배치 baked goods 제빵류　head out 출발하다　plate 접시 silverware 식기류

---

32 What is the woman getting ready for?
(A) A seasonal sale
(B) A business's reopening
(C) A book's publication
(D) A local festival

번역 여자는 무엇을 준비하는 중인가?
(A) 계절 세일
(B) 사업장의 재개점
(C) 책 출간
(D) 지역 축제

해설 **세부 사항 관련 - 여자가 준비 중인 것**
남자가 첫 대사에서 서점의 재개점을 준비하는 모습을 보니 기쁘다(I'm glad to see you're getting the bookstore ready for reopening)고 말하고 있으므로 정답은 (B)이다.

어휘 seasonal 계절적인　publication 출간

Paraphrasing
대화의 getting the bookstore ready for reopening
→ 정답의 A business's reopening

33 What new feature of the bookstore does the woman point out?
(A) Its search kiosks
(B) Its gift certificates
(C) Its author readings
(D) Its in-store café

번역 여자는 서점의 어떤 새로운 특징을 언급하는가?
(A) 검색 키오스크
(B) 상품권
(C) 저자 낭독회
(D) 매장 내 카페

해설 **세부 사항 관련 - 여자가 언급하는 서점의 새로운 특징**
여자가 첫 대사에서 저쪽 카운터에 커피와 차를 파는 직원을 둘 것(We'll have staff selling coffee and tea from that counter)이라고 말하고 있으므로 정답은 (D)이다.

어휘 point out 언급하다, 지적하다 gift certificate 상품권 reading 독서, 낭독회 in-store 매장 내의

34 What will the woman most likely do next?
(A) Purchase some supplies
(B) Start a cleaning process
(C) Hang up some signs
(D) Write a job posting

번역 여자는 다음으로 무엇을 하겠는가?
(A) 비품 구입하기
(B) 청소 시작하기
(C) 간판 걸기
(D) 구인 공고 작성하기

해설 **세부 사항 관련 - 여자가 다음에 할 일**
여자가 마지막 대사에서 필요한 접시와 식기류를 사러 지금 나갔다 와야겠다(I need to head out now to buy the plates and silverware we'll need)고 말하고 있으므로 정답은 (A)이다.

어휘 supply 물품 hang up 걸다 job posting 구인 공고

Paraphrasing
대화의 buy the plates and silverware
→ 정답의 Purchase some supplies

35-37

M-Cn Hi, this is Marco Amato. ³⁵ **I'm a new member at the gym.** Uh, ³⁶ **I was supposed to have a personal training session with Tim yesterday at seven, but I missed it because of rush-hour traffic.**

W-Am I see. Well, I'm sorry, but ³⁵ **our gym doesn't issue refunds for missed sessions.**

M-Cn Oh, I know. I was wondering if I could move my future sessions later so that this doesn't happen again.

W-Am Tim isn't available later. I could schedule you with Derek, though. ³⁷ **He has openings at eight.**

M-Cn ³⁷ **Perfect—that will give me enough time to get there after finishing work.**

남: 안녕하세요, 저는 마르코 아마토라고 합니다. 체육관의 신입 회원입니다. 음, 어제 7시에 팀과 개인 트레이닝 수업을 하기로 되어 있었는데, 러시 아워 교통 체증 때문에 수업을 놓쳤습니다.

여: 그러시군요. 죄송합니다만, 빠진 수업에 대한 환불은 해드리지 않습니다.

남: 아, 압니다. 이런 일이 다시 발생하지 않도록 앞으로의 수업 시간을 좀 늦출 수 있는지 궁금해서요.

여: 더 늦은 시간에는 팀이 안 돼요. 데릭과 시간을 잡아드릴 수는 있어요. 그는 8시에 빈 시간이 있어요.

남: 좋습니다. 그럼 퇴근 후에 거기에 갈 시간이 충분할 거예요.

어휘 miss 놓치다 issue a refund 환불해 주다 opening 빈자리

35 Where most likely does the woman work?
(A) At a bank
(B) At a medical clinic
(C) At a real estate agency
(D) At a fitness center

번역 여자는 어디서 일하겠는가?
(A) 은행
(B) 병원
(C) 부동산 중개소
(D) 피트니스 센터

해설 **전체 내용 관련 - 여자의 근무 장소**
남자가 첫 대사에서 자신을 체육관의 신입 회원(I'm a new member at the gym)이라고 했고, 여자가 빠진 수업에 대한 환불은 안 된다(our gym doesn't issue refunds for missed sessions)고 말하는 것으로 보아 여자는 체육관에서 근무하고 있다는 것을 알 수 있다. 따라서 정답은 (D)이다.

Paraphrasing
대화의 the gym → 정답의 a fitness center

36 What was the man unable to do yesterday?
(A) Locate a building
(B) Keep an appointment
(C) Transfer a payment
(D) Arrange transportation

번역　남자는 어제 무엇을 할 수 없었는가?
(A) 건물 위치 찾기
(B) 예약 시간 지키기
(C) 지불금 송금하기
(D) 교통편 준비하기

해설　**세부 사항 관련 - 남자가 어제 할 수 없었던 일**
남자가 첫 대사에서 어제 7시에 팀과 개인 트레이닝 수업을 하기로 되어 있었는데, 수업을 놓쳤다(I was supposed to have a personal training session with Tim yesterday at seven, but I missed it ~)고 말하고 있으므로 정답은 (B)이다.

어휘　locate 위치를 찾아내다　appointment (진료 등의) 예약
transfer 이체하다　arrange 준비하다

---

37 What does the man like about the woman's suggestion?
(A) It suits his schedule.
(B) It is good for his health.
(C) It will be more enjoyable.
(D) It will reduce a fee.

번역　남자는 여자의 제안에 대해 어떤 부분을 좋아하는가?
(A) 자신의 일정에 맞다.
(B) 건강에 좋다.
(C) 더 재미있을 것이다.
(D) 회비를 줄여줄 것이다.

해설　**세부 사항 관련 - 남자가 여자의 제안에 대해 좋아하는 부분**
여자가 마지막 대사에서 그는 8시에 빈 시간이 있다고 하자 남자가 좋다(Perfect)면서 퇴근 후에 거기에 갈 시간이 충분할 것(that will give me enough time to get there after finishing work)이라고 덧붙여 말하고 있으므로 정답은 (A)이다.

어휘　suit ~에게 맞다　reduce 줄이다

38-40

> W-Br　Jutaro, **38 this invoice from Turnbull Appliances just arrived in the mail. It's for the installation of our new office fridge last month.**
>
> M-Cn　That wasn't free?
>
> W-Br　The technicians had to do some extra work to set up the wiring. That isn't part of the standard installation, so it cost extra.
>
> M-Cn　Oh, that's not good. The price of the fridge was close to the limit Ms. Brent approved for the replacement. With this charge, **39 we've exceeded the budget.**
>
> W-Br　I see. **40 I'll let Ms. Brent know about the situation.**

여:　주타로, 턴불 가전제품 사에서 온 송장이 방금 우편함에 도착했어요. 지난달에 새로 들인 사무실 냉장고 설치 비용이에요.

남:　그거 무료 아니었어요?

여:　기술자들이 배선을 설치하느라 부수적인 일을 더 해야 했어요. 그 부분은 표준 설치 항목에 속하지 않아서 추가 비용이 들었어요.

남:　아, 큰일이네요. 냉장고 가격이 브렌트 씨가 교체를 위해 승인한 한도액에 가까웠어요. 이 비용이 더해지면 **예산을 초과한 거예요.**

여:　그렇군요. 제가 브렌트 씨에게 상황을 설명할게요.

어휘　appliance 가전제품　installation 설치　fridge 냉장고
technician 기술자　set up 설치하다　wiring 배선
standard 표준의　approve 승인하다　replacement 교체
exceed 초과하다　budget 예산

---

38 Why does the man say, "That wasn't free"?
(A) To show surprise
(B) To explain a refusal
(C) To request reimbursement
(D) To emphasize an item's value

번역　남자가 "그거 무료 아니었어요?"라고 말한 이유는?
(A) 놀람을 표현하려고
(B) 거절의 이유를 설명하려고
(C) 환급을 요구하려고
(D) 물건의 가치를 강조하려고

해설　**화자의 의도 파악 - 그거 무료 아니었냐는 말의 의도**
이 문장 앞에서 여자가 턴불 가전제품 사에서 온 송장이 우편함에 도착(this invoice from Turnbull Appliances just arrived in the mail)했는데 지난달에 새로 들인 사무실 냉장고 설치 비용(It's for the installation of our new office fridge last month)이라고 하자, 남자가 인용문을 언급한 것으로 보아 남자는 무료가 아닌 것에 놀라 한 말이라는 것을 알 수 있다. 따라서 정답은 (A)이다.

어휘　refusal 거절, 거부　reimbursement 환급　emphasize 강조하다　value 가치

---

39 What problem does the man report?
(A) An appliance has broken down.
(B) Some paperwork is missing.
(C) Some technicians are unavailable.
(D) A budget has been exceeded.

번역　남자는 어떤 문제를 보고하는가?
(A) 가전제품이 고장 났다.
(B) 일부 서류가 누락되었다.
(C) 일부 기술자들을 부를 수 없다.
(D) 예산이 초과되었다.

해설　**세부 사항 관련 - 남자가 보고한 문제**
남자가 마지막 대사에서 예산을 초과했다(we've exceeded the budget)고 말하고 있으므로 정답은 (D)이다.

어휘　break down 고장 나다

TEST 2

40 What does the woman say she will do?
(A) Look for a manual
(B) Cancel an order
(C) Make some copies
(D) Speak with a manager

번역 여자는 무엇을 하겠다고 말하는가?
(A) 사용 설명서 찾아보기
(B) 주문 취소하기
(C) 복사하기
(D) 관리자와 이야기하기

해설 **세부 사항 관련 - 여자가 할 일**
여자가 마지막 대사에서 브렌트 씨에게 상황을 설명하겠다(I'll let Ms. Brent know about the situation)고 말하고 있으므로 정답은 (D)이다.

어휘 make a copy 복사하다

> **Paraphrasing**
> 대화의 let Ms. Brent know
> → 정답의 Speak with a manager

41 Why is the woman calling?
(A) To check on an order
(B) To receive a cost estimate
(C) To reserve an event venue
(D) To ask for a change to a route

번역 여자가 전화를 건 이유는?
(A) 주문을 확인하려고
(B) 견적을 받으려고
(C) 행사 장소를 예약하려고
(D) 노선 변경을 요청하려고

해설 **전체 내용 관련 - 여자가 전화하는 이유**
여자가 첫 대사에서 귀사의 버스 한 대를 대여하는 데 얼마인지 알고 싶다(I'm hoping to find out how much it would cost to rent one of your buses)고 말하고 있으므로 정답은 (B)이다.

어휘 cost estimate 견적(서) reserve 예약하다 venue 장소

> **Paraphrasing**
> 대화의 how much it would cost
> → 정답의 a cost estimate

41-43

> W-Am Hi, **41 I'm hoping to find out how much it would cost to rent one of your buses** for an event next month. **42 It's a two-day company retreat for the pharmacy I own.** We'll need transportation to and from a resort on Garris Mountain.
>
> M-Cn Sure. I'll just need a few more details. But first—did you know you can request a quote through our Web site? Many customers prefer to do that.
>
> W-Am Oh, **43 I tried to use the service on your Web site, but I couldn't. I couldn't understand how to fill out the request form.**
>
> ---
>
> 여: 안녕하세요, 다음 달에 행사를 위해 **귀사의 버스 한 대를 대여하는 데 얼마인지 알고 싶은데요.** 제가 운영하는 약국에서 가는 **1박 2일 회사 수련회입니다.** 개리스 산에 있는 리조트를 왕복할 교통수단이 필요해요.
>
> 남: 네. 다만 몇 가지 세부 사항이 더 필요합니다. 하지만 우선, 저희 웹사이트를 통해 견적을 요청하실 수 있다는 사실을 알고 계셨나요? 많은 고객들이 그 방법을 선호하시거든요.
>
> 여: **아, 웹사이트에서 서비스를 이용해 보려고 했지만, 못했어요. 요청서를 어떻게 작성하는지 모르겠더라고요.**
>
> ---
>
> 어휘 retreat 야유회 pharmacy 약국 request 요청하다
> quote 견적 fill out 작성하다 request form 요청서

42 What kind of business does the woman own?
(A) A tour company
(B) A ski resort
(C) An insurance agency
(D) A pharmacy

번역 여자는 어떤 종류의 사업체를 소유하고 있는가?
(A) 여행사
(B) 스키 리조트
(C) 보험사
(D) 약국

해설 **세부 사항 관련 - 여자가 소유하고 있는 업체**
여자가 첫 대사에서 자신이 운영하는 약국에서 가는 수련회(It's a two-day company retreat for the pharmacy I own)라고 말하고 있으므로 정답은 (D)이다.

43 Why was the woman unable to use the online service?
(A) A form is confusing.
(B) She was not aware of it.
(C) A Web site was down.
(D) Her computer is outdated.

번역 여자는 왜 온라인 서비스를 이용할 수 없었는가?
(A) 양식이 헷갈려서
(B) 그것에 대해 몰라서
(C) 웹사이트가 다운돼서
(D) 컴퓨터가 오래돼서

해설 **세부 사항 관련 - 여자가 온라인 서비스를 이용할 수 없는 이유**
여자가 마지막 대사에서 웹사이트에서 서비스를 이용해 보려고 했지만, 못했다(I tried to use the service on your Web site, but I couldn't)면서 요청서를 어떻게 작성하는지 모르겠다(I couldn't

understand how to fill out the request form)고 말하고 있으므로 정답은 (A)이다.

어휘 confusing 혼란스러운   outdated 오래된, 구식의

> **Paraphrasing**
> 대화의 the service on your Web site
> → 질문의 the online service
>
> 대화의 I couldn't understand how to fill out the request form → 정답의 A form is confusing.

44-46

M-Cn	Hi, Tamara. Oh, **⁴⁴I see you're reading the new issue of the company newsletter. What's it about?**
W-Br	The main feature is an announcement about a contest to design a new company logo. Any employee can submit a design, and **⁴⁵the CEO's going to pick the winning logo next month.**
M-Cn	How interesting! I'd like to enter.
W-Br	Well, **⁴⁶the announcement includes instructions for participants. You should take a look at them.**
남	안녕하세요, 타마라. 아, **회사 뉴스레터 최신호를 읽고 계셨네요. 무슨 내용인가요?**
여	주요 기사는 새 회사 로고 디자인 경연대회에 관한 공지예요. 직원은 누구나 디자인을 제출할 수 있고, **CEO가 다음 달에 우승 로고를 고를 거예요.**
남	재미있겠네요! 저도 참여하고 싶어요.
여	**공지에 참가자를 위한 안내가 들어 있어요. 꼭 읽어 보세요.**

어휘 feature 특집 기사   submit 제출하다   enter 출전하다   instruction 설명, 지시   participant 참가자

44 What does the man ask the woman about?
(A) Who will lead a meeting
(B) Why a report is not finished
(C) What topics a newsletter covers
(D) When an executive will visit

번역 남자는 여자에게 무엇에 대해 문의하는가?
(A) 누가 회의를 주재할 건지
(B) 왜 보고서가 완성되지 않았는지
(C) 뉴스레터에 어떤 내용이 실렸는지
(D) 임원이 언제 방문할지

해설 **세부 사항 관련 - 남자의 문의 사항**
남자가 첫 대사에서 회사 뉴스레터 최신호를 읽고 계신데(I see you're reading the new issue of the company

newsletter) 무슨 내용인지(What's it about?) 묻고 있으므로 정답은 (C)이다.

어휘 lead 이끌다   cover 다루다   executive 임원, 중역

> **Paraphrasing**
> 대화의 What's ~ about → 정답의 What topics

45 What will happen next month?
(A) A new logo will be chosen.
(B) A parking area will be expanded.
(C) A department will be restructured.
(D) A review will be published.

번역 다음 달에 무슨 일이 일어나겠는가?
(A) 새 로고가 선택될 것이다.
(B) 주차장이 확장될 것이다.
(C) 부서가 개편될 것이다.
(D) 평론이 출간될 것이다.

해설 **세부 사항 관련 - 다음 달에 일어날 일**
여자가 첫 대사에서 CEO가 다음 달에 우승 로고를 고를 것(the CEO's going to pick the winning logo next month)이라고 말하고 있으므로 정답은 (A)이다.

어휘 expand 확장하다   restructure 구조를 조정하다   publish 출간하다

> **Paraphrasing**
> 대화의 the CEO's going to pick the winning logo
> → 정답의 A new logo will be chosen.

46 What does the woman say the man should look at?
(A) A revised list of names
(B) Guidelines for a competition
(C) Blueprints for a building
(D) A budget proposal

번역 여자는 남자가 무엇을 봐야 한다고 말하는가?
(A) 수정된 명단
(B) 대회를 위한 가이드라인
(C) 건물 청사진
(D) 예산 제안서

해설 **세부 사항 관련 - 남자가 봐야 하는 것**
여자가 마지막 대사에서 공지에 참가자를 위한 안내 사항이 들어 있다(the announcement includes instructions for participants)면서 꼭 읽어 봐야 한다(You should take a look at them)고 말하고 있으므로 정답은 (B)이다.

어휘 revised 수정된   competition 경쟁, 대회   blueprint 청사진

> **Paraphrasing**
> 대화의 instructions → 정답의 Guidelines

47-49

M-Au Excuse me. I'm not sure which product to buy. **47 My bathroom drain is clogged, and I need something that can clear it.** What do you recommend?

W-Br Almost any of these products would probably work, but if you want to make sure the job gets done, I'd recommend Purifine. **48 Purifine's the strongest drain cleaner on the market.**

M-Au Got it. Thank you! Is there anything I should know before using it on my drain?

W-Br Yes—these kinds of chemicals can be dangerous. **49 Make sure to look over the safety information printed on the back of the bottle** before you open it up.

남: 실례합니다. 어떤 제품을 사야 할지 모르겠어요. **화장실 배수관이 막혀서 뚫을 수 있는 게 필요해요.** 어떤 걸 추천하시나요?

여: 여기 있는 제품 중 어떤 걸 쓰시더라도 거의 다 효과가 있겠지만, 확실하게 하시려면 퓨리파인을 추천합니다. 퓨리파인은 **시중에 나와 있는 제품 중에서 가장 강력한 배수관 세척제입니다.**

남: 그렇군요. 감사합니다! 배수관에 이걸 사용하기 전에 제가 알아야 할 게 있을까요?

여: 네, 이런 화학 물질은 위험할 수 있어요. 뚜껑을 열기 전에 **병 뒷면에 적힌 안전 정보를 꼭 훑어보세요.**

어휘 drain 배수관 clog 막다, 막히다 chemicals 화학 물질
look over ~을 훑어보다 safety 안전

---

47 What does the man want to do?
(A) Clear a drain
(B) Remove a stain
(C) Protect some flooring
(D) Improve a room's odor

번역 남자는 무엇을 하기를 원하는가?
(A) 배수관 뚫기
(B) 얼룩 제거하기
(C) 바닥재 보호하기
(D) 방의 냄새 개선시키기

해설 세부 사항 관련 - 남자가 하고 싶은 것
남자가 첫 대사에서 화장실 배수관이 막혀서 뚫을 수 있는 게 필요하다(My bathroom drain is clogged, and I need something that can clear it)고 말하고 있으므로 정답은 (A)이다.

어휘 remove 제거하다 stain 얼룩 flooring 바닥재 odor 냄새

48 Why does the woman recommend a product?
(A) It is environmentally friendly.
(B) It has a variety of uses.
(C) It is powerful.
(D) It is inexpensive.

번역 여자는 왜 제품을 추천하는가?
(A) 친환경적이어서
(B) 용도가 다양해서
(C) 성능이 강력해서
(D) 저렴해서

해설 세부 사항 관련 - 여자가 제품을 추천하는 이유
여자가 첫 대사에서 퓨리파인은 시중에 나와 있는 제품 중에서 가장 강력한 배수관 세척제(Purifine's the strongest drain cleaner on the market)라고 말하고 있으므로 정답은 (C)이다.

어휘 environmentally friendly 친환경적인 a variety of 다양한
inexpensive 저렴한

> **Paraphrasing**
> 대화의 the strongest → 정답의 powerful

49 What does the woman tell the man to do?
(A) Leave some windows open
(B) Watch some videos
(C) Wear a pair of gloves
(D) Read a product label

번역 여자는 남자에게 무엇을 하라고 말하는가?
(A) 창문 열어놓기
(B) 동영상 보기
(C) 장갑 착용하기
(D) 제품 라벨 읽기

해설 세부 사항 관련 - 여자가 남자에게 하라고 한 일
여자가 마지막 대사에서 병 뒷면에 적힌 안전 정보를 꼭 훑어보라(Make sure to look over the safety information printed on the back of the bottle)고 말하고 있으므로 정답은 (D)이다.

> **Paraphrasing**
> 대화의 look over the safety information printed on the back of the bottle → 정답의 Read a product label

---

50-52 3인 대화

W-Br Hi, Tanya and George. **50 Welcome to the team here at Pritchard Airport.** We're so glad to have two more baggage handlers with our busy season coming soon. OK, do you have any questions before I begin your orientation?

W-Am Yes, I do. Are there lockers where we can leave our belongings during our shifts?

W-Br There are. **51 You'll see them when we visit the staff breakroom later this morning.**

M-Cn And—**52 we're supposed to wear a reflective vest and black pants, right? Where do we get those from?**

W-Br We supply the vest, but you'll need to wear your own pants.

W-Am Oh, OK.

여1: 안녕하세요, 타냐, 조지. **프리차드 공항의 우리 팀에 오신 것을 환영합니다.** 곧 성수기가 다가오는데 두 명의 수하물 담당자가 더 생겨서 기쁩니다. 좋습니다. 오리엔테이션을 시작하기 전에 질문이 있으신가요?

여2: 네, 있어요. 근무 시간에 소지품을 보관할 수 있는 사물함이 있나요?

여1: 있습니다. **오늘 아침 늦게 직원 휴게실을 방문할 때 보실 수 있을 거예요.**

남: 그리고, **빛반사 조끼와 검정 바지를 입어야 하는 거죠? 어디에서 받을 수 있나요?**

여1: 조끼는 제공하지만 바지는 본인 걸 입으셔야 합니다.

여2: 아, 그렇군요.

어휘 handler (직업적으로) 취급하는 사람 busy season 성수기 belongings 소지품 shift 교대 근무 시간 breakroom 휴게실 reflective 빛을 반사하는 vest 조끼

50 Where is the conversation taking place?
(A) At an appliance store
(B) At a movie theater
(C) At an airport
(D) At a school

번역 대화는 어디에서 이루어지는가?
(A) 가전제품 매장
(B) 영화관
(C) 공항
(D) 학교

해설 전체 내용 관련 - 대화의 장소
첫 번째 여자가 첫 대사에서 프리차드 공항의 우리 팀에 온 것을 환영한다(Welcome to the team here at Pritchard Airport)고 했으므로 대화 장소는 공항이라는 것을 알 수 있다. 따라서 정답은 (C)이다.

어휘 appliance 가전제품

51 Where will the speakers go later in the morning?
(A) To a staff break area
(B) To a cafeteria
(C) To a loading zone
(D) To a conference room

번역 화자들은 아침 늦게 어디로 갈 예정인가?
(A) 직원 휴게 공간
(B) 구내식당
(C) 하역장
(D) 회의실

해설 세부 사항 관련 - 화자들이 아침에 갈 예정인 곳
첫 번째 여자가 두 번째 대사에서 오늘 아침 늦게 직원 휴게실을 방문할 때(~ when we visit the staff breakroom later this morning)라고 말하고 있으므로 정답은 (A)이다.

어휘 cafeteria 구내식당 loading zone 하역장

> **Paraphrasing**
> 대화의 the staff breakroom
> → 정답의 a staff break area

52 What does the man ask about?
(A) Who is part of a team
(B) How long a certain shift is
(C) Where to submit a document
(D) How to obtain a uniform

번역 남자는 무엇에 관해 문의하는가?
(A) 누가 팀원인지
(B) 근무 시간이 얼마나 되는지
(C) 서류를 어디로 제출해야 되는지
(D) 유니폼을 어떻게 받는지

해설 세부 사항 관련 - 남자의 문의 사항
남자가 빛반사 조끼와 검정 바지를 입어야 하는 건지(we're supposed to wear a reflective vest and black pants, right?) 그리고 어디에서 받을 수 있는지(Where do we get those from?) 묻고 있으므로 정답은 (D)이다.

어휘 submit 제출하다 obtain 얻다

> **Paraphrasing**
> 대화의 get → 정답의 obtain
> 대화의 a reflective vest and black pants
> → 정답의 a uniform

53-55

M-Au Hi, Lori. **53 Did Dean let you know that I'll be giving the interview that** _Tech News Weekly_ **asked for?** He's quite busy this week, and I also know a lot about the products the interviewer wants to discuss.

W-Br Really? Last time we spoke, **54, 55 he said that he would come here to the public relations department so we could prepare him for it. 55 That was this morning.**

M-Au Well, I spoke with him after lunch. You can call him to confirm if you'd like.

남: 안녕하세요, 로리. 딘이 당신에게 제가 <테크 뉴스 위클리>에서 요청한 인터뷰를 할 거라고 말해주었나요? 그가 이번 주에 많이 바빠요. 또 저도 인터뷰 진행자가 이야기하고 싶어 하는 제품에 대해 많이 알고 있기도 하고요.

여: 정말요? 마지막으로 이야기 나눴을 때, 그가 여기 홍보부로 와서 우리가 준비할 수 있게 한다고 했었는데요. 그게 오늘 아침이었어요.

남: 아, 저는 점심 시간 이후에 그와 이야기했어요. 원하신다면 그에게 전화해서 확인해 보세요.

어휘 ask for 요청하다 interviewer 인터뷰 진행자
public relations 홍보 prepare 준비하다

---

53 What is the conversation about?
(A) A company policy
(B) A production delay
(C) A damaged machine
(D) An upcoming interview

번역 무엇에 관한 대화인가?
(A) 회사 정책
(B) 생산 지연
(C) 손상된 기계
(D) 다가오는 인터뷰

해설 **전체 내용 관련 - 대화의 주제**
남자가 첫 대사에서 인터뷰를 할 것(I'll be giving the interview ~)이라고 말하고 있으므로 정답은 (D)이다.

어휘 policy 정책 delay 지연 upcoming 다가오는

> Paraphrasing
> 대화의 I'll be giving the interview
> → 정답의 An upcoming interview

54 What department does the woman most likely work for?
(A) Security
(B) Accounting
(C) Public Relations
(D) Human Resources

번역 여자는 어느 부서에서 일하겠는가?
(A) 보안부
(B) 회계부
(C) 홍보부
(D) 인사부

해설 **전체 내용 관련 - 여자의 근무 부서**
여자가 첫 대사에서 그가 여기 홍보부로 와서 우리가 준비할 수 있게 한다고 했다(he said that he would come here to the public relations department so we could prepare him for it)고 말하는 것으로 보아 여자는 홍보부에서 근무하고 있음을 알 수 있다. 따라서 정답은 (C)이다.

55 What does the man imply when he says, "I spoke with him after lunch"?
(A) He missed a group outing.
(B) He already received some instructions.
(C) A plan changed a short time ago.
(D) A task has been completed.

번역 남자가 "저는 점심 시간 이후에 그와 이야기했어요"라고 말할 때, 그 의도는 무엇인가?
(A) 야유회에 불참했다.
(B) 이미 지시 사항을 전달받았다.
(C) 바로 조금 전에 계획이 변경되었다.
(D) 업무가 완료되었다.

해설 **화자의 의도 파악 - 점심 시간 이후에 그와 이야기했다는 말의 의도**
앞에서 여자가 그가 여기 홍보부로 와서 우리가 준비할 수 있게 한다고 했었다(he said that he would come here to the public relations department so we could prepare him for it)면서 그게 오늘 아침이었다(That was this morning)고 말한 뒤, 남자가 인용문을 언급했으므로 남자의 말이 더 최근이므로 여자가 말한 계획은 변경되었음을 확인시켜 주려는 의도로 한 말이라는 것을 알 수 있다. 따라서 정답은 (C)이다.

어휘 outing 야유회 instruction 설명, 지시 task 일, 과제

56-58 3인 대화

M-Au Scott, **56 what do you think of the company's new internal Web site?** To me, it seems to have a lot of helpful features.

M-Cn Yes, I like it. I was especially happy to see that we can share documents through it. **57 That should make it easier for teams to collaborate.**

M-Au **57 I agree. And the companywide forum page is going to improve collaboration, too.** I wonder how they thought of including that in the Web site.

M-Cn Well, Alexis might know, since she works for the IT department.

M-Au Hey, Alexis? **58 Scott and I are curious—where did the inspiration for the new Web site's forum page come from?**

W-Am I think it was proposed by Courtney Gray in Human Resources. She had a lot of good suggestions, actually.

남1: 스콧, 회사에서 새로 만든 사내 웹사이트에 대해 어떻게 생각해요? 제가 보기에는 유익한 기능이 많은 것 같아요.

남2: 네, 마음에 들어요. 이걸 통해 문서를 공유할 수 있다는 점이 특히 마음에 들어요. **팀끼리 협업하는 일이 쉬워질 거예요.**

44

남1: 맞아요. 그리고 전사가 공유할 수 있는 포럼 페이지도 협업을 향상시킬 거예요. 그걸 웹사이트에 넣을 생각을 어떻게 했는지 궁금해요.

남2: 음, 알렉시스가 알지도 몰라요. 그녀는 IT부에서 일하니까요.

남1: 저기, 알렉시스? **스콧과 제가 궁금해서 그러는데요, 새 웹사이트의 포럼 페이지를 만들자는 생각은 어디서 나왔나요?**

여: 인사부의 커트니 그레이가 제안했을걸요. 그녀는 실제로 좋은 제안을 아주 많이 했어요.

어휘 feature 기능, 특징 collaborate 협업하다
companywide 전사적인, 회사 전반의 forum 포럼, 토론회
inspiration 영감 propose 제안하다 suggestion 제안

56 What did the speakers' company recently do?
(A) It launched a Web site.
(B) It renovated its office.
(C) It hired a spokesperson.
(D) It introduced a new policy.

번역 화자들의 회사는 최근에 무엇을 했는가?
(A) 웹사이트를 개설했다.
(B) 사무실을 새단장했다.
(C) 대변인을 고용했다.
(D) 새 정책을 도입했다.

해설 **세부 사항 관련 - 회사가 최근에 한 것**
첫 번째 남자가 첫 대사에서 회사에서 새로 만든 사내 웹사이트에 대해 어떻게 생각하는지(what do you think of the company's new internal Web site?) 묻고 있으므로 정답은 (A)이다.

어휘 launch 개시하다, 출시하다 spokesperson 대변인 policy 정책

57 What do the men say is a benefit of the change?
(A) It will attract new customers.
(B) It will lower maintenance costs.
(C) It will improve staff collaboration.
(D) It will make some travel unnecessary.

번역 남자들은 변화로 인한 이득이 무엇이라고 말하는가?
(A) 신규 고객을 끌어올 것이다.
(B) 유지보수 비용을 낮출 것이다.
(C) 직원 협업을 향상시킬 것이다.
(D) 일부 여행을 불필요하게 만들 것이다.

해설 **세부 사항 관련 - 남자들이 말하는 변화로 인한 이득**
두 번째 남자가 첫 대사에서 팀끼리 협업하는 일이 쉬워질 것(That should make it easier for teams to collaborate)이라고 하자 첫 번째 남자가 맞다(I agree)고 하면서 전사가 공유할 수 있는 포럼 페이지도 협업을 향상시킬 것(And the companywide forum page is going to improve collaboration, too)이라고 호응하고 있으므로 정답은 (C)이다.

어휘 attract 끌다, 모으다 maintenance 유지보수 unnecessary 불필요한

---

58 What do the men ask the woman about?
(A) The reaction to an announcement
(B) The quality of a service
(C) The origin of an idea
(D) The status of a project

번역 남자들은 여자에게 무엇에 대해 문의하는가?
(A) 공지에 대한 반응
(B) 서비스의 품질
(C) 아이디어의 출처
(D) 프로젝트의 상태

해설 **세부 사항 관련 - 남자들의 문의 사항**
첫 번째 남자가 마지막 대사에서 새 웹사이트의 포럼 페이지를 만들자는 생각은 어디서 나왔는지(Scott and I are curious—where did the inspiration for the new Web site's forum page come from?) 스콧과 함께 묻고 있으므로 정답은 (C)이다.

어휘 reaction 반응 origin 근원, 출처 status 상태

59-61

W-Br **59 Louis, I heard that you're going to be posting about our work on social media. I think that's smart. 59 A lot of people don't know about the services that a tailor shop like this provides.**

M-Au Right! Ms. Lam made the decision when she found out that I'm active on social media. She'd been wanting to increase the shop's Internet presence. So now **60 one of my duties will be managing our accounts on social media sites.**

W-Br That's great. What kinds of content are you going to post?

M-Au Well, I definitely want to show pictures of clothes before and after tailoring. But I'm not sure what else yet. **61 If you have any ideas, please let me know!**

여: 루이스, 당신이 소셜 미디어에 우리 업무에 대한 게시물을 올릴 예정이라고 들었어요. 훌륭한 생각 같아요. 많은 사람들이 이런 맞춤 양복점이 제공하는 서비스에 대해 알지 못해요.

남: 맞아요! 램 씨가 제가 소셜 미디어에서 활발하게 활동하는 모습을 보고 결정했어요. 그녀는 우리 양복점의 인터넷상의 존재감을 높이고 싶어 했어요. 그래서 이제 **제 담당 업무 중 하나는 소셜 미디어 사이트에서 우리 계정을 관리하는 일이 될 거예요.**

여: 잘됐네요. 어떤 종류의 콘텐츠를 게시하려고요?

남: 음, 재단 전과 재단 후의 옷 사진을 꼭 올리고 싶어요. 하지만 그 외에는 아직 잘 모르겠어요. **아이디어가 있으시면, 저에게 알려주세요!**

어휘 | tailor shop 맞춤 양복점   decision 결정   active 활발한   presence 존재   duty 업무, 임무   manage 관리하다   account 계정

---

59 Where do the speakers work?
(A) At a fashion magazine
(B) At a restaurant
(C) At a Web development firm
(D) At a tailor shop

번역 | 화자들은 어디서 일하는가?
(A) 패션 잡지사
(B) 식당
(C) 웹 개발 회사
(D) 맞춤 양복점

해설 | **전체 내용 관련 - 화자들의 근무지**
여자가 첫 대사에서 남자에게 우리 업무에 대한 게시물을 올릴 예정이라고 들었다(Louis, I heard that you're going to be posting about our work on social media)고 한 뒤, 많은 사람들이 이런 맞춤 양복점의 서비스를 잘 모른다(A lot of people don't know about the services that a tailor shop like this provides)고 말하고 있으므로 정답은 (D)이다.

어휘 | development 개발

---

60 What has the man been assigned to do?
(A) Mentor some colleagues
(B) Oversee social media accounts
(C) Organize a storage space
(D) Research a competitor

번역 | 남자에게 어떤 일이 주어졌는가?
(A) 동료에게 멘토링하기
(B) 소셜 미디어 계정 감독하기
(C) 창고 공간 정리하기
(D) 경쟁업체 조사하기

해설 | **세부 사항 관련 - 남자에게 주어진 일**
남자가 첫 대사에서 자신의 담당 업무 중 하나는 소셜 미디어 사이트에서 계정을 관리하는 일이 될 것(one of my duties will be managing our accounts on social media sites)이라고 말하고 있으므로 정답은 (B)이다.

어휘 | oversee 감독하다   organize 준비하다   competitor 경쟁업체, 경쟁자

Paraphrasing
대화의 managing our accounts on social media sites
→ 정답의 Oversee social media accounts

61 What does the man ask the woman to do?
(A) Review a presentation
(B) Make some suggestions
(C) Take some pictures
(D) Pick up some food

번역 | 남자는 여자에게 무엇을 하라고 요청하는가?
(A) 발표 자료 검토하기
(B) 제안하기
(C) 사진 찍기
(D) 음식 가져오기

해설 | **세부 사항 관련 - 남자의 요청 사항**
남자가 마지막 대사에서 아이디어가 있으면 알려달라(If you have any ideas, please let me know!)고 요청하고 있으므로 정답은 (B)이다.

어휘 | suggestion 제안   pick up 와서 가져가다

Paraphrasing
대화의 If you have any ideas, please let me know
→ 정답의 Make some suggestions

62-64 대화 + 안내판

W-Br Welcome to the Beldwin Ferry East Terminal. Would you like to purchase a ticket?

M-Cn Yes, for the next ferry. I'm a photographer, and **62 I'm planning to spend the day taking pictures of the plant life on Beldwin Island.** I've heard it's beautiful.

W-Br Yes, very! **63 Four dollars, please.**

M-Cn Oh, I thought the fare was higher than that... Ah, I see.

W-Br Yes. Here's your ticket. As you can see, the next ferry departs in about half an hour.

M-Cn Hmm... In that case, is there a restaurant or cafeteria around here? **64 I'd like to grab a bite to eat before getting on the ferry.**

W-Br Yes, there's a place around that corner.

여: 벨드윈 페리 동부 터미널에 오신 것을 환영합니다. 표를 구매하시겠습니까?

남: 네, 다음 페리요. 저는 사진가예요. **오늘 하루 벨드윈 섬에서 식물 사진을 찍을 계획이에요.** 아름다운 곳이라고 들었어요.

여: 네, 정말 그래요! **4달러입니다.**

남: 아, 저는 요금이 그보다 비쌀 줄 알았어요… 알겠습니다.

여: 네, 여기 표 받으시고요. 보시다시피 다음 페리는 약 30분 후에 출발합니다.

남: 음… 그렇다면 근처에 식당이나 구내식당이 있나요? **페리를 타기 전에 간단히 좀 먹고 싶어서요.**

여: 네, 저쪽 모퉁이를 돌면 바로 하나 있습니다.

어휘 | purchase 구매하다 fare 요금 depart 출발하다
grab a bite 간단히 먹다

Beldwin Ferry

Regular Fare: $8
Discounted Fares:
$6 after 6 P.M.
63 $4 on weekends
$3 for seniors and WavePass
holders

벨드윈 페리

정가: 8달러
할인가:
오후 6시 이후 6달러
63 주말 4달러
경로우대 대상자 및 웨이브패스
소지자 3달러

어휘 | holder 소유자

62 What is the purpose of the man's trip?
(A) To get exercise outdoors
(B) To create artworks
(C) To collect samples of plants
(D) To repair electronics

번역 | 남자의 여행 목적은 무엇인가?
(A) 야외에서 운동하려고
(B) 예술 작품을 만들려고
(C) 식물을 채집하려고
(D) 전자 제품을 수리하려고

해설 | **세부 사항 관련 - 남자의 여행 목적**
남자가 첫 대사에서 오늘 벨드윈 섬에서 식물 사진을 찍을 계획(I'm planning to spend the day taking pictures of the plant life on Beldwin Island)이라고 말하고 있으므로 정답은 (B)이다.

어휘 | artwork 예술 작품 repair 수리하다 electronics 전자 제품

> **Paraphrasing**
> 대화의 taking pictures of the plant life
> → 정답의 create artworks

63 Look at the graphic. Why does the man receive a discount?
(A) It is after 6 P.M.
(B) It is a weekend day.
(C) He is a senior.
(D) He has a pass.

번역 | 시각 정보에 의하면, 남자는 왜 할인을 받는가?
(A) 오후 6시 이후라서
(B) 주말이라서
(C) 경로우대 대상자라서
(D) 이용권을 소지하고 있어서

해설 | **시각 정보 연계 - 남자가 할인을 받는 이유**
여자가 두 번째 대사에서 4달러라고 했으며, 안내판에 따르면 할인 요금으로 주말에는 4달러이므로 정답은 (B)이다.

64 What will the man most likely do next?
(A) Have a small meal
(B) Board a passenger ferry
(C) Shop for souvenirs
(D) Retrieve his bicycle

번역 | 남자는 다음으로 무엇을 하겠는가?
(A) 간단히 식사하기
(B) 여객선에 탑승하기
(C) 기념품 사기
(D) 자전거 찾아오기

해설 | **세부 사항 관련 - 남자가 다음에 할 일**
남자가 마지막 대사에서 페리를 타기 전에 간단히 좀 먹고 싶다(I'd like to grab a bite to eat before getting on the ferry)고 말하고 있으므로 정답은 (A)이다.

어휘 | board 탑승하다 souvenir 기념품 retrieve 되찾아오다

> **Paraphrasing**
> 대화의 grab a bite to eat → 정답의 Have a small meal

65-67 대화+상자

W-Br Thanks for helping me with the charity drive to collect gently used items. **65 Our patients have donated a lot, right?**

M-Au Yes. **66 Someone's just dropped off all of these board games, dolls, and blocks.** They're in great condition. And the medical staff and visitors have also been bringing things in.

W-Br Wonderful! The collection boxes are in the hall by the administration office. But don't put them in all together, as the pieces may get mixed up. **67 I brought some plastic bags to separate each item.**

여: 곱게 사용한 중고 물품을 모으는 자선 운동을 도와주어서 고마워요. **우리 환자들**이 많이 기부했죠, 그렇죠?

남: 네. **어떤 분이 방금 이 보드게임과 인형, 블록들을 모두 놓고 가셨어요.** 상태가 아주 좋아요. 그리고 의료진과 방문객들도 물건들을 가져오고 있어요.

여: 좋습니다! 수거함은 행정실 옆 복도에 있어요. 하지만 몽땅 한곳에 넣지는 마세요. 물품들이 뒤섞일지도 모르니까요. **각 물건을 분리할 비닐봉지를 좀 가져왔어요.**

<table>
<tr><td>어휘</td><td>charity drive 자선 운동 collect 모으다 gently 부드럽게
patient 환자 donate 기부하다 drop off 배달하다 doll
인형 condition 조건, 상태 administration office
행정실 get mixed up 뒤섞이다 separate 분리하다</td></tr>
</table>

Canned Food	66 Toys
Box 1	**Box 2**
Books	Clothing
Box 3	**Box 4**

통조림	66 장난감
상자 1	**상자 2**
책	옷
상자 3	상자 4

65 Where most likely are the speakers?
(A) At a travel agency
(B) At a school
(C) At a hospital
(D) At a bank

번역 화자들은 어디에 있겠는가?
(A) 여행사
(B) 학교
(C) 병원
(D) 은행

해설 **전체 내용 관련 - 대화의 장소**
여자가 첫 대사에서 우리 환자들(Our patients)이라고 말하는 것으로 보아 대화의 장소가 병원이라는 것을 알 수 있다. 따라서 정답은 (C)이다.

66 Look at the graphic. Which box will the man use?
(A) Box 1
(B) Box 2
(C) Box 3
(D) Box 4

번역 시각 정보에 의하면, 남자는 어떤 상자를 사용하겠는가?
(A) 상자 1
(B) 상자 2
(C) 상자 3
(D) 상자 4

해설 **시각 정보 연계 - 남자가 사용할 상자**
남자가 첫 대사에서 누군가 보드게임과 인형, 블록들을 모두 놓고 갔다(Someone's just dropped off all of these board games, dolls, and blocks)고 했고, 상자 표시에 따르면 장난감(Toys)은 상자 2이므로 정답은 (B)이다.

> **Paraphrasing**
> 대화의 board games, dolls, and blocks → 정답의 Toys

67 What does the woman suggest doing?
(A) Assessing the value of the contents
(B) Printing some new labels for the boxes
(C) Placing some items in individual bags
(D) Checking to see if there are missing pieces

번역 여자는 무엇을 제안하는가?
(A) 내용물의 가치 평가하기
(B) 상자에 붙일 새 라벨 출력하기
(C) 물품들을 개별 봉지에 넣기
(D) 빠진 조각이 있는지 확인해 보기

해설 **세부 사항 관련 - 여자의 제안 사항**
여자가 마지막 대사에서 각 물건을 분리할 비닐봉지를 좀 가져왔다(I brought some plastic bags to separate each item)고 말하고 있으므로 정답은 (C)이다.

어휘 assess 평가하다 value 가치 content 내용물 individual 개별적인 missing 빠진, 없어진

68-70 대화 + 평면도

M-Au Hi, could you help me?

W-Am Absolutely. What brings you to the Randholm Building today?

M-Au **69 I'm looking for the convenience store. 68 I have a job interview there in a few minutes.**

W-Am OK. Here's the floor plan for the ground floor. **69 You're here, at the information desk. Just walk around the potted trees there. The convenience store is across from Uncle Freddie's.**

M-Au I see. Thank you.

W-Am Sure. Oh, and afterwards, come back out this way. **70 The other entrance is closed today.**

M-Au That's good to know.

남: 안녕하세요, 저를 도와주실 수 있나요?
여: 물론이죠. 오늘 랜드홀름 빌딩에는 무슨 일로 오셨어요?
남: **편의점을 찾고 있습니다. 몇 분 후에 거기에서 취업 면접이 있어요.**
여: 네. 여기 1층 평면도가 있어요. **지금 여기 안내 데스크에 계시고요. 저쪽 나무 화분 쪽으로 걸어가세요. 편의점은 엉클 프레디 맞은편에 있습니다.**
남: 그렇군요. 감사합니다.
여: 별말씀요. 아 그리고 이따가 이 길로 돌아 나오세요. **다른 입구는 오늘 닫혀 있어요.**
남: 좋은 정보네요.

어휘 what brings you ~? ~에는 무슨 일로 오셨어요?
convenience store 편의점 floor plan 평면도

ground floor 1층   potted 화분에 심은   afterwards 나중에   entrance 입구

Randholm Building

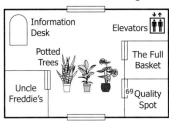

랜드홀름 빌딩

68 What does the man plan to do?
(A) Make a purchase
(B) Meet a friend
(C) Deliver a package
(D) Attend a job interview

번역　남자는 무엇을 하려고 하는가?
(A) 구매하기
(B) 친구 만나기
(C) 소포 배달하기
(D) 취업 면접 참석하기

해설　**세부 사항 관련 - 남자가 계획하는 일**
남자가 두 번째 대사에서 몇 분 후에 거기에서 취업 면접이 있다(I have a job interview there in a few minutes)고 말하고 있으므로 정답은 (D)이다.

어휘　attend 참석하다

69 Look at the graphic. Where will the man most likely go?
(A) To the Information Desk
(B) To The Full Basket
(C) To Quality Spot
(D) To Uncle Freddie's

번역　시각 정보에 의하면, 남자는 어디로 가겠는가?
(A) 안내 데스크
(B) 더 풀 배스킷
(C) 퀄리티 스팟
(D) 엉클 프레디

해설　**시각 정보 연계 - 남자가 갈 곳**
남자가 두 번째 대사에서 편의점을 찾는다(I'm looking for the

convenience store)는 말에 여자가 지금 여기 안내 데스크에 계신데(You're here, at the information desk) 저쪽 나무 화분 쪽으로 걸어가면(Just walk around the potted trees there) 편의점은 엉클 프레디 맞은편에 있다(The convenience store is across from Uncle Freddie's)고 알려주고 있으며, 평면도에 따르면 엉클 프레디 맞은편은 퀄리티 스팟이므로 정답은 (C)이다.

70 What does the woman inform the man about?
(A) An elevator skips some floors.
(B) A parking space has a time limit.
(C) A sales event is happening.
(D) An entrance is closed.

번역　여자는 남자에게 무엇에 대해 알려주는가?
(A) 승강기가 일부 층을 건너뛴다.
(B) 주차장에 시간 제한이 있다.
(C) 할인 행사가 진행 중이다.
(D) 입구가 닫혀 있다.

해설　**세부 사항 관련 - 여자가 알려주는 것**
여자가 마지막 대사에서 다른 입구는 오늘 닫혀 있다(The other entrance is closed today)고 말하고 있으므로 정답은 (D)이다.

어휘　skip 건너뛰다

PART 4

71-73 안내

M-Cn **71 Welcome to Prescott Science Museum.** I'm Hans Ulrich, the institution's volunteer program coordinator. I'll be giving you a general orientation before you're split into smaller groups for training in your specific duties. Now, **72 the museum building is massive, at over 20,000 square meters**—so we don't expect you to learn everything about its contents. However, we do want volunteers to have some familiarity with them. **73 I'll start today by showing you around the entire facility.** This is meant to be a quick overview, so please hold your questions until we're finished.

프레스콧 과학 박물관에 오신 것을 환영합니다. 저는 이 기관의 자원봉사 프로그램 담당자 한스 울리히라고 합니다. 여러분들의 구체적인 업무 교육을 위해 소그룹으로 나누기 전에 일반적인 오리엔테이션을 해드리겠습니다. 자, 이 **박물관 건물은 매우 거대합니다. 2만 평방 미터가 넘어요.** 그래서 박물관 안에 있는 모든 전시물을 다 아실 수는 없을 거예요. 하지만 자원봉사자분들은 어느 정도 익히시기를 바랍니다. **오늘은 전체 시설을 둘러보는 것으로 시작하겠습니다.** 빠르게 둘러보려고 하는 것이니 질문은 견학을 마칠 때까지 참아주세요.

어휘　institution 기관, 단체   coordinator 진행 담당자
split into (그룹을) 나누다   specific 구체적인   duty 업무, 임무

massive 거대한   familiarity 익숙함, 낯익음   entire 전체의   facility 시설   overview 개관, 개요

71 Where most likely are the listeners?
(A) At a university
(B) At a sports arena
(C) At a national park
(D) At a science museum

번역 청자들은 어디에 있겠는가?
(A) 대학교
(B) 스포츠 경기장
(C) 국립 공원
(D) 과학 박물관

해설 전체 내용 관련 - 담화의 장소
화자가 도입부에 프레스콧 과학 박물관에 오신 것을 환영한다(Welcome to Prescott Science Museum)고 했으므로 청자들은 과학 박물관에 있다는 것을 알 수 있다. 따라서 정답은 (D)이다.

72 What does the speaker emphasize about an institution?
(A) It has won awards.
(B) It has a large facility.
(C) It runs many programs.
(D) It uses new technology.

번역 화자는 기관에 대해 무엇을 강조하는가?
(A) 상을 받았다.
(B) 규모가 크다.
(C) 많은 프로그램을 운영한다.
(D) 신기술을 사용한다.

해설 세부 사항 관련 - 화자가 기관에 대해 강조하는 점
화자가 중반부에 박물관 건물은 매우 거대하며 2만 평방 미터가 넘는다(the museum building is massive, at over 20,000 square meters)고 했으므로 정답은 (B)이다.

어휘 award 상   technology 기술

> **Paraphrasing**
> 담화의 the museum building is massive
> → 정답의 a large facility

73 What will the listeners do next?
(A) Take a tour
(B) Fill out forms
(C) Introduce themselves
(D) Put on special clothing

번역 청자들은 다음으로 무엇을 하겠는가?
(A) 견학하기
(B) 양식 작성하기
(C) 자기 소개하기
(D) 특수복 입기

해설 세부 사항 관련 - 청자들이 다음에 할 일
화자가 후반부에 전체 시설을 둘러보는 것으로 시작하겠다(I'll start today by showing you around the entire facility)고 말하고 있으므로 정답은 (A)이다.

어휘 fill out ~을 작성하다   put on ~을 착용하다

> **Paraphrasing**
> 담화의 showing you around the entire facility
> → 정답의 Take a tour

74-76 공지

W-Br   Can I have everyone's attention for a moment? **74 I'm Cynthia Hughes from the IT department.** Thank you for your cooperation in using the second-floor copy machine over the last few days. **75 Tomorrow, the new copier for this floor will finally be delivered and set up.** The installation may be a little noisy, but we don't expect it to take very long. Uh, once it's complete, you'll each be assigned a four-digit code. **76 You'll have to enter that code in order to use the new copier.**

여러분 잠시만 주목해 주시겠습니까? **저는 IT부의 신시아 휴즈입니다.** 지난 며칠간 2층 복사기 사용에 협조해 주셔서 감사합니다. **내일 이 층에 놓일 새 복사기가 마침내 배송되고 설치될 겁니다.** 설치 과정에서 다소 소음이 발생할 수도 있지만, 그리 오래 걸리지는 않을 겁니다. 아, 설치가 끝나면 여러분은 각각 네 자리로 된 암호를 받으실 거예요. **새 복사기를 사용하기 위해서는 그 암호를 입력하셔야 합니다.**

어휘 cooperation 협조   copy machine 복사기   copier 복사기   installation 설치   complete 완료된   assign 할당하다   four-digit 네 자리로 된   enter 입력하다

74 Who most likely is the speaker?
(A) A technical support provider
(B) A marketing manager
(C) A legal advisor
(D) A product development specialist

번역 화자는 누구이겠는가?
(A) 기술 지원 제공자
(B) 마케팅팀 관리자
(C) 법률 고문
(D) 제품 개발 전문가

해설 전체 내용 관련 - 화자의 직업
화자가 초반부에 자신을 IT부의 신시아 휴즈(I'm Cynthia Hughes from the IT department)라고 소개했으므로 정답은 (A)이다.

어휘 technical support 기술 지원   specialist 전문가

> **Paraphrasing**
> 담화의 IT department → 정답의 technical support

75 What does the speaker say will take place tomorrow?
(A) A welcome reception
(B) An equipment installation
(C) A photography session
(D) An online seminar

번역 화자는 내일 무슨 일이 일어날 거라고 말하는가?
(A) 환영회
(B) 장비 설치
(C) 사진 촬영
(D) 온라인 세미나

해설 세부 사항 관련 - 내일 일어날 일
화자가 중반부에 내일 새 복사기가 배송되고 설치될 것(Tomorrow, the new copier for this floor will finally be delivered and set up)이라고 했으므로 정답은 (B)이다.

> **Paraphrasing**
> 담화의 the new copier ~ will finally be ~ set up
> → 정답의 An equipment installation

76 According to the speaker, why will the listeners need a number code?
(A) To receive a discount
(B) To operate a machine
(C) To log in to a Web site
(D) To enter a building

번역 화자에 따르면, 청자들은 왜 숫자 암호가 필요한가?
(A) 할인을 받기 위해
(B) 기계를 작동하기 위해
(C) 웹사이트에 로그인하기 위해
(D) 건물에 들어가기 위해

해설 세부 사항 관련 - 청자들이 숫자 암호가 필요한 이유
화자가 마지막에 새 복사기를 사용하기 위해서는 그 암호를 입력해야 한다(You'll have to enter that code in order to use the new copier)고 했으므로 정답은 (B)이다.

어휘 operate 작동하다

> **Paraphrasing**
> 담화의 in order to use the new copier
> → 정답의 To operate a machine

77-79 뉴스 보도

M-Au In local news, ⁷⁷**there is a lot of excitement for the Kiva Bledsoe concert that will be held tonight in the stadium downtown.** Ms. Bledsoe, a pop singer, is on a tour that is getting glowing reviews from attendees. ⁷⁸**Many of them have posted smartphone video footage online,** revealing that the concert features incredible costumes and sets. ⁷⁹**Tonight's show is sold out, which means that traffic around the venue will be heavy. If**

you're looking for an easier way to get to and from the stadium, the subways run until midnight.

지역 뉴스입니다. 오늘 밤 시내 경기장에서 개최될 키바 블레드소 콘서트에 대한 기대감이 높습니다. 대중 가수인 블레드소 씨는 순회 공연을 하는 중인데 참석자들에게서 호평을 받고 있습니다. 많은 사람들이 스마트폰으로 찍은 동영상을 온라인에 올리면서 그 콘서트에서 얼마나 멋진 의상과 무대를 선보였는지 공개되었습니다. 오늘 밤 공연은 매진되었습니다. 즉, 그 장소 주변에 교통 체증이 심할 거라는 뜻입니다. 경기장을 다녀올 더 쉬운 방법을 찾으신다면 지하철이 자정까지 운영합니다.

어휘 excitement 흥분 stadium 경기장 glowing 극찬하는 attendee 참석자 video footage 동영상, 비디오 영상 incredible 믿을 수 없는, 놀라운 reveal 드러내다 costume 의상 venue 장소

77 What is the main topic of the report?
(A) A music concert
(B) A sports tournament
(C) A transportation project
(D) An approaching storm

번역 보도의 주된 주제는 무엇인가?
(A) 음악 콘서트
(B) 스포츠 토너먼트
(C) 교통 프로젝트
(D) 다가오는 폭풍

해설 전체 내용 관련 - 보도의 주제
화자가 초반부에 오늘 밤 시내 경기장에서 개최될 키바 블레드소 콘서트에 대한 기대감이 높다(there is a lot of excitement for the Kiva Bledsoe concert that will be held tonight in the stadium downtown)고 했으므로 정답은 (A)이다.

어휘 transportation 교통 approach 다가오다, 접근하다

78 According to the speaker, what has been posted online?
(A) A list of road closures
(B) Contact information
(C) Video footage
(D) A technical drawing

번역 화자에 따르면, 온라인에 무엇이 게시되었는가?
(A) 통제된 도로 목록
(B) 연락처
(C) 동영상
(D) 기술 도안

해설 세부 사항 관련 - 온라인에 게시된 것
화자가 중반부에 많은 사람들이 스마트폰으로 찍은 동영상을 온라인에 올렸다(Many of them have posted smartphone video footage online)고 했으므로 정답은 (C)이다.

어휘 closure 폐쇄, 봉쇄 drawing 그림, 도안

79 What does the speaker mean when he says, "the subways run until midnight"?
(A) Subway schedules have changed recently.
(B) Attendees of an event should use the subway.
(C) Some work must take place after midnight.
(D) A city's transit services are well-funded.

번역 화자가 "지하철이 자정까지 운영합니다"라고 말할 때, 그 의도는 무엇인가?
(A) 지하철 운영 시간표가 최근에 변경되었다.
(B) 행사 참석자들은 지하철을 이용해야 한다.
(C) 일부 작업은 자정 이후에 진행해야 한다.
(D) 도시 환승 서비스는 재원이 충분하다.

해설 **화자의 의도 파악 - 지하철이 자정까지 운영한다는 말의 의도**
앞에서 오늘 밤 공연은 매진되어 그 장소 주변에 교통 체증이 심할 것 (Tonight's show is sold out, which means that traffic around the venue will be heavy)이라면서 경기장을 다녀올 더 쉬운 방법(If you're looking for an easier way to get to and from the stadium)으로 인용문을 언급한 것으로 보아, 행사 참석자들에게 대중교통인 지하철을 이용할 것을 권장하는 의도로 한 말임을 알 수 있다. 따라서 정답은 (B)이다.

어휘 take place 일어나다, 발생하다   transit 환승   well-funded 재원이 충분한

80-82 전화 메시지

W-Am Hello, Mr. Yates. **80 This is Mi-Hwa Park from Wilkett Public Radio, calling about your application for the producer position at our station.** Your résumé is very impressive. In particular, **81 I noticed that you're currently working as a producer on the podcast *Culture Week*. I'd be very interested in learning more about your contributions to the making of that show.** Uh, Human Resources handles our interview scheduling, so expect a call from them soon. **82 I'm going to send your application materials on to them now.**

안녕하세요, 예이츠 씨. 저는 윌켓 공영 라디오의 박미화입니다. 저희 방송국의 프로듀서 직책에 지원해주신 건으로 전화드립니다. 귀하의 이력서는 매우 인상적입니다. 특히, 현재 팟캐스트 <컬처 위크>에서 프로듀서로 일하고 계시네요. 그 프로그램 제작에 어떤 기여를 하고 계신지 더 알고 싶습니다. 아, 인사부에서 면접 일정을 관리하니, 그쪽에서 곧 전화를 드릴 거예요. 저는 귀하의 지원 서류를 지금 그들에게 보낼 겁니다.

어휘 position 직위, 일자리   station 방송국   résumé 이력서   impressive 인상적인   contribution 공헌, 기여   handle 다루다, 처리하다   material 자료

---

80 What job has the listener applied for?
(A) Film critic
(B) Radio producer
(C) Event coordinator
(D) Book editor

번역 청자는 무슨 일자리에 지원했는가?
(A) 영화 비평가
(B) 라디오 프로듀서
(C) 행사 기획자
(D) 책 편집자

해설 **세부 사항 관련 - 청자가 지원한 일자리**
화자가 초반부에 저는 윌켓 공영 라디오의 박미화이며 저희 방송국에 프로듀서 직책에 지원해주신 건으로 전화드린다(This is Mi-Hwa Park from Wilkett Public Radio, calling about your application for the producer position at our station)고 했으므로 정답은 (B)이다.

어휘 critic 비평가   coordinator 책임자, 담당자   editor 편집자

---

81 What does the speaker say she wants to discuss?
(A) A writing style
(B) A training process
(C) A company's goals
(D) A podcast's creation

번역 화자는 무엇에 대해 이야기하고 싶다고 말하는가?
(A) 문제
(B) 교육 과정
(C) 회사의 목표
(D) 팟캐스트의 제작

해설 **세부 사항 관련 - 화자가 원하는 이야기 주제**
화자가 중반부에 현재 팟캐스트 <컬처 위크>에서 프로듀서로 일하고 계신데(I noticed that you're currently working as a producer on the podcast *Culture Week*) 그 프로그램 제작에 어떤 기여를 하고 있는지 더 알고 싶다(I'd be very interested in learning more about your contributions to the making of that show)고 했으므로 팟캐스트의 제작에 대해 이야기하고 싶어 한다는 것을 알 수 있다. 따라서 정답은 (D)이다.

어휘 creation 창조, 창작

> **Paraphrasing**
> 담화의 the making of that show
> → 정답의 A podcast's creation

---

82 What does the speaker say she will do next?
(A) Forward some documents
(B) Leave for a business trip
(C) Confirm a pay rate
(D) Update a job advertisement

번역 화자는 자신이 다음으로 무엇을 하겠다고 말하는가?
(A) 문서 전달하기
(B) 출장 떠나기
(C) 급여율 확인하기
(D) 구인 광고 갱신하기

해설 **세부 사항 관련 - 화자가 다음에 할 일**
화자가 마지막에 귀하의 지원 서류를 지금 그들에게 보내겠다(I'm going to send your application materials on to them now)고 말하고 있으므로 정답은 (A)이다.

어휘 forward 전달하다   confirm 확인하다   pay rate 급여율(표준 시간당 임금)

> **Paraphrasing**
> 담화의 send your application materials
> → 정답의 Forward some documents

83-85 전화 메시지

> M-Cn Hello. My name is Norman Quinn, and [83] **I'm trying to reach the manager of Penver Inn and Suites.** I visited your inn last week to pick up a friend who was staying there, and I noticed that you display art in the lobby. [84] **I'm an artist—I paint colorful landscapes and portraits. They're similar to the pieces I saw in the inn. And I live nearby, in Sundale.** So I thought I'd ask... do you show works by local artists? If so, [85] **I can e-mail you some high-quality images of my work.** Just call me back at this number, 555-0167.
>
> 안녕하세요. 제 이름은 노먼 퀸이며 펜버 인 앤 스위츠의 관리자와 통화하고 싶습니다. 지난주에 그 호텔에 숙박 중이던 친구를 데리러 방문했는데요. 그때 보니 로비에 미술품을 전시하고 계시더라고요. **저는 미술가입니다. 다채로운 풍경화와 초상화를 그려요.** 귀사 호텔에서 본 작품들과 비슷해요. 그리고 저는 이 근처 선데일에 살아요. 그래서 여쭤보는데… 지역 미술가의 작품도 전시하시나요? 그러시다면 제 작품의 고화질 이미지를 이메일로 보내드릴 수 있습니다. 555-0167 번호로 전화 부탁드려요.
>
> 어휘 display 전시하다 landscape 풍경, 풍경화 portrait 초상화 piece 작품 한 점 nearby 인근에, 근처에 high-quality 고품질의

83 Who is the message intended for?
(A) A hotel manager
(B) A café owner
(C) A city official
(D) A gallery curator

번역 이 메시지는 누구에게 보낸 것인가?
(A) 호텔 관리자
(B) 카페 주인
(C) 시 공무원
(D) 갤러리 큐레이터

해설 **전체 내용 관련 - 메시지의 대상**
화자가 도입부에 펜버 인 앤 스위츠의 관리자와 통화하고 싶다(I'm trying to reach the manager of Penver Inn and Suites)고 하는 것으로 보아 메시지의 대상은 호텔 관리자임을 알 수 있다. 따라서 정답은 (A)이다.

어휘 official 공무원

> **Paraphrasing**
> 담화의 the manager of Penver Inn and Suites
> → 정답의 A hotel manager

84 What does the speaker mean when he says, "do you show works by local artists"?
(A) He wants to buy art that was made nearby.
(B) He hopes to learn about regional trends.
(C) He thinks a museum exhibit is incomplete.
(D) He wants the listener to display his work.

번역 화자가 "지역 미술가의 작품도 전시하시나요?"라고 말할 때, 그 의도는 무엇인가?
(A) 근처에서 제작된 작품을 사고 싶다.
(B) 지역의 동향에 대해 알고 싶다.
(C) 박물관 전시회가 미비하다고 생각한다.
(D) 청자가 자신의 작품을 전시해 주기를 원한다.

해설 **화자의 의도 파악 - 지역 미술가의 작품도 전시하는지 묻는 의도**
화자가 중반부에 자신은 다채로운 풍경화와 초상화를 그리는 미술가(I'm an artist—I paint colorful landscapes and portraits)이고 귀사 호텔에서 본 작품들과 비슷한 그림을 그리며(They're similar to the pieces I saw in the inn) 근처인 선데일에 산다(And I live nearby, in Sundale)고 말한 뒤 인용문을 언급하고 있으므로 자신의 작품을 호텔에 전시해 주기를 바라는 의도로 한 말임을 알 수 있다. 따라서 정답은 (D)이다.

어휘 regional 지역의   trend 동향   incomplete 불완전한

85 What does the speaker offer to do?
(A) Send some electronic files
(B) Answer the listener's questions
(C) Pay to use some images
(D) Give some driving directions

번역 화자는 무엇을 하겠다고 제안하는가?
(A) 전자 파일 보내기
(B) 청자의 질문에 답변하기
(C) 이미지 사용료 지불하기
(D) 운전 경로 정보 제공하기

해설 **세부 사항 관련 - 화자가 제안하는 일**
화자가 후반부에 자신의 작품의 고화질 이미지를 이메일로 보내줄 수 있다(I can e-mail you some high-quality images of my work)고 했으므로 정답은 (A)이다.

어휘 electronic file 전자 파일   direction 방향, 길 안내

> **Paraphrasing**
> 담화의 e-mail you some high-quality images of my work → 정답의 Send some electronic files

86-88 안내

W-Am Good morning, everyone. **86 In this seminar, I'll be teaching you how to lead meetings confidently and effectively.** By the time we're finished, you'll know how to smoothly manage difficulties ranging from technical problems to late participants. **87 I have conducted this seminar for businesses all over the country, and as you can see on my Web site, many of them say it has helped them succeed.** Now, **88 I'd like to start by telling you a few rules for the day.** I believe that seminars, like meetings, go better when the participants have clear guidelines to follow.

안녕하세요, 여러분. 이번 세미나에서 저는 회의를 자신감 있게 또 효과적으로 주재하는 방법을 알려드리겠습니다. 마칠 때쯤에는 기술적인 문제부터 지각한 참석자에 이르기까지 다양한 어려움에 순조롭게 대처하는 법을 알게 되실 겁니다. 저는 전국 곳곳에 있는 다양한 기업을 대상으로 이 세미나를 실시해 왔습니다. 제 웹사이트에서 보실 수 있듯이 그중 많은 기업들이 이 세미나가 그들이 성공하는 데 도움이 되었다고 말합니다. 자, 그럼 오늘의 규칙 몇 가지를 말씀드리며 시작하겠습니다. 저는 세미나도 회의와 마찬가지로 참석자들이 따라야 할 명확한 가이드라인이 있을 때 더 잘 진행된다고 믿습니다.

어휘 confidently 자신감 있게 effectively 효과적으로 smoothly 순조롭게 range from A to B 범위가 A에서 B에 이르다 late 지각한 participant 참석자 conduct 실시하다 go better 더 잘 되어가다

86 What is the focus of the seminar?
(A) Meeting management
(B) Cost-reduction ideas
(C) Staff recruitment
(D) Data organization

번역 세미나의 주안점은 무엇인가?
(A) 회의 관리
(B) 비용 절감 방안
(C) 직원 채용
(D) 데이터 구성

해설 전체 내용 관련 - 세미나의 주안점
화자가 초반부에 이번 세미나에서 회의를 자신감 있게 또 효과적으로 주재하는 방법을 알려주겠다(In this seminar, I'll be teaching you how to lead meetings confidently and effectively)고 말하고 있으므로 정답은 (A)이다.

어휘 cost-reduction 비용 절감 recruitment 채용 organization 조직, 구성

> Paraphrasing
> 담화의 how to lead meetings confidently and effectively
> → 정답의 Meeting management

87 According to the speaker, what can be found on a Web site?
(A) A trial version of some software
(B) A calendar of events
(C) Sample contracts
(D) Client testimonials

번역 화자에 따르면, 웹사이트에서 무엇을 찾을 수 있는가?
(A) 소프트웨어 체험판
(B) 행사 일정
(C) 계약서 견본
(D) 고객 후기

해설 세부 사항 관련 - 웹사이트에서 찾을 수 있는 것
화자가 중반부에 전국의 다양한 기업을 대상으로 세미나를 실시해 왔는데 웹사이트에서 볼 수 있듯 많은 기업들이 세미나가 그들이 성공하는 데 도움이 되었다고 말한다(I have conducted this seminar for businesses all over the country, and as you can see on my Web site, many of them say it has helped them succeed)고 했으므로 정답은 (D)이다.

어휘 trial version 체험판 testimonial 추천서, 추천의 글

88 What will the listeners most likely do next?
(A) Talk with a partner
(B) Watch a short film
(C) Listen to some rules
(D) Get some refreshments

번역 청자들은 다음으로 무엇을 하겠는가?
(A) 파트너와 이야기하기
(B) 단편 영화 감상하기
(C) 몇 가지 규칙에 대해 듣기
(D) 다과 먹기

해설 세부 사항 관련 - 청자들이 다음에 할 일
화자가 후반부에 오늘의 규칙 몇 가지를 말씀드리며 시작하겠다(I'd like to start by telling you a few rules for the day)고 했으므로 정답은 (C)이다.

어휘 refreshments 다과

> Paraphrasing
> 담화의 a few rules → 정답의 some rules

89-91 회의 발췌

W-Br **89 I called this meeting to announce an upgrade to our laboratory facility. The keypads on the doors will be replaced with keycard readers.** This means that you will no longer need to memorize key codes to unlock the doors. Instead, **90 everyone will be issued a scannable badge with their name and picture on it.** The changeover will take place this weekend, so **91 everyone needs to visit Information Technology before then to**

54

register for a badge. I've already done it, and the process only takes a few minutes.

> 우리 연구소 시설의 업그레이드 사항을 공지하기 위해 이 회의를 소집했어요. 문에 있는 키패드는 키카드 리더기로 교체될 겁니다. 이 말은 여러분이 더 이상 문의 잠금을 해제하기 위해 키 조합을 외울 필요가 없다는 뜻입니다. 대신에, **여러분은 이름과 사진이 들어간 스캔용 출입증을 받으실 겁니다.** 변경은 이번 주말에 시행될 예정이오니, 여러분은 그 전에 출입증 등록을 위해 IT부서를 방문해 주십시오. 저는 이미 했는데, 몇 분밖에 안 걸립니다.

> 어휘 laboratory 연구소, 실험실 replace 교체하다 memorize 암기하다 unlock 해제하다 issue 발급하다 scannable 스캔 가능한 badge 배지, 출입증 changeover 전환, 변경 register for ~에 등록하다 process 과정, 절차

89 What is the speaker mainly discussing?
(A) A facility tour
(B) A security upgrade
(C) An employee orientation
(D) A cleaning requirement

> 번역 화자는 주로 무엇에 관해 이야기하는가?
> (A) 시설 견학
> **(B) 보안 업그레이드**
> (C) 직원 오리엔테이션
> (D) 청소 요구 사항

> 해설 전체 내용 관련 - 담화의 주제
> 화자가 초반부에 연구소 시설의 업그레이드 사항을 공지하기 위해 회의를 소집했다(I called this meeting to announce an upgrade to our laboratory facility)고 했고, 문에 있는 키패드는 키카드 리더기로 교체될 것(The keypads on the doors will be replaced with keycard readers)이라고 말하는 것으로 보아, 보안을 위한 키패드의 업그레이드에 대해 언급하고 있음을 알 수 있다. 따라서 정답은 (B)이다.

> 어휘 security 보안 requirement 요구 사항

> **Paraphrasing**
> 담화의 an upgrade to our laboratory facility
> → 정답의 A security upgrade

90 What will the listeners receive?
(A) An identification badge
(B) A safety helmet
(C) A floor plan
(D) A computer program

> 번역 청자들은 무엇을 받을 것인가?
> **(A) 신원 확인용 출입증**
> (B) 안전모
> (C) 평면도
> (D) 컴퓨터 프로그램

> 해설 세부 사항 관련 - 청자들이 받을 것
> 화자가 중반부에 여러분은 이름과 사진이 들어간 스캔용 출입증을 받을 것(everyone will be issued a scannable badge with their name and picture on it)이라고 말하고 있으므로 정답은 (A)이다.

> 어휘 identification 신원 확인 floor plan 평면도

> **Paraphrasing**
> 담화의 a scannable badge with their name and picture on it → 정답의 An identification badge

91 Why does the speaker say, "the process only takes a few minutes"?
(A) To express concern
(B) To correct a scheduling mistake
(C) To reassure the listeners
(D) To ask for assistance

> 번역 화자가 "몇 분밖에 안 걸립니다"라고 말한 이유는?
> (A) 우려를 표현하려고
> (B) 일정 예약 실수를 바로잡으려고
> **(C) 청자들을 안심시키려고**
> (D) 도움을 청하려고

> 해설 화자의 의도 파악 - 몇 분밖에 안 걸린다는 말의 의도
> 앞에서 출입증 등록을 위해 IT부서에 방문해 줄 것(everyone needs to visit Information Technology before then to register for a badge)을 요청하면서 자신은 이미 했다(I've already done it)고 말한 뒤 인용문을 언급한 것으로 보아, 출입증 등록이 번거로울 것이라는 우려에 대해서는 걱정하지 않아도 된다고 안심시키려고 한 말임을 알 수 있다. 따라서 정답은 (C)이다.

> 어휘 concern 우려, 걱정 correct 바로잡다 reassure 안심시키다 assistance 도움

92-94 워크숍 발췌

> M-Au OK, let's move on to the next part of today's workshop. **92 This part is very important for those of you whose duties include moving inventory by hand when it's too small for the forklifts. 93 When you're lifting loads off of the ground, you must use the technique my colleague is demonstrating.** Use it even when handling empty boxes. Remember, lifting many light loads throughout the day can be as hard on your body as picking up one heavy load. **94 This technique has been proven to lower its users' risk of suffering an injury.**

> 좋습니다, 오늘 워크숍의 다음 부분으로 넘어가죠. 이 부분은 재고품이 지게차를 쓰기에는 너무 작아 손으로 옮겨야 하는 분들에게 매우 중요한 내용입니다. 짐을 땅에서 위로 들어 올릴 때는 제 동료가 시범을 보이고 있는 기술을 반드시 사용하셔야 합니다. 빈 상자를 다룰 때에도 이 기술을 사용하세요. 명심하세요. 하루 종일 가벼운 물건을 여러 개 들어

올리는 것은 한 번 무거운 물건을 들어 올릴 때만큼이나 체력적으로 힘들 수 있습니다. **이 기술은 사용자의 부상 위험을 낮춰주는 것으로 입증되었습니다.**

> 어휘   move on ~으로 넘어가다   inventory 재고, 재고품   forklift 지게차   lift 들어 올리다   load 짐, 화물   technique 기법, 기술   colleague 동료   demonstrate 시범을 보이다   prove 입증하다   lower 낮추다   risk 위험   suffer an injury 부상을 당하다

92   Where do the listeners most likely work?
(A) At a commercial laundry facility
(B) At an auto repair shop
(C) At a warehouse
(D) At a moving company

번역   청자들은 어디서 일하겠는가?
(A) 상업용 세탁 시설
(B) 자동차 정비소
(C) 물류 창고
(D) 이사업체

해설   **전체 내용 관련 - 청자들의 근무지**
화자가 초반부에 재고품들이 지게차를 쓰기에는 너무 작아 손으로 옮겨야 하는 분들(~ those of you whose duties include moving inventory by hand when it's too small for the forklifts)에게 중요한 내용이라고 했으므로 청자들은 창고에서 근무하는 사람들임을 알 수 있다. 따라서 정답은 (C)이다.

어휘   commercial 상업적인

93   What should the listeners use a certain technique for?
(A) Storing chemicals
(B) Lifting loads
(C) Packing boxes
(D) Folding fabric items

번역   청자들은 무엇을 위해 특정 기술을 사용해야 하는가?
(A) 화학 물질 보관하기
(B) 짐 들어 올리기
(C) 상자에 물건 담기
(D) 직물 제품 접기

해설   **세부 사항 관련 - 청자들이 특정 기술을 사용해야 하는 부분**
화자가 중반부에 짐을 땅에서 위로 들어 올릴 때는 동료가 시범을 보이고 있는 기술을 반드시 사용해야 한다(When you're lifting loads off of the ground, you must use the technique my colleague is demonstrating)고 말하고 있으므로 정답은 (B)이다.

어휘   chemicals 화학 물질   fold 접다   fabric 직물, 천

94   What benefit of the technique does the speaker mention?
(A) Less wasting of supplies
(B) Fewer complaints from customers
(C) Increased productivity
(D) Lower risk of injury

번역   화자는 기술의 어떤 이점을 언급하는가?
(A) 비품 낭비 감소
(B) 고객 불만 감소
(C) 향상된 생산성
(D) 부상 위험 감소

해설   **세부 사항 관련 - 화자가 언급한 기술의 이점**
화자가 마지막에 이 기술은 사용자의 부상 위험을 낮춰주는 것으로 입증되었다(This technique has been proven to lower its users' risk of suffering an injury)고 말하고 있으므로 정답은 (D)이다.

어휘   complaint 불평, 불만   productivity 생산성

> **Paraphrasing**
> 담화의 lower its users' risk of suffering an injury
> → 정답의 Lower risk of injury

95-97 방송+지도

W-Am   This is Ha-Yoon Sohn from WRN News. **95 I'm here at the Malley Station bus stop for those traveling east on Roper Street**, where the first of Oakford City's state-of-the-art bus shelters has been built. As you can see, the shelter is enclosed on all sides and includes seating. However, **96 the city's primary reason for constructing these shelters is the powerful air purification system in its roof. This filters out car exhaust and dust so that transit users can breathe clean air while waiting for their bus.** The Oakford Department of Transportation intends to put shelters at one hundred stops in the next two years. **97 Visit the department's Web site to see the planned construction dates for each site.**

WRN 뉴스의 손하윤입니다. 저는 로퍼 가의 동쪽으로 가시는 분들을 위한 맬리 역 버스 정류장에 나와 있습니다. 이곳은 오크퍼드 시에서 첫 번째 최첨단 버스 쉘터가 지어진 곳입니다. 보시다시피, 이 쉘터는 사방이 막혀 있고, 좌석도 있습니다. 하지만 **시에서 이 쉘터를 건설하는 주된 이유는 지붕에 있는 강력한 공기 정화 시스템 때문입니다. 이것은 자동차 배기가스와 먼지를 걸러내어 환승 이용객들이 버스를 기다리는 동안 깨끗한 공기를 마실 수 있도록 합니다.** 오크퍼드 교통국은 향후 2년간 100개의 정류장에 쉘터를 설치할 계획입니다. **부지별로 계획된 건설 일정을 보시려면 교통국 웹사이트를 방문하세요.**

> 어휘   state-of-the-art 최첨단의   bus shelter (지붕이 달린) 버스 정류소   enclosed 사방이 막힌   seating 좌석   primary 주된   construct 건설하다   powerful 강력한   air purification system 공기 정화 장치   filter out ~을 걸러내다   car exhaust 자동차 배기가스   dust 먼지   transit 환승, 교통   breathe 호흡하다   department 부서   transportation 교통   intend 의도하다   planned 계획된

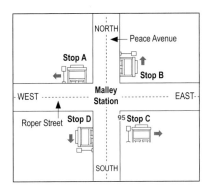

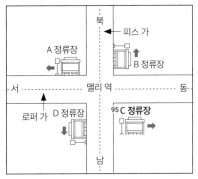

95
Look at the graphic. Where is the speaker?
(A) At Stop A
(B) At Stop B
(C) At Stop C
(D) At Stop D

번역 시각 정보에 의하면, 화자는 어디에 있는가?
(A) A 정류장
(B) B 정류장
(C) C 정류장
(D) D 정류장

해설 **시각 정보 연계 - 화자의 위치**
화자가 초반부에 자신은 로퍼 가의 동쪽으로 가는 분들을 위한 맬리 역 버스 정류장에 나와 있다(I'm here at the Malley Station bus stop for those traveling east on Roper Street)고 말하고 있고, 지도에 따르면 로퍼 가의 동쪽으로 가는 맬리 역 버스 정류장은 C 정류장이므로 정답은 (C)이다.

96
According to the speaker, what is the main reason for building the shelters?
(A) To give people a place to sit while waiting
(B) To keep people comfortable despite bad weather
(C) To protect people from air pollution
(D) To prevent traffic accidents

번역 화자에 따르면, 버스 쉘터를 건설하는 주된 이유는 무엇인가?
(A) 기다리는 동안 사람들에게 앉을 곳을 제공하려고
(B) 날씨가 안 좋을 때도 사람들을 편안하게 해주려고
(C) 대기 오염으로부터 사람들을 보호하려고
(D) 교통사고를 예방하려고

해설 **세부 사항 관련 - 버스 쉘터를 건설하는 주된 이유**
화자가 중반부에 시에서 이 쉘터를 건설하는 주된 이유는 지붕에 있는 강력한 공기 정화 시스템(the city's primary reason for constructing these shelters is the powerful air purification system in its roof)에 있다면서 이것은 자동차 배기가스와 먼지를 걸러내어 환승 이용객들이 버스를 기다리는 동안 깨끗한 공기를 마실 수 있도록 한다(This filters out car exhaust and dust so that transit users can breathe clean air ~)고 했으므로 정답은 (C)이다.

어휘 comfortable 편안한   protect 보호하다   air pollution 대기 오염   prevent 예방하다   traffic accident 교통사고

97
What is available online?
(A) A virtual tour
(B) Some statistics
(C) A feedback form
(D) A project schedule

번역 온라인에서는 무엇을 이용할 수 있는가?
(A) 가상 여행
(B) 통계 자료
(C) 피드백 양식
(D) 프로젝트 일정

해설 **세부 사항 관련 - 온라인에서 이용할 수 있는 것**
화자가 마지막에 부지별로 계획된 건설 일정을 보려면 교통국 웹사이트를 방문하라(Visit the department's Web site to see the planned construction dates for each site)고 말하고 있으므로 정답은 (D)이다.

어휘 virtual 가상의   statistics 통계 자료

> **Paraphrasing**
> 담화의 construction dates for each site
> → 정답의 A project schedule

98-100 공지+안내판

> M-Cn Attention, customers. If you love fruit-based desserts, you'll want to stop by the bakery section this afternoon. **98 Our supermarket is celebrating spring with daily specials on desserts made with fresh seasonal fruit. 99 Yesterday's cherry pie sold out well before closing time,** and today our bakers have prepared a cool treat perfect for the warm weather. Samples are available at the bakery counter, so why not head over and try some? **100 If you decide to make a purchase, our staff will be happy to provide you with forks or spoons** so that you can enjoy your dessert anywhere.
>
> 주목해 주세요, 손님 여러분. 과일 기반 후식을 좋아하신다면 오늘 오후 제빵 코너에 들러주세요. **저희 슈퍼마켓은 봄을 맞이하여 신선한 제철 과일로 만든 디저트를 매일 특별 판매하고 있습니다. 어제 체리 파이는 폐점 시간이 되기 훨씬 전에 품절되었습니다.** 오늘 우리 제빵사들은 포

근한 날씨에 안성맞춤인 시원한 간식을 준비했습니다. 제빵 코너 카운터에서 시식해 보실 수 있는데, 그쪽으로 가셔서 시식해 보시지 않겠어요? **구매하기로 결정하시면 저희 직원이 기쁜 마음으로 포크나 숟가락을 제공해 드릴 예정입니다.** 어디서든 편하게 후식을 즐기실 수 있도록이요.

어휘   stop by 잠시 들르다   celebrate 축하하다   daily special 특별 메뉴   seasonal 계절적인   baker 제빵사   available 이용 가능한   make a purchase 구매하다

98 Where does the announcement most likely take place?
(A) At a coffee shop
(B) At a fruit orchard
(C) At a grocery store
(D) At a cooking school

번역 공지는 어디에서 이루어지겠는가?
(A) 커피숍
(B) 과수원
(C) 식료품점
(D) 요리학교

해설 **전체 내용 관련 - 공지의 장소**
화자가 초반부에 저희 슈퍼마켓(Our supermarket)이라고 했으므로 공지 장소는 식료품점임을 알 수 있다. 따라서 정답은 (C)이다.

어휘   orchard 과수원   grocery store 식료품점

> **Paraphrasing**
> 담화의 supermarket → 정답의 grocery store

99 Look at the graphic. What is today's special?
(A) Cheesecake
(B) Pie
(C) Pudding
(D) Tarts

번역 시각 정보에 의하면, 오늘의 특별 메뉴는 무엇인가?
(A) 치즈케이크
(B) 파이
(C) 푸딩
(D) 타르트

해설 **시각 정보 연계 - 오늘의 특별 메뉴**
화자가 중반부에 어제 체리 파이는 폐점 시간이 되기 훨씬 전에 품절되었다(Yesterday's cherry pie sold out well before closing time)고 말하고 있고, 안내판에 따르면 체리 파이는 금요일 특별 메뉴이므로 오늘은 토요일이고, 특별 메뉴가 푸딩이라는 것을 알 수 있다. 따라서 정답은 (C)이다.

100 What is offered with a purchase?
(A) A coupon
(B) Eating utensils
(C) Gift wrapping
(D) Storage instructions

번역 구매하면 무엇이 제공되는가?
(A) 쿠폰
(B) 식사용 도구
(C) 선물 포장
(D) 보관 방법 안내문

해설 **세부 사항 관련 - 구매하면 제공되는 것**
화자가 후반부에 구매하기로 결정하면 포크나 숟가락을 제공할 예정(If you decide to make a purchase, our staff will be happy to provide you with forks or spoons)이라고 말하고 있으므로 정답은 (B)이다.

어휘   utensil (가정용) 기구   wrapping 포장, 포장지   storage 보관

> **Paraphrasing**
> 담화의 forks or spoons → 정답의 Eating utensils

TEST 3

1 (C)	2 (A)	3 (B)	4 (D)	5 (A)
6 (D)	7 (A)	8 (C)	9 (B)	10 (B)
11 (B)	12 (C)	13 (A)	14 (B)	15 (C)
16 (A)	17 (C)	18 (B)	19 (B)	20 (C)
21 (C)	22 (B)	23 (A)	24 (A)	25 (C)
26 (A)	27 (A)	28 (B)	29 (C)	30 (B)
31 (A)	32 (D)	33 (C)	34 (A)	35 (C)
36 (B)	37 (B)	38 (C)	39 (A)	40 (D)
41 (D)	42 (A)	43 (B)	44 (C)	45 (A)
46 (C)	47 (A)	48 (D)	49 (D)	50 (D)
51 (B)	52 (C)	53 (B)	54 (C)	55 (D)
56 (A)	57 (B)	58 (A)	59 (D)	60 (C)
61 (C)	62 (A)	63 (B)	64 (B)	65 (B)
66 (D)	67 (A)	68 (B)	69 (B)	70 (D)
71 (C)	72 (D)	73 (A)	74 (D)	75 (B)
76 (C)	77 (C)	78 (D)	79 (B)	80 (D)
81 (B)	82 (C)	83 (D)	84 (C)	85 (B)
86 (B)	87 (D)	88 (D)	89 (D)	90 (A)
91 (C)	92 (A)	93 (C)	94 (C)	95 (B)
96 (C)	97 (A)	98 (B)	99 (A)	100 (A)

TEST 3

PART 1

1

M-Cn

(A) She's entering a building.
(B) She's holding a toolbox.
(C) She's hammering a nail.
(D) She's putting on a hard hat.

번역　(A) 여자가 건물로 들어가고 있다.
　　　(B) 여자가 공구함을 들고 있다.
　　　(C) 여자가 망치로 못을 박고 있다.
　　　(D) 여자가 안전모를 쓰는 중이다.

해설　**1인 등장 사진**
　　　(A) 동사 오답. 여자가 건물로 들어가고 있는 모습이 아니다.
　　　(B) 사진에 없는 명사. 사진에 공구함이 보이지 않는다.
　　　(C) 정답. 여자가 망치로 못을 박고 있으므로 정답이다.
　　　(D) 동사 오답. 여자가 안전모를 착용한(wearing) 상태이지 안전모를 쓰고 있는(putting on) 동작의 모습은 아니다.

어휘　toolbox 공구함　hammer 망치로 두드리다　hard hat 안전모

2

W-Am

(A) The man is pointing out a window.
(B) The man is standing by a bridge.
(C) The man is wiping off a surface.
(D) The man is looking at his watch.

번역　**(A) 남자가 창밖을 가리키고 있다.**
　　　(B) 남자가 다리 옆에 서 있다.
　　　(C) 남자가 표면을 닦고 있다.
　　　(D) 남자가 시계를 보고 있다.

해설　**1인 등장 사진**
　　　(A) 정답. 남자가 창밖을 가리키고 있으므로 정답이다.
　　　(B) 위치 오답. 남자가 다리 옆에 서 있는 모습이 아니다.
　　　(C) 동사 오답. 남자가 표면을 닦고 있는 모습이 아니다.
　　　(D) 사진에 없는 명사. 사진에 시계가 보이지 않는다.

어휘　point out ~을 가리키다　wipe off ~을 닦다

3

W-Br

(A) The woman is hanging up a note.
(B) The man is staring at a computer.
(C) The woman is reaching for a document.
(D) The man is adjusting his glasses.

번역　(A) 여자가 메모를 게시하고 있다.
　　　(B) 남자가 컴퓨터를 응시하고 있다.
　　　(C) 여자가 문서로 손을 뻗고 있다.
　　　(D) 남자가 안경을 고쳐 쓰고 있다.

해설　**2인 이상 등장 사진**
　　　(A) 사진에 없는 명사. 사진에 메모가 보이지 않는다.
　　　(B) 정답. 남자가 컴퓨터를 보고 있으므로 정답이다.
　　　(C) 사진에 없는 명사. 사진에 문서가 보이지 않는다.
　　　(D) 동사 오답. 남자가 안경을 고쳐 쓰고 있는 모습이 아니다.

어휘　hang up ~을 걸다, 게시하다　stare 응시하다　reach for ~에 손을 뻗다　adjust 조정하다, 정돈하다

4

M-Au

(A) A presenter is writing on a whiteboard.
(B) Some people are raising their hands.
(C) A man is leaning against a podium.
(D) The audience is seated facing a screen.

번역 (A) 발표자가 화이트보드에 필기하고 있다.
(B) 몇몇 사람들이 손을 들고 있다.
(C) 한 남자가 연단에 기대어 서 있다.
(D) 청중이 화면을 마주보고 앉아 있다.

해설 **2인 이상 등장 사진**
(A) 동사 오답. 발표자가 화이트보드에 필기하고 있는 모습이 아니다.
(B) 동사 오답. 손을 들고 있는 사람들의 모습이 보이지 않는다.
(C) 동사 오답. 연단에 기대어 서 있는 남자의 모습이 보이지 않는다.
(D) 정답. 청중이 화면을 마주보고 앉아 있으므로 정답이다.

어휘 presenter 발표자 raise 올리다, 들다 lean against ~에 기대다
podium 연단 audience 청중 face 마주보다

5

W-Br

(A) Some people have gathered on a sidewalk.
(B) A bus has stopped at a traffic light.
(C) Some cars are being driven down the street.
(D) The door to a building has been opened.

번역 **(A) 사람들이 인도에 모여 있다.**
(B) 버스가 신호등 앞에 정차해 있다.
(C) 차들이 도로를 달리는 중이다.
(D) 건물 출입문이 열려 있다.

해설 **사람/사물·풍경 혼합 사진**
(A) 정답. 사람들이 인도에 모여 있는 모습이므로 정답이다.
(B) 사진에 없는 명사. 사진에 신호등이 보이지 않는다.
(C) 사진에 없는 명사. 사진에 차들이 보이지 않는다.
(D) 사진에 없는 명사. 사진에 건물 출입문이 보이지 않는다.

어휘 gather 모이다, 모으다 sidewalk 인도, 보도 traffic light 신호등

6

M-Cn

(A) A supermarket is crowded with shoppers.
(B) Vegetables are growing in a garden.
(C) Empty crates have been placed on shelves.
(D) Some produce is displayed for sale.

번역 (A) 슈퍼마켓이 쇼핑객으로 가득 차 있다.
(B) 텃밭에 채소들이 자라고 있다.
(C) 선반에 빈 상자들이 놓여 있다.
(D) 농산물이 판매를 위해 진열되어 있다.

해설 **사물·풍경 사진**
(A) 사진에 없는 명사. 사진에 쇼핑객이 보이지 않는다.
(B) 사진에 없는 명사. 사진에 밭이 보이지 않는다.
(C) 상태 오답. 상자들이 비어 있는 상태가 아니다.
(D) 정답. 농산물이 판매를 위해 진열되어 있는 모습이므로 정답이다.

어휘 be crowded with ~로 꽉 들어차다 grow 자라다, 재배하다
crate 상자 produce 농산물 display 진열하다

PART 2

7

W-Br When did you last restart your computer?
M-Au (A) A few hours ago.
(B) Because of a software update.
(C) Today's my last day.

번역 마지막으로 언제 컴퓨터를 다시 시작하셨나요?
(A) 몇 시간 전이에요.
(B) 소프트웨어 업데이트 때문에요.
(C) 오늘이 저의 마지막 날이에요.

해설 **When 의문문**
(A) 정답. 마지막으로 컴퓨터를 다시 시작한 시점을 묻는 질문에 몇 시간 전이라고 알려 주고 있으므로 정답이다.
(B) 질문과 상관없는 오답. Why 의문문에 대한 응답이므로 오답이다.
(C) 단어 반복 오답. 질문의 last를 반복 이용한 오답이다.

어휘 restart 다시 시작하다

8

W-Am Who set up the display of leather jackets?
M-Au (A) I don't mind.
(B) My jacket's in the coat room.
(C) Is there a problem with it?

번역 가죽 재킷 진열을 누가 했나요?
(A) 저는 상관없어요.
(B) 제 재킷은 외투 보관소에 있어요.
(C) 무슨 문제가 있나요?

해설 **Who 의문문**
(A) 질문과 상관없는 오답.
(B) 단어 반복 오답. 질문의 jacket을 반복 이용한 오답이다.
(C) 정답. 가죽 재킷 진열을 누가 했는지 묻는 질문에 무슨 문제가 있는지 진열과 관련된 질문을 하고 있으므로 정답이다.

어휘 set up ~을 설치하다   display 전시, 진열   leather 가죽   coat room 외투 보관소

9
M-Au Which curtains would be better for the lobby?
W-Br (A) Yes, it's an improvement.
(B) The gray ones look hard to clean.
(C) She's waiting there now.

번역 로비에 어느 커튼이 더 나을까요?
(A) 네, 나아졌네요.
(B) 회색은 청소가 어려워 보여요.
(C) 그녀는 지금 거기서 기다리는 중이에요.

해설 **Which+명사 의문문**
(A) Yes/No 불가 오답. Which 의문문에는 Yes/No 응답이 불가능하므로 오답이다.
(B) 정답. 로비에 어울리는 커튼을 묻는 질문에 회색이 청소가 어려워 보인다며 회색은 피할 것을 간접적으로 알려 주고 있으므로 정답이다. Which 의문문은 the ~ one(s)을 사용한 응답의 정답률이 높다는 점을 알아 두자.
(C) 질문과 상관없는 오답. 질문에 3인칭 대명사 She로 지칭할 인물이 언급된 적이 없으므로 오답이다.

어휘 improvement 향상, 개선

10
W-Am Would you like another cup of coffee?
M-Cn (A) On the receipt.
(B) No, thanks. I've had enough.
(C) Yes, it was.

번역 커피 한 잔 더 드시겠어요?
(A) 영수증에요.
(B) 고맙지만 사양하겠습니다. 충분히 마셨습니다.
(C) 네, 그랬어요.

해설 **요청·제안문**
(A) 연상 오답. 질문의 cup of coffee에서 연상 가능한 receipt를 이용한 오답이다.
(B) 정답. 커피 한 잔 더 마실지 묻는 제안에 고맙지만 사양하겠다는 답변과 함께 충분히 마셨다며 제안을 사양하는 이유를 덧붙이고 있으므로 정답이다.
(C) 질문과 상관없는 오답.

어휘 receipt 영수증

11
M-Au Have you received the new work uniforms?
W-Br (A) Once every two years.
(B) There's been a shipping delay.
(C) To the maintenance department.

번역 새 작업복 받으셨나요?
(A) 2년에 한 번씩이요.
(B) 배송 지연이 되고 있어요.
(C) 유지보수 부서로요.

해설 **조동사(Have) 의문문**
(A) 질문과 상관없는 오답. How often 의문문에 대한 응답이므로 오답이다.
(B) 정답. 새 작업복을 받았는지 묻는 질문에 배송이 지연되고 있다며 아니오(No)를 생략한 부정 답변을 하고 있으므로 정답이다.
(C) 질문과 상관없는 오답. Where 의문문에 대한 응답이므로 오답이다.

어휘 work uniform 작업복   shipping delay 배송 지연   maintenance 유지보수   department 부서

12
M-Cn How will the applicants' résumés be screened?
W-Br (A) He went to a public university.
(B) Is it in the conference room?
(C) We've already started interviews.

번역 지원자들의 이력서는 어떻게 심사될 건가요?
(A) 그는 공립 대학교에 다녔어요.
(B) 그것이 회의실에 있나요?
(C) 우리는 이미 면접을 시작했어요.

해설 **How 의문문**
(A) 연상 오답. 질문의 résumés에서 연상 가능한 public university를 이용한 오답이다.
(B) 연상 오답. 질문의 screened에서 연상 가능한 conference room을 이용한 오답이다.
(C) 정답. 지원자들의 이력서 심사 방법을 묻는 질문에 이미 면접을 시작했다며 이력서 심사가 완료되었음을 간접적으로 알려 주고 있으므로 정답이다.

어휘 applicant 지원자   résumé 이력서   screen 심사하다

13
W-Am When should I expect the new sofa to arrive?
M-Cn (A) Within three business days.
(B) Some quality control checks.
(C) Yes, it's really comfortable.

번역 새 소파가 언제 도착하는 걸로 알고 있으면 될까요?
(A) 영업일 기준 3일 이내요.
(B) 몇 가지 품질 관리 점검이요.
(C) 네, 굉장히 편안하네요.

해설 **When 의문문**
(A) 정답. 새 소파의 도착 시점을 묻는 질문에 영업일 기준 3일 이내라고 구체적으로 알려 주고 있으므로 정답이다.
(B) 연상 오답. 질문의 new sofa에서 연상 가능한 quality control checks를 이용한 오답이다.
(C) Yes/No 불가 오답. When 의문문에는 Yes/No 응답이 불가능하므로 오답이다.

어휘 quality control 품질 관리   check 확인, 점검   comfortable 편안한

14

M-Au Why don't you join us for dinner on Friday?
W-Br (A) A table by the windows.
(B) I just made plans with a friend.
(C) The famous Italian restaurant.

번역 금요일에 우리랑 저녁 식사 같이 하실래요?
(A) 창가 테이블이요.
(B) 방금 친구와 약속을 잡았어요.
(C) 유명한 이탈리아 식당이요.

해설 **요청·제안문**
(A) 연상 오답. 질문의 dinner에서 연상 가능한 A table을 이용한 오답이다.
(B) 정답. 금요일 저녁 식사 참여를 제안하는 질문에 방금 친구와 약속을 잡았다며 제안을 우회적으로 거절하고 있으므로 정답이다.
(C) 연상 오답. 질문의 dinner에서 연상 가능한 restaurant을 이용한 오답이다.

어휘 make a plan 계획을 세우다

15

M-Cn Tickets for the comedy show have been selling really well.
W-Am (A) In the first row of the balcony.
(B) We prefer not to.
(C) It seems we'll make a good profit.

번역 그 코미디 공연 티켓이 굉장히 잘 팔리고 있어요.
(A) 발코니석 첫 번째 줄에요.
(B) 우리는 안 하는 게 좋겠어요.
(C) 수익이 좋을 것 같아요.

해설 **사실·정보 전달의 평서문**
(A) 연상 오답. 평서문의 comedy show에서 연상 가능한 the first row of the balcony를 이용한 오답이다.
(B) 평서문과 상관없는 오답.
(C) 정답. 공연 티켓이 잘 팔리고 있다는 평서문에 수익이 좋을 것 같다며 호응하고 있으므로 정답이다.

어휘 sell well 잘 팔리다 balcony (극장 이층의) 발코니석 prefer 선호하다 profit 이윤. 수익

16

W-Am Have you found a suitable venue for our awards banquet?
M-Au (A) I'm visiting some places this week.
(B) Congratulations on your achievement!
(C) The friendly staff.

번역 시상식 연회에 적합한 장소를 찾으셨나요?
(A) 이번 주에 몇 군데 가보려고요.
(B) 당신의 업적을 축하합니다!
(C) 친절한 직원들이요.

해설 **조동사(Have) 의문문**
(A) 정답. 시상식 연회에 적합한 장소를 찾았는지 묻는 질문에 이번 주에 몇 군데 가보려 한다며 아직 찾지 못했음을 간접적으로 알려 주고 있으므로 정답이다.

(B) 연상 오답. 질문의 awards에서 연상 가능한 achievement를 이용한 오답이다.
(C) 질문과 상관없는 오답.

어휘 suitable 적합한 venue 장소 awards banquet 시상식 연회 achievement 업적. 성취

17

W-Br Nicholas plans to work overtime today, doesn't he?
M-Cn (A) Alright, I can help you.
(B) Over time it might.
(C) Yes, that's what he said.

번역 니콜라스가 오늘 초과 근무를 할 예정이죠, 그렇지 않나요?
(A) 알겠습니다, 제가 도와드릴게요.
(B) 시간이 지나면 아마도요.
(C) 네, 그가 그렇게 말했어요.

해설 **부가 의문문**
(A) 연상 오답. 질문의 work overtime에서 연상 가능한 help you를 이용한 오답이다.
(B) 유사 발음 오답. 질문의 overtime과 발음이 동일하나 두 단어인 Over time을 이용한 오답이다.
(C) 정답. 니콜라스가 오늘 초과 근무 예정인지 여부를 확인하는 질문에 네(Yes)라고 대답한 뒤, 그가 그렇게 말했다며 긍정 답변과 일관된 내용을 덧붙였으므로 정답이다.

어휘 work overtime 초과 근무하다

18

M-Au Where can I find the lunch specials?
W-Am (A) I'll probably be late.
(B) They're on the notice board.
(C) Until one o'clock.

번역 점심 특선 메뉴는 어디에서 찾을 수 있나요?
(A) 서는 아마 늦을 것 같아요.
(B) 게시판에 있어요.
(C) 1시까지요.

해설 **Where 의문문**
(A) 연상 오답. 질문의 lunch에서 연상 가능한 be late를 이용한 오답이다.
(B) 정답. 점심 특선 메뉴를 찾을 수 있는 장소를 묻는 질문에 게시판에 있다며 알 수 있는 장소를 알려 주고 있으므로 정답이다.
(C) 질문과 상관없는 오답. How long 의문문에 대한 응답이므로 오답이다.

어휘 lunch special 점심 특선 메뉴 notice board 게시판

19

W-Br What airline will you fly to the trade fair?
M-Cn (A) Amy flew to her hometown.
(B) My travel agent's taking care of that.
(C) I usually prefer a window seat.

번역 무역 박람회에 갈 때 어느 항공사를 이용할 건가요?
(A) 에이미는 비행기를 타고 고향에 갔어요.
(B) 제 여행사 담당 직원이 맡아서 처리하고 있어요.
(C) 저는 보통 창가석을 선호해요.

해설 What+명사 의문문
(A) 파생어 오답. 질문의 fly의 과거형인 flew를 이용한 오답이다.
(B) 정답. 무역 박람회에 갈 때 이용할 항공사를 묻는 질문에 여행사 담당 직원이 맡아서 처리하고 있다며 알 만한 사람을 알려 주고 있으므로 정답이다.
(C) 연상 오답. 질문의 airline에서 연상 가능한 a window seat를 이용한 오답이다.

어휘 fly to ~까지 비행기로 가다   trade fair 무역 박람회   travel agent 여행사 직원   take care of ~을 처리하다

20

M-Cn Didn't we repair this heater last week?
W-Am (A) Several complex components.
(B) Three or more workers.
(C) That was on the fifth floor.

번역 우리 지난주에 이 히터를 고치지 않았나요?
(A) 몇 가지 복잡한 부품들이요.
(B) 세 명 이상의 작업자들이요.
(C) 그건 5층에 있는 거였어요.

해설 부정 의문문
(A) 연상 오답. 질문의 repair에서 연상 가능한 components를 이용한 오답이다.
(B) 연상 오답. 질문의 repair에서 연상 가능한 workers를 이용한 오답이다.
(C) 정답. 지난주에 히터를 고치지 않았는지 묻는 질문에 그건 5층에 있는 거였다며 히터가 아직 고쳐지지 않았음을 우회적으로 알려 주고 있으므로 정답이다.

어휘 repair 수리하다   complex 복잡한   component 부품, 요소

21

W-Am When am I meeting with the bank about our loan application?
M-Au (A) Apply it daily for best results.
(B) Those books aren't out on loan.
(C) I e-mailed you the details.

번역 저희 대출 신청에 대해 언제 은행과 협의할 수 있을까요?
(A) 최상의 결과를 위해 매일 바르세요.
(B) 저 책들은 대출되지 않았어요.
(C) 세부 사항을 이메일로 보내드렸어요.

해설 When 의문문
(A) 파생어 오답. 질문의 application과 파생어 관계인 Apply를 이용한 오답.
(B) 단어 반복 오답. 질문의 loan을 반복 이용한 오답이다.
(C) 정답. 은행과 협의 가능한 시간을 묻는 질문에 세부 사항을 이메일로 보냈다며 알 수 있는 방법을 간접적으로 제시하고 있으므로 정답이다.

어휘 loan 대출   application 신청(서)   apply (페인트·크림 등을) 바르다   out on loan 대출 중인   detail 세부 사항

22

M-Au I was surprised by Mr. Seger's announcement about retiring.
W-Br (A) I'm feeling rather tired.
(B) Yes, he's still quite young.
(C) Please leave them in the packaging.

번역 시거 씨가 은퇴한다는 발표를 듣고 깜짝 놀랐어요.
(A) 저는 약간 피곤해요.
(B) 네, 그는 아직 꽤 젊은데요.
(C) 그것들의 포장을 뜯지 말아 주세요.

해설 의견·희망 사항의 평서문
(A) 유사 발음 오답. 평서문의 retiring과 부분적으로 발음이 유사한 tired를 이용한 오답이다.
(B) 정답. 시거 씨가 은퇴한다는 발표를 듣고 깜짝 놀랐다는 평서문에 네(Yes)라고 답한 뒤 그는 아직 꽤 젊다며 긍정 답변과 일관된 내용을 덧붙였으므로 정답이다.
(C) 연상 오답. 평서문의 retiring에서 연상 가능한 leave를 이용한 오답이다.

어휘 announcement 공지, 발표   retire 은퇴하다   packaging 포장재

23

M-Cn Why were extra staff called to the factory?
W-Am (A) Did you see the size of the order?
(B) When we need new machinery.
(C) Yes, a call from the client.

번역 왜 추가 인력이 공장으로 호출되었나요?
(A) 주문 규모를 보셨어요?
(B) 새 기계가 필요할 때요.
(C) 네, 고객에게 온 전화요.

해설 Why 의문문
(A) 정답. 추가 인력이 공장으로 호출된 이유를 묻는 질문에 주문 규모를 보았는지 되물으면서 발주 규모가 크기 때문이라는 이유를 간접적으로 알려 주고 있으므로 정답이다.
(B) 연상 오답. 질문의 factory에서 연상 가능한 new machinery를 이용한 오답이다.
(C) Yes/No 불가 오답. Why 의문문에는 Yes/No 응답이 불가능하므로 오답이다.

어휘 extra 추가의, 여분의   machinery 기계

24

W-Am Has the theme for the photography contest been decided?
M-Au (A) Yes, it's "Natural Landscapes".
(B) We make a good team.
(C) No, I'm not certified.

번역　사진 콘테스트의 주제가 결정되었나요?
　　　(A) 네, "자연 풍경"이에요.
　　　(B) 우리는 좋은 팀이에요.
　　　(C) 아니요, 저는 자격을 취득하지 않았어요.

해설　**조동사(Has) 의문문**
　　　(A) 정답. 사진 콘테스트의 주제가 결정되었는지 묻는 질문에 네
　　　　(Yes)라고 대답한 뒤, "자연 풍경"이라며 긍정 답변과 일관된 내
　　　　용을 덧붙였으므로 정답이다.
　　　(B) 유사 발음 오답. 질문의 theme과 부분적으로 발음이 유사한
　　　　team을 이용한 오답이다.
　　　(C) 질문과 상관없는 오답.

어휘　theme 주제　photography contest 사진 콘테스트
　　　natural landscape 자연 풍경　certified 공인된

25

W-Br　Let's hold the event on the patio instead of in the dining hall.

M-Cn　(A) Through the rear entrance.
　　　(B) A luncheon for marketers.
　　　(C) But it's supposed to be windy.

번역　그 행사를 식당 대신 테라스에서 개최합시다.
　　　(A) 후문을 통해서요.
　　　(B) 마케터들을 위한 오찬이에요.
　　　(C) 하지만 바람이 많이 불 거예요.

해설　**요청·제안문**
　　　(A) 제안문과 상관없는 오답. How 의문문에 대한 응답이므로 오답
　　　　이다.
　　　(B) 연상 오답. 제안문의 dining hall에서 연상 가능한 A luncheon
　　　　을 이용한 오답이다.
　　　(C) 정답. 행사를 테라스에서 개최하자는 제안에 바람이 많이 불 거라
　　　　며 테라스에서 개최하는 것이 어려울 것 같다는 말을 우회적으로
　　　　하고 있으므로 정답이다.

어휘　hold 열다, 개최하다　patio 테라스　instead of ~ 대신에
　　　dining hall 식당　rear entrance 후문　luncheon 오찬
　　　windy 바람이 많이 부는

26

W-Am　How long does it take to complete this survey?

M-Cn　(A) You can skip some questions if you're in a hurry.
　　　(B) We'll need at least thirty participants.
　　　(C) With a black pen, please.

번역　이 설문 조사를 완료하는 데 얼마나 걸리나요?
　　　(A) 바쁘시면 몇몇 질문은 건너뛰시면 됩니다.
　　　(B) 적어도 30명의 참가자가 필요할 거예요.
　　　(C) 검정 펜으로 부탁드립니다.

해설　**How+형용사/부사 의문문**
　　　(A) 정답. 설문 조사를 완료하는 데 걸리는 시간을 묻는 질문에 바쁘면
　　　　몇몇 질문은 건너뛰면 된다며 짧은 시간 내에 완료할 수 있음을 간
　　　　접적으로 알려 주고 있으므로 정답이다.
　　　(B) 연상 오답. 질문의 survey에서 연상 가능한 thirty participants
　　　　를 이용한 오답이다.

　　　(C) 연상 오답. 질문의 How ~ complete this survey?에서 연상
　　　　가능한 With a black pen을 이용한 오답이다.

어휘　complete 완료하다　survey 설문 조사　skip 건너뛰다
　　　in a hurry 바쁜　at least 적어도　participant 참가자

27

W-Br　We should leave these boxes in the hallway.
M-Cn　(A) There's space in the storage closet.
　　　(B) Yes, by an expert.
　　　(C) Cosmetics samples, I think.

번역　이 상자들은 복도에 남겨두어야 해요.
　　　(A) 수납장에 공간이 있어요.
　　　(B) 네, 전문가에 의해서요.
　　　(C) 화장품 견본 같아요.

해설　**요청·제안의 평서문**
　　　(A) 정답. 상자들을 복도에 남겨둘 것을 권유하는 평서문에 수납장에
　　　　공간이 있다며 다른 제안을 하고 있으므로 정답이다.
　　　(B) 평서문과 상관없는 오답.
　　　(C) 연상 오답. 평서문의 boxes에서 연상 가능한 samples를 이용
　　　　한 오답이다.

어휘　leave 그대로 두다　hallway 복도　storage closet 벽장
　　　expert 전문가　cosmetics 화장품

28

W-Br　We can park here overnight, can't we?
M-Au　(A) The office parking area.
　　　(B) I don't want to get a fine.
　　　(C) I'm free tomorrow.

번역　여기 하룻밤 주차가 가능하죠, 그렇지 않나요?
　　　(A) 사무실 주차장이요.
　　　(B) 저는 벌금을 물고 싶지 않아요.
　　　(C) 저는 내일 시간이 있어요.

해설　**부가 의문문**
　　　(A) 파생어 오답. 질문의 park와 파생어 관계인 parking을 이용한
　　　　오답이다.
　　　(B) 정답. 하룻밤 주차가 가능한지 여부를 확인하는 질문에 벌금을 물
　　　　고 싶지 않다며 부정하는 대답을 우회적으로 표현하고 있으므로
　　　　정답이다.
　　　(C) 연상 오답. 질문의 overnight에서 연상 가능한 tomorrow를 이
　　　　용한 오답이다.

어휘　overnight 하룻밤 동안　fine 벌금　free 한가한

29

M-Cn　Can employees bring their families to the picnic, or is that not allowed?
W-Br　(A) It doesn't seem loud to me.
　　　(B) Marigold Park is a good choice.
　　　(C) We'll have plenty of food.

번역　직원들은 야유회에 가족을 데려갈 수 있나요, 아니면 허용되지 않나요?
　　　(A) 저한테는 시끄럽지 않은 것 같은데요.
　　　(B) 마리골드 공원은 좋은 선택이에요.
　　　(C) 음식이 충분할 거예요.

선택 의문문
(A) 유사 발음 오답. 질문의 allowed와 부분적으로 발음이 유사한 loud를 이용한 오답이다.
(B) 연상 오답. 질문의 picnic에서 연상 가능한 Park를 이용한 오답이다.
(C) 정답. 직원들은 야유회에 가족을 데려갈 수 있는지 아니면 허용되지 않는지를 묻는 질문에 음식이 충분할 거라며 가족을 데려갈 수 있음을 우회적으로 표현하고 있으므로 정답이다.

어휘 employee 직원 allow 허용하다 loud 소리가 큰 plenty of 많은

30

M-Au Where did you live when you first moved to Boston?
W-Br (A) Is it next to the side entrance?
(B) The building's not there anymore.
(C) About three years ago.

번역 보스턴으로 처음 이사 왔을 때 어디에 사셨나요?
(A) 측면 출입구 옆에 있나요?
(B) 그 건물은 이제 거기에 없어요.
(C) 3년 전쯤이요.

해설 **Where 의문문**
(A) 연상 오답. 질문의 Where에서 연상 가능한 next to를 이용한 오답이다.
(B) 정답. 보스턴으로 처음 이사 왔을 때 살았던 곳을 묻는 질문에 그 건물은 이제 거기에 없다며 알려줄 수 없음을 간접적으로 표현하고 있으므로 정답이다.
(C) 질문과 상관없는 오답. When 의문문에 대한 응답이므로 오답이다.

어휘 side entrance 측면 출입구

31

W-Br Have you received the memo about the new layout for the Web site?
M-Cn (A) Yes, and I made an extra copy.
(B) A top graphic designer.
(C) I have a few notepads.

번역 새 웹사이트 레이아웃에 대한 회람 받으셨어요?
(A) 네, 그리고 복사본도 만들었어요.
(B) 최고의 그래픽 디자이너요.
(C) 저한테 메모장 몇 개 있어요.

해설 **조동사(Have) 의문문**
(A) 정답. 새 웹사이트 레이아웃에 대한 회람을 받았는지 묻는 질문에 네(Yes)라고 대답한 뒤, 복사본도 만들었다며 긍정 답변과 일관된 내용을 덧붙였으므로 정답이다.
(B) 연상 오답. 질문의 new layout에서 연상 가능한 graphic designer를 이용한 오답이다.
(C) 연상 오답. 질문의 memo에서 연상 가능한 notepads를 이용한 오답이다.

어휘 notepad 메모장

PART 3

32-34

W-Am Hi, Brandon. Thanks for coming in on your day off. Two of the staff members on this shift have called in sick, and ³²**we have a lot of dry cleaning to finish.**
M-Cn No problem. The only thing is that ³³**I forgot to bring my name tag with me.**
W-Am That's fine. You'll mostly be working in the back anyway.
M-Cn All right. Is there anything in particular that you want me to start on first?
W-Am Yes—the pillows from Jenkins Hotel. ³⁴**It's essential that we do a good job on that order, as they're considering giving us a permanent contract.**

여: 안녕하세요, 브랜던. 휴무일인데 와주셔서 감사해요. 오늘 근무 조인 직원들 중 두 명이 병가를 냈는데, **끝내야 할 드라이클리닝이 아주 많아요.**
남: 문제없습니다. 유일한 문제는 **제가 깜박하고 명찰을 가져오지 않았다는 것뿐이에요.**
여: 괜찮습니다. 어쨌든 주로 뒤쪽에서 일을 하실 거니까요.
남: 알겠습니다. 특별히 제가 먼저 시작했으면 하는 일이 있으세요?
여: 네, 젠킨스 호텔에서 온 베개요. **그 주문을 잘 처리하는 일은 매우 중요해요. 그들이 우리에게 영구 계약을 해주는 걸 고려 중이니까요.**

어휘 day off 휴무일 shift 교대 근무 (시간) call in sick 전화로 병가를 내다 in particular 특별히 pillow 베개 essential 매우 중요한 do a good job 일을 잘 해내다 consider 고려하다 permanent 영구적인 contract 계약, 계약서

32 Where do the speakers most likely work?
(A) At a manufacturing plant
(B) At a department store
(C) At a restaurant
(D) At a dry cleaner

번역 화자들은 어디에 종사하겠는가?
(A) 제조 공장
(B) 백화점
(C) 식당
(D) 드라이클리닝 전문점

해설 **전체 내용 관련 - 화자들의 근무지**
여자가 첫 대사에서 끝내야 할 드라이클리닝이 아주 많다(we have a lot of dry cleaning to finish)고 말하고 있으므로 화자들은 드라이클리닝 전문점에서 근무하고 있음을 알 수 있다. 따라서 정답은 (D)이다.

33 What does the man say he forgot?
(A) A handout
(B) Some safety equipment
(C) Some identification
(D) A key card

번역 남자는 무엇을 깜박했다고 말하는가?
(A) 유인물
(B) 안전 장비
(C) 신분증
(D) 카드식 열쇠

해설 **세부 사항 관련 - 남자가 깜박한 일**
남자가 첫 대사에서 깜박하고 명찰을 가져오지 않았다(I forgot to bring my name tag with me)고 말하고 있으므로 정답은 (C)이다.

> **Paraphrasing**
> 대화의 name tag → 정답의 Some identification

34 According to the woman, why is an order important?
(A) It could result in long-term business.
(B) It is for a local charity event.
(C) It is for a renowned company.
(D) It will be featured in a magazine.

번역 여자에 따르면, 주문은 왜 중요한가?
(A) 장기적인 사업 거래로 이어질 수 있어서
(B) 지역 자선 행사를 위한 거라서
(C) 명성 있는 회사를 위한 거라서
(D) 잡지에 소개될 거라서

해설 **세부 사항 관련 - 주문이 중요한 이유**
여자가 마지막 대사에서 그 주문을 잘 처리하는 일은 매우 중요한데 그들이 영구 계약을 해주는 걸 고려 중이기 때문(It's essential that we do a good job on that order, as they're considering giving us a permanent contract)이라고 말하고 있으므로 정답은 (A)이다.

어휘 long-term 장기적인   charity 자선   renowned 명성 있는
feature 특별히 포함하다

> **Paraphrasing**
> 대화의 essential → 질문의 important
> 대화의 a permanent contract
> → 정답의 long-term business

35-37

M-Cn Danielle, ³⁵ **I had a chance to look over your design for the promotional flyers we're passing out at next week's festival.** They look great. But I saw the price estimate you got from the print shop. It's a bit high, isn't it?

W-Br Well, ³⁶ **I can ask them for a discount.** It's quite a large order, so I'm sure there's room to negotiate.

M-Cn That would be great, thanks. Oh, and ³⁷ **I liked the photos that you chose, but some of them are outdated. After lunch, I'll send you the ones from our dance studio's show last week.** You can use a couple of those instead.

남: 대니엘, **다음 주 축제 때 배포할 홍보 전단 디자인하신 거 검토해 봤는데요.** 아주 좋아요. 그런데 인쇄소에서 받아온 견적서를 봤는데. 좀 비싸지 않나요?

여: 음, **할인을 요청해 볼 수 있어요.** 꽤 큰 주문이니 분명 협상의 여지가 있을 거예요.

남: 그러면 좋겠네요, 고맙습니다. 아, 그리고 당신이 고른 사진들 마음에 들긴 했지만, 그중 몇몇 개는 오래된 사진이에요. 점심시간 후에 제가 지난주에 우리 댄스교습소의 공연 때 찍은 사진을 보내드리겠습니다. 몇 장은 그걸로 교체하셔도 돼요.

어휘 look over ~을 훑어보다   promotional flyer 홍보 전단
pass out ~을 배포하다   estimate 견적서   print shop
인쇄소   room 여지   negotiate 협상하다   outdated
오래된

35 What is the conversation mainly about?
(A) A training session
(B) An event registration
(C) Some promotional materials
(D) Some festival booths

번역 대화는 주로 무엇에 관한 것인가?
(A) 교육 과정
(B) 행사 등록
(C) 홍보물
(D) 축제 부스

해설 **전체 내용 관련 - 대화의 주제**
남자가 첫 대사에서 다음 주 축제 때 배포할 홍보 전단 디자인을 검토해 봤다(I had a chance to look over your design for the promotional flyers we're passing out at next week's festival)고 대화를 시작했고, 화자들이 홍보 전단에 대한 대화를 이어가고 있으므로 정답은 (C)이다.

어휘 registration 등록   material 자료, 재료

> **Paraphrasing**
> 대화의 promotional flyers
> → 정답의 Some promotional materials

36 What does the woman offer to do?
(A) Check a Web site
(B) Request a price reduction
(C) Proofread a document
(D) Research other businesses

번역 여자는 무엇을 하겠다고 제안하는가?
(A) 웹사이트 확인하기
(B) 가격 할인 요청하기
(C) 문서 교정 보기
(D) 다른 업체 조사하기

해설 **세부 사항 관련 - 여자의 제안 사항**
여자가 첫 대사에서 할인을 요청해 볼 수 있다(I can ask them for a discount)고 말하고 있으므로 정답은 (B)이다.

어휘 reduction 감소, 할인   proofread 교정을 보다

> **Paraphrasing**
> 대화의 ask them for a discount
> → 정답의 Request a price reduction

37 What will the man send this afternoon?
(A) Schedules for upcoming shows
(B) Images of a recent event
(C) A sample contract
(D) A mailing address

번역 남자는 오늘 오후에 무엇을 보낼 것인가?
(A) 다가올 공연 일정표
(B) 최근 행사 사진
(C) 견본 계약서
(D) 우편 주소

해설 **세부 사항 관련 - 남자가 오후에 보낼 것**
남자가 마지막 대사에서 여자가 고른 사진들이 마음에 들긴 했지만, 그중 몇몇 개는 오래된 사진(I liked the photos that you chose, but some of them are outdated)이라고 하면서 점심시간 후에 지난주 공연 때 찍은 사진을 보내주겠다(After lunch, I'll send you the ones from our dance studio's show last week)고 말하고 있으므로 정답은 (B)이다.

어휘 upcoming 다가오는

> **Paraphrasing**
> 대화의 the photos ~ ones from our dance studio's show last week → 정답의 Images of a recent event

38-40

> W-Br Good morning. **38 This is Michelle from Reynolds Appliances.** I just wanted to remind you that your washing machine will be delivered today between one and two o'clock.
>
> M-Au Thank you. I'll be here. Actually, **39 I originally requested delivery only, but I'm wondering if I can have the machine installed as well.**
>
> W-Br Let me see … Yes, there's time in the schedule for that. I'll let our crew know.
>
> M-Au Thank you. And **40 please tell them they should take Lang Avenue to get here, as**

Patterson Street is currently closed for repairs.

여: 좋은 아침입니다. 저는 레이놀즈 가전의 미셸입니다. 귀하의 세탁기가 오늘 1시에서 2시 사이에 배송될 예정임을 다시 한번 알려드리고자 연락드렸습니다.

남: 감사합니다. 저는 여기 있을 거예요. 실은 원래는 배송만 요청했지만, 혹시 설치도 요청할 수 있는지 궁금합니다.

여: 잠시만요… 네, 일정상에는 시간이 가능하네요. 작업자들에게 알릴게요.

남: 감사합니다. 그리고 그들에게 여기에 오시려면 랭 가를 이용하셔야 한다고 전해주세요. 패터슨 가가 현재 수리 중이라 막혀 있거든요.

어휘 appliance 가전제품   deliver 배송하다   originally 원래   request 요청하다   delivery 배송   install 설치하다   repair 수리

38 What kind of business does the woman most likely work for?
(A) A construction firm
(B) A dental clinic
(C) An appliance store
(D) A post office

번역 여자는 어떤 종류의 업체에서 일하겠는가?
(A) 건설회사
(B) 치과
(C) 가전제품 매장
(D) 우체국

해설 **전체 내용 관련 - 여자의 근무지**
여자가 첫 대사에서 자신을 레이놀즈 가전의 미셸(This is Michelle from Reynolds Appliances)이라고 소개하는 것으로 보아 여자는 가전제품 매장에서 근무하고 있음을 알 수 있다. 따라서 정답은 (C)이다.

39 What does the man say he wants to do?
(A) Add a service request
(B) Reschedule a visit
(C) Receive an invoice
(D) Make a complaint

번역 남자는 무엇을 하고 싶다고 말하는가?
(A) 서비스 요청 추가하기
(B) 방문 날짜 다시 잡기
(C) 송장 받기
(D) 불만 제기하기

해설 **세부 사항 관련 - 남자가 하고 싶어 하는 일**
남자가 첫 대사에서 원래는 배송만 요청했지만, 혹시 설치도 요청할 수 있는지 궁금하다(I originally requested delivery only, but I'm wondering if I can have the machine installed as well)고 말하고 있으므로 정답은 (A)이다.

어휘 reschedule 일정을 변경하다 invoice 송장 complaint 불만

> **Paraphrasing**
> 대화의 have the machine installed as well
> → 정답의 Add a service request

40 What does the man offer advice about?
(A) Whom to contact
(B) When to arrive
(C) What samples to bring
(D) Which road to take

번역 남자는 무엇에 대해 충고하는가?
(A) 누구에게 연락할지
(B) 언제 도착할지
(C) 어떤 견본을 가져올지
(D) 어느 도로를 이용할지

해설 **세부 사항 관련 - 남자가 충고하는 것**
남자가 마지막 대사에서 그들에게 여기에 오려면 랭 가를 이용해야 한다고 전해줄 것(please tell them they should take Lang Avenue to get here)을 요청하면서 패터슨 가가 현재 수리 중이라 막혀 있다(as Patterson Street is currently closed for repairs)고 말하고 있으므로 정답은 (D)이다.

> **Paraphrasing**
> 대화의 Avenue, Street → 정답의 road

41-43

W-Am Walter, ⁴¹ **could you update me on the progress of our TV commercial for Marquez Athletics?** The last news I heard was that you had finished editing it.

M-Cn ⁴² **We just held a feedback session with some customers, and they loved it. They thought the animated sequence was really impressive.** They said the storyline was memorable as well.

W-Am I'm glad to hear that! It's going to be the main part of the promotional campaign, so it's important to get it right. So, how soon will it air?

M-Cn ⁴³ **It'll most likely get final approval at the management meeting, which is next Tuesday.**

여: 월터, 마케즈 애슬레틱스 TV 광고의 진행 상황에 대해 알려줄 수 있나요? 제가 들은 가장 최근 소식은 당신이 편집 작업을 마쳤다는 거였어요.

남: 방금 몇몇 소비자들과 피드백 시간을 가졌는데 다들 마음에 들어 했어요. 애니메이션 시퀀스가 굉장히 인상 깊다고 했어요. 줄거리도 기억에 남는다고 했고요.

여: 좋은 소식이네요! 이건 홍보 캠페인에서 가장 중요한 부분이 될 거니까 제대로 하는 것이 중요해요. 그럼, 얼마나 빨리 방송에 내보낼 수 있나요?

남: 간부 회의에서 최종 승인이 떨어질 것 같은데요. 회의가 다음 주 화요일이에요.

어휘 progress 진척 edit 편집하다 impressive 인상적인 storyline 줄거리 memorable 기억할 만한 get it right 제대로 하다 air 방송하다 approval 승인

41 What is mainly being discussed?
(A) A fund-raising campaign
(B) A company policy
(C) A workshop
(D) An advertisement

번역 무엇이 주로 논의되고 있는가?
(A) 모금 캠페인
(B) 회사 정책
(C) 워크숍
(D) 광고

해설 **전체 내용 관련 - 대화의 주제**
여자가 첫 대사에서 마케즈 애슬레틱스 TV 광고의 진행 상황에 대해 알려줄 수 있는지(could you update me on the progress of our TV commercial for Marquez Athletics?) 묻고 있으므로 정답은 (D)이다.

어휘 fund-raising 모금 활동 policy 정책

> **Paraphrasing**
> 대화의 TV commercial → 정답의 An advertisement

42 What good news does the man share?
(A) Some customers were impressed.
(B) A task was completed early.
(C) Product sales have increased.
(D) The company received a grant.

번역 남자는 어떤 좋은 소식을 공유하는가?
(A) 몇몇 소비자가 깊은 인상을 받았다.
(B) 업무가 일찍 완료되었다.
(C) 제품 판매량이 늘었다.
(D) 회사가 보조금을 받았다.

해설 **세부 사항 관련 - 남자가 공유하는 좋은 소식**
남자가 첫 대사에서 몇몇 소비자들과 피드백 시간을 가졌는데 다들 마음에 들어 했다(We just held a feedback session with some customers, and they loved it)면서 애니메이션 시퀀스가 굉장히 인상 깊다고 했다(They thought the animated sequence was really impressive)고 말하고 있으므로 정답은 (A)이다.

어휘 impress 깊은 인상을 주다 task 일, 과제 complete 완료하다 grant 보조금

43 What will happen next Tuesday?
(A) Some investors will visit.
(B) Some managers will meet.
(C) A winner will be announced.
(D) A business trip will begin.

번역 다음 주 화요일에 무슨 일이 있겠는가?
(A) 투자자들이 방문할 것이다.
(B) 관리자들이 만날 것이다.
(C) 수상자가 발표될 것이다.
(D) 출장이 시작될 것이다.

해설 **세부 사항 관련 - 다음 주 화요일에 일어날 일**
남자가 마지막 대사에서 간부 회의에서 최종 승인이 떨어질 것 같은데 회의가 다음 주 화요일(It'll most likely get final approval at the management meeting, which is next Tuesday)이라고 말하고 있으므로 정답은 (B)이다.

어휘 investor 투자자 winner 수상자 announce 발표하다

> **Paraphrasing**
> 대화의 the management meeting
> → 정답의 Some managers will meet.

44-46 3인 대화

> M-Au Hi, Shawn. Hey, Debbie. I'm looking for Pamela, but I haven't seen her in the office yet today. Do you know where she is?
>
> W-Am I think she had planned to take today off. **⁴⁴Would you like me to open up the staff calendar and make sure?**
>
> M-Au Thanks, but I can do that. I was just asking because **⁴⁵I know that Pamela drafts most of our press releases,** and I need one for later today.
>
> W-Am **⁴⁶You should have Shawn help you with that. He has a degree in journalism.**
>
> M-Cn That's right, I do. And I've got some time now if you want to talk about what you need.

남1: 안녕하세요, 숀. 안녕하세요, 데비. 저는 파멜라를 찾고 있는데요. 오늘 사무실에서 아직 못 봤어요. 지금 어디에 있는지 아세요?

여: 오늘 휴가를 낸다고 했던 것 같아요. **직원 달력을 열어서 확인해 드릴까요?**

남1: 감사합니다만, 제가 해도 됩니다. **파멜라가 우리 대부분의 보도 자료 초안을 작성하는 걸로 알고 있어서** 물어본 거였어요. 오늘 오후에 보도 자료가 하나 필요하거든요.

여: **숀에게 도움을 요청하세요. 그는 언론학 학위를 소지하고 있어요.**

남2: 맞습니다. 필요한 것에 대해 이야기하고 싶으시다면 저는 지금 시간이 있습니다.

어휘 take ~ off 휴가를 내다 make sure 확실하게 하다, 확인하다
draft 원고를 작성하다 press release 보도 자료
degree 학위 journalism 언론학

44 What does the woman offer to do?
(A) Wait for Pamela
(B) Contact a coworker
(C) Check a schedule
(D) Proofread a document

번역 여자는 무엇을 하겠다고 제안하는가?
(A) 파멜라 기다리기
(B) 동료에게 연락하기
(C) 일정 확인하기
(D) 문서 교정 보기

해설 **세부 사항 관련 - 여자의 제안 사항**
여자가 첫 대사에서 직원 달력을 열어서 확인해 줄 것(Would you like me to open up the staff calendar and make sure?)을 제안하고 있으므로 정답은 (C)이다.

어휘 coworker 동료 proofread 교정을 보다

> **Paraphrasing**
> 대화의 open up the staff calendar and make sure
> → 정답의 Check a schedule

45 What does Pamela usually do?
(A) Write media announcements
(B) Conduct performance evaluations
(C) Make travel arrangements
(D) Introduce new clients to the business

번역 파멜라는 보통 무엇을 하는가?
(A) 언론 발표 내용 작성하기
(B) 성과 평가 실시하기
(C) 여행 준비하기
(D) 회사에 신규 고객 소개하기

해설 **세부 사항 관련 - 파멜라가 보통 하는 일**
첫 번째 남자가 두 번째 대사에서 파멜라가 우리 대부분의 보도 자료 초안을 작성하는 걸로 알고 있다(I know that Pamela drafts most of our press releases)고 말하고 있으므로 정답은 (A)이다.

어휘 announcement 공지, 발표 conduct 실시하다
performance 성과 evaluation 평가 arrangement 준비

> **Paraphrasing**
> 대화의 drafts most of our press releases
> → 정답의 Write media announcements

46 According to the woman, why should Shawn help with a task?
(A) He used to perform it regularly.
(B) He wants to learn new skills.
(C) He has a relevant degree.
(D) He has the lightest workload.

번역 여자에 따르면, 숀은 왜 업무를 도와야 하는가?
(A) 정기적으로 했던 일이라서
(B) 새로운 기술을 배우고 싶어 해서
(C) 관련 학위가 있어서
(D) 업무량이 가장 적어서

해설 **세부 사항 관련 - 숀이 업무를 도와야 하는 이유**
여자가 마지막 대사에서 숀에게 도움을 요청하라(You should have Shawn help you with that)면서 그는 언론학 학위를 소지하고 있다(He has a degree in journalism)고 말하고 있으므로 정답은 (C)이다.

어휘 perform 수행하다 regularly 정기적으로 skill 기술, 역량 relevant 관련 있는 workload 업무량

> **Paraphrasing**
> 대화의 a degree in journalism
> → 정답의 a relevant degree

47-49

W-Br Good morning, Mr. Jeffreys. I'm calling about the plans you sent for the B70 running shoes. I can confirm that **[47] our manufacturing plant** can produce the goods for you, starting from next week.

M-Cn I'm glad to hear that. I know there was an option to send the shoes overseas, to our warehouse in Singapore. **[48] How much would the delivery costs be?**

W-Br It depends on the size of the order. **[49] I suggest taking advantage of our generous bulk discounts.**

여: 좋은 아침입니다, 제프리스 씨. B70 운동화에 대해 당신이 보내준 계획서와 관련해 전화드립니다. **우리 제조 공장에서 다음 주부터 귀하의 제품을 생산할 수 있다는 답변을 드립니다.**

남: 좋은 소식이네요. 신발을 해외로, 싱가포르에 있는 창고로 보내는 방법도 있었잖아요. **배송비가 얼마나 들까요?**

여: 발주 규모에 따라 다릅니다. **저희가 제공하는 큰 폭의 대량 주문 할인을 이용하시기를 권해드립니다.**

어휘 manufacturing plant 제조 공장 produce 생산하다 overseas 해외로 warehouse 창고 depend on ~에 달려 있다 take advantage of ~을 이용하다 generous 후한, 관대한 bulk discount 대량 주문 할인

---

47 Where most likely does the woman work?
(A) At a factory
(B) At a department store
(C) At a repair shop
(D) At a consulting firm

번역 여자는 어디에서 일하겠는가?
(A) 공장
(B) 백화점
(C) 수리점
(D) 컨설팅 회사

해설 **전체 내용 관련 - 여자의 근무지**
여자가 첫 대사에서 우리 제조 공장(our manufacturing plant)이라고 말하고 있으므로 정답은 (A)이다.

> **Paraphrasing**
> 대화의 manufacturing plant → 정답의 a factory

48 What does the man inquire about?
(A) A contract period
(B) A color option
(C) A discount offer
(D) A shipping fee

번역 남자는 무엇에 대해 문의하는가?
(A) 계약 기간
(B) 색상 옵션
(C) 할인 제안
(D) 배송비

해설 **세부 사항 관련 - 남자의 문의 사항**
남자가 첫 대사에서 배송비가 얼마나 들지(How much would the delivery costs be?) 묻고 있으므로 정답은 (D)이다.

어휘 period 기간

> **Paraphrasing**
> 대화의 the delivery costs → 정답의 A shipping fee

49 What does the woman recommend doing?
(A) Making an in-person visit
(B) Speaking to a supervisor
(C) Changing a design
(D) Placing a large order

번역 여자는 무엇을 하기를 추천하는가?
(A) 직접 방문하기
(B) 관리자와 이야기하기
(C) 디자인 변경하기
(D) 대량 주문하기

해설 **세부 사항 관련 - 여자의 추천 사항**
여자가 마지막 대사에서 대량 주문 할인을 이용하기를 권한다(I suggest taking advantage of our generous bulk discounts)고 말하고 있으므로 정답은 (D)이다.

어휘 in-person 직접   supervisor 감독관, 관리자   place an order
주문하다

> **Paraphrasing**
> 대화의 taking advantage of our generous bulk discounts
> → 정답의 Placing a large order

50-52 3인 대화

M-Au Alright, now that you're both here, let me make some introductions. ⁵⁰**This is Bethany Reeves, our new head librarian, and Clara Jackson, our new researcher.**

W-Br Nice to meet you.

W-Am You, too. I'm excited that we'll be working together.

M-Au Now, ⁵¹**you'll spend the morning together because there are lots of forms from the human resources department that you need to fill out.** Then I'll work with Bethany on plans for the summer reading program.

W-Br That sounds great. I ran the same kind of program at the Farmington branch, so I have some ideas to share.

W-Am Oh, ⁵²**how long were you at the Farmington branch, Bethany?**

W-Br Let's see... Nearly eight years.

남: 좋습니다, 이제 두 분 다 오셨으니 소개를 좀 해드리겠습니다. 이쪽은 새로 오신 수석 사서 베서니 리브스이고, 이쪽은 새로 오신 연구원 클라라 잭슨입니다.

여1: 만나서 반갑습니다.

여2: 저도요. 함께 일하게 되어 기쁩니다.

남: 자, 두 분은 오전 시간을 함께 보내실 거예요. 작성해야 하는 인사부 양식이 아주 많으니까요. 그런 다음에는 제가 베서니와 함께 여름 독서 프로그램 기획안을 준비할 거예요.

여1: 좋습니다. 파밍턴 지점에서 같은 종류의 프로그램을 운영해 봐서 공유해 드릴 만한 내용이 있어요.

여2: 아, 파밍턴 지점에 얼마나 오래 계셨어요, 베서니?

여1: 잠시만요… 거의 8년이요.

어휘 introduction 소개   librarian 사서   researcher 연구원
fill out 작성하다   reading program 독서 프로그램
branch 지사, 지점   nearly 거의

50 Where most likely are the speakers?
(A) At a bookstore
(B) At a warehouse
(C) At a medical clinic
(D) At a library

번역 화자들은 어디에 있겠는가?
(A) 서점
(B) 창고
(C) 병원
(D) 도서관

해설 **전체 내용 관련 - 대화의 장소**
남자가 첫 대사에서 이쪽은 새로 오신 수석 사서 베서니 리브스이고, 이쪽은 새로 오신 연구원 클라라 잭슨(This is Bethany Reeves, our new head librarian, and Clara Jackson, our new researcher)이라고 말하는 것으로 보아 대화의 장소가 도서관이라는 것을 알 수 있다. 따라서 정답은 (D)이다.

---

51 According to the man, what will the women do in the morning?
(A) Take a building tour
(B) Complete some paperwork
(C) Observe other colleagues
(D) Read a user manual

번역 남자에 따르면, 여자들은 오전에 무엇을 하겠는가?
(A) 건물 견학하기
(B) 서류 작성하기
(C) 동료들 관찰하기
(D) 사용 설명서 읽기

해설 **세부 사항 관련 - 여자들이 오전에 할 일**
남자가 두 번째 대사에서 두 분은 오전 시간을 함께 보내실 건데 작성해야 하는 인사부 양식이 아주 많다(you'll spend the morning together because there are lots of forms from the human resources department that you need to fill out)고 말하고 있으므로 정답은 (B)이다.

어휘 observe 관찰하다   colleague 동료

> **Paraphrasing**
> 대화의 lots of forms ~ that you need to fill out
> → 정답의 Complete some paperwork

---

52 What does Clara ask Bethany about?
(A) The usefulness of some training
(B) The number of participants in a program
(C) The duration of her previous job
(D) The reason she transferred branches

번역 클라라는 베서니에게 무엇에 대해 묻는가?
(A) 교육의 유용성
(B) 프로그램의 참가자 수
(C) 전 직장에서 일한 기간
(D) 지점을 옮긴 이유

해설 **세부 사항 관련 - 클라라가 베서니에게 묻는 것**
두 번째 여자가 마지막 대사에서 베서니에게 파밍턴 지점에 얼마나 오래 있었는지(how long were you at the Farmington branch, Bethany?) 묻고 있으므로 정답은 (C)이다.

어휘 usefulness 유용성   participant 참가자   duration 기간
previous 이전의   transfer 전근 가다

TEST 3

Paraphrasing
대화의 how long were you at the Farmington branch
→ 정답의 The duration of her previous job

53-55

M-Au Hi, ⁵³ I'm calling because I received my bill for September, and it was forty dollars more than I expected. I'm Gary Russo; account number 95039.

W-Am Let me check your account, Mr. Russo. Hmm … ⁵⁴ it looks like you got some merchandise from us in September?

M-Au ⁵⁴ Yes, I upgraded to a new smartphone model. But I thought that was free for renewing my contract.

W-Am I'm afraid not. The cost is divided over the length of your contract. ⁵⁵ That's why we advise customers to thoroughly read the contract so they understand the terms.

M-Au Hmm, I guess I'll have to have another look at it.

남: 안녕하세요, 9월 청구서를 받고서 전화드립니다. 제가 예상한 것보다 40달러가 더 많이 나왔어요. 저는 게리 루소이며, 고객 번호는 95039입니다.

여: 제가 계정을 확인해 보겠습니다, 루소 씨. 음… 9월에 저희한테 상품을 구매하신 걸로 보이는데요?

남: 네, 새 스마트폰 기종으로 바꿨어요. 하지만 계약을 갱신하면 무료인 걸로 아는데요.

여: 죄송하지만 아닙니다. 그 비용은 계약 기간에 걸쳐 분산 청구됩니다. 그게 저희가 고객님께 계약서를 철저히 읽어보시라고 말씀드리는 이유입니다. 약관을 이해하실 수 있도록요.

남: 음, 다시 한번 살펴봐야겠네요.

어휘 bill 청구서   account 계정, 계좌   merchandise 상품
renew 갱신하다   contract 계약   divide 나누다   length
길이, 기간   thoroughly 철저하게   terms 약관, 조건

53
What is the purpose of the call?
(A) To change a phone number
(B) To report a potential error
(C) To pay an outstanding bill
(D) To update an address

번역 전화를 건 목적은 무엇인가?
(A) 전화번호를 바꾸려고
(B) 오류일 수 있는 문제를 알리려고
(C) 미납 요금을 지불하려고
(D) 주소를 변경하려고

해설 **전체 내용 관련 - 전화의 목적**
남자가 첫 대사에서 9월 청구서를 받고서 전화한다면서 예상한 것보다 40달러가 더 많이 나왔다(I'm calling because I received my bill for September, and it was forty dollars more than I expected)고 말하고 있으므로 청구서 오류를 알리려고 전화를 걸었다는 것을 알 수 있다. 따라서 정답은 (B)이다.

어휘 potential 잠재적인, 가능성이 있는   error 오류, 착오
outstanding 미지불된

54
What did the man do in September?
(A) He took a trip overseas.
(B) He extended a warranty.
(C) He upgraded his phone.
(D) He downloaded a lot of files.

번역 남자는 9월에 무엇을 했는가?
(A) 해외여행을 갔다.
(B) 보증 기간을 연장했다.
(C) 전화기를 변경했다.
(D) 많은 파일을 내려받았다.

해설 **세부 사항 관련 - 남자가 9월에 한 일**
여자가 첫 대사에서 9월에 상품을 구매한 것으로 보인다(it looks like you got some merchandise from us in September?)고 하자 남자가 네(Yes)라고 대답한 뒤 새 스마트폰 기종으로 바꿨다(I upgraded to a new smartphone model)고 덧붙였으므로 정답은 (C)이다.

어휘 extend 연장하다   warranty 보증 기간

55
According to the woman, what was the man advised to do?
(A) Make a copy of a receipt
(B) Keep a product's packaging
(C) Speak to a manager
(D) Read an agreement carefully

번역 여자에 따르면, 남자는 무엇을 하라고 권고받았는가?
(A) 영수증 복사하기
(B) 제품 포장재 보관하기
(C) 관리자와 이야기하기
(D) 계약서 주의 깊게 읽기

해설 **세부 사항 관련 - 남자가 권고받은 일**
여자가 마지막 대사에서 그게 저희가 고객님께 계약서를 철저히 읽어보시라고 말씀드리는 이유(That's why we advise customers to thoroughly read the contract)라고 말하고 있으므로 정답은 (D)이다.

어휘 packaging 포장재   agreement 합의, 계약   carefully 주의 깊게

Paraphrasing
대화의 thoroughly read the contract
→ 정답의 Read an agreement carefully

56-58

M-Cn Hey, Annie. ⁵⁶ **You opened your hair salon last week, right?** How's it going?

W-Br ⁵⁶ **The first week has been stressful,** but it's exciting to finally achieve my dream. I haven't had any customers review the salon yet, but ⁵⁷ **I'm hoping to get some positive reviews soon.**

M-Cn I'm sure you will. You're very talented.

W-Br Thank you. It's a highly competitive industry, but I think my styles appeal to young professionals.

M-Cn I actually work with quite a few junior colleagues. ⁵⁸ **I can tell them about your salon, if you want.**

W-Br Oh, really? Actually... I have a stack of business cards.

M-Cn ⁵⁸ **I'd be happy to pass them out.**

남: 안녕, 애니. 지난주에 미용실을 개업하셨다고요? 잘되고 있나요?

여: 첫 번째 주는 스트레스가 많았지만 마침내 제 꿈을 이뤄서 기뻐요. 손님들이 아직 미용실에 대한 후기를 남기진 않았지만, 곧 긍정적인 후기를 받았으면 좋겠어요.

남: 당연히 그럴 거예요. 당신은 재주가 매우 뛰어나잖아요.

여: 고마워요. 굉장히 경쟁이 치열한 업종이지만, 제 스타일이 젊은 전문직 종사자들에게 잘 먹히는 것 같아요.

남: 실은 제가 꽤 많은 부하 직원들과 함께 일해요. 원한다면 그들에게 당신의 미용실에 대해 말해줄게요.

여: 오, 정말요? 실은… 명함 한 뭉치가 있어요.

남: 제가 기꺼이 그들에게 나눠줄게요.

어휘 hair salon 미용실 achieve 달성하다 review 평가하다; 평가 positive 긍정적인 talented 재능이 있는 highly 매우 competitive 경쟁이 치열한, 경쟁력이 있는 appeal to ~에 호소하다 professional 전문직 종사자, 전문가 quite a few 상당수의 a stack of 한 무더기의 pass out ~을 배포하다

56 What did the woman do last week?
(A) She started her own business.
(B) She got a book published.
(C) She relocated to a new city.
(D) She was featured in an article.

번역 여자는 지난주에 무엇을 했는가?
(A) 자영업을 시작했다.
(B) 책을 출간했다.
(C) 새로운 도시로 이사했다.
(D) 기사에 소개되었다.

해설 **세부 사항 관련 - 여자가 지난주에 한 일**
남자가 첫 대사에서 지난주 미용실 개업 여부(You opened your hair salon last week, right?)를 확인하자 여자가 첫 번째 주는 스트레스가 많았다(The first week has been stressful)고 말하고 있으므로 정답은 (A)이다.

어휘 start one's own business 자영업을 시작하다 publish 출간하다 relocate 이전하다, 이사하다 feature 특별히 포함하다 article 글, 기사

> **Paraphrasing**
> 대화의 opened ~ hair salon
> → 정답의 started ~ business

57 What does the woman say she hopes to receive?
(A) Some price estimates
(B) Some favorable reviews
(C) A local award
(D) A bank loan

번역 여자는 무엇을 받고 싶다고 말하는가?
(A) 가격 견적서
(B) 우호적인 후기
(C) 지역에서 주는 상
(D) 은행 대출

해설 **세부 사항 관련 - 여자가 받고 싶어하는 것**
여자가 첫 대사에서 곧 긍정적인 후기를 받았으면 좋겠다(I'm hoping to get some positive reviews soon)고 말하고 있으므로 정답은 (B)이다.

어휘 estimate 견적서 favorable 우호적인 loan 대출

> **Paraphrasing**
> 대화의 positive reviews → 정답의 favorable reviews

58 Why does the woman say, "I have a stack of business cards"?
(A) To ask for a favor
(B) To cancel an order
(C) To express concern
(D) To correct an error

번역 여자가 "명함 한 뭉치가 있어요"라고 말한 이유는?
(A) 부탁을 하려고
(B) 주문을 취소하려고
(C) 우려를 표현하려고
(D) 오류를 바로잡으려고

해설 **화자의 의도 파악 - 명함 한 뭉치가 있다는 말의 의도**
앞서 남자가 세 번째 대사에서 원한다면 그들에게 당신의 미용실에 대해 말해주겠다(I can tell them about your salon, if you want)고 하자 여자가 인용문을 언급하였고, 이어서 남자가 제가 기꺼이 그들에게 나눠주겠다(I'd be happy to pass them out)고 말하는 것으로 보아, 여자는 남자에게 미용실 홍보를 부탁하려는 의도로 한 말임을 알 수 있다. 따라서 정답은 (A)이다.

어휘 favor 부탁 express 표현하다 concern 우려, 걱정 correct
바로잡다

59-61

M-Au Hi, Ji-Min. ⁵⁹**I heard that you'll be representing our company at the Automotive Trade Show this year.**

W-Am Yes, that's right! In fact, ^{59,60}**I'm trying to sign up on the Web site right now.** ⁶⁰**But—I'm having a little trouble...**

M-Au Well, I did it last year. ⁶⁰**What's the problem?**

W-Am There are more participation options than I expected.

M-Au Well, we'll be exhibiting, so scroll down to that section. OK, ⁶¹**now you need to choose how large our company's booth will be. That should be our manager's decision.** Did she give you that information already?

W-Am No—⁶¹**I'll go and ask her now.** Thanks, Ravi!

남: 안녕하세요, 지민. 올해 자동차 무역 박람회에 우리 회사 대표로 참가한다고 들었어요.

여: 네, 맞아요! 실은 지금 웹사이트에 등록을 해보는 중이에요. 하지만 약간의 문제가 있어요…

남: 음, 제가 작년에 했어요. 뭐가 문제죠?

여: 제가 예상했던 것보다 더 많은 참가 옵션이 있어요.

남: 음, 우리는 전시를 할 거예요. 그러니 그 부분까지 스크롤을 내려보세요. 좋아요, 이제 우리 회사 부스의 규모를 선택해야 해요. 그건 우리 관리자가 결정할 사안이고요. 그녀가 그 정보를 벌써 알려주었나요?

여: 아니요. 지금 가서 물어볼게요. 고마워요, 라비!

어휘 represent 대표하다 automotive 자동차의 trade show
무역 박람회 sign up ~에 등록하다 have a little trouble
약간의 문제가 있다 participation 참가 exhibit 전시하다
scroll down 스크롤을 아래로 내리다 decision 결정

---

59 What are the speakers discussing?
(A) Submitting an annual report
(B) Recruiting staff for a project
(C) Taking an overseas business trip
(D) Registering for an industry event

번역 화자들은 무엇을 논의하는가?
(A) 연례 보고서 제출
(B) 프로젝트를 위한 직원 채용
(C) 해외 출장
(D) 업계 행사 등록

해설 전체 내용 관련 - 대화의 주제
남자가 첫 대사에서 올해 자동차 무역 박람회에 회사 대표로 참가한다고 들었다(I heard that you'll be representing our company at the Automotive Trade Show this year)고 대화를 시작했고, 여자가 지금 웹사이트에 등록을 해보는 중(I'm trying to sign up on the Web site right now)이라며 무역 박람회 참석 등록에 관한 대화를 이어 가고 있으므로 정답은 (D)이다.

어휘 submit 제출하다 annual 연례의 recruit 채용하다 register
등록하다

> **Paraphrasing**
> 대화의 sign up → 정답의 registering
> 대화의 Automotive Trade Show
> → 정답의 an industry event

60 What does the man imply when he says, "I did it last year"?
(A) He knows some personnel well.
(B) An experience was valuable for his career.
(C) He can provide advice on a process.
(D) A responsibility should be given to someone else.

번역 남자가 "제가 작년에 했어요"라고 말할 때, 그 의도는 무엇인가?
(A) 몇몇 직원들을 잘 안다.
(B) 경험이 자기 경력에 큰 도움이 되었다.
(C) 절차에 대해 조언을 해줄 수 있다.
(D) 책임이 다른 사람에게 주어져야 한다.

해설 화자의 의도 파악 - 자신이 작년에 했었다는 말의 의도
앞서 여자가 첫 대사에서 지금 웹사이트에 등록을 해보는 중(I'm trying to sign up on the Web site right now)이지만 약간의 문제가 있다(But—I'm having a little trouble)고 하자 남자가 인용문을 언급한 뒤 뭐가 문제인지(What's the problem?) 되묻는 것으로 보아 남자가 웹사이트 등록 절차에 대해 조언을 해 줄 수 있다는 의도로 한 말임을 알 수 있다. 따라서 정답은 (C)이다.

어휘 personnel 직원들 valuable 귀중한 responsibility 책임, 책무

61 What information will the woman ask a manager for?
(A) A sales goal
(B) A final budget
(C) A preferred size
(D) A departure time

번역 여자는 관리자에게 어떤 정보를 요청하겠는가?
(A) 판매 목표
(B) 최종 예산
(C) 선호하는 크기
(D) 출발 시각

해설 세부 사항 관련 - 여자가 관리자에게 요청할 정보
남자가 마지막 대사에서 이제 우리 회사 부스의 규모를 선택해야 하는데(now you need to choose how large our company's

booth will be) 그건 관리자가 결정할 사안(That should be our manager's decision)이라고 하자 여자가 지금 가서 물어보겠다 (I'll go and ask her now)고 말하고 있으므로 정답은 (C)이다.

어휘 goal 목표 budget 예산 preferred 선호되는 departure 출발

> **Paraphrasing**
> 대화의 choose how large our company's booth will be
> → 정답의 A preferred size

62-64 대화 + 이메일 수신함

> W-Br **62 Thanks for helping me to plan the recruiting session for finding new software developers.** I think we're going to have a good turnout.
>
> M-Cn I hope so. I'm going to order refreshments for fifty people. Does that sound about right?
>
> W-Br Yes, but **63 did you read the e-mail about caterers?** We can only use ones that have been pre-approved.
>
> M-Cn Oh, I must have missed that. I'll check it out, but while you're here, **64 why don't we rehearse the presentation we're giving at the event?** That way, we can make sure it goes smoothly.

여: 새 소프트웨어 개발자를 찾기 위한 채용 설명회 준비를 도와줘서 고마워요. 많은 지원자가 참가할 것 같아요.

남: 그러길 바라요. 50명 분의 다과를 주문할게요. 그 정도면 될까요?

여: 네, 그런데 출장 조리업체에 대한 이메일 확인하셨어요? 사전 승인된 업체만 이용할 수 있대요.

남: 아, 제가 그 부분을 놓쳤나 봐요. 확인해 보겠습니다. 그런데 여기 오신 김에 행사 때 우리가 할 발표 리허설을 하면 어떨까요? 그러면 순조롭게 진행되게 할 수 있으니까요.

어휘 recruiting session 채용 설명회 developer 개발자 turnout 참가자의 수 refreshments 다과 caterer 출장 조리업체 pre-approved 사전 승인된 miss 놓치다 presentation 발표 smoothly 순조롭게

🖂 Inbox	Subject
Tony Parsons	Volunteers needed
63Roy Martino	Approved catering companies
Beth Landrum	New extension number
Anna Cordero	Vacation request reminder

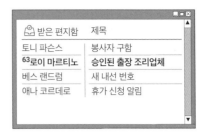

🖂 받은 편지함	제목
토니 파슨스	봉사자 구함
63로이 마르티노	승인된 출장 조리업체
베스 랜드럼	새 내선 번호
애나 코르데로	휴가 신청 알림

어휘 extension number 내선 번호 reminder 상기시키는 것

62 What are the speakers planning?
(A) A recruitment event
(B) A product launch
(C) A food festival
(D) A board meeting

번역 화자들은 무엇을 준비하는가?
(A) 채용 행사
(B) 제품 출시
(C) 음식 축제
(D) 이사회

해설 전체 내용 관련 - 화자들이 준비 중인 것
여자가 첫 대사에서 새 소프트웨어 개발자를 찾기 위한 채용 설명회 준비를 도와줘서·고맙다(Thanks for helping me to plan the recruiting session for finding new software developers)고 말하고 있으므로 정답은 (A)이다.

어휘 recruitment 채용, 모집 launch 출시

> **Paraphrasing**
> 대화의 the recruiting session
> → 정답의 A recruitment event

63 Look at the graphic. Whose e-mail does the woman refer to?
(A) Mr. Parsons's
(B) Mr. Martino's
(C) Ms. Landrum's
(D) Ms. Cordero's

번역 시각 정보에 의하면, 여자는 누구의 이메일을 언급하는가?
(A) 파슨스 씨
(B) 마르티노 씨
(C) 랜드럼 씨
(D) 코르데로 씨

해설 시각 정보 연계 - 여자가 언급하는 이메일
여자가 두 번째 대사에서 출장 조리업체에 대한 이메일 확인했는지 (did you read the e-mail about caterers?) 묻고 있고, 이메일 수신함에 따르면 출장 조리업체(~ catering companies)는 로이 마르티노(Roy Martino)의 이메일이므로 정답은 (B)이다.

64 What does the man suggest doing?
(A) Contacting technical support
(B) Practicing a presentation
(C) Checking a budget
(D) Reserving a room

번역 남자는 무엇을 제안하는가?
(A) 기술 지원부에 연락하기
(B) 발표 연습하기
(C) 예산 점검하기
(D) 방 예약하기

해설 **세부 사항 관련 - 남자의 제안 사항**
남자가 마지막 대사에서 행사 때 할 발표 리허설을 하면 어떨지(why don't we rehearse the presentation we're giving at the event?) 제안하고 있으므로 정답은 (B)이다.

어휘 technical support 기술 지원   practice 연습하다   budget 예산
reserve 예약하다

> **Paraphrasing**
> 대화의 rehearse the presentation
> → 정답의 Practicing a presentation

65-67 대화 + 표지판

M-Au	Thanks for giving me a ride to the Worthington Electronics Trade Show, Rachel. I would have had to take the bus.
W-Am	My pleasure. Anyway, **65 my house is in your neighborhood, remember?** It wasn't out of my way.
M-Au	Oh, right. But I still appreciate it. Do you know how long it will take to get to the event center? It's on Ashford Street, right?
W-Am	Yes, but the traffic report said there has been an accident on Ashford Street. **66 We need to take exit sixteen.** We can park at the south entrance.
M-Au	Okay. **67 Then I'd better text Benjamin and ask him to wait for us there instead of at the north entrance.**
W-Am	Sounds good!

남: 워딩턴 전자 제품 무역 박람회 가는 데 태워 주셔서 감사합니다, 레이첼. 아니었으면 버스를 타야 했을 거예요.

여: 천만에요. 어쨌든, **저희 집이 당신과 같은 동네잖아요, 기억하죠?** 길을 돌아가지는 않았어요.

남: 아, 맞네요. 하지만 그래도 감사드려요. 행사장까지 얼마나 걸리는지 아시나요? 애시퍼드 가에 있는 거 맞죠?

여: 네, 하지만 교통 정보에서 애시퍼드 가에 사고가 있었다고 하더라고요. **우리는 16번 출구로 나가야 해요.** 남문에 주차할 수 있어요.

남: 알겠습니다. 그럼, 제가 벤자민에게 북문 말고 거기서 우리를 기다려달라고 문자할게요.

여: 좋습니다!

어휘 give a ride 태워주다   trade show 무역 박람회
appreciate 고마워하다   traffic report 교통 정보
accident 사고

WORTHINGTON EXITS		
Oakridge Lane	Exit 11	→
Ashford Street	Exit 13	↗
Powell Street	Exit 14	↘
66 Yorkie Road	Exit 16	↑

워딩턴 출구		
오크리지 길	11번 출구	→
애시퍼드 가	13번 출구	↗
파월 가	14번 출구	↘
66 요키 로	16번 출구	↑

65 What does the woman remind the man about?
(A) She has attended the event before.
(B) She currently lives near the man.
(C) She is borrowing a company car.
(D) She has an office in the event center.

번역 여자는 남자에게 무엇에 대해 상기시키는가?
(A) 자신이 과거에 그 행사에 참석한 적이 있다.
(B) 자신이 현재 남자의 집 근처에 산다.
(C) 자신이 회사 차를 빌려 쓰고 있다.
(D) 행사장에 자신의 사무실이 있다.

해설 **세부 사항 관련 - 여자가 남자에게 상기시키는 것**
여자가 첫 대사에서 자신의 집이 같은 동네인데 기억하는지(my house is in your neighborhood, remember?) 묻고 있으므로 정답은 (B)이다.

어휘 attend 참석하다   currently 현재   borrow 빌리다

66 Look at the graphic. Which exit will the speakers use?
(A) Oakridge Lane
(B) Ashford Street
(C) Powell Street
(D) Yorkie Road

번역 시각 정보에 의하면, 화자들은 어느 출구를 이용하겠는가?
(A) 오크리지 길
(B) 애시퍼드 가
(C) 파월 가
(D) 요키 로

해설 **시각 정보 연계 - 화자들이 사용할 출구**
여자가 두 번째 대사에서 16번 출구로 나가야 한다(We need to take exit sixteen)고 말하고 있고, 표지판에 따르면 16번 출구는 요 키 로(Yorkie Road)이므로 정답은 (D)이다.

---

67 What will the man ask Benjamin to do?
(A) Meet the speakers at a different entrance
(B) Pick up some informational pamphlets
(C) Save the speakers' seats in the auditorium
(D) Approve funds for a parking fee

번역 남자는 벤자민에게 무엇을 하라고 요청하겠는가?
(A) 화자들을 다른 출입구에서 만나기
(B) 정보가 담긴 소책자 가져오기
(C) 객석에 화자들의 자리 맡아두기
(D) 주차료를 위한 자금 승인하기

해설 **세부 사항 관련 - 남자가 벤자민에게 요청하는 것**
남자가 마지막 대사에서 자신이 벤자민에게 북문 말고 거기서 기다려달라고 문자하겠다(Then I'd better text Benjamin and ask him to wait for us there instead of at the north entrance)고 말하고 있으므로 정답은 (A)이다.

어휘 informational 정보를 담은 pamphlet 소책자 save a seat 자리를 맡다 auditorium 객석, 강당 approve 승인하다

> **Paraphrasing**
> 대화의 instead of at the north entrance
> → 정답의 at a different entrance

68-70 대화+쿠폰

W-Br Hello. **68 Some friends of mine are visiting from out of town next month and staying with me.** I'd like my backyard to look its best, so I need some fertilizer.

M-Au Alright. Do you have a preference for the brand?

W-Br **69 I'd like to try Hazel fertilizer, if you have it. Everyone says it's very effective.**

M-Au I was going to suggest that. Actually, I can give you a coupon for a discount on Hazel fertilizer. The more you buy, the more you'll save.

W-Br Thank you! OK, **70 I'll get a second bag.** Based on my yard's size, it doesn't make sense to get more than that.

여: 안녕하세요. **다음 달에 제 친구들 몇 명이 타 지역에서 방문해 우리 집에서 지낼 예정이에요.** 뒷마당을 최상의 상태로 보이고 싶어서 비료가 좀 필요해요.

남: 알겠습니다. 선호하시는 브랜드가 있나요?

여: 헤이즐 비료를 써보고 싶어요. 갖고 계신다면요. 다들 효과가 아주 좋다고 말하더라고요.

남: 그 제품을 추천하려던 참이었습니다. 실은 헤이즐 비료에 적용되는 할인 쿠폰을 드릴 수 있습니다. 더 많이 구매하실수록 더 많이 절약하실 수 있습니다.

여: 감사합니다! 좋습니다, **한 포대를 더 사겠습니다.** 제 마당 크기를 감안할 때 그 이상은 살 필요 없을 것 같아요.

어휘 look one's best 가장 좋게 보이다 fertilizer 비료 preference 선호 effective 효과적인 based on ~에 근거하여

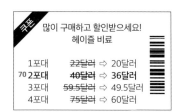

어휘 stock up 많이 사서 비축하다

68 What will the woman do next month?
(A) Start a different job
(B) Have some guests
(C) Move to a new home
(D) Teach a workshop

번역 여자는 다음 달에 무엇을 하겠는가?
(A) 새로운 일 시작하기
(B) 손님 맞이하기
(C) 새집으로 이사하기
(D) 워크숍에서 교육하기

해설 **세부 사항 관련 - 여자가 다음 달에 할 일**
여자가 첫 대사에서 다음 달에 친구들 몇 명이 타 지역에서 방문해 집에서 지낼 예정(Some friends of mine are visiting from out of town next month and staying with me)이라고 말하고 있으므로 정답은 (B)이다.

> **Paraphrasing**
> 대화의 Some friends of mine → 정답의 some guests

69 What does the woman say about Hazel fertilizer?
(A) It is often sold out.
(B) It has a good reputation.
(C) It has the cheapest price.
(D) It is environmentally friendly.

번역 여자는 헤이즐 비료에 대해 무엇을 말하는가?
(A) 자주 품절된다.
(B) 좋은 평판을 가지고 있다.
(C) 가장 저렴하다.
(D) 환경친화적이다.

해설 **세부 사항 관련 - 여자가 헤이즐 비료에 대해 언급하는 것**
여자가 두 번째 대사에서 헤이즐 비료를 써보고 싶다(I'd like to try Hazel fertilizer ~)면서 다들 효과가 아주 좋다고 말한다 (Everyone says it's very effective)고 했으므로 정답은 (B)이다.

어휘 sold out 품절된 reputation 평판 environmentally friendly 환경친화적인

> **Paraphrasing**
> 대화의 Everyone says it's very effective
> → 정답의 It has a good reputation.

70 Look at the graphic. How much will the woman pay?
(A) $20.00
(B) $36.00
(C) $49.50
(D) $60.00

번역 시각 정보에 의하면, 여자는 얼마를 내겠는가?
(A) 20달러
(B) 36달러
(C) 49.5달러
(D) 60달러

해설 **시각 정보 연계 - 여자의 지불 금액**
여자가 마지막 대사에서 한 포대를 더 사겠다(I'll get a second bag)고 말하고 있고, 쿠폰에 따르면 두 포대의 가격은 36달러이므로 정답은 (B)이다.

PART 4

71-73 광고

> M-Cn Are you looking for a way to reduce your stress and stay healthy? Working out is the key! **71 At Highland Gym, we have a wide variety of equipment and classes to suit everyone's interests and abilities.** And our friendly staff is always on hand to answer questions and show you how to use the machines. **72 We've recently extended our opening hours to make it even more convenient for our members.** And, **73 starting on November 3, we'll be building an addition that will house a pool and more class space!** Find out more about membership options by calling 555-0123. We hope to see you soon!

스트레스를 줄이고 건강을 유지하는 방법을 찾고 계십니까? 운동이 핵심입니다! 하일랜드 체육관에는 모든 분의 흥미와 능력에 맞출 수 있는 아주 다양한 장비와 수업이 있습니다. 그리고 친절한 저희 직원들이 항상 대기하며 질문에 답변해 드리고 기계를 어떻게 사용하는지 보여드립니다. 최근에는 회원 여러분이 훨씬 더 편리하게 이용하시도록 운영 시간도 연장했습니다. 더불어 11월 3일부터는 수영장과 더 많은 수업 공간을 추가할 수 있도록 증축 공사를 할 예정입니다! 555-0123으로 전화하셔서 회원권 종류에 대해 더 자세히 알아보세요. 곧 만나 뵙기를 희망합니다!

어휘 reduce 줄이다 work out 운동하다 a wide variety of 매우 다양한 equipment 장비 suit ~에게 편리하다, 맞다 ability 능력 on hand (사람이) 자리에 있는 extend 연장하다 convenient 편리한 build an addition 증축하다

71 What is the advertisement about?
(A) A pharmacy
(B) A dental clinic
(C) A fitness center
(D) A hotel

번역 무엇에 관한 광고인가?
(A) 약국
(B) 치과
(C) 피트니스 센터
(D) 호텔

해설 **전체 내용 관련 - 광고의 주제**
화자가 초반부에 하일랜드 체육관에는 모든 분의 흥미와 능력에 맞출 수 있는 아주 다양한 장비와 수업이 있다(At Highland Gym, we have a wide variety of equipment and classes to suit everyone's interests and abilities)고 말하고 있으므로 체육관을 광고하고 있다는 것을 알 수 있다. 따라서 정답은 (C)이다.

> **Paraphrasing**
> 담화의 Highland Gym → 정답의 A fitness center

72 What has the business recently changed?
(A) Its staff responsibilities
(B) Its standard fees
(C) Its cancellation policy
(D) Its hours of operation

번역 업체는 최근에 무엇을 바꿨는가?
(A) 직원의 책무
(B) 표준 요금
(C) 취소 정책
(D) 운영 시간

해설 **세부 사항 관련 - 업체가 최근에 바꾼 것**
화자가 중반부에 최근에는 운영 시간도 연장했다(We've recently extended our opening hours ~)고 했으므로 정답은 (D)이다.

어휘 responsibility 책임, 책무 standard 표준의 cancellation 취소 policy 정책 operation 운영

contribute 기여하다   goal 목표   unexpected 예기치
못한   pass out 배포하다   organizational chart
조직도   workload 업무량   assign 할당하다

73 What will happen on November 3 ?
(A) A construction project will begin.
(B) A prize drawing will be held.
(C) A newsletter will be sent.
(D) A new branch will open.

번역 11월 3일에 무슨 일이 일어나겠는가?
(A) 건설 공사가 시작될 것이다.
(B) 경품 추첨이 진행될 것이다.
(C) 뉴스레터가 전송될 것이다.
(D) 새 지점이 문을 열 것이다.

해설 **세부 사항 관련 - 11월 3일에 일어날 일**
화자가 후반부에 11월 3일부터는 수영장과 더 많은 수업 공간을 추
가할 수 있도록 증축 공사를 할 예정(starting on November 3,
we'll be building an addition that will house a pool and
more class space!)이라고 했으므로 정답은 (A)이다.

어휘 construction 건설   prize drawing 경품 추첨   branch 지점

> **Paraphrasing**
> 담화의 building an addition
> → 정답의 A construction project

74-76 회의 발췌

> W-Am **74 I called this meeting to finally discuss
> how we'll restructure some of the work teams
> here at the office.** As you know from my initial
> announcement of this plan, it's meant to help
> employees better use their talents to contribute
> to the company's goals. **75 I'm sorry that you've
> had to wait longer than planned for the details—
> I've had several unexpected visits from clients this
> week.** Uh, I'm passing out the new organizational
> chart now. **76 You'll notice that we plan to hire
> several more part-time workers, so that'll make it
> easier to finish the workload your team has been
> assigned.**

여기 사무실에서 일하는 팀들을 어떻게 개편할지 최종적으로 논의하고
자 본 회의를 소집했습니다. 이 계획에 대해 제가 최초로 공지한 내용을
기억하시겠지만, 이것은 직원들이 회사 목표에 기여하기 위해 각자의
재능을 좀 더 잘 사용할 수 있도록 돕기 위한 것입니다. **세부 사항을 알
려드리는 데 계획했던 것보다 더 오래 기다리시게 해서 죄송합니다. 이
번 주에 예기치 못한 고객 방문이 몇 건 있었어요.** 지금 새 조직도를 나
눠드릴게요. **시간제 직원을 몇 명 더 고용할 계획임을 보실 수 있을 거
예요. 이는 팀에 할당된 업무량을 더 쉽게 완료할 수 있도록 하기 위함
입니다.**

어휘 restructure 개편하다   initial 최초의   talent 재능

74 What is the speaker mainly discussing?
(A) Launching a product
(B) Relocating the office
(C) Attracting new clients
(D) Reorganizing some teams

번역 화자는 주로 무엇에 관해 이야기하는가?
(A) 제품 출시하기
(B) 사무실 이전하기
(C) 신규 고객 유치하기
(D) 팀 재편성하기

해설 **전체 내용 관련 - 담화의 주제**
화자가 도입부에 사무실에서 일하는 팀들을 어떻게 개편할지 최종
적으로 논의하고자 회의를 소집했다(I called this meeting to
finally discuss how we'll restructure some of the work
teams here at the office)고 말하는 것으로 보아 팀 개편에 대해
언급하고 있음을 알 수 있다. 따라서 정답은 (D)이다.

어휘 launch 출시하다   relocate 이전하다   attract 끌어모으다
reorganize 재편성하다

> **Paraphrasing**
> 담화의 restructure some of the work teams
> → 정답의 Reorganizing some teams

75 Why does the speaker say, "I've had several
unexpected visits from clients this week"?
(A) To issue an invitation
(B) To offer an excuse
(C) To express encouragement
(D) To request assistance

번역 화자가 "이번 주에 예기치 못한 고객 방문이 몇 건 있었어요"라고 말한
이유는?
(A) 초대장을 보내려고
(B) 변명을 하려고
(C) 격려를 표현하려고
(D) 도움을 요청하려고

해설 **화자의 의도 파악 - 이번 주에 예기치 못한 고객 방문이 몇 건
있었다는 말의 의도**
화자가 앞에서 세부 사항을 알려드리는 데 계획했던 것보다 더 오래
기다리시게 해서 죄송하다(I'm sorry that you've had to wait
longer than planned for the details)고 한 뒤 인용문을 언급한
것으로 보아, 세부 사항을 더 일찍 알려주지 못한 이유에 대해 변명을
하려는 의도로 한 말임을 알 수 있다. 따라서 정답은 (B)이다.

어휘 issue an invitation 초대장을 보내다   excuse 변명
encouragement 격려   assistance 도움

TEST 3

76 According to the speaker, what will become easier for employees?
(A) Communicating with colleagues
(B) Accessing a database
(C) Completing work assignments
(D) Receiving performance bonuses

번역 화자에 따르면, 직원들에게 무엇이 쉬워지겠는가?
(A) 동료와 소통하기
(B) 데이터베이스에 접속하기
(C) 배정된 업무 완료하기
(D) 성과급 받기

해설 **세부 사항 관련 - 직원들에게 쉬워지는 일**
화자가 후반부에 팀에 할당된 업무량을 더 쉽게 완료할 수 있도록 시간제 직원을 몇 명 더 고용할 계획임을 볼 수 있을 것(You'll notice that we plan to hire several more part-time workers, so that'll make it easier to finish the workload your team has been assigned)이라고 했으므로 정답은 (C)이다.

어휘 colleague 동료   access 접속하다   assignment 과제, 임무
performance bonus 성과급

> **Paraphrasing**
> 담화의 finish the workload your team has been assigned
> → 정답의 Completing work assignments

77-79 공지

M-Au Before we begin filming, I want to thank you all for agreeing to share the expertise you've gained **⁷⁷ during your time leading tours for our agency.** We are certain that **⁷⁸ this video featuring your expert advice for new guides** will be a valuable tool in our training program. Now, we're going to film you all having a lively discussion on the topic, hopefully to get a range of viewpoints. You can see the recording area set up here. **⁷⁹ You'll each wear a microphone that clips to your work vest. Why don't you pick those up now?** Michael has enough for everyone.

촬영을 시작하기 전에 **우리 여행사를 위해 투어를 인솔하는 동안** 습득한 전문 지식을 공유하는 데 동의해 주신 여러분 모두에게 감사의 말씀을 전합니다. **신입 가이드를 위한 전문적인 조언을 담은 이 영상은** 우리 교육 프로그램에서 귀중한 도구가 될 거라고 확신합니다. 자, 여러분이 이 주제에 대해 활기찬 토론을 하는 모습을 촬영하겠습니다. 다양한 관점을 얻을 수 있길 바라면서요. 녹화 구역은 여기에 설치되었습니다. **여러분 모두 작업 조끼에 끼우는 마이크를 착용하실 거예요. 지금 받으러 오시겠어요?** 마이클이 충분히 갖고 있어요.

어휘 film 촬영하다   expertise 전문 지식   gain 얻다   certain 확신하는   feature 특별히 포함하다   valuable 귀중한   tool 도구
lively 활기 넘치는   discussion 토론   a range of 다양한
viewpoint 관점   set up 설치하다   clip 클립으로 고정하다
vest 조끼

77 Where does the speaker most likely work?
(A) At a department store
(B) At a moving service
(C) At a tour company
(D) At a commercial airline

번역 화자는 어디서 일하겠는가?
(A) 백화점
(B) 이사업체
(C) 여행사
(D) 민간 항공사

해설 **전체 내용 관련 - 화자의 근무지**
화자가 도입부에 우리 여행사를 위해 투어를 인솔하는 동안(during your time leading tours for our agency)이라고 말하고 있으므로 화자는 여행사에서 근무하고 있음을 알 수 있다. 따라서 정답은 (C)이다.

어휘 commercial 상업적인

78 What will be the topic of the video?
(A) The history of the company
(B) Current sales territories
(C) Mandatory safety procedures
(D) Tips for new employees

번역 영상의 주제는 무엇이겠는가?
(A) 회사의 역사
(B) 현재 영업 구역
(C) 의무적인 안전 절차
(D) 신입 직원들을 위한 조언

해설 **세부 사항 관련 - 영상의 주제**
화자가 중반부에 신입 가이드를 위한 전문적인 조언을 담은 이 영상(this video featuring your expert advice for new guides)이라고 했으므로 정답은 (D)이다.

어휘 territory 영역, 구역   mandatory 의무적인   safety procedure 안전 절차

> **Paraphrasing**
> 담화의 advice for new guides
> → 정답의 Tips for new employees

79 What will the listeners probably do next?
(A) Watch a demonstration
(B) Pick up some equipment
(C) Read a script
(D) Set up some tables

번역 청자들은 다음으로 무엇을 하겠는가?
(A) 시연 보기
(B) 장비 가져오기
(C) 대본 읽기
(D) 테이블 설치하기

해설 **세부 사항 관련 - 청자들이 다음에 할 일**
화자가 후반부에 여러분 모두 작업 조끼에 끼우는 마이크를 착용할 것 (You'll each wear a microphone that clips to your work vest)이라면서 지금 받아 올 것(Why don't you pick those up now?)을 요청하고 있으므로 정답은 (B)이다.

어휘 demonstration 시연, 시범 설명   script 대본

> **Paraphrasing**
> 담화의 a microphone → 정답의 some equipment

80-82 공지

W-Am Good evening, and thanks for coming to this fundraising dinner. **80 There were supposed to be name cards at the tables, but** the print shop used the wrong address. I hope our staff helped you to find your assigned seats. **81 We had put a lot of thought into the seating plan.** Anyway, we're very thankful for the support you've given to the restoration project at the Kellerson Concert Hall. **82 I'd like to give a special thanks to Stephanie Avera, who conducted all of the research** about the building's original condition and style. More information about that is on our Web site.

좋은 저녁입니다. 그리고 본 기금 모금 만찬에 와주셔서 감사합니다. **테이블에 이름표가 준비될 예정이었습니다만,** 인쇄소에서 주소를 잘못 썼어요. 저희 직원들이 여러분의 지정 좌석을 찾는 일을 잘 도와드렸기를 바랍니다. **좌석 배치에 상당히 신경을 썼거든요.** 어쨌든 켈러슨 콘서트홀 복원 프로젝트에 여러분이 보내주신 성원에 정말 감사드립니다. 건물의 원래 상태와 양식에 대한 **조사를 전담해 주신 스테퍼니 애버라에게 특별히 감사드리고 싶습니다.** 그것에 대한 더 많은 정보는 저희 웹사이트에 있습니다.

어휘 fundraising 모금 활동   print shop 인쇄소   assigned 할당된   seating plan 좌석 배치   restoration 복원   conduct 실시하다   condition 상태

80 Why does the speaker say, "the print shop used the wrong address"?
(A) To ask for some suggestions
(B) To apologize for a delay
(C) To recommend canceling a contract
(D) To explain some missing items

번역 화자가 "인쇄소에서 주소를 잘못 썼어요"라고 말한 이유는?
(A) 제안을 부탁하려고
(B) 지연에 대해 사과하려고
(C) 계약 취소를 권고하려고
(D) 빠진 물품에 대해 설명하려고

해설 **화자의 의도 파악 - 인쇄소에서 주소를 잘못 썼다는 말의 의도**
화자가 초반부에 테이블에 이름표가 준비될 예정이었지만(There were supposed to be name cards at the tables, but ~)이라고 말한 뒤, 인용문을 언급하고 있으므로 테이블에 이름표가 빠진 것

에 대해 설명하려는 의도로 한 말임을 알 수 있다. 따라서 정답은 (D)이다.

어휘 suggestion 제안   apologize 사과하다   delay 지연   missing 없어진, 빠진

> **Paraphrasing**
> 담화의 name cards → 정답의 items

81 What does the speaker say about the seating plan?
(A) It does not need to be followed.
(B) It was carefully considered.
(C) It is the same every year.
(D) It had guests added to it.

번역 화자는 좌석 배치도에 대해 무엇을 말하는가?
(A) 따를 필요는 없다.
(B) 신중하게 고려되었다.
(C) 매년 똑같다.
(D) 손님이 추가되었다.

해설 **세부 사항 관련 - 화자가 좌석 배치에 대해 언급하는 것**
화자가 중반부에 좌석 배치도에 상당히 신경을 썼다(We had put a lot of thought into the seating plan)고 말하고 있으므로 정답은 (B)이다.

어휘 carefully 주의 깊게   consider 고려하다   add 추가하다

> **Paraphrasing**
> 담화의 We had put a lot of thought into ~
> → 정답의 It was carefully considered.

82 Who does the speaker give a special thanks to?
(A) A singer
(B) A designer
(C) A researcher
(D) A building manager

번역 화자는 누구에게 특별히 감사하는가?
(A) 가수
(B) 디자이너
(C) 조사원
(D) 건물 관리자

해설 **세부 사항 관련 - 화자가 특별히 감사해 하는 사람**
화자가 후반부에 조사를 전담한 스테퍼니 애버라에게 특별히 감사드리고 싶다(I'd like to give a special thanks to Stephanie Avera, who conducted all of the research)고 말하고 있으므로 정답은 (C)이다.

> **Paraphrasing**
> 담화의 who conducted all of the research
> → 정답의 A researcher

83-85 전화 메시지

M-Au Hi, Carolyn, this is Logan from the Exeter Gallery. First, **83 I'd like to tell you how excited I am that your exhibition is going so well. In fact, it's been our most-visited event ever. Congratulations!** We'd like to extend the duration of the exhibition for another month. **84 Since photos of your work will appear in *Art World Magazine* in July,** I think even more people will be interested in it after that. When you have time, **85 you should visit the testimonials page of our Web site. I think you'll enjoy seeing the positive comments people are leaving about your work.**

안녕하세요, 캐럴린, 저는 엑서터 화랑의 로건입니다. 먼저, 당신의 전시회가 잘되고 있어서 제가 얼마나 기쁜지 말씀드리고 싶습니다. 실은 여태껏 한 행사 중에 가장 많은 사람들이 방문한 행사가 되었습니다. 축하드립니다! 전시회 기간을 한 달 더 연장해 드리고 싶습니다. 당신의 작품 사진이 7월 〈아트 월드 매거진〉에 나올 예정이기 때문에 그 후에는 훨씬 더 많은 사람이 관심을 보일 거라고 생각합니다. 시간이 있으실 때 저희 웹사이트의 추천 후기 페이지를 꼭 방문해 보세요. 당신의 작품에 대해 사람들이 남기는 긍정적인 의견을 보시면 좋을 것 같습니다.

어휘 exhibition 전시회 most-visited 가장 많이 방문하는 congratulations 축하합니다 extend 연장하다 duration 기간 appear 나타나다, 나오다 testimonial 추천서, 추천의 글 positive 긍정적인 comment 논평, 견해

83 What does the speaker congratulate the listener for?
(A) She was given an award.
(B) She opened her own gallery.
(C) Her paintings are selling quickly.
(D) Her exhibition has been popular.

번역 화자는 무엇에 대해 청자를 축하하는가?
(A) 상을 받아서
(B) 개인 화랑을 개관해서
(C) 그림이 잘 팔리고 있어서
(D) 전시회가 인기가 많아서

해설 **세부 사항 관련 - 화자가 청자에 대해 축하하는 것**
화자가 초반부에 청자의 전시회가 잘되고 있어서 기쁘다(I'd like to tell you how excited I am that your exhibition is going so well)면서 여태껏 한 행사 중에 가장 많은 사람들이 방문한 행사가 되었다(In fact, it's been our most-visited event ever)고 말한 뒤 축하한다(Congratulations!)고 했으므로 정답은 (D)이다.

어휘 congratulate 축하하다 popular 인기 있는

> **Paraphrasing**
> 담화의 most-visited → 정답의 popular

84 According to the speaker, what will happen in July?
(A) A museum will shut down.
(B) Copies of some artwork will go on sale.
(C) Some art will be featured in a magazine.
(D) A television interview will take place.

번역 화자에 따르면, 7월에 무슨 일이 일어나겠는가?
(A) 미술관이 문을 닫을 것이다.
(B) 일부 미술품의 사본이 판매될 것이다.
(C) 일부 작품이 잡지에 소개될 것이다.
(D) TV 인터뷰가 진행될 것이다.

해설 **세부 사항 관련 - 7월에 있을 일**
화자가 중반부에 청자의 작품 사진이 7월 〈아트 월드 매거진〉에 나올 예정이기 때문(Since photos of your work will appear in *Art World Magazine* in July)이라고 말하고 있으므로 정답은 (C)이다.

어휘 shut down 문을 닫다 take place 일어나다, 발생하다

> **Paraphrasing**
> 담화의 photos of your work will appear in *Art World Magazine*
> → 정답의 Some art will be featured in a magazine.

85 Why should the listener visit a Web site?
(A) To register for an event
(B) To read some comments
(C) To upload some photographs
(D) To join a mailing list

번역 청자는 왜 웹사이트에 방문해야 하는가?
(A) 행사에 등록하려고
(B) 의견을 읽으려고
(C) 사진을 업로드하려고
(D) 메일링 리스트에 가입하려고

해설 **세부 사항 관련 - 청자가 웹사이트에 방문해야 하는 이유**
화자가 마지막에 웹사이트의 추천 후기 페이지를 꼭 방문할 것(you should visit the testimonials page of our Web site)을 권하면서 청자의 작품에 대해 사람들이 남기는 긍정적인 의견을 보면 좋을 것 같다(I think you'll enjoy seeing the positive comments people are leaving about your work)고 말하고 있으므로 정답은 (B)이다.

어휘 register for ~에 등록하다

> **Paraphrasing**
> 담화의 seeing the positive comments
> → 정답의 read some comments

86-88 방송

W-Br Good afternoon, and **86 thanks for listening to *Better Bodies*, the show that teaches you about taking good care of your health. 87 My guest today** is Dr. Max Ramirez, a food scientist working at the Kentwood Institute. He's just completed some fascinating research on almonds. **88 Did you know that eating almonds before bed helps you have better, more refreshing sleep?** We'll find out more about this and other discoveries from Dr. Ramirez's research. And we'll also be taking your questions live on the air. But first, let's have a message from our sponsor.

좋은 오후입니다. 건강을 잘 관리하는 방법을 알려드리는 프로그램인 〈베터 바디스〉를 청취해 주셔서 감사합니다. 오늘 모신 초대손님은 켄트우드 연구소에서 일하시는 식품 과학자 맥스 라미레스 박사입니다. 그는 최근에 아몬드에 관한 매우 흥미로운 연구를 마쳤습니다. **취침 전에 아몬드를 먹으면 더 잘, 더 개운하게 주무시는 데 도움이 된다는 사실을 아셨나요?** 이 내용과 더불어 라미레스 박사가 연구를 통해 발견한 다른 내용에 관해 더 알아보겠습니다. 그리고 생방송 중에 여러분의 질문도 받을 예정입니다. 하지만 먼저 광고 메시지부터 듣고 오겠습니다.

어휘 take good care of ~을 잘 관리하다   food scientist 식품 과학자   institute 연구소   fascinating 매우 흥미로운   refreshing 상쾌하게 하는   discovery 발견   sponsor 광고주, 후원자

86 Where does the speaker most likely work?
(A) At a research institute
(B) At a radio station
(C) At a manufacturing plant
(D) At a grocery store

번역 화자는 어디서 일하겠는가?
(A) 연구소
(B) 라디오 방송국
(C) 제조 공장
(D) 식료품점

해설 전체 내용 관련 - 화자의 근무지
화자가 초반부에 건강을 잘 관리하는 방법을 알려주는 프로그램인 〈베터 바디스〉를 청취해 주셔서 감사하다(thanks for listening to *Better Bodies*, the show that teaches you about taking good care of your health)고 말하는 것으로 보아 화자는 라디오 방송국에서 근무하고 있음을 알 수 있다. 따라서 정답은 (B)이다.

87 What does Dr. Ramirez specialize in?
(A) Hospital management
(B) Audio production
(C) Mechanical engineering
(D) Food science

번역 라미레스 박사의 전문 분야는 무엇인가?
(A) 병원 경영
(B) 오디오 제작
(C) 기계 공학
(D) 식품 과학

해설 세부 사항 관련 - 라미레스 박사의 전문 분야

화자가 초반부에 오늘의 초대손님은 식품 과학자 맥스 라미레스 박사(My guest today is Dr. Max Ramirez, a food scientist ~)라고 했으므로 정답은 (D)이다.

어휘 management 경영, 관리   production 제작

---

88 What benefit of an item is mentioned?
(A) It enables people to concentrate better.
(B) It helps with weight loss efforts.
(C) It can be stored for a long time.
(D) It improves the quality of people's sleep.

번역 식품의 이점으로 언급된 것은?
(A) 사람들이 더 잘 집중하게 해준다.
(B) 체중 감소를 도와준다.
(C) 오랫동안 보관될 수 있다.
(D) 사람들의 수면의 질을 향상시켜 준다.

해설 세부 사항 관련 - 식품의 이점으로 언급된 것
화자가 중반부에 취침 전에 아몬드를 먹으면 더 잘, 더 개운하게 자는 데 도움이 된다는 사실을 아는지(Did you know that eating almonds before bed helps you have better, more refreshing sleep?) 묻고 있으므로 정답은 (D)이다.

어휘 concentrate 집중하다   effort 노력   improve 향상시키다   quality 품질

> **Paraphrasing**
> 담화의 have better, more refreshing sleep
> → 정답의 improves the quality of people's sleep

89-91 회의 발췌

M-Au Let's get started, everyone. First, I'd like to report on sales of our newest wireless headphones, the BP-90. I've just reviewed the market analysis, and **89 these headphones were the top seller in their category last month. We've never done this before. 89 You should all be very proud.** This is great timing because **90 representatives from the Landry Group are visiting our offices next Monday. Their investment is essential to our operations,** so we want to make a good impression. So, before you leave on Friday, **91 don't forget to make sure your desk and cubicle are tidy.**

시작합시다, 여러분. 먼저, 가장 최신 제품인 무선 헤드폰 BP-90 판매량에 대해 보고드리고 싶습니다. 방금 시장 분석을 훑어봤는데요. **이 헤드폰은 지난달 해당 카테고리에서 가장 잘 팔리는 모델이었어요. 우리에게는 처음 있는 일이에요. 여러분 모두 자부심을 가지셔야 합니다.** 이것은 아주 좋은 타이밍이에요. 다음 주 월요일에 랜드리 그룹 대표단이 우리 사무실을 방문할 예정이니까요. 그들의 투자는 우리 회사 운영에 매우 중요하니 좋은 인상을 주어야 합니다. 그러니 금요일에 퇴근하기 전에 여러분의 책상과 자리를 잘 정돈하는 걸 잊지 마세요.

어휘   report 보고하다   analysis 분석   top seller 가장 잘 팔리는 상품   representative 대표   investment 투자   essential 매우 중요한   operation 운영   impression 인상   cubicle 칸막이로 구획된 사무 공간   tidy 잘 정돈된

89 What does the speaker mean when he says, "We've never done this before"?
(A) He can explain an error.
(B) He wants to adjust a schedule.
(C) He is nervous about a plan.
(D) He is praising an accomplishment.

번역   화자가 "우리에게는 처음 있는 일이에요"라고 말할 때, 그 의도는 무엇인가?
(A) 오류를 설명할 수 있다.
(B) 일정을 조정하기를 원한다.
(C) 계획에 대해 불안해한다.
(D) 업적을 칭찬하고 있다.

해설   **화자의 의도 파악 - 우리에게는 처음 있는 일이라는 말의 의도**
앞에서 이 헤드폰은 지난달 해당 카테고리에서 가장 잘 팔리는 모델이었다(these headphones were the top seller in their category last month)고 말한 뒤 인용문을 언급하였고, 이어서 여러분 모두 자부심을 가져야 한다(You should all be very proud)고 덧붙여 말하는 것으로 보아 직원들의 헤드폰 판매 업적을 칭찬하려는 의도로 한 말임을 알 수 있다. 따라서 정답은 (D)이다.

어휘   adjust 조정하다   nervous 불안한   praise 칭찬하다   accomplishment 업적

90 What will happen at the company next Monday?
(A) Some investors will visit.
(B) A new executive will be hired.
(C) Some training sessions will take place.
(D) A promotion will be announced.

번역   다음 주 월요일에 회사에 무슨 일이 일어나겠는가?
(A) 투자자들이 방문할 것이다.
(B) 새로운 임원이 고용될 것이다.
(C) 교육 과정이 진행될 것이다.
(D) 승진이 발표될 것이다.

해설   **세부 사항 관련 - 다음 주 월요일에 회사에 있을 일**
화자가 중반부에 다음 주 월요일에 랜드리 그룹 대표단이 우리 사무실을 방문할 예정(~ representatives from the Landry Group are visiting our offices next Monday)이라고 하면서 그들의 투자는 우리 회사 운영에 매우 중요하다(Their investment is essential to our operations)고 말하고 있으므로 정답은 (A)이다.

어휘   investor 투자자   executive 임원, 중역   promotion 승진

91 What does the speaker remind the listeners to do?
(A) Stay within a budget
(B) Review some job duties
(C) Clean up a workspace
(D) Use a sign-up sheet

번역   화자는 청자들에게 무엇을 하라고 상기시키는가?
(A) 예산 초과하지 않기
(B) 업무 분장 살펴보기
(C) 작업 공간 깨끗이 치우기
(D) 참가 신청서 사용하기

해설   **세부 사항 관련 - 청자들에게 상기시키는 것**
화자가 마지막에 책상과 자리를 잘 정돈하는 걸 잊지 말 것(don't forget to make sure your desk and cubicle are tidy)을 상기시키고 있으므로 정답은 (C)이다.

어휘   stay within a budget 예산을 초과하지 않다   duty 업무, 임무   workspace 작업 공간   sign-up sheet 참가 신청서

> **Paraphrasing**
> 담화의 make sure your desk and cubicle are tidy
> → 정답의 Clean up a workspace

92-94 안내

W-Br   **92 It's my pleasure to welcome you all to this dinner commemorating our twenty-fifth year in business.** This is a big milestone for our law firm, and we continue to look for ways to grow and improve for the next twenty-five years. **93 I would especially like to thank Kevin Diaz, the head of our IT department, who upgraded the security on our computers and other systems** to ensure that our clients' confidential documents would remain safe. This helped to attract several major clients. **94 We'll highlight other staff members' contributions throughout the night, but first, let's enjoy the delicious dishes that will be coming out shortly.**

우리 회사의 창립 25주년을 기념하기 위한 오늘 만찬에 와주신 여러분들을 환영하게 되어 기쁩니다. 우리 법률 사무소로서는 매우 뜻깊은 날입니다. 다음 25년을 위해 성장하고 향상할 방법을 계속 모색하겠습니다. 우리 고객의 기밀문서가 안전하게 보관될 수 있도록 **우리들의 컴퓨터 및 여러 시스템의 보안을 업그레이드 해주신 IT 부서장 케빈 디아스에게 특별히 감사를 표하고 싶습니다.** 그 덕분에 중요 고객을 몇 명 더 유치할 수 있었습니다. **오늘 밤 내내 다른 직원들의 공헌에 대해 강조하겠지만, 우선 곧 나올 맛있는 요리를 즐겨 봅시다.**

어휘   commemorate 기념하다   in business 영업 중인   milestone 중요한 단계나 사건   grow 성장하다   improve 향상시키다   security 보안   confidential 기밀의   attract 유치하다, 끌어모으다   highlight 강조하다   contribution 공헌, 기여

92 Why is the company holding an event?
(A) To celebrate an anniversary
(B) To promote a new product
(C) To welcome new employees
(D) To congratulate a department

번역 회사는 왜 행사를 개최하고 있는가?
(A) 기념일을 축하하려고
(B) 신상품을 홍보하려고
(C) 신입 직원을 환영하려고
(D) 부서를 축하하려고

해설 **세부 사항 관련 - 회사가 행사를 개최하는 이유**
화자가 도입부에 우리들의 창립 25주년을 기념하기 위한 오늘 만찬에 와주신 여러분들을 환영하게 되어 기쁘다(It's my pleasure to welcome you all to this dinner commemorating our twenty-fifth year in business)고 말하고 있으므로 정답은 (A)이다.

어휘 celebrate 축하하다, 기념하다 anniversary 기념일 promote 홍보하다 congratulate 축하하다

> **Paraphrasing**
> 담화의 commemorating our twenty-fifth year
> → 정답의 celebrate an anniversary

93 What does the speaker say about Mr. Diaz?
(A) He designed a training program.
(B) He oversaw a company expansion.
(C) He improved some security measures.
(D) He negotiated an important contract.

번역 화자는 디아스 씨에 대해 무엇을 말하는가?
(A) 교육 프로그램을 설계했다.
(B) 회사 확장을 감독했다.
(C) 보안 조치를 향상시켰다.
(D) 중요한 계약을 협상했다.

해설 **세부 사항 관련 - 디아스 씨에 대해 언급하는 것**
화자가 중반부에 우리들의 컴퓨터 및 여러 시스템의 보안을 업그레이드 해준 IT 부서장 케빈 디아스(Kevin Diaz, the head of our IT department, who upgraded the security on our computers and other systems)라고 말하고 있으므로 정답은 (C)이다.

어휘 oversee 감독하다 expansion 확장 measure 조치 negotiate 협상하다

> **Paraphrasing**
> 담화의 upgraded the security on our computers and other systems
> → 정답의 improved some security measures

94 According to the speaker, what will happen after a meal is served?
(A) A group photo will be taken.
(B) A series of videos will be shown.
(C) Other workers will be recognized.
(D) Messages from clients will be read.

번역 화자에 따르면, 식사가 제공된 후에 무슨 일이 일어나겠는가?
(A) 단체 사진을 찍을 것이다.
(B) 일련의 영상물을 보여줄 것이다.
(C) 다른 직원들의 공로가 인정받을 것이다.
(D) 고객으로부터 온 메시지를 읽을 것이다.

해설 **세부 사항 관련 - 식사가 제공된 후에 일어날 일**
화자가 마지막에 오늘 밤 내내 다른 직원들의 공헌에 대해 강조하겠지만, 우선 곧 나올 맛있는 요리를 즐기자(We'll highlight other staff members' contributions throughout the night, but first, let's enjoy the delicious dishes that will be coming out shortly)고 말하고 있으므로 정답은 (C)이다.

어휘 recognize (공로를) 인정하다

> **Paraphrasing**
> 담화의 We'll highlight other staff members' contributions
> → 정답의 Other workers will be recognized.

95-97 담화+지도

M-Cn I'd like to thank you once again for participating in this tour of the National Aviation Museum. **[95]I apologize that the tour did not include seeing the accessories worn by pilots. Unfortunately, that area will be closed for about ten days while some display cases are being replaced.** If you have time after this tour, **[96]I highly recommend going to the two o'clock lecture.** It's in our event room, right next to the gift shop. There, **[97]Celia Watson, a photographer for the journal *Flight Monthly*, will be discussing her collection of photos of historical planes.**

국립 항공 박물관 견학에 참여해 주셔서 다시 한번 감사드립니다. **본 견학에는 조종사들이 착용했던 액세서리를 보는 것은 포함되어 있지 않다는 점 사과드립니다. 안타깝게도, 그 구역은 진열장을 교체하는 동안 약 10일간 폐쇄될 예정입니다.** 본 견학이 끝난 후에 시간이 있으시다면, **2시에 하는 강연에 참석하실 것을 강력히 추천합니다.** 강연은 기념품 매장 바로 옆에 있는 행사실에서 열립니다. 그곳에서 **잡지 〈플라이트 먼슬리〉의 사진작가인 실리아 왓슨이 그동안 수집해 온 역사적인 항공기 사진들에 대해 이야기할 예정입니다.**

어휘 participate in ~에 참가하다 display case 진열장 replace 교체하다 lecture 강연 gift shop 기념품 매장 photographer 사진작가 journal 잡지 collection 수집품 historical 역사적인

	North Wing: Early Flights	
[95]West Wing: Pilot Accessories	Main Hall: Model Airplanes	East Wing: The Jet Age
Event Room	Gift Shop	Entrance

	북관: 초창기 비행	
95서관: 조종사 액세서리	본관: 모형 항공기	동관: 제트기 시대
행사실	기념품 매장	출입구

어휘 wing 부속 건물

95
Look at the graphic. Which area is temporarily closed?
(A) The East Wing
(B) The West Wing
(C) The North Wing
(D) The Main Hall

번역 시각 정보에 의하면, 어느 구역이 일시적으로 폐쇄되었는가?
(A) 동관
(B) 서관
(C) 북관
(D) 본관

해설 **시각 정보 연계 - 일시적으로 폐쇄된 구역**
화자가 초반부에 본 견학에는 조종사들이 착용했던 액세서리를 보는 것은 포함되어 있지 않다는 점 사과드린다(I apologize that the tour did not include seeing the accessories worn by pilots)며 교체 작업 때문에 그 구역이 10일간 폐쇄될 예정(~, that area will be closed for about ten days ~)이라고 말하고 있고, 지도에 따르면 조종사 액세서리는 서관 구역이므로 정답은 (B)이다.

> **Paraphrasing**
> 담화의 will be closed for about ten days
> → 질문의 is temporarily closed

96
What does the speaker suggest doing?
(A) Keeping a receipt
(B) Visiting a gift shop
(C) Attending a talk
(D) Taking a brochure

번역 화자는 무엇을 제안하는가?
(A) 영수증 보관하기
(B) 기념품 매장 방문하기
(C) 강연에 참석하기
(D) 안내 책자 받아 가기

해설 **세부 사항 관련 - 화자의 제안 사항**
화자가 중반부에 2시에 하는 강연에 참석할 것을 강력히 추천한다(I highly recommend going to the two o'clock lecture)고 했으므로 정답은 (C)이다.

어휘 attend 참석하다 brochure 안내 책자

> **Paraphrasing**
> 담화의 recommend → 질문의 suggest
> 담화의 going to the two o'clock lecture
> → 정답의 Attending a talk

97
Who is Celia Watson?
(A) A professional photographer
(B) A history professor
(C) A film director
(D) A commercial pilot

번역 실리아 왓슨은 누구인가?
(A) 전문 사진작가
(B) 역사학 교수
(C) 영화감독
(D) 민항기 조종사

해설 **세부 사항 관련 - 실리아 왓슨의 직업**
화자가 후반부에 잡지 〈플라이트 먼슬리〉의 사진작가인 실리아 왓슨이 그동안 수집해 온 역사적인 항공기 사진들에 대해 이야기할 예정(Celia Watson, a photographer for the journal *Flight Monthly*, will be discussing her collection of photos of historical planes)이라고 했으므로 정답은 (A)이다.

어휘 professor 교수 commercial 상업적인

98-100 전화 메시지+달력

W-Am Hi, Mr. Davis. It's Lacy. I wanted to give you an update on your appearance on the *Entertainment Daily* TV show. **98 I've scheduled it for the day before your preview screening.** That way, you'll be able to promote both the film and that event during the interview. I've also proofread and fact-checked your speech for the awards banquet in New York. **99 There are a few things that I think should be revised, so I'll send you my notes about those later.** I've reserved a room for you in New York, but **100 I wasn't able to get your first choice of hotel. Unfortunately, there were no rooms available for that night.**

안녕하세요, 데이비스 씨. 레이시입니다. 〈엔터테인먼트 데일리〉 TV 프로그램 출연 관련 추가 내용을 알려드리려고요. **당신의 사전 시사회 하루 전날로 출연 일정을 잡았습니다.** 그러면 인터뷰 동안 영화와 행사를 둘 다 홍보하실 수 있으니까요. 또 뉴욕에서 열릴 시상식 연회에서 당신이 발표할 연설문의 교정 작업과 사실 확인도 했습니다. **제가 생각하기에 수정되어야 할 부분이 몇 가지 있어서 그것에 대해 제가 메모한 내용을 나중에 보내드리겠습니다.** 뉴욕에서 당신이 머물 방을 예약했습니다만, 당신이 첫 번째로 선택한 호텔은 잡을 수 없었어요. 아쉽게도 그 날 밤에는 예약 가능한 방이 하나도 없었어요.

어휘 appearance 출연 preview screening 사전 시사회 promote 홍보하다 proofread 교정을 보다 fact-check 사실 여부를 확인하다 speech 연설 awards banquet 시상식 연회 revise 수정하다 reserve 예약하다 available 이용 가능한

OCTOBER

4	5	6
Magazine Photo Shoot		98 Preview Screening
7	**8**	**9**
	Awards Banquet	

10월

4	5	6
잡지 사진 촬영		98 사전 시사회
7	**8**	**9**
	시상식 연회	

98 Look at the graphic. For which day has the speaker scheduled a television appearance?
(A) October 4
(B) October 5
(C) October 6
(D) October 7

번역 시각 정보에 의하면, 화자는 어느 날짜에 TV 출연 일정을 잡았는가?
(A) 10월 4일
(B) 10월 5일
(C) 10월 6일
(D) 10월 7일

해설 **시각 정보 연계 - 화자가 TV 출연 일정을 잡은 날짜**
화자가 중반부에 당신의 사전 시사회 하루 전날로 출연 일정을 잡았다(I've scheduled it for the day before your preview screening)고 했으며, 달력에 따르면 사전 시사회가 10월 6일에 예정되어 있으므로 정답은 (B)이다.

99 What does the speaker say she will send?
(A) Suggestions for revisions
(B) Some driving directions
(C) A confirmation number
(D) A guest list

번역 화자는 무엇을 보내겠다고 말하는가?
(A) 수정 제안
(B) 운전 길 안내
(C) 예약 확인 번호
(D) 손님 명단

해설 **세부 사항 관련 - 화자가 보낼 것**
화자가 중반부에 수정되어야 할 부분이 몇 가지 있어서 그것에 대해 메모한 내용을 나중에 보내주겠다(There are a few things that I think should be revised, so I'll send you my notes about those later)고 했으므로 정답은 (A)이다.

어휘 suggestion 제안 revision 수정 direction 방향, 길 안내 confirmation 확인

100 What problem does the speaker mention?
(A) A hotel was fully booked.
(B) No direct flights were available.
(C) A fee has recently increased.
(D) A building is difficult to find.

번역 화자는 어떤 문제를 언급하는가?
(A) 호텔 예약이 꽉 찼다.
(B) 직항편을 예약할 수 없었다.
(C) 요금이 최근에 올랐다.
(D) 건물이 찾기가 어렵다.

해설 **세부 사항 관련 - 화자가 언급하는 문제**
화자가 마지막에 당신이 첫 번째로 선택한 호텔은 잡을 수 없었다(I wasn't able to get your first choice of hotel)면서 아쉽게도 그날 밤에는 예약 가능한 방이 하나도 없었다(Unfortunately, there were no rooms available for that night)고 했으므로 정답은 (A)이다.

어휘 fully booked 모두 예약된

> **Paraphrasing**
> 담화의 no rooms available → 정답의 fully booked

TEST 4

1 (B)	2 (D)	3 (C)	4 (D)	5 (A)
6 (B)	7 (C)	8 (A)	9 (C)	10 (B)
11 (A)	12 (C)	13 (A)	14 (B)	15 (C)
16 (B)	17 (A)	18 (C)	19 (B)	20 (A)
21 (B)	22 (B)	23 (B)	24 (B)	25 (A)
26 (A)	27 (B)	28 (C)	29 (A)	30 (C)
31 (C)	32 (A)	33 (C)	34 (D)	35 (D)
36 (C)	37 (A)	38 (B)	39 (B)	40 (C)
41 (D)	42 (A)	43 (C)	44 (D)	45 (B)
46 (A)	47 (B)	48 (A)	49 (B)	50 (A)
51 (B)	52 (C)	53 (A)	54 (B)	55 (D)
56 (B)	57 (D)	58 (D)	59 (C)	60 (D)
61 (A)	62 (A)	63 (D)	64 (C)	65 (B)
66 (D)	67 (A)	68 (A)	69 (C)	70 (B)
71 (C)	72 (A)	73 (C)	74 (B)	75 (D)
76 (D)	77 (D)	78 (D)	79 (C)	80 (C)
81 (C)	82 (B)	83 (B)	84 (C)	85 (A)
86 (C)	87 (A)	88 (C)	89 (B)	90 (A)
91 (C)	92 (A)	93 (D)	94 (D)	95 (D)
96 (C)	97 (A)	98 (B)	99 (C)	100 (B)

PART 1

1

W-Br

(A) She's putting on a pair of gloves.
(B) She's harvesting some fruit.
(C) She's holding a basket full of soil.
(D) She's watering some plants.

번역 (A) 여자가 장갑을 끼는 중이다.
(B) 여자가 과일을 수확하고 있다.
(C) 여자가 흙이 가득 담긴 바구니를 들고 있다.
(D) 여자가 식물에 물을 주고 있다.

해설 **1인 등장 사진**
(A) 동사 오답. 여자가 장갑을 착용한(wearing) 상태이지 장갑을 끼고 있는(putting on) 동작의 모습은 아니다.
(B) 정답. 여자가 과일을 수확하고 있으므로 정답이다.
(C) 동사 오답. 여자가 바구니를 들고 있는 모습이 아니다.
(D) 동사 오답. 여자가 식물에 물을 주고 있는 모습이 아니다.

어휘 harvest 수확하다 water 물을 주다

2

W-Am

(A) The man is connecting some sound equipment.
(B) The man is playing a musical instrument.
(C) The man is adjusting his headphones.
(D) The man is singing into a microphone.

번역 (A) 남자가 음향 장비를 연결하고 있다.
(B) 남자가 악기를 연주하고 있다.
(C) 남자가 헤드폰을 조절하고 있다.
(D) 남자가 마이크에 대고 노래하고 있다.

해설 **1인 등장 사진**
(A) 동사 오답. 남자가 음향 장비를 연결하고 있는 모습이 아니다.
(B) 동사 오답. 남자가 악기를 연주하고 있는 모습이 아니다.
(C) 동사 오답. 남자가 헤드폰을 조절하고 있는 모습이 아니다.
(D) 정답. 남자가 마이크에 대고 노래하고 있으므로 정답이다.

어휘 connect 연결하다 sound equipment 음향 장비
musical instrument 악기 adjust 조정하다, 정돈하다

3

M-Au

(A) Trees are being planted next to a waterway.
(B) The people are using exercise machines.
(C) There are skyscrapers in the distance.
(D) The woman is reaching down to tie her shoe.

번역 (A) 수로 옆에 나무들이 심어지고 있다.
(B) 사람들이 운동 기구를 사용하고 있다.
(C) 저 멀리 고층 건물이 있다.
(D) 여자가 운동화 끈을 매기 위해 손을 아래로 뻗고 있나.

해설 **사람/사물·풍경 혼합 사진**
(A) 동사 오답. 나무들이 심어지고 있는 모습이 아니다.
(B) 사진에 없는 명사. 사진에 운동 기구가 보이지 않는다.
(C) 정답. 저 멀리 고층 건물이 있으므로 정답이다.
(D) 동사 오답. 여자가 운동화 끈을 매기 위해 손을 아래로 뻗고 있는 모습이 아니다.

어휘 plant 심다 waterway 수로 exercise machine 운동 기구
skyscraper 고층 건물 in the distance 저 멀리 tie 매다, 묶다

4

W-Br

(A) Some outdoor steps are being swept.
(B) There are lamps on either side of a window.
(C) Some window ledges are decorated with flowerpots.
(D) Railings have been installed on a staircase.

번역 (A) 실외 계단이 청소되고 있다.
(B) 창문 양쪽에 전등이 있다.
(C) 창틀이 화분으로 장식되어 있다.
(D) 계단에 난간이 설치되어 있다.

해설 **사물·풍경 사진**
(A) 동사 오답. 실외 계단이 청소되고 있는 모습이 아니다.
(B) 위치 오답. 창문이 아닌 문 양쪽에 전등이 있으므로 오답이다.
(C) 동사 오답. 창틀이 화분으로 장식되어 있는 모습이 아니다.
(D) 정답. 계단에 난간이 설치되어 있으므로 정답이다.

어휘 sweep 쓸다, 청소하다 ledge 턱, 선반 decorate 장식하다
flowerpot 화분 railing 난간 install 설치하다
staircase 계단

5

M-Cn

(A) One of the women is carrying a handbag on her arm.
(B) One of the women is pressing a button on the wall.
(C) Some people are waiting for an elevator to arrive.
(D) The man is showing his mobile phone to the women.

번역 **(A) 여자들 중 한 명이 팔에 핸드백을 들고 있다.**
(B) 여자들 중 한 명이 벽에 있는 버튼을 누르고 있다.
(C) 사람들이 승강기가 오기를 기다리고 있다.
(D) 남자가 여자들에게 자신의 휴대 전화를 보여주고 있다.

해설 **2인 이상 등장 사진**
(A) 정답. 여자들 중 한 명이 팔에 핸드백을 들고 있으므로 정답이다.
(B) 동사 오답. 벽에 있는 버튼을 누르고 있는 여자의 모습이 보이지 않는다.
(C) 동사 오답. 승강기가 오기를 기다리고 있는 사람들의 모습이 보이지 않는다.
(D) 동사 오답. 남자가 여자들에게 자신의 휴대 전화를 보여주고 있는 모습이 아니다.

어휘 carry 나르다 press 누르다

6

M-Au

(A) Some people are lining up at a ticketing machine.
(B) Airline staff are greeting some passengers.
(C) A flight attendant is gesturing toward some curtains.
(D) Travelers are placing luggage in storage compartments.

번역 (A) 사람들이 자동발권기 앞에 줄을 서 있다.
(B) 항공사 직원들이 승객들을 맞이하고 있다.
(C) 한 승무원이 커튼 쪽을 가리키고 있다.
(D) 여행객들이 짐을 짐칸에 넣고 있다.

해설 **2인 이상 등장 사진**
(A) 사진에 없는 명사. 사진에 자동발권기가 보이지 않는다.
(B) 정답. 항공사 직원들이 승객들을 맞이하고 있으므로 정답이다.
(C) 동사 오답. 승무원이 커튼 쪽을 가리키고 있는 모습이 아니다.
(D) 동사 오답. 여행객들이 짐을 짐칸에 넣고 있는 모습이 아니다.

어휘 line up 줄을 서다 airline 항공사 greet 맞이하다, 환영하다
passenger 승객 flight attendant 승무원 gesture 몸짓으로
가리키다 storage compartment 짐칸

PART 2

7

M-Cn Who was invited to the press conference?
W-Br (A) I'd be happy to.
(B) An e-mail from the director.
(C) Everyone on this list.

번역 누가 기자 회견에 초대되었나요?
(A) 기꺼이 해드리겠습니다.
(B) 임원에게서 온 이메일이요.
(C) 이 명단에 있는 모든 사람이요.

해설 **Who 의문문**
(A) 질문과 상관없는 오답. 요청문에 대한 응답이므로 오답이다.
(B) 연상 오답. 질문의 Who에서 연상 가능한 director를 이용한 오답이다.
(C) 정답. 기자 회견에 누가 초대되었는지 묻는 질문에 이 명단에 있는 모든 사람이라고 구체적으로 알려 주고 있으므로 정답이다.

어휘 invite 초대하다 press conference 기자 회견 director 임원

8

M-Au Is Mr. Yagami thinking about moving the factory?
W-Am (A) Not that I'm aware of.
(B) Her truck is parked outside.
(C) The new manufacturing regulations.

번역 야가미 씨는 공장 이전에 대해 생각 중인가요?
(A) 제가 알기로는 그렇지 않은데요.
(B) 그녀의 트럭은 밖에 주차되어 있어요.
(C) 새 제조업 규제요.

해설 Be동사 의문문
(A) 정답. 야가미 씨가 공장 이전에 대해 생각 중인지 묻는 질문에 자신이 알기로는 그렇지 않다며 부정의 의사를 표현하고 있으므로 정답이다.
(B) 연상 오답. 질문의 moving에서 연상 가능한 truck을 이용한 오답이다.
(C) 연상 오답. 질문의 factory에서 연상 가능한 manufacturing을 이용한 오답이다.

어휘 not that I'm aware of 내가 알기로는 아니다
manufacturing 제조업   regulation 규제

9

W-Br When should I set the appetizers out?
M-Au (A) Sure, I'm starting to feel hungry.
(B) Where is the reset button?
(C) When most of the guests have arrived.

번역 전채 요리는 언제 차려야 하나요?
(A) 물론이죠, 저는 슬슬 배가 고파요.
(B) 리셋 버튼이 어디에 있나요?
(C) 대부분의 손님이 도착했을 때요.

해설 When 의문문
(A) Yes/No 불가 오답. When 의문문에는 Yes/No 응답이 불가능한데, Sure도 일종의 Yes 응답이라고 볼 수 있으므로 오답이다.
(B) 유사 발음 오답. 질문의 set과 부분적으로 발음이 유사한 reset을 이용한 오답이다.
(C) 정답. 전채 요리는 언제 차려야 하는지 묻는 질문에 대부분의 손님이 도착했을 때라고 구체적인 시기를 알려 주고 있으므로 정답이다.

어휘 set out ~을 진열하다   appetizer 전채 요리, 애피타이저
reset 재설정하다

10

W-Br Let's discuss what the consultant recommended.
M-Cn (A) It was very helpful, thanks.
(B) Do you have time right now?
(C) Along the hallway.

번역 컨설턴트가 추천한 것에 대해 의논해 봅시다.
(A) 매우 도움이 되었어요, 고마워요.
(B) 지금 시간 있으세요?
(C) 복도를 따라서 가세요.

해설 요청·제안문
(A) 연상 오답. 제안문의 consultant에서 연상 가능한 very helpful,

thanks를 이용한 오답이다.
(B) 정답. 컨설턴트가 추천한 것에 대해 의논하자는 제안에 대해 지금 시간 있는지 되물으면서 수락의 의사를 표현하고 있으므로 정답이다.
(C) 제안문과 상관없는 오답.

어휘 hallway 복도

11

W-Am Which training seminar is being held this afternoon?
M-Cn (A) I think it's "Basics of Tax Accounting."
(B) The training company has several instructors.
(C) No, in the conference room.

번역 오늘 오후에 어떤 교육 세미나가 열리나요?
(A) "세무 회계의 기초"일 거예요.
(B) 그 교육업체는 여러 명의 강사를 보유하고 있어요.
(C) 아니요, 회의실에서요.

해설 Which+명사 의문문
(A) 정답. 오후에 어떤 교육 세미나가 열리는지 묻는 질문에 "세무 회계의 기초"일 거라고 구체적으로 알려 주고 있으므로 정답이다.
(B) 단어 반복 오답. 질문의 training을 반복 이용한 오답이다.
(C) Yes/No 불가 오답. Which 의문문에는 Yes/No 응답이 불가능하므로 오답이다.

어휘 tax accounting 세무 회계   instructor 강사
conference room 회의실

12

M-Cn Why's the music in this store so loud?
M-Au (A) A collection of pop songs.
(B) OK, I'll turn them on.
(C) My manager controls the volume.

번역 이 가게의 음악 소리는 왜 이렇게 크죠?
(A) 팝송 모음이요.
(B) 알겠습니다, 제가 켜드리겠습니다.
(C) 제 관리자가 음량을 조절해요.

해설 Why 의문문
(A) 연상 오답. 질문의 music에서 연상 가능한 pop songs를 이용한 오답이다.
(B) Yes/No 불가 오답. Why 의문문에는 Yes/No 응답이 불가능한데, OK도 일종의 Yes 응답이라고 볼 수 있으므로 오답이다.
(C) 정답. 가게의 음악 소리가 크다고 불평하는 말에 관리자가 음량을 조절하므로 자신이 할 수 있는 것은 없다는 의미를 간접적으로 알려 주고 있으므로 정답이다.

어휘 loud 시끄러운   collection 모음   turn on 전원을 켜다

13

W-Am The clinic's busy today, isn't it?
M-Au (A) It certainly is.
(B) An appointment with Dr. Smith.
(C) No, my next shift is tomorrow.

번역 오늘 진료소가 붐비네요, 그렇지 않나요?
(A) 분명히 그렇네요.
(B) 스미스 박사와의 예약이요.
(C) 아니요, 제 다음 근무는 내일이에요.

해설 **부가 의문문**
(A) 정답. 오늘 진료소가 붐빈다며 동의를 구하는 질문에 분명히 그렇다며 긍정의 의사를 표현하고 있으므로 정답이다.
(B) 연상 오답. 질문의 clinic에서 연상 가능한 appointment를 이용한 오답이다.
(C) 연상 오답. 질문의 today에서 연상 가능한 tomorrow를 이용한 오답이다.

어휘 certainly 분명히 appointment 예약 shift 교대 근무

14

M-Au Why are you looking for a new apartment?
W-Br **(A) What neighborhood would you recommend?**
(B) Because my commute is terrible.
(C) On a television news program.

번역 왜 새 아파트를 구하고 있나요?
(A) 어느 동네를 추천하시나요?
(B) 통근이 너무 어려워서요.
(C) TV 뉴스 프로그램에서요.

해설 **Why 의문문**
(A) 연상 오답. 질문의 apartment에서 연상 가능한 neighborhood를 이용한 오답이다.
(B) 정답. 새 아파트를 구하는 이유를 묻는 질문에 통근이 너무 어려워서라고 구체적인 이유를 제시하고 있으므로 정답이다.
(C) 유사 발음 오답. 질문의 new와 부분적으로 발음이 유사한 news를 이용한 오답이다.

어휘 neighborhood 동네 commute 통근

15

W-Br When did your company update its logo design?
M-Cn (A) I've already signed the form.
(B) It looks like most dates are taken.
(C) After we expanded into electronics.

번역 당신 회사는 언제 로고 디자인을 갱신했나요?
(A) 저는 이미 그 양식에 서명했어요.
(B) 대부분의 날짜가 예약이 잡힌 것 같아요.
(C) 전자 제품까지 확장한 후에요.

해설 **When 의문문**
(A) 질문과 상관없는 오답.
(B) 유사 발음 오답. 질문의 update와 부분적으로 발음이 유사한 dates를 이용한 오답이다.
(C) 정답. 로고 디자인을 갱신한 시기를 묻는 질문에 전자 제품까지 확장한 후에라고 구체적으로 시기를 제시하고 있으므로 정답이다.

어휘 expand 확장하다 electronics 전자 제품

16

M-Cn Where are the workers taking those old files?
W-Am (A) No, they haven't.
(B) To a room in the basement.
(C) Sure, I can take a couple.

번역 작업자들이 저 오래된 파일들을 어디로 가져가고 있나요?
(A) 아니요, 그들은 가져가지 않았어요.
(B) 지하에 있는 방으로요.
(C) 물론이죠, 제가 두어 개 가져갈 수 있어요.

해설 **Where 의문문**
(A) Yes/No 불가 오답. Where 의문문에는 Yes/No 응답이 불가능하므로 오답이다.
(B) 정답. 오래된 파일들을 가져갈 장소를 묻는 질문에 지하에 있는 방이라고 구체적인 장소를 알려 주고 있으므로 정답이다.
(C) Yes/No 불가 오답. Where 의문문에는 Yes/No 응답이 불가능한데, Sure도 일종의 Yes 응답이라고 볼 수 있으므로 오답이다.

어휘 basement 지하층

17

M-Au You spelled my name incorrectly here.
W-Br **(A) Let me see your ID again.**
(B) There are paper towels in the cabinet.
(C) We checked the figures twice.

번역 여기 제 이름의 철자를 틀리게 쓰셨어요.
(A) 당신의 신분증을 다시 보여주세요.
(B) 수납장에 키친타월이 있어요.
(C) 우리는 수치를 두 번 확인했어요.

해설 **사실·정보 전달의 평서문**
(A) 정답. 이름의 철자를 틀리게 썼다는 평서문에 신분증을 다시 보여 줄 것을 요청하며 호응하고 있으므로 정답이다.
(B) 평서문과 상관없는 오답.
(C) 연상 오답. 평서문의 incorrectly에서 연상 가능한 checked를 이용한 오답이다.

어휘 spell 철자를 쓰다 incorrectly 부정확하게 cabinet 수납장
figure 수치

18

W-Am Won't you be conducting the interviews with us?
W-Br (A) No, I'd like a smaller one.
(B) Because she's an excellent candidate.
(C) I have an assignment due on Friday.

번역 당신은 우리와 함께 면접을 실시하지 않을 건가요?
(A) 아니요, 저는 더 작은 것이 좋아요.
(B) 그녀는 훌륭한 지원자니까요.
(C) 저는 금요일까지 해야 할 업무가 있어요.

해설 **부정 의문문**
(A) 질문과 상관없는 오답.
(B) 질문과 상관없는 오답. Why 의문문에 대한 응답이므로 오답이다.
(C) 정답. 함께 면접을 실시할 건지 여부를 확인하는 질문에 금요일까지 해야 할 업무가 있다며 아니요(No)를 생략한 부정 의사를 표현하고 있으므로 정답이다.

어휘 conduct 실시하다 excellent 훌륭한 candidate 지원자
assignment 과제, 임무 due ~하기로 되어 있는

19

W-Br You revised the employee handbook, didn't you?
M-Cn (A) A shipment of office supplies.
　　　(B) Yes, to reflect the new dress code.
　　　(C) Return them to their original locations.

번역 당신이 직원 안내서를 수정했죠, 그렇지 않나요?
　　　(A) 사무용품 배송이요.
　　　(B) 네, 새 복장 규정을 반영하려고요.
　　　(C) 그것들을 원래 자리에 갖다 놓으세요.

해설 **부가 의문문**
　　　(A) 연상 오답. 질문의 employee에서 연상 가능한 office를 이용한
　　　오답이다.
　　　(B) 정답. 직원 안내서를 수정했는지 확인하는 질문에 네(Yes)라고
　　　대답한 뒤, 새 복장 규정을 반영하려고 했다며 긍정 답변과 일관된
　　　내용을 덧붙였으므로 정답이다.
　　　(C) 연상 오답. 질문의 revised에서 연상 가능한 original을 이용한
　　　오답이다.

어휘 revise 수정하다 employee handbook 직원 안내서
shipment 배송 office supplies 사무용품 reflect 반영하다
dress code 복장 규정 original 원래의

20

W-Am Jin-Ah can help you plan the workshop.
M-Au (A) She's on vacation this week.
　　　(B) Yes, they're valuable skills.
　　　(C) Online shopping is easier.

번역 진아가 당신이 워크숍 준비하는 걸 도울 수 있어요.
　　　(A) 그녀는 이번 주에 휴가예요.
　　　(B) 네, 그것들은 유용한 기술이에요.
　　　(C) 온라인 쇼핑이 더 쉬워요.

해설 **사실·정보 전달의 평서문**
　　　(A) 정답. 진아가 워크숍 준비하는 걸 도울 수 있다는 평서문에 그녀는
　　　이번 주에 휴가라며 도와줄 수 없는 이유를 간접적으로 알려 주고
　　　있으므로 정답이다.
　　　(B) 연상 오답. 평서문의 workshop에서 연상 가능한 valuable
　　　skills를 이용한 오답이다.
　　　(C) 유사 발음 오답. 평서문의 workshop과 부분적으로 발음이 유사
　　　한 shopping을 이용한 오답이다.

어휘 valuable 귀중한 skill 기술, 역량

21

W-Br How do you adjust the height of these chairs?
M-Cn (A) Up to twenty-one inches.
　　　(B) I'll have to show you.
　　　(C) Some more comfortable seating.

번역 이 의자들의 높이를 어떻게 조정하나요?
　　　(A) 21인치까지요.
　　　(B) 제가 보여드릴게요.
　　　(C) 좀 더 편안한 좌석이요.

해설 **How 의문문**
　　　(A) 연상 오답. 질문의 height에서 연상 가능한 twenty-one
　　　inches를 이용한 오답이다.
　　　(B) 정답. 의자들의 높이 조정 방법을 묻는 질문에 직접 보여주겠다며
　　　제안하고 있으므로 정답이다.
　　　(C) 연상 오답. 질문의 chairs에서 연상 가능한 seating을 이용한 오
　　　답이다.

어휘 adjust 조정하다, 정돈하다 comfortable 편안한 seating 좌석

22

M-Cn Shouldn't the text on these slides be in a larger
　　　font?
W-Am (A) I'll put away the textbooks.
　　　(B) That's what I told the presenter.
　　　(C) Yes, the biggest box you have.

번역 이 슬라이드에 있는 글자를 더 크게 해야 하지 않을까요?
　　　(A) 제가 교과서들을 치울게요.
　　　(B) 그게 제가 발표자에게 했던 말이에요.
　　　(C) 네, 당신이 가진 것 중에 가장 큰 상자요.

해설 **부정 의문문**
　　　(A) 유사 발음 오답. 질문의 text와 부분적으로 발음이 유사한
　　　textbooks를 이용한 오답이다.
　　　(B) 정답. 슬라이드에 있는 글자를 더 크게 해야 하지 않냐는 부정 의
　　　문문에 그게 자신이 발표자에게 했던 말이라며 동의하는 의사를
　　　간접적으로 표현하고 있으므로 정답이다.
　　　(C) 연상 오답. 질문의 larger에서 연상 가능한 biggest를 이용한 오
　　　답이다.

어휘 put away 치우다 textbook 교과서 presenter 발표자

23

W-Br Do you go to the botanical gardens often?
M-Cn (A) People who love nature.
　　　(B) My house is just a short walk away.
　　　(C) Oh, I'll be out of town then.

번역 당신은 그 식물원에 자주 가나요?
　　　(A) 자연을 사랑하는 사람들이요.
　　　(B) 저희 집이 걸어갈 만큼 가까워요.
　　　(C) 아, 제가 그때는 여기 없을 거예요.

해설 **조동사(Do) 의문문**
　　　(A) 연상 오답. 질문의 botanical gardens에서 연상 가능한
　　　nature를 이용한 오답이다.
　　　(B) 정답. 식물원에 자주 가는지 묻는 질문에 자신의 집이 걸어갈 만
　　　큼 가깝다며 긍정의 답변을 간접적으로 알려 주고 있으므로 정답
　　　이다.
　　　(C) 질문과 상관없는 오답.

어휘 botanical garden 식물원 out of town (도시를 떠나) 외출 중인

24

W-Am How do I join the company book club?

M-Au (A) No, we already paid the membership fee.
(B) I can give you the leader's e-mail address.
(C) She chose a book on teamwork.

번역 사내 독서 모임에 어떻게 가입하나요?
(A) 아니요, 우리는 이미 회비를 지불했어요.
(B) 제가 운영자의 이메일 주소를 알려드릴게요.
(C) 그녀는 팀워크에 관한 책을 골랐어요.

해설 **How 의문문**
(A) Yes/No 불가 오답. How 의문문에는 Yes/No 응답이 불가능하므로 오답이다.
(B) 정답. 사내 독서 모임의 가입 방법을 묻는 질문에 운영자의 이메일 주소를 알려주겠다며 알 수 있는 방법을 알려 주고 있으므로 정답이다.
(C) 단어 반복 오답. 질문의 book을 반복 이용한 오답이다.

어휘 membership fee 회비

25

M-Cn Isn't there going to be traffic on the highway?

W-Am (A) It's almost nine o'clock at night.
(B) The highway expansion project.
(C) An air traffic controller.

번역 고속도로가 많이 막히지 않을까요?
(A) 지금은 거의 밤 9시예요.
(B) 고속도로 확장 공사요.
(C) 항공 교통 관제사요.

해설 **부정 의문문**
(A) 정답. 고속도로가 많이 막히지 않을지 염려하며 묻는 질문에 지금은 거의 밤 9시라며 막히지 않을 것이라는 부정 답변을 간접적으로 표현하고 있으므로 정답이다.
(B) 단어 반복 오답. 질문의 highway를 반복 이용한 오답이다.
(C) 단어 반복 오답. 질문의 traffic을 반복 이용한 오답이다.

어휘 expansion 확장 air traffic controller 항공 교통 관제사

26

M-Au Excuse me—my suitcase still hasn't arrived at baggage claim.

W-Am (A) It can take a while to fully unload the plane.
(B) OK, I'll tie this special tag on it.
(C) I fly pretty frequently.

번역 실례합니다. 제 여행 가방이 아직 짐 찾는 곳에 도착하지 않았어요.
(A) 비행기에서 짐을 완전히 내리려면 시간이 좀 걸릴 수 있습니다.
(B) 알겠습니다, 이 특별 꼬리표를 달아드리겠습니다.
(C) 저는 꽤 자주 비행기를 이용해요.

해설 **사실 · 정보 전달의 평서문**
(A) 정답. 여행 가방이 아직 짐 찾는 곳에 도착하지 않았다는 평서문에 비행기에서 짐을 완전히 내리려면 시간이 좀 걸릴 수 있다며 여행 가방을 찾는 것이 늦어질 수 있음을 간접적으로 알려 주고 있으므로 정답이다.

(B) 연상 오답. 평서문의 suitcase에서 연상 가능한 tag를 이용한 오답이다.
(C) 연상 오답. 평서문의 baggage에서 연상 가능한 fly를 이용한 오답이다.

어휘 suitcase 여행 가방 baggage claim 짐 찾는 곳 unload ~에서 짐을 내리다 frequently 자주

27

M-Cn Where should I submit my monthly expense report?

W-Br (A) No, I haven't.
(B) I'm on my way to a meeting, sorry.
(C) No more than fifty dollars.

번역 제 월별 지출 보고서를 어디에 제출해야 하나요?
(A) 아니요, 저는 하지 않았어요.
(B) 저는 회의에 가는 길이에요, 죄송해요.
(C) 50달러 이하요.

해설 **Where 의문문**
(A) Yes/No 불가 오답. Where 의문문에는 Yes/No 응답이 불가능하므로 오답이다.
(B) 정답. 지출 보고서 제출 장소를 묻는 질문에 회의에 가는 길이라며 바빠서 알려 줄 수 없음을 간접적으로 표현하고 있으므로 정답이다.
(C) 연상 오답. 질문의 expense에서 연상 가능한 fifty dollars를 이용한 오답이다.

어휘 submit 제출하다 monthly 월간의 expense 경비, 지출 no more than ~ 이하

28

W-Br Could you post a reply to this customer review of our café?

M-Au (A) The patio has a nice view.
(B) The sign on the front door.
(C) Can you send me the link?

번역 우리 카페에 대한 이 고객의 후기에 답변을 게시해 줄 수 있나요?
(A) 그 테라스는 전망이 좋아요.
(B) 정문에 있는 표지판이요.
(C) 링크를 보내주실 수 있나요?

해설 **요청 · 제안문**
(A) 유사 발음 오답. 질문의 review와 부분적으로 발음이 유사한 view를 이용한 오답.
(B) 연상 오답. 질문의 post에서 연상 가능한 sign을 이용한 오답이다.
(C) 정답. 고객의 후기에 답변을 달아달라는 요청에 링크를 보내달라는 것은 요청을 들어주겠다는 의미를 내포하므로 정답이다.

어휘 post 게시하다 review 후기, 평가 patio 테라스

29

W-Am Shall I buy a flower arrangement or a nice card?

M-Cn (A) Could you get both, please?
(B) It was a lovely idea.
(C) Because the receptionist is retiring.

번역 꽃다발을 살까요, 아니면 예쁜 카드를 살까요?
(A) 둘 다 살 수 있으세요?
(B) 아주 좋은 생각이었어요.
(C) 접수원이 곧 퇴직하니까요.

해설 선택 의문문
(A) 정답. 꽃다발과 예쁜 카드 중 살 것을 묻는 질문에 둘 다 살 수 있는 지 되묻고 있으므로 정답이다.
(B) 연상 오답. 질문의 Shall I buy에서 연상 가능한 a lovely idea 를 이용한 오답이다.
(C) 질문과 상관없는 오답. Why 의문문에 대한 응답이므로 오답이다.

어휘 flower arrangement 꽃다발, 꽃꽂이   receptionist 접수원
retire 은퇴하다, 퇴직하다

30
M-Au Do you know where the elevators are?
W-Am (A) Yes, I know her too.
(B) Just a routine inspection.
(C) Our client's office is on the ground floor.

번역 승강기가 어디에 있는지 아세요?
(A) 네, 저도 그녀를 알아요.
(B) 그냥 정기 점검이에요.
(C) 우리 고객의 사무실은 1층에 있어요.

해설 간접 의문문
(A) 질문과 상관없는 오답. 질문에 3인칭 대명사 her로 지칭할 인물이 언급된 적이 없으므로 오답이다.
(B) 연상 오답. 질문의 elevators에서 연상 가능한 a routine inspection을 이용한 오답이다.
(C) 정답. 승강기가 어디에 있는지 묻는 질문에 고객의 사무실은 1층 에 있다며 승강기를 타지 않아도 된다는 것을 간접적으로 알려 주고 있으므로 정답이다.

어휘 routine inspection 정기 점검   ground floor 1층

31
M-Au Should we reserve a booth near the entrance to the hall or near the catering terrace?
W-Br (A) Yes, that's a great location.
(B) The floor plan for the exhibition.
(C) The terrace does get a lot of visitors.

번역 행사장 쪽 출입문 근처 부스를 예약해야 할까요? 아니면 음식이 차려 진 테라스 근처 부스를 예약해야 할까요?
(A) 네, 그곳은 훌륭한 장소예요.
(B) 전시회 평면도요.
(C) 테라스는 방문자들이 많이 와요.

해설 선택 의문문
(A) 연상 오답. 질문의 near the entrance에서 연상 가능한 location을 이용한 오답이다.
(B) 연상 오답. 질문의 booth에서 연상 가능한 exhibition을 이용한 오답이다.
(C) 정답. 행사장 출입문 근처 부스와 음식이 차려진 테라스 근처 부스 중 어디를 예약할지 묻는 질문에 테라스가 방문객들이 많이 오므 로 테라스 쪽이 더 좋다는 의미를 간접적으로 표현하고 있으므로 정답이다.

어휘 reserve 예약하다   catering (행사, 연회 등에서) 제공되는 음식
floor plan 평면도   exhibition 전시회

32-34

M-Cn Theresa, [32] I finished my drawings for the back entrance of the Orosco Building.

W-Am Let me take a look at them… good work! [32] These nicely complement our overall design for the structure.

M-Cn Thanks! Also, I'm not sure how to write up my research into concrete options for the Kirby Street parking garage. [33] It would be helpful to have a sample report to refer to…

W-Am Sure, [33] here's a good one that Lloyd wrote recently.

M-Cn Thank you. I'll get to work on that now.

W-Am Oh, no hurry—[34] that project is on pause. The client is short on funding right now because one of their investors dropped out.

남: 테레사, 오로스코 빌딩의 후문을 위한 도면을 완성했어요.
여: 제가 좀 볼게요… 잘했어요! 이것들은 건축물의 전반적인 디자 인을 멋지게 보완하네요.
남: 감사합니다! 또, 커비 가의 주차 빌딩을 위한 콘크리트 종류에 대 한 조사 결과를 어떻게 작성해야 할지 모르겠어요. 참고할 만한 견본 보고서가 있으면 도움이 될 텐데…
여: 물론이죠, 여기 로이드가 최근에 작성한 훌륭한 보고서가 있 어요.
남: 감사합니다. 지금 바로 착수할게요.
여: 아, 서두를 필요 없어요, 그 프로젝트는 보류 중이에요. 이 고객 사는 투자자 중 한 명이 빠졌기 때문에 지금 당장은 자금이 부족 하대요.

어휘 drawing 도면   complement 보완하다   overall 전반적인
structure 구조, 건축물   concrete 콘크리트   parking
garage 주차 빌딩   refer to ~을 참고하다   get to work
일을 시작하다   on pause 보류 중인   be short on
~이 부족하다   investor 투자자   drop out 빠지다, 손을 떼다

32 Who most likely are the speakers?
(A) Architects
(B) Real estate agents
(C) Property managers
(D) City officials

번역 화자들은 누구이겠는가?
(A) 건축가
(B) 부동산 중개인
(C) 자산 관리자
(D) 시 공무원

해설 **전체 내용 관련 - 화자들의 직업**
남자가 첫 대사에서 오로스코 빌딩의 후문을 위한 도면을 완성했다
(I finished my drawings for the back entrance of the
Orosco Building)고 하자, 여자가 이것들은 건축물의 전반적인 디
자인을 멋지게 보완한다(~ complement our overall design for
the structure)고 말하는 것으로 보아 화자들은 건축가임을 알 수 있
다. 따라서 정답은 (A)이다.

어휘 property 자산, 부동산   official 공무원

---

33 What does the woman give the man?
(A) Some safety gear
(B) Some blueprints
(C) A report
(D) A tool

번역 여자는 남자에게 무엇을 주는가?
(A) 안전 장비
(B) 청사진
(C) 보고서
(D) 도구

해설 **세부 사항 관련 - 여자가 남자에게 제공하는 것**
남자가 두 번째 대사에서 참고할 만한 견본 보고서가 있으면 도움
이 될 텐데(It would be helpful to have a sample report to
refer to…)라고 하자 여자가 로이드가 최근에 작성한 훌륭한 보고서
(here's a good one that Lloyd wrote recently)라고 말하면서
건네고 있으므로 정답은 (C)이다.

---

34 Why has a project been postponed?
(A) The weather is unfavorable for it.
(B) The client has not provided some information.
(C) An inspection must be carried out first.
(D) Some financing is no longer available.

번역 프로젝트는 왜 미루어졌는가?
(A) 날씨가 좋지 않아서
(B) 고객이 일부 정보를 제공해 주지 않아서
(C) 점검이 먼저 진행되어야 해서
(D) 일부 자금을 더 이상 끌어올 수 없어서

해설 **세부 사항 관련 - 프로젝트가 미루어진 이유**
여자가 마지막 대사에서 그 프로젝트는 보류 중(that project is on
pause)이라고 하면서 고객사는 투자자 중 한 명이 빠졌기 때문에
지금 당장은 자금이 부족하다(The client is short on funding
right now because one of their investors dropped out)고
말하고 있으므로 정답은 (D)이다.

어휘 unfavorable 호의적이 아닌   inspection 점검   carry out
수행하다   financing 자금   available 이용 가능한

Paraphrasing
대화의 on pause → 질문의 postponed

대화의 one of their investors dropped out
→ 정답의 Some financing is no longer available.

35-37

W-Br Hi, this is Satomi at Satomi's Coffee. **35 I'm
having trouble with the lighting your company
installed in my café.** Is this the right number
to call?

M-Au Yes, **36 this is our customer helpline.** Let's
see, our records say we put in hanging LED
lamps for you. What's the problem you're
experiencing?

W-Br They've been making an annoying buzzing
sound. And it gets louder when we use the
dimmer switch.

M-Au Hmm, there are at least two potential causes
for that issue. **37 I'll arrange for one of our
technicians to come by and check it out.**

여: 안녕하세요, 저는 사토미 커피의 사토미입니다. **귀사에서 제 카
페에 설치해 주신 조명등에 문제가 있어요.** 이쪽 번호로 전화하
는 게 맞나요?

남: 네, **여기가 고객 상담실 맞습니다.** 잠시만요, 기록을 보니 걸이식
LED 램프를 설치해 드렸네요. 어떤 문제를 겪고 계시죠?

여: 신경을 거스르는 윙윙 소리가 계속 나고 있어요. 조광 스위치를
사용하면 더 커지고요.

남: 음, 그 문제에 대해서는 적어도 두 가지 잠재적인 원인이 있습니
다. **저희 기술자 한 명이 들러서 확인해 보도록 조치를 취하겠습
니다.**

어휘 install 설치하다   helpline 전화 상담 서비스   put in (장비,
가구 등을) 설치하다   hanging 매달린   annoying 성가신
buzzing 윙윙거리는   loud 시끄러운   dimmer switch
조광 스위치   potential 잠재적인   cause 원인   arrange
준비하다   technician 기술자   come by 잠깐 들르다

---

35 What product are the speakers discussing?
(A) Refrigerators
(B) Display cases
(C) Coffee makers
(D) Light fixtures

번역 화자들은 어떤 제품에 대해 이야기하는가?
(A) 냉장고
(B) 진열장
(C) 커피 메이커
(D) 조명 기구

해설 **전체 내용 관련 - 화자들이 논의 중인 제품**
여자가 첫 대사에서 카페에 설치해 준 조명등에 문제가 있다(I'm having trouble with the lighting your company installed in my café)고 하면서 조명 기구에 대해 언급하고 있으므로 정답은 (D)이다.

> **Paraphrasing**
> 대화의 the lighting → 정답의 Light fixtures

36 What department does the man most likely work in?
(A) Sales
(B) Accounting
(C) Customer Support
(D) Product Development

번역 남자는 어느 부서에서 일하겠는가?
(A) 영업부
(B) 회계부
(C) 고객 지원부
(D) 제품 개발부

해설 **전체 내용 관련 - 남자의 근무 부서**
남자가 첫 대사에서 여기가 고객 상담실이 맞다(this is our customer helpline)고 말하고 있으므로 정답은 (C)이다.

어휘 support 지원   development 개발

> **Paraphrasing**
> 대화의 customer helpline → 정답의 Customer Support

37 What will the man do next?
(A) Schedule a site visit
(B) Correct an invoice
(C) Test some equipment himself
(D) Add a note to a file

번역 남자는 다음으로 무엇을 하겠는가?
(A) 현장 방문 일정 잡기
(B) 송장 수정하기
(C) 직접 장비 테스트해 보기
(D) 파일에 메모 추가하기

해설 **세부 사항 관련 - 남자가 다음에 할 일**
남자가 마지막 대사에서 기술자가 들러서 확인해 보도록 조치를 취하겠다(I'll arrange for one of our technicians to come by and check it out)고 말하고 있으므로 정답은 (A)이다.

어휘 site visit 현장 방문   correct 바로잡다   invoice 송장
equipment 장비

> **Paraphrasing**
> 대화의 arrange for one of our technicians to come by
> → 정답의 Schedule a site visit

M-Cn **38 Thanks again for agreeing to do our annual banquet. The food was so disappointing last year—we're glad to have someone new handling it.** Now, where do you want to start the walk-through?

W-Br **39 I'd like to see the banquet hall** so that I can plan the set-up of the buffet. Your main dishes need to be kept warm, so I'll need to find power outlets for our serving equipment.

M-Cn OK, follow me. But that reminds me—**40 could you put the drinks and dessert tables in other corners of the room?** When all of the refreshments are concentrated in one area, there's too much crowding.

남 저희 연례 연회 준비를 맡아주셔서 다시 한번 감사드립니다. 작년에는 음식이 너무 실망스러웠거든요. 새로운 분이 이 일을 맡게 되어 기쁩니다. 자, 어디서부터 자세한 설명을 시작할까요?

여 연회장을 보고 싶어요. 그래야 뷔페 구성을 계획할 수 있으니까요. 주요리는 따뜻한 상태로 보관해야 하니 저희 서빙 장비를 꽂을 전기 콘센트도 찾아야 하고요.

남 알겠습니다, 저를 따라오세요. 하지만 그 얘길 들으니 생각이 나는데, 음료 테이블과 후식 테이블을 서로 다른 쪽 코너에 놓아주실 수 있나요? 모든 다과가 한 곳에 집중되어 있으면 사람들이 너무 몰리더라고요.

어휘 annual 연례의   banquet 연회   disappointing
실망스러운   handle 다루다, 처리하다   walk-through
자세한 설명   power outlet 전기 콘센트   equipment 장비
remind 상기시키다   refreshments 다과   concentrate
집중하다   crowding 혼잡

38 Who most likely is the woman?
(A) A florist
(B) A caterer
(C) A musician
(D) A photographer

번역 여자는 누구이겠는가?
(A) 플로리스트
(B) 출장 요리 연회사
(C) 음악가
(D) 사진가

해설 **전체 내용 관련 - 여자의 직업**
남자가 첫 대사에서 연회 준비를 맡아줘서 감사하다(Thanks again for agreeing to do our annual banquet)고 하면서 작년에는 음식이 너무 실망스러웠는데 새로운 분이 이 일을 맡게 되어 기쁘다(The food was so disappointing last year—we're glad to have someone new handling it)고 말하는 것으로 보아 여자는 출장 요리 연회를 취급하는 사람임을 알 수 있다. 따라서 정답은 (B)이다.

39 Where does the woman want to go first?
(A) To an outdoor patio
(B) To a dining space
(C) To a loading area
(D) To a commercial kitchen

번역 여자는 가장 먼저 어디로 가기를 원하는가?
(A) 옥외 테라스
(B) 식사 공간
(C) 하역장
(D) 상업용 주방

해설 **세부 사항 관련 - 여자가 가장 먼저 가기를 원하는 곳**
여자가 첫 대사에서 연회장을 보고 싶다(I'd like to see the banquet hall)고 했으므로 정답은 (B)이다.

어휘 patio 테라스   commercial 상업적인

> **Paraphrasing**
> 대화의 the banquet hall → 정답의 a dining space

40 According to the man, what should the woman do?
(A) Bring extra supplies
(B) Use lightweight equipment
(C) Place tables in separate locations
(D) Revise a set-up timeline

번역 남자에 따르면, 여자는 무엇을 해야 하는가?
(A) 추가 용품 가져오기
(B) 가벼운 장비 사용하기
(C) 각각 별도의 위치에 테이블 배치하기
(D) 준비 시간표 수정하기

해설 **세부 사항 관련 - 여자가 해야 할 일**
남자가 마지막 대사에서 음료 테이블과 후식 테이블을 다른 쪽 코너에 놓아줄 것(could you put the drinks and dessert tables in other corners of the room?)을 요청하고 있으므로 정답은 (C)이다.

어휘 extra 추가의   lightweight 가벼운   separate 분리된   revise 수정하다

> **Paraphrasing**
> 대화의 put ~ tables in other corners of the room
> → 정답의 Place tables in separate locations

41-43 3인 대화

> W-Am Mr. Gwon and Mr. McBride, welcome to our bank. **41 I understand you're planning to apply for a loan for your print shop.**
>
> M-Au Yes, we'd like to use the money to invest in a fast, wide-format printer. It would allow us to print large signs and posters quickly.

M-Cn **42 We need to make the purchase soon because another print shop near ours just bought that kind of printer.**

M-Au **42 Right—it's important for us to offer similar technology to remain competitive.**

W-Am That makes sense. But... **43 I see that your shop just opened last January. We don't often approve loans to companies that have been in operation for less than two years.** With that in mind, would you still like to apply?

여: 권 씨, 맥브라이드 씨, 저희 은행에 오신 것을 환영합니다. 두 분이 인쇄소를 위해 대출을 신청하려고 하신다고 알고 있습니다.

남1: 네, 그 돈을 고속 와이드 포맷 프린터에 투자하고 싶습니다. 그러면 대형 간판이나 포스터를 신속하게 인쇄할 수 있거든요.

남2: 저희 가게 근처에 있는 다른 인쇄소에서 최근에 그런 종류의 프린터를 구매했기 때문에 저희도 빨리 구매해야 합니다.

남1: 맞습니다. 경쟁력을 유지하려면 비슷한 기술을 제공하는 것이 중요하거든요.

여: 일리가 있네요. 하지만… 보니까 두 분의 인쇄소는 겨우 지난 1월에 개업하셨네요. 저희는 운영 기간이 2년 이하인 회사에는 대출을 잘 승인해 드리지 않습니다. 그 점을 염두에 두시고, 그래도 신청을 원하십니까?

어휘 apply for ~을 신청하다   loan 대출   invest in ~에 투자하다   make a purchase 구매하다   remain 유지하다   competitive 경쟁력 있는   make sense 타당하다   approve 승인하다   in operation 운영 중인

41 What is the conversation mostly about?
(A) Expanding a workforce
(B) Repairing some machinery
(C) Participating in a trade show
(D) Arranging a business loan

번역 대화는 주로 무엇에 관한 것인가?
(A) 노동력 충원
(B) 기계 수리
(C) 무역 박람회 참석
(D) 사업 대출 신청

해설 **전체 내용 관련 - 대화의 주제**
여자가 첫 대사에서 남자들에게 인쇄소를 위해 대출을 신청하려고 한다고 알고 있다(I understand you're planning to apply for a loan for your print shop)고 말하고 있으므로 정답은 (D)이다.

어휘 expand 확장하다   workforce 노동력   repair 수리하다   machinery 기계   participate in ~에 참여하다   trade show 무역 박람회

> **Paraphrasing**
> 대화의 apply for a loan for your print shop
> → 정답의 Arranging a business loan

42 What do the men say is important?
(A) Keeping up with a competitor
(B) Addressing employee feedback
(C) Increasing brand recognition
(D) Avoiding legal issues

번역 남자들은 무엇이 중요하다고 말하는가?
(A) 경쟁업체 따라잡기
(B) 직원 피드백 대응하기
(C) 브랜드 인지도 높이기
(D) 법적 문제 피하기

해설 **세부 사항 관련 - 남자들이 중요하다고 말하는 것**
두 번째 남자가 첫 대사에서 근처에 있는 다른 인쇄소에서 최근에 그런 종류의 프린터를 구매했기 때문에 자신들도 빨리 구매해야 한다(We need to make the purchase soon because another print shop near ours just bought that kind of printer)고 하자, 첫 번째 남자가 맞다(Right)고 말한 뒤, 경쟁력을 유지하려면 비슷한 기술을 제공하는 것이 중요하다(it's important for us to offer similar technology to remain competitive)고 덧붙여 말하고 있으므로 정답은 (A)이다.

어휘 keep up with ~을 따라잡다   address 다루다, 고심하다
increase 증가시키다   brand recognition 브랜드 인지도
legal 법률과 관련된

> **Paraphrasing**
> 대화의 another print shop near ours
> → 정답의 a competitor
>
> 대화의 to remain competitive
> → 정답의 keeping up with a competitor

43 What problem does the woman mention?
(A) A decision-making process is slow.
(B) A cost estimate may be incorrect.
(C) An application might be rejected.
(D) A new technology is difficult to use.

번역 여자는 어떤 문제를 언급하는가?
(A) 의사 결정 절차가 느리다.
(B) 비용 견적서가 부정확할 수도 있다.
(C) 신청이 거부될 수도 있다.
(D) 새로운 기술은 사용하기가 어렵다.

해설 **세부 사항 관련 - 여자가 언급하는 문제**
여자가 마지막 대사에서 남자들의 인쇄소는 겨우 지난 1월에 개업했다(I see that your shop just opened last January)면서 운영 기간이 2년 이하인 회사에는 대출을 잘 승인해 주지 않는다(We don't often approve loans to companies that have been in operation for less than two years)고 말하고 있으므로 정답은 (C)이다.

어휘 decision-making 의사 결정   cost estimate 비용 견적
incorrect 부정확한   reject 거부하다

> **Paraphrasing**
> 대화의 We don't often approve loans ~
> → 정답의 An application might be rejected.

44-46

M-Au OK, before we start boarding this flight, we have an overbooking issue to take care of. **44 The economy section is seven people over capacity.** We'll need to make other arrangements for some passengers.

W-Br Well, **45 there's space in business class. I'll choose two passengers who are members of our loyalty program and move them up there.**

M-Au That's good. Then we'll only have to find five people who are willing to wait for a later flight. I'll make the announcement now and **46 let them know that volunteers will receive four hundred Euros for their trouble.**

남: 자, 이 비행기에 탑승을 시작하기 전에 처리해야 할 초과 예약 문제가 있습니다. **이코노미석이 정원보다 일곱 명 초과되었습니다.** 일부 승객들을 위해 다른 방법을 찾아야 합니다.

여: 음, 비즈니스석에는 자리가 있어요. 충성 고객 프로그램 회원인 승객 두 명을 골라 승급해 드리겠습니다.

남: 좋습니다. 그러면 더 늦은 항공편을 기다릴 의향이 있는 다섯 명만 찾으면 되겠네요. 제가 지금 안내 방송을 해서 자원하시는 분은 불편에 대한 보상으로 400유로를 받게 되실 거라고 알리겠습니다.

어휘 board 탑승하다   overbooking 초과 예약   take care of ~을 처리하다   capacity 용량, 수용력   arrangement 준비   passenger 승객   loyalty program 충성 고객 프로그램   volunteer 자원하는 사람

44 Why does the man talk to the woman?
(A) To question a baggage policy
(B) To share a passenger complaint
(C) To explain a new boarding procedure
(D) To discuss a seating shortage

번역 남자는 왜 여자에게 말을 거는가?
(A) 수하물 정책에 대해 문의하려고
(B) 승객 불만을 공유하려고
(C) 새로운 탑승 절차를 설명하려고
(D) 좌석 부족에 대해 상의하려고

해설 **전체 내용 관련 - 남자가 여자에게 말을 거는 이유**
남자가 첫 대사에서 이코노미석이 정원보다 일곱 명 초과되었다(The economy section is seven people over capacity)고 말하고 있으므로 정답은 (D)이다.

어휘 baggage 짐, 수하물   policy 정책   complaint 불평, 불만   procedure 절차   shortage 부족

> **Paraphrasing**
> 대화의 The economy section is seven people over capacity → 정답의 a seating shortage

45 What does the woman say she will do?
(A) Search in an employee handbook
(B) Give upgrades to some passengers
(C) Inform flight attendants of a problem
(D) Change the text on a digital sign

번역 여자는 무엇을 하겠다고 말하는가?
(A) 직원 안내서에서 찾아보기
(B) 일부 승객들에게 좌석 승급해 주기
(C) 승무원들에게 문제 알리기
(D) 디지털 전광판의 문구 변경하기

해설 **세부 사항 관련 - 여자가 할 일**
여자가 첫 대사에서 비즈니스석에는 자리가 있다(there's space in business class)면서 충성 고객 프로그램 회원인 승객 두 명을 골라 승급해 주겠다(I'll choose two passengers who are members of our loyalty program and move them up there)고 말하고 있으므로 정답은 (B)이다.

어휘 handbook 안내서 inform 알리다 flight attendant 승무원

> **Paraphrasing**
> 대화의 move ~ up → 정답의 Give upgrades

46 What does the man plan to do?
(A) Offer compensation for an inconvenience
(B) Continue monitoring an entrance
(C) Instruct some travelers to form a line
(D) Ask for assistance with moving an object

번역 남자는 무엇을 할 계획인가?
(A) 불편에 대한 보상 제공하기
(B) 출입구 모니터링 지속하기
(C) 여행객들에게 줄을 서도록 안내하기
(D) 물건을 옮기는 데 도움 요청하기

해설 **세부 사항 관련 - 남자가 계획한 일**
남자가 마지막 대사에서 자원하시는 분은 불편에 대한 보상으로 400유로를 받게 될 거라고 알리겠다(let them know that volunteers will receive four hundred Euros for their trouble)고 말하고 있으므로 정답은 (A)이다.

어휘 compensation 보상 inconvenience 불편 entrance 출입구 instruct 지시하다, 안내하다 form a line 한 줄로 서다 assistance 도움 object 물건, 물체

> **Paraphrasing**
> 대화의 four hundred Euros for their trouble
> → 정답의 compensation for an inconvenience

47-49

W-Am Hi. I'd like to become a member of your gym. **⁴⁷ I just moved here to start university,** and I want to keep up my exercise routine from back home.

M-Au Great! **⁴⁷ Welcome to Australia.** We'll just need you to fill out this registration form.

W-Am OK. Oh… it asks for my contact information, but **⁴⁸ I don't have my mailing address memorized yet.** I only know the name of my dormitory building.

M-Au Well, could you look it up with your smartphone? **⁴⁹ I can give you the password to access our Wi-Fi if you need it.**

여: 안녕하세요. 이 체육관의 회원이 되고 싶은데요. **대학 입학을 위해 최근에 여기로 이사 왔는데,** 원래 살던 곳에서 하던 운동 일과를 유지하고 싶어서요.

남: 좋습니다! **호주에 오신 것을 환영합니다.** 이 등록 신청서만 작성해 주시면 됩니다.

여: 알겠습니다. 아… 제 연락처를 적어야 하네요, 하지만 **제 우편 주소를 아직 외우지 못했어요.** 제 기숙사 건물의 이름만 알아요.

남: 음, 그럼 스마트폰으로 찾아보시겠어요? **필요하시다면 저희 와이파이에 접속할 수 있는 암호를 드리겠습니다.**

어휘 keep up ~을 계속하다 fill out ~을 작성하다 registration 등록 memorize 암기하다 dormitory 기숙사 look up ~을 찾아보다 access 접속하다

47 Why has the woman come to Australia?
(A) For a business trip
(B) For a study program
(C) For a visit with family
(D) For some sightseeing

번역 여자는 왜 호주로 왔는가?
(A) 출장을 위해
(B) 학업 프로그램을 위해
(C) 가족 방문을 위해
(D) 관광을 위해

해설 **세부 사항 관련 - 여자가 호주로 온 이유**
여자가 첫 대사에서 대학교에 입학하려고 최근에 여기로 이사 왔다(I just moved here to start university)고 했고, 남자가 호주에 온 것을 환영한다(Welcome to Australia)고 말하고 있으므로 정답은 (B)이다.

어휘 sightseeing 관광

> **Paraphrasing**
> 대화의 to start university
> → 정답의 For a study program

48 What problem does the woman have?
(A) She does not remember an address.
(B) She forgot to bring some identification.
(C) She cannot log in to an e-mail account.
(D) She does not have a local phone number.

번역 여자는 어떤 문제를 가지고 있는가?
(A) 주소를 기억하지 못한다.
(B) 신분증을 깜박하고 가져오지 않았다.
(C) 이메일 계정에 로그인을 할 수 없다.
(D) 현지 전화번호가 없다.

해설 **세부 사항 관련 - 여자가 가진 문제**
여자가 두 번째 대사에서 우편 주소를 아직 외우지 못했다(I don't have my mailing address memorized yet)고 말하고 있으므로 정답은 (A)이다.

어휘 identification 신분 증명 자료

> **Paraphrasing**
> 대화의 don't have my mailing address memorized
> → 정답의 does not remember an address

49 What does the man offer the woman?
(A) A map of the area
(B) An Internet connection
(C) A trial membership
(D) A facility tour

번역 남자는 여자에게 무엇을 제공하는가?
(A) 지역 지도
(B) 인터넷 접속
(C) 체험 회원권
(D) 시설 견학

해설 **세부 사항 관련 - 남자가 제공하는 것**
남자가 마지막 대사에서 필요하면 와이파이에 접속할 수 있는 암호를 주겠다(I can give you the password to access our Wi-Fi if you need it)고 말하고 있으므로 정답은 (B)이다.

어휘 connection 연결   trial 시험, 시도   facility 시설

> **Paraphrasing**
> 대화의 access ~ Wi-Fi → 정답의 An Internet connection

50-52

M-Au	Laverne, **50 I'd like to order special food on the upcoming holiday to show appreciation for the doctors and nurses working that day. 51 What do you think they would like?**
W-Br	Well, **51 the pizza that Nelson chose for his retirement party was delicious.** I believe it was from Pizzeria Moretti. All of the pieces were gone in minutes.
M-Au	That pizza was very good. Thanks for the reminder!
W-Br	No problem. **52 Just make sure a few pizzas are set aside for the people on the night shift.** Sometimes they miss out on treats like this.

남: 러번, 다가오는 휴일에 그날 근무하는 의사와 간호사들에게 감사를 표하기 위해 특별한 음식을 주문하고 싶은데요. 그들이 뭘 좋아할 거라고 생각해요?

여: 음, 넬슨이 은퇴 기념식 때 골랐던 피자 맛있었어요. 피제리아 모레티에서 사 온 것이었을 거예요. 모든 조각이 몇 분 만에 다 없어졌었죠.

남: 그 피자 정말 괜찮았어요. 상기시켜 줘서 고마워요!

여: 별말씀을요. 야간 조에 근무하는 사람들을 위해 몇 조각을 따로 챙겨놓는 거 잊지 마세요. 가끔 그들은 이런 간식을 놓치니까요.

어휘 upcoming 다가오는   appreciation 감사   retirement 은퇴, 퇴직   set aside 따로 챙겨두다   miss out on ~을 놓치다

50 Where most likely do the speakers work?
(A) At a hospital
(B) At a university
(C) At a restaurant
(D) At a factory

번역 화자들은 어디서 일하겠는가?
(A) 병원
(B) 대학교
(C) 식당
(D) 공장

해설 **전체 내용 관련 - 화자들의 근무 장소**
남자가 첫 대사에서 다가오는 휴일에 그날 근무하는 의사와 간호사들에게 감사를 표하기 위해 특별한 음식을 주문하고 싶다(I'd like to order special food on the upcoming holiday to show appreciation for the doctors and nurses working that day)고 말하는 것으로 보아 화자들은 병원에서 근무하고 있다는 것을 알 수 있다. 따라서 정답은 (A)이다.

51 What does the man mean when he says, "That pizza was very good"?
(A) The taste of a dish has changed.
(B) A dish should be ordered again.
(C) A business deserves a positive review.
(D) He is disappointed to miss a party.

번역 남자가 "그 피자 정말 괜찮았어요"라고 말할 때, 그 의도는 무엇인가?
(A) 요리의 맛이 변했다.
(B) 요리를 또 주문해야 한다.
(C) 가게가 긍정적인 후기를 받을 만하다.
(D) 파티에 참석하지 못해서 아쉬워한다.

해설 **화자의 의도 파악 - 그 피자 정말 괜찮았다는 말의 의도**
앞에서 남자가 그들이 뭘 좋아할 거라고 생각하는지(What do you think they would like?) 묻자, 여자가 넬슨이 은퇴 기념식 때 골랐던 피자가 맛있었다(the pizza that Nelson chose for his retirement party was delicious)고 말한 뒤 인용문을 언급했으므로 피자를 또 주문해야 한다는 의도로 한 말이라는 것을 알 수 있다. 따라서 정답은 (B)이다.

어휘 deserve ~을 받을 만하다   positive 긍정적인   disappointed
실망한

---

52 What is the woman concerned about?
(A) Staying under a budget
(B) Starting her shift on time
(C) Providing food to everyone
(D) Following a complicated recipe

번역 여자는 무엇에 대해 걱정하는가?
(A) 예산을 초과하지 않는 것
(B) 제시간에 교대 근무를 시작하는 것
(C) 음식을 모두에게 제공하는 것
(D) 복잡한 조리법을 따라 하는 것

해설 세부 사항 관련 - 여자의 우려 사항
여자가 마지막 대사에서 야간 조에 근무하는 사람들을 위해 몇 조각을
따로 챙겨놓는 거 잊지 말라(Just make sure a few pizzas are
set aside for the people on the night shift)면서 가끔 그들은
이런 간식을 놓친다(Sometimes they miss out on treats like
this)고 말하고 있으므로 정답은 (C)이다.

어휘 budget 예산   on time 제시간에   provide 제공하다
complicated 복잡한   recipe 조리법

> **Paraphrasing**
> 대화의 a few pizzas → 정답의 food

53-55

> M-Cn Delia, **53 did you run into a problem in the
> north hallway during your patrol?** I saw on
> our video feed that you put out a safety sign
> there.
>
> W-Am Yes, **54 the floor's wet—it seems the air
> conditioner is leaking. I let the facilities
> department know about it over the radio.**
>
> M-Cn Hmm. **55 They may not be able to get around
> to repairing that soon. I was told that Brian in
> Facilities called in sick this morning.**
>
> W-Am Oh, then let's keep an eye on the area today.
>
> 남: 델리아, 순찰 중 북쪽 복도에서 문제가 발생했나요? CCTV 화면
> 비디오 피드에서 당신이 거기에 안전 표지판을 내놓는 모습을
> 보았어요.
>
> 여: 네, 바닥이 젖었어요. 에어컨에서 누수가 있는 것 같아요. 이 문
> 제에 대해 무전으로 시설부에 알렸어요.
>
> 남: 음. 그들은 어쩌면 빨리 수리하러 오지 못할 수도 있어요. 시설부
> 의 브라이언이 오늘 아침에 병가를 냈다고 들었어요.
>
> 여: 아, 그럼 오늘 그 구역을 계속 주시하도록 하죠.
>
> 어휘 run into ~와 우연히 만나다, 겪다   hallway 복도   patrol
> 순찰   put out 내놓다   leak (물 등이) 새다   facility 시설

over the radio 무전을 통해   get around to ~을 할 시간을
내다   call in sick 병가를 내다   keep an eye on ~을 계속
지켜보다

53 Who most likely are the speakers?
(A) Security guards
(B) Plumbers
(C) Office cleaners
(D) Mailroom staff

번역 화자들은 누구이겠는가?
(A) 경비원
(B) 배관공
(C) 사무실 청소원
(D) 우편물실 직원

해설 전체 내용 관련 - 화자들의 직업
남자가 첫 대사에서 순찰 중 북쪽 복도에서 문제가 발생했는지(did
you run into a problem in the north hallway during your
patrol?) 묻는 것으로 보아 화자들은 경비원임을 알 수 있다. 따라서
정답은 (A)이다.

어휘 mailroom 우편물실

---

54 What does the woman say she did?
(A) Consulted a manual
(B) Reported a safety problem
(C) Turned on an air conditioner
(D) Disposed of some waste

번역 여자는 무엇을 했다고 말하는가?
(A) 사용 설명서를 찾아보았다.
(B) 안전 문제를 보고했다.
(C) 에어컨을 켰다.
(D) 폐기물을 버렸다.

해설 세부 사항 관련 - 여자가 한 일
여자가 첫 대사에서 바닥이 젖었다(the floor's wet)며 에어컨에서
누수가 있는 것 같다(it seems the air conditioner is leaking)
면서 이 문제에 대해 무전으로 시설부에 알렸다(I let the facilities
department know about it over the radio)고 했으므로 정답
은 (B)이다.

어휘 consult 찾아보다, 상담하다   report 보고하다   turn on
~의 전원을 켜다   dispose of ~을 없애다   waste 폐기물

> **Paraphrasing**
> 대화의 let ~ know → 정답의 Reported

---

55 What does the man say may cause a delay?
(A) The nearest parking area is closed.
(B) A special telephone line is down.
(C) A product warranty cannot be located.
(D) A worker in another department is absent.

번역 남자는 무엇이 지연을 유발할 수 있다고 말하는가?
(A) 가장 가까운 주차장이 폐쇄된 것
(B) 특별한 전화선이 먹통이 된 것
(C) 제품 품질 보증서를 찾을 수 없는 것
(D) 다른 부서 직원이 결근한 것

해설 **세부 사항 관련 - 남자가 말하는 지연 이유**
남자가 마지막 대사에서 그들은 어쩌면 빨리 수리하러 오지 못할 수도 있다(They may not be able to get around to repairing that soon)면서 시설부의 브라이언이 오늘 아침에 병가를 냈다고 들었다(I was told that Brian in Facilities called in sick this morning)고 말하고 있으므로 정답은 (D)이다.

어휘 warranty 품질 보증서 locate ~의 위치를 찾아내다 absent 결근한

> **Paraphrasing**
> 대화의 Brian in Facilities called in sick
> → 정답의 A worker in another department is absent.

56-58 3인 대화

M-Au **56 Thank you for coming all the way out to my home,** Ms. Castillo.

W-Br Of course, Mr. Suzuki. While I'm mostly involved in the records review part of our firm's surveys, I do like to see the land. Uh, **57 let me introduce my colleague, Iris Clayton, who would lead our on-site archaeological team here.** She'd handle tasks like using ground-penetrating radar to check for buried objects.

W-Am It's nice to meet you, Mr. Suzuki. So, why are you having your property surveyed?

M-Au **58 I'm hoping to add an access road connecting my driveway to Upton Lane.** As I'm sure you know, the local planning authorities require confirmation that the work area doesn't include any historic sites.

남: 저희 집까지 먼 길을 와주셔서 감사합니다, 카스티요 씨.

여1: 물론이죠, 스즈키 씨. 저는 주로 회사의 측량 업무에서 기록 검토를 담당하고 있지만, 땅을 보는 것을 좋아합니다. 아, **여기 저희 현장 고고학팀을 이끌 제 동료 아이리스 클레이턴을 소개할게요.** 그녀는 지표 투과 레이더를 사용하여 매설물을 확인하는 등의 작업을 담당할 거예요.

여2: 만나 뵈어 반갑습니다, 스즈키 씨. 그런데 왜 부동산을 측량하시는 건가요?

남: 저희 집 진입로와 업턴 길을 연결하는 연결 도로를 추가하고 싶은데요. 아시다시피, 지역 계획 당국은 공사 구역에 유적지가 포함되어 있지 않다는 확인을 요구하죠.

어휘 be involved in ~에 관여하다 survey 측량 on-site 현장의 archaeological 고고학의 handle 다루다

ground-penetrating radar 지표 투과 레이더 buried 묻힌 object 물건, 물체 property 재산, 부동산 connect 연결하다 driveway 진입로 authorities 당국 confirmation 확인 historic site 유적지

56 Where does the conversation take place?
(A) At a history exhibition
(B) At a private residence
(C) At a storage facility
(D) At a local park

번역 대화는 어디에서 이루어지는가?
(A) 역사 전시회
(B) 개인 주택
(C) 보관 시설
(D) 지역 공원

해설 **전체 내용 관련 - 대화의 장소**
남자가 첫 대사에서 자신의 집까지 먼 길을 와줘서 감사하다(Thank you for coming all the way out to my home)고 말하고 있으므로 정답은 (B)이다.

어휘 exhibition 전시회 residence 주택, 거주지 storage 보관

> **Paraphrasing**
> 대화의 my home → 정답의 a private residence

57 Who are the women?
(A) Museum curators
(B) Tour guides
(C) Restoration experts
(D) Archaeological surveyors

번역 여자들은 누구인가?
(A) 박물관 큐레이터
(B) 여행 인솔자
(C) 복원 전문가
(D) 고고학 측량사

해설 **전체 내용 관련 - 여자들의 직업**
첫 번째 여자가 첫 대사에서 현장 고고학팀을 이끌 동료 아이리스 클레이턴을 소개한다(let me introduce my colleague, Iris Clayton, who would lead our on-site archaeological team here)고 말하는 것으로 보아 여자들은 고고학팀에서 근무한다는 것을 알 수 있다. 따라서 정답은 (D)이다.

어휘 restoration 복원 expert 전문가 surveyor 측량사

58 What does the man say he hopes to do?
(A) Sell some artifacts
(B) Write a fiction book
(C) Plan an outdoor event
(D) Build a new road

번역 남자는 무엇을 하기를 원한다고 말하는가?
(A) 유물 판매
(B) 소설책 집필
(C) 옥외 행사 기획
(D) 새로운 도로 건설

해설 **세부 사항 관련 - 남자가 원하는 일**
남자가 마지막 대사에서 자기 집의 진입로와 업턴 길을 연결하는 연결 도로를 추가하고 싶다(I'm hoping to add an access road connecting my driveway to Upton Lane)고 말하고 있으므로 정답은 (D)이다.

어휘 artifact 유물, 공예품 fiction 소설

> **Paraphrasing**
> 대화의 add an access road → 정답의 Build a new road

59-61

W-Am Kevin, I just got off the phone with a representative from Gamboa Sports.

M-Cn **59 Do they want me to wear their clothing during my matches?**

W-Am Even better—they want you to be an official spokesperson for a new line of tennis wear.

M-Cn Wow! But... I don't want my name attached to anything that isn't high-quality, so I'd have to check out the clothes first. **60 Can I get a few sample pieces before I agree to anything?**

W-Am I don't think that would be a problem. **60 I'll put in the request.** Then, **61 once you've given your approval, we can begin discussing contract terms.**

M-Cn OK, but **61 I'll be on vacation for the next few weeks.**

W-Am Oh, they're still in the design stage.

여: 케빈, 방금 감보아 스포츠의 담당자와 통화를 끝냈어요.
남: **제가 경기 때 그들의 옷을 입기를 원하던 가요?**
여: 훨씬 더 좋은 제안이에요. 새로 나오는 테니스 의류 제품군의 공식 모델이 되어주기를 원해요.
남: 우와! 하지만… 제 이름이 고품질이 아닌 어떤 것에 붙여지는 게 싫으니 우선 그 옷부터 확인해 봐야겠어요. **동의하기 전에 견본을 몇 점 받을 수 있을까요?**
여: 그건 문제없을 것 같아요. **제가 요청할게요.** 그런 다음에 **당신이 승인하면 계약 조건에 대한 논의를 시작하면 됩니다.**
남: 알겠습니다, 하지만 **다음 몇 주 동안 제가 휴가를 갈 예정이에요.**
여: 아, 아직 디자인 단계예요.

어휘 get off the phone 전화를 끊다 representative 담당자, 대리인 match 경기, 시합 official 공식적인

---

spokesperson 대표자, 대변인 attach 붙이다
high-quality 고품질의 put in 제출하다 approval 승인
contract terms 계약 조건 stage 단계

59 Who most likely is the man?
(A) An advertising executive
(B) A fashion photographer
(C) A professional athlete
(D) An event organizer

번역 남자는 누구이겠는가?
(A) 광고 책임자
(B) 패션 사진작가
(C) 전문 운동선수
(D) 행사 기획자

해설 **전체 내용 관련 - 남자의 직업**
남자가 첫 대사에서 자신의 경기 때(during my matches)라고 말하고 있으므로 남자는 운동선수임을 알 수 있다. 따라서 정답은 (C)이다.

어휘 athlete 운동선수 organizer 주최자

60 What does the woman say she will request?
(A) Sales projections
(B) A venue recommendation
(C) A long-term contract
(D) Clothing samples

번역 여자는 무엇을 요청하겠다고 말하는가?
(A) 판매 예상 수치
(B) 장소 추천
(C) 장기 계약
(D) 의류 견본

해설 **세부 사항 관련 - 여자의 요청 사항**
남자가 두번째 대사에서 동의하기 전에 견본을 몇 점 받을 수 있는지(Can I get a few sample pieces before I agree to anything?) 묻자 여자가 자신이 요청하겠다(I'll put in the request)고 했으므로 정답은 (D)이다.

어휘 projection 예상 venue 장소 long-term 장기적인

61 Why does the woman say, "they're still in the design stage"?
(A) To indicate that the man's input is not needed yet
(B) To encourage the man to suggest some changes
(C) To show frustration about a lack of progress
(D) To explain why some accessories are not being used

번역 여자가 "아직 디자인 단계예요"라고 말한 이유는?
(A) 남자의 개입이 아직 필요하지 않다는 사실을 알리려고
(B) 남자가 수정을 제안하도록 장려하려고
(C) 진척이 없다는 점에 대해 답답함을 표현하려고
(D) 일부 액세서리가 사용되지 않고 있는 이유를 설명하려고

해설 **화자의 의도 파악 - 아직 디자인 단계라는 말의 의도**
앞에서 여자가 당신이 승인하면 계약 조건에 대한 논의를 시작하면 된다(once you've given your approval, we can begin discussing contract terms)고 했고 남자가 다음 몇 주 동안 휴가를 갈 예정(I'll be on vacation for the next few weeks)이라고 말하자 여자가 인용문을 언급한 것으로 보아, 아직 초기 단계로 남자의 개입이 필요하지 않다는 것을 알려주려는 의도로 한 말임을 알 수 있다. 따라서 정답은 (A)이다.

어휘 input 투입, 제공 encourage 장려하다 frustration 좌절 progress 진척

62-64 대화+평면도

W-Br	Welcome to Avalos Electronics. Is there anything I can help you with today?
M-Au	Yes, **62 I've just agreed to take a sales position that will involve a lot of travel**, and I'd like to buy a good e-reader to bring along.
W-Br	I'm happy to walk you through the options. Are you planning to only read e-books, or do you want something that can browse the Internet, too?
M-Au	Just e-books. I'm trying to spend less time online.
W-Br	I understand. **63 Let's head over to the mobile devices section.** It's in the center of our store. Now, **64 I want you to know that all of the products you're going to see can run the Litera public library app.**

여: 아발로스 전자에 오신 것을 환영합니다. 제가 도와드릴 일이 있으신가요?

남: 네, 제가 출장을 많이 다녀야 하는 영업직 일자리를 수락하기로 했거든요. 그래서 갖고 다닐 좋은 전자책 단말기를 사고 싶어요.

여: 몇 가지 제품들을 차근차근 보여드리겠습니다. 전자책만 읽으실 건가요? 아니면 인터넷 검색도 할 수 있는 제품을 원하시나요?

남: 전자책만요. 인터넷을 덜 하려고 노력 중이거든요.

여: 알겠습니다. 모바일 기기 코너로 가실게요. 저희 매장 중앙에 있어요. 자, 앞으로 보실 모든 제품에서 리테라 공공 도서관 앱을 사용하실 수 있다는 점을 알려드려요.

어휘 position 일자리 involve 포함하다 e-reader 전자책 단말기 bring along 가지고 가다 walk through 차근차근 도와주다 browse 검색하다 head over to ~으로 향하다

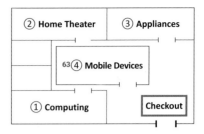

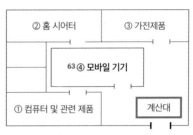

62 What did the man do recently?
(A) He accepted a job offer.
(B) He moved to a new city.
(C) He started writing a book.
(D) He attended a presentation.

번역 남자는 최근에 무엇을 했는가?
(A) 일자리 제안을 수락했다.
(B) 새로운 도시로 이사했다.
(C) 책 집필을 시작했다.
(D) 발표회에 참석했다.

해설 **세부 사항 관련 - 남자가 최근에 한 일**
남자가 첫 대사에서 출장을 많이 다녀야 하는 영업직 일자리를 수락하기로 했다(I've just agreed to take a sales position that will involve a lot of travel)고 말하고 있으므로 정답은 (A)이다.

어휘 accept 수락하다 job offer 일자리 제안 attend 참석하다 presentation 발표

> **Paraphrasing**
> 내화의 agreed to take a sales position
> → 정답의 accepted a job offer

63 Look at the graphic. Where will the speakers go next?
(A) To Section 1
(B) To Section 2
(C) To Section 3
(D) To Section 4

번역 시각 정보에 의하면, 화자들은 다음에 어디로 가겠는가?
(A) 1번 코너로
(B) 2번 코너로
(C) 3번 코너로
(D) 4번 코너로

해설 **시각 정보 연계 - 화자들이 다음에 갈 곳**
여자가 마지막 대사에서 모바일 기기 코너로 갈 것(Let's head over to

the mobile devices section)을 제안하고 있고, 평면도에 따르면 모바일 기기(Mobile Devices)는 4번 코너이므로 정답은 (D)이다.

---

64 What does the woman mention about the products?
(A) They come with a warranty.
(B) They are part of a sales promotion.
(C) They are compatible with an app.
(D) They were released recently.

번역 여자는 제품에 대해 무엇을 언급하는가?
(A) 품질 보증서가 딸려 나온다.
(B) 판촉 행사의 일환이다.
(C) 앱과 호환된다.
(D) 최근에 출시되었다.

해설 **세부 사항 관련 - 여자가 제품에 대해 언급하는 것**
여자가 마지막 대사에서 앞으로 볼 모든 제품에서 리테라 공공 도서관 앱을 사용할 수 있다(I want you to know that all of the products you're going to see can run the Litera public library app)고 말하고 있으므로 정답은 (C)이다.

어휘 warranty 품질 보증서 be compatible with ~와 호환되다
release 출시하다

65-67 대화+프로그램 발췌

W-Am **65 I just finished making the program for the library's anniversary celebration.** Here's the sample.

M-Cn Looks great! Wow, it's wonderful that so many people are coming together to commemorate our fiftieth year, isn't it?

W-Am Yes, it is.

M-Cn Oh wait, I see that I forgot to tell you about a change to the author readings section. **66 It's Arletta DeWitt—she decided she's going to read from *A Joyous World.***

W-Am Got it. After I make that correction, can I send this to the printers?

M-Cn Yes. Oh, and—**67 don't forget to change Ms. DeWitt's book on the event's Web page, too.**

여: **도서관의 기념일 축하 행사를 위한 프로그램을 방금 다 만들었어요.** 여기 견본이에요.

남: 좋아 보이네요! 우와, 이렇게 많은 사람들이 우리 50주년을 기념하기 위해 모인다니 정말 멋지네요, 안 그래요?

여: 네, 정말 그래요.

남: 아 잠깐만요, 저자 낭독회 시간 중에 변동 사항이 있는데 제가 깜박하고 말씀을 안 드렸나 보네요. **알레타 드윗이에요. 그녀가 〈어 조이어스 월드〉를 낭독하기로 결정했어요.**

여: 알겠습니다. 수정한 다음에 이 파일을 인쇄소로 보내면 될까요?

남: 네. 아, 그리고, **행사 웹페이지에도 드윗 씨의 책을 수정하는 것 잊지 마세요.**

어휘 anniversary 기념일 celebration 축하 commemorate 기념하다 author 저자 reading 낭독 correction 수정 printer 인쇄소, 인쇄업자

Readings	
Author	**Book**
Eun-Young Cho	*Silver Flame*
Conrad Morris	*My Father's Hands*
Break	
Igor Bartosz	*Nights on the Oder*
66 Arletta DeWitt	*Let Us Run*

낭독회	
저자	도서
조은영	〈실버 플레임〉
콘래드 모리스	〈마이 파더스 핸즈〉
휴식 시간	
이고리 바르토시	〈나이츠 온 디 오데르〉
66 알레타 드윗	〈렛 어스 런〉

65 What are the speakers organizing?
(A) A birthday celebration for an author
(B) An anniversary party for a library
(C) A special event for a book festival
(D) The grand opening of a bookstore

번역 화자들은 무엇을 준비하는가?
(A) 저자를 위한 생일 파티
(B) 도서관을 위한 기념 파티
(C) 도서 축제를 위한 특별 행사
(D) 서점의 개장

해설 **전체 내용 관련 - 화자들이 준비하는 것**
여자가 첫 대사에서 도서관의 기념일 축하 행사를 위한 프로그램을 만들었다(I just finished making the program for the library's anniversary celebration)고 말하고 있으므로 정답은 (B)이다.

어휘 grand opening 개업, 개점

> **Paraphrasing**
> 대화의 the library's anniversary celebration
> → 정답의 An anniversary party for a library

66 Look at the graphic. Which book title will be replaced?
(A) *Silver Flame*
(B) *My Father's Hands*
(C) *Nights on the Oder*
(D) *Let Us Run*

번역 시각 정보에 의하면, 어떤 책 제목이 교체되겠는가?
(A) <실버 플레임>
(B) <마이 파더스 핸즈>
(C) <나이츠 온 디 오데르>
(D) <렛 어스 런>

해설 **시각 정보 연계 - 교체될 책 제목**
남자가 두 번째 대사에서 알레타 드윗이 <어 조이어스 월드>를 낭독하기로 결정했다(It's Arletta DeWitt—she decided she's going to read from *A Joyous World*)고 말하고 있고, 프로그램 발췌에 따르면 알레타 드윗은 <렛 어스 런>을 낭독할 예정이므로 정답은 (D)이다.

어휘 replace 교체하다

---

67 What does the man remind the woman to do?
(A) Update a Web page
(B) Buy refreshments
(C) Change a window display
(D) Contact a newspaper company

번역 남자는 여자에게 무엇을 하라고 상기시키는가?
(A) 웹페이지 수정
(B) 다과 구입
(C) 창가 진열 변경
(D) 신문사 연락

해설 **세부 사항 관련 - 남자가 상기시키는 것**
남자가 마지막 대사에서 행사 웹페이지에 드윗 씨의 책을 수정하는 것도 잊지 말 것(don't forget to change Ms. DeWitt's book on the event's Web page, too)을 상기시키고 있으므로 정답은 (A)이다.

어휘 refreshments 다과   display 전시, 진열

> **Paraphrasing**
> 대화의 change ~ on the event's Web page
> → 정답의 Update a Web page

68-70 대화+목록

W-Br Hi, Nicholas. I'm looking over the editorial calendar for our magazine's July issue, and— **68 how's your article on energy bars coming along?** It was due yesterday.

M-Cn Yes, sorry. **69 It was hard to find a variety of energy bars without nuts. But I finally did, and I'm writing up my paragraph on the best one now**. The rest of the piece is already finished.

W-Br I'm glad to hear that. Send it over soon.

M-Cn Will do. Uh, I had to order those bars online instead of just buying them in person, though. **70 How do I request reimbursement in that case?**

W-Br The store e-mailed you an order confirmation, right? Print that out and submit it with your request.

여: 안녕하세요, 니콜라스. 우리 잡지의 7월호를 위해 편집 일정표를 살펴보는 중인데요, 에너지 바에 관한 기사는 잘 되어가나요? 마감이 어제까지였네요.

남: 네, 죄송합니다. 견과류가 없는 다양한 에너지 바를 찾기가 어려웠어요. 하지만 마침내 찾았어요. 최고의 제품에 대한 단락을 지금 쓰는 중이에요. 나머지는 이미 끝마쳤고요.

여: 다행이네요. 빨리 보내주세요.

남: 알겠습니다. 참, 그 에너지 바는 가서 직접 사는 대신 온라인으로 주문해야 했어요. 그런 경우에는 어떻게 환급을 신청하나요?

여: 그 상점에서 주문 확인서를 이메일로 보내줬죠, 그렇죠? 그걸 출력해서 신청서와 함께 제출하세요.

어휘 editorial 편집의   issue (잡지 등의) 호   article 기사, 글   come along 일이 되어가다   due 하기로 되어 있는   a variety of 다양한   write up 작성하다   paragraph 단락   in person 직접   reimbursement 환급   confirmation 확인서   submit 제출하다

The Best Energy Bars Following Dietary Restrictions	
Category	**Winner**
Vegan	YouFuel
Dairy-free	Savorette
69 Nut-free	Power Crunch
Gluten-free	The Go Bar

식이 제한별 최고의 에너지 바	
범주	수상 제품
비건	유퓨얼
유제품 무함유	세이보릿
69 견과류 무함유	파워 크런치
글루텐 무함유	더 고 바

어휘 dietary 식이의   restriction 제한

68 Why is the woman calling?
(A) To check on the status of an article
(B) To cancel an editorial meeting
(C) To suggest some relevant products
(D) To discuss the theme of an upcoming issue

번역 여자는 왜 전화를 걸고 있는가?
(A) 기사의 진행 상황을 확인하려고
(B) 편집 회의를 취소하려고
(C) 적절한 제품을 제안하려고
(D) 다음 호의 주제를 상의하려고

해설 **전체 내용 관련 - 여자가 전화 건 이유**
여자가 첫 대사에서 에너지 바에 관한 기사는 잘 되어가는지(how's your article on energy bars coming along?) 묻고 있으므로 정답은 (A)이다.

어휘 status 진행 상황 relevant 관련 있는, 적절한 theme 주제
upcoming 다가오는

> **Paraphrasing**
> 대화의 how's your article ~ coming along?
> → 정답의 the status of an article

69 Look at the graphic. Which energy bar is the man currently writing about?
(A) YouFuel
(B) Savorette
(C) Power Crunch
(D) The Go Bar

번역 시각 정보에 의하면, 남자는 현재 어떤 에너지 바에 대해 글을 쓰고 있는가?
(A) 유퓨얼
(B) 세이보릿
(C) 파워 크런치
(D) 더 고 바

해설 **시각 정보 연계 - 남자가 현재 글을 쓰고 있는 에너지 바**
남자가 첫 대사에서 견과류가 없는 다양한 에너지 바를 찾기가 어려웠지만(It was hard to find a variety of energy bars without nuts) 마침내 찾아 최고의 제품에 대한 단락을 지금 쓰는 중(But I finally did, and I'm writing up my paragraph on the best one now)이라고 말하고 있고, 목록에 따르면 견과류가 없는 에너지 바는 파워 크런치(Power Crunch)이므로 정답은 (C)이다.

70 What does the man ask about?
(A) A request from a reader
(B) A reimbursement process
(C) The word limit for a review
(D) The previous work of a journalist

번역 남자는 무엇에 대해 물어보는가?
(A) 독자로부터의 요청 사항
(B) 환급 절차
(C) 후기의 글자 수 제한
(D) 기자가 이전에 쓴 기사

해설 **세부 사항 관련 - 남자의 문의 사항**
남자가 마지막 대사에서 어떻게 환급을 신청하는지(How do I request reimbursement ~?) 묻고 있으므로 정답은 (B)이다.

어휘 previous 이전의 journalist 기자

PART 4

71-73 전화 메시지

> W-Am Hello. **71 This is Sun-Mi from Vanover Landscape Contractors**. I'm calling about your backyard renovation. **72 We just confirmed receipt of your deposit payment**, so we'll begin work on the sixteenth as scheduled. Please make sure the yard is ready for our crew. Also, I should warn you that **73 our trucks take up quite a bit of space**, so it's a good idea to move your car out of your driveway before they arrive.
>
> 안녕하세요. **배노버 조경업체의 선미입니다.** 뒷마당 보수 공사 때문에 전화드립니다. 당신의 **계약금 지불 영수증을 방금 확인했으니**, 예정대로 16일에 공사를 시작하겠습니다. 마당을 작업자들이 일할 수 있도록 준비해 주십시오. 그리고 미리 말씀드려야 하는 부분이 있는데 **저희 트럭들이 자리를 꽤 많이 차지할 테니**, 작업자들이 도착하기 전에 진입로에 있는 차량을 이동하시는 게 좋을 겁니다.
>
> 어휘 landscape contractor 조경업체 renovation 보수 confirm 확인하다 receipt 영수증 deposit 계약금 payment 지불 as scheduled 예정대로 take up 차지하다 driveway 진입로

71 Where does the speaker work?
(A) At a moving company
(B) At an apartment complex
(C) At a landscaping firm
(D) At a hardware store

번역 화자는 어디서 일하는가?
(A) 이사업체
(B) 아파트 단지
(C) 조경회사
(D) 철물점

해설 **전체 내용 관련 - 화자의 근무지**
화자가 초반부에 배노버 조경업체의 선미(This is Sun-Mi from Vanover Landscape Contractors)라고 말하고 있으므로 정답은 (C)이다.

72 According to the speaker, what has the business received?
(A) An advance deposit
(B) A signed agreement
(C) A product shipment
(D) A repair request

번역 화자에 따르면, 업체는 무엇을 받았는가?
(A) 선수금
(B) 서명된 계약서
(C) 제품 배송
(D) 수리 요청서

TEST 4

화자가 중반부에 계약금 지불 영수증을 방금 확인했다(We just confirmed receipt of your deposit payment)고 말하고 있으므로 정답은 (A)이다.

어휘 advance deposit 선수금 agreement 계약서 repair 수리

> **Paraphrasing**
> 담화의 deposit payment → 정답의 An advance deposit

73 What does the speaker say about the business's vehicles?
(A) They are easy to recognize.
(B) They make a lot of noise.
(C) They are large in size.
(D) They have tracking devices.

번역 화자는 업체의 차량에 대해 뭐라고 말하는가?
(A) 알아보기 쉽다.
(B) 소음이 많이 난다.
(C) 크기가 크다.
(D) 추적 장치가 달려 있다.

해설 세부 사항 관련 - 화자가 업체의 차량에 대해 하는 말
화자가 마지막에 트럭들이 자리를 꽤 많이 차지한다(our trucks take up quite a bit of space)고 했으므로 정답은 (C)이다.

어휘 recognize 알아보다 tracking device 추적 장치

> **Paraphrasing**
> 담화의 take up quite a bit of space
> → 정답의 large in size

74-76 공지

M-Au Can I have everyone's attention? I have an update on the process of hiring our new office manager. Obviously, It has taken longer than expected. **74 The job's scope had expanded, and we didn't realize until after reviewing applications that we needed to revise the description.** But, the hiring team has now met with several candidates. **75 Tomorrow we're going to offer the position to our top choice.** We hope he'll accept and be able to start soon. With that in mind, **76 I've noticed that the office manager's cubicle has become a kind of storage area. Can anyone who's keeping stuff there go and clear it out now?**

여러분 주목해 주시겠습니까? 새로운 사무장을 고용하는 과정에 관해 새로 알려드릴 내용이 있습니다. 확실히 예상보다 오래 걸렸습니다. **직무의 범위가 늘어났는데, 설명을 수정해야 한다는 사실을 지원서를 검토한 후에야 알게 된 거였어요.** 하지만 이제 채용팀에서 몇몇 지원자를 만났습니다. **내일 그 자리를 저희가 1순위로 뽑은 지원자에게 제안**

할 예정입니다. 그가 수락해서 빨리 일을 시작할 수 있으면 좋겠네요. 그 점을 염두에 두시고, **사무장의 자리가 거의 보관 창고가 되었더라고요. 거기에 물건을 갖다 놓으신 분은 지금 가서 치워주시겠습니까?**

어휘 hire 고용하다 office manager 사무장 obviously 확실히 scope 범위 expand 확장하다 revise 수정하다 description 설명 candidate 지원자 position 일자리, 직위 accept 수락하다 cubicle 칸막이로 구획된 사무 공간 storage 보관 clear out 청소하다

74 According to the speaker, why is a hiring process behind schedule?
(A) A manager was out of the office.
(B) A job description was outdated.
(C) A posting received too few responses.
(D) Some funding had to be secured.

번역 화자에 따르면, 채용 과정은 왜 일정보다 늦어졌는가?
(A) 관리자가 사무실에 없어서
(B) 직무 설명이 오래된 것이어서
(C) 채용 공고에 대한 반응이 너무 적어서
(D) 자금이 확보되어야 해서

해설 세부 사항 관련 - 채용 과정이 일정보다 늦어진 이유
화자가 초반부에 직무의 범위가 늘어났는데, 설명을 수정해야 한다는 사실을 지원서를 검토한 후에야 알게 되었다(The job's scope had expanded, and we didn't realize until after reviewing applications that we needed to revise the description)고 말하고 있으므로 정답은 (B)이다.

어휘 behind schedule 예정보다 늦은 outdated 오래된 response 응답, 반응 funding 자금 secure 확보하다

75 What does the speaker say will happen tomorrow?
(A) Some interviews will take place.
(B) An office tour will be given.
(C) An orientation will begin.
(D) A job offer will be extended.

번역 화자는 내일 무슨 일이 일어날 거라고 말하는가?
(A) 면접이 진행될 것이다.
(B) 사무실 견학이 진행될 것이다.
(C) 오리엔테이션이 시작될 것이다.
(D) 일자리 제안이 전달될 것이다.

해설 세부 사항 관련 - 내일 일어날 일
화자가 중반부에 내일 그 자리를 1순위로 뽑은 지원자에게 제안할 예정(Tomorrow we're going to offer the position to our top choice)이라고 말하고 있으므로 정답은 (D)이다.

어휘 take place 일어나다 job offer 일자리 제안 extend 주다, 베풀다

> **Paraphrasing**
> 담화의 offer the position → 정답의 A job offer

76 What will some of the listeners most likely do next?
(A) Read a handout
(B) Greet a new colleague
(C) Go to a conference room
(D) Clean up a work space

번역 청자들 중 일부는 다음으로 무엇을 하겠는가?
(A) 유인물 읽기
(B) 새로운 동료 환영하기
(C) 회의실로 가기
(D) **사무 공간 청소하기**

해설 **세부 사항 관련 - 청자들이 다음에 할 일**
화자가 후반부에 사무장의 자리가 거의 보관 창고가 되었다(I've noticed that the office manager's cubicle has become a kind of storage area)면서 지금 가서 치워줄 것(Can anyone ~ go and clear it out now?)을 요청하고 있으므로 정답은 (D)이다.

어휘 handout 유인물, 인쇄물 greet 환영하다 colleague 동료

> **Paraphrasing**
> 담화의 clear it out → 정답의 Clean up

77-79 회의 발췌

> W-Br Alright, ⁷⁷ **we're now just one month away from the career fair.** As usual, let's start today's planning meeting by sharing updates on our assigned tasks. I'll go first. Um, unfortunately, ⁷⁸ **I'm having trouble finding a place to rent the tables and chairs from.** The company we used last year doesn't have enough available for the date of the fair, and other companies I've found charge higher rates. But—I remember that there were some empty tables at last year's event. ⁷⁹ **Could we check that all of the employers who've registered this time are still planning to come?**
>
> 좋습니다, **취업 박람회가 겨우 한 달 앞으로 다가왔습니다.** 평소처럼, 맡은 업무에 대한 진행 상황을 공유하는 것으로 오늘의 기획 회의를 시작합시다. 제가 먼저 하죠. 음, 안타깝게도 **테이블과 의자를 대여할 곳을 찾는 데 어려움을 겪고 있어요.** 작년에 이용했던 회사는 박람회 날짜에 수량이 부족하다고 하고, 제가 찾은 다른 회사들은 더 높은 금액을 청구해요. 하지만, 작년 행사 때 빈 테이블이 좀 있었던 걸 기억해요. **이번에 등록한 고용주들이 모두 여전히 올 계획인지 확인할 수 있을까요?**
>
> 어휘 career fair 취업 박람회 assigned 할당된 task 과제, 일 enough 충분한 만큼의 수 available 이용 가능한 charge 청구하다 employer 고용주 register 등록하다

77 What event is being planned?
(A) A festival
(B) A fund-raiser
(C) An awards ceremony
(D) A job fair

번역 어떤 행사가 계획되고 있는가?
(A) 축제
(B) 모금 행사
(C) 시상식
(D) **채용 박람회**

해설 **세부 사항 관련 - 계획되고 있는 행사**
화자가 도입부에 취업 박람회가 겨우 한 달 앞으로 다가왔다(we're now just one month away from the career fair)고 말하고 있으므로 정답은 (D)이다.

> **Paraphrasing**
> 담화의 the career fair → 정답의 A job fair

78 What task is the speaker having difficulty with?
(A) Obtaining a permit
(B) Recruiting volunteers
(C) Creating advertisements
(D) Renting furniture

번역 화자는 어떤 업무에 어려움을 겪고 있는가?
(A) 허가 얻기
(B) 자원봉사자 모집하기
(C) 광고 제작하기
(D) **가구 대여하기**

해설 **세부 사항 관련 - 화자가 어려움을 겪고 있는 업무**
화자가 중반부에 테이블과 의자를 대여할 곳을 찾는 데 어려움을 겪고 있다(I'm having trouble finding a place to rent the tables and chairs from)고 했으므로 정답은 (D)이다.

어휘 obtain 얻다, 획득하다 permit 허가 recruit 모집하다 advertisement 광고 furniture 가구

> **Paraphrasing**
> 담화의 tables and chairs → 정답의 furniture

79 What does the speaker propose doing?
(A) Changing the event date
(B) Hiring an outside specialist
(C) Confirming some attendees
(D) Reviewing records from last year

번역 화자는 무엇을 하기로 제안하는가?
(A) 행사 날짜 변경하기
(B) 외부 전문가 고용하기
(C) **참석자 확인하기**
(D) 작년 기록 살펴보기

해설 **세부 사항 관련 - 화자의 제안 사항**
화자가 마지막에 등록한 고용주들이 여전히 올 계획인지 확인하자(Could we check that all of the employers who've registered this time are still planning to come?)고 제안하고 있으므로 정답은 (C)이다.

어휘 specialist 전문가 attendee 참석자

80-82 방송

M-Cn Welcome back to the *Channel 8 News*. We'll now turn our attention to entertainment. **80 *Wave Cruiser 3*, the final film in the Wave Cruiser trilogy, will arrive on screens next Thursday. 81 Rockwell Theaters released tickets online for its first few days of screenings this morning,** and the number of visitors overloaded its Web site! Fans reported waiting for as long as three hours for their purchases to go through. By mid-afternoon, however, **82 the theater chain had announced through its social media accounts that tickets were successfully sold out.**

〈채널 8 뉴스〉에 다시 오신 것을 환영합니다. 이제 연예계 쪽을 살펴보겠습니다. 웨이브 크루저 3부작 중 마지막 영화인 〈웨이브 크루저 3〉가 다음 주 목요일에 개봉될 예정입니다. 로크웰 극장은 오늘 아침에 첫 며칠 상영분에 대한 온라인 티켓 판매를 시작했습니다. 방문자 수로 인해 웹사이트에 과부하가 걸렸습니다! 팬들은 구매가 완료되는 데까지 세 시간이나 기다렸다고 말했습니다. 하지만 오후 중반쯤 극장 측은 자체 소셜 미디어 계정을 통해 티켓이 성공적으로 매진되었다고 발표했습니다.

어휘 turn one's attention to ~으로 주의를 돌리다 trilogy 3부작 release 출시하다 screening 상영 visitor 방문자 overload 과부하를 주다 purchase 구매 go through 성사되다 account 계정 sold out 매진된

80 What is the topic of the broadcast?
(A) Holiday travel
(B) A sports tournament
(C) The opening of a movie
(D) A sales promotion at a store

번역 방송의 주제는 무엇인가?
(A) 휴가 여행
(B) 스포츠 토너먼트
(C) 영화 개봉
(D) 상점의 판촉 행사

해설 전체 내용 관련 - 방송의 주제
화자가 초반부에 웨이브 크루저 3부작 중 마지막 영화인 〈웨이브 크루저 3〉가 다음 주 목요일에 개봉될 예정(*Wave Cruiser 3*, the final film in the Wave Cruiser trilogy, will arrive on screens next Thursday)이라고 했으므로 정답은 (C)이다.

어휘 opening 개봉, 개점 promotion 촉진

81 What does the speaker imply when he says, "the number of visitors overloaded its Web site"?
(A) A service is currently unavailable.
(B) It is better to make a purchase in person.
(C) There is high demand for some tickets.
(D) Many people received a special discount.

번역 화자가 "방문자 수로 인해 웹사이트에 과부하가 걸렸습니다"라고 말할 때, 그 의도는 무엇인가?
(A) 서비스가 현재 이용 불가 상태이다.
(B) 직접 가서 구매하는 것이 낫다.
(C) 티켓에 대한 수요가 높다.
(D) 많은 사람들이 특별 할인을 받았다.

해설 화자의 의도 파악 - 방문자 수로 인해 웹사이트에 과부하가 걸렸다는 말의 의도
앞에서 로크웰 극장은 오늘 아침에 첫 며칠 상영분에 대한 온라인 티켓 판매를 시작했다(Rockwell Theaters released tickets online for its first few days of screenings this morning)고 말한 뒤 인용문을 언급한 것으로 보아, 티켓에 대한 방문자 수요가 높다는 의도로 한 말임을 알 수 있다. 따라서 정답은 (C)이다.

어휘 unavailable 이용 불가능한 in person 직접 demand 수요

82 According to the speaker, how did a company make an announcement?
(A) By issuing text messages
(B) By posting on social media
(C) By holding a press conference
(D) By sending a mass e-mail

번역 화자에 따르면, 회사는 어떻게 공지를 했는가?
(A) 문자 메시지를 보내서
(B) 소셜 미디어에 올려서
(C) 기자 회견을 열어서
(D) 대량 이메일을 발송해서

해설 세부 사항 관련 - 회사가 공지를 한 방법
화자가 마지막에 극장 측은 자체 소셜 미디어 계정을 통해 티켓이 성공적으로 매진되었다고 발표했다(the theater chain had announced through its social media accounts that tickets were successfully sold out)고 말하고 있으므로 정답은 (B)이다.

어휘 issue 발행하다 post 게시하다 press conference 기자 회견

83-85 여행 정보

W-Br I'm glad you all could join me for this tour of London's Southwark district. **83 I'm Wanda Bailey, your guide. Throughout the morning, don't hesitate to ask me your questions about this fascinating city**—my family has lived here for generations. Now, **84 I'm glad to see that you all followed our instructions to choose shoes you**

can walk comfortably in. We have a long way to go before lunch. ⁸⁵ **Let's start by heading toward that monument decorated with striking sculptures.**

여러분 모두 런던의 서더크 지구 투어에 함께해 주셔서 기뻐요. 저는 여러분의 인솔자 완다 베일리입니다. 오전 중 언제든지 이 매력적인 도시에 대해 질문이 있으시면 망설이지 말고 얘기해 주세요. 저희 가족은 대대로 이곳에서 살았답니다. 자, 여러분 모두 편히 걸을 수 있는 신발을 고르시라는 저희 안내에 잘 따라주셔서 기쁘네요. 점심시간까지 갈 길이 멉니다. 그럼 인상적인 조각으로 장식된 저 기념물을 향해 출발함으로써 투어를 시작합시다.

어휘   district 지구, 구역   hesitate 망설이다   fascinating 매력적인   for generations 대대로   instruction 지시, 안내   comfortably 편안하게   monument 기념물   decorate 장식하다   striking 눈에 띄는, 인상적인   sculpture 조각

83 What does the speaker mean when she says, "my family has lived here for generations"?
(A) She recommends moving to the city.
(B) She has a useful background for her job.
(C) She prefers to vacation in other places.
(D) She is unhappy about a redevelopment plan.

번역   화자가 "저희 가족은 대대로 이곳에서 살았답니다"라고 말할 때, 그 의도는 무엇인가?
(A) 이 도시로 이사하는 것을 추천한다.
(B) 자신의 일에 유용한 배경을 갖고 있다.
(C) 다른 곳에서 휴가 보내는 것을 선호한다.
(D) 재개발 계획이 마음에 들지 않는다.

해설   화자의 의도 파악 - 가족이 대대로 이곳에서 살았다는 말의 의도
앞에서 자신은 인솔자 완다 베일리(I'm Wanda Bailey, your guide)라면서 매력적인 도시에 대해 질문이 있으면 망설이지 말고 얘기할 것(~ don't hesitate to ask me your questions about this fascinating city)을 상기시킨 뒤 인용문을 언급한 것으로 보아, 지역에 대해 잘 알고 있는 인솔자라는 것을 알리려고 한 말임을 알 수 있다. 따라서 정답은 (B)이다.

어휘   useful 유용한   redevelopment 재개발

84 What were listeners instructed to do?
(A) Bring a bottle of water
(B) Arrive a few minutes early
(C) Wear comfortable shoes
(D) Place a lunch order

번역   청자들은 무엇을 하도록 지시받았는가?
(A) 생수 한 병 가져오기
(B) 몇 분 일찍 도착하기
(C) 편안한 신발 신기
(D) 점심 주문하기

해설   세부 사항 관련 - 청자들이 지시받은 것
화자가 중반부에 편히 걸을 수 있는 신발을 고르라는 안내에 잘 따라줘서 기쁘다(I'm glad to see that you all followed our instructions to choose shoes you can walk comfortably

---

in)고 말하고 있으므로 정답은 (C)이다.

어휘   place an order 주문하다

> **Paraphrasing**
> 담화의 shoes you can walk comfortably in
> → 정답의 comfortable shoes

85 What will the listeners see first?
(A) Some public art
(B) A government building
(C) An outdoor market
(D) A waterway

번역   청자들은 가장 먼저 무엇을 보겠는가?
(A) 공공 미술 작품
(B) 정부 청사
(C) 노천 시장
(D) 수로

해설   세부 사항 관련 - 청자들이 가장 먼저 볼 것
화자가 마지막에 인상적인 조각으로 장식된 기념물을 향해 출발함으로써 투어를 시작하자(Let's start by heading toward that monument decorated with striking sculptures)고 말하고 있으므로 정답은 (A)이다.

> **Paraphrasing**
> 담화의 that monument decorated with striking sculptures → 정답의 Some public art

86-88 전화 메시지

> M-Cn Hi, this is Elijah in Accounting. As you've probably heard, ⁸⁶ **a team will be coming here to headquarters soon to conduct our company's first external audit.** We're trying to prepare well so that the process goes smoothly. In addition to our financial records, ⁸⁷ **we expect that the audit team will need some things from your department— namely, the employee handbook and all recent versions of our organizational chart.** ⁸⁸ **Could you get those documents together this week?** Thanks.
>
> 안녕하세요, 회계부의 일라이자입니다. 아마도 들으셨겠지만 우리 회사의 첫 외부 감사를 실시하기 위해 감사단이 곧 이곳 본사로 올 예정입니다. 절차가 순조롭게 진행될 수 있도록 열심히 준비하는 중이에요. 우리 재무 기록 외에도 감사단이 당신의 부서에서 뭔가 필요로 할 수도 있을 겁니다. 즉, 직원 안내서와 우리 조직도의 최신 버전이요. 그 문서들을 이번 주에 취합해 줄 수 있나요? 고맙습니다.
>
> ---
>
> 어휘   accounting 회계   headquarters 본사, 본부   conduct 실시하다   external audit 외부 감사   smoothly 순조롭게   financial 금융의   namely 즉, 다시 말해   handbook 안내서   organizational chart 조직도   get together 합치다, 정리하다

86 What is the company preparing to do?
(A) Relocate its headquarters
(B) Negotiate a merger
(C) Undergo an audit
(D) Launch a product line

번역 회사는 무엇을 준비 중인가?
(A) 본사 이전
(B) 합병 협상
(C) 감사 받기
(D) 제품군 출시

해설 **세부 사항 관련 - 회사가 준비 중인 것**
화자가 초반부에 회사의 첫 외부 감사를 실시하기 위해 감사단이 곧 이곳 본사로 올 예정(a team will be coming here to headquarters soon to conduct our company's first external audit)이라고 말하고 있으므로 정답은 (C)이다.

어휘 relocate 이전하다 negotiate 협상하다 merger 합병 undergo 겪다 launch 출시하다

> **Paraphrasing**
> 담화의 conduct our company's first external audit
> → 정답의 Undergo an audit

87 What department does the listener most likely work for?
(A) Human Resources
(B) Finance
(C) Public Relations
(D) Security

번역 청자는 어느 부서에서 일하겠는가?
(A) 인사부
(B) 재무부
(C) 홍보부
(D) 경비실

해설 **선체 내용 관련 - 청자의 근무 부서**
화자가 중반부에 감사단이 청자의 부서에서 뭔가 필요로 할 수도 있는데 직원 안내서와 조직도의 최신 버전(we expect that the audit team will need some things from your department—namely, the employee handbook and all recent versions of our organizational chart)이라고 말하고 있으므로 청자는 인사부에서 근무 중이라는 것을 알 수 있다. 따라서 정답은 (A)이다.

88 What does the speaker ask the listener to do?
(A) Revise a proposal
(B) Organize a meeting
(C) Gather some documents
(D) Postpone an announcement

번역 화자는 청자에게 무엇을 하라고 요청하는가?
(A) 제안 수정하기
(B) 회의 준비하기
(C) 문서 취합하기
(D) 공지 연기하기

해설 **세부 사항 관련 - 화자의 요청 사항**
화자가 후반부에 그 문서들을 이번 주에 취합해 줄 것(Could you get those documents together this week?)을 요청하고 있으므로 정답은 (C)이다.

어휘 revise 수정하다 proposal 제안 organize 조직하다 gather 모으다 postpone 연기하다 announcement 공지, 발표

> **Paraphrasing**
> 담화의 get those documents together
> → 정답의 Gather some documents

89-91 회의 발췌

M-Au At this meeting, **89 I'd like to talk about ways to build our furniture more efficiently without sacrificing quality or safety.** As you know, **90 last month we started storing many tools on wall hooks instead of keeping them hidden away in drawers,** and it has noticeably helped our productivity. Another idea I've had is automating the preparation of some materials. **91 I've brought a few pieces of wood sanded by a robot. Feel them and tell me what you think of the quality.**

본 회의에서 저는 품질이나 안전을 희생하지 않고 더 효율적으로 우리 가구를 제작하는 방법들에 대해 이야기하고자 합니다. 아시다시피 지난달에 우리는 많은 도구를 서랍에 숨겨놓는 대신 벽에 걸어서 보관하기 시작했고, 눈에 띄게 생산성에 도움이 되었습니다. 제가 생각해 본 또 다른 아이디어는 일부 재료의 준비를 자동화하는 것입니다. 제가 로봇이 사포질한 나무 조각들을 몇 개 가져왔습니다. 만져보시고 품질에 대해 어떻게 생각하시는지 말씀해 주세요.

어휘 furniture 가구 efficiently 효율적으로 sacrifice 희생하다 quality 품질 safety 안전 store 보관하다 tool 도구 hide away 숨기다 drawer 서랍 noticeably 현저하게 productivity 생산성 automate 자동화하다 preparation 준비 material 재료 sand 사포로 밀다

89 What is the meeting mainly about?
(A) Finding uses for some waste
(B) Improving manufacturing practices
(C) Increasing staff retention rates
(D) Replacing a supplies vendor

번역 회의는 주로 무엇에 관한 것인가?
(A) 폐기물의 용도 찾기
(B) 제조 관행 개선하기
(C) 직원 유지율 높이기
(D) 공급업체 바꾸기

해설 **전체 내용 관련 - 회의의 주제**
화자가 초반부에 더 효율적으로 가구를 제작하는 방법들에 대해 이야기하고자 한다(I'd like to talk about ways to build our furniture more efficiently ~)고 말하고 있으므로 정답은 (B)이다.

어휘 waste 폐기물 manufacturing practice 제조 관행 retention rate 유지율 replace 교체하다 supplies vendor 공급업체

> **Paraphrasing**
> 담화의 ways to build our furniture more efficiently
> → 정답의 Improving manufacturing practices

90 What has recently changed?
(A) A storage method
(B) A training period
(C) A uniform policy
(D) A safety regulation

번역 최근에 무엇이 변경되었는가?
(A) 보관 방법
(B) 연수 기간
(C) 작업복 정책
(D) 안전 규정

해설 **세부 사항 관련 - 최근에 변경된 것**
화자가 중반부에 지난달에 많은 도구를 서랍에 숨겨놓는 대신 벽에 걸어서 보관하기 시작했다(last month we started storing many tools on wall hooks instead of keeping them hidden away in drawers)고 말하고 있으므로 정답은 (A)이다.

어휘 storage 보관 method 방법 policy 정책 regulation 규정

---

91 What will the listeners do next?
(A) Watch a slide presentation
(B) Report on their activities
(C) Handle some materials
(D) Establish a project team

번역 청자들은 다음으로 무엇을 하겠는가?
(A) 슬라이드 발표 자료를 본다.
(B) 활동에 대해 보고한다.
(C) 재료를 만져본다.
(D) 프로젝트팀을 꾸린다.

해설 **세부 사항 관련 - 청자들이 다음에 할 일**
화자가 후반부에 로봇이 사포질한 나무 조각들을 몇 개 가져왔다(I've brought a few pieces of wood sanded by a robot)면서 만져보고 품질에 대해 어떻게 생각하는지 말해줄 것(Feel them and tell me what you think of the quality)을 요청하고 있으므로 정답은 (C)이다.

어휘 activity 활동 handle 다루다, 만지다 establish 설립하다

> **Paraphrasing**
> 담화의 a few pieces of wood → 정답의 some materials

92-94 회의 발췌

> W-Am Thank you all for coming to this team meeting. Overall, **⁹² I'm pleased with how our study's going.** We've made some interesting findings about the consumer behavior of grocery shoppers. **⁹³ And I'd like to call attention to Masato's success in convincingly acting like a participant in the experiment. You've all been doing a great job,** but he has the hardest role in the project. Well done, Masato. However, there's one outside issue that has come up. **⁹⁴ A similar study was just published in a major journal. Here, I've made copies for everyone.**

> 본 팀 회의에 참석해 주신 모든 분께 감사드립니다. 전반적으로 **우리 연구가 잘 진행되고 있어서 기쁩니다.** 우리는 식료품 구매자의 소비자 행동에 대한 몇 가지 흥미로운 사실을 발견했죠. **또 그 실험에서 그럴듯하게 참가자처럼 행동해 주신 마사토의 성공에 주목하고 싶어요. 여러분 모두 잘해주셨지만,** 그는 이 프로젝트에서 가장 힘든 역할을 맡으셨어요. 수고하셨습니다, 마사토. 그런데 외부적인 문제가 하나 발생했어요. 유사한 연구가 주요 학술지에 최근에 게재되었어요. 여기 모두에게 나눠줄 사본을 준비해 왔습니다.

> 어휘 overall 전반적으로 finding 발견, 결과 consumer behavior 소비자 행동 call attention to ~에 주의를 환기하다 convincingly 설득력 있게 participant 참가자 experiment 실험 role 역할 come up 발생하다 journal 저널, 학술지 make a copy 사본을 만들다

92 Who most likely are the listeners?
(A) Research team members
(B) Grocery store workers
(C) Theater actors
(D) Publishing staff

번역 청자들은 누구이겠는가?
(A) 연구팀의 팀원
(B) 식료품점 직원
(C) 연극배우
(D) 출판사 직원

해설 **전체 내용 관련 - 청자들의 직업**
화자가 초반부에 우리 연구가 잘 진행되고 있어서 기쁘다(I'm pleased with how our study's going)고 말하고 있으므로 정답은 (A)이다.

---

93 What does the speaker imply when she says, "he has the hardest role in the project"?
(A) An employee needs more assistance.
(B) An initial deadline may be missed.
(C) A personnel decision was easy to make.
(D) An accomplishment is especially impressive.

번역 화자가 "그는 이 프로젝트에서 가장 힘든 역할을 맡았어요"라고 말할 때, 그 의도는 무엇인가?
(A) 직원은 더 많은 도움이 필요하다.
(B) 처음에 정한 마감 시한을 지킬 수 없을지도 모른다.
(C) 인사 결정은 쉽게 내릴 수 있었다.
(D) 업적이 특히 인상적이다.

해설 **화자의 의도 파악 - 그는 이 프로젝트에서 가장 힘든 역할을 맡았다는 말의 의도**
앞에서 또 그 실험에서 그럴듯하게 참가자처럼 행동해 주신 마사토의 성공에 주목하고 싶다(And I'd like to call attention to Masato's success in convincingly acting like a participant in the experiment)면서 여러분 모두 잘해주셨지만 (You've all been doing a great job)이라고 한 후, 인용문을 언급하고 있는 것으로 보아, 마사토의 업적이 특히 크고 인상적이라는 것을 강조하기 위한 의도로 한 말임을 알 수 있다. 따라서 정답은 (D)이다.

어휘 assistance 도움 deadline 마감 시한 miss 놓치다
accomplishment 업적. 성취 impressive 인상적인

---

94 What did the speaker make copies of?
(A) A list of incomplete tasks
(B) Images of similar products
(C) The floor plan of a building
(D) A recent journal article

번역 화자는 무엇의 사본을 만들었는가?
(A) 미완료 업무 목록
(B) 유사 상품의 이미지
(C) 건물의 평면도
(D) 최근 학술지 기사

해설 **세부 사항 관련 - 화자가 만든 사본**
화자가 마지막에 유사한 연구가 주요 학술지에 최근에 게재되었다(A similar study was just published in a major journal)면서 모두에게 나눠줄 사본을 준비해 왔다(Here, I've made copies for everyone)고 말하고 있으므로 정답은 (D)이다.

어휘 incomplete 불완전한, 미완성의 floor plan 평면도 article 기사

95-97 담화+셔틀버스 노선도

W-Br Good morning! The shuttle bus will be departing our resort in just a moment. In case you don't know, **95 the Hagan Valley Ski Tournament kicks off today. 96 This means that we'll experience quite a bit of traffic, particularly between the far edge of town and the base of Hagan Mountain.** That section could take much longer than the schedule estimates. Oh, and for safety reasons, **97 please put your bags on your laps and keep a hand on them while we're on the road.**

좋은 아침입니다! 셔틀버스는 잠시 후에 리조트를 출발할 예정입니다. 혹시 모르실까 봐 말씀드리자면 **헤이건 밸리 스키 토너먼트가 오늘 시작합니다.** 그 말은 특히 도시 최외곽에서 헤이건 산 입구까지 교통 체증이 꽤 심할 거라는 뜻입니다. 해당 구간은 예상 도착 시간보다 훨씬 더 오래 걸릴 수 있습니다. 아, 그리고 안전상의 이유로 **이동 중에는 가방을 무릎 위에 놓으시고 손으로 잡고 계십시오.**

어휘 depart 출발하다 kick off 시작하다 particularly 특히
edge 끝, 가장자리 base 맨 아래 부분 estimate 추정 safety
안전 on the road 이동 중인

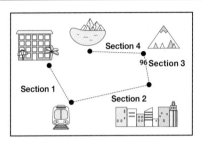

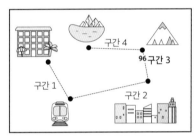

95 What does the speaker say will happen today?
(A) Snow will fall periodically.
(B) A road will be resurfaced.
(C) A public facility will reopen.
(D) A competition will begin.

번역 화자는 오늘 무슨 일이 일어날 거라고 말하는가?
(A) 눈이 가헐적으로 내릴 것이다.
(B) 도로가 재포장될 것이다.
(C) 공공시설이 다시 문을 열 것이다.
(D) 대회가 시작될 것이다.

해설 **세부 사항 관련 - 오늘 있을 일**
화자가 초반부에 헤이건 밸리 스키 토너먼트가 오늘 시작할 것(the Hagan Valley Ski Tournament kicks off today)이라고 말하고 있으므로 정답은 (D)이다.

어휘 periodically 주기적으로, 간헐적으로 resurface 표면 처리를 다시 하다 public facility 공공시설 competition 경쟁, 대회

> **Paraphrasing**
> 담화의 the Hagan Valley Ski Tournament kicks off
> → 정답의 A competition will begin

96 Look at the graphic. Which section of the route does the speaker warn the listeners about?
(A) Section 1
(B) Section 2
(C) Section 3
(D) Section 4

번역 시각 정보에 의하면, 화자는 청자들에게 노선 중 어떤 구간에 대해 경고하는가?
(A) 구간 1
(B) 구간 2
(C) 구간 3
(D) 구간 4

해설 **시각 정보 연계 - 화자가 경고하는 노선 구간**
화자가 중반부에 특히 도시 최외곽에서 헤이건 산 입구까지 교통 체증이 꽤 심할 것(This means that we'll experience quite a bit of traffic, particularly between the far edge of town and the base of Hagan Mountain)이라고 말하고 있고, 셔틀버스 노선도에 따르면 도시 최외곽에서 산 입구까지는 3번 구간이므로 정답은 (C)이다.

---

97 What are the listeners asked to do?
(A) Hold on to their belongings
(B) Silence their mobile phones
(C) Press a button before their stop
(D) Move to the back of the vehicle

번역 청자들은 무엇을 하라고 요청받았는가?
(A) 소지품을 계속 잡고 있기
(B) 휴대 전화 무음 설정하기
(C) 내릴 정류장 전에 버튼 누르기
(D) 차량 뒤쪽으로 이동하기

해설 **세부 사항 관련 - 청자들이 요청받은 일**
화자가 후반부에 이동 중에는 가방을 무릎 위에 놓고 손으로 잡고 있을 것(please put your bags on your laps and keep a hand on them while we're on the road)을 요청하고 있으므로 정답은 (A)이다.

어휘 hold on to ~을 계속 잡고 있다 belongings 소지품 silence ~의 소리를 없애다

> **Paraphrasing**
> 담화의 keep a hand on them(your bags)
> → 정답의 Hold on to their belongings

98-100 방송+영상 리스트

M-Au OK, that's how you play the guitar part in the Carl Brady Band's song "*Dance City*." I showed you the chords and gave you some tips on playing technique. You probably noticed this song has a lot of strumming—**98 if you'd like to work on that skill** **some more, check out my video on strumming technique.** You can find it in my playlist. As always, **99 I'd like to thank Natalie Newman of Newman Productions for filming and editing this video.** Scroll down to the notes below for a link to her Web site. Finally, **100 if there's a topic that I haven't covered yet that you would like to see a video about, feel free to leave a comment requesting it.** I'm always open to suggestions.

자, 칼 브레이디 밴드의 노래 〈댄스 시티〉에서 기타 부분은 이런 식으로 연주하시면 됩니다. 코드를 보여드렸고 연주 기법에 대한 팁도 알려드렸습니다. 여러분은 아마도 이 노래가 스트럼 주법이 많이 필요하다는 점을 알아채셨을 겁니다. **그 기술을 좀 더 연습하고 싶으시다면, 스트럼 주법을 다룬 제 영상을 확인해 보세요.** 제 재생목록에서 찾으실 수 있습니다. 늘 그렇듯이, **이 영상을 촬영하고 편집해 주신 뉴먼 프로덕션스의 나탈리 뉴먼에게 감사드립니다.** 스크롤을 내리시면 그녀의 웹사이트 링크가 보일 겁니다. 마지막으로, **여러분이 영상으로 보고 싶은데 제가 아직 다루지 못한 주제가 있다면, 부담 갖지 마시고 요청하는 댓글을 남겨주세요.** 제안은 언제나 환영합니다.

어휘 chord 코드 technique 기법 strumming 스트럼 (손이나 피크로 여러 개의 기타 줄을 동시에 튕기는 기법) work on 노력하다 skill 기술, 역량 scroll down 스크롤을 아래로 내리다 cover 다루다 leave 남기다 comment 댓글, 논평 be open to ~에 열려 있다 suggestion 제안

Video	Length
▶ Choosing the Right Guitar	11:25
▶ **98 Improve your Strumming Technique**	6:10
▶ Practice Exercises for Beginners	14:35
▶ How to Hold the Pick	4:50
⋮	

영상	길이
▶ 올바른 기타 고르기	11:25
▶ **98 스트럼 주법 향상시키기**	6:10
▶ 초보자를 위한 연습 방법	14:35
▶ 피크를 쥐는 방법	4:50
⋮	

98 Look at the graphic. What is the length of the video that the speaker recommends?
(A) 11:25
(B) 6:10
(C) 14:35
(D) 4:50

번역 시각 정보에 의하면, 화자가 추천한 영상의 길이는 무엇인가?
(A) 11분 25초
(B) 6분 10초
(C) 14분 35초
(D) 4분 50초

TEST 4

시각 정보 연계 - 화자가 추천한 영상의 길이

화자가 중반부에 그 기술을 좀 더 연습하고 싶다면, 스트럼 주법을 다룬 자신의 영상을 확인해 볼 것(if you'd like to work on that skill some more, check out my video on strumming technique)을 추천하고 있고, 영상 리스트에 따르면 스트럼 주법 향상시키기의 영상 길이는 6:10이므로 정답은 (B)이다.

---

99 Who most likely is Natalie Newman?
(A) The composer of a song
(B) A recording studio owner
(C) A professional videographer
(D) A fan of the speaker's videos

번역 나탈리 뉴먼은 누구이겠는가?
(A) 노래의 작곡가
(B) 녹음실 주인
(C) 전문 영상 촬영 기술자
(D) 화자의 영상을 좋아하는 팬

해설 **세부 사항 관련 - 나탈리 뉴먼의 직업**

화자가 중반부에서 이 영상을 촬영하고 편집해 준 뉴먼 프로덕션스의 나탈리 뉴먼에게 감사드린다(I'd like to thank Natalie Newman of Newman Productions for filming and editing this video)고 말하고 있으므로 나탈리 뉴먼은 영상 촬영 기술자임을 알 수 있다. 따라서 정답은 (C)이다.

어휘 composer 작곡가 recording studio 녹음실 videographer 영상 촬영 기술자

---

100 What does the speaker encourage the listeners to give him?
(A) Positive ratings
(B) Topic suggestions
(C) Monetary donations
(D) Used musical instruments

번역 화자는 청자들에게 사신에게 무엇을 달라고 권유하는가?
(A) 긍정적인 평가
(B) 주제 제안
(C) 금전적인 기부
(D) 중고 악기

해설 **세부 사항 관련 - 화자의 요청 사항**

화자가 마지막에 영상으로 보고 싶은데 자신이 아직 다루지 못한 주제가 있다면, 부담 갖지 말고 요청하는 댓글을 남겨달라(if there's a topic that I haven't covered yet that you would like to see a video about, feel free to leave a comment requesting it)고 말하고 있으므로 정답은 (B)이다.

어휘 positive 긍정적인 rating 순위, 평가 monetary 금전의 donation 기부 used 중고의 musical instrument 악기

TEST 5

1 (C)	2 (C)	3 (D)	4 (D)	5 (B)
6 (B)	7 (C)	8 (B)	9 (A)	10 (B)
11 (C)	12 (A)	13 (B)	14 (A)	15 (A)
16 (C)	17 (C)	18 (C)	19 (B)	20 (B)
21 (A)	22 (C)	23 (C)	24 (A)	25 (C)
26 (B)	27 (C)	28 (C)	29 (C)	30 (B)
31 (B)	32 (B)	33 (D)	34 (D)	35 (C)
36 (B)	37 (C)	38 (C)	39 (A)	40 (D)
41 (C)	42 (D)	43 (B)	44 (D)	45 (A)
46 (B)	47 (D)	48 (B)	49 (D)	50 (A)
51 (C)	52 (B)	53 (A)	54 (A)	55 (B)
56 (C)	57 (B)	58 (C)	59 (B)	60 (B)
61 (C)	62 (D)	63 (C)	64 (B)	65 (B)
66 (C)	67 (C)	68 (D)	69 (C)	70 (B)
71 (D)	72 (A)	73 (A)	74 (C)	75 (B)
76 (B)	77 (B)	78 (D)	79 (D)	80 (C)
81 (A)	82 (B)	83 (A)	84 (B)	85 (D)
86 (B)	87 (A)	88 (D)	89 (C)	90 (D)
91 (C)	92 (D)	93 (C)	94 (A)	95 (D)
96 (C)	97 (A)	98 (B)	99 (C)	100 (A)

PART 1

1

W-Am

(A) He is delivering a package.
(B) He is wrapping a container in paper.
(C) He is looking into a cardboard box.
(D) He is wiping off the surface of a kitchen table.

번역 (A) 남자가 소포를 배달하고 있다.
(B) 남자가 종이로 용기를 포장하고 있다.
(C) **남자가 판지 상자 안을 들여다보고 있다.**
(D) 남자가 식탁 표면을 닦고 있다.

해설 **1인 등장 사진**
(A) 동사 오답. 남자가 소포를 배달하고 있는 모습이 아니다.
(B) 동사 오답. 남자가 종이로 포장하고 있는 모습이 아니다.
(C) 정답. 남자가 판지 상자 안을 들여다보고 있으므로 정답이다.
(D) 동사 오답. 남자가 식탁 표면을 닦고 있는 모습이 아니다.

어휘 deliver 배달하다   package 소포   wrap 싸다, 포장하다
container 그릇, 용기   cardboard box 판지 상자   wipe off
~을 닦다   surface 표면

2

W-Br

(A) He is stacking items on a supermarket shelf.
(B) He is placing some products into a bag.
(C) He is holding the handle of a shopping cart.
(D) He is labeling some merchandise with price tags.

번역 (A) 남자가 슈퍼마켓 선반에 물품을 쌓고 있다.
(B) 남자가 상품들을 가방에 넣고 있다.
(C) **남자가 쇼핑 카트의 손잡이를 잡고 있다.**
(D) 남자가 상품에 가격표를 붙이고 있다.

해설 **1인 등장 사진**
(A) 동사 오답. 남자가 슈퍼마켓 선반에 물품을 쌓고 있는 모습이 아니다.
(B) 동사 오답. 남자가 상품들을 가방에 넣고 있는 모습이 아니다.
(C) 정답. 남자가 쇼핑 카트의 손잡이를 잡고 있으므로 정답이다.
(D) 동사 오답. 남자가 상품에 가격표를 붙이고 있는 모습이 아니다.

어휘 stack 쌓다, 포개다   shelf 선반   place 놓다, 두다   handle
손잡이   label 라벨을 붙이다   merchandise 상품   price tag
가격표

3

M-Cn

(A) The man is plugging in a laptop.
(B) The man is leaning against a wall.
(C) One of the women is pointing at a binder.
(D) One of the women is talking on a mobile phone.

번역 (A) 남자가 노트북의 플러그를 꽂고 있다.
(B) 남자가 벽에 기대어 서 있다.
(C) 여자들 중 한 명이 바인더를 가리키고 있다.
(D) **여자들 중 한 명이 휴대 전화로 통화를 하고 있다.**

해설 **2인 이상 등장 사진**
(A) 동사 오답. 남자가 노트북의 플러그를 꽂고 있는 모습이 아니다.
(B) 동사 오답. 남자가 벽에 기대어 서 있는 모습이 아니다.
(C) 동사 오답. 바인더를 가리키고 있는 여자의 모습이 보이지 않는다.
(D) 정답. 여자가 휴대 전화로 통화를 하고 있으므로 정답이다.

어휘 plug in ~의 플러그를 꽂다   lean against ~에 기대다

4

M-Au

(A) A woman is rolling up a hose.
(B) Some water has been left in a bucket.
(C) A woman is digging up flowers from the ground.
(D) Some bushes have been planted outdoors.

번역 (A) 여자가 호스를 돌돌 말고 있다.
(B) 양동이에 물이 남아 있다.
(C) 여자가 땅에서 꽃을 파내고 있다.
(D) 야외에 관목들이 심어져 있다.

해설 **사람/사물·풍경 혼합 사진**
(A) 동사 오답. 여자가 호스를 돌돌 말고 있는 모습이 아니다.
(B) 사진에 없는 명사. 사진에 양동이가 보이지 않는다.
(C) 동사 오답. 여자가 땅에서 꽃을 파내고 있는 모습이 아니다.
(D) 정답. 야외에 관목들이 심어져 있으므로 정답이다.

어휘 roll up 돌돌 말다   bucket 양동이   dig up ~을 땅에서 파내다
bush 관목   plant 심다   outdoors 야외에서

5

M-Au

(A) One of the workers is hanging up a lab coat.
(B) One of the workers is operating some laboratory equipment.
(C) One of the workers is unpacking a microscope.
(D) One of the workers is filling a glass bottle with a liquid.

번역 (A) 작업자들 중 한 명이 실험복을 걸고 있다.
(B) **작업자들 중 한 명이 실험실 장비를 작동하고 있다.**
(C) 작업자들 중 한 명이 현미경을 꺼내고 있다.
(D) 작업자들 중 한 명이 유리병에 액체를 붓고 있다.

해설 **2인 이상 등장 사진**
(A) 동사 오답. 실험복을 걸고 있는 모습이 보이지 않는다.
(B) 정답. 작업자들 중 한 명이 실험실 장비를 작동하고 있으므로 정답이다.
(C) 동사 오답. 현미경을 꺼내고 있는 모습이 보이지 않는다.
(D) 동사 오답. 유리병에 액체를 붓고 있는 모습이 보이지 않는다.

어휘 hang up ~을 걸다   lab coat 실험복   operate 작동하다
laboratory 실험실   equipment 장비   unpack 꺼내다
microscope 현미경   liquid 액체

6

W-Am

(A) A waiting area is crowded with customers.
(B) A television is mounted on the wall.
(C) Some chairs are arranged in a circle.
(D) Some windows are covered with curtains.

번역 (A) 대기실이 손님으로 꽉 차 있다.
(B) **벽에 텔레비전이 걸려 있다.**
(C) 의자들이 원형으로 배치되어 있다.
(D) 창문들이 커튼으로 덮여 있다.

해설 **사물·풍경 사진**
(A) 사진에 없는 명사. 사진에 손님이 보이지 않는다.
(B) 정답. 벽에 텔레비전이 걸려 있으므로 정답이다.
(C) 상태 오답. 의자들은 원 모양(in a circle)이 아니라 나란히(side by side) 놓여 있다.
(D) 사진에 없는 명사. 사진에 커튼이 보이지 않는다.

어휘 be crowded with ~으로 붐비다   be mounted on ~에 설치되어
있다   arrange 배열하다   cover 씌우다, 덮다

PART 2

7

W-Br Why are you traveling to Melbourne next week?
M-Cn (A) Probably the international airport.
(B) On an eight o'clock flight.
(C) I have to inspect the manufacturing facility.

번역 다음 주에 멜버른에 왜 가시나요?
(A) 아마도 국제공항이요.
(B) 8시 비행기로요.
(C) **제조 시설을 점검해야 해요.**

해설 **Why 의문문**
(A) 연상 오답. 질문의 traveling에서 연상 가능한 international airport를 이용한 오답이다.
(B) 연상 오답. 질문의 traveling에서 연상 가능한 flight를 이용한 오답이다.
(C) 정답. 다음 주에 멜버른에 가는 이유를 묻는 질문에 제조 시설을 점검해야 한다고 구체적인 이유를 제시하고 있으므로 정답이다.

어휘 inspect 점검하다   manufacturing facility 제조 시설

8

M-Cn Who will add graphics to the slides?
W-Br (A) For the meeting with Bayne Enterprises.
(B) **Helen is in charge of that.**
(C) Download the new software package.

번역 누가 슬라이드에 그래픽을 추가할 건가요?
(A) 베인 엔터프라이즈와의 회의를 위해서요.
(B) 헬렌이 담당이에요.
(C) 새 소프트웨어 패키지를 다운받으세요.

해설 **Who 의문문**
(A) 질문과 상관없는 오답. Why 의문문에 대한 응답이므로 오답이다.
(B) 정답. 슬라이드에 그래픽을 추가할 사람이 누군지 묻는 질문에 헬렌이 담당이라고 알려 주고 있으므로 정답이다.
(C) 연상 오답. 질문의 graphics에서 연상 가능한 software를 이용한 오답이다.

어휘 be in charge of ~을 담당하다

9

M-Au Where is the maintenance office?
W-Am **(A) At the end of the hallway.**
(B) Because the window is broken.
(C) I think his name is Christopher.

번역 관리 사무소는 어디에 있나요?
(A) 복도 끝이에요.
(B) 창문이 깨져서요.
(C) 그의 이름은 크리스토퍼일 거예요.

해설 **Where 의문문**
(A) 정답. 관리 사무소의 위치를 묻는 질문에 복도 끝이라고 구체적인 위치를 알려 주고 있으므로 정답이다.
(B) 질문과 상관없는 오답. Why 의문문에 대한 응답이므로 오답이다.
(C) 질문과 상관없는 오답. 질문에 3인칭 대명사 his로 지칭할 인물이 언급된 적이 없으므로 오답이다.

어휘 maintenance 유지보수 hallway 복도 broken 깨진, 고장 난

10

M-Au Would you like to pay for your sofa in monthly installments?
M-Cn (A) Is there a leather one in stock?
(B) Yes, that would be better.
(C) My new two-bedroom apartment.

번역 소파를 월 할부로 지불하기를 원하십니까?
(A) 가죽으로 된 것의 재고가 있나요?
(B) 네, 그게 더 좋겠어요.
(C) 저의 침실 2개짜리 새 아파트요.

해설 **요청·제안문**
(A) 연상 오답. 질문의 sofa에서 연상 가능한 leather를 이용한 오답이다.
(B) 정답. 소파를 월 할부로 지불하고 싶은지 묻는 제안에 그게 더 좋겠다며 호응하고 있으므로 정답이다.
(C) 연상 오답. 질문의 pay ~ monthly에서 연상 가능한 apartment를 이용한 오답이다.

어휘 monthly installments 월 할부 leather 가죽 in stock 재고가 있는

11

W-Br When will the security software be installed?
M-Cn (A) To reduce computer viruses.
(B) A soft and durable fabric, please.
(C) Probably later this month.

번역 보안 소프트웨어가 언제 설치될 건가요?
(A) 컴퓨터 바이러스를 줄이기 위해서요.
(B) 부드럽고 내구성이 있는 직물로 부탁드려요.
(C) 아마도 이달 말예요.

해설 **When 의문문**
(A) 질문과 상관없는 오답. Why 의문문에 대한 응답이므로 오답이다.
(B) 유사 발음 오답. 질문의 software와 부분적으로 발음이 유사한 soft를 이용한 오답이다.
(C) 정답. 보안 소프트웨어의 설치 시점을 묻는 질문에 아마도 이달 말이라고 알려 주고 있으므로 정답이다.

어휘 security 보안 install 설치하다 reduce 줄이다 durable 내구성이 있는 fabric 직물

12

M-Cn Why has the annual company retreat been postponed?
W-Br **(A) Because the venue had been double-booked.**
(B) To the last weekend in July.
(C) Everyone enjoyed the team-building activities.

번역 연례 회사 야유회는 왜 연기되었나요?
(A) 장소가 중복으로 예약되어서요.
(B) 7월 마지막 주 주말로요.
(C) 모두 팀워크 강화 활동을 즐거워했어요.

해설 **Why 의문문**
(A) 정답. 연례 회사 야유회가 연기된 이유를 묻는 질문에 장소가 중복으로 예약되어서라고 구체적인 이유를 제시하고 있으므로 정답이다.
(B) 질문과 상관없는 오답. When 의문문에 대한 응답이므로 오답이다.
(C) 연상 오답. 질문의 company retreat에서 연상 가능한 team-building activities를 이용한 오답이다.

어휘 company retreat 회사 야유회 postpone 미루다 venue 장소 double-book 중복으로 예약을 받다 team-building activity 팀워크 강화 활동

13

W-Am Does Ms. Bradford teach music classes online or just in person?
M-Cn (A) Preparing for a music recital.
(B) Only in person, I think.
(C) She plays the piano well.

번역 브래드퍼드 씨는 음악 수업을 온라인으로 하나요? 아니면 대면으로만 하나요?
(A) 연주회를 준비 중이에요.
(B) 대면으로만 할 걸요.
(C) 그녀는 피아노 연주를 잘해요.

해설 **선택 의문문**
(A) 단어 반복 오답. 질문의 music을 반복 이용한 오답이다.
(B) 정답. 브래드퍼드 씨가 음악 수업을 온라인과 대면 중 어떻게 하는지 묻는 질문에 대면으로만 할 거라고 둘 중 하나를 선택해 응답하고 있으므로 정답이다.
(C) 연상 오답. 질문의 music에서 연상 가능한 piano를 이용한 오답이다.

어휘 in person 직접 prepare for ~을 준비하다 recital 연주회

14
M-Au What's the fastest way to get to the new furniture outlet store downtown?
W-Am (A) I'll check the map application on my phone.
(B) The deadline has already passed, unfortunately.
(C) It had a lot of fantastic deals.

번역 시내에 있는 새 가구 할인점까지 가는 가장 빠른 방법이 뭔가요?
(A) 제 전화기에서 지도 앱을 확인해 볼게요.
(B) 안타깝지만 마감 시한이 이미 지났습니다.
(C) 정말 괜찮은 특가 상품이 많았어요.

해설 **What 의문문**
(A) 정답. 시내에 있는 새 가구 할인점까지 가는 가장 빠른 방법에 대해 묻는 질문에 전화기에서 지도 앱을 확인해보겠다며 자신도 알지 못함을 우회적으로 말하고 있으므로 정답이다.
(B) 질문과 상관없는 오답.
(C) 연상 오답. 질문의 outlet store에서 연상 가능한 deals를 이용한 오답이다.

어휘 furniture 가구 outlet 할인점 deadline 마감 시한 unfortunately 유감스럽게도 deal 거래

15
W-Br Did you forget to order more disposable coffee cups in the large size?
M-Au (A) They should have arrived earlier this week.
(B) Oh, would you like milk or sugar?
(C) Just sign the form at the bottom.

번역 큰 일회용 커피 컵 더 주문하는 것을 잊으셨나요?
(A) 이번 주 초에 도착했어야 했는데요.
(B) 아, 우유나 설탕을 드릴까요?
(C) 양식 아랫부분에 서명해 주세요.

해설 **조동사(Did) 의문문**
(A) 정답. 큰 일회용 커피 컵을 더 주문하는 것을 잊었는지 확인하는 질문에 이번 주 초에 도착했어야 했다며 잊지 않고 주문했음을 우회적으로 알려 주고 있으므로 정답이다.
(B) 연상 오답. 질문의 coffee에서 연상 가능한 milk와 sugar를 이용한 오답이다.
(C) 연상 오답. 질문의 order에서 연상 가능한 sign the form을 이용한 오답이다.

어휘 disposable 일회용의 bottom 아랫부분

16
M-Cn How long does it take for the wallpaper glue to dry?
W-Br (A) It comes in a variety of patterns.
(B) The hallway and the largest bedroom.
(C) I've never used this brand before.

번역 벽지 풀이 마르는 데 얼마나 걸리나요?
(A) 이 제품은 다양한 무늬로 나와요.
(B) 복도와 가장 큰 침실이요.
(C) 이 브랜드는 처음 써보네요.

해설 **How+형용사/부사 의문문**
(A) 연상 오답. 질문의 wallpaper에서 연상 가능한 patterns를 이용한 오답이다.
(B) 질문과 상관없는 오답.
(C) 정답. 벽지 풀이 마르는 데 걸리는 기간을 묻는 질문에 이 브랜드는 처음 써본다며 알지 못함을 우회적으로 알려 주고 있으므로 정답이다.

어휘 wallpaper 벽지 glue 풀, 접착제 come in (제품 등이) 들어오다 a variety of 다양한

17
W-Am Doesn't this phone come with a free charger?
M-Au (A) We charge an hourly rate.
(B) No, she's not here today.
(C) You're right; let me find one.

번역 이 전화기는 무료 충전기가 딸려 있지 않나요?
(A) 우리는 시간당 요금을 청구해요.
(B) 아니요, 그녀는 오늘 여기에 오지 않았어요.
(C) 맞습니다. 제가 찾아보겠습니다.

해설 **부정 의문문**
(A) 유사 발음 오답. 질문의 charger와 발음이 유사한 charge를 이용한 오답이다.
(B) 질문과 상관없는 오답. 질문에 3인칭 대명사 she로 지칭할 인물이 언급된 적이 없으므로 오답이다.
(C) 정답. 전화기에 무료 충전기가 딸려 있는지 여부를 묻는 질문에 맞다(You're right)고 대답한 뒤 자신이 찾아보겠냐며 긍정 답변과 일관된 내용을 덧붙이고 있으므로 정답이다.

어휘 come with ~이 딸려 있다 charger 충전기 charge 충전하다, 청구하다 hourly rate 시간당 요금

18
W-Br Who's going to hang up the promotional banners?
W-Am (A) No, he hasn't gone there.
(B) To advertise our upcoming show.
(C) One of the interns can handle that.

번역 홍보 배너를 누가 걸 예정인가요?
(A) 아니요, 그는 거기에 가지 않았어요.
(B) 다가오는 공연을 광고하기 위해서요.
(C) 인턴들 중 한 명이 할 수 있어요.

해설 **Who 의문문**
(A) Yes/No 불가 오답. Who 의문문에는 Yes/No 응답이 불가능하므로 오답이다.

120

(B) 질문과 상관없는 오답. Why 의문문에 대한 응답이므로 오답이다.

(C) 정답. 홍보 배너를 걸 사람을 묻는 질문에 인턴들 중 한 명이 할 수 있다고 응답하고 있으므로 정답이다.

어휘 hang up 걸다 promotional 홍보의 advertise 광고하다
upcoming 다가오는 handle 다루다, 처리하다

19

W-Br How do you change the machine's power settings?

M-Cn (A) Because it might start to overheat.
(B) There's a helpful video online.
(C) No, the power cables are down.

번역 그 기계의 전원 설정을 어떻게 바꾸나요?
(A) 과열될 수 있어서요.
(B) 온라인에 유용한 영상이 있어요.
(C) 아니요, 전원 케이블이 고장 났어요.

해설 How 의문문
(A) 질문과 상관없는 오답. Why 의문문에 대한 응답이므로 오답이다.
(B) 정답. 기계의 전원 설정을 바꾸는 방법을 묻는 질문에 온라인에 유용한 영상이 있다며 알 수 있는 방법을 알려 주고 있으므로 정답이다.
(C) Yes/No 불가 오답. How 의문문에는 Yes/No 응답이 불가능하므로 오답이다.

어휘 setting 설정 overheat 과열되다 helpful 유용한
down 작동이 안 되는

20

W-Am I'm ordering coffee for the team after lunch.

W-Br (A) I'm in charge of the team.
(B) Oh, I'm taking the afternoon off.
(C) She ordered more copies of the book.

번역 점심 먹고 제가 팀원들 커피를 주문할게요.
(A) 제가 그 팀을 책임지고 있어요.
(B) 아, 저는 오후에 반차를 쓸 거예요.
(C) 그녀가 책을 몇 권 더 주문했어요.

해설 사실·정보 전달의 평서문
(A) 단어 반복 오답. 평서문의 team을 반복 이용한 오답이다.
(B) 정답. 점심 먹고 팀원들 커피를 주문하겠다는 말에 자신은 오후에 반차를 쓸 거라며 본인의 커피는 주문하지 않아도 됨을 우회적으로 알려 주고 있으므로 정답이다.
(C) 단어 반복 오답. 평서문의 order를 반복 이용한 오답이다.

어휘 be in charge of ~을 담당하다 take off 휴가를 쓰다

21

M-Cn They're planning to offer vegetarian dishes at the staff dinner, right?

W-Am (A) I'd better check the menu again.
(B) No, I've already had a meal.
(C) I'll help you wash them now.

번역 그들은 직원 회식 때 채식 요리를 제공할 예정이죠, 맞죠?
(A) 메뉴를 다시 확인해 볼게요.
(B) 아니요, 저는 이미 식사를 했어요.
(C) 지금 그것들 씻는 걸 도와드릴게요.

해설 부가 의문문
(A) 정답. 회식 때 채식 요리를 제공할 예정인지를 확인하는 질문에 메뉴를 다시 확인해 보겠다며 알지 못함을 간접적으로 표현하고 있으므로 정답이다.
(B) 연상 오답. 질문의 dishes와 dinner에서 연상 가능한 a meal을 이용한 오답이다.
(C) 연상 오답. 질문의 dishes를 접시로 이해했을 경우 연상 가능한 wash를 이용한 오답이다.

어휘 vegetarian 채식의 staff dinner 회식 meal 식사

22

W-Am Oh, this Web site requires a password.

M-Cn (A) It's quieter than usual.
(B) The confidential financial records.
(C) You can sign in as a guest.

번역 아, 이 웹사이트는 비밀번호를 요구하네요.
(A) 평소보다 조용하네요.
(B) 기밀 재무 기록이요.
(C) 게스트로 들어갈 수 있어요.

해설 사실·정보 전달의 평서문
(A) 유사 발음 오답. 평서문의 requires와 부분적으로 발음이 유사한 quieter를 이용한 오답이다.
(B) 연상 오답. 평서문의 password에서 연상 가능한 confidential을 이용한 오답이다.
(C) 정답. 웹사이트가 비밀번호를 요구한다는 평서문에 게스트로 들어갈 수 있다며 비밀번호가 필요하지 않음을 알려 주고 있으므로 정답이다.

어휘 require 요구하다 confidential 기밀의 financial record 재무 기록 sign in ~에 서명하고 들어가다

23

M-Au What can I do to give back to the community?

W-Am (A) Yes, there's a 60-day return policy.
(B) A population of about thirty thousand.
(C) The library has some volunteer opportunities.

번역 지역사회에 보답하기 위해 제가 무엇을 할 수 있을까요?
(A) 네, 60일 반품 정책이 있어요.
(B) 약 3만 명의 인구요.
(C) 도서관에서 자원봉사자를 모집하고 있어요.

해설 What 의문문
(A) Yes/No 불가 오답. What 의문문에는 Yes/No 응답이 불가능하므로 오답이다.
(B) 연상 오답. 질문의 community에서 연상 가능한 population을 이용한 오답이다.
(C) 정답. 지역사회에 기여하기 위해 할 수 있는 일에 대해 묻는 질문에 도서관에서 자원봉사자를 모집하고 있다고 구체적으로 알려 주고 있으므로 정답이다.

어휘　give back ~을 돌려주다　community 지역사회, 공동체　return
반품　policy 정책　population 인구　opportunity 기회

24

W-Am　Can you move the podium further away from the room's entrance?

M-Au　(A) Of course, no problem.
(B) There's room for luggage.
(C) On the table, please.

번역　연단을 방 입구에서 더 멀리 옮겨주실 수 있나요?
(A) 물론이죠, 문제없습니다.
(B) 짐을 놓을 공간이 있어요.
(C) 탁자 위로 부탁드려요.

해설　요청·제안문
(A) 정답. 연단을 방 입구에서 더 멀리 옮겨달라는 요청에 그럼요(Of course)라고 말한 뒤 문제없다고 수락하고 있으므로 정답이다.
(B) 단어 반복 오답. 질문의 room을 반복 이용한 오답이다.
(C) 연상 오답. 질문의 move에서 연상 가능한 On the table을 이용한 오답이다.

어휘　podium 연단　entrance 입구　luggage 짐, 가방

25

W-Br　Do we have any qualified applicants for the marketing position?

M-Au　(A) It's a high-quality product.
(B) He bought some office supplies.
(C) I'll speak to the recruiter again.

번역　마케팅 직책에 적합한 지원자가 있나요?
(A) 이건 고급 제품이에요.
(B) 그는 사무용품을 구입했어요.
(C) 제가 인사 담당자와 다시 이야기해 볼게요.

해설　조동사(Do) 의문문
(A) 유사 발음 오답. 질문의 qualified와 부분적으로 발음이 유사한 quality를 이용한 오답이다.
(B) 질문과 상관없는 오답. 질문에 3인칭 대명사 He로 지칭할 인물이 언급된 적이 없으므로 오답이다.
(C) 정답. 마케팅 직책에 적합한 지원자가 있는지 여부를 확인하는 질문에 자신이 인사 담당자와 다시 이야기해보겠다며 알지 못함을 우회적으로 알려 주고 있으므로 정답이다.

어휘　qualified 자격을 갖춘　applicant 지원자　position 직책, 일자리
high-quality 고급의　recruiter 인사 담당자

26

W-Br　I can be compensated for unused vacation days, right?

W-Am　(A) Yes, they had a wonderful time.
(B) The procedure is not straightforward.
(C) I haven't selected a destination.

번역　저는 미사용 연차에 대한 수당을 받을 수 있죠, 맞죠?
(A) 네, 그들은 좋은 시간을 보냈어요.
(B) 절차가 간단하지는 않아요.
(C) 아직 목적지를 고르지 못했어요.

해설　부가 의문문
(A) 연상 오답. 질문의 vacation에서 연상 가능한 wonderful time을 이용한 오답이다.
(B) 정답. 미사용 연차에 대한 수당을 받을 수 있는지 확인하는 질문에 절차가 간단하지는 않다며 관련된 정보를 알려 주고 있으므로 정답이다.
(C) 연상 오답. 질문의 vacation에서 연상 가능한 destination을 이용한 오답이다.

어휘　compensate 보상하다　procedure 절차　straightforward
간단한, 쉬운　select 고르다　destination 목적지

27

W-Br　Where can I get my parking pass renewed for the company lot?

M-Au　(A) At least two weeks in advance.
(B) No, there are plenty of spots available.
(C) I don't drive to work.

번역　회사 주차장의 주차권은 어디에서 갱신받을 수 있나요?
(A) 최소 2주 전에요.
(B) 아니요, 이용할 수 있는 자리가 많아요.
(C) 저는 차로 출근하지 않아요.

해설　Where 의문문
(A) 질문과 상관없는 오답. When 의문문에 대한 응답이므로 오답이다.
(B) Yes/No 불가 오답. Where 의문문에는 Yes/No 응답이 불가능하므로 오답이다.
(C) 정답. 주차권 갱신 장소를 묻는 질문에 자신은 차로 출근하지 않는다며 알지 못함을 우회적으로 알려 주고 있으므로 정답이다.

어휘　renew 갱신하다　in advance 미리　plenty of 많은　available
이용 가능한　drive to work 차로 출근하다

28

M-Cn　When does the company usually conduct employee performance reviews?

W-Br　(A) We were impressed by the show.
(B) Above average ratings.
(C) Around the end of the fourth quarter.

번역　그 회사는 직원 성과 평가를 보통 언제 실시하나요?
(A) 우리는 그 공연에 깊은 감명을 받았어요.
(B) 평균 점수 이상이요.
(C) 4사분기 말쯤에요.

해설　When 의문문
(A) 연상 오답. 질문의 performance에서 연상 가능한 show를 이용한 오답이다.
(B) 연상 오답. 질문의 performance reviews에서 연상 가능한 average ratings를 이용한 오답이다.
(C) 정답. 회사의 직원 성과 평가 실시 시기를 묻는 질문에 4사분기 말쯤이라고 알려 주고 있으므로 정답이다.

어휘　conduct 실시하다　performance review 성과 평가　impress
깊은 인상을 남기다　average rating 평균 점수　quarter 사분기,
4분의 1

29

M-Au To use the advanced hiking trail, can I go by myself, or do I need a guide?

W-Am (A) The national park opens soon.
(B) A gorgeous view from the top.
(C) Sign up for a group hike.

번역 상급 등산로를 이용하려면 혼자서도 갈 수 있나요? 아니면 가이드가 필요한가요?
(A) 그 국립공원은 곧 개장해요.
(B) 정상에서 볼 수 있는 훌륭한 전망이요.
(C) 단체 등산을 신청하세요.

해설 선택 의문문
(A) 연상 오답. 질문의 hiking trail에서 연상 가능한 The national park를 이용한 오답이다.
(B) 연상 오답. 질문의 hiking에서 연상 가능한 view를 이용한 오답이다.
(C) 정답. 상급 등산로를 이용하려면 혼자 갈 수 있는지 아니면 가이드가 필요한지 묻는 질문에 단체 등산을 신청하라며 두 선택지를 제외한 제3의 안을 제시하고 있으므로 정답이다.

어휘 advanced 상급의 by oneself 혼자 gorgeous 아주 멋진 sign up for ~을 신청하다

30

W-Am Can you forward me the itinerary for the trip overseas?

M-Au (A) Sure, she oversees construction projects.
(B) It has not been finalized yet.
(C) A window seat, please.

번역 해외여행 일정표를 저에게 보내주실 수 있나요?
(A) 그럼요, 그녀는 건설 공사를 감독해요.
(B) 아직 완성되지 않았어요.
(C) 창가석으로 부탁드려요.

해설 요청·제안문
(A) 유사 발음 오답. 질문의 overseas와 발음이 유사한 oversees를 이용한 오답이다.
(B) 정답. 해외여행 일정표를 보내달라는 요청에 아직 완성되지 않았다며 요청을 수락할 수 없음을 우회적으로 표현하고 있으므로 정답이다.
(C) 연상 오답. 질문의 trip에서 연상 가능한 A window seat를 이용한 오답이다.

어휘 forward 보내다, 전달하다 itinerary 일정표 overseas 해외로 oversee 감독하다 construction 건설 finalize 완성하다

31

M-Au Don't the building's doors lock automatically after nine P.M.?

W-Br (A) He works at an automobile factory.
(B) No, it's not the most reliable system.
(C) I like the building's design.

번역 건물 출입문은 밤 9시 이후에 자동으로 잠기지 않나요?
(A) 그는 자동차 공장에서 일해요.
(B) 아니요, 그다지 신뢰할 만한 시스템이 아니에요.
(C) 저는 건물 디자인이 마음에 들어요.

해설 부정 의문문
(A) 질문의 automatically와 부분적으로 발음이 비슷한 automobile을 이용한 오답.
(B) 정답. 건물 출입문이 밤 9시 이후에 자동으로 잠기는지 확인하는 질문에 아니요(No)라고 대답한 뒤, 그다지 신뢰할 만한 시스템이 아니라며 부정 답변과 일관된 내용을 덧붙이고 있으므로 정답이다.
(C) 단어 반복 오답. 질문의 building을 반복 이용한 오답이다.

어휘 lock 잠기다, 잠그다 automatically 자동으로 automobile 자동차 reliable 신뢰할 만한

PART 3

32-34

M-Au Ms. Calvert, as you requested, **[32] I've just moved you to an earlier flight for your business trip to Manchester.** You're now departing at eight A.M. instead of ten-thirty.

W-Am Thank you! That will be much better.

M-Au Happy to help. And **[33] remember to bring along your company credit card** for purchases while you're away.

W-Am Yes, of course. Oh, and **[34] does the hotel offer a shuttle from the airport?** That would be easier than trying to figure out which public bus to take.

남 캘버트 씨, 요청하신 대로 **맨체스터 출장을 위한 항공편을 더 빠른 항공편으로 방금 옮겨드렸어요.** 10시 30분이 아니라 오전 8시에 출발하시게 돼요.

여 감사합니다! 훨씬 좋네요.

남 별말씀을요. 그리고 출장 중 구매를 위해 **법인 카드를 가져가시는 거 잊지 마세요.**

여 네, 물론이죠. 아, 그런데 **그 호텔은 공항에서 셔틀버스를 제공하나요?** 어떤 대중 버스를 타야 할지 알아내는 것보다 그게 훨씬 쉬울 거예요.

어휘 depart 출발하다 bring along 가져가다 purchase 구매 figure out 알아내다

32 What did the man just do?
(A) He selected a rental car.
(B) He changed a travel itinerary.
(C) He upgraded a hotel reservation.
(D) He approved some vacation time.

번역　남자는 방금 무엇을 했는가?
(A) 렌터카를 골랐다.
(B) 여행 일정을 바꿨다.
(C) 호텔 예약을 업그레이드했다.
(D) 휴가를 승인했다.

해설　**세부 사항 관련 - 남자가 방금 한 일**
남자가 첫 대사에서 출장을 위한 항공편을 더 빠른 항공편으로 방금 옮겨드렸다(I've just moved you to an earlier flight for your business trip ~)고 말하고 있으므로 정답은 (B)이다.

어휘　select 고르다　travel itinerary 여행 일정　reservation 예약
approve 승인하다

> **Paraphrasing**
> 대화의 moved you to an earlier flight
> → 정답의 changed a travel itinerary

33 What does the man remind the woman about?
(A) Weighing her luggage carefully
(B) Purchasing some travel insurance
(C) Saving receipts for purchases
(D) Bringing a company credit card

번역　남자는 여자에게 무엇에 대해 상기시키는가?
(A) 수하물 무게 꼼꼼히 확인하기
(B) 여행 보험 구매하기
(C) 구매 영수증 보관하기
(D) 법인 카드 가져가기

해설　**세부 사항 관련 - 남자가 여자에게 상기시키는 것**
남자가 두 번째 대사에서 법인 카드를 가져가는 거 잊지 말라(remember to bring along your company credit card)고 말하고 있으므로 정답은 (D)이다.

어휘　weigh 무게를 재다　luggage 수하물　carefully 주의 깊게
insurance 보험　receipt 영수증

34 What does the woman inquire about?
(A) A job requirement
(B) A dining establishment
(C) A business center
(D) A shuttle service

번역　여자는 무엇에 대해 문의하는가?
(A) 직무 요구사항
(B) 음식점
(C) 상업 중심지
(D) 셔틀 서비스

해설　**세부 사항 관련 - 여자의 문의 사항**
여자가 마지막 대사에서 그 호텔은 공항에서 셔틀버스를 제공하는지(does the hotel offer a shuttle from the airport?) 묻고 있으므로 정답은 (D)이다.

어휘　requirement 요구사항

35-37

W-Br　Sean, I'm wondering if you have any ideas for improving ³⁵ **the sales of our smart TV.**

M-Cn　³⁶ **How about having employees show shoppers how to use the different features it has?** Once people see how easy it is to use, I think they'll want to buy it.

W-Br　Hmm... that's a good idea, but ³⁷ **there isn't any room on the shop floor for people to gather to watch something like that.** We would have to move some items around. Let's go to that area now and see if we can adjust the layout.

여:　**선, 우리 스마트 TV 판매를 증진할 아이디어가 있는지 궁금해요.**
남:　**직원들이 쇼핑객들에게 TV의 다양한 기능을 사용하는 법을 보여주게 하면 어떨까요?** 사람들이 사용법이 얼마나 쉬운지 보고 나면 구매하고 싶어질 거예요.
여:　음… 좋은 생각이지만, **사람들이 그런 것을 보기 위해 모일 수 있는 공간이 매장에는 없어요.** 일부 물품을 옮겨야 할 거예요. 지금 그곳으로 가서 배치를 바꿀 수 있는지 알아봅시다.

어휘　improve 향상시키다　feature 기능　gather 모이다. 모으다
adjust 조정하다　layout 배치

35 What industry do the speakers most likely work in?
(A) Finance
(B) Publishing
(C) Technology
(D) Pharmaceutical

번역　화자들은 어떤 업계에 종사하겠는가?
(A) 금융
(B) 출판
(C) 기술
(D) 제약

해설　**전체 내용 관련 - 화자들의 근무 업종**
여자가 첫 대사에서 우리 스마트 TV 판매(the sales of our smart TV)라고 했으므로 화자들은 가전 기술 분야에서 근무하고 있음을 알 수 있다. 따라서 정답은 (C)이다.

36 What does the man suggest doing?
(A) Consulting employees from other branches
(B) Giving demonstrations in the store
(C) Creating a smartphone application for customers
(D) Featuring an item in a magazine advertisement

번역 남자는 무엇을 제안하는가?
(A) 다른 지점에서 온 직원들과 상의하기
(B) 매장에서 시연하기
(C) 고객용 스마트폰 앱 만들기
(D) 잡지 광고에 제품 소개하기

해설 **세부 사항 관련 - 남자의 제안 사항**
남자가 첫 대사에서 직원들이 쇼핑객들에게 TV의 다양한 기능을 사용하는 법을 보여줄 것(How about having employees show shoppers how to use the different features it has?)을 제안하고 있으므로 정답은 (B)이다.

어휘 consult 상의하다 branch 지사, 지점 demonstration 시연
feature 특별히 포함하다 advertisement 광고

> **Paraphrasing**
> 대화의 show shoppers how to use ~
> → 정답의 Giving demonstrations

---

37 What is the woman worried about?
(A) The business will relocate soon.
(B) The suggested plan will cost too much.
(C) An activity requires too much space.
(D) A room needs to be redecorated.

번역 여자는 무엇에 대해 걱정하는가?
(A) 사업체가 곧 이전할 것이다.
(B) 제안된 계획은 비용이 너무 많이 들 것이다.
(C) 활동이 너무 많은 공간을 필요로 한다.
(D) 방을 재단장해야 한다.

해설 **세부 사항 관련 - 여자의 우려 사항**
여자가 마지막 대사에서 사람들이 그런 것을 보기 위해 모일 수 있는 공간이 매장에는 없다(there isn't any room on the shop floor for people to gather to watch something like that)고 말하고 있으므로 정답은 (C)이다.

어휘 relocate 이전하다 activity 활동 redecorate 실내 장식을 새로 하다

> **Paraphrasing**
> 대화의 room → 정답의 space

38-40

> M-Au Hi, Cassandra. **38 This Friday, I want to do something special for Ms. Wilkins at our department meeting. As she just received a promotion last week, I'd like to order her a cake.** Can you recommend a local bakery?
>
> W-Br Whenever I'm celebrating a special occasion, **39 I use Maxwell Bakery. It's located just a few doors down, opposite Marietta Pharmacy.**
>
> M-Au Thanks! **40 I just have to check these financial reports, and then I'll stop by on my lunch break.**

남 안녕하세요, 커샌드라. **이번 금요일 부서 회의 때 윌킨스 씨를 위해 특별한 것을 하고 싶어요. 그녀가 지난주에 승진했으니 케이크를 주문해 주고 싶어요.** 동네 제과점을 추천해 줄 수 있나요?

여 특별한 날을 기념할 때마다 제가 이용하는 곳은 **맥스웰 제과점**이에요. **길 아래쪽으로 몇 집만 내려가면 있어요. 매리에타 약국 맞은편이에요.**

남 고맙습니다! **이 재무 보고서 확인만 하고 나서 점심시간에 잠깐 들러야겠네요.**

어휘 department 부서 receive 받다 promotion 승진
celebrate 기념하다 occasion 경우, 행사 pharmacy 약국 financial 금융의, 재무의 stop by 잠깐 들르다

---

38 Why does the man want to order a cake for Ms. Wilkins?
(A) She has received an award.
(B) She will celebrate her birthday.
(C) She has recently been promoted.
(D) She will leave the company soon.

번역 남자는 왜 윌킨스 씨를 위한 케이크를 주문하려고 하는가?
(A) 그녀가 상을 받아서
(B) 그녀가 생일을 맞아서
(C) 그녀가 최근에 승진해서
(D) 그녀가 곧 회사를 떠날 예정이어서

해설 **세부 사항 관련 - 남자가 케이크를 주문하는 이유**
남자가 첫 대사에서 이번 금요일 부서 회의 때 윌킨스 씨를 위해 특별한 것을 하고 싶다(This Friday, I want to do something special for Ms. Wilkins at our department meeting)면서 그녀가 지난주에 승진했으니 케이크를 주문해 주고 싶다(As she just received a promotion last week, I'd like to order her a cake)고 말하고 있으므로 정답은 (C)이다.

어휘 award 상 recently 최근에 leave 떠나다

> **Paraphrasing**
> 대화의 she just received a promotion last week
> → 정답의 She has recently been promoted.

---

39 According to the woman, where is Maxwell Bakery?
(A) Across from a pharmacy
(B) Next to the office
(C) In a shopping mall
(D) Behind a bank

번역 여자에 따르면, 맥스웰 제과점은 어디에 있는가?
(A) 약국 맞은편에
(B) 사무실 옆에
(C) 쇼핑몰에
(D) 은행 뒤에

해설 **세부 사항 관련 - 맥스웰 제과점의 위치**
여자가 첫 대사에서 자신이 이용하는 곳은 맥스웰 제과점(I use Maxwell Bakery)이라면서 길 아래쪽으로 몇 집만 내려가면 매리에타 약국 맞은편에 있다(It's located just a few doors down,

opposite Marietta Pharmacy)고 말하고 있으므로 정답은 (A)이다.

어휘   across from ~의 맞은편에

> **Paraphrasing**
> 대화의 opposite Marietta Pharmacy
> → 정답의 Across from a pharmacy

40   What does the man plan to do before taking a lunch break?
(A) Ask Ms. Wilkins for a preference
(B) Check a department's budget
(C) Set up a job interview
(D) Review some documents

번역   남자는 점심시간이 되기 전에 무엇을 할 계획인가?
(A) 윌킨스 씨에게 원하는 것 물어보기
(B) 부서 예산 점검하기
(C) 채용 면접 일정 잡기
(D) 문서 검토하기

해설   **세부 사항 관련 - 남자가 점심시간이 되기 전에 할 일**
남자가 마지막 대사에서 재무 보고서 확인만 하고 나서 점심시간에 잠깐 들러야겠다(I just have to check these financial reports, and then I'll stop by on my lunch break)고 말하고 있으므로 정답은 (D)이다.

어휘   preference 선호하는 것   budget 예산   set up 일정을 잡다

> **Paraphrasing**
> 대화의 check these financial reports
> → 정답의 Review some documents

41-43 3인 대화

> M-Au   Cheryl and Reiko, have you heard back from the city representative about **[41] the contract for our company to move their office items to the new site?**
>
> W-Am   Well, a committee has to make the decision, and **[42] we are not the only company they are looking at.**
>
> W-Br   Right. I spoke to Patricia Walsh, our point of contact, this morning, and **[42] she said they are accepting bids from some of our competitors.**
>
> M-Au   Hmm... this could be a big job. **[43] We could tell them we can throw in the shelf assembly service at no charge.** That might make our package more attractive.

남: 세릴, 레이코, 시 담당자에게서 **우리 회사가 그들의 사무용 집기를 새 장소로 옮기는 계약 건에 대한 회신**이 왔나요?

여1:   음, 위원회가 결정해야 하는데, **그들이 알아보고 있는 회사가 우리 회사만은 아니에요.**

여2:   맞아요. 제가 오늘 아침에 우리와 연락 중인 패트리샤 월시와 이야기해 보았는데, **경쟁업체들로부터 입찰을 받고 있다**고 했어요.

남: 음… 이거 큰일이네요. **선반 조립 서비스를 무료로 해줄 수 있다고 말해봅시다.** 우리 패키지가 더 매력적으로 보일지도 몰라요.

어휘   representative 담당자   contract 계약   committee 위원회   make a decision 결정하다   point of contact 연락 중인 사람   accept 받아들이다   bid 입찰   competitor 경쟁업체   a big job 큰일   throw in ~을 덤으로 주다   shelf 선반   assembly 조립   at no charge 무료로   attractive 매력적인

41   Where do the speakers most likely work?
(A) At a real estate agency
(B) At a cleaning service
(C) At a moving company
(D) At an architecture firm

번역   화자들은 어디서 일하겠는가?
(A) 부동산 중개소
(B) 청소업체
(C) 이사업체
(D) 건축회사

해설   **전체 내용 관련 - 화자들의 근무지**
남자가 첫 대사에서 우리 회사가 그들의 사무용 집기를 새 장소로 옮기는 계약 건(the contract for our company to move their office items to the new site)이라고 말하고 있으므로 화자들은 이사업체에서 근무하고 있음을 알 수 있다. 따라서 정답은 (C)이다.

42   What problem do the women mention?
(A) Some employees do not have enough experience.
(B) The area has been experiencing bad weather.
(C) A requested item is not currently available.
(D) Potential clients are considering other options.

번역   여자들은 어떤 문제를 언급하는가?
(A) 일부 직원들은 경험이 충분하지 않다.
(B) 그 지역은 계속 날씨가 안 좋다.
(C) 요청된 물품은 현재 수급이 가능하지 않다.
(D) 잠재 고객이 다른 업체들을 고려 중이다.

해설   **세부 사항 관련 - 여자들이 언급하는 문제점**
첫 번째 여자가 첫 대사에서 그들이 알아보고 있는 회사가 우리 회사만은 아니(we are not the only company they are looking at)라고 했고, 두 번째 여자가 경쟁업체들로부터 입찰을 받고 있다(she said they are accepting bids from some of our competitors)고 말하고 있으므로 정답은 (D)이다.

어휘 experience 경험; 경험하다 currently 현재, 지금 potential
잠재적인 consider 고려하다

43 What does the man suggest doing?
(A) Canceling a business contract
(B) Offering a free service
(C) Updating a software package
(D) Extending a proposed deadline

번역 남자는 무엇을 제안하는가?
(A) 사업 계약 취소
(B) 무료 서비스 제공
(C) 소프트웨어 패키지 업데이트
(D) 제안된 마감 시한 연장

해설 세부 사항 관련 - 남자의 제안 사항
남자가 마지막 대사에서 선반 조립 서비스를 무료로 해줄 수 있다
고 말해보자(We could tell them we can throw in the shelf
assembly service at no charge)고 했으므로 정답은 (B)이다.

어휘 cancel 취소하다 extend 연장하다 proposed 제안된
deadline 마감 시한

> **Paraphrasing**
> 대화의 throw in the ~ service at no charge
> → 정답의 Offering a free service

44-46

M-Cn Ms. Fleming, **44 I've finished ironing the shirts for today.**

W-Br Great. **44 And were you able to get the stain out of Mr. Morgan's suit?**

M-Cn Yes. And I just need to put a few more clothes in bags for pickup tomorrow. That'll be finished before closing time. That's at seven o'clock, right?

W-Br Yes, that's correct.

M-Cn Hmm... I know I've just transferred here, but **45 I'm wondering why other branches of our business are open until nine o'clock and we're not.** Wouldn't that be more convenient for customers?

W-Br Well, there are not many apartment buildings around here. **45 This neighborhood is empty after office hours.**

M-Cn That makes sense. Thanks! Now I won't have to ask **46 at tomorrow's staff meeting.**

남: 플레밍 씨, 오늘 해야 하는 셔츠들 다림질을 끝냈어요.
여: 좋습니다. 모건 씨의 양복에서 얼룩을 제거할 수 있었나요?

남: 네. 그리고 내일 찾아갈 옷들 몇 벌만 더 봉지에 넣기만 하면 됩니다. 폐점 시간 전에 끝날 거예요. 폐점 시간이 7시 맞죠?

여: 네, 맞습니다.

남: 음… 제가 이곳으로 전근 온 지 얼마 되지 않은 것은 알지만, 우리 회사의 다른 지점들은 9시까지 문을 여는데 왜 우리는 그렇게 안 하는지 궁금합니다. 그게 고객들에게 더 편리하지 않을까요?

여: 음, 이 주변에는 아파트 건물이 그리 많지 않아요. 이 동네는 퇴근 시간 이후에는 사람이 없어요.

남: 이해가 되네요. 고맙습니다! 이제 내일 직원회의 때 물어보지 않아도 되겠네요.

어휘 iron 다림질하다 stain 얼룩 suit 양복 transfer 전근하다
branch 지사, 지점 convenient 편리한 empty 비어 있는

44 Where most likely are the speakers?
(A) At a shipping company
(B) At a clothing shop
(C) At a fitness club
(D) At a dry cleaner's

번역 화자들은 어디에 있겠는가?
(A) 운송회사
(B) 옷 가게
(C) 피트니스 클럽
(D) 세탁소

해설 전체 내용 관련 - 대화의 장소
남자가 첫 대사에서 오늘 해야 하는 셔츠들 다림질을 끝냈다(I've
finished ironing the shirts for today)고 하자 여자가 모건 씨의
양복에서 얼룩을 제거할 수 있었는지(And were you able to get
the stain out of Mr. Morgan's suit?) 묻고 있는 것으로 보아 대
화 장소는 세탁소라는 것을 알 수 있다. 따라서 정답은 (D)이다.

어휘 shipping 운송

45 Why does the woman say, "there are not many apartment buildings around here"?
(A) To explain why a closing time is earlier
(B) To suggest searching for a new home
(C) To complain about a long commute
(D) To apologize for a lack of available parking

번역 여자가 "이 주변에는 아파트 건물이 그리 많지 않아요"라고 말한 이
유는?
(A) 폐점 시간이 왜 더 이른지 설명하려고
(B) 새집을 찾아보라고 제안하려고
(C) 긴 통근 시간에 대해 불평하려고
(D) 주차할 곳이 부족한 점에 대해 사과하려고

해설 화자의 의도 파악 - 주변에 아파트 건물이 그리 많지 않다는 말
의 의도
앞에서 남자가 우리 회사의 다른 지점들은 9시까지 문을 여는데 왜
우리는 그렇게 안 하는지 궁금하다(I'm wondering why other
branches of our business are open until nine o'clock
and we're not)고 하자 여자가 인용문을 언급하고 이어서 이 동네는
퇴근 시간 이후에는 사람이 없다(This neighborhood is empty

after office hours)고 말하는 것으로 보아, 다른 지점보다 더 일찍 문을 닫는 이유를 알려주려는 의도로 한 말임을 알 수 있다. 따라서 정답은 (A)이다.

어휘 search for ~을 찾다   commute 통근 시간   a lack of ~의 부족

---

46 What will happen tomorrow?
(A) Staff evaluations will be carried out.
(B) Some employees will attend a meeting.
(C) A new company policy will go into effect.
(D) A staff member will transfer from another branch.

번역 내일 무슨 일이 일어나겠는가?
(A) 직원 평가가 수행될 것이다.
(B) 직원들이 회의에 참석할 것이다.
(C) 새 회사 정책이 발효될 것이다.
(D) 한 직원이 다른 지점에서 전근해 올 것이다.

해설 **세부 사항 관련 - 내일 일어날 일**
남자가 마지막 대사에서 내일 직원회의 때(at tomorrow's staff meeting)라고 말하고 있으므로 정답은 (B)이다.

어휘 evaluation 평가   carry out ~을 수행하다   attend 참석하다   policy 정책   go into effect 효력이 발생되다

47-49

W-Br ⁴⁷ **Brennan Institute.** How can I help you?

M-Cn Hi, I'm a manager at Melville Sales. ⁴⁷ **I'd like to book a private painting class** for my team. There are seven people in our group, and we would prefer to come on June 5, in the afternoon.

W-Br I'm very sorry, but ⁴⁸ **we'll be closed on June 5 because we're having some damaged ceiling tiles fixed in our hallway.**

M-Cn Oh, I see. Would you have anything available later that week?

W-Br How about June 6 at three o'clock? Tammy Orozco could work with your group then.

M-Cn That sounds good. What would be the fee per person?

W-Br I'll need to double-check that, so ⁴⁹ **please wait on the line while I look it up.**

여: 브레넌 학원입니다. 무엇을 도와드릴까요?
남: 안녕하세요. 저는 멜빌 세일즈의 관리자입니다. 저희 팀을 위한 **맞춤형 회화 수업을 예약하고 싶습니다.** 모두 7명이고 6월 5일 오후에 가기를 희망합니다.
여: 너무 죄송합니다만, 저희가 6월 5일에 문을 닫을 예정이에요. 복도의 파손된 천장 타일을 수리해야 하거든요.

남: 아, 그러시군요. 그 주 후반에는 가능한 시간대가 있나요?
여: 6월 6일 3시는 어떠세요? 그날은 태미 오로스코가 귀하의 단체를 맡을 수 있어요.
남: 좋습니다. 1인당 수업료는 얼마인가요?
여: 다시 한번 확인해 보아야 하니, **제가 찾아보는 동안 끊지 말고 잠시 기다려주세요.**

어휘 institute 기관, 학원   private 전용의   damaged 파손된   ceiling 천장   fix 고치다, 바로잡다   fee 수업료, 요금   double-check 재확인하다   wait on the line 전화를 끊지 않고 기다리다   look up ~을 찾아보다

---

47 Where does the woman work?
(A) At a department store
(B) At a law office
(C) At a recruitment firm
(D) At an art institute

번역 여자는 어디서 일하는가?
(A) 백화점
(B) 법률 사무소
(C) 채용 중개업체
(D) 미술 학원

해설 **전체 내용 관련 - 여자의 근무지**
여자가 첫 대사에서 브레넌 학원(Brennan Institute)이라고 소개를 한 후, 남자가 맞춤형 회화 수업을 예약하고 싶다(I'd like to book a private painting class)고 말하는 것으로 보아 여자는 미술학원에서 근무하고 있음을 알 수 있다. 따라서 정답은 (D)이다.

어휘 recruitment 채용

> **Paraphrasing**
> 대화의 painting → 정답의 art

---

48 Why is the man unable to use a service on June 5?
(A) Some employees will be trained.
(B) Some tiles will be repaired.
(C) An entrance will be blocked.
(D) A schedule is already full.

번역 남자는 왜 6월 5일에 서비스를 이용할 수 없는가?
(A) 직원들이 교육을 받을 예정이라서
(B) 타일이 수리될 예정이라서
(C) 출입구가 폐쇄될 예정이라서
(D) 일정이 이미 꽉 차서

해설 **세부 사항 관련 - 남자가 6월 5일에 서비스를 이용할 수 없는 이유**
여자가 두 번째 대사에서 6월 5일에 문을 닫을 예정인데 복도의 파손된 천장 타일을 수리해야 한다(we'll be closed on June 5 because we're having some damaged ceiling tiles fixed in our hallway)고 말하는 것으로 보아 정답은 (B)이다.

어휘 train 교육시키다   repair 수리하다   block 차단하다

49 What will the man most likely do next?
(A) Select a payment method
(B) Provide a list of attendees
(C) Confirm a mailing address
(D) Wait for some information

번역 남자는 다음으로 무엇을 하겠는가?
(A) 결제 방법 고르기
(B) 참석자 명단 제공하기
(C) 우편 주소 확인하기
(D) 정보 기다리기

해설 **세부 사항 관련 - 남자가 다음에 할 일**
여자가 마지막 대사에서 자신이 찾아보는 동안 끊지 말고 잠시 기다려
줄 것(please wait on the line while I look it up)을 요청하고
있으므로 정답은 (D)이다.

어휘 select 고르다   payment 지불   method 방법, 수단   attendee
참석자

50-52 3인 대화

W-Br Hi, Takeshi. Are you busy? ⁵⁰ **Jasmine and I
are having trouble getting supplies for our
department.**

M-Au I've got some time now. What's going on?

W-Br ⁵⁰ **When we try to place the order, it says
there are insufficient funds.**

W-Am Right. But we're not requesting more than we
usually do each quarter.

M-Au Well, ⁵¹ **all of us on the accounting team** have
been getting a lot of questions about this.
Didn't you get the memo saying that funds
will be allocated monthly from now on? You
probably exceeded the monthly budget.

W-Am Oh, we've been away on business. ⁵² **We'd
better catch up on the e-mails and memos
we missed now.**

여1: 안녕하세요, 다케시. 바쁘세요? 재스민과 내가 우리 부서의 용품
을 구입하는 데 어려움을 겪고 있어요.

남: 지금은 시간이 좀 있습니다. 무슨 일인가요?

여1: **주문을 하려고 하면 자금이 부족하다고 나와요.**

여2: 맞아요. 하지만 매 분기에 사용하는 것보다 더 많이 신청하지는
않았어요.

남: 음, **회계부에 있는 저희 모두**가 이 문제와 관련해 많은 문의를 받
고 있는데요. 이제부터 자금이 매월 할당될 거라는 회람을 못 받
으셨나요? 아마도 월 예산을 초과하셨을 거예요.

여2: 아, 우리는 출장 중이었어요. **읽지 못한 이메일과 회람을 먼저 읽
어보는 게 좋겠네요.**

어휘 have trouble -ing ~하는 데 어려움이 있다   place an
order 주문하다   insufficient 불충분한   fund 자금
quarter 분기, 4분의 1   accounting 회계   memo 회람
allocate 할당하다   exceed 초과하다   budget 예산
away on business 출장 중인   catch up on ~을 따라잡다
miss 놓치다

---

50 What problem are the speakers discussing?
(A) An order for supplies is not being processed.
(B) An employee handbook is missing
information.
(C) Some equipment has broken components.
(D) Some team members were not assigned
tasks.

번역 화자들은 어떤 문제를 논의하고 있는가?
(A) 용품 주문이 처리되지 않고 있다.
(B) 직원 안내서에 정보가 빠져 있다.
(C) 일부 장비에 고장 난 부품이 있다.
(D) 일부 팀원들이 업무를 배정받지 못했다.

해설 **전체 내용 관련 - 화자들이 논의하는 문제점**
첫 번째 여자가 첫 대사에서 부서의 용품을 구입하는 데 어려움을 겪
고 있다(Jasmine and I are having trouble getting supplies
for our department)고 했고, 두 번째 대사에서 주문을 하려고 하
면 자금이 부족하다고 나온다(When we try to place the order,
it says there are insufficient funds)고 말하고 있으므로 화자
들은 부서의 용품 주문에 어려움을 겪고 있다는 것을 알 수 있다. 따라
서 정답은 (A)이다.

어휘 process 처리하다   handbook 안내서   component 부품
assign 할당하다   task 일, 업무

---

51 Who most likely is the man?
(A) A product designer
(B) A sales manager
(C) A company accountant
(D) A delivery person

번역 남자는 누구이겠는가?
(A) 제품 디자이너
(B) 영업부 관리자
(C) 회계 담당자
(D) 배달 기사

해설 **전체 내용 관련 - 남자의 직업**
남자가 두 번째 대사에서 회계부에 있는 저희 모두(all of us on the
accounting team)라고 했으므로 남자는 회계 담당자임을 알 수 있
다. 따라서 정답은 (C)이다.

어휘 accountant 회계사   delivery 배달

52 What will the women most likely do next?
(A) Update their computer passwords
(B) Read some work-related messages
(C) Depart for a business trip
(D) Print a budget report

번역 여자들은 다음으로 무엇을 하겠는가?
(A) 컴퓨터 비밀번호 변경하기
(B) 업무와 관련된 메시지 읽기
(C) 출장 떠나기
(D) 예산 보고서 출력하기

해설 **세부 사항 관련 - 여자들이 다음에 할 일**
두 번째 여자가 마지막 대사에서 읽지 못한 이메일과 회람을 먼저 읽어보는 게 좋겠다(We'd better catch up on the e-mails and memos we missed now)고 말하고 있으므로 정답은 (B)이다.

어휘 work-related 업무와 관련된   depart 떠나다

> **Paraphrasing**
> 대화의 catch up on the e-mails and memos
> → 정답의 Read some work-related messages

53-55

M-Cn Hi, Ms. Frazier. **53 This is Ivan Ellis, the caterer who hosted the tasting event last week.** You're preparing for a company celebration, right?

W-Am Yes. Next month will be our company's thirtieth anniversary, so we're holding a dinner.

M-Cn Great! I'm calling because we've added a few more appetizer options. **54 If you're still considering your menu, I'd love for you to try them.**

W-Am We signed a contract with Newton Services.

M-Cn Oh, I see. Well, I hope we can work together in the future.

W-Am Actually, it's good that you called. We have an orientation session for employees this Thursday. Our lunch reservation was canceled, so **55 I wonder if you can make a meal at the last minute.**

남: 안녕하세요, 프레이저 씨. 저는 지난주에 시식회를 주최했던 **출장 요리 연회사인 이반 엘리스입니다.** 회사 기념행사를 준비 중이시죠?

여: 네. 다음 달이 저희 회사의 30주년이라서 만찬을 열려고 해요.

남: 좋습니다! 전채 요리를 몇 가지 더 추가했음을 알려드리려고 전화드렸습니다. **여전히 메뉴를 고민 중이시라면 그것들을 맛보시면 좋을 것 같아요.**

여: 저희는 뉴턴 서비스와 계약을 했어요.

남: 아, 그러시군요. 그럼, 나중에 함께 일할 수 있기를 바랍니다.

여: 실은, 마침 전화 잘 주셨어요. 이번 주 목요일에 직원들을 위한 오리엔테이션이 있는데요. 점심 예약이 취소되어서, **시간이 촉박하지만 식사를 준비해 주실 수 있는지 궁금해요.**

어휘 caterer 출장 요리 연회사   tasting event 시식회, 시음회   prepare for ~을 준비하다   celebration 기념행사   anniversary 기념일   appetizer 전채 요리, 애피타이저   consider 고려하다   sign a contract 계약을 맺다   reservation 예약   cancel 취소하다   at the last minute 마지막 순간에

53 Who is the man?
(A) A caterer
(B) A driver
(C) A journalist
(D) A florist

번역 남자는 누구인가?
(A) 출장 요리 연회사
(B) 운전사
(C) 기자
(D) 플로리스트

해설 **전체 내용 관련 - 남자의 직업**
남자가 첫 대사에서 출장 요리 연회사인 이반 엘리스(This is Ivan Ellis, the caterer)라고 자신을 소개하고 있으므로 정답은 (A)이다.

54 Why does the woman say, "We signed a contract with Newton Services"?
(A) To reject an offer
(B) To apologize for a delay
(C) To recommend a company
(D) To reassure the man

번역 여자가 "저희는 뉴턴 서비스와 계약을 했어요"라고 말한 이유는?
(A) 제안을 거절하려고
(B) 지연에 대해 사과하려고
(C) 회사를 추천하려고
(D) 남자를 안심시키려고

해설 **화자의 의도 파악 - 뉴턴 서비스와 계약을 했다는 말의 의도**
앞에서 남자가 여전히 메뉴를 고민 중이라면 그것들을 맛보면 좋을 것 같다(If you're still considering your menu, I'd love for you to try them)고 하자 여자가 인용문을 언급한 것으로 보아, 남자의 제안을 거절하려는 의도로 한 말임을 알 수 있다. 따라서 정답은 (A)이다.

어휘 reject 거절하다   apologize 사과하다   reassure 안심시키다

55 What does the woman ask the man to do?
(A) Plan an orientation session
(B) Fulfill a last-minute request
(C) Suggest a day to meet
(D) Provide a bulk discount

번역 여자는 남자에게 무엇을 요청하는가?
(A) 오리엔테이션 준비
(B) 시간이 촉박한 요청 완수
(C) 만날 날짜 제안
(D) 대량 구매 할인 제공

해설 **세부 사항 관련 - 여자의 요청 사항**
여자가 마지막 대사에서 시간이 촉박하지만 식사를 준비해 줄 수 있
는지 궁금하다(I wonder if you can make a meal at the last
minute)고 했으므로 정답은 (B)이다.

어휘 fulfill 완수하다　provide 제공하다　bulk discount
대량 구입 시의 가격 할인

56-58

W-Am　Thanks for seeing me today, Lucas. **⁵⁶ Our company is running into some problems with the building models for the documentary.** Some scenes require a tower from a century ago, but the model is not ready yet.

M-Cn　Hmm... We have other models from previous projects, but **⁵⁷ I don't think those will look authentic.** They need to fit the period.

W-Am　Actually, there is some room in the travel budget. We could shoot footage in person at a real structure.

M-Cn　That might be our only choice.

W-Am　**⁵⁸ Could you do some research on the architecture of the time and see if anything in the area matches what we need?**

M-Cn　Sure.

여:　오늘 만나주셔서 감사합니다, 루커스. **저희 회사는 다큐멘터리를 위한 건축 모형과 관련된 문제를 겪고 있습니다.** 일부 장면은 100년 전 탑이 필요한데 모형이 아직 준비되지 않았습니다.

남:　음… 예전 프로젝트 때 만든 다른 모형들이 있긴 하지만, **진짜처럼 보이지는 않을 것 같습니다.** 시대에 맞아야 하니까요.

여:　실은, 여행 예산에 약간 여유가 있어요. 실제 구조물에서 직접 촬영할 수도 있습니다.

남:　그게 유일한 방법일 것 같네요.

여:　**당신이 그 시대 건축물에 대해 조사를 좀 해서 그 지역에 우리가 필요로 하는 것과 일치하는 것이 있는지 알아봐 주실 수 있나요?**

남:　물론이죠.

어휘 run into (곤경 등을) 겪다　require 요구하다　century
100년　previous 이전의　authentic 진짜의, 진품인
fit 맞다　period 기간, 시대　budget 예산　shoot 촬영하다
footage 장면, 화면　in person 직접　structure 구조,
구조물　architecture 건축　match 어울리다, 맞다

---

56 Which industry do the speakers most likely work in?
(A) Interior design
(B) Construction
(C) Film production
(D) Tourism

번역 화자들은 어떤 업계에 종사하겠는가?
(A) 실내 디자인
(B) 건축
(C) 영화 제작
(D) 관광

해설 **전체 내용 관련 - 화자들의 근무 업종**
여자가 첫 대사에서 저희 회사는 다큐멘터리를 위한 건축 모형
과 관련해서 문제를 겪고 있다(Our company is running
into some problems with the building models for the
documentary)고 말하고 있으므로 화자들은 영화 제작 업계에서 일
하고 있다는 것을 알 수 있다. 따라서 정답은 (C)이다.

어휘 production 제작

> **Paraphrasing**
> 대화의 the documentary → 정답의 Film

---

57 What is the man concerned about?
(A) Saving space
(B) Maintaining authenticity
(C) Reducing expenses
(D) Following regulations

번역 남자는 무엇에 대해 걱정하는가?
(A) 공간 절약하기
(B) 진정성 유지하기
(C) 지출 줄이기
(D) 규정 준수하기

해설 **세부 사항 관련 - 남자의 우려 사항**
남자가 첫 대사에서 진짜처럼 보이지는 않을 것 같다(I don't think
those will look authentic)고 말하고 있으므로 정답은 (B)이다.

어휘 maintain 유지하다　authenticity 진정성　reduce 줄이다
expense 지출　regulation 규제

---

58 What does the woman ask the man to do?
(A) Look into hiring some temporary workers
(B) Perform photo editing on some images
(C) Research architecture in the area
(D) Find some colors to match a logo

번역 여자는 남자에게 무엇을 하라고 요청하는가?
(A) 임시직 직원 고용에 대해 알아보기
(B) 일부 이미지 편집하기
(C) 그 지역의 건축물 조사하기
(D) 로고와 어울리는 색상 찾기

해설 **세부 사항 관련 - 여자의 요청 사항**
여자가 마지막 대사에서 그 시대 건축물에 대해 조사를 해 줄 것

(Could you do some research on the architecture of the time ~?)을 요청하고 있으므로 정답은 (C)이다.

어휘   look into ~을 조사하다   hire 고용하다   temporary 임시적인   perform 수행하다   photo editing 사진 편집

59-61

M-Cn   Good morning, Ms. Hawthorne. ⁵⁹ **Thanks for coming to give your feedback on our new line of cookware.**

W-Am   I think it will be fun. So, will I actually get a chance to cook with the items?

M-Cn   Yes. We have a test kitchen on the second floor. Before we go there, ⁶⁰ **could you please put on this visitor ID badge?** It will help our security team to know that you are supposed to be in the building.

W-Am   Of course. Do you need me to do anything else?

M-Cn   We have your contact information, but ⁶¹ **we do need you to sign some non-disclosure forms.** I've got them right here.

남: 좋은 아침입니다, 호손 씨. **저희 조리 도구 신제품군에 대한 피드백을 주시기 위해 와주셔서 감사합니다.**

여: 재미있을 것 같아요. 그럼, 실제로 그 제품들로 요리해 볼 기회가 있을까요?

남: 네. 2층에 연습용 주방이 있습니다. 거기로 가기 전에 **이 방문자 명찰을 착용해 주시겠습니까?** 그러면 저희 보안팀에서 당신이 이 건물에 출입하기로 되어 있다는 사실을 아는 데 도움이 됩니다.

여: 물론이죠. 제가 그밖에 더 해야 할 일이 있나요?

남: 연락처는 받았지만, **기밀 유지 서약서에 서명을 해주셔야 합니다.** 여기 준비해 놓았어요.

어휘   feedback 피드백   cookware 조리 도구   get a chance 기회를 얻다   put on ~을 착용하다   security 보안   be supposed to ~하기로 되어 있다   non-disclosure 기밀 유지

---

59   Why did the woman visit the man's business?
(A) To repair some cooking equipment
(B) To share her opinions about products
(C) To meet with some investors
(D) To lead a business strategy seminar

번역   여자는 왜 남자의 사업체에 방문했는가?
(A) 조리 장비를 수리하려고
(B) 제품에 대한 의견을 공유하려고
(C) 투자자들을 만나려고
(D) 경영 전략 세미나를 주관하려고

해설   **세부 사항 관련 - 여자가 남자의 사업체에 방문한 이유**
남자가 첫 대사에서 저희 조리 도구 신제품군에 대한 피드백을 위해 와 줘서 감사하다(Thanks for coming to give your feedback on our new line of cookware)고 말하고 있으므로 정답은 (B)이다.

어휘   repair 수리하다   equipment 장비   investor 투자자   strategy 전략

> **Paraphrasing**
> 대화의 to give your feedback on our new line of cookware → 정답의 To share her opinions about products

60   What does the man ask the woman to put on?
(A) A staff uniform
(B) An ID badge
(C) A safety vest
(D) A hard hat

번역   남자는 여자에게 무엇을 착용하라고 요청하는가?
(A) 근무복
(B) 신분 명찰
(C) 안전 조끼
(D) 안전모

해설   **세부 사항 관련 - 남자가 착용을 요청하는 것**
남자가 두 번째 대사에서 방문자 명찰을 착용해 줄 것(could you please put on this visitor ID badge?)을 요청하고 있으므로 정답은 (B)이다.

61   What will the woman probably do next?
(A) Take a building tour
(B) Enjoy a meal
(C) Sign some paperwork
(D) Provide her contact information

번역   여자는 다음으로 무엇을 하겠는가?
(A) 건물 견학하기
(B) 식사하기
(C) 서류에 서명하기
(D) 연락처 제공하기

해설   **세부 사항 관련 - 여자가 다음에 할 일**
남자가 마지막 대사에서 기밀 유지 서약서에 서명을 해야 한다(we do need you to sign some non-disclosure forms)고 말하고 있으므로 정답은 (C)이다.

어휘   take a tour 견학하다   provide 제공하다

> **Paraphrasing**
> 대화의 sign some non-disclosure forms → 정답의 Sign some paperwork

개발 과정

1단계:
의뢰인과
상담하기

➡

2단계:
아이디어
생성하기

⬇

63 3단계:
의뢰인에게 선택
지 보여주기

➡

4단계:
선택된 콘셉트
완성하기

어휘 consult 상담하다 generate 만들어내다 selected 선택된

W-Br Tae-Soo, I'm glad to run into you. **62 I heard you hired an agency to develop an advertising campaign for the car dealership.**

M-Au That's right. I felt like professionals could help us reach new customers.

W-Br That makes sense. **63 How far along in the development process are you?**

M-Au **63 They've just presented me with three potential concepts. Once I choose one, they'll begin to finalize it.**

W-Br I see. Well, let me know if you'd like me to look over them. I'd be very interested to see the agency's work.

M-Au Sure, I'd appreciate your input. Today won't work, though. **64 The financing department needs me to sign off on their latest set of contracts.**

여: 태수, 우연히 만나니 반갑네요. **자동차 대리점을 위한 광고 캠페인을 개발해 줄 대행사를 고용하셨다고 들었어요.**

남: 맞아요. 전문가들이 신규 고객에게 다가가는 데 도움을 줄 거라고 생각했어요.

여: 그럴 거예요. **개발 과정은 얼마나 진행되었나요?**

남: **그들이 막 세 가지 시안을 보여줬어요. 제가 하나를 고르면 그들이 마무리 작업을 시작할 거예요.**

여: 그렇군요. 음, 제가 봐주기를 바라신다면 알려주세요. 대행사의 작업물이 매우 궁금하네요.

남: 물론이에요, 의견을 주시면 감사하죠. 오늘은 안 되겠지만요. **경리부에서 최신 계약서에 사인을 하러 오라네요.**

어휘 run into ~와 우연히 만나다 develop 개발하다
dealership 대리점 professional 전문가 present
제시하다 potential 잠재적인 finalize 마무리 짓다
appreciate 감사하다 input 조언 sign off 서명으로
승인하다 contract 계약서

Development Process

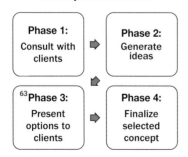

Phase 1:
Consult with
clients

➡

Phase 2:
Generate
ideas

⬇

63 Phase 3:
Present
options to
clients

➡

Phase 4:
Finalize
selected
concept

---

62 What is the conversation mainly about?
(A) Hiring methods
(B) Vehicle designs
(C) Safety regulations
(D) Marketing plans

번역 대화는 주로 무엇에 관한 것인가?
(A) 채용 방법
(B) 자동차 디자인
(C) 안전 규정
(D) 마케팅 계획

해설 **전체 내용 관련 - 대화의 주제**
여자가 첫 대사에서 남자에게 자동차 대리점을 위한 광고 캠페인을 개발해 줄 대행사를 고용했다고 들었다(I heard you hired an agency to develop an advertising campaign for the car dealership)며 광고 캠페인에 대해 말하고 있으므로 정답은 (D)이다.

어휘 method 수단, 방법 regulation 규제, 규정

> **Paraphrasing**
> 대화의 an advertising campaign
> → 정답의 Marketing plans

63 Look at the graphic. What phase is the project currently in?
(A) Phase 1
(B) Phase 2
(C) Phase 3
(D) Phase 4

번역 시각 정보에 의하면, 프로젝트는 현재 몇 단계에 있는가?
(A) 1단계
(B) 2단계
(C) 3단계
(D) 4단계

해설 **시각 정보 연계 - 프로젝트의 현재 단계**
여자가 두 번째 대사에서 개발 과정은 얼마나 진행되었는지(How far along in the development process are you?) 묻자 남자가 그들이 막 세 가지 시안을 보여줬는데(They've just presented me with three potential concepts) 하나를 고르면 그들이 마무리 작업을 시작할 것(Once I choose one, they'll begin to finalize it)이라고 했으며, 업무 흐름도에 따르면 의뢰인에게 선택지 보여주기가 3단계이므로 정답은 (C)이다.

TEST 5

64 What does the man say he has to do today?
(A) Arrange a quality inspection
(B) Approve some legal agreements
(C) Draft a financial report
(D) Check the business's inventory

번역 남자는 자신이 오늘 무엇을 해야 한다고 말하는가?
(A) 품질 검사 준비하기
(B) 법적 계약 승인하기
(C) 재무 보고서 초안 작성하기
(D) 사업장의 재고 확인하기

해설 **세부 사항 관련 - 남자가 오늘 해야 할 일**
남자가 마지막 대사에서 경리부에서 최신 계약서에 사인을 하러 오라고 한다(The financing department needs me to sign off on their latest set of contracts)고 말하고 있으므로 정답은 (B)이다.

어휘 arrange 준비하다 inspection 검사 legal agreement 법적 계약 draft 초안을 작성하다 financial 재무의, 재정의 inventory 재고

> **Paraphrasing**
> 대화의 sign off on their latest set of contracts
> → 정답의 Approve some legal agreements

65-67 대화 + 초대장

W-Am Do you have a minute, Blake? ⁶⁵ **The ceremony to honor our top-performing employees is coming soon,** and I'm designing the invitations. What do you think of this first draft?

M-Au Hmm... Everything looks fine, but ⁶⁶ **I think the slideshow should start at the same time as the live music.** It's quite long, so we don't want the event to run too late.

W-Am True. Any other suggestions?

M-Au You know, it's not a very well-known venue. ⁶⁷ **How about adding a line telling people how to get to the banquet hall by car?**

W-Am Good idea. I'll do that.

여: 잠깐 시간 있나요, 블레이크? **최우수 직원 시상식이 곧 열릴 예정이라서** 제가 초대장을 만들고 있어요. 이 1차 시안에 대해 어떻게 생각해요?

남: 음… 다 괜찮은데, **제 생각엔 슬라이드쇼가 라이브 음악과 동시에 시작해야 해요.** 꽤 긴데, 행사가 너무 길어지는 건 바라지 않잖아요.

여: 그렇죠. 다른 의견은요?

남: 아시다시피, 그곳이 그다지 유명한 장소가 아니잖아요. **차로 연회장까지 오는 방법에 대한 설명을 한 줄 추가하면 어떨까요?**

여: 좋은 생각이에요. 그렇게 할게요.

어휘 ceremony 의식 honor 수여하다 top-performing 가장 실적이 뛰어난 invitation 초대장 draft 초안 run late 늦어지다 suggestion 제안 well-known 유명한 venue 장소 add 추가하다 banquet hall 연회장

Invitation: First draft

Date: Saturday, December 7
Location: Hillhaven Banquet Hall

✦ ✦ ✦

✦ 6:30 P.M. Dinner
✦ 7:30 P.M. Main Program
66 ✦ 8:30 P.M. Live Music
✦ 9:30 P.M. Photo Slideshow

초대장: 1차 시안

날짜: 12월 7일 토요일
장소: 힐헤이븐 연회장

✦ ✦ ✦

✦ 오후 6시 30분 만찬
✦ 오후 7시 30분 본 행사
66 ✦ **오후 8시 30분 라이브 음악**
✦ 오후 9시 30분 사진 슬라이드쇼

---

65 What kind of event is being planned?
(A) A coworker's birthday celebration
(B) A company awards ceremony
(C) A new employee training session
(D) A colleague's retirement dinner

번역 어떤 종류의 행사를 기획하는 중인가?
(A) 동료의 생일 축하 파티
(B) 회사의 시상식
(C) 신입 직원 교육
(D) 동료의 은퇴 기념 만찬

해설 **전체 내용 관련 - 기획 중인 행사**
여자가 첫 대사에서 최우수 직원 시상식이 곧 열릴 예정(The ceremony to honor our top-performing employees is coming soon)이라고 말하고 있으므로 정답은 (B)이다.

어휘 coworker 동료 celebration 기념행사 award 상 colleague 동료 retirement 은퇴, 퇴직

> **Paraphrasing**
> 대화의 The ceremony to honor our top-performing
> employees → 정답의 A company awards ceremony

66 Look at the graphic. What time does the man think the photo slideshow should begin?
(A) At 6:30 P.M.
(B) At 7:30 P.M.
(C) At 8:30 P.M.
(D) At 9:30 P.M.

번역 시각 정보에 의하면, 남자는 사진 슬라이드쇼가 몇 시에 시작되어야 한다고 생각하는가?
(A) 오후 6시 30분
(B) 오후 7시 30분
(C) **오후 8시 30분**
(D) 오후 9시 30분

해설 **시각 정보 연계 - 남자가 생각하는 사진 슬라이드쇼 시작 시간**
남자가 첫 대사에서 슬라이드쇼가 라이브 음악과 동시에 시작해야 한다(I think the slideshow should start at the same time as the live music)고 했고, 초대장에 따르면 라이브 음악(Live Music)이 오후 8시 30분이므로 정답은 (C)이다.

67 What does the man suggest adding to the invitation?
(A) A list of menu options
(B) The venue's phone number
(C) **Some driving directions**
(D) Some employees' job titles

번역 남자는 초대장에 무엇을 추가하라고 제안하는가?
(A) 메뉴 목록
(B) 장소의 전화번호
(C) **운전자용 길 안내**
(D) 직원들의 직함

해설 **세부 사항 관련 - 남자가 초대장에 추가하라고 제안하는 것**
남자가 마지막 대사에서 차로 연회장까지 오는 방법에 대한 설명을 한 줄 추가할 것(How about adding a line telling people how to get to the banquet hall by car?)을 제안하고 있으므로 정답은 (C)이다.

어휘 direction 방향 job title 직함

> **Paraphrasing**
> 대화의 how to get to the banquet hall by car
> → 정답의 Some driving directions

68-70 대화+평면도

M-Au Hi, I got a call saying that **68 there's a problem with one of your air conditioning units. I'm here to fix that.**

W-Am Oh, you arrived sooner than I expected. Do you need help bringing in your equipment?

M-Au Well, I'd like to take a look at it first to see what I'm dealing with.

W-Am Of course. It's in Mr. Griffith's office, **69 which is the room nearest to the elevator, just past the copy room.**

M-Au Thanks. **70 Do I need to put on a visitor ID badge?**

W-Am Yes, I've got one right here for you. **70 Please don't forget to drop it off with me when you leave.**

남: 안녕하세요. 제가 전화를 받았는데, **귀사의 에어컨 중 하나에 문제가 생겼다면서요. 제가 고쳐드리려고 왔습니다.**

여: 아, 제가 예상했던 것보다 일찍 도착하셨네요. 장비를 가져오는 데 도움이 필요하신가요?

남: 음, 제가 처리해야 하는 문제가 뭔지 알아보기 위해 에어컨을 먼저 살펴보고 싶은데요.

여: 물론이죠. 그리피스 씨의 사무실에 있어요. **승강기에서 가장 가까운 방이에요. 복사실 바로 지나서요.**

남: 감사합니다. 방문자 명찰을 착용해야 하나요?

여: 네, 여기 있습니다. **가실 때 저에게 돌려주시는 거 잊지 마세요.**

어휘 fix 고치다, 바로잡다 equipment 장비 deal with ~을 다루다, 처리하다 drop off 가져다주다 leave 떠나다

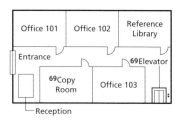

68 Why is the man visiting the business?
(A) To pick up some brochures
(B) To give a sales pitch
(C) To sign a contract
(D) **To make a repair**

번역 남자는 왜 이 회사에 방문하는가?
(A) 안내 책자를 받아 가려고
(B) 판매를 위한 설득을 하려고
(C) 계약서에 서명하려고
(D) **수리를 하려고**

해설 **세부 사항 관련 - 남자가 회사에 방문하는 이유**
남자가 첫 대사에서 에어컨에 문제가 생겼다는 말을 듣고 고치러 왔다(there's a problem with one of your air conditioning units. I'm here to fix that)고 말하고 있으므로 정답은 (D)이다.

어휘 pick up 와서 가져가다 brochure 안내 책자 sales pitch 판매를 위한 설득

Paraphrasing
대화의 fix → 정답의 make a repair

69 Look at the graphic. Where does the woman direct the man to go?
(A) Office 101
(B) Office 102
(C) Office 103
(D) Copy room

번역 시각 정보에 의하면, 여자는 남자에게 어디로 가라고 알려주는가?
(A) 사무실 101호
(B) 사무실 102호
(C) 사무실 103호
(D) 복사실

해설 **시각 정보 연계 - 여자가 남자에게 안내하는 곳**
여자가 두 번째 대사에서 승강기에서 가장 가까운 방이며 복사실 바로 지나서(which is the room nearest to the elevator, just past the copy room)라고 말하고 있다. 평면도에 따르면 승강기에서 가까우면서 복사실 바로 지나서 위치하고 있는 방이 사무실 103호(Office 103)이므로 정답은 (C)이다.

70 What does the woman ask the man to do?
(A) Avoid using an elevator
(B) Return a badge later
(C) Leave his business card
(D) Remove his outerwear

번역 여자는 남자에게 무엇을 하라고 요청하는가?
(A) 승강기 사용 피하기
(B) 명찰 나중에 반납하기
(C) 명함 두고 가기
(D) 외투 벗기

해설 **세부 사항 관련 - 여자의 요청 사항**
남자가 마지막 대사에서 방문자 명찰을 착용해야 하는지(Do I need to put on a visitor ID badge?) 묻자 여자가 갈 때 돌려주는 거 잊지 말 것(Please don't forget to drop it off with me when you leave)을 요청하고 있으므로 정답은 (B)이다.

어휘 avoid 피하다 remove 없애다, 제거하다 outerwear 외투

> **Paraphrasing**
> 대화의 drop it off with me when you leave
> → 정답의 Return ~ later

PART 4

71-73 회의 발췌

M-Au The last thing I'd like to discuss today is ensuring the best quality while making [71] **our energy drinks and sodas** here at Kinney Company. Before you add any ingredients, [72] **please make sure that they have not expired.** We have recently received some outdated goods from our supplier, so we can't let these get into our final products. And, if you do find anything that cannot be used, please place it in [73] **the yellow box in the main corridor. We would like to collect everything in the same place** so we can make a return. Thank you for your cooperation.

오늘 마지막으로 의논하고 싶은 사항은 이곳 키니 컴퍼니에서 **우리 에너지 드링크와 탄산음료를** 만드는 동안 최상의 품질을 유지하는 것입니다. 원료를 추가하기 전에 **유통 기한이 지나지 않았는지 반드시 확인해 주십시오.** 우리는 최근에 공급업체로부터 유통 기한이 지난 상품을 받았으므로 그것들이 최종 완제품에 들어가게 하면 안 됩니다. 그리고 사용할 수 없는 것을 발견한다면 그것을 **중앙 복도에 있는 노란 상자에** 넣어주십시오. 모두 한곳에 모아야 반품할 수 있으니까요. 여러분의 협조에 감사드립니다.

어휘 ensure 보장하다 quality 품질 add 추가하다
ingredient 재료, 성분 expire 만료되다 outdated 유효 기간이 지난 supplier 공급업체 corridor 복도 collect 모으다
make a return 반품하다 cooperation 협조

71 What does the speaker's company produce?
(A) Exercise equipment
(B) Light fixtures
(C) Automobiles
(D) Beverages

번역 화자의 회사는 무엇을 생산하는가?
(A) 운동 기구
(B) 조명 기구
(C) 자동차
(D) 음료

해설 **전체 내용 관련 - 화자의 회사가 생산하는 것**
화자가 초반부에 우리 에너지 드링크와 탄산음료(our energy drinks and sodas)라고 했으므로 정답은 (D)이다.

> **Paraphrasing**
> 담화의 energy drinks and sodas → 정답의 Beverages

72 What does the speaker remind the listeners to do?
(A) Check some expiration dates
(B) Update their contact information
(C) Review a purchasing agreement
(D) Record their working hours

번역 화자는 청자들에게 무엇을 하라고 상기시키는가?
(A) 유통 기한 확인하기
(B) 연락처 업데이트하기
(C) 구매 계약서 검토하기
(D) 근무 시간 기록하기

해설 **세부 사항 관련 - 화자가 청자들에게 상기시키는 것**
화자가 중반부에 유통 기한이 지나지 않았는지 반드시 확인하라 (please make sure that they have not expired)고 했으므로 정답은 (A)이다.

어휘 expiration date 유통 기한, 유효 기간 agreement 합의, 계약 record 기록하다

---

73 What can be found in the main corridor?
(A) A collection container
(B) A box of tools
(C) An order form
(D) An employee directory

번역 중앙 복도에는 무엇이 있겠는가?
(A) 수거 용기
(B) 공구 상자
(C) 주문서
(D) 직원 명부

해설 **세부 사항 관련 - 중앙 복도에 있는 것**
화자가 후반부에 중앙 복도에 있는 노란 상자(the yellow box in the main corridor)를 언급하며, 반품할 수 있도록 모두 한곳에 모으고자 한다(We would like to collect everything in the same place)고 했으므로 정답은 (A)이다.

어휘 container 그릇, 용기 directory 명단, 목록

> **Paraphrasing**
> 담화의 yellow box → 정답의 container

74-76 전화 메시지

> W-Br Hi, Monica. I've arrived here at the community center. **74 I've just set up the photo booth so I can take group shots of people attending the food festival.** The organizers have assigned me a spot near the live band. **75 I know you were worried that I wouldn't be able to plug in all of the extra lights I brought,** but I can see several power outlets. Anyway, **76 I'm actually calling to remind you to put up the posting for the assistant photographer job today on the Web sites** we discussed. We need to get that role filled as soon as possible.

안녕하세요, 모니카. 저 여기 지역 문화 센터에 도착했어요. **사진 부스를 방금 설치해서 음식 축제에 참석한 사람들의 단체 사진을 찍을 수 있어요.** 주최자들이 라이브 밴드 옆자리를 지정해 주었어요. **제가 가져온 모든 추가 조명들의 플러그를 꽂을 수 없을까 봐 걱정하셨잖아요.** 하지만 전기 콘센트 몇 개가 보여요. 어쨌든, 상의했던 대로 웹사이트에 오늘 보조 사진가 구인 공고를 올리는 걸 상기시켜 드리려고 전화드렸어

요. 최대한 빨리 그 자리를 채워야 해요.

어휘 set up 설치하다 booth 부스 take a shot of ~의 사진을 찍다 attend 참석하다 organizer 주최자 assign 할당하다 spot 자리 plug in ~의 플러그를 꽂다 extra 추가의 power outlet 전기 콘센트 remind 상기시키다 put up ~을 게시하다 posting 게시물 assistant 조수, 보조 role 역할

---

74 What will the speaker do at the community center?
(A) Serve some food samples
(B) Give a public speech
(C) Take people's photographs
(D) Advertise a family vacation

번역 화자는 지역 문화 센터에서 무엇을 할 것인가?
(A) 시식용 음식 서빙하기
(B) 공개 연설하기
(C) 사람들의 사진 찍기
(D) 가족 휴가 광고하기

해설 **세부 사항 관련 - 화자가 지역 문화 센터에서 할 일**
화자가 초반부에 사진 부스를 방금 설치해서 음식 축제에 참석한 사람들의 단체 사진을 찍을 수 있다(I've just set up the photo booth so I can take group shots of people attending the food festival)고 했으므로 정답은 (C)이다.

어휘 public speech 공개 연설 photograph 사진 advertise 광고하다

> **Paraphrasing**
> 담화의 take group shots of people
> → 정답의 Take people's photographs

---

75 Why does the speaker say, "I can see several power outlets"?
(A) To reject an offer of assistance
(B) To provide reassurance to the listener
(C) To complain about an unfinished task
(D) To ask for some clarification

번역 화자가 "전기 콘센트 몇 개가 보여요"라고 말한 이유는?
(A) 도움을 거절하려고
(B) 청자를 안심시키려고
(C) 완료되지 않은 일에 대해 불평하려고
(D) 좀 더 자세한 설명을 요구하려고

해설 **화자의 의도 파악 - 전기 콘센트 몇 개가 보인다는 말의 의도**
앞에서 모든 추가 조명들의 플러그를 꽂을 수 없을까 봐 걱정하셨잖아요(I know you were worried that I wouldn't be able to plug in all of the extra lights I brought)라고 말한 뒤 인용문을 언급하고 있으므로, 플러그를 다 꽂지 못할까 봐 걱정 안 해도 된다고 청자를 안심시키려는 의도로 한 말임을 알 수 있다. 따라서 정답은 (B)이다.

어휘 reject 거절하다 assistance 도움 reassurance 안심시키는 말[행동] unfinished 완료되지 않은 clarification 설명, 해명

76 What does the speaker remind the listener to do?
(A) Proofread some brochures
(B) Post some information online
(C) Fill out a reimbursement request
(D) Renew a business license

번역 화자는 청자에게 무엇을 하라고 상기시키는가?
(A) 안내 책자 교정하기
(B) 온라인에 정보 게시하기
(C) 환급 신청서 작성하기
(D) 사업자 등록증 갱신하기

해설 **세부 사항 관련 - 화자가 청자에게 상기시키는 것**
화자가 후반부에 웹사이트에 오늘 보조 사진가 구인 공고를 올리는 걸 상기시켜 주려고 전화했다(I'm actually calling to remind you to put up the posting for the assistant photographer job today on the Web sites)고 말하고 있으므로 정답은 (B)이다.

어휘 proofread 교정을 보다   brochure 안내 책자   fill out 작성하다
reimbursement 환급   renew 갱신하다

> **Paraphrasing**
> 담화의 put up the posting ~ on the Web sites
> → 정답의 Post some information online

77-79 방송

> M-Cn Thanks for tuning in to the business report on KRRT radio. **77 Earlier this week, Rinehart Manufacturing moved its headquarters from New York to Boston. 78 Rinehart Manufacturing is known for the refrigerators, washing machines, and dryers that it makes.** A Rinehart spokesperson reported that the move allowed the company to expand and upgrade its facilities. To see the new building for yourself, **79 visit Rinehart Manufacturing's Web site, where you can browse the company's online photo gallery.**
>
> KRRT 라디오의 경제 뉴스를 청취해 주셔서 감사합니다. **이번 주 초에 라인하트 제조사가 본사를 뉴욕에서 보스턴으로 이전했습니다. 라인하트 제조사는 직접 생산하는 냉장고와 세탁기, 건조기로 유명합니다.** 라인하트 대변인은 이번 이전으로 회사가 시설을 확충하고 개선할 수 있었다고 말했습니다. 새 건물을 직접 보고 싶으시다면 **라인하트 제조사의 웹사이트를 방문하세요. 웹사이트에서 이 회사의 온라인 사진첩을 보실 수 있습니다.**
>
> 어휘 tune in to ~을 청취하다   manufacturing 제조
> headquarters 본사, 본부   be known for ~으로 유명하다
> refrigerator 냉장고   washing machine 세탁기   dryer 건조기
> spokesperson 대변인   allow 허용하다   facility 시설

77 What did Rinehart Manufacturing recently do?
(A) It passed an annual factory safety inspection.
(B) It changed the location of its headquarters.
(C) It hired a new CEO to lead the company.
(D) It introduced a popular new line of products.

번역 라인하트 제조사는 최근에 무엇을 했는가?
(A) 연례 공장 안전 점검을 통과했다.
(B) 본사의 위치를 바꿨다.
(C) 회사를 이끌 새 CEO를 고용했다.
(D) 인기 있는 신제품군을 출시했다.

해설 **세부 사항 관련 - 라인하트 제조사가 최근에 한 일**
화자가 초반부에 이번 주에 라인하트 제조사가 본사를 뉴욕에서 보스턴으로 이전했다(Earlier this week, Rinehart Manufacturing moved its headquarters from New York to Boston)고 말하고 있으므로 정답은 (B)이다.

어휘 pass 통과하다   annual 연례의   safety 안전   inspection 점검

> **Paraphrasing**
> 담화의 Earlier this week → 질문의 recently
> 담화의 moved its headquarters
> → 정답의 changed the location of its headquarters

78 What kind of product does Rinehart Manufacturing make?
(A) Tools
(B) Automobiles
(C) Clothing
(D) Appliances

번역 라인하트 제조사는 어떤 종류의 제품을 생산하는가?
(A) 공구
(B) 자동차
(C) 의류
(D) 가전제품

해설 **세부 사항 관련 - 라인하트 제조사가 생산하는 제품**
화사가 중빈부에 라인하트 제조사는 직접 생산하는 냉장고와 세탁기, 건조기로 유명하다(Rinehart Manufacturing is known for the refrigerators, washing machines, and dryers that it makes)고 말하고 있으므로 정답은 (D)이다.

> **Paraphrasing**
> 담화의 refrigerators, washing machines, and dryers
> → 정답의 Appliances

79 What can the listeners find online?
(A) Some job descriptions
(B) Some driving directions
(C) An updated staff directory
(D) A collection of images

번역 청자들은 온라인에서 무엇을 찾을 수 있는가?
(A) 직무 설명
(B) 운전자용 길 안내
(C) 최신 직원 명단
(D) 이미지 모음

해설 **세부 사항 관련 - 청자들이 온라인에서 찾을 수 있는 것**
화자가 마지막에 라인하트 제조사의 온라인 사진첩을 볼 수 있는 웹사이트를 방문하라(visit Rinehart Manufacturing's Web site, where you can browse the company's online photo gallery)고 권하고 있으므로 정답은 (D)이다.

어휘 description 설명 direction 방향 directory 명단, 목록 collection 수집품, 모음집

> **Paraphrasing**
> 담화의 photo gallery → 정답의 A collection of images

80-82 연설

W-Br Thank you all for being here for today's event. I would especially like to welcome city officials as well as one of our sponsors, Michael Rowley of Rowley Tech. I know I'm not alone in saying that **80 this new library is essential for our community.** In addition to books, magazines, and newspapers, **81 we have a computer lab with twenty computers donated by Mr. Rowley's shop.** Now, before you start browsing, **82 I've had pens custom-printed with the library's hours of operation.** Don't forget to pick one up.

오늘 행사를 위해 참석해 주신 모든 분께 감사드립니다. 특히 시 공무원분들 뿐만 아니라 후원자 중 한 분인 롤리 테크의 마이클 롤리도 환영합니다. 이 신설 도서관이 우리 지역사회에 꼭 필요하다고 말하는 사람은 저만이 아닐 겁니다. 도서와 잡지, 신문뿐 아니라 **롤리 씨의 가게에서 기부해 주신 컴퓨터 20대를 구비한 컴퓨터실도 있습니다.** 자, 둘러보시기 전에 제가 도서관의 운영 시간이 맞춤 인쇄된 펜을 준비했습니다. 잊지 말고 하나씩 받아 가세요.

어휘 city official 시 공무원 sponsor 후원자, 광고주 essential 매우 중요한 community 지역사회, 공동체 donate 기부하다 browse 검색하다, 둘러보다 custom-printed 맞춤 인쇄된 hours of operation 운영 시간

80 What event is taking place?
(A) A retirement party
(B) A company picnic
(C) A grand opening
(D) A writing competition

번역 어떤 행사가 진행되고 있는가?
(A) 은퇴 기념식
(B) 회사 야유회
(C) 개관식
(D) 글쓰기 대회

해설 **전체 내용 관련 - 진행 중인 행사**
화자가 초반부에 이 신설 도서관이 우리 지역사회에 꼭 필요하다(this new library is essential for our community)고 말하고 있으므로 정답은 (C)이다.

어휘 retirement 은퇴, 퇴직 grand opening 개점, 개장

81 What kind of business does Mr. Rowley most likely own?
(A) An electronics store
(B) A clothing shop
(C) A car dealership
(D) An insurance company

번역 롤리 씨는 어떤 종류의 사업체를 소유하고 있겠는가?
(A) 전자 제품 판매점
(B) 옷 가게
(C) 자동차 대리점
(D) 보험 회사

해설 **세부 사항 관련 - 롤리 씨가 소유하고 있는 사업체의 종류**
화자가 중반부에 롤리 씨의 가게에서 기부해 준 컴퓨터 20대를 구비한 컴퓨터실도 있다(we have a computer lab with twenty computers donated by Mr. Rowley's shop)고 말하고 있으므로 정답은 (A)이다.

어휘 electronics 전자 제품 dealership 대리점 insurance 보험

82 What has the speaker prepared for attendees?
(A) Some tote bags
(B) Some pens
(C) Some business cards
(D) Some printed calendars

번역 화자는 참석자들을 위해 무엇을 준비했는가?
(A) 토트백
(B) 펜
(C) 명함
(D) 인쇄된 달력

해설 **세부 사항 관련 - 참석자들을 위해 준비한 것**
화자가 마지막에 도서관의 운영 시간이 맞춤 인쇄된 펜을 준비했다(I've had pens custom-printed with the library's hours of operation)고 했으므로 정답은 (B)이다.

어휘 tote bag 토트백(손잡이 2개가 마주 달린 큰 가방)

83-85 회의 발췌

W-Am The last thing that I would like to talk about is our annual recruitment event. Just like last year, **83 our gym** will invite the public to take a tour of our facilities and learn about the exercise classes we offer. This is a great way to increase our membership. **84 So far, three employees have** volunteered to give tours. Five or six would be better. I'll give you all the information you need, so please talk to me after this meeting if you can help. **85 I know that some of you had ideas for what kinds of refreshments we should serve at the event. So, I'd like to take some time to hear those now.**

마지막으로 이야기하고 싶은 사항은 연례 모집 행사입니다. 작년과 마찬가지로 **우리 체육관은** 일반인들을 초대해 시설을 견학하고 우리가 제공하는 운동 수업에 대해 알아볼 기회를 제공할 겁니다. 이것은 회원을 늘리는 데 매우 좋은 방법입니다. **지금까지 세 명의 직원이 견학을 진행할 수 있다고 자원했습니다. 대여섯이면 더 좋을 것 같아요.** 필요한 정보는 모두 드릴 테니 도울 수 있는 분은 이 회의가 끝나고 저에게 말씀해 주세요. 여러분 중에 이 행사 때 어떤 종류의 다과를 제공해야 하는지에 대해 아이디어가 있는 분이 있을 겁니다. 그러니 지금은 그것들부터 들어보고 싶군요.

어휘 annual 연례의 recruitment 모집 invite 초대하다 take a tour 견학하다 facility 시설 offer 제공하다 increase 증가시키다 membership 회원, 회원의 수 volunteer 자원하다 refreshments 다과 serve (식당 등에서 음식을) 제공하다

83 Where do the listeners work?
(A) At a fitness facility
(B) At a clothing store
(C) At a dental clinic
(D) At a financial institution

번역 청자들은 어디서 일하는가?
(A) 피트니스 시설
(B) 옷 가게
(C) 치과
(D) 금융 기관

해설 **전체 내용 관련 - 청자들의 근무 장소**
화자가 초반부에 우리 체육관(our gym)이라고 말하고 있으므로 청자들은 피트니스 시설에서 근무하고 있다는 것을 알 수 있다. 따라서 정답은 (A)이다.

> Paraphrasing
> 담화의 our gym → 정답의 a fitness facility

84 What does the speaker imply when she says, "Five or six would be better"?
(A) The length of an event is too short.
(B) A task requires more people.
(C) More tables need to be set up.
(D) Pages should be added to a tour brochure.

번역 화자가 "대여섯이면 더 좋을 것 같아요"라고 말할 때, 그 의도는 무엇인가?
(A) 행사 기간이 너무 짧다.
(B) 일을 하기 위해 더 많은 사람이 필요하다.
(C) 더 많은 탁자가 설치되어야 한다.
(D) 관광 안내 책자에 페이지가 추가되어야 한다.

해설 **화자의 의도 파악 - 대여섯이면 더 좋겠다는 말의 의도**
앞에서 지금까지 세 명의 직원이 견학을 진행할 수 있다고 자원했다 (So far, three employees have volunteered to give tours)고 말한 후, 인용문을 언급하고 있으므로 견학을 진행할 직원이 더 필요하다는 의도로 한 말임을 알 수 있다. 따라서 정답은 (B)이다.

어휘 length 길이 require 필요로 하다, 요구하다 set up 설치하다 brochure 안내 책자

85 What will the listeners probably do next?
(A) Watch a sales presentation
(B) Enjoy some free refreshments
(C) Sign a membership contract
(D) Share some of their suggestions

번역 청자들은 다음으로 무엇을 하겠는가?
(A) 영업 프리젠테이션 보기
(B) 무료 다과 맛보기
(C) 회원 계약서에 서명하기
(D) 제안을 공유하기

해설 **세부 사항 관련 - 청자들이 다음에 할 일**
화자가 마지막에 여러분 중에 이 행사 때 어떤 종류의 다과를 제공해야 하는지에 대해 아이디어가 있는 분이 있을 것(I know that some of you had ideas for what kinds of refreshments we should serve at the event)이라면서 지금은 그것들부터 들어보고 싶다(So, I'd like to take some time to hear those now)고 말하고 있으므로 정답은 (D)이다.

어휘 sales presentation 제품 또는 서비스 소개 발표 suggestion 제안

> Paraphrasing
> 담화의 ideas → 정답의 suggestions

86-88 전화 메시지

M-Au Hi, Nicole. This is Eun-Seok. **86 I'm calling about the meeting preparations for next Monday. First, I'd like to thank you for agreeing to speak to the board members about the specialty lab equipment with a voice command feature. 87 I know that you were nervous about their reaction to the proposed investment,** whether they think our company should be involved. Well, don't forget that this device will be the first of its kind. Second, **88 Carl can advise you about the approach you should take**. He has worked directly with some of the members before, so his insights will be invaluable.

안녕하세요, 니콜. 은석이에요. 다음 주 월요일 회의 준비 때문에 전화 드려요. 먼저, 음성 명령 기능을 갖춘 특수 실험 장비에 대해 이사들에게 설명하는 데 동의해 주셔서 감사합니다. 투자 제안에 대한 그들의 반응에 대해 걱정하셨다는 점을 알고 있습니다. 그들이 우리 회사가 참여해야 한다고 생각하든 그렇지 않든 간에요. 음, 잊지 마세요. 이 기기는

이런 유형으로는 **최초입니다**. 두 번째로, **칼은 당신이 취해야 할 접근법에 대해 조언을 해줄 수 있어요**. 그는 몇몇 이사들과 직접 일해본 적이 있으니 그의 통찰력은 매우 유용할 거예요.

> 어휘 preparation 준비 board member 이사 specialty 특수, 전문 equipment 장비 command 명령 feature 기능 reaction 반응 proposed 제안된 investment 투자 involve 참여시키다 device 기기 advise 조언하다 approach 접근법 insight 통찰력 invaluable 매우 유용한

86 What is scheduled for next Monday?
(A) A group interview session
(B) A corporate board meeting
(C) An annual factory inspection
(D) An industry trade fair

번역 다음 주 월요일에 무엇이 예정되어 있는가?
(A) 집단 면접
(B) 기업 이사회 회의
(C) 연례 공장 점검
(D) 산업 무역 박람회

해설 **세부 사항 관련 - 다음 주 월요일로 예정된 일**
화자가 초반부에 다음 주 월요일 회의 준비 때문에 전화한다(I'm calling about the meeting preparations for next Monday)면서 음성 명령 기능을 갖춘 특수 실험 장비에 대해 이사들에게 설명하는 데 동의해 줘서 감사하다(First, I'd like to thank you for agreeing to speak to the board members about the specialty lab equipment with a voice command feature)고 말하고 있으므로 정답은 (B)이다.

어휘 corporate 기업의 board meeting 이사회 annual 연례의 inspection 점검 industry 산업 trade fair 무역 박람회

87 Why does the speaker say, "this device will be the first of its kind"?
(A) To express confidence in a proposal
(B) To request more time for a project
(C) To show concern about an investment
(D) To correct an error in a business report

번역 화자가 "이 기기는 이런 유형으로는 최초입니다"라고 말한 이유는?
(A) 제안에 대한 자신감을 표현하려고
(B) 프로젝트에 더 많은 시간을 요청하려고
(C) 투자에 대한 우려를 표현하려고
(D) 사업 보고서에서 오류를 바로잡으려고

해설 **화자의 의도 파악 - 이 기기는 이런 유형으로는 최초라는 말의 의도**
화자가 앞에서 투자 제안에 대한 그들의 반응에 대해 걱정했다는 점을 알고 있다(I know that you were nervous about their reaction to the proposed investment)고 한 뒤 인용문을 언급하는 것으로 보아, 최초라는 것을 강조하면서 제안에 대한 자신감을 표현하기 위해 한 말임을 알 수 있다. 따라서 정답은 (A)이다.

어휘 confidence 자신감 proposal 제안 concern 우려, 걱정 correct 바로잡다

88 What does the speaker say about Carl?
(A) He was involved in recruiting members.
(B) He has given a demonstration for a device.
(C) He will be the director of a project.
(D) He can provide some helpful advice.

번역 화자는 칼에 대해 뭐라고 말하는가?
(A) 회원을 모집하는 일에 참여했다.
(B) 기기를 시연해 보았다.
(C) 프로젝트의 책임자가 될 것이다.
(D) 유용한 조언을 해줄 수 있다.

해설 **세부 사항 관련 - 화자가 칼에 대해 하는 말**
화자가 후반부에서 칼은 당신이 취해야 할 접근법에 대해 조언을 해줄 수 있다(Carl can advise you about the approach you should take)고 말하고 있으므로 정답은 (D)이다.

어휘 recruit 모집하다 demonstration 시연 helpful 유용한

> **Paraphrasing**
> 담화의 advise you about the approach
> → 정답의 provide some helpful advice

89-91 담화

M-Cn Good afternoon, everyone. **89 I appreciate all of your hard work in helping customers find the right necklaces, rings, and bracelets to suit their style.** Unfortunately, despite these efforts, **90 our business is struggling due to several shops opening nearby. They sell very similar products to ours,** though I believe our merchandise is of much better quality. I'm looking for ways to combat this problem. As an initial strategy, **91 I'd like to give 10% off to first-time buyers**. We can advertise this deal on social media. I hope it will attract more people to our store. Of course, if you have any other ideas that might help, please feel free to share them with me anytime.

좋은 오후입니다, 여러분. **고객들이 자신의 취향에 맞는 목걸이와 반지, 팔찌를 찾을 수 있도록 도와주신 여러분의 노고에 감사드립니다**. 안타깝게도 이러한 노력에도 불구하고 **우리 사업은 근처에 문을 여는 가게들 때문에 어려움을 겪고 있습니다. 그들은 우리와 매우 비슷한 제품을 판매합니다**. 그래도 저는 우리 상품의 품질이 훨씬 더 좋다고 믿지만요. 이 문제를 해결할 방법을 찾고 있습니다. 초기 전략으로서 **저는 최초 구매자들에게 10% 할인을 제공하고 싶습니다**. 이 내용을 소셜 미디어에 광고합시다. 이를 통해 더 많은 사람을 우리 가게로 끌어모을 수 있으면 좋겠어요. 물론 도움이 될 만한 다른 아이디어가 있다면 언제든 저에게 편하게 공유해 주십시오.

어휘 appreciate 고마워하다 necklace 목걸이 bracelet 팔찌 suit 어울리다 effort 노력 struggle 투쟁하다, 싸우다 due to ~ 때문에 merchandise 상품 quality 품질 combat 싸우다 initial 초기의 strategy 전략 first-time buyer 최초 구매자 advertise 광고하다 attract 끌어모으다

89 What kind of business does the speaker most likely work for?
(A) A home improvement store
(B) A flower shop
(C) A jewelry store
(D) A hair salon

번역 화자는 어떤 종류의 사업체에서 일하겠는가?
(A) 주택 개조 용품점
(B) 꽃 가게
(C) 보석 가게
(D) 미용실

해설 전체 내용 관련 - 화자의 근무 업종
화자가 초반부에서 고객들이 자신의 취향에 맞는 목걸이와 반지, 팔찌를 찾을 수 있도록 도와준 여러분의 노고에 감사드린다(I appreciate all of your hard work in helping customers find the right necklaces, rings, and bracelets to suit their style)고 말하는 것으로 보아 화자는 보석 가게에서 근무하고 있음을 알 수 있다. 따라서 정답은 (C)이다.

어휘 improvement 향상 jewelry 보석

> **Paraphrasing**
> 담화의 necklaces, rings, and bracelets
> → 정답의 jewelry

90 What is the speaker concerned about?
(A) Several nearby roads will be closed.
(B) Some merchandise was damaged in transit.
(C) An advertising campaign was expensive.
(D) Competition in the market has increased.

번역 화자는 무엇에 대해 걱정하는가?
(A) 인근 도로 몇 개가 폐쇄될 것이다.
(B) 일부 상품이 운송 중에 파손되었다.
(C) 광고 캠페인 비용이 많이 들었다.
(D) 시장 내 경쟁이 치열해졌다.

해설 세부 사항 관련 - 화자의 우려 사항
화자가 중반부에 우리 사업은 근처에 문을 여는 가게들 때문에 어려움을 겪고 있다(our business is struggling due to several shops opening nearby)면서 그들은 우리와 매우 비슷한 제품을 판매한다(They sell very similar products to ours)고 말하고 있으므로 정답은 (D)이다.

어휘 damage 손상을 주다 in transit 운송 중에 competition 경쟁 increase 증가시키다

91 What does the speaker say he will do?
(A) Purchase more attractive display cases
(B) Hire an experienced marketing consultant
(C) Offer a discount to new customers
(D) Provide free shipping on all orders

번역 화자는 무엇을 하겠다고 말하는가?
(A) 더 눈길을 끄는 진열장 구입하기
(B) 경험이 풍부한 마케팅 컨설턴트 고용하기
(C) 신규 고객에게 할인 제공하기
(D) 모든 주문 건에 대해 무료 배송하기

해설 세부 사항 관련 - 화자가 할 일
화자가 중반부에 최초 구매자들에게 10% 할인을 제공하고 싶다(I'd like to give 10% off to first-time buyers)고 말하고 있으므로 정답은 (C)이다.

어휘 attractive 매력적인 display case 진열장 experienced 경험이 풍부한

> **Paraphrasing**
> 담화의 give 10% off to first-time buyers
> → 정답의 Offer a discount to new customers

92-94 공지

M-Au Attention, please, **92 warehouse employees.** We have several large trucks arriving on Wednesday morning that must be unloaded quickly. Therefore, we need some of you to come in early that day, at 5:30 A.M. **93 After your shift is over today, please stop by my office** to let me know if you're available. You'll be paid the overtime rate for the additional hours. **94 I know that some of you have signed up for the equipment repair workshop on Wednesday,** but this task will be finished before then.

주목해 주십시오, **창고 직원 여러분.** 수요일 아침에 빨리 하역 작업을 해야 하는 큰 트럭들이 몇 대 올 겁니다. 따라서 여러분 중 일부는 그날 일찍 오전 5시 30분에 오셔야 합니다. **오늘 여러분의 근무가 끝난 후에 제 사무실에 들르셔서 가능한지 알려주세요.** 추가 시간에 대해서는 초과 근무 수당을 받으실 겁니다. **여러분 중 일부가 수요일에 열릴 장비 수리 워크숍을 신청하셨다는 사실을 알고 있지만,** 이 작업은 그 전에 끝날 겁니다.

어휘 warehouse 창고 unload 짐을 내리다 shift 교대 근무 stop by 잠깐 들르다 overtime rate 초과 근무 수당 additional 추가적인 sign up for ~을 신청하다 equipment 장비 repair 수리

92 Where is the announcement taking place?
(A) At a repair shop
(B) At a construction site
(C) At an airport
(D) At a warehouse

번역 공지는 어디서 이루어지고 있는가?
(A) 수리점
(B) 건설 현장
(C) 공항
(D) 창고

해설 **전체 내용 관련 - 공지 장소**
화자가 초반부에 창고 직원 여러분(warehouse employees)이라고 말하고 있는 것으로 보아 공지가 나오는 장소는 창고라는 것을 알 수 있다. 따라서 정답은 (D)이다.

어휘 construction 건설

---

93 Where should some listeners go after completing their shifts?
(A) To the security desk
(B) To the loading dock
(C) To the speaker's office
(D) To the conference room

번역 청자들은 근무 시간이 끝난 후에 어디로 가야 하는가?
(A) 경비실
(B) 하역장
(C) **화자의 사무실**
(D) 회의실

해설 **세부 사항 관련 - 청자들이 근무 시간 후에 갈 곳**
화자가 중반부에 오늘 근무가 끝난 후에 사무실에 들를 것(After your shift is over today, please stop by my office ~)을 요청하고 있으므로 정답은 (C)이다.

어휘 complete 완료하다 loading dock 하역장

---

94 What will happen on Wednesday?
(A) A training session will be held.
(B) A new policy will be implemented.
(C) Some electronic equipment will be purchased.
(D) Some promotions will be announced.

번역 수요일에는 무슨 일이 일어나겠는가?
(A) **교육이 진행될 것이다.**
(B) 새로운 정책이 시행될 것이다.
(C) 전자 장비가 구매될 것이다.
(D) 승진이 발표될 것이다.

해설 **세부 사항 관련 - 수요일에 있을 일**
화자가 마지막에 여러분 중 일부가 수요일에 열릴 장비 수리 워크숍을 신청하셨다는 사실을 알고 있다(I know that some of you have signed up for the equipment repair workshop on Wednesday)고 말하고 있으므로 정답은 (A)이다.

어휘 policy 정책 implement 시행하다 purchase 구매하다 promotion 승진

> **Paraphrasing**
> 담화의 the equipment repair workshop
> → 정답의 A training session

95-97 회의 발췌 + 일정표

M-Cn I'd like to start today's meeting of the event planning team with some happy news.

---

[95]Yesterday I got an e-mail from the company president about what a fun time she had at the picnic—so again, well done, everyone! Now, there's been an update to our schedule. [96]Mr. Kim has pushed his retirement back, so his party will now be November third. This is a problem, because Gwangju Grill is already booked for that evening. [97]Damien, can you work with Mr. Kim to find another place we could hold the event?

오늘 행사 기획팀 회의를 좋은 소식으로 시작하고 싶습니다. 어제 회사 회장님으로부터 야유회 때 정말 즐거우셨다는 이메일을 받았습니다. 그래서 다시 한번 말씀드리는데, 수고 많으셨어요, 여러분! 자, 이제 우리 일정에 변경 사항이 있습니다. 김 씨가 은퇴를 미뤘기 때문에 그의 은퇴 기념식은 11월 3일이 될 것입니다. 이것은 문제입니다. 왜냐하면 광주 그릴은 그날 저녁에 이미 예약이 차 있거든요. 데미안, 김 씨와 함께 행사를 열 수 있는 다른 장소를 찾아줄 수 있나요?

어휘 event planning 행사 기획 president 회장 push back ~을 미루다 retirement 은퇴, 퇴직 hold 개최하다

Date	Event
Saturday, September 9	Company picnic
Wednesday, September 27	Board meeting
[96]Friday, October 6	Retirement party
Thursday, October 19	Awards dinner

날짜	행사
9월 9일 토요일	회사 야유회
9월 27일 수요일	이사회 회의
[96]10월 6일 금요일	은퇴 기념식
10월 19일 목요일	시상식 만찬

95 Why does the speaker praise the listeners?
(A) Some invitations are attractive.
(B) Some tasks were done in a short time.
(C) The company saved some money.
(D) An executive enjoyed an event.

번역 화자는 왜 청자들을 칭찬하는가?
(A) 초대장이 멋지게 나왔기 때문에
(B) 업무가 단시간에 완료되었기 때문에
(C) 회사가 비용을 절약했기 때문에
(D) **임원이 행사를 즐겼기 때문에**

해설 **세부 사항 관련 - 청자들을 칭찬하는 이유**
화자가 초반부에 회사 회장님으로부터 야유회 때 정말 즐거웠다는 이메일을 받았다(Yesterday I got an e-mail from the company

TEST 5

president about what a fun time she had at the picnic)면서 수고 많았다(so again, well done, everyone!)고 청자들을 칭찬하고 있으므로 정답은 (D)이다.

어휘 praise 칭찬하다 invitation 초대장 attractive 매력적인 executive 임원, 중역

> **Paraphrasing**
> 담화의 the company president → 정답의 An executive

96 Look at the graphic. Which date is no longer correct?
(A) September 9
(B) September 27
(C) October 6
(D) October 19

번역 시각 정보에 의하면, 어떤 날짜가 더 이상 정확하지 않은가?
(A) 9월 9일
(B) 9월 27일
(C) 10월 6일
(D) 10월 19일

해설 **시각 정보 연계 - 정확하지 않은 날짜**
화자가 중반부에 김 씨가 은퇴를 미뤘기 때문에 그의 은퇴 기념식은 11월 3일이 될 것(Mr. Kim has pushed his retirement back, so his party will now be November third)이라고 말하고 있고, 일정표에 따르면 은퇴 기념식(Retirement party)은 10월 6일이므로 정답은 (C)이다.

---

97 What does the speaker ask Damien to do with a coworker?
(A) Choose a venue
(B) Work on a presentation
(C) Search for some decorations
(D) Draft a guest list

번역 화자는 데미안에게 동료와 함께 무엇을 하라고 요청하는가?
(A) 장소 고르기
(B) 발표 자료 만들기
(C) 장식품 찾아보기
(D) 손님 명단 초안 작성하기

해설 **세부 사항 관련 - 화자가 데미안에게 동료와 함께 하라고 요청하는 일**
화자가 마지막에 데미안에게 김 씨와 함께 행사를 열 수 있는 다른 장소를 찾아줄 것(Damien, can you work with Mr. Kim to find another place we could hold the event?)을 요청하고 있으므로 정답은 (A)이다.

어휘 venue 장소 decoration 장식품 draft 초안을 작성하다

> **Paraphrasing**
> 담화의 find another place → 정답의 Choose a venue

98-100 전화 메시지 + 목록

W-Am Hello, Mr. Abner. This is Sylvia Clement. **98 I wanted to let you know that I've finalized the paperwork for the construction of the extension for your house.** I'll send you a digital as well as a paper copy. **99 Please remember that the thirty-five dollar fee has to be paid directly to the city through their Web site.** We accept payment for the remaining fees by credit card over the phone or by bank transfer. Once the city approves your permit, we can begin the work. And **100 don't forget to try our complimentary consultation service. One of our designers can advise you on paint color options.**

안녕하세요, 애브너 씨. 저는 실비아 클레멘트입니다. **귀하의 주택 확장 공사를 위한 서류 작업을 완료했음을 알려드리려고요.** 실물 사본뿐만 아니라 디지털 사본도 보내드리겠습니다. **35달러 수수료는 웹사이트를 통해 시청으로 직접 납부하셔야 한다는 점을 명심해 주십시오.** 잔금 지불은 전화를 통해 신용카드로 하실 수도 있고 은행 이체로 하실 수도 있습니다. 일단 시청에서 허가를 승인하면 공사를 시작할 수 있습니다. 그리고 저희가 제공하는 무료 상담 서비스도 잊지 마세요. 저희 디자이너 중 한 명이 페인트 색상 옵션에 대해 조언을 해드릴 수 있습니다.

어휘 finalize 완성하다 construction 공사 extension 확장 copy 사본 fee 수수료 accept 받아들이다 payment 지불 remaining 남아 있는 transfer 이체 approve 승인하다 permit 허가 complimentary 무료의 consultation 상담 advise 조언하다

Summary of Fees		Due
Deposit:	$350	June 8
Site assessment:	$90	June 15
99Filing:	$35	June 15
Phase 1:	$1,200	June 21

요금 요약서		납기일
계약금	350달러	6월 8일
현장 평가	90달러	6월 15일
99서류 작업	35달러	6월 15일
1차 공사	1,200달러	6월 21일

어휘 summary 요약 deposit 계약금 assessment 평가 filing 서류 정리 phase 단계

98 Who most likely is the speaker?
(A) A real estate agent
(B) A building contractor
(C) A vehicle repair person
(D) A corporate attorney

번역 화자는 누구이겠는가?
(A) 부동산 중개인
(B) 건축 도급업자
(C) 차량 정비사
(D) 기업 변호사

해설 **전체 내용 관련 - 화자의 직업**
화자가 초반부에 귀하의 주택 확장 공사를 위한 서류 작업을 완료했다(I wanted to let you know that I've finalized the paperwork for the construction of the extension for your house)고 말하고 있으므로 화자는 건축 도급업자임을 알 수 있다. 따라서 정답은 (B)이다.

어휘 contractor 도급업자 vehicle 차량 repair 수리

99 Look at the graphic. Which fee must be paid online?
(A) Deposit
(B) Site assessment
(C) Filing
(D) Phase 1

번역 시각 정보에 의하면, 어떤 요금이 온라인으로 지불되어야 하는가?
(A) 계약금
(B) 현장 평가
(C) 서류 작업
(D) 1차 공사

해설 **시각 정보 연계 - 온라인으로 지불되어야 하는 요금**
화자가 중반부에서 35달러 수수료는 웹사이트를 통해 납부해야 한다는 점(Please remember that the thirty-five dollar fee has to be paid ~ through their Web site)을 상기시키고 있고, 목록에 따르면 서류 작업(Filing)이 35달러이므로 정답은 (C)이다.

100 What service does the speaker tell the listener about?
(A) A free color consultation
(B) An extended warranty
(C) An annual membership
(D) An overnight delivery

번역 화자는 청자에게 어떤 서비스에 대해 말하는가?
(A) 무료 색상 상담
(B) 보증 기간 연장
(C) 연간 회원권
(D) 익일 배송

해설 **세부 사항 관련 - 화자가 언급하는 서비스**
화자가 마지막 부분에서 우리가 제공하는 무료 상담 서비스도 잊지 말라(don't forget to try our complimentary consultation service)면서 디자이너 중 한 명이 페인트 색상 옵션에 대해 조언을 해줄 수 있다(One of our designers can advise you on paint color options)고 말하고 있으므로 정답은 (A)이다.

어휘 extended 연장된 warranty 보증 기간 annual membership 연간 회원권 overnight delivery 익일 배송

> Paraphrasing
> 담화의 our complimentary consultation service
> → A free ~ consultation

TEST 6

1 (B)	2 (D)	3 (B)	4 (A)	5 (C)
6 (C)	7 (C)	8 (B)	9 (C)	10 (C)
11 (A)	12 (A)	13 (A)	14 (A)	15 (B)
16 (C)	17 (C)	18 (A)	19 (C)	20 (A)
21 (A)	22 (A)	23 (C)	24 (B)	25 (B)
26 (B)	27 (C)	28 (B)	29 (C)	30 (B)
31 (B)	32 (A)	33 (D)	34 (C)	35 (B)
36 (D)	37 (A)	38 (D)	39 (C)	40 (B)
41 (C)	42 (D)	43 (B)	44 (A)	45 (B)
46 (D)	47 (C)	48 (A)	49 (B)	50 (D)
51 (C)	52 (D)	53 (A)	54 (B)	55 (C)
56 (A)	57 (C)	58 (D)	59 (A)	60 (B)
61 (B)	62 (D)	63 (C)	64 (B)	65 (A)
66 (C)	67 (D)	68 (B)	69 (C)	70 (D)
71 (D)	72 (C)	73 (A)	74 (C)	75 (D)
76 (B)	77 (B)	78 (D)	79 (A)	80 (C)
81 (A)	82 (B)	83 (B)	84 (D)	85 (D)
86 (D)	87 (A)	88 (C)	89 (B)	90 (A)
91 (C)	92 (A)	93 (B)	94 (A)	95 (C)
96 (D)	97 (B)	98 (A)	99 (B)	100 (D)

PART 1

1

W-Am

(A) The woman is rinsing a paintbrush in a sink.
(B) The woman is painting a picture on an easel.
(C) The woman is visiting an art gallery.
(D) The woman is holding a tube of paint.

번역 (A) 여자가 싱크대에서 붓을 헹구고 있다.
(B) **여자가 이젤에 대고 그림을 그리고 있다.**
(C) 여자가 미술관을 방문하고 있다.
(D) 여자가 물감 한 개를 들고 있다.

해설 1인 등장 사진
(A) 사진에 없는 명사. 사진에 싱크대가 보이지 않는다.
(B) 정답. 여자가 이젤에 대고 그림을 그리고 있으므로 정답이다.
(C) 동사 오답. 여자가 미술관을 방문하고 있는 모습이 아니다.
(D) 동사 오답. 여자가 물감 한 개를 들고 있는 모습이 아니다.

어휘 rinse 헹구다   paintbrush 붓   sink 싱크대   paint 그리다.
페인트를 칠하다   easel 이젤   art gallery 미술관, 화랑   tube
(치약 등을 넣는) 통, 튜브

2

M-Cn

(A) He's tying a cloth apron.
(B) He's pouring beans into a coffee machine.
(C) He's handing a beverage to a customer.
(D) He's picking up an empty cup.

번역 (A) 남자가 천 앞치마를 묶고 있다.
(B) 남자가 커피 제조기에 원두를 붓고 있다.
(C) 남자가 손님에게 음료를 건네고 있다.
(D) **남자가 빈 컵을 집어 들고 있다.**

해설 1인 등장 사진
(A) 동사 오답. 남자가 천 앞치마를 묶는 동작을 하고 있는 모습이 아니다.
(B) 동사 오답. 남자가 커피 제조기에 원두를 붓고 있는 모습이 아니다.
(C) 사진에 없는 명사. 사진에 손님이 보이지 않는다.
(D) 정답. 남자가 빈 컵을 집어 들고 있으므로 정답이다.

어휘 tie 매다. 묶다   cloth 천   apron 앞치마   pour 붓다   hand
건네주다   beverage 음료   pick up 집어 들다

3

W-Br

(A) A food truck has been parked in a field.
(B) A seating area has been set up outside.
(C) Some people are waiting in line to place
    orders.
(D) There is a row of lampposts behind a building.

번역 (A) 푸드 트럭 한 대가 들판에 주차되어 있다.
(B) **야외에 앉을 수 있는 공간이 설치되어 있다.**
(C) 사람들이 주문을 하기 위해 줄을 서 있다.
(D) 건물 뒤에 가로등이 일렬로 서 있다.

해설 사람/사물·풍경 혼합 사진
(A) 위치 오답. 푸드 트럭 한 대가 들판에 주차되어 있는 모습이 아니다.
(B) 정답. 야외에 앉을 수 있는 공간이 설치되어 있으므로 정답이다.
(C) 동사 오답. 사람들이 주문하기 위해 줄을 서 있는 모습이 아니다.
(D) 사진에 없는 명사. 사진에 건물이 보이지 않는다.

어휘 field 들판   set up 설치하다   wait in line 줄을 서서 기다리다
place an order 주문하다   lamppost 가로등

4

M-Au

(A) Some of the shoes are lined up on the floor.
(B) Clothing has been folded and stacked.
(C) A handbag has been left on top of a basket.
(D) Hats are being stored on some shelves.

번역 **(A) 신발들 중 일부가 바닥에 나란히 놓여 있다.**
(B) 옷이 개어진 상태로 쌓여 있다.
(C) 핸드백 한 개가 바구니 위에 놓여 있다.
(D) 모자들이 선반에 보관되어 있다.

해설 사물·풍경 사진
(A) 정답. 신발들 중 일부가 바닥에 나란히 놓여 있으므로 정답이다.
(B) 동사 오답. 옷이 개어진 상태로 쌓여 있는 모습이 아니다.
(C) 동사 오답. 핸드백 한 개가 바구니 위에 놓여 있는 모습이 아니다.
(D) 동사 오답. 모자들이 선반에 보관되어 있는 모습이 아니다.

어휘 line up 한 줄로 세우다 fold 접다 stack 쌓다, 포개다
on top of ~의 위에 hat 모자

5

W-Br

(A) A moving van has been driven into a garage.
(B) Boxes have been piled on a cart.
(C) A sofa is being carried across a driveway.
(D) Workers are unloading some packing materials.

번역 (A) 이삿짐 트럭 한 대가 차고 안으로 들어왔다.
(B) 상자들이 카트 위에 쌓여 있다.
(C) 진입로를 가로질러 소파 한 개가 운반되고 있다.
(D) 인부들이 포장재를 내리고 있다.

해설 사람/사물·풍경 혼합 사진
(A) 위치 오답. 이삿짐 트럭 한 대가 차고 안으로 들어온 모습이 아니다.
(B) 사진에 없는 명사. 사진에 카트가 보이지 않는다.
(C) 정답. 진입로를 가로질러 소파 한 개가 운반되고 있으므로 정답이다.
(D) 동사 오답. 인부들이 포장재를 내리고 있는 모습이 아니다.

어휘 moving van 이삿짐 트럭 garage 차고 pile 쌓다, 포개다
carry 나르다 driveway 진입로 unload 짐을 내리다 packing
material 포장재

6

M-Cn

(A) The woman is climbing a staircase in a bookstore.
(B) The woman is adjusting the height of a stepladder.
(C) Some display furniture has been placed by a window.
(D) Some books are being removed from a backpack.

번역 (A) 여자가 서점에 있는 계단을 오르고 있다.
(B) 여자가 발판 사다리의 높이를 조절하고 있다.
(C) 진열장들이 창가에 놓여 있다.
(D) 책들이 배낭에서 꺼내어지고 있다.

해설 사람/사물·풍경 혼합 사진
(A) 사진에 없는 명사. 사진에 계단이 보이지 않는다.
(B) 동사 오답. 여자가 발판 사다리의 높이를 조절하고 있는 모습이 아니다.
(C) 정답. 진열장들이 창가에 놓여 있으므로 정답이다.
(D) 동사 오답. 책들이 배낭에서 꺼내어지고 있는 모습이 아니다.

어휘 climb 오르다 staircase 계단 adjust 조정하다 stepladder
발판 사다리 display furniture 진열장 remove 제거하다,
옮기다 backpack 배낭

PART 2

7

M-Cn How did you like the book?
M-Au (A) Around three hundred pages.
(B) A friend recommended it.
(C) The ending was surprising!

번역 그 책은 어땠나요?
(A) 약 300쪽이요.
(B) 한 친구가 그것을 추천했어요.
(C) 결말이 놀라웠어요!

해설 How 의문문
(A) 연상 오답. 질문의 book에서 연상 가능한 pages를 이용한 오답이다.
(B) 질문과 상관없는 오답.
(C) 정답. 책에 대한 의견을 묻는 질문에 결말이 놀라웠다고 구체적으로 응답하고 있으므로 정답이다.

어휘 recommend 추천하다 ending 결말 surprising 놀라운

어휘 demonstration 시연 exposition 전시회, 박람회 accept 받아들이다 donation 기부 public speaking 공개 연설

8

W-Br Where is the security office?
M-Au (A) For a visitor's badge.
　　　(B) At the back of the lobby.
　　　(C) The security report is done.

번역 경비실은 어디에 있나요?
　　　(A) 방문자 배지 때문에요.
　　　(B) 로비 뒤편에요.
　　　(C) 보안 보고서가 완성되었어요.

해설 Where 의문문
　　　(A) 연상 오답. 질문의 security office에서 연상 가능한 badge를 이용한 오답이다.
　　　(B) 정답. 경비실의 위치를 묻는 질문에 로비 뒤편이라고 구체적으로 응답하고 있으므로 정답이다.
　　　(C) 단어 반복 오답. 질문의 security를 반복 이용한 오답이다.

어휘 security office 경비실 report 보고서

9

W-Am What did you think of the orientation video?
W-Br (A) On my first day at the company.
　　　(B) You can start recording at any time.
　　　(C) It had a lot of helpful information.

번역 오리엔테이션 영상에 대해 어떻게 생각했어요?
　　　(A) 회사 첫 근무일에요.
　　　(B) 언제든지 녹화를 시작하실 수 있습니다.
　　　(C) 유용한 정보가 많았습니다.

해설 What 의문문
　　　(A) 질문과 상관없는 오답. When 의문문에 대한 응답이므로 오답이다.
　　　(B) 연상 오답. 질문의 video에서 연상 가능한 recording을 이용한 오답이다.
　　　(C) 정답. 오리엔테이션 영상에 대한 의견을 묻는 질문에 유용한 정보가 많았다고 의견을 제시하고 있으므로 정답이다.

어휘 recording 녹화, 녹음 helpful 유용한

10

W-Am Should we ask Donna to give the product demonstration?
M-Cn (A) At the exposition in Seoul.
　　　(B) They only accept cash donations.
　　　(C) Yes, she's great at public speaking.

번역 도나에게 제품 시연을 해달라고 부탁해야 할까요?
　　　(A) 서울에서 열리는 전시회에서요.
　　　(B) 그들은 현금 기부만 받아요.
　　　(C) 네, 그녀는 공개 연설을 아주 잘해요.

해설 조동사(Should) 의문문
　　　(A) 질문과 상관없는 오답. Where 의문문에 대한 응답이므로 오답이다.
　　　(B) 질문과 상관없는 오답.
　　　(C) 정답. 도나에게 제품 시연을 해달라고 부탁해야 할지 묻는 질문에 네(Yes)라고 대답한 뒤, 긍정 답변과 일관된 내용을 덧붙이고 있으므로 정답이다.

11

M-Au What is that interesting building across the river?
W-Am (A) A concert hall.
　　　(B) Take Calhoun Bridge, please.
　　　(C) From the top floor.

번역 강 건너에 있는 저 흥미로운 건물은 무엇인가요?
　　　(A) 콘서트홀이요.
　　　(B) 캘훈 다리로 가주세요.
　　　(C) 꼭대기 층에서요.

해설 What 의문문
　　　(A) 정답. 강 건너에 있는 건물이 무엇인지 묻는 질문에 콘서트홀이라고 구체적으로 알려 주고 있으므로 정답이다.
　　　(B) 연상 오답. 질문의 across the river에서 연상 가능한 Bridge를 이용한 오답이다.
　　　(C) 연상 오답. 질문의 building에서 연상 가능한 top floor를 이용한 오답이다.

어휘 interesting 흥미로운 top floor 꼭대기 층

12

M-Au Will the clinic stay open while the road is being repaired?
W-Br (A) Yes, we'll be seeing patients.
　　　(B) It's a load of disposable gloves.
　　　(C) Because of damage from heavy trucks.

번역 도로가 보수되는 동안 이 병원은 계속 문을 열 건가요?
　　　(A) 네, 저희는 계속 환자를 볼 겁니다.
　　　(B) 일회용 장갑이 한가득입니다.
　　　(C) 대형 트럭으로 인한 피해 때문에요.

해설 조동사(Will) 의문문
　　　(A) 정답. 도로가 보수되는 동안 병원이 문을 열 것인지 묻는 질문에 네(Yes)라고 대답한 뒤, 계속 환자를 볼 거라며 긍정 답변과 일관된 내용을 덧붙이고 있으므로 정답이다.
　　　(B) 유사 발음 오답. 질문의 road와 부분적으로 발음이 유사한 load를 이용한 오답이다.
　　　(C) 질문과 상관없는 오답. Why 의문문에 대한 응답이므로 오답이다.

어휘 repair 수리하다 patient 환자 a load of 한 짐의, 많은 disposable 일회용의 damage 피해, 손상

13

M-Cn When will the inspection take place?
W-Br (A) Sometime this week.
　　　(B) The corner by the dishwashers.
　　　(C) No, I brought my own.

번역 그 점검은 언제 진행되나요?
　　　(A) 이번 주 중에요.
　　　(B) 식기세척기들 옆 구석이요.
　　　(C) 아니요, 저는 제 것을 가져왔어요.

해설 When 의문문
(A) 정답. 점검 진행 시기를 묻는 질문에 이번 주 중이라고 구체적으로 알려 주고 있으므로 정답이다.
(B) 연상 오답. 질문의 place에서 연상 가능한 The corner를 이용한 오답이다.
(C) Yes/No 불가 오답. When 의문문에는 Yes/No 응답이 불가능하므로 오답이다.

어휘 inspection 점검 take place 일어나다, 발생하다 dishwasher 식기세척기

14

M-Au It's going to start raining soon.
W-Am (A) I'll bring the sidewalk display inside.
(B) Yes, that was a good start.
(C) With a professional trainer.

번역 곧 비가 올 거예요.
(A) 입간판을 안으로 들여야겠어요.
(B) 네, 좋은 출발이었어요.
(C) 전문 트레이너와 함께요.

해설 사실·정보 전달의 평서문
(A) 정답. 곧 비가 올 거라는 평서문에 입간판을 안으로 들여야겠다며 관련된 응답을 하고 있으므로 정답이다.
(B) 단어 반복 오답. 평서문의 start를 반복 이용한 오답이다.
(C) 유사 발음 및 파생어 오답. 평서문의 start raining과 부분적으로 발음이 비슷한 training의 파생어인 trainer를 이용한 오답이다.

어휘 sidewalk display 입간판 professional 전문적인

15

W-Br Why did the candidate turn down our offer?
M-Cn (A) Yes, unfortunately.
(B) He had already taken another job.
(C) Do you want me to turn it up again?

번역 그 지원자는 왜 우리 제안을 거절했나요?
(A) 네, 안타깝게도요.
(B) 그는 이미 다른 일자리를 구했대요.
(C) 제가 그것을 다시 올리기를 원하시나요?

해설 Why 의문문
(A) Yes/No 불가 오답. Why 의문문에는 Yes/No 응답이 불가능하므로 오답이다.
(B) 정답. 지원자가 제안을 거절한 이유를 묻는 질문에 그는 이미 다른 일자리를 구했다며 이유를 제시하고 있으므로 정답이다.
(C) 연상 오답. 질문의 turn down에서 연상 가능한 turn ~ up을 이용한 오답이다.

어휘 candidate 지원자 turn down 거절하다 turn up (소리 등을) 높이다, 올리다

16

M-Au Which project is our crew working on next?
W-Br (A) The concrete was already safe to walk on.
(B) That's not what I've heard.
(C) The Miller family's kitchen renovation.

번역 우리 팀은 다음으로 어떤 프로젝트를 수행할까요?
(A) 콘크리트 바닥은 이미 걸어다니기 안전했어요.
(B) 제가 들은 것과는 다르네요.
(C) 밀러 가족의 주방 보수 공사요.

해설 Which+명사 의문문
(A) 유사 발음 오답. 질문의 working과 부분적으로 발음이 유사한 walk를 이용한 오답이다.
(B) 질문과 상관없는 오답.
(C) 정답. 팀이 다음으로 수행할 프로젝트에 대해 묻는 질문에 밀러 가족의 주방 보수 공사라고 구체적으로 알려 주고 있으므로 정답이다.

어휘 renovation 보수 공사

17

M-Cn Aren't you supposed to be leaving for your business trip?
W-Am (A) I already left it with the front desk.
(B) Actually, it's a very successful business.
(C) My flight isn't until seven P.M.

번역 당신은 출장을 떠나야 하지 않나요?
(A) 이미 프론트 데스크에 맡겼어요.
(B) 실은 매우 성공적인 사업이에요.
(C) 제 비행기는 오후 7시예요.

해설 부정 의문문
(A) 파생어 오답. 질문의 leaving의 과거형인 left를 이용한 오답이다. leave는 다의어로, 질문에서는 '떠나다'라는 의미이지만 답변에서는 '맡기다'라는 의미로 쓰였다.
(B) 단어 반복 오답. 질문의 business를 반복 이용한 오답이다.
(C) 정답. 출장을 떠나야 하지 않냐는 질문에 비행기는 오후 7시라며 아직 시간적 여유가 있음을 우회적으로 표현한 정답이다.

어휘 leave for ~로 떠나다

18

W-Am Why don't we redesign our sandals this year?
M-Au (A) This style is still selling pretty well.
(B) She goes to the beach every summer.
(C) A famous shoe designer.

번역 올해에는 우리 샌들을 새로 디자인하면 어떨까요?
(A) 이 스타일은 여전히 꽤 잘 팔려요.
(B) 그녀는 매년 여름 해변에 가요.
(C) 유명한 신발 디자이너요.

해설 요청·제안문
(A) 정답. 올해에 샌들을 새로 디자인하자는 제안에 이 스타일은 여전히 꽤 잘 팔린다며 거절하는 의사를 우회적으로 표현하고 있으므로 정답이다.
(B) 질문과 상관없는 오답. 질문에 3인칭 대명사 She로 지칭할 인물이 언급된 적이 없으므로 오답이다.
(C) 연상 오답. 질문의 redesign our sandals에서 연상 가능한 shoe designer를 이용한 오답이다.

어휘 redesign 디자인을 새로 하다 sandal 샌들

TEST 6

TEST 6 **149**

19

W-Br How many buses will we need to take everyone to the retreat site?

M-Au (A) No, you can't park here on weekdays.
(B) Over thirty miles away.
(C) We have a hundred and twenty people on staff.

번역 야유회 장소까지 모두 데려가려면 몇 대의 버스가 필요할까요?
(A) 아니요, 평일에는 여기에 주차하실 수 없습니다.
(B) 30마일 이상 떨어져 있어요.
(C) 직원이 총 120명이에요.

해설 How+형용사/부사 의문문
(A) Yes/No 불가 오답. How 의문문에는 Yes/No 응답이 불가능하므로 오답이다.
(B) 질문과 상관없는 오답. 거리를 묻는 How far 의문문에 대한 응답이므로 오답이다.
(C) 정답. 야유회 장소까지 모두 데려가기 위해 필요한 버스의 대수를 묻는 질문에 직원이 총 120명이라며 필요한 버스 대수와 관련된 정보를 제공하고 있으므로 정답이다.

어휘 retreat 야유회

20

W-Br Are we giving our clients wall calendars or desk calendars this year?

M-Cn (A) I thought you ordered the gifts.
(B) To show our appreciation for them.
(C) No, not according to my calendar.

번역 올해는 우리 고객들에게 벽걸이 달력을 증정하나요? 아니면 탁상 달력을 증정하나요?
(A) 당신이 선물을 주문한 줄 알았어요.
(B) 그들에게 감사를 표현하려고요.
(C) 아니요, 제 일정표에 따르면 아니에요.

해설 선택 의문문
(A) 정답. 올해 고객에게 증정할 달력을 묻는 선택 의문문에 당신이 선물을 주문한 줄 알았다며 알지 못함을 우회적으로 알려 주고 있으므로 정답이다.
(B) 질문과 상관없는 오답. Why 의문문에 대한 응답이므로 오답이다.
(C) Yes/No 불가 오답. 문장과 문장을 연결하는 경우를 제외하고는 선택 의문문에는 Yes/No 응답이 불가능하므로 오답이다.

어휘 calendar 달력, 일정표   appreciation 감사

21

W-Am Wasn't that food festival postponed again?

M-Au (A) It's been pushed back to June.
(B) Some of it was quite spicy.
(C) I put one on the bulletin board.

번역 그 음식 축제는 또 연기되지 않았나요?
(A) 6월로 미뤄졌어요.
(B) 그것 중 일부는 아주 매웠어요.
(C) 게시판에 하나 붙여두었어요.

해설 부정 의문문
(A) 정답. 음식 축제가 또 연기되었는지 여부를 확인하는 질문에 6월로 미뤄졌다고 네(Yes)를 생략한 긍정 답변을 하고 있으므로 정답이다.
(B) 연상 오답. 질문의 food에서 연상 가능한 spicy를 이용한 오답이다.
(C) 질문과 상관없는 오답.

어휘 postpone 미루다   push back 미루다   spicy 매운   bulletin board 게시판

22

W-Am The office relocation is taking longer than we hoped.

M-Cn (A) We do have a lot of electronics to set up.
(B) Our official logo.
(C) I could cut a few words here.

번역 사무실 이전이 예상했던 것보다 오래 걸리네요.
(A) 설치해야 할 전자 제품이 아주 많아요.
(B) 우리 공식 로고요.
(C) 여기서 몇 단어 지울게요.

해설 사실·정보 전달의 평서문
(A) 정답. 사무실 이전이 예상했던 것보다 오래 걸린다는 평서문에 설치해야 할 전자 제품이 아주 많다며 오래 걸리는 이유를 제시하고 있으므로 정답이다.
(B) 파생어 오답. 평서문의 office와 파생어 관계인 official을 이용한 오답이다.
(C) 연상 오답. 평서문의 longer에서 연상 가능한 cut을 이용한 오답이다.

어휘 relocation 이전   electronics 전자 제품   set up 설치하다   official 공식적인

23

W-Br Why did Mayor Shin call a press conference?

M-Cn (A) Just a few hours ago.
(B) It's been called that for years.
(C) She's announcing a new policy.

번역 신 시장은 왜 기자 회견을 소집했나요?
(A) 바로 몇 시간 전에요.
(B) 오랫동안 그렇게 불렸어요.
(C) 그녀는 새 정책을 발표할 예정이에요.

해설 Why 의문문
(A) 질문과 상관없는 오답. When 의문문에 대한 응답이므로 오답이다.
(B) 단어 반복 오답. 질문의 call을 반복 이용한 오답이다.
(C) 정답. 신 시장이 기자 회견을 소집한 이유를 묻는 질문에 그녀는 새 정책을 발표할 예정이라며 구체적인 이유를 제시하고 있으므로 정답이다.

어휘 press conference 기자 회견   announce 발표하다   policy 정책

24

W-Am The projector in that conference room is still out of order, isn't it?

M-Au (A) They should be in alphabetical order.
(B) Just print out your presentation slides.
(C) On a rolling cart outside the door.

번역 회의실 프로젝터는 여전히 고장이 나 있죠, 그렇지 않나요?
(A) 알파벳 순으로 나열해야 합니다.
(B) 그냥 발표 슬라이드를 출력하세요.
(C) 문밖에 있는 바퀴 달린 카트 위에요.

해설 부가 의문문
(A) 단어 반복 오답. 질문의 order를 반복 이용한 오답이다.
(B) 정답. 회의실 프로젝터가 여전히 고장 나 있는지 여부를 확인하는 질문에 발표 슬라이드를 출력하라며 여전히 고장 나 있음을 우회적으로 표현하고 있으므로 정답이다.
(C) 질문과 상관없는 오답. Where 의문문에 대한 응답이므로 오답이다.

어휘 out of order 고장이 난   in alphabetical order 알파벳순으로
presentation 발표   rolling cart 바퀴 달린 카트

25

M-Cn Who knows how to report a maintenance issue?

W-Am (A) Some routine elevator maintenance.
(B) Sheldon has done it before.
(C) Yes, we have copies of every issue.

번역 유지보수 문제를 보고하는 방법을 누가 알고 있나요?
(A) 승강기 정기 유지보수요.
(B) 셸던이 전에 해본 적이 있어요.
(C) 네, 모든 호의 사본을 모아두고 있어요.

해설 Who 의문문
(A) 단어 반복 오답. 질문의 maintenance를 반복 이용한 오답이다.
(B) 정답. 유지보수 문제를 보고하는 방법을 알고 있는 사람을 묻는 질문에 셸던이 전에 해본 적이 있다고 알 수 있는 사람을 언급하고 있으므로 정답이다.
(C) Yes/No 불가 오답. Who 의문문에는 Yes/No 응답이 불가능하므로 오답이다.

어휘 maintenance 유지보수   issue 문제, (잡지·신문 등의) 호
routine 정기적인

26

W-Br Why is the exhibit on European painting closed?

M-Cn (A) There's an art supply store on Martin Street.
(B) Didn't you read the notice at the museum entrance?
(C) Yes, the very next room.

번역 유럽 회화 전시회는 왜 닫혀 있나요?
(A) 마틴 가에 미술용품점이 있어요.
(B) 박물관 입구에 있는 공지 못 보셨어요?
(C) 네, 바로 옆방이요.

해설 Why 의문문
(A) 연상 오답. 질문의 painting에서 연상 가능한 art를 이용한 오답이다.
(B) 정답. 유럽 회화 전시회가 닫혀 있는 이유를 묻는 질문에 박물관 입구에 있는 공지를 언급하며 닫힌 이유를 알 수 있는 방법을 제시하고 있으므로 정답이다.
(C) Yes/No 불가 오답. Why 의문문에는 Yes/No 응답이 불가능하므로 오답이다.

어휘 exhibit 전시회   art supply store 미술용품점   entrance 출입구

27

M-Au When do you want to meet to sign the contract?

W-Am (A) Yes, she sent out the agenda.
(B) I believe that's correct.
(C) I'd like to see more apartments first.

번역 계약서에 서명하기 위해 언제 만나기를 원하시나요?
(A) 네, 그녀가 안건을 보냈어요.
(B) 맞는 것 같은데요.
(C) 먼저 더 많은 아파트를 보고 싶어요.

해설 When 의문문
(A) Yes/No 불가 오답. When 의문문에는 Yes/No 응답이 불가능하므로 오답이다.
(B) 질문과 상관없는 오답.
(C) 정답. 계약서에 서명하기 위해 언제 만날지 묻는 질문에 먼저 더 많은 아파트를 보고 싶다며 아직 계약할 때가 아님을 우회적으로 알려 주고 있으므로 정답이다.

어휘 contract 계약서   agenda 안건   correct 정확한

28

W-Br What should I do with these old bank statements?

M-Cn (A) No, they really shouldn't.
(B) Put them through the shredder.
(C) Once a year, in January.

번역 이 오래된 입출금 내역서들을 어떻게 하면 좋을까요?
(A) 아니요, 그들은 정말 그러지 말아야 해요.
(B) 문서 파쇄기에 넣으세요.
(C) 일 년에 한 번, 1월에요.

해설 What 의문문
(A) Yes/No 불가 오답. What 의문문에는 Yes/No 응답이 불가능하므로 오답이다.
(B) 정답. 오래된 입출금 내역서들의 처리 방법을 묻는 질문에 문서 파쇄기에 넣으라고 구체적으로 알려 주고 있으므로 정답이다.
(C) 질문과 상관없는 오답. How often 의문문에 대한 응답이므로 오답이다.

어휘 bank statement 입출금 내역서   shredder 문서 파쇄기

29

M-Au I'd be happy to pick up the executives at the airport.

W-Br (A) We hired a car service.
(B) Yes, a round-trip ticket.
(C) Some shipments from overseas.

번역　제가 기꺼이 공항에서 임원들을 모시고 올게요.
　　　(A) 차량 서비스를 예약했어요.
　　　(B) 네, 왕복으로요.
　　　(C) 해외에서 온 배송품이요.

해설　의견·희망 사항의 평서문
　　　(A) 정답. 기꺼이 공항에서 임원들을 모시고 오겠다는 평서문에 차량 서비스를 예약했다며 공항에 갈 필요가 없음을 우회적으로 알려주고 있으므로 정답이다.
　　　(B) 연상 오답. 평서문의 airport에서 연상 가능한 a round-trip ticket을 이용한 오답이다.
　　　(C) 연상 오답. 평서문의 airport에서 연상 가능한 overseas를 이용한 오답이다.

어휘　executive 임원, 중역　hire 빌리다, 고용하다　shipment 배송품　overseas 해외: 해외의

30
M-Cn This credit card's annual fee is quite high.
W-Am (A) A monthly list of charges.
　　　(B) It offers great user rewards.
　　　(C) Let me get you a stepladder.

번역　이 신용카드의 연회비는 꽤 비싸네요.
　　　(A) 월별 요금 청구서요.
　　　(B) 사용자 혜택이 좋아요.
　　　(C) 발판 사다리를 갖다드릴게요.

해설　사실·정보 전달의 평서문
　　　(A) 연상 오답. 평서문의 credit card에서 연상 가능한 charges를 이용한 오답이다.
　　　(B) 정답. 신용카드의 연회비는 꽤 비싸다는 평서문에 사용자 혜택이 좋다며 비싼 이유를 제시하고 있으므로 정답이다.
　　　(C) 연상 오답. 평서문의 high에서 연상 가능한 stepladder를 이용한 오답이다.

어휘　annual fee 연회비　charge 청구　reward 보상　stepladder 발판 사다리

31
M-Cn Selma, could you order more file folders?
W-Br (A) Yes, he filed the permit yesterday.
　　　(B) Tatsu found some extras in the cabinet.
　　　(C) One of our major shareholders.

번역　셀마, 서류철을 좀 더 주문해 주실 수 있나요?
　　　(A) 네, 그는 어제 허가증을 제출했어요.
　　　(B) 타츠가 수납장에서 여분을 몇 개 찾았어요.
　　　(C) 우리 대주주 중 한 명이요.

해설　요청·제안문
　　　(A) 유사 발음 오답. 질문의 file과 부분적으로 발음이 유사한 filed를 이용한 오답이다.
　　　(B) 정답. 서류철 추가 주문을 요청하는 질문에 타츠가 수납장에서 여분을 몇 개 찾았다며 추가 주문할 필요가 없음을 간접적으로 알려주고 있으므로 정답이다.
　　　(C) 유사 발음 오답. 질문의 folders와 부분적으로 발음이 유사한 shareholders를 이용한 오답이다.

어휘　file folder 서류철　file 제출하다　permit 허가증　cabinet 수납장　major shareholder 대주주

PART 3

32-34

M-Au Hi, Kira, it's Nate in Sales. **32 I'm calling because I'm having a problem with the Conversa software program.** I can get instant messages from other people, but my replies aren't going through.

W-Br Oh, I see. Have you tried updating the program? **33 The latest version was released just this week.**

M-Au Yes, I just did that, but it didn't help. I also tried restarting my computer.

W-Br OK, then **34 I'll need to come over and take a look at your computer myself.** Is now a good time?

M-Au Now would be great. Thank you.

남:　안녕하세요, 키라. 영업팀의 네이트입니다. **컨버사 소프트웨어에 문제가 있어서 전화드렸어요.** 다른 사람들에게서 인스턴트 메시지를 받을 수는 있는데, 제 응답은 전송이 되지 않고 있어요.

여:　아, 그렇군요. 업데이트를 해보셨나요? **최신 버전이 바로 이번 주에 배포되었거든요.**

남:　네, 방금 해봤는데, 소용이 없었어요. 컴퓨터를 껐다 켜보기도 했어요.

여:　알겠습니다. 그럼 **제가 직접 가서 컴퓨터를 살펴봐야겠네요.** 지금 가도 괜찮을까요?

남:　지금 좋습니다. 감사합니다.

어휘　instant message 인스턴트 메시지　reply 응답, 답장　go through 통과하다　release 공개하다, 출시하다　restart 다시 시작하다

---

32 Why is the man calling the woman?
　　　(A) To receive help with a technical issue
　　　(B) To ask her to make an announcement
　　　(C) To explain why he missed a meeting
　　　(D) To confirm that he read a message

번역　남자는 왜 여자에게 전화를 걸고 있는가?
　　　(A) 기술적인 문제에 도움을 받으려고
　　　(B) 여자에게 안내 방송을 부탁하려고
　　　(C) 자신이 왜 회의에 빠졌는지 설명하려고
　　　(D) 메시지를 읽었다고 확인해 주려고

해설 전체 내용 관련 - 남자가 여자에게 전화를 건 이유

남자가 첫 대사에서 컨버사 소프트웨어에 문제가 있어서 전화했다(I'm calling because I'm having a problem with the Conversa software program)고 말하고 있으므로 정답은 (A)이다.

어휘 receive 받다   technical 기술적인   make an announcement 발표하다   miss 놓치다

> **Paraphrasing**
> 대화의 a problem with ~ software program
> → 정답의 a technical issue

33 What does the woman inform the man about?
(A) A sales catalog has not been updated.
(B) A computer system is currently down.
(C) A request must be approved by a supervisor.
(D) A new version of some software is available.

번역 여자는 남자에게 무엇에 대해 알려주는가?
(A) 판매 카탈로그가 업데이트되지 않았다.
(B) 컴퓨터 시스템이 현재 먹통이다.
(C) 요청 사항은 관리자의 승인을 받아야 한다.
(D) 소프트웨어의 새 버전이 이용 가능하다.

해설 세부 사항 관련 - 여자가 남자에게 알려주는 것

여자가 첫 대사에서 최신 버전이 바로 이번 주에 배포되었다(The latest version was released just this week)고 말하고 있으므로 정답은 (D)이다.

어휘 currently 현재   down 작동이 안 되는   approve 승인하다
supervisor 관리자   available 이용 가능한

> **Paraphrasing**
> 대화의 The latest version → 정답의 A new version

34 What does the woman say she will have to do?
(A) Wait until tomorrow to start a task
(B) Look through a product manual
(C) Visit the man's workstation
(D) Dispose of some equipment

번역 여자는 자신이 무엇을 해야 한다고 말하는가?
(A) 업무를 시작하기 위해 내일까지 기다리기
(B) 제품 사용 설명서 훑어보기
(C) 남자의 사무 공간 방문하기
(D) 장비 처분하기

해설 세부 사항 관련 - 여자가 할 일

여자가 마지막 대사에서 직접 가서 컴퓨터를 살펴봐야겠다(I'll need to come over and take a look at your computer myself)고 말하고 있으므로 정답은 (C)이다.

어휘 look through 훑어보다   manual 사용 설명서   workstation 사무 공간   dispose of ~을 없애다   equipment 장비

35-37

W-Am Hi! Are you opening soon? **35 I was just hoping to get a new set of brakes for my bike.**

M-Cn Yes, we've been open since nine! Let me know if you need help finding the right pair.

W-Am Oh! Then I should let you know—**37 the sign on the front doors says you're closed.**

M-Cn Ah, **36 sorry about that. We often forget to turn that sign around when we come in in the mornings. 37 I'll go and fix that now.**

여: 안녕하세요! 곧 문을 여시나요? 제 자전거에 필요한 새 브레이크 세트를 사려고 하는데요.

남: 네, 9시부터 문을 열었습니다! 적합한 부품을 찾는 데 도움이 필요하시면 말씀하세요.

여: 아! 그럼 알려드려야겠네요. 정문에 있는 표지판에는 영업 종료라고 적혀 있어요.

남: 아, 죄송합니다. 아침에 들어올 때 종종 표지판 돌려놓는 걸 깜박할 때가 있네요. 지금 가서 바꿔놓을게요.

어휘 brake 브레이크   pair 짝   sign 간판, 표지판   turn around 회전하다   fix 바로잡다

35 What does the woman want to do?
(A) Rent some bicycles
(B) Purchase some parts
(C) Check on a repair
(D) Join a riding club

번역 여자는 무엇을 하기를 원하는가?
(A) 자전거 대여
(B) 부품 구매
(C) 수리 진행 상황 확인
(D) 자전거 동호회 가입

해설 세부 사항 관련 - 여자가 하기를 원하는 것

여자가 첫 대사에서 자전거에 필요한 새 브레이크 세트를 사려고 한다(I was just hoping to get a new set of brakes for my bike)고 말하고 있으므로 정답은 (B)이다.

어휘 purchase 구매하다   part 부품   repair 수리   riding club 자전거 동호회, 승마 동호회

> **Paraphrasing**
> 대화의 get a new set of brakes for my bike
> → 정답의 Purchase some parts

36 Why does the man apologize?
(A) A message was not sent.
(B) A shelf was not restocked.
(C) The business is closed.
(D) A sign is wrong.

번역　남자는 왜 사과하는가?
　　　(A) 메시지가 전송되지 않아서
　　　(B) 선반에 물건을 채워두지 않아서
　　　(C) 사업장이 문을 닫아서
　　　(D) 표지판이 잘못되어서

해설　**세부 사항 관련 - 남자가 사과하는 이유**
　　　남자가 두 번째 대사에서 죄송하다(sorry about that)면서 아침에
　　　들어올 때 종종 표지판을 돌려놓는 걸 깜박할 때가 있다(We often
　　　forget to turn that sign around when we come in in the
　　　mornings)고 말하고 있으므로 정답은 (D)이다.

어휘　shelf 선반　restock 다시 채우다

37　What will the man most likely do next?
　　　(A) Go to the front entrance
　　　(B) Search a stockroom
　　　(C) Consult with a mechanic
　　　(D) Wait at a checkout counter

번역　남자는 다음으로 무엇을 하겠는가?
　　　(A) 정문으로 가기
　　　(B) 창고 뒤지기
　　　(C) 정비사와 상담하기
　　　(D) 계산대에서 기다리기

해설　**세부 사항 관련 - 남자가 다음에 할 일**
　　　여자가 마지막 대사에서 정문에 있는 표지판에는 영업 종료라고 적혀
　　　있다(the sign on the front doors says you're closed)고 하
　　　자, 남자가 지금 가서 바꿔놓겠다(I'll go and fix that now)고 말하
　　　는 것으로 보아 정문에 있는 표지판을 돌려놓겠다는 것이므로 정답은
　　　(A)이다.

어휘　stockroom 창고　mechanic 정비공　checkout counter
　　　계산대

> **Paraphrasing**
> 대화의 the front doors → 정답의 the front entrance

38-40 3인 대화

W-Am　Worthington Print Shop. This is Darlene
　　　speaking.

M-Au　Hi, this is Pasquale Cafaro. **38 I ordered
　　　custom T-shirts from your shop for the
　　　soccer tournament I'm putting together this
　　　month.**

W-Am　OK, uh... our records show that all four boxes
　　　arrived yesterday. Is there a problem?

M-Au　Yes—shouldn't there be five boxes? **39 I didn't
　　　get the size extra-small shirts that I ordered.**

W-Am　**40 Let me connect you with Sheila**, the
　　　employee who filled your order. Please hold.

W-Br　Hi, Mr. Cafaro. Darlene told me about your
　　　issue. **40 We often group smaller-quantity
　　　items together to cut down on the number of
　　　shipments.** So try checking the bottom of the
　　　box of small-size T-shirts.

여:　워딩턴 인쇄소입니다. 저는 달린입니다.

남:　안녕하세요, 저는 파스콸레 카파로입니다. **제가 이번 달에 준비
　　　중인 축구 토너먼트 경기를 위한 맞춤 티셔츠를 주문했는데요.**

여1:　아, 네… 저희 기록을 보니 네 상자가 모두 어제 도착했네요. 문
　　　제가 있나요?

남:　네, 다섯 상자여야 하지 않나요? **제가 주문한 엑스스몰 사이즈
　　　티셔츠를 받지 못했어요.**

여1:　고객님의 주문을 처리한 직원 **실라를 바꿔드릴게요.** 잠시만 기
　　　다려주세요.

여2:　안녕하세요, 카파로 씨. 달린이 문제에 대해 말해줬어요. **저희는
　　　종종 배송품의 개수를 줄이기 위해 소량인 품목을 한데 합치거
　　　든요.** 그러니 스몰 사이즈 티셔츠가 든 상자의 하단을 확인해 보
　　　세요.

어휘　custom 주문 제작한　tournament 토너먼트(승자끼리
　　　맞붙는 경기 방식)　put together 준비하다　connect
　　　(전화를) 연결하다　fill an order 주문을 처리하다　group
　　　모으다　quantity 양　cut down on ~을 줄이다
　　　shipment 배송품

38　What is the man doing this month?
　　　(A) Taking a group vacation
　　　(B) Celebrating an anniversary
　　　(C) Putting up holiday decorations
　　　(D) Organizing an athletic event

번역　남자는 이번 달에 무엇을 할 예정인가?
　　　(A) 단체 여행 가기
　　　(B) 기념일 축하하기
　　　(C) 명절 장식 설치하기
　　　(D) 체육 행사 수최하기

해설　**세부 사항 관련 - 남자가 이번 달에 할 일**
　　　남자가 첫 대사에서 이번 달에 준비 중인 축구 토너먼트 경기를 위한
　　　맞춤 티셔츠를 주문했다(I ordered custom T-shirts from your
　　　shop for the soccer tournament I'm putting together
　　　this month)고 말하고 있으므로 정답은 (D)이다.

어휘　celebrate 축하하다　anniversary 기념일　put up 설치하다
　　　decoration 장식　organize 주최하다　athletic event 체육
　　　행사

> **Paraphrasing**
> 대화의 the soccer tournament I'm putting together
> → 정답의 Organizing an athletic event

39 What concern does the man express?
(A) His order arrived later than scheduled.
(B) A product is the wrong size.
(C) Some purchased items are missing.
(D) Some boxes broke open.

번역 남자는 어떤 우려를 표현하는가?
(A) 주문품이 예정보다 늦게 도착했다.
(B) 제품의 치수가 잘못되었다.
(C) 일부 구매한 품목이 빠져 있다.
(D) 일부 상자가 뜯어졌다.

해설 세부 사항 관련 - 남자의 우려 사항
남자가 두 번째 대사에서 주문한 엑스스몰 사이즈 티셔츠를 받지 못했다(I didn't get the size extra-small shirts that I ordered)고 말하고 있으므로 정답은 (C)이다.

어휘 missing 없어진, 빠진   break open 뜯어지다

---

40 What does Sheila explain to the man?
(A) How to repair some damage
(B) How shipments are packed
(C) How to request a refund
(D) How long a process took

번역 실라는 남자에게 무엇을 설명하는가?
(A) 손상된 부분을 어떻게 수리하는지
(B) 배송품이 어떻게 포장되었는지
(C) 어떻게 환불을 요청하는지
(D) 절차가 얼마나 오래 걸렸는지

해설 세부 사항 관련 - 실라가 남자에게 설명하는 것
첫 번째 여자가 세 번째 대사에서 실라를 바꿔주겠다(Let me connect you with Sheila)고 했고, 두 번째 여자가 종종 배송품의 개수를 줄이기 위해 소량인 품목을 한데 합친다(We often group smaller-quantity items together to cut down on the number of shipments)고 말하고 있으므로 정답은 (B)이다.

어휘 repair 수리하다   damage 손상   pack 포장하다   request 요청하다   refund 환불

41-43

M-Cn Bernice, your team's in charge of monitoring customer satisfaction with our products. **41 How's the response to the new packaging for our socks?**

W-Br We're seeing mostly positive mentions of it in online reviews. **42 People appreciate that we got rid of the plastic fasteners in order to reduce plastic pollution.** However, a few have complained that it's harder to remove the thread loops that now hold the socks together.

M-Cn OK. I'd like you to post replies to those reviews. Express sympathy for the customers'

frustration and then **43 direct them to the page on our Web site that explains why we changed the packaging.**

남: 버니스, 당신의 팀이 제품에 대한 고객 만족도를 모니터링하는 일을 맡고 있잖아요. **양말 새 포장재에 대한 반응은 어때요?**

여: 온라인 후기에서는 주로 긍정적인 언급이 달리고 있어요. **사람들은 플라스틱 오염을 줄이기 위해 플라스틱 고리를 제거한 것에 대해 환영하고 있어요.** 하지만 몇몇 사람들은 양말을 고정하는 실 고리를 제거하기가 더 어렵다고 불평했어요.

남: 알겠습니다. 당신이 그 후기들에 답변을 달아주셨으면 좋겠어요. 고객들의 불만에 대해 공감을 표현하고 난 다음에 **우리가 왜 포장재를 바꿨는지 설명이 담긴 웹사이트 페이지를 방문하도록 안내해 주세요.**

어휘 be in charge of ~을 담당하다   satisfaction 만족   response 응답, 반응   packaging 포장재   positive 긍정적인   mention 언급   review 후기   appreciate 고마워하다, 환영하다   get rid of ~을 제거하다   fastener 조임 장치   reduce 줄이다   pollution 오염   remove 제거하다   thread 실   sympathy 공감   frustration 불만, 좌절감   direct 안내하다

---

41 What industry do the speakers work in?
(A) Electronics
(B) Cosmetics
(C) Clothing
(D) Pharmaceutical

번역 화자들은 어떤 업계에 종사하는가?
(A) 전자 제품
(B) 화장품
(C) 의류
(D) 제약

해설 전체 내용 관련 - 화자들의 근무 업계
남자가 첫 대사에서 양말 새 포장재에 대한 반응은 어떤지(How's the response to the new packaging for our socks?) 묻고 있으므로 화자들은 의류 업계에 종사함을 알 수 있다. 따라서 정답은 (C)이다.

Paraphrasing
대화의 socks → 정답의 Clothing

---

42 Why did the company change its product packaging?
(A) To make the packaging easier to remove
(B) To prevent damage to some goods
(C) To reduce production expenses
(D) To become more environmentally friendly

번역 회사는 왜 제품 포장재를 바꿨는가?
(A) 포장재를 더 쉽게 제거하게 하려고
(B) 제품 손상을 방지하려고
(C) 생산 비용을 절감하려고
(D) 더 환경친화적이 되려고

해설　세부 사항 관련 - 회사가 제품 포장재를 바꾼 이유
여자가 첫 대사에서 사람들은 플라스틱 오염을 줄이기 위해 플라스틱 고리를 제거한 것에 대해 환영하고 있다(People appreciate that we got rid of the plastic fasteners in order to reduce plastic pollution)고 말하고 있으므로 정답은 (D)이다.

어휘　prevent 방지하다　damage 손상　production 생산
expense 지출, 비용　environmentally friendly 환경친화적인

> Paraphrasing
> 대화의 to reduce plastic pollution
> → 정답의 To become more environmentally friendly

43 What will the woman most likely do in her replies to some reviews?
(A) Offer a one-time discount
(B) Post a link to a Web page
(C) Direct customers to a help line
(D) Express gratitude for feedback

번역　여자는 일부 후기에 대한 답변에서 무엇을 하겠는가?
(A) 일회성 할인 제공하기
(B) 웹페이지 링크 게시하기
(C) 고객을 고객 센터로 안내하기
(D) 피드백에 대한 감사 표현하기

해설　세부 사항 관련 - 여자가 일부 후기에 대한 답변에서 할 일
남자가 마지막 대사에서 우리가 왜 포장재를 바꿨는지 설명이 담긴 웹사이트 페이지를 방문하도록 안내해 줄 것(direct them to the page on our Web site that explains why we changed the packaging)을 요청하고 있으므로 정답은 (B)이다.

어휘　one-time 일회성의　help line 고객 센터　gratitude 감사

44-46

W-Am　Min-Seok, **44 thanks for suggesting that tagline for our ad campaign for the career consultancy.** The clients love it.

M-Au　Glad to hear it! Oh, and Ms. West? I was just wondering—**45 are we going to have an end-of-the-year staff party in the office again this December?**

W-Am　It's a company tradition. **45 Why wouldn't we?**

M-Au　A lot of employees are remote now.

W-Am　Oh, good point. But… some of those employees might enjoy the chance to see everyone in person again.

M-Au　That's true.

W-Am　Well, now I'm also curious about what we'll do. **46 Next time I see the president, I'll ask her what the plan for this year is.**

여:　민석, 커리어 컨설팅 회사용 광고 캠페인을 위한 태그라인을 제안해 줘서 고마워요. 고객들이 매우 마음에 든대요.

남:　다행이네요! 아, 그런데 웨스트 씨? 궁금한 게 있는데, **이번 12월에도 사무실에서 연말 회식을 할 예정인가요?**

여:　그건 회사 전통이죠. 하지 않을 이유가 있겠어요?

남:　많은 직원들이 지금 원격으로 일하잖아요.

여:　아, 좋은 지적이에요. 하지만… 그 직원들 중 일부는 다시 한 번 모두를 직접 만나볼 기회를 원할지도 몰라요.

남:　그건 그렇죠.

여:　음, 그러고 보니 저도 우리가 무엇을 할지 궁금해지네요. 다음번에 회장님을 만나면 올해 계획이 무엇인지 여쭤볼게요.

어휘　tagline 태그라인(브랜드를 표현하는 함축적인 문구)　career 경력　consultancy 자문 회사　end-of-the-year 연말의 staff party 회식　tradition 전통　employee 직원 remote 원격으로 근무하는　in person 직접　president 회장

44 What type of business do the speakers most likely work at?
(A) An advertising agency
(B) An accounting firm
(C) An insurance company
(D) A career coaching service

번역　화자들은 어떤 유형의 사업체에서 일하겠는가?
(A) 광고 대행사
(B) 회계 사무소
(C) 보험 회사
(D) 커리어 코칭 서비스 회사

해설　전체 내용 관련 - 화자들의 근무 업종
여자가 첫 대사에서 커리어 컨설팅 회사용 광고 캠페인(our ad campaign for the career consultancy)이라고 했으므로 화자들은 광고 대행사에서 근무하고 있다는 것을 알 수 있다. 따라서 정답은 (A)이다.

어휘　accounting 회계　insurance 보험　coaching 지도

45 What does the man most likely mean when he says, "A lot of employees are remote now"?
(A) Some office space could be used in a different way.
(B) A company event might not be well-attended.
(C) Fewer supplies will be needed for a break room.
(D) It will be difficult to train some new staff members.

번역　남자가 "많은 직원들이 지금 원격으로 일하잖아요"라고 말할 때, 그 의도는 무엇인가?
(A) 일부 사무 공간이 다른 방식으로 사용될 수 있다.
(B) 회사 행사의 참석률이 높지 않을 수 있다.
(C) 휴게실에 필요한 물품이 감소할 것이다.
(D) 신입 직원을 교육하는 일이 어려울 것이다.

해설 **화자의 의도 파악 - 많은 직원들이 지금 원격으로 일한다는 말의 의도**
앞에서 남자가 이번 12월에도 사무실에서 연말 회식을 할 예정인지(are we going to have an end-of-the-year staff party in the office again this December?) 묻자 여자가 하지 않을 이유가 있는지(Why wouldn't we?) 되물은 후, 남자가 인용문을 언급한 것으로 보아, 원격 근무 때문에 연말 회식 참석률이 낮을 수 있다는 의도로 한 말임을 알 수 있다. 따라서 정답은 (B)이다.

어휘 well-attended 많은 사람이 참석한 break room 휴게실

---

46 What does the woman decide to do?
(A) Send out a survey
(B) Plan a virtual celebration
(C) Make revisions to a food order
(D) Ask a question to an executive

번역 여자는 무엇을 하기로 결정하는가?
(A) 설문 조사 발송하기
(B) 온라인 기념행사 계획하기
(C) 음식 주문 변경하기
(D) 임원에게 질문하기

해설 **세부 사항 관련 - 여자가 결정한 일**
여자가 마지막 대사에서 다음번에 회장님을 만나면 올해 계획이 무엇인지 여쭤보겠다(Next time I see the president, I'll ask her what the plan for this year is)고 말하고 있으므로 정답은 (D)이다.

어휘 survey 설문 조사 virtual 가상의 celebration 기념행사 revision 수정, 변경 executive 임원, 중역

> **Paraphrasing**
> 대화의 the president → 정답의 an executive

47-49 3인 대화

> M-Au This construction exposition is really well-organized. **47 I like how the vendors that sell the same types of products are placed near each other.**
>
> M-Cn Yeah, **47 that'll make it easy for us to talk to all the companies that sell site-clearing supplies.** Let's see… they're in this block. Let's start with this one.
>
> W-Br Good morning! What brings you to our booth today?
>
> M-Au We're interested in hearing about **48 your company's heavy equipment for clearing land**—like the large machines that cut up tree stumps.
>
> W-Br Sure. We have five stump cutters in our product lineup. **49 Do you already know what kind of cutting power or wheel size you'll want?**

남1: 이 건축 박람회는 정말 준비가 잘 되어 있네요. **같은 유형의 제품을 파는 업체들이 서로 가까이 붙어 있는 점이 마음에 들어요.**

남2: 맞아요, **대지 정리 용품을 파는 모든 업체와 상담을 하기가 더 수월할 거예요.** 어디 보자… 그 업체들은 이 블록에 있네요. 이곳부터 시작합시다.

여: 좋은 아침입니다! 오늘 어떤 일로 저희 부스를 찾아주셨나요?

남1: **귀사의 대지 정리용 중장비에** 대해 관심이 있습니다. 그러니까 나무 밑동을 잘라내는 대형 기계 같은 거죠.

여: 네. 저희 제품 라인업에는 다섯 가지 밑동 절단기가 있습니다. **원하시는 절삭력이나 바퀴 크기를 이미 알고 계시나요?**

어휘 construction 건축, 건설 exposition 박람회, 전시회 well-organized 준비가 잘 된 vendor 판매 업체 site-clearing 대지 정리 heavy equipment 중장비 cut up 자르다 stump 나무 밑동 cutter 절단기 cutting power 절삭력

---

47 What do the men like about the exposition?
(A) It lasts for several days.
(B) Its organizers are responsive.
(C) Its layout is convenient.
(D) It has many vendors.

번역 남자들은 박람회에 대해서 어떤 점을 마음에 들어 하는가?
(A) 며칠간 열린다.
(B) 주최자들의 응답이 빠르다.
(C) 배치가 편리하다.
(D) 공급업체가 많다.

해설 **세부 사항 관련 - 남자들이 박람회에 대해 마음에 들어 하는 점**
첫 번째 남자가 첫 대사에서 같은 유형의 제품을 파는 공급업체들이 서로 가까이 붙어 있는 점이 마음에 든다(I like how the vendors that sell the same types of products are placed near each other)고 하자, 두 번째 남자가 대지 정리 용품을 파는 모든 업체와 상담을 하기가 더 수월할 것(that'll make it easy for us to talk to all the companies that sell site-clearing supplies)이라고 말하고 있으므로 정답은 (C)이다.

어휘 last 지속되다 organizer 주최자 responsive 응답이 빠른 layout 배치 convenient 편리한

> **Paraphrasing**
> 대화의 easy → 정답의 convenient

---

48 What does the woman sell?
(A) Heavy machinery
(B) Building materials
(C) Safety gear
(D) Hand tools

번역 여자는 무엇을 판매하는가?
(A) 중장비
(B) 건축 자재
(C) 안전 장비
(D) 수공구

첫 번째 남자가 두 번째 대사에서 귀사의 대지 정리용 중장비(your company's heavy equipment for clearing land)라고 말하고 있으므로 정답은 (A)이다.

어휘 material 재료

> **Paraphrasing**
> 대화의 heavy equipment → 정답의 Heavy machinery

49 What does the woman ask the men about?
(A) The brand of products they currently use
(B) Their desired product specifications
(C) The number of products they need
(D) Their interest in a product demonstration

번역 여자는 남자들에게 무엇에 대해 문의하는가?
(A) 그들이 현재 사용하는 제품 브랜드
(B) 그들이 원하는 제품 사양
(C) 그들이 필요한 제품의 개수
(D) 제품 시연에 대한 관심

해설 세부 사항 관련 - 여자의 문의 사항
여자가 마지막 대사에서 원하는 절삭력이나 바퀴 크기를 이미 알고 있는지(Do you already know what kind of cutting power or wheel size you'll want?) 묻고 있으므로 정답은 (B)이다.

어휘 currently 현재 desired 원하는 specification 사양 demonstration 시연

> **Paraphrasing**
> 대화의 what kind of cutting power or wheel size you'll want → 정답의 Their desired product specifications

50-52

> M-Au Good morning. **50 I've just become the owner of a small apartment nearby, and I was wondering if your agency could help me list it for rental.**
>
> W-Am Absolutely. Where is the apartment?
>
> M-Au In the building at 470 Boone Avenue, close to the elevated train line. In fact, **51 the sound of the train passing by can be quite loud even with the windows closed.** Will that be a big problem?
>
> W-Am No, we should still be able to find someone willing to live there. **52 It does mean you probably won't be able to collect a very high rent fee, though.**

남: 좋은 아침입니다. 제가 얼마 전 이 근처에 있는 작은 아파트의 소유주가 되었는데요. 귀하의 중개소에서 임대 매물로 내놓는 일을 도와주실 수 있는지 궁금합니다.

여: 물론이죠. 아파트가 어디에 있나요?

남: 분 가 470번지에 있는 건물입니다. 고가 열차 노선에서 가까워요. 실은 **지나가는 열차에서 나는 소리가 창문을 닫아도 꽤 시끄러울 수 있습니다.** 이게 큰 문제가 될까요?

여: 아니요, 그래도 거기에 살려는 사람을 찾을 수 있을 거예요. **아주 높은 임대료를 받을 수는 없으실 테지만요.**

어휘 list for rental 임대 매물로 내놓다 elevated (주변이나 지면보다) 높은 pass by 옆을 지나가다 loud 시끄러운 collect 수집하다, 수금하다 rent fee 임대료

50 What are the speakers mainly discussing?
(A) Choosing a venue for a talk
(B) Arranging renovations to a building
(C) Becoming investors in a business
(D) Finding a tenant for a property

번역 화자들은 주로 무엇에 관해 이야기하는가?
(A) 연설을 위한 장소 고르기
(B) 건물 보수 공사 준비하기
(C) 사업 투자자 되기
(D) 부동산 세입자 찾기

해설 전체 내용 관련 - 대화의 주제
남자가 첫 대사에서 얼마 전 근처 아파트의 소유주가 되었는데 임대 매물로 내놓는 일을 도와줄 수 있는지 궁금하다(I've just become the owner of a small apartment nearby, and I was wondering if your agency could help me list it for rental)고 말하고 있으므로 정답은 (D)이다.

어휘 venue 장소 arrange 준비하다 renovation 보수 공사 investor 투자자 tenant 세입자 property 부동산

> **Paraphrasing**
> 대화의 a small apartment → 정답의 a property

51 According to the man, what might cause a problem?
(A) A lack of access to public transportation
(B) A scheduling conflict
(C) A disruptive noise
(D) Confusion about some regulations

번역 남자에 따르면, 무엇이 문제를 일으킬 수 있는가?
(A) 대중교통에 대한 접근성 부족
(B) 일정 충돌
(C) 지장을 주는 소음
(D) 일부 규정에 대한 혼동

해설 세부 사항 관련 - 남자가 문제를 일으킬 수 있다고 하는 것
남자가 두 번째 대사에서 지나가는 열차에서 나는 소리가 창문을 닫아도 꽤 시끄러울 수 있다(the sound of the train passing by can be quite loud even with the windows closed)고 말하고 있으므로 정답은 (C)이다.

어휘 lack 부족 access 접근 public transportation 대중교통 scheduling conflict 일정 충돌 disruptive 지장을 주는 confusion 혼동 regulation 규제

52 What does the woman warn the man about?
(A) Some earnings may be low.
(B) A manager may reject a proposal.
(C) It will take time to collect some data.
(D) A location may need to be changed.

번역 여자는 남자에게 무엇에 대해 경고하는가?
(A) 수익이 낮을지도 모른다.
(B) 관리자가 제안을 거부할지도 모른다.
(C) 자료를 수집하는 데 시간이 걸릴 것이다.
(D) 장소가 변경되어야 할지도 모른다.

해설 세부 사항 관련 - 여자가 경고하는 것
여자가 마지막 대사에서 아주 높은 임대료를 받을 수는 없을 것(It does mean you probably won't be able to collect a very high rent fee, though)이라고 말하고 있으므로 정답은 (A)이다.

어휘 earnings 소득 reject 거부하다 proposal 제안

> **Paraphrasing**
> 대화의 rent fee → 정답의 earnings

53-55

> W-Br Hi, Mr. Myers. Thank you for making time for this call. **53 I'm excited to tell you more about how partnering with Sonore Group would benefit your company.**
>
> M-Au I look forward to hearing it.
>
> W-Br So, what we'd like to do is buy the rights to several of **54 your popular podcast series.** We would then re-record the series in French and release them to our subscribers here in France.
>
> M-Au I see. To be honest, we've also been contacted by another French distributor—Podtastique. Why should we choose your company over them?
>
> W-Br Well, they're new to this area, whereas **55 Sonore Group has been translating podcasts for the French-speaking market for over five years.**

여: 안녕하세요, 마이어스 씨. 시간을 내주셔서 감사합니다. **서노어 그룹과의 파트너십이 귀사에 어떤 이점이 있는지 좀 더 설명해 드릴 수 있어서 기쁩니다.**

남: 빨리 듣고 싶군요.

여: 그러니까, 저희가 하고자 하는 것은 **귀사의 인기 팟캐스트 시리즈** 중 몇 개에 대한 판권을 구입하는 것입니다. 그런 다음 그 시리즈를 프랑스어로 다시 녹음해서 이곳 프랑스에 있는 저희 구독자들에게 공개하겠습니다.

남: 그렇군요. 솔직히 말씀드리자면, 저희는 다른 프랑스 배급사인 팟타스틱에서도 연락을 받았어요. 저희가 왜 그들을 제치고 귀사를 선택해야 할까요?

여: 음, 그들은 이 분야에 이제 막 들어온 반면, **서노어 그룹은 프랑스어권 시장을 위해 팟캐스트를 번역한 지 5년이 넘었습니다.**

어휘 partner with ~와 협력하다 benefit 이득을 주다 right 판권, 권리 popular 인기 있는 re-record 다시 녹음하다 release 공개하다, 출시하다 subscriber 구독자 contact 연락하다 distributor 배급사 translate 번역하다

53 Why is the woman calling the man?
(A) To discuss a potential deal
(B) To inquire about a job applicant
(C) To announce a price change
(D) To extend an event invitation

번역 여자는 왜 남자에게 전화를 걸고 있는가?
(A) 잠재적인 거래에 대해 의논하려고
(B) 입사 지원자에 대해 문의하려고
(C) 가격 변경을 알리려고
(D) 행사에 초대하려고

해설 전체 내용 관련 - 여자가 전화한 이유
여자가 첫 대사에서 서노어 그룹과의 파트너십이 남자의 회사에 어떤 이점이 있는지 좀 더 설명해 줄 수 있어서 기쁘다(I'm excited to tell you more about how partnering with Sonore Group would benefit your company)고 말하고 있으므로 정답은 (A)이다.

어휘 potential 잠재적인 applicant 지원자 extend an invitation 초대하다

54 What does the man's company do?
(A) International travel planning
(B) Audio content creation
(C) Foreign language education
(D) Recording equipment manufacturing

번역 남자의 회사는 무엇을 하는가?
(A) 해외여행 기획
(B) 오디오 콘텐츠 제작
(C) 외국어 교육
(D) 녹음 장비 제조

해설 세부 사항 관련 - 남자의 회사가 하는 일
여자가 두 번째 대사에서 귀사의 인기 팟캐스트 시리즈(your popular podcast series)라고 말하고 있으므로 정답은 (B)이다.

어휘 creation 창조, 제작 education 교육 equipment 장비 manufacturing 제조

> **Paraphrasing**
> 대화의 podcast → 정답의 Audio content

55 What does the woman say about Sonore Group?
(A) It has a large customer base.
(B) It has offices throughout the area.
(C) It has a lot of relevant experience.
(D) It has a prestigious certification.

번역　여자는 서노어 그룹에 대해 뭐라고 말하는가?
　　(A) 고객층이 넓다.
　　(B) 지역 곳곳에 사무실이 있다.
　　(C) 관련 경험이 풍부하다.
　　(D) 권위 있는 증명서를 보유하고 있다.

해설　세부 사항 관련 - 여자가 서노어 그룹에 대해 하는 말
　　여자가 마지막 대사에서 서노어 그룹은 프랑스어권 시장을 위해 팟캐스트를 번역한 지 5년이 넘었다(Sonore Group has been translating podcasts for the French-speaking market for over five years)고 말하고 있으므로 정답은 (C)이다.

어휘　customer base 고객층　relevant 관련 있는　prestigious 권위 있는　certification 증명서

56-58

> M-Cn　Ms. Chen, welcome! We really appreciate your agreeing to talk to **56 our agricultural engineering students.** They're very eager to hear about one of the jobs open to them after graduation.
>
> W-Am　It's my pleasure. I've really enjoyed working as an irrigation technician. And I know that **57 the industry's expected to keep adding jobs in the future, so it's a great long-term career option.**
>
> M-Cn　Excellent. So, as I said in my e-mail, you'll have thirty minutes to speak, and then there'll be a fifteen-minute question-and-answer session. Oh, and **58 would you be willing to share your e-mail address** in case students have additional questions later?
>
> W-Am　**58 Sure,** I'll write it on this whiteboard.

남：　첸 씨, 어서 오세요! **농업공학과 학생들**과의 대화를 수락해 주셔서 정말 감사드립니다. 학생들은 졸업 후에 그들에게 기회가 열려 있는 직업들 중 하나에 대해 듣기를 간절히 원하고 있습니다.

여：　도움이 될 수 있어서 저도 기뻐요. 관개 기술자로 일하는 것은 정말 즐거워요. 그리고 제가 알기로 **이 산업 분야는 앞으로 일자리가 계속 늘어날 전망이므로 장기적으로 봤을 때 훌륭한 직업입니다.**

남：　훌륭합니다. 그럼, 이메일에서 말씀드린 것처럼 30분 동안 말씀하신 후에 15분 동안 질의응답 시간을 가지겠습니다. 아, 그리고 학생들이 나중에 추가 질문이 있을 경우를 대비해 **이메일 주소를 공유해 주시겠습니까?**

여：　**그럼요,** 화이트보드에 적어놓을게요.

어휘　agricultural engineering 농업 공학　be eager to 간절히 바라다　graduation 졸업　irrigation 관개　technician 기술자　long-term 장기적인　session 시간　in case ~할 경우를 대비해　additional 추가의

---

56 Who most likely is the man?
(A) A university employee
(B) A television reporter
(C) A public librarian
(D) A newspaper editor

번역　남자는 누구이겠는가?
　　(A) 대학교 직원
　　(B) TV 리포터
　　(C) 공공 도서관 사서
　　(D) 신문 편집자

해설　전체 내용 관련 - 남자의 직업
　　남자가 첫 대사에서 우리 농업공학과 학생들(our agricultural engineering students)이라고 말하는 것으로 보아 남자는 대학에서 근무하고 있음을 알 수 있다. 따라서 정답은 (A)이다.

어휘　public 공공의　librarian 사서　editor 편집자

---

57 What does the woman mention about her industry?
(A) It is not related to her degree.
(B) It is difficult to enter.
(C) It is predicted to grow.
(D) It has not existed for long.

번역　여자는 자신의 산업 분야에 대해 무엇을 언급하는가?
　　(A) 자신의 학위와 관련이 없다.
　　(B) 진입하기가 어렵다.
　　(C) 성장할 것으로 예측된다.
　　(D) 그리 오래되지 않았다.

해설　세부 사항 관련 - 여자가 자신의 산업 분야에 대해 언급하는 것
　　여자가 첫 대사에서 이 산업 분야는 앞으로 일자리가 계속 늘어날 전망이므로 장기적으로 봤을 때 훌륭한 직업(the industry's expected to keep adding jobs in the future, so it's a great long-term career option)이라고 말하고 있으므로 정답은 (C)이다.

어휘　be related to ~와 관련이 있다　degree 학위　enter 진입하다　predict 예측하다　grow 성장하다　exist 존재하다

> **Paraphrasing**
> 대화의 the industry's expected to keep adding jobs in the future → 정답의 It is predicted to grow.

---

58 What does the woman agree to do?
(A) Sign a consent form
(B) Pose for a photograph
(C) Write an opinion column
(D) Provide some contact information

번역　여자는 무엇을 하기로 동의하는가?
　　(A) 동의서에 서명하기
　　(B) 사진을 위해 자세 잡기
　　(C) 사설 쓰기
　　(D) 연락처 제공하기

해설 **세부 사항 관련 - 여자가 동의한 일**

남자가 마지막 대사에서 이메일 주소를 공유해 줄 것(would you be willing to share your e-mail address ~?)을 요청하자 여자가 그럼요(Sure)라고 수락하고 있으므로 정답은 (D)이다.

어휘 consent 동의 form 양식 opinion 의견, 견해 column 칼럼

> **Paraphrasing**
> 대화의 share your e-mail address
> → 정답의 Provide some contact information

59-61

M-Cn	Hi, Ms. Newton? This is Dennis Hendricks calling from Powell Health. **⁵⁹ I'm sorry to tell you that Dr. Diaz has had to take a leave of absence because of an urgent family matter.** He'll be unavailable for the next month.
W-Br	Oh… so I won't be able to have my knee surgery next week?
M-Cn	Well, **⁶⁰ we do have another surgeon who could perform the procedure as scheduled— Dr. Kelvin.**
W-Br	Hmm… but Dr. Diaz is the best-rated surgeon in the area…
M-Cn	Sure, I understand. Then **⁶¹ I'll move your surgery date to early April.** You should get a text message confirmation within a few minutes.

남: 안녕하세요, 뉴턴 씨? 저는 파월 헬스 병원의 데니스 헨드릭스입니다. 유감스럽게도 디아스 선생님이 급한 집안일로 인해 휴가를 내시게 되었습니다. 다음 달까지는 못 나오실 거예요.

여: 아… 그럼 다음 주에 제 무릎 수술을 받을 수 없는 건가요?

남: 음, 예정대로 그 수술을 할 수 있는 다른 외과의가 있습니다. 켈빈 선생님이요.

여: 음… 하지만 디아스 선생님이 이 분야에서 가장 높은 평가를 받는 외과의잖아요…

남: 맞습니다, 이해합니다. 그럼 **수술 날짜를 4월 초로 변경해 드리겠습니다.** 몇 분 내로 확인 문자를 받으실 거예요.

어휘 take a leave of absence 휴가를 내다 urgent 긴급한 unavailable (사람과) 만날 수 없는 surgery 수술 surgeon 외과의 perform 수행하다 procedure 절차, 수술 best-rated 가장 높은 평가를 받는 confirmation 확인

59 What problem does the man describe?
(A) A colleague has gone on leave.
(B) A member of his family has been injured.
(C) A medication is not working.
(D) A speaker has canceled.

번역 남자는 어떤 문제를 설명하는가?
(A) 동료가 휴가를 갔다.
(B) 자신의 가족 중 누군가가 다쳤다.
(C) 약효가 없다.
(D) 연사가 취소했다.

해설 **세부 사항 관련 - 남자가 언급한 문제**

남자가 첫 대사에서 유감스럽게도 디아스 선생님이 급한 집안일로 인해 휴가를 내시게 됐다(I'm sorry to tell you that Dr. Diaz has had to take a leave of absence ~)고 말하고 있으므로 정답은 (A)이다.

어휘 go on leave 휴가 가다 injure 부상을 입히다 medication 약물 speaker 연사

> **Paraphrasing**
> 대화의 take a leave of absence
> → 정답의 has gone on leave

60 Why most likely does the woman say, "Dr. Diaz is the best-rated surgeon in the area"?
(A) To show surprise
(B) To refuse an offer
(C) To make a suggestion
(D) To complain about a decision

번역 여자가 "디아스 선생님이 이 분야에서 가장 높은 평가를 받는 외과의잖아요"라고 말한 이유는?
(A) 놀람을 표현하려고
(B) 제의를 거절하려고
(C) 제안을 하려고
(D) 결정에 대해 불평하려고

해설 **화자의 의도 파악 - 디아스 선생님이 이 분야에서 가장 높은 평가를 받는 외과의라는 말의 의도**

앞에서 남자가 예정대로 그 수술을 할 수 있는 다른 외과의 켈빈 선생님이 있다(we do have another surgeon who could perform the procedure as scheduled—Dr. Kelvin)고 하자, 여자가 인용문을 언급하고 있으므로 다른 외과의 제안을 거절하려는 의도로 한 말임을 알 수 있다. 따라서 정답은 (B)이다.

어휘 refuse 거절하다 suggestion 제안 complain 불평하다 decision 결정

61 What does the man say he will do next?
(A) Update a Web site
(B) Reschedule an appointment
(C) Send a message to Dr. Diaz
(D) Research a surgical procedure

번역 남자는 다음으로 무엇을 하겠다고 말하는가?
(A) 웹사이트 갱신하기
(B) 예약 일정 조정하기
(C) 디아스 선생님에게 메시지 보내기
(D) 외과 수술 절차 조사하기

해설 세부 사항 관련 - 남자가 다음에 할 일
남자가 마지막 대사에서 수술 날짜를 4월 초로 변경해 주겠다(I'll move your surgery date to early April)고 말하고 있으므로 정답은 (B)이다.

어휘 reschedule 일정을 조정하다　appointment (진료 등의) 예약
surgical 외과의

> **Paraphrasing**
> 대화의 move your surgery date to early April
> → 정답의 Reschedule an appointment

62-64 대화 + 카탈로그

M-Au Anna, I'm thinking of buying one of these countertop refrigerators so that we can sell cold drinks.

W-Am That's a great idea. **⁶² It's been so hot and humid outside since last week.**

M-Au Exactly. Now, we don't have that much counter space, so **⁶³ one of these tall fridges with three shelves would be best, right? But what's this large block at the top of this one?**

W-Am **⁶³ It's a display panel.** You can put advertising there.

M-Au **⁶³ Oh, we don't need that. I'll order this one instead.**

W-Am That seems like a good choice. And about the drinks—since we're a pharmacy, **⁶⁴ I think we should only sell healthy ones**, like sugar-free juices with lots of vitamins.

남: 애나, 차가운 음료를 팔 수 있도록 이 카운터탑 냉장고들 중 하나를 구매할까요?

여: 좋은 생각이에요. **지난주부터 바깥 날씨가 엄청 덥고 습해졌네요.**

남: 그러게요. 이제, 카운터 공간이 별로 남아 있지 않으니, **3단 선반이 있는 이 키 큰 냉장고 중 하나가 가장 낫겠죠?** 그런데 상단에 있는 이 커다란 사각형 부분은 뭘까요?

여: 그건 디스플레이 패널이에요. 거기에 광고를 넣을 수 있어요.

남: 아, 그건 필요가 없어요. 그럼 그거 말고 이걸로 주문하겠어요.

여: 좋은 선택 같네요. 그리고 음료에 대해서는, 우리가 약국이다 보니, **건강 음료만 팔아야 할 것 같아요.** 비타민이 풍부한 무설탕 주스 같은 거요.

어휘 countertop 카운터 상판　refrigerator 냉장고　humid 습도가 높은　fridge 냉장고　shelf 선반　advertising 광고　pharmacy 약국　sugar-free 무설탕의　vitamin 비타민

#2061

- short, square
- 2 shelves
- swinging door

#2077
- short, wide
- 2 shelves
- 2 sliding doors

#2084

- ⁶³ tall, thin
- ⁶³ 3 shelves
- swinging door

#2095
- tall, thin
- 3 shelves
- swinging door
- ⁶³ display part on top

#2061

- 키 작음, 사각형
- 2단 선반
- 반회전문

#2077

- 키 작음, 와이드형
- 2단 선반
- 쌍미닫이문

#2084

- ⁶³ 키 큼, 폭이 좁음
- ⁶³ 3단 선반
- 반회전문

#2095

- 키 큼, 폭이 좁음
- 3단 선반
- 반회전문
- ⁶³ 상단 디스플레이

62 According to the woman, what happened recently?
(A) A refrigerator broke down.
(B) The business's sales decreased.
(C) New countertops were installed.
(D) The weather changed.

번역 여자에 따르면, 최근에 어떤 일이 일어났는가?
(A) 냉장고가 고장이 났다.
(B) 사업체의 매출이 감소했다.
(C) 새 카운터 상판이 설치되었다.
(D) 날씨가 바뀌었다.

해설 **세부 사항 관련 - 최근에 있었던 일**
여자가 첫 대사에서 지난주부터 바깥 날씨가 엄청 덥고 습해졌다(It's been so hot and humid outside since last week)고 했으므로 정답은 (D)이다.

어휘 break down 고장이 나다 decrease 감소하다 install 설치하다

> **Paraphrasing**
> 대화의 since last week → 질문의 recently

---

63 Look at the graphic. Which refrigerator will the man order?
(A) #2061
(B) #2077
(C) #2084
(D) #2095

번역 시각 정보에 의하면, 남자는 어떤 냉장고를 주문할 것인가?
(A) #2061
(B) #2077
(C) #2084
(D) #2095

해설 **시각 정보 연계 - 남자가 주문할 냉장고**
남자가 두 번째 대사에서 3단 선반이 있는 키 큰 냉장고 중 하나가 좋을 것 같다(one of these tall fridges with three shelves would be best, right?)면서 상단에 있는 커다란 사각형 부분이 무엇인지(But what's this large block at the top of this one?) 묻자 여자가 디스플레이 패널(It's a display panel)이라고 대답했고, 남자가 그건 필요 없다(we don't need that)면서 그거 말고 이걸로 주문하겠다(I'll order this one instead)고 말하고 있다. 카탈로그에 따르면 3단 선반이 있는 키 큰 냉장고는 #2084와 #2095인데 #2095의 디스플레이 패널은 필요 없다고 했으므로 정답은 (C)이다.

---

64 What does the woman suggest about some drinks?
(A) They should be inexpensive.
(B) They should promote health.
(C) They should have a variety of flavors.
(D) They should come in small containers.

번역 여자는 일부 음료에 대해 무엇을 제안하는가?
(A) 비싸지 않아야 한다.
(B) 건강을 증진해야 한다.
(C) 다양한 맛이어야 한다.
(D) 작은 용기로 나와야 한다.

해설 **세부 사항 관련 - 여자가 일부 음료에 대해 제안하는 것**
여자가 마지막 대사에서 건강 음료만 팔아야 할 것 같다(I think we should only sell healthy ones)고 말하고 있으므로 정답은 (B)이다.

어휘 inexpensive 비싸지 않은 promote 촉진하다 a variety of 다양한 flavor 맛 container 그릇, 용기

65-67 대화+목차

M-Cn Eun-Young, the orientation packets you made are great! **65 They're really going to help the firm's new junior accountants get settled quickly.** I especially like how you created the list of contents so it's easy to check whether anything has been left out.

W-Br Thanks! **66 That's something I learned in my first job in human resources. Orientations are an important introduction to the company. You have to plan carefully to make sure that all the necessary information is included.**

M-Cn I agree. Uh, I did notice one issue with the packets, though—**67 I'm afraid these directions for setting up a workstation will be a little confusing for the new hires.** I suggest adding some visual aids, like equipment photos and screenshots.

남: 은영, 당신이 만든 오리엔테이션 자료집은 정말 훌륭해요! **사내 신입 하급 회계사들이 빨리 적응하는 데 정말 도움이 될 거예요.** 특히 목차를 정리한 방식이 뭐가 빠졌는지 확인하기 쉬워서 마음에 들어요.

여: 감사합니다! **첫 직장 인사부에서 일할 때 배운 거예요. 오리엔테이션은 중요한 회사 소개예요. 필요한 정보가 모두 포함되도록 세심하게 준비해야 해요.**

남: 맞아요. 아, 그런데 자료집에서 한 가지 문제를 발견했어요. **워크스테이션을 설치하는 방법이 신입 사원들에게는 조금 헷갈릴까 봐 걱정이 돼요.** 장비 사진이나 스크린샷 같은 시각 보조 자료를 덧붙이면 좋을 것 같아요.

어휘 packet 꾸러미 junior accountant 하급 회계사 get settled 자리 잡다 list of contents 목차 leave out 빼다, 생략하다 human resources 인사부 introduction 소개 set up 세우다, 설치하다 workstation 워크스테이션(전문직 종사자들이 사용하는 전용 컴퓨터) confusing 헷갈리는 hire 신입 사원 visual aid 시각 보조 자료 equipment 장비

> **Paraphrasing**
> 대화의 only sell healthy ones → 정답의 promote health

Orientation Packet
Item 1 – Welcome Message
Item 2 – Organization Chart
Item 3 – Employee Handbook
Item 4 – Human Resources Paperwork
67 Item 5 – Workstation Setup
      Instructions

TEST 6

```
┌─────────────────────────────────┐
│ ┌───────────────────────────┐   │
│ │  오리엔테이션 자료집           │   │
│ │  항목 1 - 환영 인사           │   │
│ │  항목 2 - 조직도             │   │
│ │  항목 3 - 직원 안내서         │   │
│ │  항목 4 - 인사기록부          │   │
│ │ 67 항목 5 - 워크스테이션 설치 안내 │   │
│ └───────────────────────────┘   │
└─────────────────────────────────┘
```

어휘 handbook 안내서 instruction 설명, 지시

65 What kind of business do the speakers work for?
(A) An accounting firm
(B) A graphic design company
(C) A translation service
(D) A travel agency

번역 화자들은 어떤 종류의 회사에서 일하는가?
(A) 회계 사무소
(B) 그래픽 디자인 회사
(C) 번역 서비스 회사
(D) 여행사

해설 전체 내용 관련 - 화자들의 근무지
남자가 첫 번째 대사에서 여자가 만든 자료집이 회사의 신입 하급 회계
사들이 빨리 적응하는 데 정말 도움이 될 것(They're really going
to help the firm's new junior accountants get settled
quickly)이라고 말하고 있으므로 정답은 (A)이다.

66 What does the woman say she learned in a previous job?
(A) How to set work performance goals
(B) How to recruit talented job candidates
(C) How to ensure an orientation is thorough
(D) How to keep employee information confidential

번역 여자는 이전 직장에서 무엇을 배웠다고 말하는가?
(A) 업무 성과 목표를 세우는 법
(R) 유능한 입사 지원자를 모집하는 법
(C) 오리엔테이션을 철저하게 준비하는 법
(D) 사원 정보를 기밀로 유지하는 법

해설 세부 사항 관련 - 여자가 이전 직장에서 배웠다고 말하는 것
여자가 첫 번째 대사에서 첫 직장 인사부에서 일할 때 배운 것(That's
something I learned in my first job in human resources)
이라고 말하며 오리엔테이션은 중요한 회사 소개이기 때문에 필요
한 정보가 모두 포함되도록 세심하게 준비해야 한다(Orientations
are an important introduction ~ all the necessary
information is included)고 말하고 있으므로 정답은 (C)이다.

어휘 work performance 업무 성과 recruit 모집하다 talented
유능한 job candidate 입사 지원자 thorough 철저한
confidential 기밀의

67 Look at the graphic. Which item in the orientation packet does the man express concern about?
(A) Item 2
(B) Item 3
(C) Item 4
(D) Item 5

번역 시각 정보에 의하면, 오리엔테이션 자료집에서 어떤 항목에 대해 남자
가 우려를 표하는가?
(A) 항목 2
(B) 항목 3
(C) 항목 4
(D) 항목 5

해설 시각 정보 연계 - 남자가 우려하는 것
남자가 마지막 대사에서 워크스테이션을 설치하는 방법이 신입 사
원들에게는 조금 헷갈릴까 봐 걱정이 된다(I'm afraid these
directions for setting up a workstation will be a little
confusing for the new hires)고 말했고, 목차에 따르면 워크스테이
션 설치 방법은 항목 5에 나와 있으므로 정답은 (D)이다.

68-70 대화+영수증

┌──┐
│ M-Cn Good morning! How can I help you?   │
│   │
│ W-Am Hi, 68 **I just finished checking out with one of** │
│   **your store's self-service machines, but I see**   │
│   **on my receipt that I made a mistake with one**   │
│   **of the fruit items. I put in the wrong quantity**   │
│   **for it.**   │
│   │
│ M-Cn I'm happy to fix that for you. Which item was   │
│   it?   │
│   │
│ W-Am This one here. 69 **There are three of them in**   │
│   **the bag I picked up, so I entered "three," but**   │
│   **this is not the price that was on the sign. I**   │
│   **guess the bag is one unit.**   │
│   │
│ M-Cn 69 **Yes, that's right. OK, I'll refund the extra**│
│   **money you paid.** 70 **May I have the credit card** │
│   **you used for the purchase?**   │
└──┘

남: 좋은 아침입니다! 무엇을 도와드릴까요?

여: 안녕하세요, 방금 당신의 상점에 있는 무인 계산기 중 하나에서
결제를 마쳤는데, 영수증을 보니 과일 품목 하나에 제가 실수를
했더라고요. 수량을 잘못 입력했어요.

남: 기꺼이 처리해 드리겠습니다. 어떤 품목이었나요?

여: 여기 이거요. 제가 집어 온 봉지에 세 개가 들어 있길래 '세 개'라
고 입력했는데 가격표에 있는 가격이 아니더라구요. 봉지가 하
나의 단위인 것 같아요.

남: 네, 맞습니다. 그럼 제가 지불하신 초과 금액을 환불해 드리겠습
니다. 구매에 사용하신 신용카드를 주시겠어요?

┌──┐
│ 어휘 check out 결제하다 receipt 영수증 quantity 양 fix│
│   바로잡다 enter 입력하다 sign 간판, 표지판 refund │
│   환불하다 extra 추가의 purchase 구매   │
└──┘

RECEIPT

Item	Quantity	Price
Bananas	1	$3.00
Spinach	1	$4.50
Avocados	**69** 3	$6.30
Watermelon	2	$10.10
		Total: $23.90

영수증

품목	수량	가격
바나나	1	3달러
시금치	1	4.5달러
아보카도	**69** 3	6.3달러
수박	2	10.1달러
		합계: 23.9달러

68 What problem does the woman describe?
(A) A checkout machine is malfunctioning.
(B) An item's quantity was entered incorrectly.
(C) An available discount was not applied.
(D) Some fruit is in poor condition.

번역 여자는 어떤 문제를 설명하는가?
(A) 무인 계산기가 오작동하고 있다.
(B) 품목의 수량이 부정확하게 입력되었다.
(C) 해당하는 할인이 적용되지 않았다.
(D) 일부 과일의 상태가 좋지 않다.

해설 세부 사항 관련 - 여자가 언급하는 문제
여자가 첫 대사에서 방금 무인 계산기에서 결제를 마쳤는데, 영수증을 보니 과일 품목 하나에 자신이 실수를 했다(I just finished checking out with one of your store's self-service machines, but I see on my receipt that I made a mistake with one of the fruit items)면서 수량을 잘못 입력했다(I put in the wrong quantity for it)고 말하고 있으므로 정답은 (B)이다.

어휘 malfunction 오작동하다 incorrectly 부정확하게 apply 적용하다 be in poor condition 상태가 좋지 않다

> **Paraphrasing**
> 대화의 I put in the wrong quantity for it.
> → 정답의 An item's quantity was entered incorrectly.

69 Look at the graphic. Which amount will be partially refunded?
(A) $3.00
(B) $4.50
(C) $6.30
(D) $10.10

번역 시각 정보에 의하면, 어떤 금액에서 일부 환불이 될 것인가?
(A) 3달러
(B) 4.5달러
(C) 6.3달러
(D) 10.1달러

해설 시각 정보 연계 - 일부 환불될 금액
여자가 두 번째 대사에서 집어 온 봉지에 세 개가 들어 있길래 '세 개'라고 입력했는데 가격표에 나와 있는 가격이 아니며 봉지가 하나의 단위인 것 같다(There are three of them in the bag I picked up, so I entered "three," but this is not the price that was on the sign. I guess the bag is one unit)고 하자, 남자가 맞다(Yes, that's right)면서 지불한 초과 금액을 환불해 주겠다(I'll refund the extra money you paid)고 말하고 있고, 영수증에 따르면 수량이 3인 것은 아보카도로 가격이 6.3달러이므로 정답은 (C)이다.

어휘 partially 부분적으로

70 What does the man ask the woman for?
(A) A coupon code
(B) A container of produce
(C) A rewards card
(D) A payment method

번역 남자는 여자에게 무엇을 요청하는가?
(A) 쿠폰 코드
(B) 농산물을 담을 용기
(C) 멤버십 카드
(D) 결제 수단

해설 세부 사항 관련 - 남자의 요청 사항
남자가 마지막 대사에서 구매에 사용한 신용카드를 요청(May I have the credit card you used for the purchase?)하고 있으므로 정답은 (D)이다.

어휘 container 그릇, 용기 produce 농산물 payment 지불 method 방법, 수단

> **Paraphrasing**
> 대화의 the credit card you used for the purchase
> → 정답의 A payment method

PART 4

71-73 전화 메시지

M-Cn Hi, Ms. Bailey. It's Diego Medero from Bader Motorcycles. **71 Our company is having an issue that we'd like your professional legal advice on.** Uh, I'll give you the basics now. **72 We're concerned because another company, Rinford Services, recently adopted a logo that looks very similar to ours**—a golden wing on top of the company name written in black letters. I'm sending you an e-mail with images of both so you can see for yourself. Now, you should know that [73] **Rinford is a shipping company, so it's not one of our competitors.** But we'd still prefer not to have our brands confused. Could you call me back to discuss our options for handling this matter? Thanks.

안녕하세요, 베일리 씨. 저는 베이더 모터사이클의 디에고 메데로입니다. 저희 회사는 귀하의 전문적인 법률 자문을 구하고 싶은 문제가 하나 있습니다. 음, 지금 기본적인 사실을 설명드리겠습니다. 린퍼드 서비스라는 다른 회사에서 최근에 저희 로고와 매우 유사한 로고를 채택해서 걱정이 됩니다. 검은색 글자로 쓴 회사명 위에 금색 날개가 달린 로고입니다. 직접 보실 수 있도록 두 이미지를 이메일로 보내드리겠습니다. 자, 린퍼드가 해운회사이므로 저희 경쟁업체가 아니라는 점은 아실 겁니다. 하지만 여전히 저희 브랜드에 혼동이 생기지 않기를 바랍니다. 이 문제를 해결할 수 있는 방안에 대해 의논하기 위해 저에게 전화를 주실 수 있을까요? 감사합니다.

어휘 professional 전문적인 legal 법적의 advice 조언 adopt 채택하다 shipping 해상 운송 competitor 경쟁업체 confuse 혼동시키다 handle 처리하다

71 Who is the speaker calling?
(A) A publicist
(B) A graphic designer
(C) A property manager
(D) A corporate attorney

번역 화자는 누구에게 전화를 걸고 있는가?
(A) 홍보 담당자
(B) 그래픽 디자이너
(C) 부동산 관리자
(D) 기업 변호사

해설 전체 내용 관련 - 화자가 전화를 건 대상
화자가 초반부에서 저희 회사는 귀하의 전문적인 법률 자문을 구하고 싶은 문제가 하나 있다(Our company is having an issue that we'd like your professional legal advice on)고 하므로 전화 수신인은 기업의 변호사임을 알 수 있다. 따라서 정답은 (D)이다.

어휘 property 자산, 부동산

72 What is the speaker concerned about?
(A) The terms of a contract
(B) A building directory
(C) A logo design
(D) A shipping method

번역 화자는 무엇에 대해 우려하는가?
(A) 계약의 조건
(B) 건물 안내도
(C) 로고 디자인
(D) 운송 방법

해설 세부 사항 관련 - 화자의 우려 사항
화자가 중반부에서 린퍼드 서비스라는 다른 회사에서 최근에 저희 로고와 매우 유사한 로고를 택했기 때문에 우려스럽다(We're concerned because another company, Rinford Services,

recently adopted a logo that looks very similar to ours ~)고 말하고 있으므로 정답은 (C)이다.

어휘 terms 조건 contract 계약 directory 안내도 method 방법, 수단

73 What does the speaker say about Rinford Services?
(A) It is in a different field.
(B) It was recently founded.
(C) It is based overseas.
(D) It is well-known.

번역 화자는 린퍼드 서비스에 대해 뭐라고 말하는가?
(A) 다른 분야에 있다.
(B) 최근에 설립되었다.
(C) 해외에 본사가 있다.
(D) 유명하다.

해설 세부 사항 관련 - 화자가 린퍼드 서비스에 대해 언급하는 것
화자가 후반부에 린퍼드가 해운회사이므로 저희 경쟁업체가 아니다(Rinford is a shipping company, so it's not one of our competitors)라고 말하고 있으므로 정답은 (A)이다.

어휘 field 분야 found 설립하다 base ~에 본부를 두다 well-known 유명한

74-76 광고

W-Br Are you planning to make some improvements to your home this fall? Make sure to stop by Barnett Brothers beforehand to pick up the supplies and equipment you'll need. [74] **We carry everything from power tools to paint, and light fixtures to building materials.** Not sure what to look for? We're happy to help! [75] **Barnett Brothers is famous for the expert advice provided by our friendly floor staff.** And, throughout October, [76] **we'll be offering discounts on weatherproofing supplies to help you prepare your house for winter.** Visit BarnettBrothers.com to learn more.

이번 가을에 당신의 집을 개선할 계획이신가요? 필요한 용품과 장비를 구매하기 위해 미리 바넷 브라더스에 들러주세요. 저희는 전동 공구에서 페인트, 조명 기구, 건축 자재까지 모든 것을 취급합니다. 무엇을 찾아야 할지 모르시겠다고요? 기꺼이 도와드리겠습니다! 바넷 브라더스는 친절한 매장 직원들이 제공하는 전문가 조언으로 유명합니다. 그리고 10월 한 달 동안 집의 월동 준비를 돕기 위해 내후성 용품 할인을 제공합니다. 자세한 내용은 BarnettBrothers.com을 방문하세요.

어휘 improvement 개선 stop by 잠깐 들르다 beforehand 사전에 equipment 장비 carry (가게에서 물건을) 취급하다 power tool 전동 공구 light fixture 조명 기구 material 재료 be famous for ~으로 유명하다 expert 전문가 advice 조언 friendly 친절한 floor staff 매장 직원 weatherproofing 내후성의(다양한 기상 조건에 견딜 수 있는) prepare 준비하다

74 What most likely is being advertised?
(A) A construction company
(B) A real estate Web site
(C) A hardware store
(D) An interior design firm

번역 어떤 것이 광고되고 있는가?
(A) 건설회사
(B) 부동산 웹사이트
(C) 철물점
(D) 실내 디자인 회사

해설 전체 내용 관련 - 광고되고 있는 것
화자가 초반부에 전동 공구에서 페인트, 조명 기구, 건축 자재까지 모든 것을 취급한다(We carry everything from power tools to paint, and light fixtures to building materials)고 했으므로 철물점을 광고하고 있다는 것을 알 수 있다. 따라서 정답은 (C)이다.

어휘 construction 건설, 공사   real estate 부동산, 부동산 중개업

---

75 What is the business known for?
(A) Its pricing
(B) Its speed
(C) Its creativity
(D) Its customer service

번역 이 사업체는 무엇으로 알려져 있는가?
(A) 가격 책정
(B) 속도
(C) 창의성
(D) 고객 서비스

해설 세부 사항 관련 - 이 사업체가 알려져 있는 것
화자가 중반부에 바넷 브라더스는 친절한 매장 직원들이 제공하는 전문가 조언으로 유명하다(Barnett Brothers is famous for the expert advice provided by our friendly floor staff)고 말하고 있으므로 정답은 (D)이다.

어휘 be known for ~으로 알려져 있다

> **Paraphrasing**
> 담화의 famous for → 질문의 known for
> 담화의 the expert advice provided by our friendly floor staff → 정답의 Its customer service

---

76 What does the speaker say is on a Web site?
(A) Hours of operation
(B) Details about a sale
(C) Pictures of houses
(D) Positive reviews

번역 화자는 웹사이트에 무엇이 있다고 말하는가?
(A) 영업 시간
(B) 할인 행사에 대한 세부 내용
(C) 주택 사진
(D) 긍정적인 후기

해설 세부 사항 관련 - 웹사이트에 있다고 말하는 것
화자가 마지막에 내후성 용품들에 대해 할인을 제공할 것(we'll be offering discounts on weatherproofing supplies ~)이라면서 자세한 내용은 BarnettBrothers.com을 방문하라(Visit BarnettBrothers.com to learn more)고 하고 있으므로 정답은 (B)이다.

어휘 operation 운영   positive 긍정적인

> **Paraphrasing**
> 담화의 discounts → 정답의 a sale

77-79 전화 메시지

M-Au Hi, Robin. **77 This is Noah Adkins from Lakeside Dental.** We're looking forward to speaking to you about the hygienist position on Thursday. **78 I'm calling to make sure you know that this first interview will just be a conversation about your skills and experience.** You won't be interacting with patients. There's been some confusion about this among our other candidates. All right, then **79 we'll see you at two on Thursday.** Oh, and—you should probably start heading over quite early. It can be hard to find parking around here.

안녕하세요, 로빈. 저는 레이크사이드 치과의 노아 애드킨스입니다. 목요일에 치위생사직에 대해 당신과 이야기를 나누기를 고대하고 있습니다. 이 첫 번째 면접은 단지 당신의 역량과 경험에 대한 대화가 될 것임을 알려드리려고 전화드렸습니다. 환자들과 소통은 하지 않으실 겁니다. 그동안 다른 지원자들 사이에서 이 점에 대한 혼동이 좀 있었습니다. 자 그럼, 목요일 두 시에 뵙겠습니다. 아, 그리고, 꽤 일찍 출발하시는 게 좋을 거예요. 이 근처에 주차할 곳을 찾기가 어려울 수 있습니다.

어휘 hygienist 치위생사   position 일자리   skill 기술, 역량   experience 경험   interact with ~와 상호작용하다   patient 환자   confusion 혼동   candidate 지원자   head over ~로 향하다

---

77 Where most likely does the speaker work?
(A) At a hair salon
(B) At a dentist's office
(C) At an auto repair shop
(D) At a dry cleaning business

번역 화자는 어디에서 일하겠는가?
(A) 미용실
(B) 치과
(C) 자동차 정비소
(D) 세탁소

해설 전체 내용 관련 - 화자의 근무지
화자가 초반부에 자신을 레이크사이드 치과의 노아 애드킨스(This is Noah Adkins from Lakeside Dental)라고 말하는 것으로 보아 화자는 치과에서 근무하고 있음을 알 수 있다. 따라서 정답은 (B)이다.

어휘 dentist 치과 의사

78 What is the speaker calling about?
(A) An appliance delivery
(B) A customer appointment
(C) A safety inspection
(D) A job interview

번역 화자는 무슨 일로 전화를 걸고 있는가?
(A) 가전제품 배송
(B) 고객 예약
(C) 안전 점검
(D) 취업 면접

해설 전체 내용 관련 - 전화를 건 이유
화자가 중반부에 이 첫 번째 면접은 단지 당신의 역량과 경험에 대한 대화가 될 것임을 알려드리려고 전화드렸다(I'm calling to make sure you know that this first interview will just be a conversation about your skills and experience)고 말하고 있으므로 정답은 (D)이다.

어휘 appointment (진료 등의) 예약

79 Why does the speaker say, "It can be hard to find parking around here"?
(A) To explain a recommendation
(B) To justify an expense
(C) To express doubt about a plan
(D) To request patience with a delay

번역 화자가 "이 근처에 주차할 곳을 찾기가 어려울 수 있습니다"라고 말한 이유는?
(A) 권장 사항을 설명하려고
(B) 비용을 정당화하려고
(C) 계획에 대한 의구심을 표현하려고
(D) 지연에 대한 양해를 부탁하려고

해설 화자의 의도 파악 - 이 근처에 주차할 곳을 찾기가 어려울 수 있다는 말의 의도
앞에서 목요일 두 시에 뵙겠다(we'll see you at two on Thursday)면서 꽤 일찍 출발하는 게 좋을 것(you should probably start heading over quite early)이라고 말한 뒤 인용문을 언급한 것으로 보아, 주차가 어려울 수 있어 일찍 출발할 것을 권장하려는 의도로 한 말임을 알 수 있다. 따라서 정답은 (A)이다.

어휘 recommendation 권고, 추천 justify 정당화하다 expense 비용, 지출 doubt 의구심 patience 인내심 delay 지연

80-82 팟캐스트

W-Am Today's episode of *Tech Insider* is for some of you who aren't part of the technology industry yet, but want to be. Specifically, [80] **I'll be talking**

about intensive courses in computer coding, and how to choose the one that best suits your goals and existing skills. These days, there are many options for coding courses. [81] **It's important to carry out detailed research on several factors before enrolling.** I'll tell you what information you need to know and how to find it—with some help from my guest today. [82] **His name is Hinata Kondo, and he has written extensively about coding courses for TechNation.com and other sites.** Hinata, welcome.

<테크 인사이더>의 오늘 에피소드는 아직 기술 산업에 종사하지는 않지만 그러기를 원하는 분들을 위해 마련되었습니다. 구체적으로 말하자면, 컴퓨터 코딩 집중 과정에 대해, 그리고 여러분의 목표와 기존 역량에 가장 잘 맞는 과정을 고르는 법에 대해 이야기하겠습니다. 요즘 정말 많은 코딩 강좌가 있습니다. 등록을 하기 전에 몇 가지 요소에 대해 상세한 조사를 하는 것이 중요합니다. 어떤 정보를 알아야 하는지, 그리고 그것을 어떻게 찾아야 하는지 알려드리겠습니다. 오늘 초대 손님의 도움을 받아서요. 그의 이름은 히나타 콘도이며 그는 TechNation.com을 비롯한 여러 웹사이트에 코딩 강좌에 대해 광범위하게 글을 써왔습니다. 히나타, 어서 오세요.

어휘 technology 기술 industry 산업 specifically 구체적으로 말하자면 intensive 집중적인 best suit 가장 적합하다 goal 목표 existing 기존의 skill 기술, 역량 carry out 수행하다 factor 요인 enroll 등록하다 extensively 광범위하게

80 What is the focus of the episode?
(A) Developing a mobile application
(B) Taking advantage of a new technology
(C) Selecting a training program
(D) Evaluating job candidates

번역 에피소드의 주제는 무엇인가?
(A) 모바일 앱 개발하기
(B) 신기술 활용하기
(C) 교육 프로그램 선택하기
(D) 입사 지원자 평가하기

해설 전체 내용 관련 - 에피소드의 주제
화자가 초반부에 컴퓨터 코딩 집중 과정에 대해, 그리고 여러분의 목표와 기존 역량에 가장 잘 맞는 과정을 고르는 법에 대해 이야기하겠다(I'll be talking about intensive courses in computer coding, and how to choose the one that best suits your goals and existing skills)고 말하고 있으므로 정답은 (C)이다.

어휘 develop 개발하다 take advantage of ~을 이용하다 select 고르다 evaluate 평가하다 candidate 지원자

Paraphrasing
담화의 intensive courses in computer coding
→ 정답의 a training program

81 What does the speaker say is important?
(A) Conducting thorough research
(B) Specifying a set of goals
(C) Joining an industry association
(D) Asking others for recommendations

번역 화자는 무엇이 중요하다고 말하는가?
(A) 철저한 조사 실시하기
(B) 일련의 목표들 명시하기
(C) 산업 협회에 가입하기
(D) 다른 사람들에게 추천 부탁하기

해설 **세부 사항 관련 - 화자가 중요하다고 하는 것**
화자가 중반부에 등록을 하기 전에 몇 가지 요소에 대해 상세한 조사를 하는 것이 중요하다(It's important to carry out detailed research on several factors before enrolling)고 말하고 있으므로 정답은 (A)이다.

어휘 conduct 실시하다 thorough 철저한 specify 명시하다
association 협회 recommendation 권고, 추천

> **Paraphrasing**
> 담화의 carry out detailed research
> → 정답의 Conducting thorough research

82 Who most likely is Hinata Kondo?
(A) A professional recruiter
(B) An online journalist
(C) A business consultant
(D) A computer programmer

번역 히나타 콘도는 누구이겠는가?
(A) 채용 전문가
(B) 온라인 저널리스트
(C) 경영 컨설턴트
(D) 컴퓨터 프로그래머

해설 **세부 사항 관련 - 히나타 콘도의 직업**
화자가 마지막에 그의 이름은 히나타 콘도이며 그는 TechNation.com을 비롯한 여러 웹사이트에 코딩 강좌에 대해 광범위하게 글을 써왔다(His name is Hinata Kondo, and he has written extensively about coding courses for TechNation.com and other sites)고 말하는 것으로 보아 히나타 콘도는 온라인에서 활동하는 저널리스트라는 것을 알 수 있다. 따라서 정답은 (B)이다.

어휘 recruiter 채용 담당자 journalist 기자

83-85 관광 정보

M-Cn **83 Welcome to today's tour of Fox Canyon, one of the highlights of Hodges National Park.** I'm Eric, your guide. I'll also be driving the UTV, or utility terrain vehicle, that will take us to the canyon. It's about a twenty-minute drive across the desert. You can take pictures and video along the way—**84 just make sure to keep your seat belt fastened until**

we've come to a complete stop at the canyon. Also, for anyone who's interested, I have a few copies of a park vegetation guide. **85 It's just one page, but it shows a lot of the trees, cacti, and wildflowers you'll be able to see today.**

호지스 국립 공원의 하이라이트 중 하나인 폭스 협곡 투어에 오신 것을 환영합니다. 저는 여러분의 인솔자 에릭입니다. 저는 또한 협곡까지 이동하기 위한 UTV, 즉 다목적 전지형 차량도 운전할 겁니다. 사막을 가로질러 차로 약 20분 정도 걸립니다. 가는 길에 사진과 영상을 찍으실 수 있습니다. 다만 협곡에 완전히 정차할 때까지는 안전띠를 꼭 매고 계셔야 합니다. 또한 관심이 있는 분을 위해 제가 공원 식물 안내서를 몇 부 가지고 있습니다. 달랑 한 장짜리이지만, 오늘 볼 수 있는 많은 나무와 선인장, 야생화가 소개되어 있습니다.

어휘 canyon 협곡 highlight 하이라이트, 가장 좋은 부분 utility terrain vehicle(UTV) 다목적 전지형 차량 desert 사막 fasten 매다 come to a complete stop 완전히 정차하다 vegetation 식물, 초목 cacti 선인장류 wildflower 야생화

83 Where is the tour taking place?
(A) At a city zoo
(B) At a national park
(C) At a vegetable farm
(D) At a historical site

번역 투어는 어디에서 진행되고 있는가?
(A) 도시 동물원
(B) 국립 공원
(C) 채소 농장
(D) 유적지

해설 **전체 내용 관련 - 투어의 진행 장소**
화자가 도입부에 호지스 국립 공원의 하이라이트 중 하나인 폭스 협곡 투어에 오신 것을 환영한다(Welcome to today's tour of Fox Canyon, one of the highlights of Hodges National Park)고 말하고 있으므로 투어는 국립 공원에서 진행되고 있다는 것을 알 수 있다. 따라서 정답은 (B)이다.

84 What does the speaker tell the listeners to do during a drive?
(A) Refrain from speaking
(B) Handle some electronics carefully
(C) Watch out for some animals
(D) Leave their seat belts on

번역 화자는 청자들에게 차로 이동 중에 무엇을 하라고 말하는가?
(A) 말하지 않기
(B) 전자 제품들을 조심스럽게 다루기
(C) 일부 동물들을 조심하기
(D) 안전띠 매고 있기

해설 **세부 사항 관련 - 차로 이동 중에 화자의 요청 사항**
화자가 중반부에 협곡에 완전히 정차할 때까지는 안전띠를 꼭 매고 있어야 한다(just make sure to keep your seat belt fastened until we've come to a complete stop at the canyon)고 말하고 있으므로 정답은 (D)이다.

어휘 refrain from ~을 삼가다 handle 다루다 electronics 전자 제품
carefully 조심스럽게 watch out for ~을 조심하다

> **Paraphrasing**
> 담화의 keep your seat belt fastened
> → 정답의 Leave their seat belts on

85 According to a speaker, what is shown on a
handout?
(A) A route map
(B) Meal options
(C) Operating instructions
(D) Images of plants

번역 화자에 따르면, 유인물에는 무엇이 보이겠는가?
(A) 노선도
(B) 식사 메뉴
(C) 사용 설명서
(D) 식물 이미지

해설 세부 사항 관련 - 유인물에 보이는 것
화자가 마지막에 달랑 한 장짜리이지만, 오늘 볼 수 있는 많은 나무
와 선인장, 야생화가 소개되어 있다(It's just one page, but it
shows a lot of the trees, cacti, and wildflowers you'll be
able to see today)고 말하고 있으므로 정답은 (D)이다.

어휘 handout 유인물

> **Paraphrasing**
> 담화의 a lot of the trees, cacti, and wildflowers
> → 정답의 Images of plants

86-88 공지

W-Br Thank you all for coming in early. As you
know, **86 our bookstore chain has been losing
customers since Internet booksellers became
popular. Management has come to the conclusion
that what our stores need is a unique, local
flavor**—after all, you can't get that online. So,
**87 headquarters just let us know that each location
no longer has to follow strict guidelines about
brand identity.** We can make changes to our
store's interior and even inventory. Exciting, isn't it?
And please know that your input will be welcome.
In fact, **88 I'm going to form an "Improvements
Committee." Those of you who have time should
sign up.**

일찍 와주신 여러분께 감사드립니다. 아시다시피, 우리 서점 체인점은
인터넷 서점이 대중화된 이후로 고객을 잃고 있습니다. 경영진은 우리
서점에 필요한 것이 독특하고 지역적인 특색이라는 결론에 도달했습
니다. 어쨌든 온라인에서는 그것을 얻을 수 없잖아요. 따라서, 본사에서
방금 알려주기를 각 지점은 더 이상 브랜드 정체성에 대한 엄격한 지침
을 따를 필요가 없다고 합니다. 우리 서점의 내부도, 심지어 재고 목록

도 바꿀 수 있습니다. 설레지 않나요? 그리고 여러분의 의견도 환영한
다는 점을 알아주세요. 실은, '개선 위원회'를 구성할 계획입니다. 여러
분 중에서 시간이 있는 분은 가입해 주세요.

어휘 popular 인기 있는 management 경영진 come to the
conclusion that ~이라는 결론에 도달하다 flavor 특색
headquarters 본사, 본부 strict 엄격한 identity 정체성
inventory 재고 목록 input 조언, 입력 form 구성하다
improvement 개선 committee 위원회 sign up ~에 가입하다

86 What does the speaker imply when she says, "you
can't get that online"?
(A) It is becoming difficult to obtain some
merchandise.
(B) She is proud of the high-quality service
provided at the store.
(C) Some news has not been communicated to
the public yet.
(D) The company will differentiate itself from
some competitors.

번역 화자가 "온라인에서는 그것을 얻을 수 없잖아요"라고 말할 때, 그 의도
는 무엇인가?
(A) 일부 상품을 구하기가 점점 어려워지고 있다.
(B) 상점에서 제공하는 고품질 서비스에 자부심이 있다.
(C) 일부 소식이 아직 대중에게 전달되지 않았다.
(D) 회사는 경쟁업체들과 차별화할 것이다.

해설 화자의 의도 파악 - 온라인에서는 그것을 얻을 수 없다는 말의 의
도
앞에서 우리 서점 체인점은 인터넷 서점이 대중화된 이후로 고객을 잃
고 있다(our bookstore chain has been losing customers
since Internet booksellers became popular)면서 경영진
은 우리 서점에 필요한 것은 독특하고 지역적인 특색이라는 결론에
도달했다(Management has come to the conclusion that
what our stores need is a unique, local flavor)고 말한 뒤,
인용문을 언급하고 있으므로 회사는 독특하고 지역적인 색깔을 가져
경쟁사들과 차별화할 것이라는 의도로 한 말임을 알 수 있다. 따라서
정답은 (D)이다.

어휘 obtain 획득하다 merchandise 상품 high-quality 고품질의
differentiate 차별화하다 competitor 경쟁업체

87 What is the main topic of the announcement?
(A) A revision to a corporate policy
(B) The relocation of a store branch
(C) A search for a new supplier
(D) The launch of a marketing campaign

번역 공지의 주제는 무엇인가?
(A) 회사 정책의 변경
(B) 지점의 이전
(C) 새 공급업체 검색
(D) 마케팅 캠페인 개시

해설 전체 내용 관련 - 공지의 주제
화자가 중반부에 본사에서 방금 알려주기를 각 지점은 더 이상

브랜드 정체성에 대한 엄격한 지침을 따를 필요가 없다고 한다 (headquarters just let us know that each location no longer has to follow strict guidelines about brand identity)고 했으므로 정답은 (A)이다.

어휘 revision 변경 corporate 기업의 policy 정책 relocation 이전 supplier 공급업체 launch 개시, 출시

> **Paraphrasing**
> 담화의 no longer has to follow strict guidelines
> → 정답의 A revision to a corporate policy

88 What are some of the listeners asked to do?
(A) Check some inventory
(B) Visit some retail spaces
(C) Join a committee
(D) Set up a display

번역 청자들 중 일부는 무엇을 하라고 요청받았는가?
(A) 재고 목록 확인하기
(B) 소매점 방문하기
(C) 위원회 가입하기
(D) 진열하기

해설 세부 사항 관련 - 일부 청자들이 요청받는 일
화자가 마지막에 '개선 위원회'를 구성할 계획(I'm going to form an "Improvements Committee.")이라면서 시간이 있는 분은 가입해 줄 것을 요청(Those of you who have time should sign up)하고 있으므로 정답은 (C)이다.

어휘 retail space 소매점 set up 설치하다 display 진열

> **Paraphrasing**
> 담화의 sign up → 정답의 Join

89-91 연설

M-Au **89 It's great to see everyone gathered here to say goodbye to Angela Thorne.** Our hotel has been lucky to have her as our head of human resources for the past five years. In that time, **90 she did wonderful work in fostering a culture of transparency and teamwork here.** Let's hope that she can make a similar impact on our other locations as the new regional vice president of HR. Now, we'd usually present Angela with a gift at this point, but she's asked that we give money to one of her favorite causes, animal welfare, instead. So, I'm proud to announce that **91 I've sent a generous check to Herrick Animal Shelter.**

안젤라 쏜에게 작별 인사를 하기 위해 모여주신 여러분 반갑습니다. 우리 호텔로서는 그녀가 인사부장으로 지난 5년간 일해주신 것이 행운이었습니다. 그동안 **그녀는 이곳에 투명성과 팀워크의 문화를 조성하는 데 훌륭한 역할을 했습니다.** 그녀가 새로운 지역의 인사 담당 부사장으

로서 다른 지점들에서도 같은 영향력을 펼치기를 바랍니다. 자, 보통 이 시점에서 안젤라에게 선물을 증정해야 하지만, 그녀는 선물 대신에 그녀가 좋아하는 관심사 중 하나인 동물 복지에 돈을 기부해 달라고 부탁했습니다. 그래서 **헤릭 동물 보호소에 넉넉한 후원금을 보냈음을** 자랑스럽게 알려드립니다.

어휘 gather 모이다 human resources 인사부 foster 조성하다 transparency 투명성 impact 영향 regional 지역의 vice president 부사장, 부회장 present 수여하다 cause 대의명분 welfare 복지 send a check 수표를 보내다 generous 넉넉한, 관대한

89 What event is taking place?
(A) A community fund-raiser
(B) A going-away party
(C) An awards dinner
(D) A press conference

번역 어떤 행사가 열리고 있는가?
(A) 지역 사회 모금 행사
(B) 송별회
(C) 시상식 만찬
(D) 기자 회견

해설 전체 내용 관련 - 열리고 있는 행사
화자가 도입부에 안젤라 쏜에게 작별 인사를 하기 위해 모여주신 여러분 반갑다(It's great to see everyone gathered here to say goodbye to Angela Thorne)고 말하고 있으므로 정답은 (B)이다.

90 What does the speaker praise Angela Thorne for?
(A) Improving a workplace's culture
(B) Increasing awareness of a local issue
(C) Forming an effective project team
(D) Managing a budget wisely

번역 화자는 무엇에 대해 안젤라 쏜을 칭찬하는가?
(A) 직장 문화를 개선한 것
(B) 지역 문제에 대한 인식을 높인 것
(C) 효과적인 프로젝트팀을 구성한 것
(D) 예산을 현명하게 관리한 것

해설 세부 사항 관련 - 화자가 안젤라 쏜에 대해 칭찬하는 부분
화자가 초반부에 그녀는 이곳에 투명성과 팀워크의 문화를 조성하는 데 훌륭한 역할을 했다(she did wonderful work in fostering a culture of transparency and teamwork here)고 말하고 있으므로 정답은 (A)이다.

어휘 improve 향상시키다 workplace 직장, 일터 awareness 인식 form 구성하다 effective 효과적인 budget 예산 wisely 현명하게

> **Paraphrasing**
> 담화의 fostering a culture of transparency and teamwork → 정답의 Improving a workplace's culture

91 What does the speaker say he has done?
(A) Prepared a visual presentation
(B) Invited another person to speak
(C) Made a charitable donation
(D) Purchased a personal gift

번역 화자는 자신이 무엇을 했다고 말하는가?
(A) 시각적 발표 자료를 준비했다.
(B) 연설해 줄 사람을 초대했다.
(C) 자선 기부금을 냈다.
(D) 개인적인 선물을 구매했다.

해설 세부 사항 관련 - 화자가 했다고 말하는 것
화자가 마지막에 헤릭 동물 보호소에 넉넉한 후원금을 보냈다(I've sent a generous check to Herrick Animal Shelter)고 말하고 있으므로 정답은 (C)이다.

어휘 prepare 준비하다   visual 시각적인   charitable 자선의   donation 기부금   personal 개인적인

> **Paraphrasing**
> 담화의 sent a generous check to Herrick Animal Shelter → 정답의 Made a charitable donation

92-94 회의 발췌

> W-Br   Since we're speaking of plans for our new manufacturing plant, I'd like to bring up an idea I had. ⁹² **During my family vacation last week, we toured a chocolate factory**, and the best part was an enclosed walkway that went right over the production floor. We could see everything that was going on, and we weren't bothering the workers. I believe that people would be interested in seeing how our products are made— ⁹³ **especially our baseballs and baseball gloves.** ⁹⁴ **Why don't we include a walkway like that in the new plant and start offering tours? It seems to me like it wouldn't be hard to have that feature added to the plans,** but I'm not an architect.

> 우리의 새 제조 공장 설립 계획에 대해 이야기하는 김에 제가 가진 의견을 하나 제시하고 싶어요. **지난주에 가족 휴가를 갔을 때 초콜릿 공장을 견학했었는데요.** 가장 좋았던 부분은 생산 현장 바로 위를 가로 지르는 밀폐형 통로였어요. 진행되는 모든 것을 볼 수 있었고, 작업자들을 방해하지도 않았어요. 사람들은 우리 제품이 어떻게 만들어지는지 보는 데 관심이 있을 것 같아요. **특히 우리 야구공과 야구 장갑이요. 새 공장에 그런 통로를 넣어서 견학을 시작하면 어떨까요? 저에게는 그런 장치를 설계도에 추가하는 일이 어려울 것 같지 않지만,** 제가 건축가는 아니죠.

> 어휘   manufacturing plant 제조 공장   bring up (의견 등을) 제시하다   tour 견학하다   factory 공장   enclosed 사방이 막힌   walkway 통로   production floor 생산 현장   bother 성가시게 하다   include 포함하다   feature 특징   add 추가하다   architect 건축가

92 What did the speaker recently do?
(A) She took a factory tour.
(B) She read a journal article.
(C) She spoke with some workers.
(D) She hosted some visitors.

번역 화자는 최근에 무슨 일을 했는가?
(A) 공장 견학을 했다.
(B) 학술지 기사를 읽었다.
(C) 근로자들과 이야기했다.
(D) 방문자들을 접대했다.

해설 세부 사항 관련 - 화자가 최근에 한 일
화자가 초반부에 지난주에 가족 휴가를 갔을 때 초콜릿 공장을 견학했다(During my family vacation last week, we toured a chocolate factory)고 했으므로 정답은 (A)이다.

어휘 journal 학술지   article 글, 기사   host (행사 등을) 주최하다   visitor 방문자

> **Paraphrasing**
> 담화의 last week → 질문의 recently
>
> 담화의 toured a chocolate factory → 정답의 took a factory tour

93 What does the speaker's company make?
(A) Musical instruments
(B) Sporting goods
(C) Snack foods
(D) Wooden furniture

번역 화자의 회사는 무엇을 만드는가?
(A) 악기
(B) 스포츠용품
(C) 간식
(D) 목제 가구

해설 세부 사항 관련 - 화자의 회사가 만드는 제품
화자가 후반부에 특히 우리 야구공과 야구 장갑(especially our baseballs and baseball gloves)이라고 했으므로 정답은 (B)이다.

어휘 wooden 나무로 된

> **Paraphrasing**
> 담화의 baseballs and baseball gloves → 정답의 Sporting goods

94 What does the speaker mean when she says, "I'm not an architect"?
(A) She does not know if a proposal is reasonable.
(B) She will need assistance with an assignment.
(C) She is not interested in the details of a building plan.
(D) She is concerned that the listeners have been misled.

번역　화자가 "제가 건축가는 아니죠"라고 말할 때, 그 의도는 무엇인가?
(A) 제안이 합리적인지 잘 모르겠다.
(B) 많은 일에 도움이 필요할 것이다.
(C) 건축 계획의 세부 내용에는 관심이 없다.
(D) 청자들이 오해했을까 봐 걱정된다.

해설　화자의 의도 파악 - 자신이 건축가는 아니라는 말의 의도
화자가 마지막에 새 공장에 그런 통로를 넣어서 견학을 시작할 것(Why don't we include a walkway like that in the new plant and start offering tours?)을 제안하면서 자신은 그런 장치를 설계도에 추가하는 일이 어려울 것 같지 않다(It seems to me like it wouldn't be hard to have that feature added to the plans)고 말한 뒤, 인용문을 언급하고 있으므로, 건축가가 아니어서 제안이 합리적인지 잘 모르겠다는 의도로 한 말임을 알 수 있다. 따라서 정답은 (A)이다.

어휘　proposal 제안　reasonable 타당한　assistance 도움
assignment 과제, 임무　mislead 호도하다

95-97 안내＋일정표

W-Am Thank you all for coming to Venegas Fashion's development day for store staff. Today you'll have the chance to develop your skills as retail professionals and consider the futures of your careers. Uh, if you didn't do so when you arrived, 95 **please sign in now by writing your name on the sheet near the door.** We want to know who's in attendance today. As you can see, we have four workshops scheduled. 96 **Each will last fifty minutes, except the four o'clock workshop. That will last just half an hour,** so it will end around four-thirty. Now, I have a special guest to introduce. 97 **This is Yuko Ikeda, the company's director of personnel for more than ten years. She would like to say a few words before we begin the first workshop.**

베네가스 패션의 매장 직원 연수회에 와주신 모든 분께 감사드립니다. 오늘은 소매 전문가로서 여러분의 자질을 발전시키고 여러분의 미래 진로에 대해 고민해 볼 기회가 되실 겁니다. 아, 도착했을 때 하지 않으셨다면, 지금 문 옆에 있는 종이에 여러분의 이름을 적어 주십시오. 오늘 누가 참석하셨는지 알아야 하니까요. 보시다시피 네 가지 워크숍이 준비되어 있습니다. 4시 워크숍을 제외하고는 각각 50분씩 진행될 겁니다. 4시 워크숍은 30분만 진행될 겁니다. 그래서 4시 30분쯤에 끝날 겁니다. 자, 그럼 특별한 손님을 소개하겠습니다. 10년 이상 인사부장을 맡고 계신 유코 이케다입니다. 첫 번째 워크숍을 시작하기 전에 그녀가 짧게 인사말을 하고 싶다고 합니다.

어휘　development day 연수일　retail 소매　sign in 서명으로 기록하다　be in attendance 참석하다　last 계속되다　director of personnel 인사부장

Venegas Fashion Store
Staff Development Day

Introduction to Upcoming Products	1:00 P.M.
Good Customer Service	2:00 P.M.
How to Arrange Displays	3:00 P.M.
96 Career Paths at Venegas Fashion	4:00 P.M.

베네가스 패션 매장
직원 연수일

곧 나올 신제품 소개	오후 1시
좋은 고객 서비스	오후 2시
진열 방법	오후 3시
96 베네가스 패션에서의 커리어 진로	오후 4시

어휘　upcoming 다가오는　career path 커리어 진로

95 What are the listeners asked to do?
(A) Put on name tags
(B) Silence their mobile phones
(C) Sign an attendance sheet
(D) Take their seats

번역　청자들은 무엇을 하도록 요청받았는가?
(A) 이름표 착용하기
(B) 휴대전화 무음으로 바꾸기
(C) 출석부에 서명하기
(D) 좌석에 앉기

해설　세부 사항 관련 - 청자들이 요청받는 일
화자가 중반부에 지금 문 옆에 있는 종이에 이름을 적을 것(please sign in now by writing your name on the sheet ~)을 요청하고 있으므로 정답은 (C)이다.

어휘　put on 착용하다, 입다　silence 조용하게 하다　attendance sheet 출석부

> **Paraphrasing**
> 담화의 sign in ~ by writing your name on the sheet
> → 정답의 Sign an attendance sheet

96 Look at the graphic. Which workshop will be shorter than the others?
(A) Introduction to Upcoming Products
(B) Good Customer Service
(C) How to Arrange Displays
(D) Career Paths at Venegas Fashion

번역　시각 정보에 의하면, 어떤 워크숍이 다른 것들보다 짧을 것인가?
(A) 곧 나올 신제품 소개
(B) 좋은 고객 서비스
(C) 진열 방법
(D) 베네가스 패션에서의 커리어 진로

해설　시각 정보 연계 - 다른 것들보다 짧은 워크숍
화자가 중반부에 4시 워크숍을 제외하고는 각각 50분씩 진행될 것(Each will last fifty minutes, except the four o'clock worksho)이라고 하면서 4시 워크숍은 30분만 진행될 것(That will

last just half an hour)이라고 말하고 있다. 일정표에 따르면 4시 워크숍은 베네가스 패션에서의 커리어 진로이므로 정답은 (D)이다.

97 According to the speaker, what will Ms. Ikeda do?
(A) Make an audio recording
(B) Give a short speech
(C) Lead one of the workshops
(D) Distribute an employee survey

번역　화자에 따르면, 이케다 씨는 무엇을 하겠는가?
(A) 오디오 녹음하기
(B) 짧게 연설하기
(C) 워크숍 중 하나 주재하기
(D) 직원 설문지 나눠주기

해설　세부 사항 관련 - 이케다 씨가 할 일
화자가 마지막에 유코 이케다(This is Yuko Ikeda, ~)를 소개하면서 그녀가 짧게 인사말을 하고 싶어 한다(She would like to say a few words ~)고 말하고 있으므로 정답은 (B)이다.

어휘　distribute 배포하다　survey 설문지, 설문조사

> **Paraphrasing**
> 담화의 say a few words → 정답의 Give a short speech

98-100 회의 발췌 + 도표

M-Cn　All right, everyone, I have the latest results from our customer exit survey—the one we ask them to take when they cancel our meal kit service. **98 To make the survey easier to complete, we recently cut it down to just one question about their reason for canceling.** I'm happy to say that this has resulted in a better response rate. So, what have we found out? Well, **99 you'll see here that a surprisingly high percentage of people are canceling because they're not satisfied with the food.** It seems we need new and better recipes. Perhaps we should try asking popular food bloggers to develop some, like other services have done. **100 What do you all think of that idea?**

좋습니다, 여러분, 제가 고객 이탈 설문 조사의 최신 결과를 갖고 있습니다. 고객이 우리 밀키트 서비스를 취소할 때 작성을 부탁한 것입니다. **설문 조사를 더 쉽게 작성하게 하려고 우리는 최근에 취소 사유에 대한 질문을 한 개로 줄였습니다.** 이로써 응답률이 더 나아졌다고 말할 수 있어서 기쁩니다. 자, 무엇을 알아냈을까요? 음, **여기 보시면 놀라울 정도로 높은 비율의 사람들이 음식에 만족하지 않기 때문에 취소한다고 합니다.** 새롭고 더 나은 조리법이 필요한 것 같습니다. 아마도 다른 회사들이 했던 것처럼 인기 있는 음식 블로거에게 몇 가지 조리법을 개발해 달라고 부탁해야 할 것 같습니다. **이 방안에 대해 모두 어떻게 생각하시나요?**

어휘　exit 출구, 이탈　survey 설문 조사　cancel 취소하다　complete 완료하다　cut down 줄이다　result in ~하는 결과를 낳다　response rate 응답률　surprisingly 놀랍도록　be satisfied with ~에 만족하다　recipe 조리법　popular 인기 있는　develop 개발하다

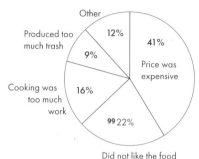

Main Reason for Cancellation

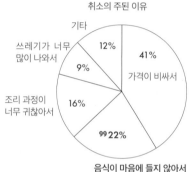

취소의 주된 이유

어휘　cancellation 취소　produce 생산하다　trash 쓰레기

98 What does the speaker mention about the survey?
(A) It has been simplified.
(B) It does not receive many responses.
(C) A question has been added to it.
(D) It is delivered by e-mail.

번역　화자는 설문 조사에 대해 무엇을 언급하는가?
(A) 간소화되었다.
(B) 많은 응답을 받지 못했다.
(C) 질문 한 개가 추가되었다.
(D) 이메일로 전달된다.

해설　세부 사항 관련 - 설문 조사에 대해 언급하는 것
화자가 초반부에서 설문 조사를 더 쉽게 작성하게 하려고 취소 사유에 대한 질문을 한 개로 줄였다(To make the survey easier to complete, we recently cut it down to just one question about their reason for canceling)고 했으므로 정답은 (A)이다.

어휘　simplify 간소화하다　add 추가하다　deliver 전달하다

99 Look at the graphic. Which figure does the speaker call attention to?
(A) 41%
(B) 22%
(C) 16%
(D) 9%

번역 시각 정보에 의하면, 화자는 어떤 수치에 관심을 가지는가?
(A) 41%
(B) 22%
(C) 16%
(D) 9%

해설 시각 정보 연계 - 화자가 관심을 가지는 수치
화자가 중반부에서 놀라울 정도로 높은 비율의 사람들이 음식에 만족하지 않기 때문에 취소한다고 한다(you'll see here that a surprisingly high percentage of people are canceling because they're not satisfied with the food)고 했으며, 도표에 따르면 음식에 만족하지 않는(Did not like the food) 사람들의 비율이 22%이므로 정답은 (B)이다.

어휘 call attention to ~에 주의를 환기하다

---

100 What will the listeners most likely do next?
(A) Divide into groups
(B) Look at more data
(C) Sample some food
(D) Give their opinions

번역 청자들은 다음으로 무엇을 하겠는가?
(A) 그룹별로 나누기
(B) 더 많은 자료 보기
(C) 음식 시식하기
(D) 의견 내기

해설 세부 사항 관련 - 청자들이 다음에 할 일
화자가 마지막에 이 방안에 대해 모두 어떻게 생각하는지(What do you all think of that idea?) 의견을 묻고 있으므로 정답은 (C)이다.

어휘 divide into ~으로 나누다   sample 시식하다   opinion 의견

TEST 6

TEST 7

1 (C)	2 (A)	3 (C)	4 (D)	5 (A)
6 (B)	7 (C)	8 (A)	9 (A)	10 (C)
11 (A)	12 (B)	13 (B)	14 (C)	15 (A)
16 (A)	17 (C)	18 (B)	19 (B)	20 (A)
21 (C)	22 (B)	23 (A)	24 (A)	25 (C)
26 (B)	27 (C)	28 (C)	29 (C)	30 (A)
31 (C)	32 (C)	33 (B)	34 (C)	35 (C)
36 (B)	37 (D)	38 (B)	39 (C)	40 (D)
41 (C)	42 (B)	43 (A)	44 (C)	45 (B)
46 (A)	47 (C)	48 (C)	49 (A)	50 (A)
51 (C)	52 (B)	53 (B)	54 (B)	55 (B)
56 (D)	57 (D)	58 (C)	59 (A)	60 (C)
61 (D)	62 (B)	63 (A)	64 (B)	65 (C)
66 (B)	67 (B)	68 (B)	69 (C)	70 (B)
71 (C)	72 (A)	73 (A)	74 (C)	75 (B)
76 (B)	77 (C)	78 (B)	79 (A)	80 (C)
81 (D)	82 (A)	83 (C)	84 (D)	85 (B)
86 (D)	87 (A)	88 (B)	89 (D)	90 (D)
91 (D)	92 (B)	93 (C)	94 (B)	95 (B)
96 (C)	97 (A)	98 (C)	99 (B)	100 (B)

PART 1

1

M-Au

(A) The man is carrying pieces of wood.
(B) The man is charging a power tool.
(C) The man is assembling some furniture.
(D) The man is cleaning up a workshop.

번역 (A) 남자가 나무토막을 나르고 있다.
(B) 남자가 전동 공구를 충전하고 있다.
(C) 남자가 가구를 조립하고 있다.
(D) 남자가 작업장을 청소하고 있다.

해설 **1인 등장 사진**
(A) 동사 오답. 남자가 나무토막을 나르고 있는 모습이 아니다.
(B) 동사 오답. 남자가 전동 공구를 충전하고 있는 모습이 아니다.
(C) 정답. 남자가 가구를 조립하고 있으므로 정답이다.
(D) 동사 오답. 남자가 작업장을 청소하고 있는 모습이 아니다.

어휘 carry 나르다   charge 충전하다   power tool 전동 공구
assemble 조립하다   furniture 가구   workshop 작업장

2

W-Br

(A) Some people are gathered on a balcony.
(B) Someone is polishing the sliding doors.
(C) Some tree branches have been trimmed.
(D) Some outdoor railings have been removed.

번역 **(A) 사람들이 발코니에 모여 있다.**
(B) 한 사람이 미닫이문을 닦고 있다.
(C) 나뭇가지들이 다듬어져 있다.
(D) 외부 난간이 제거되어 있다.

해설 **사람/사물·풍경 혼합 사진**
(A) 정답. 사람들이 발코니에 모여 있으므로 정답이다.
(B) 동사 오답. 미닫이문을 닦고 있는 사람의 모습이 보이지 않는다.
(C) 동사 오답. 나뭇가지들이 다듬어져 있는 모습이 아니다.
(D) 동사 오답. 외부 난간이 제거되어 있는 모습이 아니다.

어휘 gather 모으다, 모이다   polish 닦다, 광택을 내다   sliding door
미닫이문   trim 다듬다   railing 난간   remove 제거하다

3

M-Cn

(A) One of the women is addressing a group.
(B) The man is removing his jacket.
(C) Some of the people are waiting in a line.
(D) One of the women is plugging in a machine.

번역 (A) 여자들 중 한 명이 군중에게 연설하고 있다.
(B) 남자가 재킷을 벗고 있다.
(C) 사람들이 줄을 서서 기다리고 있다.
(D) 여자들 중 한 명이 기계에 플러그를 꽂고 있다.

해설 **2인 이상 등장 사진**
(A) 동사 오답. 군중에게 연설하고 있는 여자의 모습이 보이지 않는다.
(B) 동사 오답. 남자가 재킷을 벗고 있는 모습이 아니다.
(C) 정답. 사람들이 줄을 서서 기다리고 있으므로 정답이다.
(D) 동사 오답. 기계에 플러그를 꽂고 있는 여자의 모습이 보이지 않는다.

어휘 address 연설하다   remove (옷 등을) 벗다   plug in ~의 플러그를
꽂다   machine 기계

4

W-Am

(A) A wheel is being stored in a cabinet.
(B) The man is sitting on a bench outdoors.
(C) A tree has fallen across a bike path.
(D) The man is inspecting a wheel.

번역 (A) 바퀴가 수납장에 보관되어 있다.
(B) 남자가 야외에서 벤치에 앉아 있다.
(C) 나무가 자전거 도로를 가로질러 넘어져 있다.
(D) 남자가 바퀴를 점검하고 있다.

해설 **사람/사물·풍경 혼합 사진**
(A) 사진에 없는 명사. 사진에 수납장이 보이지 않는다.
(B) 동사 오답. 남자가 벤치에 앉아 있는 모습이 아니다.
(C) 동사 오답. 나무가 넘어져 있는 모습이 보이지 않는다.
(D) 정답. 남자가 바퀴를 점검하고 있으므로 정답이다.

어휘 wheel 바퀴 cabinet 수납장 path 길 inspect 점검하다

5

M-Au

(A) Some artwork is hanging on a wall.
(B) Reading materials have been left on a sofa.
(C) Some windows are being installed.
(D) Some potted plants have fallen on the floor.

번역 **(A) 미술품들이 벽에 걸려 있다.**
(B) 읽을거리가 소파에 놓여 있다.
(C) 창문들이 설치되고 있다.
(D) 화분들이 바닥에 떨어져 있다.

해설 **사물·풍경 사진**
(A) 정답. 미술품들이 벽에 걸려 있으므로 정답이다.
(B) 위치 오답. 읽을거리는 소파가 아니라 탁자 위에 놓여 있다.
(C) 동사 오답. 창문들이 설치되고 있는 모습이 아니다.
(D) 동사 오답. 화분들이 바닥에 떨어져 있는 모습이 아니다.

어휘 artwork 미술품 reading material 읽을거리 install 설치하다
potted plant 화분

6

W-Br

(A) There are some restaurant menus stacked in
a pile.
(B) There's an awning stretching over a walkway.
(C) He is wiping his hands on his apron.
(D) He's spraying water on the pavement.

번역 (A) 식당 메뉴판이 무더기로 쌓여 있다.
(B) 차양이 인도 위로 뻗어 있다.
(C) 남자가 앞치마에 손을 닦고 있다.
(D) 남자가 인도에 물을 뿌리고 있다.

해설 **사람/사물·풍경 혼합 사진**
(A) 동사 오답. 식당 메뉴판이 무더기로 쌓여 있는 모습이 아니다.
(B) 정답. 차양이 인도 위로 뻗어 있으므로 정답이다.
(C) 동사 오답. 남자가 앞치마에 손을 닦고 있는 모습이 아니다.
(D) 사진에 없는 명사. 사진에 물이 보이지 않는다.

어휘 stack 쌓다, 포개다 in a pile 무더기로 awning 차양
walkway 인도, 통행로 wipe 닦다 apron 앞치마
pavement 인도

PART 2

7

W-Br You get your dry cleaning delivered, don't you?
M-Cn (A) Please make sure it is completely dry.
(B) We clean the floor after closing time.
(C) Yes, once in a while.

번역 당신은 드라이클리닝 세탁물을 배달 받으시죠, 그렇지 않나요?
(A) 완전히 말랐는지 꼭 확인하세요.
(B) 저희는 폐점 시간 이후에 바닥을 청소합니다.
(C) 네, 가끔씩이요.

해설 **부가 의문문**
(A) 단어 반복 오답. 질문의 dry를 반복 이용한 오답이다.
(B) 파생어 오답. 질문의 cleaning과 파생어 관계인 clean을 이용한
오답이다.
(C) 정답. 세탁물을 배달 받는지 여부를 확인하는 질문에 네(Yes)라
고 대답한 뒤, 가끔씩이라며 긍정 답변과 일관된 내용을 덧붙였으
므로 정답이다.

어휘 deliver 배달하다 completely 완전히 once in a while 가끔씩

8

W-Am　Did you get your business cards from the printing department yet?

M-Au　(A) No, they've had numerous requests lately.
(B) Alright, that looks much better actually.
(C) A shipment of toner.

번역　인쇄부에서 당신 명함을 아직 못 받았나요?
(A) 못 받았어요, 최근에 신청이 몰렸대요.
(B) 괜찮아요, 실은 그게 훨씬 더 보기 좋네요.
(C) 토너 배송품이요.

해설　**조동사(Did) 의문문**
(A) 정답. 인쇄부에서 명함을 아직 못 받았는지 여부를 묻는 질문에 못 받았다(No)고 대답한 뒤, 최근에 신청이 몰렸다며 부정 답변과 일관된 내용을 덧붙이고 있으므로 정답이다.
(B) 질문과 상관없는 오답.
(C) 연상 오답. 질문의 printing에서 연상 가능한 toner를 이용한 오답이다.

어휘　department 부서　numerous 많은　request 요청, 신청
shipment 배송품　toner (복사기의) 토너

9

M-Au　Why was the ferry service canceled today?

W-Br　(A) Because the high winds are causing rough waters.
(B) Let's take the earliest journey that we can.
(C) From the observation deck, I think.

번역　오늘 페리 운항이 왜 취소되었나요?
(A) 강풍으로 파도가 거칠어져서요.
(B) 최대한 빠른 여정을 택합시다.
(C) 아마도 전망대에서요.

해설　**Why 의문문**
(A) 정답. 페리 운항이 취소된 이유를 묻는 질문에 강풍으로 파도가 거칠어져서라고 구체적인 이유를 제시하고 있으므로 정답이다.
(B) 연상 오답. 질문의 ferry에서 연상 가능한 journey를 이용한 오답이다.
(C) 연상 오답. 질문의 ferry에서 연상 가능한 deck(갑판)을 이용한 오답이다.

어휘　high wind 강풍　rough 거친　observation deck 전망대

10

M-Cn　How often can we request office supplies for the team?

W-Br　(A) No, I'm not surprised at all.
(B) Mainly staples and paper clips.
(C) You're allowed to do it every month.

번역　팀에 필요한 사무용품을 얼마나 자주 신청할 수 있나요?
(A) 아니요, 저는 전혀 놀랍지 않아요.
(B) 주로 철심과 클립이요.
(C) 매달 신청할 수 있어요.

해설　**How+형용사/부사 의문문**
(A) Yes/No 불가 오답. How 의문문에는 Yes/No 응답이 불가능하므로 오답이다.

(B) 연상 오답. 질문의 office supplies에서 연상 가능한 staples와 paper clips를 이용한 오답이다.
(C) 정답. 사무용품을 얼마나 자주 신청할 수 있는지 묻는 질문에 매달 신청할 수 있다며 구체적인 빈도를 제시하고 있으므로 정답이다.

어휘　office supplies 사무용품　be allowed to ~하는 것이 허용되다

11

M-Cn　When are you giving your speech at the conference?

W-Am　(A) The timetable hasn't been finalized.
(B) At least one hour, including questions.
(C) A speech about literacy rates.

번역　컨퍼런스에서 당신은 언제 연설을 하실 건가요?
(A) 시간표가 확정되지 않았어요.
(B) 질문을 포함해서 적어도 한 시간이요.
(C) 문해율에 대한 연설이요.

해설　**When 의문문**
(A) 정답. 컨퍼런스에서 연설을 할 시간을 묻는 질문에 시간표가 확정되지 않았다며 알 수 없음을 우회적으로 알려 주고 있으므로 정답이다.
(B) 연상 오답. 질문의 speech에서 연상 가능한 one hour와 questions를 이용한 오답이다.
(C) 단어 반복 오답. 질문의 speech를 반복 이용한 오답이다.

어휘　finalize 완성하다　literacy 읽고 쓸 수 있는 능력　rate 비율

12

M-Au　Have you emptied the boxes that arrived from the vendor?

W-Am　(A) Is this box large enough?
(B) Yes, the contents are unpacked and organized.
(C) I can pour you another one.

번역　공급업체에서 배송받은 상자를 비웠나요?
(A) 이 상자는 충분히 큰가요?
(B) 네, 내용물은 다 꺼내서 정리했어요.
(C) 한 잔 더 드릴 수 있어요.

해설　**조동사(Have) 의문문**
(A) 단어 반복 오답. 질문의 box를 반복 이용한 오답이다.
(B) 정답. 공급업체에서 배송받은 상자를 비웠는지 여부를 묻는 질문에 네(Yes)라고 대답한 뒤, 내용물은 다 꺼내서 정리했다며 긍정 답변과 일관된 내용을 덧붙이고 있으므로 정답이다.
(C) 연상 오답. 질문의 emptied에서 연상 가능한 pour를 이용한 오답이다.

어휘　empty 비우다　vendor 공급업체　content 내용물　unpack (짐 등을) 꺼내다, 풀다　organize 정리정돈하다　pour (액체를) 붓다

13

W-Am　Would you like to try the online photo-editing software?

M-Au　(A) Did you wait in the line?
(B) Sure, I'll make some time for that.
(C) Images from our company retreat.

번역 온라인 사진 편집 소프트웨어를 써보시겠어요?
(A) 줄을 서서 기다리셨나요?
(B) 그럼요, 시간을 내볼게요.
(C) 회사 야유회 때 찍은 사진들이에요.

해설 요청·제안문
(A) 유사 발음 오답. 질문의 online과 부분적으로 발음이 유사한 line을 이용한 오답이다.
(B) 정답. 온라인 사진 편집 소프트웨어를 써보겠냐는 제안에 그럼요 (Sure)라고 답한 뒤, 시간을 내보겠다며 수락의 의사를 표현하고 있으므로 정답이다.
(C) 연상 오답. 질문의 photo-editing에서 연상 가능한 Images를 이용한 오답이다.

어휘 company retreat 회사 야유회

14

W-Br Don't we need a navigation system for the rental car?
M-Cn (A) The station is closed for repairs.
(B) The standard size should be suitable.
(C) No, I'm familiar with the city.

번역 렌터카에 내비게이션이 필요하지 않나요?
(A) 그 역은 수리를 위해 폐쇄되었어요.
(B) 표준 크기가 맞을 거예요.
(C) 아니요, 저는 이 도시에 대해 잘 알아요.

해설 부정 의문문
(A) 연상 오답. 질문의 rental car에서 연상 가능한 repairs를 이용한 오답이다.
(B) 연상 오답. 질문의 rental car에서 연상 가능한 size를 이용한 오답이다.
(C) 정답. 렌터카에 내비게이션이 필요한지 확인하는 질문에 아니요 (No)라고 대답한 뒤, 이 도시에 대해 잘 안다며 부정 답변과 일관된 내용을 덧붙이고 있으므로 정답이다.

어휘 repair 수리 standard 표준의 suitable 적합한
be familiar with ~에 대해 잘 알다

15

M-Au Could you check that the door to the side entrance has been secured?
M-Cn (A) Would you rather I checked all of them?
(B) They were printed earlier this morning.
(C) A master key for the whole building.

번역 옆 출입문이 단단히 잠겨 있는지 확인해 줄 수 있나요?
(A) 전부 다 확인해 보는 걸 원하세요?
(B) 오늘 아침에 인쇄되었어요.
(C) 건물 전체에 사용하는 마스터 열쇠요.

해설 요청·제안문
(A) 정답. 옆 출입문이 단단히 잠겨 있는지 확인해 줄 것을 요청하는 질문에 전부 다 확인하길 원하는지 물으며 출입문과 관련된 내용을 묻고 있으므로 정답이다.
(B) 질문과 상관없는 오답.
(C) 연상 오답. 질문의 the door에서 연상 가능한 key를 이용한 오답이다.

16

W-Br I can return the items for a full refund, right?
M-Cn (A) Yes, within thirty days.
(B) A seat for my return flight.
(C) I think that's a good price.

번역 물건을 반품하면 전액 환불을 받을 수 있죠, 맞죠?
(A) 네, 30일 이내예요.
(B) 귀국 항공편을 위한 좌석이요.
(C) 좋은 가격 같은데요.

해설 부가 의문문
(A) 정답. 물건을 반품하면 전액 환불을 받을 수 있는지 여부를 확인하는 질문에 네(Yes)라고 대답한 뒤, 30일 이내라고 긍정 답변과 일관된 내용을 덧붙였으므로 정답이다.
(B) 단어 반복 오답. 질문의 return을 반복 이용한 오답이다.
(C) 연상 오답. 질문의 refund에서 연상 가능한 price를 이용한 오답이다.

어휘 return 반품하다 full refund 전액 환불

17

W-Br What's the fee for the hotel's breakfast buffet?
W-Am (A) Every morning from 6 A.M.
(B) Coffee and tea are included.
(C) It's free with a one-night stay or more.

번역 호텔의 조식 뷔페 요금은 얼마인가요?
(A) 매일 아침 6시부터요.
(B) 커피와 차는 포함돼 있어요.
(C) 1박 이상 하실 경우 무료입니다.

해설 What 의문문
(A) 연상 오답. 질문의 breakfast에서 연상 가능한 morning을 이용한 오답이다.
(B) 연상 오답. 질문의 buffet에서 연상 가능한 Coffee와 tea를 이용한 오답이다.
(C) 정답. 호텔의 조식 뷔페 요금을 묻는 질문에 1박 이상 할 경우 무료라고 구체적으로 알려 주고 있으므로 정답이다.

어휘 include 포함하다

18

M-Cn Is the office's new air conditioning system quiet?
W-Br (A) Poor weather conditions are expected.
(B) I didn't even notice it was on.
(C) Yes, he's fitting in well.

번역 사무실의 새 에어컨은 조용한가요?
(A) 안 좋은 날씨가 예상돼요.
(B) 켜져 있는지도 몰랐어요.
(C) 네, 그는 잘 적응하고 있어요.

해설 Be동사 의문문
(A) 파생어 오답. 질문의 conditioning과 파생어 관계인 conditions를 이용한 오답이다.

(B) 정답. 사무실의 새 에어컨은 조용한지 묻는 질문에 켜져 있는지도 몰랐다며 조용하다는 것을 우회적으로 알려 주고 있으므로 정답이다.

(C) 질문과 상관없는 오답. 질문에 3인칭 대명사 he로 지칭할 인물이 언급된 적이 없으므로 오답이다.

어휘   quiet 조용한   notice 알아차리다   fit in well 잘 적응하다

19

W-Am   Where can I get some colored paper for printing?

M-Au   (A) The payment is collected by bank transfer.
(B) Only department managers can place supply orders.
(C) The printer frequently runs out of ink.

번역   인쇄용 색지를 어디에서 구할 수 있을까요?
(A) 결제는 은행 송금으로 이루어져요.
(B) 부서장만 용품 주문을 할 수 있어요.
(C) 그 프린터는 자주 잉크가 떨어져요.

해설   Where 의문문
(A) 질문과 상관없는 오답.
(B) 정답. 인쇄용 색지를 구할 수 있는 곳을 묻는 질문에 부서장만 용품 주문을 할 수 있다며 부서장에게 문의해야 함을 우회적으로 알려 주고 있으므로 정답이다.
(C) 파생어 오답. 질문의 printing과 파생어 관계인 printer를 이용한 오답이다.

어휘   payment 지불   collect 수금하다   bank transfer 은행 계좌이체   frequently 자주   run out of ~을 다 써버리다

20

M-Au   Would you like some black tea or coffee after your meal?

W-Am   (A) It's too late to have caffeine.
(B) Because the café is well known.
(C) Yes, I'm feeling quite full.

번역   식사 후에 홍차나 커피를 드시겠습니까?
(A) 카페인을 마시기에는 너무 늦은 시간이에요.
(B) 그 카페는 유명하니까요.
(C) 네, 정말 배가 불러요.

해설   선택 의문문
(A) 정답. 식사 후에 홍차와 커피 중 무엇을 마실지 묻는 질문에 카페인을 마시기에는 너무 늦은 시간이라며 둘 다 마시지 않겠다는 의사를 우회적으로 알려 주고 있으므로 정답이다.
(B) 연상 오답. 질문의 black tea or coffee에서 연상 가능한 café를 이용한 오답이다.
(C) 연상 오답. 질문의 meal에서 연상 가능한 feeling quite full을 이용한 오답이다.

어휘   caffeine 카페인   well known 유명한

21

M-Cn   How do I renew my newspaper subscription?

W-Am   (A) Thanks for showing me the article.
(B) No later than the last day of April.
(C) You should contact the customer service team.

번역   신문 구독은 어떻게 갱신하나요?
(A) 이 기사를 나에게 보여줘서 고마워요.
(B) 늦어도 4월 말일까지요.
(C) 고객 서비스팀에 연락하셔야 해요.

해설   How 의문문
(A) 연상 오답. 질문의 newspaper에서 연상 가능한 article을 이용한 오답이다.
(B) 질문과 상관없는 오답.
(C) 정답. 신문 구독을 갱신할 방법을 묻는 질문에 고객 서비스팀에 연락해야 한다며 알 수 있는 방법을 간접적으로 알려 주고 있으므로 정답이다.

어휘   renew 갱신하다   subscription 구독   article 글, 기사   no later than 늦어도 ~까지는

22

M-Cn   Your department will undergo a financial audit next month.

W-Br   (A) Five thousand dollars is enough.
(B) The bookkeeping is well organized, thankfully.
(C) I wasn't able to attend it.

번역   당신의 부서는 다음 달에 재무 감사를 받을 거예요.
(A) 5천 달러면 충분해요.
(B) 다행히 장부 정리는 잘 정리돼 있어요.
(C) 저는 참석할 수 없었어요.

해설   사실·정보 전달의 평서문
(A) 연상 오답. 평서문의 financial에서 연상 가능한 dollars를 이용한 오답이다.
(B) 정답. 다음 달에 재무 감사를 받을 거라는 평서문에 다행히 장부 정리는 잘 정리되어 있다며 재무 감사와 관련된 내용으로 답변을 하고 있으므로 정답이다.
(C) 평서문과 상관없는 오답.

어휘   undergo 겪다, 받다   financial audit 재무 감사   bookkeeping 부기, 장부 정리   well organized 잘 정리된   attend 참석하다

23

W-Am   Would you like to help select the recipients of the employee awards?

M-Cn   (A) Sure, I know the staff members well.
(B) Every year in late December.
(C) The newly elected vice president.

번역   직원상 수상자를 선정하는 일을 도와주시겠어요?
(A) 물론이죠, 저는 직원들을 잘 알아요.
(B) 매년 12월 말에요.
(C) 새로 선출된 부사장이요.

해설   요청·제안문
(A) 정답. 직원상 수상자를 선정하는 일을 도와줄 것을 요청하는 말에 물론이죠(Sure)라고 수락한 뒤, 직원들을 잘 안다며 긍정 답변과 일관된 내용을 덧붙이고 있으므로 정답이다.
(B) 연상 오답. 질문의 employee awards에서 연상 가능한 late December를 이용한 오답이다.

(C) 유사 발음 오답. 질문의 select와 부분적으로 발음이 유사한 elected를 이용한 오답이다.

어휘 select 선택하다 recipient 수령인 award 상 newly elected 새로 선출된 vice president 부사장, 부회장

24

M-Au How about renting a private venue for the welcome reception?

W-Br (A) I'm afraid we've got a tight budget.
(B) It says it can be renewed annually.
(C) Sure, I've decorated the space.

번역 환영회를 위해 우리끼리 사용할 수 있는 장소를 빌리면 어떨까요?
(A) 안타깝게도 예산이 빠듯해요.
(B) 해마다 갱신할 수 있다고 쓰여 있어요.
(C) 그럼요, 제가 그 장소를 꾸몄어요.

해설 요청·제안문
(A) 정답. 환영회를 위한 단독 장소를 빌리면 어떨지 의견을 묻는 질문에 예산이 빠듯하다며 빌릴 수 없음을 간접적으로 표현하고 있으므로 정답이다.
(B) 연상 오답. 질문의 renting에서 연상 가능한 renewed를 이용한 오답이다.
(C) 연상 오답. 질문의 private venue에서 연상 가능한 decorated the space를 이용한 오답이다.

어휘 private 사적인, (특정 개인·집단) 전용의 venue 장소 welcome reception 환영회 tight 빠듯한 budget 예산 renew 갱신하다 annually 해마다 decorate 장식하다

25

W-Br Who's setting up the conference room on Monday?

M-Au (A) All of the board members are invited.
(B) The meeting ran long, I'm afraid.
(C) I'm working from home that entire week.

번역 월요일에 누가 회의실을 준비하나요?
(A) 이사회 구성원 모두가 초대되었어요.
(B) 안타깝게도 회의가 너무 길어졌어요.
(C) 저는 그 주 내내 재택근무 해요.

해설 Who 의문문
(A) 연상 오답. 질문의 Who에서 연상 가능한 All of the board members를 이용한 오답이다.
(B) 연상 오답. 질문의 conference에서 연상 가능한 meeting을 이용한 오답이다.
(C) 정답. 월요일에 누가 회의실을 준비하는지 묻는 질문에 그 주 내내 재택근무 한다며 본인이 할 수 없음을 우회적으로 알려 주고 있으므로 정답이다.

어휘 set up 준비하다 invite 초대하다 entire 전체의

26

M-Cn Isn't the portfolio supposed to be provided in digital form?

W-Am (A) This is a promising business opportunity.
(B) Yes, I'm working on the electronic copy.
(C) We should digitize the patient records.

번역 포트폴리오를 디지털 형태로 제공해야 하지 않나요?
(A) 이건 유망한 사업 기회예요.
(B) 네, 지금 전자 사본을 준비 중이에요.
(C) 환자 기록을 전산화해야 해요.

해설 부정 의문문
(A) 질문과 상관없는 오답.
(B) 정답. 포트폴리오를 디지털 형태로 제출해야 하는지 여부를 묻는 질문에 네(Yes)라고 대답한 뒤, 지금 전자 사본을 준비 중이라며 긍정 답변과 일관된 내용을 덧붙이고 있으므로 정답이다.
(C) 파생어 오답. 질문의 digital과 파생어 관계인 digitize를 이용한 오답이다.

어휘 portfolio 포트폴리오 promising 유망한 opportunity 기회 electronic 전자의 digitize 전산화하다 patient 환자 record 기록

27

W-Br Don't you sell these hiking boots in brown?

M-Au (A) The cell phones are a good price.
(B) There's a high level of customer satisfaction.
(C) We're restocking that section later this week.

번역 이 등산화 갈색도 있나요?
(A) 그 휴대전화는 좋은 가격이에요.
(B) 고객 만족도가 아주 높아요.
(C) 이번 주 후반에 그 섹션에 물건을 다시 채울 거예요.

해설 부정 의문문
(A) 유사 발음 오답. 질문의 sell과 발음이 유사한 cell을 이용한 오답이다.
(B) 연상 오답. 질문의 sell에서 연상 가능한 customer를 이용한 오답이다.
(C) 정답. 등산화가 갈색도 있는지를 묻는 질문에 이번 주 후반에 그 섹션에 물건을 다시 채울 거라며 아니요(No)를 생략한 부정 답변을 하고 있으므로 정답이다.

어휘 hiking boots 등산화 satisfaction 만족 restock 다시 채우다

28

W-Am Should we get a one-year subscription for the software or pay monthly?

M-Cn (A) She downloaded the files.
(B) Last year, in June.
(C) Monthly, at first.

번역 그 소프트웨어의 1년 구독권을 사야 할까요? 아니면 매달 지불해야 할까요?
(A) 그녀가 파일을 내려받았어요.
(B) 작년 6월에요.
(C) 우선은 매달요.

해설 **선택 의문문**
(A) 연상 오답. 질문의 software에서 연상 가능한 downloaded the files를 이용한 오답이다.
(B) 단어 반복 오답. 질문의 year를 반복 이용한 오답이다.
(C) 정답. 소프트웨어의 1년 구독권과 매달 지불을 묻는 질문에 우선은 매달이라며 둘 중 하나를 선택해 응답하고 있으므로 정답이다.

어휘 subscription 구독   monthly 매달

29

M-Cn Ellie designed the invitations for the networking luncheon, didn't she?

W-Am (A) The system is working again.
(B) I'm grateful to be invited.
(C) Actually, one of the interns did.

번역 엘리가 네트워킹 오찬 초대장을 디자인했죠?
(A) 그 시스템은 다시 작동하고 있어요.
(B) 초대받아서 감사해요.
(C) 실은 인턴 중 한 명이 했어요.

해설 **부가 의문문**
(A) 유사 발음 오답. 질문의 networking과 부분적으로 발음이 유사한 working을 이용한 오답이다.
(B) 파생어 오답. 질문의 invitations와 파생어 관계인 invited를 이용한 오답이다.
(C) 정답. 엘리가 네트워킹 오찬 초대장을 디자인했는지 여부를 확인하는 질문에 실은 인턴 중 한 명이 했다며 아니요(No)를 생략한 부정 답변을 하고 있으므로 정답이다.

어휘 invitation 초대장   networking 네트워킹(사람들이 모여 정보를 교류하고 인맥을 형성하는 자리)   luncheon 오찬   grateful 감사하는

30

M-Cn These containers should have been cleared from the loading dock.

W-Br (A) I thought that they were meant to be refilled.
(B) No thanks, I still have a good deal of space.
(C) The contract contains sensitive information.

번역 이 컨테이너들은 하역장에서 치워졌어야 해요.
(A) 저는 그것들에 다시 물건을 채울 예정인 줄 알았어요.
(B) 고맙지만 사양할게요, 아직 공간이 충분해요.
(C) 그 계약서에는 민감한 정보가 들어 있어요.

해설 **의견·희망 사항의 평서문**
(A) 정답. 컨테이너들이 하역장에서 치워졌어야 한다는 평서문에 자신은 그것들에 물건을 채울 예정인 줄 알았다며 잘못 알고 있었음을 표현하고 있으므로 정답이다.
(B) 연상 오답. 평서문의 containers에서 연상 가능한 space를 이용한 오답이다.
(C) 파생어 오답. 평서문의 containers와 파생어 관계인 contains를 이용한 오답이다.

어휘 loading dock 하역장   be meant to ~할 예정이다   refill 다시 채우다   a good deal of 많은   sensitive 민감한

31

M-Au Who will be in charge of testing the health-monitoring equipment?

W-Br (A) On the first few days of each month.
(B) Yes, I was impressed with its functionality.
(C) The chief engineer oversees all aspects of the project.

번역 건강 모니터링 장비를 시험하는 일은 누가 담당할 건가요?
(A) 매달 초에요.
(B) 네, 저는 이것의 기능에 깊은 인상을 받았어요.
(C) 수석 기술자가 그 프로젝트 전반을 감독해요.

해설 **Who 의문문**
(A) 질문과 상관없는 오답. When 의문에 대한 응답이므로 오답이다.
(B) Yes/No 불가 오답. Who 의문문에는 Yes/No 응답이 불가능하므로 오답이다.
(C) 정답. 건강 모니터링 장비를 시험하는 일의 담당자를 묻는 질문에 수석 기술자가 그 프로젝트 전반을 감독한다며 구체적으로 알려주고 있으므로 정답이다.

어휘 be in charge of ~을 담당하다   be impressed with ~에 깊은 인상을 받다   functionality 기능   oversee 감독하다   aspect 측면

PART 3

32-34

W-Br Thank you for calling Monroe Art Museum. How can I help you?

M-Cn Hello. **32 I work for Home Hearted, which helps build affordable housing for low-income families. We are looking for a site for our charity's annual fundraiser,** and we're interested in the museum.

W-Br Well, we recently held a private event like that here, but... um, **33 one of our paintings was scratched. I'm worried that would happen at another event.**

M-Cn I understand, but it would be a fairly small group.

W-Br I see. Well, **34 you would be welcome to put forward a written proposal to our board of directors**. Their approval would be required for an after-hours event.

여: 먼로 미술관에 전화 주셔서 감사합니다. 무엇을 도와드릴까요?

남: 안녕하세요. **저는 홈 하티드에서 일해요. 저소득 가구를 위한 저렴한 주택을 짓는 일을 돕는 곳인데요. 저희 자선단체의 연례 모금행사를 위한 장소를 찾는 중이에요.** 그런데 저희가 이 미술관에 관심이 있어서요.

여: 음, 저희가 최근에 그런 비공개 행사를 여기에서 한 적이 있어요, 그런데… 음, 저희 그림 중 한 점이 긁혔어요. 또 다른 행사 때 그런 일이 또 생길까 봐 우려가 됩니다.

남: 이해합니다, 하지만 상당히 작은 규모일 거예요.

여: 그렇군요. 그럼, **이사회에 서면 제안서를 올려보셔도 좋습니다.** 폐관 이후 행사에는 이사회의 승인이 필요하거든요.

어휘 affordable 가격이 적당한 housing 주택 low-income 저소득층의 charity 자선단체 annual 연례의 fundraiser 모금행사 painting 그림 scratch 긁다 fairly 상당히 put forward 제안하다 proposal 제안 approval 승인 after-hours 영업시간 이후의

32 Where does the man most likely work?
(A) At a real estate company
(B) At an art auction house
(C) At a non-profit organization
(D) At a financial institution

번역 남자는 어디서 일하겠는가?
(A) 부동산 회사
(B) 미술품 경매장
(C) 비영리 단체
(D) 금융기관

해설 **전체 내용 관련 - 남자의 근무지**
남자가 첫 대사에서 홈 하티드에서 일하는데 저소득 가구를 위한 저렴한 주택을 짓는 일을 돕는 곳(I work for Home Hearted, which helps build affordable housing for low-income families)이라고 하면서 자선단체의 연례 모금행사를 위한 장소를 찾는 중(We are looking for a site for our charity's annual fundraiser ~)이라고 말하는 것으로 보아 남자는 자선단체에서 근무하고 있다는 것을 알 수 있다. 따라서 정답은 (C)이다.

어휘 real estate 부동산 auction 경매

> **Paraphrasing**
> 대화의 charity → 정답의 a non-profit organization

33 What does the woman express concern about?
(A) The lack of after-hours staff
(B) The risk of damage to items
(C) The cost of hosting an event
(D) The timeline for getting approval

번역 여자는 무엇에 대해 우려를 표하는가?
(A) 폐관 시간 이후 직원의 부족
(B) 물건에 손상이 갈 위험
(C) 행사를 주최하는 비용
(D) 승인을 받기 위한 일정

해설 **세부 사항 관련 - 여자의 우려 사항**
여자가 두 번째 대사에서 그림 중 한 점이 긁혔다(one of our paintings was scratched)면서 또 다른 행사 때 그런 일이 또 생길까 봐 우려가 된다(I'm worried that would happen at another event)고 말하고 있으므로 정답은 (B)이다.

어휘 lack 부족 damage 손상 host 주최하다 timeline 일정

> **Paraphrasing**
> 대화의 one of our paintings was scratched
> → 정답의 damage to items

34 What does the woman suggest that the man do?
(A) Decorate a room
(B) Review the museum's policies
(C) Submit a proposal
(D) Attend a board meeting

번역 여자는 남자에게 무엇을 하라고 제안하는가?
(A) 방 장식
(B) 미술관 정책 검토
(C) 제안서 제출
(D) 이사회 참석

해설 **세부 사항 관련 - 여자의 제안 사항**
여자가 마지막 대사에서 이사회에 서면 제안서를 올려볼 것(you would be welcome to put forward a written proposal to our board of directors)을 제안하고 있으므로 정답은 (C)이다.

어휘 decorate 장식하다 policy 정책 submit 제출하다 attend 참석하다

> **Paraphrasing**
> 대화의 put forward a written proposal
> → 정답의 Submit a proposal

35-37

M-Cn Welcome to Bradberry Luggage. Can I help you find anything?

W-Am Hi. **35 I'm flying to Seoul for work next week, so I need to get a new suitcase.**

M-Cn I can help you find something. What size did you have in mind?

W-Am Well, I like the size of the one displayed by the entrance. But **36 the pattern is too bold for my taste.**

M-Cn No problem. That particular model is also available in solid black, navy blue, or red. It has spinner wheels that can move three hundred sixty degrees, and the handle is retractable.

W-Am That sounds great. It's on sale for one hundred forty dollars, right?

M-Cn Yes, that's right. And **37 that price includes a two-year warranty on all parts.**

남: 브래드베리 러기지에 오신 것을 환영합니다. 찾는 걸 도와드릴까요?

여:	안녕하세요. **제가 다음 주에 일 때문에 비행기를 타고 서울에 가는데요, 새 여행 가방을 사야 해요.**
남:	제가 찾는 걸 도와드릴 수 있어요. 어떤 크기를 생각하셨어요?
여:	음, 입구 옆에 진열된 것과 같은 크기가 좋아요. 하지만 **무늬가 제 취향에 비해 너무 눈에 띄어요.**
남:	걱정 마세요. 그 모델은 완전 검정색, 남색, 빨간색으로도 나와요. 360도 회전하는 바퀴가 있고요. 손잡이는 집어넣을 수 있어요.
여:	좋네요. 그게 140달러로 할인 판매 중인 거죠?
남:	네, 맞습니다. 그리고 **그 금액에는 모든 부품에 대한 2년 품질 보증서가 포함되어 있습니다.**

어휘	suitcase 여행 가방　have ~ in mind ~을 염두에 두다　display 진열하다　entrance 입구　bold 선명한　taste 취향　particular 특정한　solid 단색의　retratable 집어넣을 수 있는　warranty 품질 보증서

35 What does the woman need a suitcase for?
(A) A family trip
(B) A friend's birthday
(C) A business trip
(D) A house move

번역 여자는 무엇 때문에 여행 가방이 필요한가?
(A) 가족 여행
(B) 친구 생일
(C) 출장
(D) 주택 이사

해설 **세부 사항 관련 - 여자가 여행 가방이 필요한 이유**
여자가 첫 대사에서 다음 주에 일 때문에 비행기를 타고 서울에 가는데 새 여행 가방을 사야 한다(I'm flying to Seoul for work next week, so I need to get a new suitcase)고 말하고 있으므로 정답은 (C)이다.

> Paraphrasing
> 대화의 flying to Seoul for work
> → 정답의 A business trip

36 What does the woman dislike about the display suitcase?
(A) Its size
(B) Its pattern
(C) Its price
(D) Its fabric

번역 여자는 진열된 여행 가방에 대해 어떤 점을 좋아하지 않는가?
(A) 크기
(B) 무늬
(C) 가격
(D) 직물

해설 **세부 사항 관련 - 여자가 진열된 여행 가방에 대해 좋아하지 않는 점**
여자가 두 번째 대사에서 무늬가 자신의 취향에 비해 너무 눈에 띈다

(the pattern is too bold for my taste)고 말하고 있으므로 정답은 (B)이다.

---

37 According to the man, what is included in the price?
(A) Spare wheels
(B) A tracking device
(C) Free shipping
(D) A warranty

번역 남자에 따르면, 무엇이 금액에 포함되어 있는가?
(A) 여분의 바퀴
(B) 추적 장치
(C) 무료 배송
(D) 품질 보증서

해설 **세부 사항 관련 - 금액에 포함된 것**
남자가 마지막 대사에서 그 금액에는 모든 부품에 대한 2년 품질 보증서가 포함되어 있다(that price includes a two-year warranty on all parts)고 말하고 있으므로 정답은 (D)이다.

어휘 spare 여분의　shipping 배송

38-40

W-Am	Theo, **[38] have you finalized the schedule for the employee retreat next month?**
M-Au	I've been really busy, so **[38] I've just started working on it.**
W-Am	That's great, actually. **[39] I would like to put something on the schedule for the first day, August 4. It's a quiz game to help employees work together and get to know each other.** I don't mind hosting it and coming up with the questions that we'll need.
M-Au	That sounds like fun. **[40] Could you just let me know about how long that will take?** Then I'll make sure to leave enough time for it.

여:	테오, **다음 달 직원 야유회 일정 완성했나요?**
남:	제가 그동안 정말 바빠서 **방금 그 일을 시작했어요.**
여:	실은 잘됐네요. **제가 첫날인 8월 4일 일정에 추가하고 싶은 게 있어요. 직원들이 함께 일하고 서로 알게 되는 데 도움이 될 만한 퀴즈 게임이에요.** 제가 진행해도 상관없고 필요한 질문을 만들 수 있어요.
남:	재미있겠네요. **시간이 얼마나 걸릴지만 알려주시겠어요?** 그럼 제가 충분한 시간을 남겨둘게요.

어휘	finalize 완성하다　retreat 야유회　host 진행하다　come up with ~을 제시하다　leave 남겨두다

38 What task is the man in charge of?
(A) Organizing a trade fair schedule
(B) Planning a staff retreat
(C) Analyzing customer feedback
(D) Recruiting new company employees

번역 남자는 어떤 업무를 담당하는가?
(A) 무역 박람회 일정 잡기
(B) **직원 야유회 기획하기**
(C) 고객 피드백 분석하기
(D) 신입사원 채용하기

해설 **전체 내용 관련 - 남자의 담당 업무**
여자가 첫 대사에서 다음 달 직원 야유회 일정 완성했는지(have you finalized the schedule for the employee retreat next month?) 묻자 남자가 방금 그 일을 시작했다(I've just started working on it)고 답하는 것으로 보아 남자는 직원 야유회를 기획하는 업무를 담당하고 있음을 알 수 있다. 따라서 정답은 (B)이다.

어휘 organize 조직하다   trade fair 무역 박람회   analyze 분석하다
recruit 채용하다

> **Paraphrasing**
> 대화의 the employee retreat → 정답의 a staff retreat

39 What does the woman want to do on August 4 ?
(A) Give out achievement awards
(B) Introduce some new products
(C) Lead a team-building activity
(D) Answer questions from the staff

번역 여자는 8월 4일에 무엇을 하길 원하는가?
(A) 공로상 주기
(B) 신제품 소개하기
(C) **팀워크 강화 활동 이끌기**
(D) 직원들의 질문에 답변하기

해설 **세부 사항 관련 - 여자가 8월 4일에 하길 원하는 일**
여자가 두 번째 대사에서 첫날인 8월 4일 일정에 추가하고 싶은 게 있다(I would like to put something on the schedule for the first day, August 4)면서 직원들이 함께 일하고 서로 알게 되는 데 도움이 될 만한 퀴즈 게임(It's a quiz game to help employees work together and get to know each other)이라고 말하고 있으므로 정답은 (C)이다.

어휘 achievement award 공로상   team-building activity 팀워크
강화 활동

> **Paraphrasing**
> 대화의 a quiz game to help employees work together and get to know each other
> → 정답의 a team-building activity

40 What is the woman asked to do?
(A) Review employee performance
(B) Check a list of attendees
(C) Give a welcome address
(D) Provide a time estimate

번역 여자는 무엇을 해달라고 요청받았는가?
(A) 직원 성과 검토하기
(B) 참석자 명단 확인하기
(C) 환영사하기
(D) **예상 시간 알려주기**

해설 **세부 사항 관련 - 여자가 요청받은 일**
남자가 마지막 대사에서 시간이 얼마나 걸릴지 알려줄 것(Could you just let me know about how long that will take)을 요청하고 있으므로 정답은 (D)이다.

어휘 performance 성과   attendee 참석자   welcome address
환영사   estimate 추정

> **Paraphrasing**
> 대화의 let me know about how long that will take
> → 정답의 Provide a time estimate

41-43

> W-Br Hi, it's Lucy from the Sales Department. **41 I need some equipment for the meeting with the prospective investors from Milan on Thursday at 1 P.M.**
>
> M-Cn Of course. What do you need?
>
> W-Br Just a laptop and projector, please. We'll start at 1 P.M.
>
> M-Cn Alright. **42 I can set the computer up for you. Do you need any special software installed?**
>
> W-Br I don't think so. **43 I'll just have a slideshow presentation saved on an external hard drive. Can I give that to you on Thursday morning?**
>
> M-Cn Sure. I'll make sure everything's working in advance.
>
> ---
>
> 여: 안녕하세요. 저는 영업부의 루시예요. 목요일 오후 1시에 밀라노에서 오는 잠재적 투자자들과의 회의를 위해 장비가 좀 필요해요.
>
> 남: 물론이죠. 뭐가 필요하세요?
>
> 여: 노트북과 프로젝터만 있으면 돼요. 오후 1시에 시작할 거예요.
>
> 남: 좋습니다. 제가 컴퓨터를 준비해 드릴 수 있어요. 특별한 소프트웨어의 설치가 필요하신가요?
>
> 여: 아니요. 외장하드에 저장한 슬라이드쇼 자료만 사용할 거라서요. 그걸 목요일 아침에 보내드리면 될까요?
>
> 남: 그럼요. 모든 것이 작동하는지 미리 확인해 두겠습니다.
>
> ---
>
> 어휘 equipment 장비   prospective 유망한   investor 투자자
> install 설치하다   save 저장하다   external 외부의, 외장형의
> in advance 미리

41 What does the woman have to prepare for?
(A) A session to test new products
(B) An inspection by a government official
(C) A visit from potential investors
(D) A training workshop for employees

번역 여자는 무엇을 준비해야 하는가?
(A) 신제품을 시험해 보는 시간
(B) 공무원의 점검
(C) 잠재적 투자자들의 방문
(D) 직원들을 위한 연수 워크숍

해설 **세부 사항 관련 - 여자가 준비해야 할 것**
여자가 첫 대사에서 목요일 오후 1시에 밀라노에서 오는 잠재적 투자자들과의 회의를 위해 장비가 필요하다(I need some equipment for the meeting with the prospective investors from Milan on Thursday at 1 P.M.)고 말하고 있으므로 정답은 (C)이다.

어휘 prepare for ~을 준비하다 session 시간 inspection 점검 government official 공무원 potential 잠재적인

> **Paraphrasing**
> 대화의 the prospective investors
> → 정답의 potential investors

42 Who most likely is the man?
(A) A company owner
(B) A computer technician
(C) A financial advisor
(D) A sales director

번역 남자는 누구이겠는가?
(A) 회사 소유주
(B) 컴퓨터 기술자
(C) 재정 고문
(D) 영업부장

해설 **전체 내용 관련 - 남자의 직업**
남자가 두 번째 대사에서 컴퓨터를 준비해 드릴 수 있다(I can set the computer up for you)면서 특별한 소프트웨어의 설치가 필요한지(Do you need any special software installed?)를 묻고 있는 것으로 보아 남자는 컴퓨터 기술자임을 알 수 있다. 따라서 정답은 (B)이다.

어휘 technician 기술자

43 What does the woman plan to give the man on Thursday morning?
(A) A hard drive
(B) A meeting agenda
(C) A lunch menu
(D) A cost estimate

번역 여자는 목요일 아침에 남자에게 무엇을 줄 계획인가?
(A) 하드디스크 드라이브
(B) 회의 안건
(C) 점심 메뉴
(D) 비용 견적서

해설 **세부 사항 관련 - 여자가 목요일 아침에 남자에게 줄 것**
여자가 마지막 대사에서 외장하드에 저장한 슬라이드쇼 자료만 사용할 것(I'll just have a slideshow presentation saved on an external hard drive)이라면서 그걸 목요일 아침에 보내주면 될지(Can I give that to you on Thursday morning?)를 묻고 있으므로 정답은 (A)이다.

어휘 agenda 안건

44-46

W-Br Hi, Taichi. Are you finding the new sales summary forms confusing? They require a lot more information about the details for each product, like adding the energy usage for **⁴⁴our toasters and blenders.**

M-Au Right. I thought I could get most of those details from the database, but it's incomplete. **⁴⁵I had to ask my team leader to push back the due date for this assignment.**

W-Br **⁴⁵Did you really?** You're always so prompt with your work.

M-Au Well, this is too time-consuming. **⁴⁶I think we need to bring this up with one of the managers.**

W-Br Ms. Adkins is always willing to listen. I just saw her go into her office.

여: 안녕하세요, 타이치. 새 영업 요약 보고서 양식이 헷갈리나요? 이 양식에는 각 상품의 상세 정보에 대한 훨씬 더 많은 정보가 필요해요. **우리 토스터와 믹서기의 전력 사용량을 추가하는 것**처럼요.

남: 맞아요. 상세 정보를 대부분 데이터베이스에서 찾을 수 있을 거라 생각했는데, 부족하더라고요. **팀장에게 이 업무에 대한 마감일을 미뤄달라고 부탁해야 했어요.**

여: **정말요?** 당신은 언제나 업무를 신속하게 마치잖아요.

남: 음, 이건 너무 시간을 많이 잡아먹는 일이에요. **관리자들 중 한 명에게 이 문제를 제기해야 할 것 같아요.**

여: 애드킨스 씨는 언제나 기꺼이 경청해주세요. 방금 그녀가 사무실로 들어가는 걸 봤어요.

어휘 summary 요약 confusing 헷갈리는 usage 사용량 blender 믹서기 incomplete 불충분한 push back 미루다 due date 만기일 assignment 과제, 임무 prompt 신속한, 시간을 엄수하는 time-consuming 시간 소모가 큰 bring up 화제를 꺼내다

44 What kind of product does the speakers' company most likely sell?
(A) Gardening equipment
(B) Casual clothing
(C) Kitchen appliances
(D) Light fixtures

번역 화자들의 회사는 어떤 종류의 제품을 팔겠는가?
(A) 정원 손질용 장비
(B) 캐주얼 의류
(C) 주방 가전제품
(D) 조명 기구

해설 전체 내용 관련 - 화자들의 회사가 판매하는 제품
여자가 첫 대사에서 우리 토스터와 믹서기(our toasters and blenders)라고 말하고 있으므로 화자들의 회사는 주방 가전제품을 판매하는 회사라는 것을 알 수 있다. 따라서 정답은 (C)이다.

어휘 gardening 정원 손질 appliance 가전제품

> **Paraphrasing**
> 대화의 toasters, blenders → 정답의 Kitchen appliances

45 Why is the woman surprised?
(A) The man could not access a database.
(B) The man requested a deadline extension.
(C) The price of some items has changed.
(D) Some devices use a lot of energy.

번역 여자는 왜 놀랐는가?
(A) 남자가 데이터베이스에 접속할 수 없었기 때문에
(B) 남자가 마감 시한 연장을 요청했기 때문에
(C) 일부 상품들의 가격이 바뀌었기 때문에
(D) 일부 기기들이 많은 전력을 사용하기 때문에

해설 세부 사항 관련 - 여자가 놀란 이유
남자가 첫 대사에서 팀장에게 이 업무에 대한 마감일을 미뤄달라고 부탁해야 했다(I had to ask my team leader to push back the due date for this assignment)고 하자, 여자가 정말요(Did you really?)라면서 놀라고 있으므로 정답은 (B)이다.

어휘 access 접속하다 deadline 마감 시한 extension 연장
device 기기

> **Paraphrasing**
> 대화의 push back the due date
> → 정답의 a deadline extension

46 Why does the woman say, "I just saw her go into her office"?
(A) To suggest discussing an issue with a supervisor
(B) To indicate that a meeting has finished early
(C) To express disagreement about an absence
(D) To confirm that a task has been completed

번역 여자가 "방금 그녀가 사무실로 들어가는 걸 봤어요"라고 말한 이유는?
(A) 관리자와 문제를 상의해 보라고 제안하려고
(B) 회의가 일찍 끝났음을 알려주려고
(C) 불참에 대한 의견이 다름을 표현하려고
(D) 업무가 완료되었음을 확인하려고

해설 화자의 의도 파악 - 방금 그녀가 사무실로 들어가는 걸 봤다는 말의 의도
앞에서 남자가 관리자들 중 한 명에게 이 문제를 제기해야 할 것 같다(I think we need to bring this up with one of the managers)고 말하자 여자가 인용문을 언급하고 있는 것으로 보아, 방금 사무실로 들어간 관리자와 상의해 볼 것을 제안하려는 의도로 한 말임을 알 수 있다. 따라서 정답은 (A)이다.

어휘 supervisor 관리자 disagreement 불일치 absence 불참, 결근

47-49

M-Au ⁴⁷**I wanted to ask you about the hair products we sell.** They're... ⁴⁷**Oh, sorry, Michelle. You're in the middle of something.**

W-Am These reports are not urgent.

M-Au Okay, great. Well, when I was dusting our display stand by the window, ⁴⁸**I noticed that some of the shampoo has turned a strange color.**

W-Am Hmm... our hair salon customers haven't been buying it, so it's been sitting in the sun for a long time. It's probably unusable now, unfortunately.

M-Au Then ⁴⁹**we should probably relocate the stand to somewhere out of the light.** It would be more noticeable near the reception desk anyway.

남: 우리가 파는 모발 관리 제품에 대해 물어볼 게 있었는데요. 그게… 아, 죄송해요, 미셸. 한창 뭔가 하시는 중이군요.

여: 이 보고서들은 급하지 않아요.

남: 아, 잘됐네요. 음, 창가에 있는 진열대의 먼지를 털다 보니 **일부 샴푸가 이상한 색깔로 변해 있는 게 보였어요.**

여: 음… 우리 미용실 고객들이 사 가지 않다 보니 햇빛에 너무 오래 노출되었네요. 안타깝게도 더 이상 사용할 수 없을 거예요.

남: 그럼 **아무래도 진열대를 햇빛이 안 닿는 다른 곳으로 옮겨야겠네요.** 어쨌든 접수 데스크 근처가 눈에 더 잘 띌 거고요.

어휘 be in the middle of something 바쁘게 뭔가 하는 중이다
urgent 긴급한 dust 먼지를 털다 display stand 진열대
unusable 사용할 수 없는 relocate 다시 배치하다
noticeable 눈에 잘 띄는 reception 접수처

47 What does the woman imply when she says, "These reports are not urgent"?
(A) She wants to rearrange a schedule.
(B) She does not need the man's assistance.
(C) She can respond to a question.
(D) She plans to take a day off.

번역 여자가 "이 보고서들은 급하지 않아요"라고 말할 때, 그 의도는 무엇인가?
(A) 일정을 다시 잡기를 원한다.
(B) 남자의 도움이 필요하지 않다.
(C) 질문에 응답할 수 있다.
(D) 하루 휴가를 쓸 계획이다.

해설 **화자의 의도 파악 - 이 보고서들은 급하지 않다는 말의 의도**
앞에서 남자가 물어볼 게 있었다(I wanted to ask you about ~)면서 한창 뭔가 하는 중(Oh, sorry, Michelle. You're in the middle of something)이냐며 미안해하자 여자가 인용문을 언급하고 있는 것으로 보아, 보고서가 급하지 않기에 남자의 질문에 응답해 줄 수 있다는 의도로 한 말임을 알 수 있다. 따라서 정답은 (C)이다.

어휘 rearrange 재조정하다   assistance 도움   take a day off 하루 휴가를 쓰다

---

48 What did the man notice about some shampoo?
(A) Its bottles have cracked.
(B) Its labels are faded.
(C) Its appearance has changed.
(D) Its ingredients are harmful.

번역 남자는 일부 샴푸에 대해 무엇을 발견했는가?
(A) 병에 금이 갔다.
(B) 라벨의 색이 바랬다.
(C) 겉모습이 바뀌었다.
(D) 성분이 해롭다.

해설 **세부 사항 관련 - 남자가 일부 샴푸에 대해 발견한 점**
남자가 두 번째 대사에서 일부 샴푸가 이상한 색깔로 변해 있는 게 보였다(I noticed that some of the shampoo has turned a strange color)고 말하고 있으므로 정답은 (C)이다.

어휘 crack 금이 가다   fade 색깔이 바래다   appearance 겉모습   ingredient 성분   harmful 해로운

> **Paraphrasing**
> 대화의 some of the shampoo has turned a strange color → 정답의 Its appearance has changed.

49 What does the man suggest that the business do in the future?
(A) Move items to a different place
(B) Offer discounts to customers
(C) Hire a full-time receptionist
(D) Use a more reliable supplier

번역 남자는 사업체가 앞으로 무엇을 해야 한다고 제안하는가?
(A) 물건들을 다른 장소로 옮겨야 한다.
(B) 고객들에게 할인을 제공해야 한다.
(C) 전일제 접수원을 고용해야 한다.
(D) 더 신뢰할 수 있는 공급업체를 이용해야 한다.

해설 **세부 사항 관련 - 사업체에 대한 남자의 제안 사항**
남자가 마지막 대사에서 진열대를 햇빛이 안 닿는 다른 곳으로 옮길 것(we should probably relocate the stand to somewhere out of the light)을 제안하고 있으므로 정답은 (A)이다.

어휘 full-time 전일제   receptionist 접수원   reliable 신뢰할 만한   supplier 공급업체

> **Paraphrasing**
> 대화의 relocate the stand to somewhere
> → 정답의 Move items to a different place

50-52

> M-Au Excuse me, could you please help me find **50 Amy Ogren's novel** entitled *Daybreak is Calling*?
>
> W-Br Actually, the book just came out, but the library hasn't been able to order it yet. **51 We are waiting for our finance committee to decide the budget for this quarter** before we can place the next book order.
>
> M-Au Oh, what a shame. I was hoping to check it out today.
>
> W-Br I'm sorry for the inconvenience. We don't have a waiting list, but **52 updates are in the library's monthly newsletter. You can register for it for free.**
>
> ---
> 남: 실례합니다만, 제목이 <데이브레이크 이즈 콜링>인 에이미 오그렌의 소설 찾는 일을 도와주시겠어요?
>
> 여: 실은, 그 책은 최근에 나왔지만 도서관에서 아직 주문을 하지 못했어요. 다음 도서 주문을 하기 전에 **이번 분기 예산을 재정 위원회에서 결정하기를 기다리고 있어요.**
>
> 남: 아, 아쉽네요. 오늘 대출받고 싶었는데요.
>
> 여: 불편을 끼쳐 죄송합니다. 저희가 대기자 명단은 없지만, **도서관 월간 뉴스레터에 최신 소식이 실려요. 무료로 신청하실 수 있어요.**
>
> ---
> 어휘 entitle 제목을 붙이다   committee 위원회   budget 예산   quarter 4분의 1, 사분기   place an order 주문하다   What a shame 아쉽네요   check out (책을) 대출받다   inconvenience 불편   register for ~에 등록하다

50 Who most likely is Amy Ogren?
(A) An author
(B) A librarian
(C) A painter
(D) A reporter

번역 에이미 오그렌은 누구이겠는가?
(A) 저자
(B) 도서관 사서
(C) 화가
(D) 기자

해설 **세부 사항 관련 - 에이미 오그렌의 직업**
남자가 첫 대사에서 에이미 오그렌의 소설(Amy Ogren's novel)이
라고 말하는 것으로 보아 에이미 오그렌은 저자임을 알 수 있다. 따라
서 정답은 (A)이다.

51 What does the woman mention about a
committee?
(A) It is recruiting new members.
(B) It has rejected an order.
(C) It must finalize a budget.
(D) It meets every quarter.

번역 여자는 위원회에 대해 무엇을 언급하는가?
(A) 신입 위원을 채용 중이다.
(B) 주문을 거부했다.
(C) 예산을 확정해야 한다.
(D) 분기마다 회의를 한다.

해설 **세부 사항 관련 - 여자가 위원회에 대해 언급하는 것**
여자가 첫 대사에서 이번 분기 예산을 재정 위원회에서 결정하기를 기
다리고 있다(We are waiting for our finance committee to
decide the budget for this quarter)고 말하고 있으므로 정답은
(C)이다.

어휘 recruit 채용하다 reject 거부하다 finalize 완성하다

52 What does the woman suggest doing?
(A) Joining a waiting list
(B) Signing up for a newsletter
(C) Attending a monthly talk
(D) Participating in a book club

번역 여자는 무엇을 제안하는가?
(A) 대기자 명단에 이름 올리기
(B) 뉴스레터 신청하기
(C) 월례 회담에 참석하기
(D) 독서 모임에 참여하기

해설 **세부 사항 관련 - 여자가 제안하는 것**
여자가 마지막 대사에서 도서관 월간 뉴스레터에 최신 소식이 실린다
(updates are in the library's monthly newsletter)면서 무료
로 신청하실 수 있다(You can register for it for free)고 월간 뉴
스레터 신청을 제안하고 있으므로 정답은 (B)이다.

어휘 sign up for ~을 신청하다 attend 참석하다 participate in ~에
참여하다

> **Paraphrasing**
> 대화의 register → 정답의 Signing up

53-55 3인 대화

M-Cn Well, Ms. Harper, your business plan looks
excellent. **⁵³ Based on the sales projections,
I think I can approve you for your business
loan within a few weeks.**

W-Am That's good news, but... um, I didn't realize it
would take that long. I thought I would have
the funds within a few days.

M-Cn **⁵⁴ I'm sorry. The person who booked this
appointment should have gone over the
estimated timeline in more detail.**

W-Am That's okay. I understand.

M-Cn Ms. Flores, is there anything else we need?

W-Br Actually, yes. Ms. Harper, you mentioned that
you recently moved, so **⁵⁵ could you please fill
out these forms with the address of where
we should send everything?** That'll prevent
delays.

W-Am Of course.

남: 저, 하퍼 씨, 당신의 사업 계획은 훌륭해 보여요. **예상 매출에 근
거해 당신의 사업 대출을 몇 주 내로 승인해 드릴 수 있을 것 같
아요.**

여1: 좋은 소식이네요. 하지만… 음, 그렇게 오래 걸릴 줄은 몰랐어요.
며칠 내로 자금을 받을 수 있을 거라 생각했어요.

남: **죄송합니다. 이 예약을 진행한 담당자가 더 자세히 예상 일정을
검토해 드렸어야 했는데.**

여1: 괜찮습니다. 이해합니다.

남: 플로레스 씨, 우리가 더 필요한 게 있나요?

여2: 실은 있어요. 하퍼 씨, 최근에 이사하셨다고 말씀하셨잖아요.
**이 양식들에 저희가 어디로 모든 자료를 보내드려야 하는지 그
주소를 기재해 주시겠어요?** 그럼 시간 지체를 막을 수 있을 거
예요.

여1: 물론이죠.

어휘 excellent 우수한 based on ~에 근거해 projection 예상
approve 승인하다 loan 대출 appointment (진료 등의)
예약 go over ~을 검토하다 estimated 예상되는 fill out
~을 작성하다 prevent 방지하다 delay 지연

53 Who is the man?
(A) A politician
(B) A banker
(C) A lawyer
(D) A journalist

번역 남자는 누구인가?
(A) 정치인
(B) 은행가
(C) 변호사
(D) 언론인

해설 **전체 내용 관련 - 남자의 직업**
남자가 첫 대사에서 예상 매출에 근거해 사업 대출을 몇 주 내로 승인해 줄 수 있을 것 같다(Based on the sales projections, I think I can approve you for your business loan within a few weeks)고 말하고 있으므로 정답은 (B)이다.

54 Why does the man apologize?
(A) A cost will be higher than expected.
(B) A timeline was not explained well.
(C) Some staff members are absent.
(D) Some services are no longer available.

번역 남자는 왜 사과하는가?
(A) 비용이 예상보다 높게 나올 거라서
(B) 일정이 잘 설명되지 않아서
(C) 일부 직원들이 결근해서
(D) 일부 서비스를 더 이상 이용할 수 없어서

해설 **세부 사항 관련 - 남자가 사과하는 이유**
남자가 두 번째 대사에서 죄송하다(I'm sorry)고 사과하면서 이 예약을 진행한 담당자가 더 자세히 예상 일정을 검토해 드렸어야 했다(The person who booked this appointment should have gone over the estimated timeline in more detail)고 말하고 있으므로 정답은 (B)이다.

어휘 absent 결근한 available 이용 가능한

55 Why should Ms. Harper complete some paperwork?
(A) To apply for a temporary position
(B) To update her mailing address
(C) To use an express service
(D) To open a new account

번역 하퍼 씨는 왜 서류를 작성해야 하는가?
(A) 임시직에 지원하려고
(B) 우편 주소를 갱신하려고
(C) 빠른 배송 서비스를 이용하려고
(D) 신규 계좌를 개설하려고

해설 **세부 사항 관련 - 하퍼 씨가 서류를 작성해야 하는 이유**
두 번째 여자가 마지막 대사에서 최근 이사에 대해 언급하며, 자료를 보낼 그 주소를 기재해 줄 것(could you please fill out these forms with the address of where we should send everything?)을 요청하고 있으므로 정답은 (B)이다.

어휘 apply for ~에 지원하다 temporary 임시의 position 일자리 express service 빠른 배송 서비스 account 계좌

> **Paraphrasing**
> 대화의 the address of where we should send everything
> → 정답의 mailing address

56-58

W-Am	Thanks for stopping by, Calvin. As I'm sure you know, **56 Jan Eckles will be moved to the London branch at the beginning of June.** As a result, we have an opening for a field sales executive. Do you know anyone who would be suitable for the role?
M-Cn	That would be a great opportunity. I have a few colleagues that I could recommend. However, **57 does the person need a degree or any specific qualifications?**
W-Am	A business degree is preferred but experience counts for a lot. And **58 the position has a lot of benefits, like a company car and generous commission payments.**

여: 들러줘서 고마워요, 캘빈. 아시겠지만, 잰 에클스가 6월 초에 런던 지점으로 전근 갈 예정이에요. 그래서 현장 영업 임원 자리에 공석이 생기는데, 그 역할에 적합한 사람을 알고 있나요?

남: 좋은 기회가 되겠군요. 추천할 수 있는 동료가 몇 명 있어요. 그런데, 학위나 특정한 자격 요건이 필요한가요?

여: 경영학 학위를 우대하지만 경험이 매우 중요해요. 그리고 이 자리는 회사 차라든가 후한 수당 지급 같은 많은 복리후생이 있어요.

어휘 stop by 잠깐 들르다 opening 공석 field sales 현장 영업 executive 중역, 임원 suitable 적합한 role 역할 opportunity 기회 colleague 동료 recommend 추천하다 degree 학위 qualification 자격 요건 preferred 선호되는 count for 중요하다 benefit 혜택, 복리후생 generous 관대한, 후한 commission 수당 payment 지불, 지급

56 According to the woman, what will happen in June?
(A) A product will go on the market.
(B) A new office will open overseas.
(C) A branch will undergo renovations.
(D) A staff member will be transferred.

번역 여자에 따르면, 6월에 무슨 일이 일어나겠는가?
(A) 한 제품이 시장에 유통될 것이다.
(B) 새 사무실이 해외에서 문을 열 것이다.
(C) 한 지점이 보수 공사를 할 것이다.
(D) 한 직원이 전근될 것이다.

해설 **세부 사항 관련 - 6월에 일어날 일**
여자가 첫 대사에서 잰 에클스가 6월 초에 런던 지점으로 전근 갈 예정 (Jan Eckles will be moved to the London branch at the beginning of June)이라고 말하고 있으므로 정답은 (D)이다.

어휘 go on the market 시장에 유통되다   overseas 해외에
undergo 겪다   renovation 보수 공사   transfer 전근 가다

> **Paraphrasing**
> 대화의 Jan Eckles will be moved to the London
> branch → 정답의 A staff member will be transferred.

57 What does the man want to know about?
(A) When an assignment must be submitted
(B) Where he should upload a file
(C) Who will be leading a project
(D) What is required for a position

번역 남자는 무엇에 대해 알고 싶어 하는가?
(A) 할당 과제가 언제까지 제출되어야 하는지
(B) 파일을 어디에 업로드해야 하는지
(C) 누가 프로젝트를 이끌 것인지
(D) 일자리에 무엇이 요구되는지

해설 **세부 사항 관련 - 남자가 알고 싶어 하는 것**
남자가 첫 대사에서 학위나 특정한 자격 요건이 필요한지(does the person need a degree or any specific qualifications?) 묻고 있으므로 정답은 (D)이다.

어휘 assignment 과제, 임무   submit 제출하다   lead 이끌다

> **Paraphrasing**
> 대화의 does the person need a degree or any
> specific qualifications
> → 정답의 What is required for a position

58 What does the woman say the company will provide?
(A) Paid vacation days
(B) On-site meals
(C) A work vehicle
(D) A credit card

번역 여자는 회사가 무엇을 제공할 거라고 말하는가?
(A) 유급 휴가
(B) 급식
(C) 업무용 차량
(D) 신용카드

해설 **세부 사항 관련 - 회사가 제공하는 것**
여자가 마지막 대사에서 이 자리는 회사 차량든가 많은 복리후생이 있다(the position has a lot of benefits, like a company car ~)고 말하고 있으므로 정답은 (C)이다.

어휘 vehicle 차량

> **Paraphrasing**
> 대화의 a company car → 정답의 A work vehicle

59-61 3인 대화

> M-Cn Hey, Elena! **⁵⁹I heard that your team won the bid to design the bridge over Broadbeck River.** That's amazing! Congratulations!
>
> W-Br Thanks, Jorge. This project will be fantastic exposure for our firm. And **⁶⁰once the bridge is in use, it will significantly cut down on commuting times for people in the area.**
>
> M-Cn That's true. When will you start working on it?
>
> W-Br I'm not quite sure. But I can ask Eric, our team leader. He'll know... Eric, when will the Broadbeck River project begin?
>
> M-Au Well, **⁶¹that depends on how long it takes to measure the site initially.** We're still waiting on that information.

> 남1: 안녕하세요, 엘레나! 당신의 팀이 브로드벡 강 위에 지을 교량 설계 입찰을 따냈다고 들었어요. 대단해요! 축하해요!
>
> 여: 고마워요, 호르헤. 이 프로젝트는 우리 회사를 위한 굉장히 좋은 광고가 될 거예요. 그리고 다리가 완공되면, 이 지역 주민들의 통근 시간이 상당히 줄어들 거예요.
>
> 남1: 맞아요. 언제 착수할 건가요?
>
> 여: 정확히 모르겠어요. 하지만 팀장인 에릭에게 물어볼 수 있어요. 그는 알 거예요… 에릭, 브로드벡 강 프로젝트는 언제 시작하나요?
>
> 남2: 음, 초기에 현장을 측량하는 일이 얼마나 걸릴지에 달렸어요. 아직 그 정보를 기다리는 중이에요.

> 어휘 win the bid 입찰을 따내다   exposure 노출, 광고되기
> significantly 상당히   cut down on ~을 줄이다
> commuting 통근   depend on ~에 달려 있다   measure
> 측정하다   initially 초기에

59 What industry do the speakers most likely work in?
(A) Architecture
(B) Tourism
(C) Agriculture
(D) Electronics

번역 화자들은 어떤 업계에 종사하겠는가?
(A) 건축
(B) 관광
(C) 농업
(D) 전자 제품

전체 내용 관련 - 화자들의 근무 업종

첫 번째 남자가 첫 대사에서 당신의 팀이 브로드벡 강 위에 지을 교량 설계 입찰을 따냈다고 들었다(I heard that your team won the bid to design the bridge over Broadbeck River)고 말하고 있으므로 화자들은 건축 업종에서 근무하고 있음을 알 수 있다. 따라서 정답은 (A)이다.

| Paraphrasing
| 대화의 design the bridge → 정답의 Architecture

60 What does the woman say a project will do in the area?
(A) Protect historic buildings
(B) Promote local businesses
(C) Reduce travel times
(D) Increase tax revenue

번역 여자는 프로젝트가 지역에서 무엇을 할 거라고 말하는가?
(A) 역사적 건물 보호
(B) 지역 기업 활성화
(C) 이동 시간 단축
(D) 조세 수입 증가

해설 **세부 사항 관련 - 프로젝트가 지역에서 할 일**

여자가 첫 대사에서 다리가 완공되면, 이 지역 주민들의 통근 시간이 상당히 줄어들 거(once the bridge is in use, it will significantly cut down on commuting times for people in the area)라고 말하고 있으므로 정답은 (C)이다.

어휘 protect 보호하다   historic 역사적인   promote 촉진하다
reduce 줄이다   increase 증가시키다   tax revenue 조세 수입

| Paraphrasing
| 대화의 cut down on commuting times
| → 정답의 Reduce travel times

61 What does Eric say needs to happen?
(A) Equipment needs to be rented.
(B) Materials need to be delivered.
(C) A team leader needs to be selected.
(D) Measurements need to be taken.

번역 에릭은 무슨 일이 일어나야 한다고 말하는가?
(A) 장비가 대여되어야 한다.
(B) 자재가 배송되어야 한다.
(C) 팀장이 선출되어야 한다.
(D) 측량이 이루어져야 한다.

해설 **세부 사항 관련 - 에릭이 말하는 일어날 일**

두 번째 남자가 마지막 대사에서 초기에 현장을 측량하는 일이 얼마나 걸릴지에 달렸다(that depends on how long it takes to measure the site initially)고 말하고 있으므로 정답은 (D)이다.

어휘 material 재료, 자재   measurement 측량, 측정

62-64 대화+선반

M-Cn Hi, Louise! **62 How's your first day at our warehouse going?**

W-Am Oh hi, Mr. Okada. I think it's going well. I'm taking care to pack each product securely, so it won't get damaged during shipping.

M-Cn That's good to hear! Just don't forget that your packing speed is important, too.

W-Am Right, I won't. Actually, I have a question related to that—are we allowed to rearrange our packing stations? I'm left-handed, so **63 I could work a little faster if the tape were on that side of this shelf.**

M-Cn Sure—**63 go ahead and swap it with the labels.** And I see you're almost out of the wide packing tape. Do you know how to get more?

W-Am Yes, **64 my supervisor showed me where the supplies are stored.**

남: 안녕하세요, 루이즈! 우리 창고에서의 첫날은 어때요?

여: 안녕하세요, 오카다 씨. 잘되고 있는 것 같아요. 각 제품을 단단하게 포장하려고 각별히 신경 쓰고 있어요. 그래야 운송 중에 손상되지 않을 테니까요.

남: 다행이네요! 포장 속도도 중요하다는 사실만 잊지 마세요.

여: 네, 그럴게요. 실은 그것과 관련해서 궁금한 게 하나 있는데요, 포장 작업대를 다시 배열해도 될까요? 제가 왼손잡이라서요. 테이프가 이 선반의 저쪽에 있으면 일을 좀 더 빨리할 수 있거든요.

남: 물론이죠. 그렇게 하시고 테이프와 라벨을 바꿔주세요. 그리고 넓은 포장 테이프가 거의 다 떨어졌네요. 어떻게 더 가져오는지는 아시나요?

여: 네, 제 관리자가 비품이 어디에 보관되어 있는지 보여줬어요.

어휘 warehouse 창고   take care to 각별히 신경 쓰다   pack 포장하다   securely 단단하게   get damaged 손상되다   shipping 운송   rearrange 다시 배열하다   left-handed 왼손잡이인   swap 바꾸다   supervisor 감독관, 관리자   supplies 비품   store 보관하다

63Section 1: Labels	Section 2: Markers	Section 3: Scissors	63Section 4: Tape

631구역: 라벨	2구역: 마커	3구역: 가위	634구역: 테이프

62 Where does the conversation take place?
(A) At a gift shop
(B) At a warehouse
(C) At an office-supply store
(D) At a post office

번역 대화는 어디서 이루어지는가?
(A) 기념품점
(B) 창고
(C) 사무용품점
(D) 우체국

해설 **전체 내용 관련 - 대화의 장소**
남자가 첫 대사에서 창고에서의 첫날은 어떤지(How's your first day at our warehouse going?) 묻고 있으므로 대화 장소는 창고라는 것을 알 수 있다. 따라서 정답은 (B)이다.

어휘 office-supply 사무용품

63 Look at the graphic. Where will the tape be moved to?
(A) To section 1
(B) To section 2
(C) To section 3
(D) To section 4

번역 시각 정보에 의하면, 테이프는 어디로 옮겨지겠는가?
(A) 1구역으로
(B) 2구역으로
(C) 3구역으로
(D) 4구역으로

해설 **시각 정보 연계 - 테이프가 옮겨지는 장소**
여자가 두 번째 대사에서 테이프가 이 선반의 저쪽에 있으면 일을 좀 더 빨리할 수 있다(I could work a little faster if the tape were on that side of this shelf)고 말하자, 남자가 그렇게 하고 테이프와 라벨을 바꿔달라(go ahead and swap it with the labels)고 하고 있다. 선반을 보면 라벨은 1구역이므로 정답은 (A)이다.

64 What does the woman say her supervisor did for her?
(A) Let her borrow an item
(B) Showed her a storage area
(C) Approved a special request
(D) Packed some large boxes

번역 여자는 관리자가 자신을 위해 무엇을 했다고 말하는가?
(A) 물건을 빌려주었다.
(B) 보관 구역을 보여주었다.
(C) 특별한 요청을 승인해 주었다.
(D) 큰 상자를 포장해 주었다.

해설 **세부 사항 관련 - 관리자가 여자를 위해 한 일**
여자가 마지막 대사에서 관리자가 비품이 어디에 보관되어 있는지 보여줬다(my supervisor showed me where the supplies are stored)고 말하고 있으므로 정답은 (B)이다.

어휘 storage area 보관 구역 approve 승인하다

> **Paraphrasing**
> 대화의 where the supplies are stored
> → 정답의 a storage area

65-67 대화 + 지출 명세서

M-Au Ms. Provost, the last few dinner guests are heading out now. I'm going to start packing up, unless you need anything else.

W-Br No, thanks. It's all fine. ⁶⁵**I hope you got a lot of great shots of the guests** and the different parts of the event.

M-Au I certainly did, and I can send you some sample images within the next few days. Also, ⁶⁶**I'm very sorry that I didn't remember to bring some of the props from my studio.**

W-Br Don't worry about that. ⁶⁷**This is a historic hotel, so it's just gorgeous inside.** We had plenty of different backdrops to use.

남: 프로보스트 씨, 마지막 만찬 손님들이 지금 떠나시네요. 뭔가 더 필요한 게 없으시다면 이제 짐을 챙기려고 합니다.

여: 없어요, 감사합니다. 다 좋습니다. **손님들의 멋진 사진을 많이 찍으셨기를 바라요.** 행사의 여러 부분도요.

남: 물론 그랬습니다. 며칠 내로 견본 사진을 보내드릴 수 있어요. 또 제 작업실에서 몇몇 소품을 깜박하고 안 가져와서 너무 죄송해요.

여: 걱정하지 마세요. **여기는 역사적인 호텔이라서 내부가 충분히 아름답잖아요.** 사용할 만한 다양한 배경이 많았어요.

어휘 head out 출발하다 pack up 짐을 챙기다 prop 소품
historic 역사적인 gorgeous 아름다운 backdrop 배경

Provost Anniversary Dinner	
Service	**Cost**
Food and servers	$8,175
Flowers	$1,750
⁶⁵Photography	$1,200
Live Music	$680
Total	$11,805

프로보스트 기념일 만찬	
서비스	비용
음식 및 서빙	8,175달러
꽃	1,750달러
⁶⁵사진 촬영	**1,200달러**
라이브 음악	680달러
합계	11,805달러

어휘 anniversary 기념일

65 Look at the graphic. What was the fee for the services provided by the man?
(A) $8,175
(B) $1,750
(C) $1,200
(D) $680

번역 시각 정보에 의하면, 남자에 의해 제공된 서비스의 요금은 얼마인가?
(A) 8,175달러
(B) 1,750달러
(C) 1,200달러
(D) 680달러

해설 **시각 정보 연계 - 남자에 의해 제공된 서비스의 요금**
여자가 첫 대사에서 손님들의 멋진 사진을 많이 찍었기를 바란다(I hope you got a lot of great shots of the guests)고 했고, 지출 명세서에 따르면 사진 촬영(Photography)은 $1,200이므로 정답은 (C)이다.

66 Why does the man apologize to the woman?
(A) He did not answer a phone call.
(B) Some items were forgotten.
(C) A start time was delayed.
(D) An invoice contained an error.

번역 남자는 왜 여자에게 사과하는가?
(A) 전화를 받지 못해서
(B) 일부 물품을 빠뜨려서
(C) 시작 시간이 늦어져서
(D) 송장에 오류가 있어서

해설 **세부 사항 관련 - 남자가 사과하는 이유**
남자가 두 번째 대사에서 작업실에서 몇몇 소품을 깜박하고 안 가져와서 너무 죄송하다(I'm very sorry that I didn't remember to bring some of the props from my studio)고 사과하고 있으므로 정답은 (B)이다.

어휘 delay 지연시키다   invoice 송장   contain 들어 있다

> **Paraphrasing**
> 대화의 I didn't remember to bring some of the props → 정답의 Some items were forgotten.

67 What does the woman like about the hotel?
(A) It has affordable rental rates.
(B) It has a beautiful interior.
(C) It is near a major roadway.
(D) It has several meeting spaces.

번역 여자는 호텔에 대해 어떤 점을 좋아하는가?
(A) 대여료가 저렴하다.
(B) 실내장식이 아름답다.
(C) 주요 도로 근처에 있다.
(D) 여러 회의 공간이 있다.

해설 **세부 사항 관련 - 여자가 호텔에 대해 좋아하는 점**
여자가 마지막 대사에서 여기는 역사적인 호텔이라서 내부가 충분

히 아름답다(This is a historic hotel, so it's just gorgeous inside)고 말하고 있으므로 정답은 (B)이다.

어휘 affordable 가격이 적당한   rental rate 대여료   roadway 도로

> **Paraphrasing**
> 대화의 gorgeous inside → 정답의 a beautiful interior

68-70 대화+좌석 배치도

> W-Am Hi, Edward. Do you want to go to the Greenway Jazz Band concert this Saturday? I have an extra ticket.
>
> M-Au **68 This Saturday? That's surprising! I thought the show was on Friday.** I tried to get tickets, but they were sold out.
>
> W-Am **68 They decided to add another show for Saturday because of the high demand.** And the seats I got aren't too bad. **69 They're far from the stage, but they're in the middle section.**
>
> M-Au I'd love to go. Thank you so much!
>
> W-Am Fantastic! I actually couldn't have gone to the Friday show anyway because **70 my friend is showing her paintings at the Dolby Gallery, and Friday is the opening night.**

여: 안녕하세요, 에드워드. 이번 주 토요일에 그린웨이 재즈 밴드 콘서트 가고 싶으세요? 저한테 여분의 표가 있어요.

남: 이번 주 토요일이요? 놀랍네요! 저는 공연이 금요일인 줄 알았어요. 표를 사려고 했는데 매진이었어요.

여: 높은 수요 때문에 토요일 공연을 추가하기로 결정했대요. 그리고 제가 구한 좌석이 나쁘지 않아요. 무대에서는 멀지만 그래도 가운데 구역이에요.

남: 정말 가고 싶어요. 성말 고마워요!

여: 좋아요! 실은 저는 어쨌든 금요일 공연은 갈 수가 없었어요. 제 친구가 돌비 화랑에서 그림을 전시하는데 금요일이 개막의 밤이거든요.

어휘 extra 여분의   be sold out 매진되다   add 추가하다
demand 수요   painting 그림

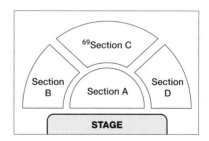

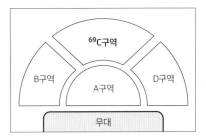

B구역　　　C구역　　　D구역

A구역

무대

68 What is the man surprised about?
(A) The woman has joined a jazz band.
(B) A group is offering a second performance.
(C) The price of some tickets has changed.
(D) A new venue for an event was announced.

번역　남자는 무엇에 대해 놀랐는가?
(A) 여자가 재즈 밴드에 가입했다.
(B) 한 그룹이 두 번째 공연을 할 예정이다.
(C) 일부 표의 가격이 변경되었다.
(D) 행사를 위한 새로운 장소가 발표되었다.

해설　**세부 사항 관련 - 남자가 놀란 것**
남자가 첫 대사에서 이번 주 토요일(This Saturday?)인 것에 놀라면서(That's surprising!) 공연이 금요일인 줄 알았다(I thought the show was on Friday)고 하자, 여자가 높은 수요 때문에 토요일 공연을 추가하기로 결정했다고 한다(They decided to add another show for Saturday because of the high demand)고 말하고 있으므로 정답은 (B)이다.

어휘　performance 공연　venue 장소　announce 발표하다

69 Look at the graphic. For which section does the woman have tickets?
(A) Section A
(B) Section B
(C) Section C
(D) Section D

번역　시각 정보에 의하면, 여자는 어떤 구역의 표를 가지고 있는가?
(A) A구역
(B) B구역
(C) C구역
(D) D구역

해설　**시각 정보 연계 - 여자가 가지고 있는 표의 구역**
여자가 두 번째 대사에서 무대에서는 멀지만 그래도 가운데 구역(They're far from the stage, but they're in the middle section)이라고 말하고 있고, 좌석 배치도에 따르면 무대에서는 멀지만 가운데 구역은 C구역(Section C)이므로 정답은 (C)이다.

70 What will the woman do this Friday?
(A) Help her friend move
(B) Attend an art exhibition
(C) Host a holiday party
(D) Do some home repair tasks

번역　여자는 이번 주 금요일에 무엇을 하겠는가?
(A) 친구의 이사를 돕는다.
(B) 미술 전시회에 참석한다.
(C) 휴일 파티를 주최한다.
(D) 집수리 작업을 한다.

해설　**세부 사항 관련 - 여자가 이번 주 금요일에 할 일**
여자가 마지막 대사에서 친구가 돌비 화랑에서 그림을 전시하는데 금요일이 개막의 밤(my friend is showing her paintings at the Dolby Gallery, and Friday is the opening night)이라고 말하고 있으므로 정답은 (B)이다.

어휘　attend 참석하다　exhibition 전시회　host 주최하다　repair 수리

> **Paraphrasing**
> 대화의 the Dolby Gallery → 정답의 an art exhibition

PART 4

71-73 공지

> W-Br　May I have your attention, please? **[71] Now that the orchestra has completed the first half of its performance**, it is time for intermission. You probably noticed that **[72] some of the stage lights were flickering, and we will try to get these repaired during intermission. We are sorry for any inconvenience or discomfort.** By way of apology, **[73] please come to the box office on your way out to receive a coupon for ten percent off your next ticket purchase.** Thank you for your understanding.
>
> 주목해 주시겠습니까? 오케스트라가 공연의 전반부를 마쳤으므로 중간 휴식 시간을 갖겠습니다. 아마도 알아차리셨겠지만 무대 조명 일부가 깜박거렸는데 저희가 중간 휴식 시간 동안 고쳐보려고 합니다. 불편을 드려 죄송합니다. 사죄의 뜻으로, 나가실 때 매표소에 들러 다음 표 구입시 10% 할인을 받을 수 있는 쿠폰을 받아가 주십시오. 양해해 주셔서 감사합니다.
>
> 어휘　performance 공연　intermission 중간 휴식 시간　flicker 깜박거리다　repair 수리하다　inconvenience 불편　discomfort 불편　by way of apology 사죄의 뜻으로　purchase 구매

71 Where is the announcement taking place?
(A) At a public library
(B) At a history museum
(C) At a concert hall
(D) At a sports stadium

번역　이 공지는 어디에서 이루어지고 있는가?
(A) 공공 도서관
(B) 역사 박물관
(C) 콘서트홀
(D) 스포츠 경기장

화자가 초반부에 오케스트라가 공연의 전반부를 마쳤다(Now that the orchestra has completed the first half of its performance)고 말하고 있는 것으로 보아 공지가 나오는 장소는 콘서트홀이라는 것을 알 수 있다. 따라서 정답은 (C)이다.

---

72 Why does the speaker apologize to the listeners?
(A) Some lights were malfunctioning.
(B) The building is hotter than usual.
(C) An event began later than scheduled.
(D) Some tickets had a misprint.

번역 화자는 왜 청자들에게 사과하는가?
(A) 일부 조명이 오작동했기 때문에
(B) 건물이 평소보다 더웠기 때문에
(C) 행사가 예정보다 늦게 시작했기 때문에
(D) 표에 잘못 인쇄된 부분이 있었기 때문에

해설 **세부 사항 관련 - 화자가 사과하는 이유**
화자가 중반부에 무대 조명이 깜박거렸는데 중간 휴식 시간 동안 고쳐보려고 한다(some of the stage lights were flickering, and we will try to get these repaired during intermission)면서 불편을 드려서 죄송하다(We are sorry for any inconvenience or discomfort)고 사과하고 있으므로 정답은 (A)이다.

어휘 malfunction 오작동하다 misprint 인쇄 실수

> **Paraphrasing**
> 담화의 some of the stage lights were flickering
> → 정답의 Some lights were malfunctioning.

---

73 What is offered to the listeners?
(A) A discount coupon
(B) A partial refund
(C) A complimentary beverage
(D) A gift shop voucher

번역 청자들에게 무엇이 제공되는가?
(A) 할인 쿠폰
(B) 부분 환불
(C) 무료 음료
(D) 기념품점 교환권

해설 **세부 사항 관련 - 청자들에게 제공되는 것**
화자가 후반부에 나가실 때 매표소에 들러 다음 표 구입시 10% 할인을 받을 수 있는 쿠폰을 받아갈 것(please come to the box office on your way out to receive a coupon for ten percent off your next ticket purchase)을 요청하고 있으므로 정답은 (A)이다.

어휘 partial 부분적인 refund 환불 complimentary 무료의 beverage 음료 gift shop 기념품점 voucher 교환권

> **Paraphrasing**
> 담화의 a coupon for ten percent off
> → 정답의 A discount coupon

74-76 전화 메시지

W-Am Hi, this is Melanie Chong. [74] **I booked an appointment with Dr. Sharma for my annual checkup and teeth cleaning for Wednesday.** Unfortunately, that day doesn't work for me anymore. [75] **I need to change it to a later date** due to an unexpected trip for my job. Is there anything available on Friday? Also, [76] **I've recently changed the insurance company I use, so I'm wondering about the best way to give you their details.** Please call me back at 555-3944.

안녕하세요, 멜라니 청입니다. **수요일에 연례 검진과 스케일링을 위해 샤르마 선생님께 예약을 했는데요.** 안타깝게도 그날 제가 안 됩니다. 예기치 못한 출장 때문에 **날짜를 더 나중으로 바꿔야 하는데요.** 금요일에 가능한 시간이 있을까요? 또, **제가 최근에 사용하는 보험회사를 바꿔서 세부 내용을 전달할 가장 좋은 방법이 무엇인지 궁금합니다.** 555-3944로 회신 전화 부탁드립니다.

어휘 appointment (진료 등의) 예약 annual 연례의 checkup 건강 검진 unexpected 예기치 못한 insurance 보험

---

74 What type of business is the speaker most likely calling?
(A) An employment agency
(B) A vehicle repair shop
(C) A dental office
(D) A hair salon

번역 화자는 어떤 유형의 사업체에 전화를 걸고 있겠는가?
(A) 직업소개소
(B) 차량 정비소
(C) 치과
(D) 미용실

해설 **전체 내용 관련 - 화자가 전화를 건 업체 유형**
화자가 초반부에서 수요일에 연례 검진과 스케일링을 위해 샤르마 선생님께 예약을 했다(I booked an appointment with Dr. Sharma for my annual checkup and teeth cleaning for Wednesday)고 하므로 전화 수신업체는 치과임을 추론할 수 있다. 따라서 정답은 (C)이다.

---

75 What does the speaker mention about her appointment?
(A) It was booked with the wrong person.
(B) It has to be postponed.
(C) It must be at another branch.
(D) It includes a new customer discount.

번역 화자는 자신의 예약에 대해 무엇을 언급하는가?
(A) 사람을 잘못 예약했다.
(B) 미뤄져야 한다.
(C) 다른 지점으로 되어야 한다.
(D) 신규 고객 할인이 포함되어 있다.

해설 **세부 사항 관련 - 화자가 자신의 예약에 대해 언급한 것**
화자가 중반부에서 날짜를 더 나중으로 바꿔야 한다(I need to change it to a later date)고 하므로 정답은 (B)이다.

어휘 postpone 미루다 branch 지사, 지점

> **Paraphrasing**
> 담화의 I need to change it to a later date
> → 정답의 It has to be postponed.

76 What does the speaker want to find out about?
(A) Taking public transportation
(B) Updating insurance information
(C) Receiving an employee discount
(D) Handling unexpected charges

번역 화자는 무엇에 대해 알고 싶어 하는가?
(A) 대중교통 타기
(B) 보험 정보 갱신하기
(C) 직원 할인 받기
(D) 예치기 못한 요금 처리하기

해설 **세부 사항 관련 - 화자가 알고 싶어 하는 것**
화자가 후반부에서 최근에 사용하는 보험회사를 바꿔서 세부 내용을 전달할 가장 좋은 방법이 무엇인지 궁금하다(I've recently changed the insurance company I use, so I'm wondering about the best way to give you their details)고 하므로 정답은 (B)이다.

어휘 public transportation 대중교통 handle 다루다, 처리하다

77-79 광고

M-Cn Do you want to experience all that Irvine Bay has to offer? Then [77]**book a tour with Wonderful Waves! Our boats depart daily at 9 A.M. and 4 P.M.,** with our launch site conveniently located near the Boone Street parking area. During the tour, we'll take you by boat to all of the top sites in the area. [78]**Everyone will receive a catered lunch or dinner upon returning from the tour,** and we serve free sodas and bottled water on the boat. And for the month of April, [79]**you can book online to get an exclusive offer of 15% off for parties of five or more.**

어빈 만이 제공할 수 있는 모든 것을 경험하고 싶으세요? 그렇다면 **원더풀 웨이브스에서 투어를 예약하세요! 저희 배는 매일 오전 9시와 오후 4시에 출발하며,** 승선장은 분 가 주차장 근처에 편리하게 위치해 있습니다. 투어가 진행되는 동안 이 지역에서 가장 좋은 장소들을 모두 들를 겁니다. **투어에서 돌아자마자 모든 분은 출장 준비된 점심 식사나 저녁 식사를 제공받으실 겁니다.** 배 위에서는 탄산음료와 생수를 무료로 제공해 드립니다. 4월 한 달 동안 **5인 이상 단체인 경우 온라인으로 예약하시면 15% 할인이라는 특별한 혜택을 받으실 수 있습니다.**

어휘 depart 출발하다 launch site 출발 지점 conveniently 편리하게 catered 출장 요리로 준비된 upon -ing ~을 하자마자 serve 제공하다 exclusive 특별한, 고급의 party 단체

77 What is the advertisement about?
(A) An art festival
(B) A museum tour
(C) A boat ride
(D) A holiday parade

번역 광고는 무엇에 관한 것인가?
(A) 예술 축제
(B) 박물관 견학
(C) 배 타기
(D) 휴일 퍼레이드

해설 **전체 내용 관련 - 광고하는 것**
화자가 초반부에서 원더풀 웨이브스에서 투어를 예약하라(book a tour with Wonderful Waves!)면서 배는 매일 출발한다(Our boats depart daily)고 하므로 정답은 (C)이다.

어휘 ride (말, 차량 등을) 타기

78 What will participants be given?
(A) A tote bag
(B) A prepared meal
(C) A group photograph
(D) An area map

번역 참가자들은 무엇을 받을 것인가?
(A) 토트백
(B) 준비된 식사
(C) 단체 사진
(D) 지역 지도

해설 **세부 사항 관련 - 참가자들이 받을 것**
화자가 중반부에서 투어에서 돌아자마자 모든 분은 출장 준비된 점심 식사나 저녁 식사를 제공받을 것(Everyone will receive a catered lunch or dinner upon returning from the tour)이라고 하므로 정답은 (B)이다.

어휘 participant 참가자 tote bag 토트백(손잡이 2개가 마주 달린 큰 가방) prepared 준비된

> **Paraphrasing**
> 담화의 a catered lunch or dinner
> → 정답의 A prepared meal

79 What does the speaker say can be done on a Web site?
(A) Accessing a group discount
(B) Viewing videos of the area
(C) Making a dinner reservation
(D) Watching a safety video

번역 화자는 웹사이트에서 무엇이 진행될 수 있다고 말하는가?
(A) 단체 할인 받기
(B) 지역 영상 보기
(C) 저녁 식사 예약하기
(D) 안전 교육 영상 시청하기

해설 **세부 사항 관련 - 웹사이트에서 진행될 것**
화자가 마지막에 5인 이상 단체인 경우 온라인으로 예약하면 15% 할인이라는 특별한 혜택을 받을 수 있다(you can book online to get an exclusive offer of 15% off for parties of five or more)고 말하고 있으므로 정답은 (A)이다.

어휘 access 이용하다, 접속하다 reservation 예약 safety 안전

> **Paraphrasing**
> 담화의 online → 질문의 Web site
> 담화의 get an exclusive offer of 15% off for parties of five or more → 정답의 Accessing a group discount

80-82 전화 메시지

W-Am This is Mindy Harper, **80 head of the R&D division** at the Nashville branch. I'm calling about our rechargeable battery project. I know that you are not able to commute to our branch, but your supervisor said that **81 you would be willing to do the project on the days that you work from home. Normally, we don't allow that,** but we know that you're highly experienced. So, please call me back so that we can make the necessary arrangements. **82 We would need to figure out what day you could begin the project.** Thanks a lot!

저는 내슈빌 지점의 **연구 개발부장** 민디 하퍼입니다. 충전식 배터리 프로젝트 건으로 전화드리는데요. 당신이 저희 지점으로 통근할 수 없다는 사실을 알고 있습니다만, 당신의 관리자가 말씀하시길 당신이 재택 근무하는 날에는 이 프로젝트를 수행할 의향이 있을 거라고 해서요. 보통은 저희가 그걸 허용하지 않지만 당신이 매우 경험이 풍부하다는 걸 알아요. 그러니 저희 쪽에서 필요한 준비를 할 수 있도록 회신 전화 부탁드려요. 당신이 언제부터 프로젝트를 시작할 수 있을지 파악해야 하니까요. 고맙습니다!

어휘 division (조직의) 분과 rechargeable 충전 가능한 commute 통근하다 supervisor 관리자 allow 허용하다 experienced 경험이 풍부한 necessary 필요한 arrangement 준비 figure out 알아내다

80 Which department does the speaker work in?
(A) Human resources
(B) Building maintenance
(C) Research and development
(D) Information technology

번역 화자는 어떤 부서에서 일하는가?
(A) 인사부
(B) 건물 유지보수부
(C) 연구 개발부
(D) 정보 기술부

해설 **전체 내용 관련 - 화자의 근무 부서**
화자가 도입부에 연구 개발부장(head of the R&D division)이라고 자신을 소개하고 있으므로 정답은 (C)이다.

어휘 maintenance 유지보수

> **Paraphrasing**
> 담화의 division → 질문의 department

81 Why does the speaker say, "we know that you're highly experienced"?
(A) To explain the reason for a promotion
(B) To accept a request for a pay raise
(C) To show understanding of a busy schedule
(D) To approve working remotely for a task

번역 화자가 "당신이 매우 경험이 풍부하다는 걸 알아요"라고 말한 이유는?
(A) 승진 이유를 설명하려고
(B) 봉급 인상 요구를 수락하려고
(C) 바쁜 일정에 대한 이해심을 보이려고
(D) 업무를 위해 원격으로 근무하는 것을 승인하려고

해설 **화자의 의도 파악 - 당신이 매우 경험이 풍부하다는 걸 안다는 말의 의도**
앞에서 당신이 재택 근무하는 날에는 이 프로젝트를 수행할 의향이 있을 것(you would be willing to do the project on the days that you work from home)이라고 하면서 보통은 그걸 허용하지 않는다(Normally, we don't allow that)고 말한 뒤 인용문을 언급하는 것으로 보아, 재택 근무를 승인하려는 의도로 한 말임을 알 수 있다. 따라서 정답은 (D)이다.

어휘 promotion 승진 accept 받아들이다 pay raise 봉급 인상 approve 승인하다 work remotely 원격으로 근무하다

82 What does the speaker want to discuss with the listener?
(A) A start date
(B) A payment method
(C) Some necessary tools
(D) Some coworkers' skills

번역 화자는 청자와 무엇에 대해 상의하고 싶어 하는가?
(A) 시작일
(B) 결제 방법
(C) 필요한 도구들
(D) 동료들의 역량

해설 **세부 사항 관련 - 화자가 상의하고 싶어 하는 것**
화자가 마지막에 당신이 언제부터 프로젝트를 시작할 수 있을지 파악해야 한다(We would need to figure out what day you could begin the project)고 말하고 있으므로 정답은 (A)이다.

어휘 method 방법, 수단 tool 도구 skill 기술, 역량

> **Paraphrasing**
> 담화의 what day you could begin the project
> → 질문의 a start date

83-85 연설

> W-Br **83 Welcome to Gilbert International's fifth annual conference on preventative medicine. 84 Last year we had nearly five hundred people in attendance at the venue, but you'll notice we have about half as much this year.** Well, for the first time ever, we've added an online option. Now, the first talk will begin in just a moment. And, **85 if you've signed up for an afternoon workshop, just make sure you confirm which room you're going to.** Our staff can direct you if needed.
>
> 길버트 인터내셔널의 제5회 연례 예방 의학 학회에 오신 것을 환영합니다. 작년에는 이 장소에 거의 500명이 참석했지만 올해에는 약 절반 수준임을 알아차리셨을 겁니다. 음, 처음으로 저희가 온라인 옵션을 추가했습니다. 이제 첫 번째 발표가 곧 시작될 겁니다. 그리고, **오후 워크숍을 신청하셨다면 어느 호실로 가셔야 하는지 꼭 확인하시기 바랍니다.** 필요하다면 저희 직원이 안내해 드릴 수 있습니다.
>
> 어휘 annual 연례의 preventative medicine 예방 의학 in attendance 참석한 venue 장소 add 추가하다 sign up for ~을 신청하다 direct 길을 안내하다

83 What kind of event is taking place?
(A) A product launch
(B) A group interview session
(C) A medical conference
(D) A film festival

번역 어떤 종류의 행사가 진행되고 있는가?
(A) 제품 출시
(B) 집단 면접
(C) 의학 학회
(D) 영화제

해설 **전체 내용 관련 - 진행 중인 행사**
화자가 도입부에 길버트 인터내셔널의 제5회 연례 예방 의학 학회에 오신 것을 환영한다(Welcome to Gilbert International's fifth annual conference on preventative medicine)고 말하고 있으므로 의학 학회가 진행 중이라는 것을 알 수 있다. 따라서 정답은 (C)이다.

어휘 launch 출시

> **Paraphrasing**
> 담화의 conference on preventative medicine
> → 정답의 A medical conference

84 Why does the speaker say, "we've added an online option"?
(A) To encourage listeners to make a purchase
(B) To apologize for some technical difficulties
(C) To demonstrate that listeners' ideas are being used
(D) To explain why a group is smaller in size

번역 화자가 "저희가 온라인 옵션을 추가했습니다"라고 말한 이유는?
(A) 청자들이 구매하도록 장려하려고
(B) 기술적 문제에 대해 사과하려고
(C) 청자들의 아이디어가 사용되고 있음을 보여주려고
(D) 인원이 왜 축소되었는지 설명하려고

해설 **화자의 의도 파악 - 온라인 옵션을 추가했다는 말의 의도**
앞에서 작년에는 이 장소에 거의 500명이 참석했지만 올해에는 약 절반 수준임을 알아차렸을 것(Last year we had nearly five hundred people in attendance at the venue, but you'll notice we have about half as much this year)이라고 한 뒤 인용문을 언급하는 것으로 보아, 나머지 절반 인원은 온라인으로 참가했다는 의미이므로 작년에 비해 올해 참석 인원이 적은 이유를 설명하려는 의도로 한 말임을 알 수 있다. 따라서 정답은 (D)이다.

어휘 make a purchase 구매하다 apologize 사과하다 technical 기술적인 difficulty 어려움 demonstrate 시연하다

85 What are the listeners asked to do?
(A) Turn off their phones temporarily
(B) Check the locations of some activities
(C) Complete a form to provide feedback
(D) Wear a name tag during the event

번역 청자들은 무엇을 하도록 요청받았는가?
(A) 잠시 전화기를 꺼두기
(B) 활동이 진행될 장소 확인하기
(C) 피드백을 제공하기 위해 양식 작성하기
(D) 행사가 진행되는 동안 명찰 달기

해설 **세부 사항 관련 - 청자들이 요청받은 일**
화자가 후반부에 오후 워크숍을 신청했다면 어느 호실로 가야 하는지 꼭 확인하기 바란다(if you've signed up for an afternoon workshop, just make sure you confirm which room you're going to)고 했으므로 정답은 (B)이다.

어휘 turn off 전원을 끄다 temporarily 일시적으로 activity 활동 complete 작성하다

> **Paraphrasing**
> 담화의 confirm which room you're going to
> → 정답의 Check the locations

86-88 담화

Thank you for stopping by our booth at the expo! **86 We're thrilled to introduce our new line of kitchen flooring today.** It looks like wood, but it is actually made of plastic. With our unique design, you can get the look and feel of wood, but **87 this new plastic is much tougher.** Even after years of walking on it, it will still look like new. There are a variety of shades to choose from. **88 I'll pass out our catalog now, which shows everything we sell and the color options that are available.**

본 박람회에서 저희 부스에 들러주셔서 감사합니다! **오늘 주방 바닥재 신제품군을 소개할 수 있어서 매우 기쁩니다.** 이것은 나무처럼 보이지만 실은 플라스틱으로 만들어졌습니다. 저희의 독특한 디자인으로 나무 같은 외형과 촉감을 느끼실 수 있지만, **이 새 플라스틱은 훨씬 견고합니다.** 수년을 밟고 다니신 후에도 여전히 새것처럼 보일 겁니다. 다양한 색상 중에서 고르실 수 있습니다. **지금 저희 카탈로그를 나눠드리겠습니다.** 여기에서 저희가 파는 모든 제품과 구매 가능한 색상을 보실 수 있습니다.

어휘 stop by 잠깐 들르다 expo 박람회 be thrilled to ~하는 것이 신이 나다 introduce 소개하다 flooring 바닥재 unique 독특한 tough 튼튼한 shade 그늘, 색조 pass out 나눠주다 available 이용 가능한

86 What kind of business does the speaker work for?
(A) A package delivery service
(B) A computer software distributor
(C) A fashion design company
(D) A flooring manufacturer

번역 화자는 어떤 종류의 사업체에서 일하는가?
(A) 택배 회사
(B) 컴퓨터 소프트웨어 유통업체
(C) 패션 디자인 회사
(D) 바닥재 제조업체

해설 **전체 내용 관련 - 화자의 근무 업종**
화자가 초반부에 오늘 주방 바닥재 신제품군을 소개할 수 있어서 매우 기쁘다(We're thrilled to introduce our new line of kitchen flooring today)고 말하고 있으므로 정답은 (D)이다.

어휘 distributor 유통업체 manufacturer 제조업체

87 What advantage of the new material does the speaker mention?
(A) It is very durable.
(B) It is inexpensive.
(C) It is available in many sizes.
(D) It is good for the environment.

번역 화자는 새 재료의 어떤 장점에 대해 언급하는가?
(A) 매우 견고하다.
(B) 저렴하다.
(C) 다양한 사이즈가 있다.
(D) 환경에 이롭다.

해설 **세부 사항 관련 - 화자가 언급하는 새 재료의 장점**
화자가 중반부에서 이 새 플라스틱은 훨씬 견고하다(this new plastic is much tougher)고 말하고 있으므로 정답은 (A)이다.

어휘 durable 견고한 inexpensive 저렴한 environment 환경

> **Paraphrasing**
> 담화의 much tougher → 정답의 very durable

88 What will the speaker do next?
(A) Respond to listeners' questions
(B) Distribute a product catalog
(C) Show the listeners a chart
(D) Introduce one of her colleagues

번역 화자는 다음으로 무엇을 하겠는가?
(A) 청자들의 질문에 응답하기
(B) 제품 카탈로그 배포하기
(C) 청자들에게 차트 보여주기
(D) 동료들 중 한 명 소개하기

해설 **세부 사항 관련 - 화자가 다음에 할 일**
화자가 마지막에 지금 카탈로그를 나눠드릴 건데 저희가 파는 모든 제품과 구매 가능한 색상을 보실 수 있다(I'll pass out our catalog now, which shows everything we sell and the color options that are available)고 말하고 있으므로 정답은 (B)이다.

어휘 respond 응답하다 distribute 배포하다 colleague 동료

> **Paraphrasing**
> 담화의 pass out → 정답의 Distribute
> 담화의 everything we sell → 정답의 product

89-91 방송

You're listening to *Community Corner* on Radio 22. On Saturday, June 29, **89 the town's annual cooking contest will take place at Blossom Hall.** **90 Even if you don't make anything, don't forget that attendees get to try the food after the judging is completed.** There will be plenty to go around. There are several categories for entry, including stews, grilled meat, pasta, and more. **91 Tomorrow, the event's planner, Ayako Yano, will visit the studio to share the details about the entry requirements. She'll also let us know what prizes will be given to the winners of the event,** which I'm sure everyone will want to hear about. Be sure to tune in!

여러분은 지금 라디오 22의 <커뮤니티 코너>를 듣고 계십니다. 6월 29일 토요일 우리 시의 연례 요리 경연대회가 블러섬 홀에서 열릴 예정입니다. 요리를 하지 않으시더라도 참석자들은 심사가 끝난 후에 음식을 맛볼 수 있다는 사실을 잊지 마십시오. 음식은 충분할 겁니다. 출전 부문은 스튜, 구운 고기, 파스타 등 다양합니다. 내일, 행사 기획자인 아야코 야노가 스튜디오를 방문해 출전 자격 요건에 대한 세부 내용을 공유해 줄 겁니다. 그녀는 우승자에게 어떤 상품이 주어지는지도 알려줄 겁니다. 이건 모든 분이 궁금하신 부분이겠죠. 꼭 청취해 주세요!

> 어휘　annual 연례의　attendee 참석자　judging 심사　complete 완료하다　go around (사람들에게 많이) 돌아가다　entry 출전　requirement 자격 요건　winner 우승자　tune in 청취하다

89　What event does the speaker mention?
(A) A comedy show
(B) A graduation ceremony
(C) A theater performance
(D) A cooking competition

번역　화자는 어떤 행사를 언급하는가?
(A) 코미디 공연
(B) 졸업식
(C) 연극 공연
(D) 요리 대회

해설　**전체 내용 관련 - 화자가 언급하는 행사**
화자가 초반부에 우리 시의 연례 요리 경연대회가 블러섬 홀에서 열릴 예정(the town's annual cooking contest will take place at Blossom Hall)이라고 말하고 있으므로 정답은 (D)이다.

어휘　graduation 졸업　ceremony 식　performance 공연　competition 경쟁, 대회

> **Paraphrasing**
> 담화의 the town's annual cooking contest
> → 정답의 A cooking competition

90　Why does the speaker say, "There will be plenty to go around"?
(A) To ask people to be patient when receiving items
(B) To confirm that the selected venue is large enough
(C) To explain that tickets will probably not sell out
(D) To encourage the listeners to attend an event

번역　화자가 "음식은 충분할 겁니다"라고 말한 이유는?
(A) 물건을 받을 때 인내심을 가져달라고 부탁하려고
(B) 선택된 장소가 충분히 큰지 확인하려고
(C) 표가 다 팔리지는 않을 거라고 설명하려고
(D) 청자들이 행사에 참석하도록 장려하려고

해설　**화자의 의도 파악 - 음식은 충분할 것이라는 말의 의도**
앞에서 요리를 하지 않더라도 참석자들은 심사가 끝난 후에 음식

을 맛볼 수 있다는 사실을 잊지 말라(Even if you don't make anything, don't forget that attendees get to try the food after the judging is completed)고 한 뒤 인용문을 언급하는 것으로 보아, 청자들이 요리 경연대회 행사에 참석하도록 독려하려는 의도로 한 말임을 알 수 있다. 따라서 정답은 (D)이다.

어휘　patient 인내심 있는　selected 선택된　attend 참석하다

91　What will happen tomorrow?
(A) An enrollment period will begin.
(B) A discount on tickets will be offered.
(C) A Web site will be launched.
(D) A list of prizes will be announced.

번역　내일 무슨 일이 일어나겠는가?
(A) 등록 기간이 시작될 것이다.
(B) 표 할인이 제공될 것이다.
(C) 웹사이트가 개시될 것이다.
(D) 상품이 발표될 것이다.

해설　**세부 사항 관련 - 내일 일어날 일**
화자가 마지막에 내일 행사 기획자인 아야코 야노가 스튜디오를 방문해 출전 자격 요건에 대한 세부 내용을 공유할 것(Tomorrow, the event's planner, Ayako Yano, will visit the studio to share the details about the entry requirements)이라며 그녀는 우승자에게 어떤 상품이 주어지는지도 알려줄 것(She'll also let us know what prizes will be given to the winners of the event)이라고 말하고 있으므로 정답은 (D)이다.

어휘　enrollment 등록　launch 출시하다

> **Paraphrasing**
> 담화의 She'll also let us know what prizes will be given to the winners of the event
> → 정답의 A list of prizes will be announced.

92-94 담화

> M-Au　Good morning, everyone. The Flynn City Planning Committee is pleased to announce the approval of a project to build twenty-five miles of bicycle lanes in our city. **[92] We hope this will encourage people to get more exercise**, which is good for their overall health. Upon completion of the project, **[93] we will run a series of advertisements to inform out-of-town visitors about the new bicycle lanes.** Thanks to mainly using existing roadways, the lanes will be open by August, and **[94] next year we will evaluate the success of the project** to see if further expansion of the network is justified.
>
> 좋은 아침입니다, 여러분. 플린 도시계획위원회는 우리 시에 25마일짜리 자전거 도로를 짓는 프로젝트가 승인되었음을 발표하게 되어 기쁩니다. **우리는 이 프로젝트를 통해 사람들이 운동을 더 많이 하기를 바랍**

니다. 운동은 전반적인 건강에 도움이 되니까요. 프로젝트가 완공되는 대로 우리는 타지에서 온 방문자들에게 새 자전거 도로에 대해 알리는 일련의 광고를 게재할 겁니다. 주로 기존 도로를 사용하기 때문에 자전거 도로는 8월까지는 완공될 겁니다. 그리고 도로망의 추가 확장이 타당한지 확인하기 위해 **내년에 이 프로젝트의 성공 여부를 평가할 겁니다.**

어휘 committee 위원회 approval 승인 overall 전반적인 completion 완료 advertisement 광고 out-of-town 타지에서 온 visitor 방문자 existing 기존의, 현재 사용되는 roadway 도로 evaluate 평가하다 success 성공 expansion 확장 justify 타당함을 보여 주다

92 According to the speaker, what is the purpose of the project?
(A) To cut public spending
(B) To promote a healthy habit
(C) To reduce road accidents
(D) To attract more businesses

번역 화자에 따르면, 프로젝트의 목적은 무엇인가?
(A) 공공 지출을 삭감하는 것
(B) 건강한 습관을 장려하는 것
(C) 도로 사고를 줄이는 것
(D) 더 많은 기업을 유치하는 것

해설 **세부 사항 관련 - 프로젝트의 목적**
화자가 초반부에서 이 프로젝트를 통해 사람들이 운동을 더 많이 하기를 바란다(We hope this will encourage people to get more exercise)고 말하고 있으므로 정답은 (B)이다.

어휘 cut 삭감하다 public spending 공공 지출 promote 촉진하다 habit 습관 reduce 줄이다 attract 끌어들이다

> **Paraphrasing**
> 담화의 encourage people to get more exercise
> → 정답의 promote a healthy habit

93 Who will be targeted in an ad campaign?
(A) Students
(B) Business owners
(C) Tourists
(D) Prospective investors

번역 광고 캠페인은 누구를 대상으로 하겠는가?
(A) 학생
(B) 업체 소유주
(C) 관광객
(D) 잠재적 투자자

해설 **세부 사항 관련 - 광고 캠페인의 대상**
화자가 중반부에서 우리는 타지에서 온 방문자들에게 새 자전거 도로에 대해 알리는 일련의 광고를 게재할 것(we will run a series of advertisements to inform out-of-town visitors about the new bicycle lanes)이라고 말하고 있으므로 정답은 (C)이다.

어휘 prospective 유망한 investor 투자자

> **Paraphrasing**
> 담화의 out-of-town visitors → 정답의 Tourists

94 What will happen next year?
(A) A communication network will be upgraded.
(B) An assessment will be carried out.
(C) Voters will elect a new mayor.
(D) The city will host a bicycle race.

번역 내년에는 무슨 일이 일어나겠는가?
(A) 통신망이 업그레이드될 것이다.
(B) 평가가 실시될 것이다.
(C) 유권자들이 새 시장을 선출할 것이다.
(D) 시에서 자전거 경주 대회를 주최할 것이다.

해설 **세부 사항 관련 - 내년에 일어날 일**
화자가 마지막에 내년에 이 프로젝트의 성공 여부를 평가할 것(next year we will evaluate the success of the project)이라고 말하고 있으므로 정답은 (B)이다.

어휘 assessment 평가 carry out 수행하다 voter 유권자 elect 선출하다 mayor 시장

> **Paraphrasing**
> 담화의 we will evaluate the success of the project
> → 정답의 An assessment will be carried out

95-97 전화 메시지 + 지도

M-Cn Hello, Ms. Nakano. This is Damon Arroyo at Pruitt Insurance. **95 I'm calling about the workshop on sales techniques that you'll be conducting at our office.** Some staff from anoτher branch are going to join, so the total number of participants will now be eighteen. Also, **96 can you let me know your car's license plate number?** I need it to request your parking permit from our business complex's parking office. **97 With a permit, you'll be able to park in the visitors' lot between the Hastings Building and the Levine Building, instead of on the street.**

안녕하세요, 나카노 씨. 저는 프루잇 보험의 데이먼 아로요입니다. 귀하께서 저희 사무실에서 실시하실 영업 기법 워크숍 건으로 전화드립니다. 다른 지점의 직원들이 참석할 예정이라서, 총 참가자 수가 18명이 될 겁니다. 또한, **귀하의 차량 번호를 알려주시겠습니까?** 저희 복합업무단지의 주차 관리소에서 주차 허가를 신청하는 데 필요하거든요. 주차 허가가 있으면 길에 주차하지 않고 헤이스팅스 빌딩과 러빈 빌딩 사이에 있는 방문자 주차장에 주차하실 수 있습니다.

어휘 insurance 보험 technique 기법 conduct 실시하다 branch 지사, 지점 participant 참가자 license plate number 차량 번호 permit 허가

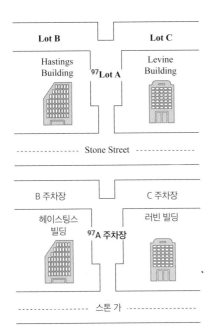

Lot B

Lot C

Hastings Building

Levine Building

⁹⁷Lot A

------- Stone Street -------

B 주차장

C 주차장

헤이스팅스 빌딩

러빈 빌딩

⁹⁷A 주차장

------- 스톤 가 -------

95 Who most likely is the listener?
(A) A potential customer
(B) A corporate trainer
(C) A truck driver
(D) A repair technician

번역 청자는 누구이겠는가?
(A) 잠재 고객
(B) **기업체 교육 강사**
(C) 트럭 운전사
(D) 수리 기술자

해설 **전체 내용 관련 - 청자의 직업**
화자가 초반부에 귀하께서 저희 사무실에서 실시하실 영업 기법 워크숍 건으로 전화드린다(I'm calling about the workshop on sales techniques that you'll be conducting at our office)고 말한 것으로 보아 청자는 기업체 교육 강사임을 알 수 있다. 따라서 정답은 (B)이다.

어휘 potential 잠재적인   corporate 기업의

96 What should the listener inform the speaker of?
(A) Her technology needs
(B) Her meal preference
(C) Her vehicle information
(D) Her expected arrival time

번역 청자는 화자에게 무엇을 알려야 하는가?
(A) 기술 관련 요구
(B) 선호하는 식사 메뉴
(C) **차량 정보**
(D) 예상 도착 시간

해설 **세부 사항 관련 - 청자가 화자에게 알려야 하는 것**
화자가 중반부에 차량 번호를 알려줄 것(can you let me know

your car's license plate number)을 요청하고 있으므로 정답은 (C)이다.

어휘 technology 기술   preference 선호, 특히 좋아하는 것

> **Paraphrasing**
> 담화의 car's license plate number
> → 정답의 vehicle information

97 Look at the graphic. According to the speaker, where can visitors with parking permits park?.
(A) In Lot A
(B) In Lot B
(C) In Lot C
(D) Along Stone Street

번역 시각 정보에 의하면, 화자에 따르면, 주차 허가가 있는 방문자들은 어디에 주차할 수 있는가?
(A) **A 주차장에**
(B) B 주차장에
(C) C 주차장에
(D) 스톤 가를 따라

해설 **시각 정보 연계 - 주차 허가가 있는 방문자들의 주차 장소**
화자가 마지막에 주차 허가가 있으면 헤이스팅스 빌딩과 러빈 빌딩 사이에 있는 방문자 주차장에 주차할 수 있다(With a permit, you'll be able to park in the visitors' lot between the Hastings Building and the Levine Building ~)고 했고, 지도에 따르면 헤이스팅스 빌딩과 러빈 빌딩 사이에 있는 방문자 주차장은 A 주차장이므로 정답은 (A)이다.

98-100 방송+일정표

M-Au Thanks for tuning in to *Daily Steps* with Amish Punja. In each episode, ⁹⁸**I welcome a new guest to share the latest advice on staying fit and healthy.** Our two-hundredth episode will be broadcast on March 16. To celebrate this milestone, ⁹⁹**we are giving away a number of great prizes. For a chance to win, simply register for the drawing on our Web site.** The winners will be announced on March 16. Alright, now, ¹⁰⁰**I would like to welcome Maya Mendoza to the studio.** I'm sure you'll find her comments useful.

아미시 푼자와 함께하는 <데일리 스텝스>를 청취해 주셔서 감사합니다. 매 에피소드에서는 **건강을 유지하는 법에 대한 최신 조언을 공유해 줄 새로운 초대 손님을 모십니다.** 200번째 에피소드는 3월 16일에 방송될 예정입니다. 이 특별한 날을 기념하기 위해 **많은 상품을 나눠드릴 예정입니다. 기회를 얻기 위해서는 저희 웹사이트에서 경품 추첨 행사에 등록만 해주시면 됩니다.** 당첨자는 3월 16일에 발표될 겁니다. 자, 이제, **마야 멘도사를 스튜디오로 모시겠습니다.** 그녀가 해줄 말은 매우 유용할 거라고 확신합니다.

```
◎ ◎ ◎ ◎ ◎ ◎ ◎ ◎ ◎ ◎ ◎ ◎ ◎
          Interviews This Week
```

Monday:	Ravi Dayal
100Tuesday:	Maya Mendoza
Wednesday:	Kami Foster
Thursday:	Yun Bai – Part 1
Friday:	Yun Bai – Part 2

```
◎ ◎ ◎ ◎ ◎ ◎ ◎ ◎ ◎ ◎ ◎ ◎ ◎
             이번 주 인터뷰
```

월요일:	라비 다얄
100화요일:	마야 멘도사
수요일:	카미 포스터
목요일:	윤 바이 - 1부
금요일:	윤 바이 - 2부

98 Why are guests included on the radio show?
(A) To offer financial advice
(B) To talk about business opportunities
(C) To provide health tips
(D) To discuss a hospital expansion

번역　초대 손님들은 왜 라디오 프로그램에 출연하는가?
(A) 재정 관련 조언을 제공하려고
(B) 사업 기회에 대해 이야기하려고
(C) 건강 조언을 제공하려고
(D) 병원 확장을 상의하려고

해설　**세부 사항 관련 - 초대 손님들이 라디오 프로그램에 출연하는
이유**
화자가 초반부에 건강을 유지하는 법에 대한 최신 조언을 공유해 줄 새
로운 초대 손님을 모신다(I welcome a new guest to share the
latest advice on staying fit and healthy)고 말하고 있으므로
정답은 (C)이다.

어휘　opportunity 기회　expansion 확장

> **Paraphrasing**
> 담화의 to share the latest advice on staying fit and
> healthy → 정답의 To provide health tips

99 According to the speaker, what can listeners do
on a Web site?
(A) Read product reviews from the host
(B) Enter an upcoming prize drawing
(C) Download full episodes of the show
(D) Get guests' contact details

번역　화자에 따르면, 청자들은 웹사이트에서 무엇을 할 수 있는가?
(A) 진행자가 작성한 제품 후기 읽기
(B) 다가오는 경품 행사 참가하기
(C) 방송 전체 에피소드 내려받기
(D) 초대 손님들의 연락처 받기

해설　**세부 사항 관련 - 청자들이 웹사이트에서 할 수 있는 일**
화자가 중반부에 많은 상품을 나눠줄 예정(we are giving away a
number of great prizes)이라면서 기회를 얻기 위해서는 저희 웹
사이트에서 경품 추첨 행사에 등록만 하면 된다(For a chance to
win, simply register for the drawing on our Web site)고
말하고 있으므로 정답은 (B)이다.

어휘　enter 참가하다　upcoming 다가오는

100 Look at the graphic. When is this episode being
broadcast?
(A) On Monday
(B) On Tuesday
(C) On Wednesday
(D) On Thursday

번역　시각 정보에 의하면, 이 에피소드는 언제 방송되겠는가?
(A) 월요일
(B) 화요일
(C) 수요일
(D) 목요일

해설　**시각 정보 연계 - 이번 에피소드의 방송일**
화자가 후반부에 마야 멘도사를 스튜디오로 모시겠다(I would like
to welcome Maya Mendoza to the studio)고 말하고 있고,
일정표에 따르면 마야 멘도사의 인터뷰는 화요일(Tuesday)에 예정
되어 있으므로 정답은 (R)이다.

TEST 8

1 (B)	2 (D)	3 (A)	4 (C)	5 (A)
6 (C)	7 (A)	8 (A)	9 (B)	10 (C)
11 (A)	12 (B)	13 (A)	14 (A)	15 (A)
16 (C)	17 (B)	18 (C)	19 (A)	20 (C)
21 (B)	22 (C)	23 (B)	24 (B)	25 (B)
26 (A)	27 (C)	28 (C)	29 (A)	30 (B)
31 (C)	32 (D)	33 (D)	34 (A)	35 (A)
36 (C)	37 (B)	38 (C)	39 (B)	40 (A)
41 (B)	42 (B)	43 (C)	44 (D)	45 (C)
46 (B)	47 (A)	48 (C)	49 (D)	50 (C)
51 (A)	52 (C)	53 (D)	54 (B)	55 (D)
56 (B)	57 (A)	58 (B)	59 (C)	60 (B)
61 (C)	62 (B)	63 (D)	64 (A)	65 (D)
66 (B)	67 (C)	68 (B)	69 (A)	70 (B)
71 (A)	72 (C)	73 (D)	74 (D)	75 (B)
76 (A)	77 (D)	78 (B)	79 (C)	80 (A)
81 (C)	82 (B)	83 (A)	84 (D)	85 (B)
86 (C)	87 (A)	88 (D)	89 (B)	90 (D)
91 (A)	92 (C)	93 (A)	94 (D)	95 (D)
96 (B)	97 (C)	98 (B)	99 (D)	100 (C)

PART 1

1

W-Br

(A) He's glancing at a window.
(B) He's reading a posted notice.
(C) He's lifting a paper off of a printer.
(D) He's pointing at a bulletin board.

번역 (A) 남자가 창문을 보고 있다.
(B) 남자가 게시된 공지를 읽고 있다.
(C) 남자가 프린터에서 종이를 들어 올리고 있다.
(D) 남자가 게시판을 가리키고 있다.

해설 **1인 등장 사진**
(A) 동사 오답. 남자가 창문을 보고 있는 모습이 아니다.
(B) 정답. 남자가 게시된 공지를 읽고 있으므로 정답이다.
(C) 사진에 없는 명사. 사진에 프린터가 보이지 않는다.
(D) 동사 오답. 남자가 게시판을 가리키고 있는 모습이 아니다.

어휘 glance 흘끗 보다   posted 게시된   notice 공지   lift 들어
올리다   bulletin board 게시판

2

M-Au

(A) The counter is covered with gardening tools.
(B) Some potted plants are being watered.
(C) Some baskets are lined up against the wall.
(D) A floral arrangement is being assembled.

번역 (A) 카운터가 원예용 도구로 가득 차 있다.
(B) 화분들에 물이 뿌려지고 있다.
(C) 바구니들이 벽을 따라 줄지어 놓여 있다.
(D) 꽃꽂이가 완성되고 있다.

해설 **사람/사물·풍경 혼합 사진**
(A) 사진에 없는 명사. 사진에 원예용 도구가 보이지 않는다.
(B) 동사 오답. 화분들에 물이 뿌려지고 있는 모습이 아니다.
(C) 위치 오답. 바구니들이 벽을 따라 한 줄로 놓여 있는 모습이 아니다.
(D) 정답. 꽃꽂이가 완성되고 있으므로 정답이다.

어휘 be covered with ~으로 뒤덮이다   gardening tool 원예용 도구
potted plant 화분   be lined up 줄지어 있다   against the wall
벽을 따라   floral arrangement 꽃꽂이   assemble 조립하다

3

W-Am

(A) The woman is walking past some storefronts.
(B) The woman is crossing an intersection.
(C) The woman is chaining her bicycle to a bench.
(D) The woman is pushing a glass door.

번역 **(A) 여자가 상점 앞을 지나가고 있다.**
(B) 여자가 교차로를 건너고 있다.
(C) 여자가 자전거를 벤치에 묶고 있다.
(D) 여자가 유리문을 밀고 있다.

해설 **1인 등장 사진**
(A) 정답. 여자가 상점 앞을 걸어서 지나가고 있으므로 정답이다.
(B) 사진에 없는 명사. 사진에 교차로가 보이지 않는다.
(C) 동사 오답. 여자가 자전거를 벤치에 묶고 있는 모습이 아니다.
(D) 동사 오답. 여자가 유리문을 밀고 있는 모습이 아니다.

어휘 storefront (거리) 상점   intersection 교차로   chain (사슬로)
묶다

4

M-Cn

(A) A hotel employee is assisting a guest.
(B) Some luggage is being organized on a cart.
(C) A light fixture has been suspended over a desk.
(D) Some travelers are standing in front of an elevator.

번역 (A) 호텔 직원이 손님을 돕고 있다.
(B) 짐이 카트에 정리되고 있다.
(C) 조명 기구가 책상 위에 매달려 있다.
(D) 여행객들이 승강기 앞에 서 있다.

해설 **사람/사물·풍경 혼합 사진**
(A) 동사 오답. 호텔 직원이 손님을 돕고 있는 모습이 보이지 않는다.
(B) 사진에 없는 명사. 사진에 카트가 보이지 않는다.
(C) 정답. 조명 기구가 책상 위에 매달려 있으므로 정답이다.
(D) 사진에 없는 명사. 사진에 승강기가 보이지 않는다.

어휘 assist 돕다 luggage 짐 organize 정리정돈을 하다
light fixture 조명 기구 suspend 매달다

5

W-Br

(A) One of the men is holding a kitchen knife.
(B) One of the men is stacking bowls in a sink.
(C) Food is being cooked on a stove.
(D) They're sorting vegetables into containers.

번역 **(A) 남자들 중 한 명이 부엌칼을 잡고 있다.**
(B) 남자들 중 한 명이 싱크대에 그릇을 쌓고 있다.
(C) 음식이 가스레인지에서 조리되고 있다.
(D) 사람들이 채소를 종류별로 용기에 담고 있다.

해설 **2인 이상 등장 사진**
(A) 정답. 부엌칼을 잡고 있는 남자의 모습이 보이므로 정답이다.
(B) 동사 오답. 싱크대에 그릇을 쌓고 있는 남자의 모습이 보이지 않는다.
(C) 사진에 없는 명사. 사진에 가스레인지가 보이지 않는다.
(D) 동사 오답. 채소를 종류별로 용기에 담고 있는 사람들의 모습이 아니다.

어휘 stack 쌓다, 포개다 bowl 그릇 sort into ~으로 분류하다
container 그릇, 용기

6

W-Am

(A) A toolbox has been left open.
(B) Rolls of fabric are propped against a wall.
(C) Some power cords have been plugged in.
(D) Machines have been set up at a construction site.

번역 (A) 공구함이 열려 있다.
(B) 둘둘 말린 원단들이 벽에 기대어 놓여 있다.
(C) 전선들의 플러그가 꽂혀 있다.
(D) 공사 현장에 기계들이 설치되어 있다.

해설 **사물·풍경 사진**
(A) 사진에 없는 명사. 사진에 공구함이 보이지 않는다.
(B) 사진에 없는 명사. 사진에 둘둘 말린 원단들이 보이지 않는다.
(C) 정답. 전선들의 플러그가 꽂혀 있으므로 정답이다.
(D) 장소 오답. 공사 현장의 모습이 아니다.

어휘 toolbox 공구함 fabric 직물, 천 prop against ~에 받쳐 놓다
power cord 전선 plug in ~의 플러그를 꽂다 construction site 공사 현장

PART 2

7

M-Au When will the new water cooler be delivered?
W-Br (A) Later this week.
(B) The employee lounge.
(C) Eight degrees Celsius.

번역 새 정수기는 언제 배달될까요?
(A) 이번 주 중으로요.
(B) 직원 휴게실이요.
(C) 섭씨 8도요.

해설 **When 의문문**
(A) 정답. 새 정수기의 배달 시기를 묻는 질문에 이번 주 중이라고 구체적으로 응답하고 있으므로 정답이다.
(B) 연상 오답. 질문의 water cooler에서 연상 가능한 employee lounge를 이용한 오답이다.
(C) 연상 오답. 질문의 water cooler에서 연상 가능한 Eight degrees를 이용한 오답이다.

어휘 water cooler 정수기 lounge 휴게실, 대합실 Celsius 섭씨

8

M-Cn Can you post the job advertisement?

W-Am (A) Sure, I'll do that this afternoon.
(B) She saw our billboards.
(C) Some advice on interviewing.

번역 그 구인 광고를 올려줄 수 있나요?
(A) 물론이죠, 오늘 오후에 할게요.
(B) 그녀가 우리 옥외 광고판을 봤어요.
(C) 면접에 대한 조언이요.

해설 요청·제안문
(A) 정답. 구인 광고를 올려 달라는 요청에 물론이죠(Sure)라고 수락한 뒤, 오늘 오후에 하겠다며 긍정 답변과 일관된 내용을 덧붙이고 있으므로 정답이다.
(B) 연상 오답. 질문의 advertisement에서 연상 가능한 billboards를 이용한 오답이다.
(C) 연상 오답. 질문의 job에서 연상 가능한 interviewing을 이용한 오답이다.

어휘 billboard 옥외 광고판 advice 조언, 충고 interviewing 면접

9

W-Br What pieces will the orchestra perform?

M-Au (A) The concert hall by the harbor.
(B) The program is on its Web site.
(C) Yes, for the first time in years.

번역 그 오케스트라는 어떤 곡들을 연주할 건가요?
(A) 항구 옆 콘서트홀이요.
(B) 프로그램은 웹사이트에 있어요.
(C) 네, 몇 년 만에 처음이에요.

해설 What+명사 의문문
(A) 연상 오답. 질문의 orchestra에서 연상 가능한 concert hall을 이용한 오답이다.
(B) 정답. 오케스트라가 연주할 곡을 묻는 질문에 프로그램은 웹사이트에 있다며 알 수 있는 곳을 알려 주고 있으므로 정답이다.
(C) Yes/No 불가 오답. What 의문문에는 Yes/No 응답이 불가능하므로 오답이다.

어휘 piece 작품, 곡 perform 공연하다 harbor 항구

10

M-Cn Why did we switch paper suppliers?

W-Br (A) Newspaper subscriptions.
(B) It controls the hallway lights.
(C) Because we needed to cut expenses.

번역 종이 공급업체를 왜 바꿨나요?
(A) 신문 구독이요.
(B) 이것은 복도 조명을 조절해요.
(C) 비용을 줄여야 했기 때문에요.

해설 Why 의문문
(A) 유사 발음 오답. 질문의 paper와 부분적으로 발음이 유사한 Newspaper를 이용한 오답이다.
(B) 연상 오답. 질문의 switch를 명사 어휘 스위치로 잘못 이해했을 때 연상 가능한 lights를 이용한 오답이다.
(C) 정답. 종이 공급업체를 바꾼 이유를 묻는 질문에 비용을 줄여야 했기 때문이라고 구체적인 이유를 제시하고 있으므로 정답이다.

어휘 switch 바꾸다 subscription 구독 cut 삭감하다 expense 비용, 지출

11

W-Am The prototype has been completed, right?

M-Cn (A) Yes, I believe so.
(B) The next competition.
(C) Let's talk more then.

번역 그 시제품은 완성되었죠, 맞죠?
(A) 네, 그럴 거예요.
(B) 다음 대회요.
(C) 그때 더 이야기해 봅시다.

해설 부가 의문문
(A) 정답. 시제품의 완성 여부를 확인하는 질문에 네(Yes)라고 대답한 뒤, 그럴 거라며 긍정 답변과 일관된 내용을 덧붙였으므로 정답이다.
(B) 유사 발음 오답. 질문의 completed와 부분적으로 발음이 유사한 competition을 이용한 오답이다.
(C) 질문과 상관없는 오답.

어휘 prototype 시제품 complete 완성하다 competition 대회

12

W-Br Where could I get a haircut?

W-Am (A) On Thursday evening.
(B) I like the salon on Pine Street.
(C) Tina might have some extras.

번역 어디에서 머리를 자를 수 있을까요?
(A) 목요일 저녁에요.
(B) 저는 파인 가에 있는 미용실이 좋더라고요.
(C) 티나가 여분을 좀 갖고 있을 거예요.

해설 Where 의문문
(A) 질문과 상관없는 오답. When 의문문에 대한 응답이므로 오답이다.
(B) 정답. 머리를 자를 수 있는 곳을 묻는 질문에 파인 가에 있는 미용실이 좋더라며 미용실을 추천하고 있으므로 정답이다.
(C) 질문과 상관없는 오답.

어휘 get a haircut 머리를 자르다 extra 여분의 것

13

M-Cn How many brochures should I bring to the exposition?

W-Br (A) That's a question for Ethan.
(B) By five P.M. the day before.
(C) Yes, I just registered.

번역 전시회에 안내 책자를 몇 부나 가져가야 할까요?
(A) 그건 이선에게 물어야 할 질문이에요.
(B) 하루 전날 오후 5시까지요.
(C) 네, 방금 등록했어요.

해설　How+형용사/부사 의문문
(A) 정답. 전시회에 가져가야 할 안내 책자 부수를 묻는 질문에 그건 이선에게 물어야 할 질문이라며 대답해줄 수 있는 사람을 알려 주고 있으므로 정답이다.
(B) 질문과 상관없는 오답. When 의문문에 대한 응답이므로 오답이다.
(C) Yes/No 불가 오답. How 의문문에는 Yes/No 응답이 불가능하므로 오답이다.

어휘　brochure 안내 책자　exposition 전시회, 박람회　register 등록하다

14

M-Au　Did you make your time-off request in person or over e-mail?
M-Cn　(A) I've decided to work from home instead.
(B) I'm interested in personal training.
(C) Please delete messages over one year old.

번역　휴가 신청을 직접 방문해서 하셨나요, 아니면 이메일로 하셨나요?
(A) 저는 대신 재택근무를 하기로 했어요.
(B) 저는 개인 지도에 관심이 있어요.
(C) 1년이 지난 메시지는 삭제하세요.

해설　선택 의문문
(A) 정답. 휴가 신청 방식을 묻는 질문에 재택근무를 하기로 했다며 두 선택지를 제외한 제3의 답변을 제시하고 있는 정답이다.
(B) 파생어 오답. 질문의 person과 파생어 관계인 personal을 이용한 오답이다.
(C) 연상 오답. 질문의 e-mail에서 연상 가능한 messages를 이용한 오답이다.

어휘　time-off 휴가　in person 직접　delete 삭제하다

15

W-Am　This rental fee includes utilities, doesn't it?
M-Au　(A) Only electricity and gas.
(B) The property's owner.
(C) No, it's still on the market.

번역　이 임대료에는 공과금이 포함되어 있죠, 그렇지 않나요?
(A) 전기와 가스만요.
(B) 부동산의 소유주요.
(C) 아니요, 아직 안 팔렸어요.

해설　부가 의문문
(A) 정답. 임대료에 공과금의 포함 여부를 확인하는 질문에 전기와 가스만이라며 일부만 포함되어 있다는 것을 알려주고 있으므로 정답이다.
(B) 연상 오답. 질문의 rental에서 연상 가능한 property를 이용한 오답이다.
(C) 질문과 상관없는 오답.

어휘　rental fee 대여료　utilities 공과금　property 부동산

16

W-Am　Don't we have to mail the party invitations?
M-Cn　(A) A book of stamps.
(B) Do you host other types of events?
(C) Thank you for reminding me.

번역　우리 파티 초대장을 우편으로 보내야 하지 않나요?
(A) 우표 한 묶음이요.
(B) 다른 종류의 행사도 주최하시나요?
(C) 상기시켜 줘서 고마워요.

해설　부정 의문문
(A) 연상 오답. 질문의 mail에서 연상 가능한 stamps를 이용한 오답이다.
(B) 연상 오답. 질문의 party에서 연상 가능한 events를 이용한 오답이다.
(C) 정답. 파티 초대장을 우편으로 보내야 하는지 묻는 질문에 상기시켜 줘서 고맙다며, 네(Yes)를 생략한 긍정 답변을 하고 있으므로 정답이다.

어휘　invitation 초대장　stamp 우표　remind 상기시키다

17

W-Am　Who's coming to the four P.M. meeting?
M-Au　(A) I only took two.
(B) Kenji won't be able to make it.
(C) A special project.

번역　오후 4시 회의에 누가 오나요?
(A) 저는 두 개만 가져갔어요.
(B) 켄지는 못 올 거예요.
(C) 특별한 프로젝트요.

해설　Who 의문문
(A) 연상 오답. 질문의 four에서 연상 가능한 숫자 two를 이용한 오답이다.
(B) 정답. 오후 4시 회의에 올 사람을 묻는 질문에 켄지는 못 올 거라고 미리 알려 주고 있으므로 정답이다.
(C) 연상 오답. 질문의 meeting에서 연상 가능한 project를 이용한 오답이다.

어휘　make it (모임 등에) 참석하다, 해내다

18

W-Br　Should we all attend the presentation?
M-Au　(A) Here's my attendance certificate.
(B) No presents, please.
(C) It's not mandatory.

번역　우리 모두 발표에 참석해야 하나요?
(A) 여기 제 출석 증명서예요.
(B) 선물은 사절할게요.
(C) 의무는 아니에요.

해설　조동사(Should) 의문문
(A) 파생어 오답. 질문의 attend와 파생어 관계인 attendance를 이용한 오답이다.
(B) 유사 발음 오답. 질문의 presentation과 부분적으로 발음이 유사한 presents를 이용한 오답이다.

(C) 정답. 모두가 발표에 참석해야 할지 묻는 질문에 의무는 아니라며, 아니오(No)를 생략한 부정의 답변을 간접적으로 하고 있으므로 정답이다.

어휘 attend 참석하다   attendance 참석   certificate 증명서   present 선물   mandatory 의무적인

19

M-Cn How many study participants do you have?
W-Br (A) I could use a few more!
(B) A short survey.
(C) It's for one of my university courses.

번역 몇 명의 연구 참여자를 확보하셨나요?
(A) 몇 명 더 필요해요!
(B) 짧은 설문지요.
(C) 대학 수업 중 하나를 위한 거예요.

해설 How+형용사/부사 의문문
(A) 정답. 확보한 연구 참여자 수를 묻는 질문에 몇 명 더 필요하다며 아직 사람이 부족함을 나타내고 있으므로 정답이다.
(B) 연상 오답. 질문의 study participants에서 연상 가능한 survey를 이용한 오답이다.
(C) 연상 오답. 질문의 study에서 연상 가능한 university를 이용한 오답이다.

어휘 study 연구   participant 참가자, 참여자   survey 설문 조사

20

M-Au Are you planning on buying a new tractor or a used one?
W-Am (A) I'd prefer a specialized contractor.
(B) No, not immediately.
(C) Well, I have a limited budget.

번역 새 트랙터를 살 계획인가요, 아니면 중고 트랙터를 살 계획인가요?
(A) 저는 전문 도급업체를 선호해요.
(B) 아니요, 당장은 아니에요.
(C) 음, 예산이 한정되어 있어요.

해설 선택 의문문
(A) 유사 발음 오답. 질문의 tractor와 부분적으로 발음이 유사한 contractor를 이용한 오답이다.
(B) 질문과 상관없는 오답. 문장과 문장을 연결하는 경우를 제외하고는 선택 의문문에는 Yes/No 응답이 불가능하므로 오답이다.
(C) 정답. 어떤 트랙터를 살 계획인지 묻는 질문에 예산이 한정되어 있다며, 새 트랙터를 사는 것은 어려울 수 있음을 나타내고 있으므로 정답이다.

어휘 specialized 전문화된   contractor 도급업체   immediately 당장   limited 한정된   budget 예산

21

W-Br Who's leading the networking workshop for the interns?
M-Cn (A) No, I'm not a member of the organization.
(B) That's been postponed to August.
(C) You can use the network to share files.

번역 인턴들을 위한 네트워킹 워크숍은 누가 진행하나요?
(A) 아니요, 저는 그 단체의 회원이 아니에요.
(B) 그거 8월로 미뤄졌어요.
(C) 당신은 그 네트워크를 이용해 파일을 공유할 수 있어요.

해설 Who 의문문
(A) Yes/No 불가 오답. Who 의문문에는 Yes/No 응답이 불가능하므로 오답이다.
(B) 정답. 네트워킹 워크숍의 진행자를 묻는 질문에 8월로 미뤄졌다며, 현재는 진행자를 알 수 없음을 우회적으로 알려 주고 있으므로 정답이다.
(C) 파생어 오답. 질문의 networking과 파생어 관계인 network를 이용한 오답이다.

어휘 lead 이끌다   networking 네트워킹(사람들이 모여 정보를 교류하고 인맥을 형성하는 자리)   organization 단체   postpone 미루다

22

M-Au Could you tell me where the reference books are kept?
W-Br (A) Any of the librarians.
(B) They certainly are.
(C) The shelves on your left.

번역 참고 도서가 어디에 보관되어 있는지 알려주실 수 있나요?
(A) 사서들 중 아무나요.
(B) 분명 그래요.
(C) 왼쪽 선반이요.

해설 간접 의문문
(A) 연상 오답. 질문의 reference books에서 연상 가능한 librarians를 이용한 오답이다.
(B) 질문과 상관없는 오답.
(C) 정답. 참고 도서가 보관된 장소를 묻는 질문에 왼쪽 선반이라고 구체적으로 알려주고 있으므로 정답이다.

어휘 reference book 참고 도서   librarian 사서   shelf 선반

23

M-Au What's your store's policy on refunds?
W-Am (A) We stock several major brands.
(B) You have to show your original receipt.
(C) I have access to more funds.

번역 귀 가게의 환불 정책은 무엇인가요?
(A) 저희는 여러 주요 브랜드 제품을 판매해요.
(B) 영수증 원본을 보여주셔야 해요.
(C) 저는 더 많은 자금을 이용할 수 있어요.

해설 What 의문문
(A) 연상 오답. 질문의 store에서 연상 가능한 stock을 이용한 오답이다.
(B) 정답. 환불 정책을 묻는 질문에 영수증 원본을 보여줘야 한다고 구체적으로 알려주고 있으므로 정답이다.
(C) 유사 발음 오답. 질문의 refunds와 부분적으로 발음이 유사한 funds를 이용한 오답이다.

어휘 policy 정책   refund 환불   stock (판매할 상품을) 가지고 있다   original 원본의   receipt 영수증   have access to ~을 이용할 수 있다   fund 자금

24

W-Br All the information in the staff directory is up-to-date, isn't it?

M-Au (A) OK, I'll mark the event dates on the calendar.
(B) Some extension numbers may have changed.
(C) The first line on the form is for your job title.

번역 직원 명부에 있는 모든 정보는 최신의 것이죠, 그렇지 않나요?
(A) 알겠습니다, 달력에 그 행사 날짜들을 표시해 놓을게요.
(B) 일부 내선 번호들이 바뀌었을걸요.
(C) 양식의 첫 번째 줄에는 직함을 쓰세요.

해설 부가 의문문
(A) 단어 반복 오답. 질문의 date를 반복 이용한 오답이다.
(B) 정답. 직원 명부에 있는 모든 정보가 최신의 것인지 확인하는 질문에 일부 내선 번호들이 바뀌었을 거라며, 아니오(No)를 생략한 부정의 답변을 우회적으로 하고 있으므로 정답이다.
(C) 연상 오답. 질문의 the staff directory에서 연상 가능한 job title을 이용한 오답이다.

어휘 directory 명부, 목록 up-to-date (정보가) 최신인 extension number 내선 번호 job title 직함

25

W-Am When does the market research report need to be submitted?

M-Cn (A) A promising product idea, usually.
(B) The director keeps moving the deadline.
(C) Yes, I can see that.

번역 그 시장 조사 보고서는 언제 제출되어야 하나요?
(A) 유망한 제품 아이디어죠, 보통은.
(B) 부장이 마감 시한을 계속 바꾸네요.
(C) 네, 그런 것 같네요.

해설 When 의문문
(A) 연상 오답. 질문의 market research report에서 연상 가능한 product idea를 이용한 오답이다.
(B) 정답. 보고서 제출 시기를 묻는 질문에 부장이 마감 시한을 계속 바꾼다며, 시기를 알 수 없음을 우회적으로 나타내고 있으므로 정답이다.
(C) Yes/No 불가 오답. When 의문문에는 Yes/No 응답이 불가능하므로 오답이다.

어휘 submit 제출하다 promising 유망한 deadline 마감 시한

26

W-Am There's a refreshments table in the hallway.

M-Au (A) I'm still full from breakfast.
(B) He reserved a table for six.
(C) The conference organizers.

번역 복도에 다과 테이블이 있어요.
(A) 저는 아침 먹은 배가 아직 안 꺼졌어요.
(B) 그가 6인용 테이블을 예약했어요.
(C) 회의 주최자들이요.

해설 사실·정보 전달의 평서문
(A) 정답. 복도에 다과 테이블이 있다는 평서문에 아침 먹은 배가 아직

안 꺼졌다며 배가 불러 다과를 먹을 수 없다는 의미를 내포하고 있으므로 정답이다.
(B) 단어 반복 오답. 평서문의 table을 반복 이용한 오답이다.
(C) 연상 오답. 평서문의 refreshments table에서 연상 가능한 conference를 이용한 오답이다.

어휘 refreshments 다과 reserve 예약하다 organizer 주최자

27

W-Br Why don't we share a taxi to the airport?

M-Cn (A) At the entrance to the terminal.
(B) Last year's tax forms.
(C) Would there be room for Na-Young, too?

번역 우리 공항까지 택시를 같이 타고 가면 어때요?
(A) 터미널 입구에서요.
(B) 작년의 세금 신고서요.
(C) 나영이 탈 자리도 있을까요?

해설 요청·제안문
(A) 연상 오답. 질문의 airport에서 연상 가능한 terminal을 이용한 오답이다.
(B) 유사 발음 오답. 질문의 taxi와 부분적으로 발음이 유사한 tax를 이용한 오답이다.
(C) 정답. 공항까지 택시를 함께 탈 것을 제안하는 질문에 나영이 탈 자리도 있는지 택시 자리와 관련된 내용을 묻고 있으므로 정답이다.

어휘 entrance 입구 tax form 세금 신고서 room 자리, 공간

28

M-Au Have you decided what you're going to do with your annual bonus?

W-Am (A) It's the last Friday of the month.
(B) I think she's going to the parking lot.
(C) I'm putting it in my savings account.

번역 연례 상여금으로 뭘 할지 결정했어요?
(A) 그 달의 마지막 금요일이요.
(B) 그녀는 주차장으로 가고 있을걸요.
(C) 저는 그것을 예금 계좌에 넣을 거예요.

해설 조동사(Have) 의문문
(A) 질문과 상관없는 오답. When 의문문에 대한 응답이므로 오답이다.
(B) 단어 반복 오답. 질문의 going to를 반복 이용한 오답이다.
(C) 정답. 연례 상여금으로 뭘 할지 결정했냐고 묻는 질문에 예금 계좌에 넣을 거라며 상여금의 사용 용도를 구체적으로 제시하고 있으므로 정답이다.

어휘 decide 결정하다 annual 연례의 savings account 예금 계좌

29

M-Cn Should I visit a pharmacy or a health food store to get vitamin supplements?

W-Am (A) Supermarkets sell them, too.
(B) The recommended amount.
(C) Your updated medical records.

번역 비타민 영양제를 사려면 약국에 가야 할까요, 아니면 건강 식품점에 가야 할까요?
  (A) 슈퍼마켓에서도 팔아요.
  (B) 권장량이요.
  (C) 당신의 최신 의료 기록이요.

해설 선택 의문문
  (A) 정답. 비타민 영양제를 구매할 장소를 묻는 질문에 슈퍼마켓에서도 판다며 두 선택지를 제외한 제3의 안을 제시하고 있으므로 정답이다.
  (B) 연상 오답. 질문의 vitamin supplements에서 연상 가능한 amount를 이용한 오답이다.
  (C) 연상 오답. 질문의 pharmacy에서 연상 가능한 medical records를 이용한 오답이다.

어휘 pharmacy 약국 supplement 영양제, 보충제
  recommended amount 권장량

30

W-Am The video needs to be uploaded to social media today.
M-Au (A) It was quite informative.
  (B) We haven't added the music yet.
  (C) I mostly watch TV programs.

번역 그 영상을 오늘 소셜 미디어에 올려야 해요.
  (A) 그것은 꽤 유익했어요.
  (B) 아직 음악을 넣지 못했어요.
  (C) 저는 주로 TV 프로그램을 봐요.

해설 의견·희망 사항의 평서문
  (A) 연상 오답. 평서문의 video에서 연상 가능한 informative를 이용한 오답이다.
  (B) 정답. 그 영상을 오늘 소셜 미디어에 올려야 한다는 평서문에 아직 음악을 넣지 못했다며 관련된 내용으로 응답하고 있으므로 정답이다.
  (C) 연상 오답. 평서문의 social media에서 연상 가능한 TV programs를 이용한 오답이다.

어휘 informative 유익한 add 추가하다

31

M-Cn Why does Leonard have so many plants in his office?
W-Br (A) No, you don't have to anymore.
  (B) Try this scheduling app for smartphones.
  (C) Everyone gets to decorate their own space.

번역 레너드는 사무실에 왜 그렇게 많은 화분을 가지고 있나요?
  (A) 아니요, 더 이상 안 하셔도 돼요.
  (B) 이 스마트폰용 일정 관리 앱을 사용해 보세요.
  (C) 모두 자신만의 공간을 꾸미게 되죠.

해설 Why 의문문
  (A) Yes/No 불가 오답. Why 의문문에는 Yes/No 응답이 불가능하므로 오답이다.
  (B) 질문과 상관없는 오답.

(C) 정답. 레너드가 사무실에 많은 화분을 가지고 있는 이유를 묻는 질문에 모두 자신만의 공간을 꾸미게 된다고 그 이유에 대한 자신의 의견을 제시하고 있으므로 정답이다.

어휘 decorate 장식하다

32-34

W-Am Matteo, ³² **the waiting list for our custom-made shoes is now over six months long.**

M-Au Ever since that musician was photographed wearing a pair, we've had more business than we could handle.

W-Am I was thinking it might be time to hire one or two employees to help us work a little faster.

M-Au OK… ³³ **I'm just worried that the quality of our shoes could suffer**, since new workers probably won't be as skilled as we are.

W-Am Well, we could start by only giving them the easiest jobs, like polishing the finished shoes.

M-Au Yes, that could work. ³⁴ **Let's write out everything involved in the process, from start to finish.** That will make it easy to see which tasks could be delegated.

여: 마테오, **주문 제작 신발 대기 명단이 이제 6개월 치를 넘어섰어요.**
남: 그 음악가가 신발을 신은 모습이 사진에 찍힌 후로 우리가 감당할 수 있는 것보다 주문량이 많아졌어요.
여: 안 그래도 일을 좀 더 빨리할 수 있도록 한두 명의 직원을 새로 뽑아야 할 시기일지도 모른다고 생각 중이었어요.
남: 알겠습니다… **저는 단지 우리 신발의 품질이 나빠질까 봐 걱정이에요.** 새 직원들은 아마 우리만큼 숙련되지는 않았을 테니까요.
여: 음, 처음에는 완성된 신발에 광을 내는 작업 같은 쉬운 일만 주면 되죠.
남: 그래요, 그러면 되겠네요. **처음부터 끝까지 생산 과정에 포함된 모든 것을 적어봅시다.** 그러면 어떤 일을 넘길 수 있을지 파악하기 쉬워질 거예요.

어휘 custom-made 주문 제작한 handle 감당하다 hire 고용하다 quality 품질 suffer 나빠지다, 악화되다 skilled 숙련된 polish 광을 내다 involved in ~에 관련된 delegate 위임하다

TEST 8

32 What are the speakers discussing?
(A) Appointing a spokesperson
(B) Relocating a storefront
(C) Postponing some repairs
(D) Meeting customer demand

번역 화자들은 무엇을 논의하는가?
(A) 대변인 임명하기
(B) 매장 이전하기
(C) 수리 공사 연기하기
(D) 고객 수요 충족시키기

해설 **전체 내용 관련 - 대화의 주제**
여자가 첫 대사에서 주문 제작 신발 대기 명단이 이제 6개월 치를 넘어섰다(the waiting list for our custom-made shoes is now over six months long)며 신발 주문 고객의 수요를 충족시키는 것에 대해 이야기하고 있으므로 정답은 (D)이다.

어휘 appoint 임명하다   spokesperson 대변인   relocate 이전하다   storefront (거리) 상점   postpone 미루다   demand 수요

---

33 What is the man concerned about?
(A) Paying for some expenses
(B) Unpredictable market trends
(C) Inconvenience to employees
(D) A decrease in product quality

번역 남자는 무엇에 대해 걱정하는가?
(A) 비용 지불하기
(B) 예측할 수 없는 시장 동향
(C) 직원들의 불편
(D) 제품 품질의 저하

해설 **세부 사항 관련 - 남자의 우려 사항**
남자가 두 번째 대사에서 신발의 품질이 나빠질까 봐 걱정(I'm just worried that the quality of our shoes could suffer)이라고 말하고 있으므로 정답은 (D)이다.

어휘 expense 비용, 지출   unpredictable 예측할 수 없는   trend 동향   inconvenience 불편   decrease 감소

> **Paraphrasing**
> 대화의 worried → 질문의 concerned
> 대화의 the quality of our shoes could suffer
> → 정답의 A decrease in product quality

34 What does the man suggest doing?
(A) Listing the steps of a process
(B) Determining a budget limit
(C) Involving staff in a decision
(D) Attending an upcoming event

번역 남자는 무엇을 제안하는가?
(A) 생산 과정의 절차 나열하기
(B) 예산 한도 정하기
(C) 의사결정에 직원 참여시키기
(D) 다가오는 행사에 참석하기

해설 **세부 사항 관련 - 남자의 제안 사항**
남자가 마지막 대사에서 처음부터 끝까지 생산 과정에 포함된 모든 것을 적어볼 것(Let's write out everything involved in the process, from start to finish)을 제안하고 있으므로 정답은 (A)이다.

어휘 list 나열하다   determine 결정하다   budget limit 예산 한도   decision 결정   attend 참석하다   upcoming 다가오는

> **Paraphrasing**
> 대화의 write out everything involved in the process, from start to finish
> → 정답의 Listing the steps of a process

35-37

M-Cn	Patricia, [35] **do you have any pasta meals left? I just handed out my last one, but there are a lot of people left to serve.**
W-Br	Sorry, I'm out too. I guess the new meal uptake prediction software isn't working very well.
M-Cn	No kidding. [36] **There's going to be a lot of disappointed passengers at the back of the plane.** We should give them some extra snacks to make up for it.
W-Br	That's a good idea. [37] **I'll try to memorize where the people who ask for pasta are sitting**, so that I can bring them something later.

남:	패트리샤, 파스타 남은 것 좀 있어요? 저는 방금 마지막 것을 드렸는데, 아직 음식을 드려야 할 분들이 많이 남았어요.
여:	죄송하지만, 저도 다 떨어졌어요. 새로운 식사 예측 소프트웨어가 잘 작동하지 않는 것 같아요.
남:	정말요. 비행기 뒤쪽에 실망하는 탑승객들이 많겠네요. 보상 차원에서 간식을 좀 더 드려야겠어요.
여:	좋은 생각이에요. 파스타를 원하시는 분들이 어디에 앉아 계신지 기억하도록 할게요. 그래야 이따가 뭔가 가져다드릴 수 있으니까요.

어휘 hand out 나눠주다   serve 음식을 제공하다   uptake 채택   prediction 예측   disappointed 실망한   passenger 탑승객   extra 여분의   make up for ~에 대해 보상하다   memorize 암기하다

35 What problem does the man report?
(A) He has run out of some meals.
(B) He is unfamiliar with some software.
(C) An Internet connection is slow.
(D) Some utensils are missing.

번역 남자는 어떤 문제를 보고하는가?
(A) 일부 음식이 다 떨어졌다.
(B) 일부 소프트웨어에 대해 잘 모른다.
(C) 인터넷 연결이 느리다.
(D) 식기구들이 없어졌다.

해설 **세부 사항 관련 - 남자가 언급하는 문제**
남자가 첫 대사에서 파스타 남은 것이 좀 있는지(do you have any pasta meals left?) 물은 뒤, 방금 마지막 것을 드렸는데, 아직 음식을 드려야 할 분들이 많이 남았다(I just handed out my last one, but there are a lot of people left to serve)고 말하고 있으므로 정답은 (A)이다.

어휘 run out of ~이 다 떨어지다   be unfamiliar with ~에 친숙하지 않다   connection 연결   utensil (수저 등의) 식기구   missing 없어진, 빠진

> **Paraphrasing**
> 대화의 pasta meals → 정답의 some meals

36 Who most likely are the speakers?
(A) Caterers
(B) Tour guides
(C) Flight attendants
(D) Conference organizers

번역 화자들은 누구이겠는가?
(A) 출장 요리 연회사
(B) 관광 안내원
(C) 비행기 승무원
(D) 회의 주최자

해설 **전체 내용 관련 - 화자들의 직업**
남자가 두 번째 대사에서 비행기 뒤쪽에 실망하는 탑승객들이 많겠다(There's going to be a lot of disappointed passengers at the back of the plane)고 말하는 것으로 보아 화자들은 비행기 승무원임을 알 수 있다. 따라서 정답은 (C)이다.

어휘 caterer 출장 요리 연회사   flight attendant 비행기 승무원   organizer 주최자

37 What does the woman say she will try to do?
(A) Inform some coworkers
(B) Remember some seat locations
(C) Find an extra box of supplies
(D) Reset an electronic device

번역 여자는 무엇을 노력해 보겠다고 말하는가?
(A) 동료들에게 알리기
(B) 좌석 위치를 기억하기
(C) 여분의 비품 상자 찾기
(D) 전자 기기 재설정하기

해설 **세부 사항 관련 - 여자가 노력할 일**
여자가 마지막 대사에서 파스타를 원하시는 분들이 어디에 앉아 있는지 기억하도록 하겠다(I'll try to memorize where the people who ask for pasta are sitting)고 말하고 있으므로 정답은 (B)이다.

어휘 inform 알리다   reset 재설정하다   electronic device 전자 기기

> **Paraphrasing**
> 대화의 memorize where the people ~ are sitting
> → 정답의 Remember some seat locations

38-40

M-Au ³⁸**Welcome to Sungshin Leather. Would you like help finding anything?**

W-Br Yes, ³⁹**I'm interested in buying a briefcase for my new job. I like how they have more carrying space than most handbags.** My files would fit in there more easily.

M-Au OK. This one here—the Wilkes Elite—is very popular with our female customers.

W-Br Hmm… I see it doesn't have a separate compartment for a laptop. I wouldn't feel comfortable carrying my laptop in this.

M-Au Well, ⁴⁰**you could buy a soft laptop cover to use inside the briefcase**. That would provide enough protection.

남: 성신 가죽에 오신 것을 환영합니다. 상품 찾는 것을 도와드릴까요?

여: 네, 저는 새 직장에서 사용할 서류 가방을 사는 데 관심이 있어요. 서류 가방이 대부분의 핸드백보다 더 많은 수납공간이 있다는 점이 마음에 들거든요. 제 서류들이 더 쉽게 들어갈 거예요.

남: 알겠습니다. 여기 이 제품은 윌크스 엘리트라는 제품인데요, 여성 고객분들께 매우 인기가 많습니다.

여: 음… 이건 노트북용으로 따로 분리된 칸이 없네요. 제 노트북을 여기에 담아 가지고 다니기에는 불안할 것 같아요.

남: 그럼, 서류 가방 안에 넣어 사용할 수 있는 부드러운 노트북 커버를 구매하시면 돼요. 그 제품이 충분한 보호 기능을 제공할 거예요.

어휘 briefcase 서류 가방   fit in ~에 들어가다   popular 인기 있는   separate 분리된   compartment 칸   provide 제공하다   protection 보호

38 Who most likely is the man?
(A) A market researcher
(B) A cleaning professional
(C) A sales associate
(D) A business journalist

번역 남자는 누구이겠는가?
(A) 시장 조사원
(B) 청소 전문가
(C) 영업 사원
(D) 경제부 기자

전체 내용 관련 - 남자의 직업
남자가 첫 대사에서 성신 가죽에 오신 것을 환영한다(Welcome to Sungshin Leather)면서 상품 찾는 것을 도와드릴지(Would you like help finding anything?) 묻고 있으므로 남자는 영업 사원이라는 것을 알 수 있다. 따라서 정답은 (C)이다.

어휘 journalist 기자

---

39 What does the woman say she likes about a briefcase?
(A) Its durable material
(B) Its large capacity
(C) Its attractive color
(D) Its reasonable price

번역 여자는 서류 가방의 어떤 점이 마음에 든다고 말하는가?
(A) 견고한 재질
(B) 큰 용량
(C) 매력적인 색상
(D) 합리적인 가격

해설 **세부 사항 관련 - 여자가 서류 가방에 대해 마음에 든다고 하는 것**
여자가 첫 대사에서 서류 가방을 사는 데 관심이 있다(I'm interested in buying a briefcase ~)면서 서류 가방이 대부분의 핸드백보다 더 많은 수납공간이 있다는 점이 마음에 든다(I like how they have more carrying space than most handbags)고 말하고 있는 것으로 보아 정답은 (B)이다.

어휘 durable 견고한 capacity 용량 attractive 매력적인
reasonable 합리적인

> **Paraphrasing**
> 대화의 how they have more carrying space than
> most handbags → 정답의 Its large capacity

40 What does the man recommend doing?
(A) Purchasing an extra item
(B) Visiting a special Web site
(C) Speaking with his colleague
(D) Trying out several briefcases

번역 남자는 무엇을 하기를 추천하는가?
(A) 추가 물품 구매하기
(B) 특별한 웹사이트 방문하기
(C) 자신의 동료와 이야기하기
(D) 여러 개의 서류 가방 사용해보기

해설 **세부 사항 관련 - 남자의 추천 사항**
남자가 마지막 대사에서 부드러운 노트북 커버를 구매하면 된다(you could buy a soft laptop cover ~)고 했으므로 정답은 (A)이다.

어휘 purchase 구매하다 colleague 동료 try out 시험 삼아 해보다

> **Paraphrasing**
> 대화의 buy a soft laptop cover
> → 정답의 Purchasing an extra item

41-43 3인 대화

M-Cn Uh oh… **41 I don't see our bus listed on this sign.**

M-Au Really? But the hotel clerk said it passes by here.

M-Cn Excuse me, ma'am, can we catch Bus 403 here?

W-Am I'm not sure, but **42 I could use the transportation app on my phone to find out.**

M-Au That would be great.

W-Am OK… Oh, it stops at that platform in the middle of the street. And the next one's in fifteen minutes.

M-Cn Ah! Thank you. Well, **43 Min-Jae, we're going to be a little late to dinner. You'd better ask your friend to order for us.**

M-Au Yes, I'll message him.

남1: 이런… 우리가 탈 버스가 표지판에 안 보이네요.
남2: 정말이요? 하지만 호텔 직원이 여기를 지나간다고 말했는데요.
남1: 실례합니다, 403번 버스를 여기서 탈 수 있나요?
여: 잘 모르겠어요. 하지만 제 휴대 전화에 있는 교통 앱을 이용해 찾아볼 수 있어요.
남2: 그래 주시면 감사하겠습니다.
여: 알겠어요… 아, 그 버스는 도로 중앙 승강장에 정차하네요. 그리고 다음 버스는 15분 후에 도착하고요.
남1: 아! 감사합니다. 음, 민재, 우리 저녁 식사 시간에 조금 늦을 것 같아요. 당신의 친구에게 우리 것을 주문해 달라고 부탁하는 게 좋겠어요.
남2: 네, 그에게 문자를 보낼게요.

어휘 sign 간판, 표지판 clerk 직원 catch (버스 등을) 타다
transportation 교통 platform 승차대 order 주문하다

41 Where does the conversation most likely take place?
(A) On a train
(B) At a bus stop
(C) At a taxi stand
(D) In an elevator

번역 대화는 어디서 이루어지겠는가?
(A) 기차에서
(B) 버스 정류장에서
(C) 택시 승차장에서
(D) 승강기 안에서

첫 번째 남자가 첫 대사에서 우리가 탈 버스가 표지판에 안 보인다(I don't see our bus listed on this sign)고 말하는 것으로 보아 대화 장소는 버스 정류장임을 알 수 있다. 따라서 정답은 (B)이다.

---

42 What does the woman offer to do?
(A) Drive to a destination
(B) Check a mobile app
(C) Make a phone call
(D) Draw a map

번역　여자는 무엇을 하겠다고 제안하는가?
(A) 목적지까지 운전해 주기
(B) 모바일 앱 확인해 주기
(C) 전화 걸기
(D) 약도 그리기

해설　세부 사항 관련 - 여자의 제안 사항
여자가 첫 번째 대사에서 휴대 전화에 있는 교통 앱을 이용해 찾아볼 수 있다(I could use the transportation app on my phone to find out)고 말하는 것으로 보아, 여자는 모바일 교통 앱을 확인해 주겠다고 제안하고 있음을 알 수 있다. 따라서 정답은 (B)이다.

어휘　destination 목적지　draw 그리다

> **Paraphrasing**
> 대화의 use the transportation app on my phone
> → 정답의 Check a mobile app

43 What will Min-Jae ask his friend to do?
(A) Stand outside a venue
(B) Buy tickets for a show
(C) Choose dishes for a meal
(D) Confirm a street's name

번역　민재는 자신의 친구에게 무엇을 해달라고 부탁하겠는가?
(A) 장소 밖에서 있기
(B) 공연 입장권 구매하기
(C) 식사를 위한 요리 고르기
(D) 도로 이름 확인하기

해설　세부 사항 관련 - 민재가 친구에게 부탁할 일
첫 번째 남자가 마지막 대사에서 민재에게 저녁 식사 시간에 조금 늦을 것 같다(Min-Jae, we're going to be a little late to dinner)면서 친구에게 우리 것을 주문해 달라고 부탁하는 게 좋겠다(You'd better ask your friend to order for us)고 말하고 있으므로 정답은 (C)이다.

어휘　venue 장소　dish 요리

44-46

> M-Au　Nora, **⁴⁴I heard you went to a seminar yesterday**—how was it? **⁴⁴Did you pick up**

anything that'll be useful for the Bradbury project?

W-Br　No, but **⁴⁵some of the information might come in handy in the future. The topic was designing lightweight bridges.** We learned the latest recommendations for materials and structural forms.

M-Au　Interesting! I know some people find our continuing education requirements annoying, but I always enjoy fulfilling them. Oh, and **⁴⁶you know you have to write an attendance report, right?**

W-Br　Yes, but... this is my first time writing one.

M-Au　Gilberto on the compliance team can walk you through it.

남:　노라, 어제 세미나에 갔었다고 들었어요. 어땠어요? 브래드버리 프로젝트에 유용할 만한 걸 좀 배우고 왔나요?

여:　아니요, 하지만 일부 정보는 앞으로 쓸모가 있을 것 같아요. 주제는 경량 교량 설계였어요. 자재 및 구조 양식에 대한 최신 권장 사항을 알게 되었죠.

남:　흥미롭군요! 일부 사람들은 우리의 지속적인 교육 이수 요건을 귀찮은 일로 생각한다는 걸 알고 있어요. 하지만 저는 교육을 수료하는 일이 늘 즐거워요. 아, 그런데 참석 보고서를 작성해야 하는 건 알고 계시죠?

여:　네, 하지만⋯ 그걸 작성하는 건 이번이 처음이에요.

남:　컴플라이언스팀의 질베르토가 차근차근 요령을 알려드릴 수 있을 거예요.

어휘　pick up 배우다　useful 쓸모 있는　come in handy 쓸모가 있다　lightweight 경량의　latest 최신의　recommendation 권고 사항　material 자재, 재료　structural 구조적인　form 형태　requirement 요건　annoying 성가신　fulfill 수행하다, 완료하다　attendance 참석　compliance (법 등의) 준수　walk through 차근차근 요령을 알려주다

---

44 What did the woman do yesterday?
(A) She drafted a project proposal.
(B) She applied for a mentorship program.
(C) She finished conducting some research.
(D) She took a professional development seminar.

번역　여자는 어제 무엇을 했는가?
(A) 프로젝트 제안서 초안을 작성했다.
(B) 멘토링 프로그램에 지원했다.
(C) 조사를 끝마쳤다.
(D) 전문성 개발 세미나에 참석했다.

해설　세부 사항 관련 - 여자가 어제 한 일
남자가 첫 대사에서 어제 세미나에 갔었다고 들었다(I heard you went to a seminar yesterday)면서 브래드버리 프로젝트에 유

용할 만한 걸 좀 배우고 왔는지(Did you pick up anything that'll be useful for the Bradbury project?) 묻고 있으므로 정답은 (D)이다.

어휘 draft 초안을 작성하다 proposal 제안 mentorship program 멘토링 프로그램 conduct 실시하다 professional 전문적인 development 개발

> **Paraphrasing**
> 대화의 a seminar ~ that'll be useful for the Bradbury project
> → 정답의 a professional development seminar

45 What kind of business do the speakers most likely work for?
(A) An employment agency
(B) A publishing company
(C) An engineering firm
(D) A financial institution

번역 화자들은 어떤 종류의 사업체에서 일하겠는가?
(A) 직업소개소
(B) 출판사
(C) 토목 회사
(D) 금융 기관

해설 **전체 내용 관련 - 화자들의 근무 업체**
여자가 첫 대사에서 일부 정보는 앞으로 쓸모가 있을 것 같다 (some of the information might come in handy in the future)면서 주제는 경량 교량 설계(The topic was designing lightweight bridges)였다고 말하고 있으므로 화자들은 토목과 관련된 회사에서 근무 중이라는 것을 알 수 있다. 따라서 정답은 (C)이다.

46 Why does the woman say, "this is my first time writing one"?
(A) To express excitement
(B) To request some assistance
(C) To complain about an assignment
(D) To explain some mistakes

번역 여자가 "그걸 작성하는 건 이번이 처음이에요"라고 말한 이유는?
(A) 흥분한 마음을 표현하려고
(B) 도움을 요청하려고
(C) 할당된 일에 대해 불평하려고
(D) 실수에 대해 설명하려고

해설 **화자의 의도 파악 - 그걸 작성하는 건 이번이 처음이라는 말의 의도**
앞에서 남자가 참석 보고서를 작성해야 하는 건 알고 있는지(you know you have to write an attendance report, right?) 묻자 여자가 인용문을 언급한 것으로 보아, 보고서를 작성하는 데 도움을 요청하려는 의도로 한 말임을 알 수 있다. 따라서 정답은 (B)이다.

어휘 excitement 흥분 assistance 도움 assignment 할당된 일

47-49

W-Br Whew, that was a busy morning, wasn't it? Hi, I'm Etsuko Mori. **47 I run the Mori's Berries booth at this farmer's market.** Could I chat with you for a moment about your business's booth?

M-Cn Sure. **47 I could use a break from loading these produce crates.**

W-Br Well, **48 I'm very impressed by this beautiful "Blackbird Farms" banner you've started hanging over the booth recently.**

M-Cn Thank you! It wasn't cheap, but it seems to be worth the expense—we've had considerably more customers since putting it up.

W-Br Oh, really? That's what I wanted to ask about. I'm considering making a similar investment.

M-Cn Well, **49 we were very happy with the print shop we used.** Would you like its name?

여: 휴, 정말 바쁜 아침이었어요, 안 그래요? 안녕하세요, 저는 에츠코 모리예요. 저는 이 농산물 직거래 장터에서 모리스 베리스 부스를 운영해요. 당신 업체의 부스에 대해 잠깐 이야기 좀 나눌 수 있을까요?

남: 물론이죠. 이 농산물 상자들을 싣는 일에서 잠시 쉬어야겠어요.

여: 음, 저는 당신이 최근에 부스 위에 매달기 시작한, 이 예쁜 "블랙버드 농장" 배너를 보고 매우 감탄했어요.

남: 감사합니다! 저렴하지는 않았지만, 투자한 가치가 있는 것 같아요. 이걸 매단 이후에 손님이 훨씬 더 많이 늘었거든요.

여: 어머, 정말요? 바로 그게 제가 물어보고 싶은 거였어요. 저도 비슷한 투자를 할까 생각 중이에요.

남: 음, 저희는 이용했던 인쇄소에 매우 만족했어요. 이름을 알려 드릴까요?

어휘 run 운영하다 load 짐을 싣다 produce 농산물 crate 상자 be impressed by ~에 깊은 인상을 받다 hang 걸다, 매달다 considerably 상당히 put up 게시하다 investment 투자 print shop 인쇄소

47 What industry do the speakers most likely work in?
(A) Agriculture
(B) Hospitality
(C) Electronics
(D) Construction

번역 화자들은 어떤 업계에 종사하겠는가?
(A) 농업
(B) 접객 서비스
(C) 전자 제품
(D) 건설

해설　**전체 내용 관련 - 화자들의 근무 업계**

여자가 첫 대사에서 이 농산물 직거래 장터에서 모리스 베리스 부스를 운영한다(I run the Mori's Berries booth at this farmer's market)고 했고, 남자가 이 농산물 상자들을 싣는 일에서 잠시 쉬어야겠다(I could use a break from loading these produce crates)고 말하는 것으로 보아 화자들은 농업에 종사한다는 것을 알 수 있다. 따라서 정답은 (A)이다.

---

48 According to the woman, what happened at a business recently?
(A) An executive retired.
(B) A Web site was upgraded.
(C) A new sign was put on display.
(D) A famous product was discontinued.

번역　여자에 따르면, 최근에 한 사업체에 무슨 일이 생겼는가?
(A) 한 임원이 퇴직했다.
(B) 웹사이트가 업그레이드되었다.
(C) 새로운 간판이 전시되었다.
(D) 유명한 제품이 단종되었다.

해설　**세부 사항 관련 - 최근에 한 사업체에 발생한 일**

여자가 두 번째 대사에서 당신이 최근에 부스 위에 매달기 시작한, 이 예쁜 "블랙버드 농장" 배너를 보고 매우 감탄했다(I'm very impressed by this beautiful "Blackbird Farms" banner you've started hanging over the booth recently)고 말하고 있으므로 정답은 (C)이다.

어휘　executive 임원, 중역　retire 퇴직하다, 은퇴하다　be put on display 전시되다　discontinue 중단되다

> **Paraphrasing**
> 대화의 banner you've started hanging over the booth
> → 정답의 A new sign was put on display

---

49 What does the man offer the woman?
(A) Some printouts
(B) Some samples
(C) A special discount
(D) A business referral

번역　남자는 여자에게 무엇을 제공하는가?
(A) 인쇄물
(B) 견본
(C) 특별 할인
(D) 업체 소개

해설　**세부 사항 관련 - 남자가 여자에게 제공할 것**

남자가 마지막 대사에서 이용했던 인쇄소에 매우 만족했다(we were very happy with the print shop we used)면서 인쇄소 이름을 알고 싶은지(Would you like its name?) 묻고 있으므로 정답은 (D)이다.

어휘　referral 소개

50-52

W-Am　Alvin, ⁵⁰ **what's your opinion on the big change that the owner told us about this morning?**

M-Au　I was late to work today.

W-Am　Ah, I didn't realize that. Well, ⁵¹ **she's going to hire a Spanish-speaking driving instructor so that we can expand our customer base.**

M-Au　Interesting! Hmm… ⁵² **my only concern would be the level of customer service we could provide to Spanish-speaking students.** Because of the language barrier, our office staff wouldn't be able to do things like answering their inquiries.

여:　앨빈, 오늘 아침에 사장님이 이야기한 큰 변화에 대한 당신 의견은 어때요?

남:　저는 오늘 지각했어요.

여:　아, 몰랐네요. 음. 그녀는 우리 고객층을 넓힐 수 있도록 스페인어를 구사하는 운전 교습 강사를 고용할 예정이래요.

남:　흥미롭네요! 음… 스페인어를 사용하는 학생들에게 우리가 제공할 수 있는 고객 서비스 수준이 걱정될 뿐입니다. 언어 장벽 때문에 우리 사무직원들이 그들의 문의에 대한 답변과 같은 일을 해줄 수 없을 테니까요.

어휘　opinion 의견　Spanish-speaking 스페인어를 구사하는　driving instructor 운전 교습 강사　expand 확장하다　customer base 고객층　concern 걱정　provide 제공하다　language barrier 언어 장벽　inquiry 문의

---

50 What does the man mean when he says, "I was late to work today"?
(A) He has not met a new colleague yet.
(B) He was negatively affected by a change.
(C) He was not present for an announcement.
(D) He is behind schedule on an assignment.

번역　남자가 "저는 오늘 지각했어요"라고 말할 때, 그 의도는 무엇인가?
(A) 새로 온 동료를 아직 만나보지 못했다.
(B) 변화에 의해 부정적으로 영향받았다.
(C) 발표할 때 참석하지 못했다.
(D) 할당된 일의 일정이 늦어졌다.

해설　**화자의 의도 파악 - 오늘 지각했다는 말의 의도**

앞에서 여자가 오늘 아침에 사장님이 이야기한 큰 변화에 대한 남자의 의견은 어떤지(what's your opinion on the big change that the owner told us about this morning?) 묻자 남자가 인용문을 언급한 것으로 보아, 사장님의 발표에 불참했음을 설명하려는 의도로 한 말임을 알 수 있다. 따라서 정답은 (C)이다.

어휘　negatively 부정적으로　affect 영향을 미치다　present 참석한　behind schedule 예정보다 늦은　assignment 할당된 일

51 Where do the speakers most likely work?
(A) At a driving school
(B) At a recording studio
(C) At a translation firm
(D) At a medical clinic

번역 화자들은 어디서 일하겠는가?
(A) 운전 학원
(B) 녹음실
(C) 번역회사
(D) 병원

해설 **전체 내용 관련 - 화자들의 근무지**
여자가 첫 대사에서 그녀는 우리 고객층을 넓힐 수 있도록 스페인어를 구사하는 운전 교습 강사를 고용할 예정(she's going to hire a Spanish-speaking driving instructor so that we can expand our customer base)이라고 말하는 것으로 보아 화자들은 운전 학원에서 근무한다는 것을 알 수 있다. 따라서 정답은 (A)이다.

어휘 translation 번역

---

52 What does the man say he is worried about?
(A) Hiring too many workers
(B) Obtaining enough supplies
(C) Offering poor customer service
(D) Revising some materials quickly

번역 남자는 무엇에 대해 걱정스럽다고 말하는가?
(A) 너무 많은 직원을 고용하는 것
(B) 충분한 비품을 확보하는 것
(C) 미흡한 고객 서비스를 제공하는 것
(D) 일부 자료를 빨리 수정하는 것

해설 **세부 사항 관련 - 남자의 우려 사항**
남자가 마지막 대사에서 스페인어를 사용하는 학생들에게 우리가 제공할 수 있는 고객 서비스 수준이 걱정될 뿐(my only concern would be the level of customer service we could provide to Spanish-speaking students)이라고 말하고 있으므로 정답은 (C)이다.

어휘 obtain 획득하다 poor 형편없는 revise 수정하다

53-55 3인 대화

> M-Cn OK, Yoo-Jin and Sheryl. **53 You've now learned how to use our factory's machines to make fabric. 54 Today, we're going to talk about what to do to keep them in good condition.**
>
> W-Am We're supposed to apply oil to some of the parts before each shift, right?
>
> W-Br Oh yes—because the oil keeps those parts from grinding against each other.

M-Cn That's correct. But it's important to note that the parts will eventually wear out anyway. So another important task is inspecting them to determine whether they should be replaced.

W-Am How will we be able to tell if they're worn out?

M-Cn Well, let's start with the cutter component. **55 Here're some photos of its blade taken a few weeks apart. Tell me what differences you see between them.**

남: 알겠습니다, 유진, 세릴. 두 분은 이제 공장의 기계를 사용하여 원단을 만드는 방법을 배우셨습니다. 오늘은 기계를 좋은 상태로 유지하기 위해 해야 할 일에 관해 이야기하려고 합니다.

여1: 근무 교대 시간이 되기 전에 부품들에 기름칠을 해야 하는 거 맞죠?

여2: 네 맞아요. 기름이 부품들이 서로 부딪혀 닳는 걸 막아주니까요.

남: 맞습니다. 하지만 부품들은 결국 마모된다는 점을 기억하는 것이 중요합니다. 따라서 또 다른 중요한 일은 부품들을 점검해 교체가 필요한지를 결정하는 것입니다.

여1: 마모되었는지를 어떻게 알 수 있나요?

남: 음, 절단기 부품부터 시작합시다. 여기 몇 주 간격으로 촬영된 칼날 사진들이에요. 사진들 간에 어떤 차이점이 보이는지 말씀해 보세요.

어휘 fabric 섬유, 직물 in good condition 상태가 좋은 apply 바르다 part 부품 shift 교대 근무 시간 grind 갈다 eventually 결국 wear out 마모되다 inspect 점검하다 determine 결정하다 replace 교체하다 cutter 절단기 component 부품 blade 칼날, 톱날 difference 차이점

---

53 What industry are the women training to work in?
(A) Fashion retail
(B) Laundry services
(C) Clothing alteration
(D) Textile manufacturing

번역 여자들은 어떤 업계에 종사하기 위해 교육을 받는 중인가?
(A) 패션 소매업
(B) 세탁업
(C) 의류 수선업
(D) 섬유 제조업

해설 **세부 사항 관련 - 여자들이 교육을 받는 업종**
남자가 첫 대사에서 이제 공장의 기계를 사용하여 원단을 만드는 방법을 배웠다(You've now learned how to use our factory's machines to make fabric)고 말하는 것으로 보아 여자들은 섬유 제조업에 종사하기 위해 교육을 받는 중이라는 것을 알 수 있다. 따라서 정답은 (D)이다.

어휘 retail 소매

> **Paraphrasing**
> 대화의 make fabric → 정답의 Textile manufacturing

54 What are the speakers mainly discussing?
(A) Customer complaints
(B) Equipment maintenance
(C) Workspace layouts
(D) Shift scheduling

번역 화자들은 주로 무엇에 관해 이야기하는가?
(A) 고객 불만
(B) 장비 유지보수
(C) 사무 공간 배치
(D) 근무 일정 배정

해설 **전체 내용 관련 - 대화의 주제**
남자가 첫 대사에서 오늘은 기계를 좋은 상태로 유지하기 위해 해야 할 일에 관해 이야기하려고 한다(Today, we're going to talk about what to do to keep them in good condition)며 기계 유지보수에 대한 대화를 이어 가고 있으므로 정답은 (B)이다.

어휘 complaint 불평, 불만   equipment 장비   maintenance 유지보수   workspace 사무 공간   layout 배치

> **Paraphrasing**
> 대화의 keep them in good condition
> → 정답의 maintenance

55 What will the women do next?
(A) Practice a procedure
(B) Watch a demonstration
(C) Read some instructions
(D) Look at some photographs

번역 여자들은 다음으로 무엇을 하겠는가?
(A) 절차 연습하기
(B) 시연 보기
(C) 설명서 읽기
(D) 사진 보기

해설 **세부 사항 관련 - 여자들이 다음에 할 일**
남자가 마지막 대사에서 칼날 사진들(Here're some photos of its blade ~)을 언급하면서 두 사진에서 어떤 차이점이 보이는지 말해 줄 것(Tell me what differences you see between them)을 요청하고 있으므로 정답은 (D)이다.

어휘 practice 연습하다   procedure 절차   demonstration 시연   instruction 설명, 지시

> **Paraphrasing**
> 대화의 photos → 정답의 photographs

56-58

> W-Am Hello, Mr. Brock. This is Julia Bailey from Bailey Antiques. **56 I'm calling about the appraisal service you requested. Would Wednesday at four P.M. work for you?**
>
> M-Au Yes, I can be home then.

W-Am Excellent. When we finish this call, **57 please send me your address by text message.**

M-Au OK, but I'll include some directions too, because our house can be hard to find the first time.

W-Am I see. Oh, and along with your antiques, **58 don't forget to prepare any documentation you have for the age or authenticity of the items.**

여: 안녕하세요, 브록 씨. 저는 베일리 골동품의 줄리아 베일리입니다. 요청하신 감정 서비스 건으로 전화드립니다. 수요일 오후 4시에 시간 되실까요?

남: 네, 그때 집에 있을 수 있어요.

여: 좋습니다. 이 통화가 끝나면 **귀하의 주소를 저에게 문자로 보내 주세요.**

남: 알겠습니다. 그런데 길 안내도 같이 보낼게요. 저희 집이 처음에는 찾기가 좀 어려울 수 있거든요.

여: 알겠습니다. 아, 그리고 귀하의 골동품과 함께 **그 물품의 연대나 진품 여부를 알 수 있는 서류를 준비하시는 것도 잊지 마세요.**

어휘 antique 골동품   appraisal 평가   request 요청하다   include 포함하다   direction 방향, 길 안내   prepare 준비하다   documentation 서류   authenticity 진품 여부

56 Why is the woman calling the man?
(A) To discuss a payment
(B) To arrange a consultation
(C) To provide an order update
(D) To follow up on some feedback

번역 여자는 왜 남자에게 전화를 걸고 있는가?
(A) 지불에 대해 상의하려고
(B) 상담 일정을 정하려고
(C) 주문 관련 새로운 내용을 제공하려고
(D) 피드백에 대해 후속 조치를 하려고

해설 **전체 내용 관련 - 여자가 전화하는 이유**
여자가 첫 대사에서 요청하신 감정 서비스 건으로 전화드린다(I'm calling about the appraisal service you requested)면서 수요일 오후 4시에 시간 되는지(Would Wednesday at four P.M. work for you?) 묻고 있으므로 정답은 (B)이다.

어휘 payment 지불   arrange 일정을 잡다   consultation 상담   follow up on ~에 대해 후속 조치를 하다

> **Paraphrasing**
> 대화의 the appraisal service → 정답의 a consultation

57 What information does the woman ask the man to send her?
(A) A home address
(B) A credit card number
(C) Design preferences
(D) Space measurements

번역 여자는 남자에게 어떤 정보를 보내라고 요청하는가?
(A) 집 주소
(B) 신용카드 번호
(C) 디자인 선호도
(D) 공간 치수

해설 **세부 사항 관련 - 여자가 남자에게 요청하는 정보**
여자가 두 번째 대사에서 남자의 주소를 문자로 보내줄 것(please send me your address by text message)을 요청하고 있으므로 정답은 (A)이다.

어휘 preference 선호도　measurement 측정, 치수

---

58 What does the woman remind the man to do?
(A) Move any parked vehicles
(B) Prepare some paperwork
(C) Complete a transaction
(D) Check his mail frequently

번역 여자는 남자에게 무엇을 하라고 상기시키는가?
(A) 주차된 차량 이동하기
(B) 서류 준비하기
(C) 거래 완료하기
(D) 우편함 자주 확인하기

해설 **세부 사항 관련 - 여자가 남자에게 상기시키는 것**
여자가 마지막 대사에서 그 물품의 연대나 진품 여부를 알 수 있는 서류를 준비할 것(don't forget to prepare any documentation you have for the age or authenticity of the items)을 상기시키고 있으므로 정답은 (B)이다.

어휘 transaction 거래　frequently 자주

> **Paraphrasing**
> 대화의 any documentation → 정답의 some paperwork

59-61

> M-Cn Denniston Historic Estate visitors' assistance.
>
> W-Br Hi, I'm hoping to visit the estate, but **⁵⁹I can't seem to reserve a tour spot through your Web site.** Nothing happens when I click the green button.
>
> M-Cn **⁶⁰Are you using Exult to access our site? If so, you need to uncheck the box next to the address bar.** Otherwise, the program won't allow pop-up windows.
>
> W-Br OK… yes, that solved the problem. Thank you! Oh, and just to check—the tour will include a visit to the estate's guest cottage, right?
>
> M-Cn Yes, near the end.
>
> W-Br Good. **⁶¹A client asked me to use the cottage's style as inspiration while redecorating his house,** so I really need to see it.

남: 데니스턴 유적지 방문자 도움 서비스입니다.

여: 안녕하세요, 유적지를 방문하고 싶은데, **귀사의 웹사이트를 통한 관람 예약이 안 되는 것 같아요.** 녹색 버튼을 클릭하면 아무 일도 일어나지 않아요.

남: **저희 웹사이트에 접속하는 데 Exult를 사용하고 계신가요? 그렇다면 주소창 옆에 있는 네모 칸의 선택을 취소하셔야 해요.** 안 그러면, 프로그램에서 팝업창을 차단할 거예요.

여: 알겠습니다… 네, 그걸로 문제가 해결되었네요. 감사합니다! 아, 그리고 확인할 게 있는데요, 관람에 유적지의 손님 별장 방문도 포함되는 거 맞죠?

남: 네, 끝날 무렵에요.

여: 잘됐네요. **한 고객이 집을 새로 꾸미면서 그 별장 스타일을 참고해 달라고 하셔서 제가 그걸 꼭 봐야 하거든요.**

어휘 historic 역사적인　estate 사유지, 재산　assistance 도움　can't seem to ~할 수 없는 것 같다　reserve 예약하다　access 접속하다　uncheck 선택을 취소하다　allow 허용하다　solve 해결하다　include 포함하다　cottage 작은 별장　inspiration 영감　redecorate 실내 장식을 새로 하다

59 Why is the woman calling?
(A) She is disappointed with a virtual tour.
(B) She found inaccurate information on a Web site.
(C) She cannot make a reservation online.
(D) She did not receive a confirmation e-mail.

번역 여자는 왜 전화를 걸고 있는가?
(A) 가상 관람에 실망해서
(B) 웹사이트에서 부정확한 정보를 발견해서
(C) 온라인으로 예약을 할 수 없어서
(D) 확인 이메일을 받지 못해서

해설 **전체 내용 관련 - 여자가 전화하는 이유**
여자가 첫 대사에서 귀사의 웹사이트를 통한 관람 예약이 안 되는 것 같다(I can't seem to reserve a tour spot through your Web site)고 말하고 있으므로 정답은 (C)이다.

어휘 be disappointed with ~에 실망하다　inaccurate 부정확한　make a reservation 예약하다　confirmation 확인

> **Paraphrasing**
> 대화의 reserve a tour spot through your Web site
> → 정답의 make a reservation online

60 What does the man tell the woman about?
(A) An improvement project
(B) A computer program setting
(C) A membership requirement
(D) A cancellation policy

번역　남자는 여자에게 무엇에 대해 말하는가?
(A) 개조 공사
(B) 컴퓨터 프로그램 설정
(C) 회원 가입을 위한 요건
(D) 취소 정책

해설　**세부 사항 관련 - 남자가 여자에게 알려주는 것**
남자가 두 번째 대사에서 웹사이트에 접속하는 데 Exult를 사용하고 있는지(Are you using Exult to access our site?) 물어면서 그렇다면 주소창 옆에 있는 네모 칸의 선택을 취소해야 한다(If so, you need to uncheck the box next to the address bar)고 컴퓨터 프로그램 설정에 대해 말하고 있으므로 정답은 (B)이다.

어휘　improvement 개선, 개조　setting 설정　requirement 요건
cancellation 취소　policy 정책

---

61 What most likely is the woman's job?
(A) Historian
(B) Landscaper
(C) Interior decorator
(D) Event planner

번역　여자의 직업은 무엇이겠는가?
(A) 역사가
(B) 조경사
(C) 실내 장식가
(D) 행사 기획자

해설　**전체 내용 관련 - 여자의 직업**
여자가 마지막 대사에서 한 고객이 집을 새로 꾸미면서 그 별장 스타일을 참고해 달라고 했다(A client asked me to use the cottage's style as inspiration while redecorating his house)고 말하는 것으로 보아 여자는 실내 장식가임을 알 수 있다. 따라서 정답은 (C)이다.

62-64 대화+패키지 종류

M-Au　Fredericks Photography, Akio speaking.

W-Am　Hi, **62 I'm interested in getting some new acting headshots taken**. I don't think my current photos give a good sense of my abilities as an actress.

M-Au　Our photographers can certainly work with you to get some shots you're happy with. **63 How many different images do you want?**

W-Am　**63 Four should be enough.** And just digital files, please.

M-Au　Alright. Uh, I'll need to book your studio session for over an hour... I see an opening on Thursday at three.

W-Am　Perfect. Oh, and **64 do you provide hair and makeup services?** If so, I'd like to book those as well.

남:　프레드릭스 사진관의 아키오입니다.

여:　안녕하세요. **배우 프로필 사진을 새로 찍고 싶은데요.** 현재 제 사진으로는 여배우로서 제 능력을 제대로 보여주지 못하는 것 같아요.

남:　저희 사진사들이 당신이 마음에 드는 사진이 나올 수 있도록 확실히 도와드릴 수 있습니다. **몇 장의 사진을 원하시나요?**

여:　**네 장이면 충분할 거예요.** 그리고 디지털 파일만요.

남:　알겠습니다. 음, 1시간 이상 예약 시간을 잡아드려야 하는데… 목요일 세 시에 빈자리가 있네요.

여:　아주 좋아요. 아, 그리고 **머리 손질과 화장 서비스도 제공하시나요?** 그렇다면 그것도 같이 예약하고 싶습니다.

어휘　acting headshot 배우 프로필 사진　current 현재의
ability 능력　actress 여배우　session 시간　opening
빈자리　provide 제공하다

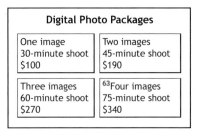

Digital Photo Packages

One image 30-minute shoot $100	Two images 45-minute shoot $190
Three images 60-minute shoot $270	63Four images 75-minute shoot $340

디지털 사진 패키지

1장 30분 촬영 100달러	2장 45분 촬영 190달러
3장 60분 촬영 270달러	634장 75분 촬영 **340달러**

---

62 What field does the woman work in?
(A) Photography
(B) Entertainment
(C) Real estate
(D) Law

번역　여자는 어떤 분야에서 일하는가?
(A) 사진
(B) 연예
(C) 부동산
(D) 법률

해설　**전체 내용 관련 - 여자의 근무 업종**
여자가 첫 대사에서 배우 프로필 사진을 새로 찍고 싶다(I'm interested in getting some new acting headshots taken)고 말하고 있으므로 정답은 (B)이다.

63 Look at the graphic. How much will the woman pay for her photo package?
(A) $100
(B) $190
(C) $270
(D) $340

번역 시각 정보에 의하면, 여자는 사진 패키지에 얼마를 지불하겠는가?
(A) 100달러
(B) 190달러
(C) 270달러
(D) 340달러

해설 **시각 정보 연계 - 여자가 사진 패키지에 지불할 금액**
남자가 두 번째 대사에서 몇 장의 사진을 원하는지(How many different images do you want?) 묻자, 여자가 네 장이면 충분할 거(Four should be enough)라고 말하고 있고, 패키지 종류에 따르면 4장(Four images)은 340달러이므로 정답은 (D)이다.

64 What does the woman ask the man about?
(A) Additional services
(B) Payment methods
(C) A wait time
(D) A clothing choice

번역 여자는 남자에게 무엇에 대해 문의하는가?
(A) 추가 서비스
(B) 결제 방법
(C) 대기 시간
(D) 의상 선택

해설 **세부 사항 관련 - 여자의 문의 사항**
여자가 마지막 대사에서 머리 손질과 화장 서비스도 제공하는지(do you provide hair and makeup services?) 묻고 있으므로 정답은 (A)이다.

어휘 additional 부가적인 payment 지불 method 방법, 수단

65-67 대화+목록

M-Cn Thanks for agreeing to come in on your usual day off, Amber.

W-Br No problem. ⁶⁵I understand that it takes a lot of effort to get the store ready for holidays like this one.

M-Cn Right. So, I made a list of what we need to get done today. Here it is.

W-Br Hmm… making an attractive window display is important, right? Why don't you focus on that while I tackle these other tasks?

M-Cn OK, but ⁶⁶I need the new holiday merchandise to put into the display, so I'll unpack that first.

W-Br Got it. And—⁶⁷before we start, why don't I put

on some music for us to listen to?

남: 당신의 정기 휴무일인데 기꺼이 와주셔서 감사합니다, 앰버.

여: 괜찮아요. **이번 같은 명절 연휴를 위해 매장을 준비하려면 많은 수고가 들어간다는 것을 잘 알고 있습니다.**

남: 맞아요. 그래서 우리가 오늘 해야 할 일의 목록을 만들었어요. 여기요.

여: 음… 매력적으로 창가를 진열하는 것이 중요한 거죠? 제가 여기 다른 일들을 처리하는 동안 당신은 그 일에 집중하면 어때요?

남: 알겠습니다, 그런데 **진열대에 넣을 새 명절 상품이 필요하니 그것부터 먼저 포장을 풀게요.**

여: 알았어요. 그리고, **시작하기 전에 제가 음악을 좀 틀어도 될까요?**

어휘 usual 평소의 day off 쉬는 날 effort 노력 attractive 매력적인 display 진열 tackle (문제 등을) 다루다 merchandise 상품 unpack 꺼내다 put on some music 음악을 틀다

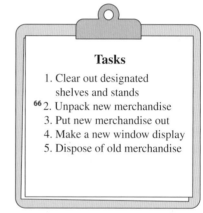

Tasks
1. Clear out designated shelves and stands
⁶⁶2. Unpack new merchandise
3. Put new merchandise out
4. Make a new window display
5. Dispose of old merchandise

할 일
1. 지정된 선반과 진열대 치우기
⁶⁶2. 새 상품 포장 풀기
3. 새 상품 내놓기
4. 창가 진열 새로 꾸미기
5. 오래된 상품 폐기하기

어휘 designated 지정된 put out 내놓다 dispose of ~을 폐기하다

65 Why did the man ask the woman to work today?
(A) A lot of customers are expected today.
(B) He wants to teach her how to do a task.
(C) Another worker had to take a day off.
(D) They need to prepare the store for a holiday.

222

번역 남자는 왜 여자에게 오늘 일해 달라고 부탁했는가?
(A) 오늘 많은 손님이 올 것으로 예상되어서
(B) 여자에게 일하는 방법을 가르쳐주고 싶어서
(C) 다른 직원이 쉬어야 해서
(D) 명절을 위해 가게를 준비해야 해서

해설 **세부 사항 관련 - 남자가 여자에게 오늘 일해 달라고 부탁한 이유**
여자가 첫 대사에서 이번 같은 명절 연휴를 위해 매장을 준비하려면 많은 수고가 들어간다는 것을 잘 알고 있다(I understand that it takes a lot of effort to get the store ready for holidays like this one)고 말하고 있으므로 정답은 (D)이다.

어휘 prepare 준비하다

> **Paraphrasing**
> 대화의 get the store ready for holidays like this one
> → 정답의 prepare the store for a holiday

66 Look at the graphic. Which task will the man do first?
(A) Task 1
(B) Task 2
(C) Task 3
(D) Task 4

번역 시각 정보에 의하면, 남자는 먼저 어떤 일을 하겠는가?
(A) 할 일 1
(B) 할 일 2
(C) 할 일 3
(D) 할 일 4

해설 **시각 정보 연계 - 남자가 먼저 할 일**
남자가 마지막 대사에서 진열대에 넣을 새 명절 상품이 필요하니 그것부터 먼저 포장을 풀겠다(I need the new holiday merchandise to put into the display, so I'll unpack that first)고 말하고 있고, 목록에 따르면 새 상품 포장 풀기(Unpack new merchandise)는 할 일 2이므로 정답은 (B)이다.

67 What does the woman suggest doing before they start?
(A) Buying some refreshments
(B) Opening the windows
(C) Turning on some music
(D) Putting on gloves

번역 여자는 시작하기 전에 무엇을 하겠다고 제안하는가?
(A) 다과 사기
(B) 창문 열기
(C) 음악 틀기
(D) 장갑 끼기

해설 **세부 사항 관련 - 여자가 시작하기 전에 제안하는 것**
여자가 마지막 대사에서 시작하기 전에 음악을 좀 틀어도 되는지(before we start, why don't I put on some music for us to listen to?) 묻고 있으므로 정답은 (C)이다.

어휘 refreshments 다과 turn on 전원을 켜다 put on ~을 착용하다

> **Paraphrasing**
> 대화의 put on some music
> → 정답의 Turning on some music

68-70 대화 + 호텔 안내도

M-Cn Welcome to Upshaw Hotel. Are you checking in?

W-Am No, **68,69 I'm here to have dinner with a business associate who's staying with you.** But my mobile phone's out of power. **69 Would you mind calling her and letting her know I've arrived?** She's in Room 306.

M-Cn **69 Sure.** Could you give me your name? I'll need to tell her who's waiting for her in the lobby.

W-Am Oh, actually, **70 we're eating in your restaurant,** so ask her to meet me there. And my name's Lydia Fisher.

남: 업쇼 호텔에 오신 것을 환영합니다. 체크인 하시게요?
여: 아니요. 이 호텔에 머물고 있는 거래처 사람과 저녁을 먹으려고 왔는데요. 제 휴대전화가 꺼졌어요. 그녀에게 전화를 걸어서 제가 도착했다고 좀 전해 주실 수 있나요? 그녀가 묵는 방은 306호실이에요.
남: 물론이죠. 당신의 이름도 알려주시겠어요? 로비에서 누가 기다리는지 말씀드려야 해서요.
여: 아, 실은 호텔 식당에서 식사를 할 예정이니 거기서 만나자고 전해 주세요. 그리고 제 이름은 리디아 피셔입니다.

어휘 business associate 거래처 사람, 동업자 out of power 방전된

UPSHAW HOTEL

UPSHAW HOTEL	
Floor 4	Suites
Floor 3	Rooms
70Floor 2	Restaurant
Floor 1	Lobby

업쇼 호텔	
4층 특실	
3층 객실	
70 2층 식당	
1층 로비	

68 Why has the woman come to the hotel?
(A) For a job interview
(B) For a business dinner
(C) For an equipment repair
(D) For an overnight stay

번역 여자는 왜 호텔에 왔는가?
(A) 취업 면접을 위해
(B) 사업상 저녁 식사를 위해
(C) 장비 수리를 위해
(D) 숙박을 위해

해설 **세부 사항 관련 - 여자가 호텔에 온 이유**
여자가 첫 대사에서 이 호텔에 머물고 있는 거래처 사람과 저녁을 먹으려고 왔다(I'm here to have dinner with a business associate who's staying with you)고 말하고 있으므로 정답은 (B)이다.

어휘 equipment 장비 repair 수리 overnight 하룻밤 동안의

> **Paraphrasing**
> 대화의 dinner with a business associate
> → 정답의 a business dinner

69 Who does the man agree to contact?
(A) A current guest
(B) A maintenance supervisor
(C) A parking attendant
(D) A hotel manager

번역 남자는 누구에게 연락하기로 동의하는가?
(A) 현재 투숙객
(B) 유지보수 관리자
(C) 주차 보조원
(D) 호텔 지배인

해설 **세부 사항 관련 - 남자가 연락하기로 동의한 대상**
여자가 첫 대사에서 이 호텔에 머물고 있는 거래처 사람과 저녁을 먹으려고 왔다(I'm here to have dinner with a business associate who's staying with you)고 말한 뒤, 그녀에게 전화를 걸어서 도착했다고 좀 전해줄 것(Would you mind calling her and letting her know I've arrived?)을 요청하자 남자가 물론(Sure)이라고 수락하고 있으므로 정답은 (A)이다.

어휘 maintenance 유지보수 supervisor 감독관, 관리자 attendant 안내원, 종업원

70 Look at the graphic. Which floor will the woman most likely go to next?
(A) Floor 1
(B) Floor 2
(C) Floor 3
(D) Floor 4

번역 시각 정보에 의하면, 여자는 다음으로 어느 층으로 가겠는가?
(A) 1층
(B) 2층
(C) 3층
(D) 4층

해설 **시각 정보 연계 - 여자가 다음에 갈 층**
여자가 마지막 대사에서 호텔 식당에서 식사를 할 예정(we're eating in your restaurant)이라고 말하고 있고, 호텔 안내도에 따르면 식당은 2층에 위치해 있으므로 정답은 (B)이다.

PART 4

71-73 담화

> M-Au First, I want to thank Wenston Bookstore for holding this reading. **71 It's always a pleasure to come here and introduce my books to this enthusiastic audience.** I'm especially excited to be bringing you this one. It's titled *Write for Yourself*, and **72 it's a collection of helpful tips I've picked up over the decades.** While it's mainly for aspiring writers, I think my fans will also enjoy its insights into the creation of some of my stories. Alright, let's dive in. **73 Here's an excerpt from the introduction.**

> 먼저 이 낭독회를 주최해 주신 웬스턴 서점에 감사드리고 싶습니다. **이곳에 와서 이 열정적인 독자들께 제 책을 소개하는 것은 언제나 즐거운 일입니다.** 이번 책을 소개하려니 유난히 마음이 들뜹니다. 이 책의 제목은 〈자신을 위한 글쓰기〉이며, **수십 년 동안 제가 터득한 유용한 팁을 모아놓은 책입니다.** 주로 작가 지망생들을 위한 것이지만, 제 팬들도 제 이야기 창작에 대한 통찰력을 즐겁게 읽으실 수 있을 거라고 생각합니다. 자 그럼, 본격적으로 시작하겠습니다. **이것은 서문에서 발췌한 내용입니다.**

> 어휘 hold 주최하다 reading 낭독회 introduce 소개하다 enthusiastic 열정적인 audience 독자 collection 모음 helpful 유용한 pick up 배우다 aspiring writer 작가 지망생 insight 통찰력 creation 창작 dive in 본격적으로 시작하다 excerpt 발췌 introduction 서문

71 Who most likely is the speaker?
(A) An author
(B) A bookstore clerk
(C) A university professor
(D) A museum guide

번역 화자는 누구이겠는가?
(A) 저자
(B) 서점 직원
(C) 대학 교수
(D) 박물관 안내인

해설 **전체 내용 관련 - 화자의 직업**
화자가 초반부에 이곳에 와서 독자들에게 자신의 책을 소개하는 것은 언제나 즐거운 일(It's always a pleasure to come here and introduce my books to this enthusiastic audience)이라고 말하는 것으로 보아 화자는 저자임을 알 수 있다. 따라서 정답은 (A)이다.

어휘 clerk 직원   professor 교수

---

72 What does the speaker mention about the book?
(A) It is unusually old.
(B) It is in good condition.
(C) It contains useful advice.
(D) It is very popular.

번역 화자는 책에 대해 무엇을 언급하는가?
(A) 몹시 오래되었다.
(B) 상태가 좋다.
(C) 유용한 조언을 담고 있다.
(D) 매우 인기가 있다.

해설 **세부 사항 관련 - 화자가 책에 대해 언급하는 것**
화자가 중반부에 이것은 수십 년 동안 자신이 터득한 유용한 팁을 모아 놓은 책(it's a collection of helpful tips I've picked up over the decades)이라고 말하고 있으므로 정답은 (C)이다.

어휘 unusually 몹시, 이례적으로   in good condition 상태가 좋은
contain 들어 있다   advice 조언, 충고   popular 인기 있는

> **Paraphrasing**
> 담화의 helpful tips → 정답의 useful advice

---

73 What will the listeners do next?
(A) Look at some shelves
(B) Ask some questions
(C) Introduce themselves
(D) Listen to a reading

번역 청자들은 다음으로 무엇을 하겠는가?
(A) 선반을 본다.
(B) 질문을 한다.
(C) 자신을 소개한다.
(D) 낭독을 듣는다.

해설 **세부 사항 관련 - 청자들이 다음에 할 일**
화자가 마지막에 이것은 서문에서 발췌한 내용(Here's an excerpt from the introduction)이라며 낭독을 시작하려고 하고 있으므로 정답은 (D)이다.

74-76 회의 발췌

W-Br **74 I know you're all tired from a long day in your collection trucks,** but I want to address an issue that some of you have asked about. **74, 75 For those who don't know—from next year,**

---

city residents will be required to set their trash out for us in plastic or metal bins. Now, you're right to be concerned that this change will make your job harder. **76 The cans will be heavier to lift than the plastic bags you're used to. But don't worry— within a few months, we're going to get new trucks that can empty the bins automatically.**

쓰레기 수거 트럭에서 긴 하루를 보냈기 때문에 여러분 모두 피곤하시다는 점을 알고 있습니다만, 여러분 중 몇 분이 물어보았던 문제에 대해 이야기하고 싶습니다. 모르시는 분들을 위해 말씀드리자면, 내년부터 시 거주민들은 쓰레기를 플라스틱 또는 철제 쓰레기통에 담아 배출하도록 요구될 것입니다. 자, 이 변화가 여러분의 일을 더 힘들게 만들 거라고 걱정하실 만도 합니다. 이 통들은 여러분에게 익숙한 비닐봉지보다 들기에 무거울 것입니다. 하지만 걱정하지 마세요. 몇 달 내로 우리는 수거함을 자동으로 비울 수 있는 새 트럭을 구매할 것입니다.

어휘 collection truck 쓰레기 수거 트럭   address 다루다
resident 거주민   be required to ~하도록 요구되다   bin 쓰레기통
be right to be concerned 걱정할 만도 하다   can 통
lift 들어 올리다   be used to ~에 익숙하다   empty 비우다
automatically 자동으로

---

74 Where does the speaker most likely work?
(A) A chemical factory
(B) A vegetable farm
(C) An auto-mechanic shop
(D) A waste disposal company

번역 화자는 어디서 일하겠는가?
(A) 화학 공장
(B) 채소 농장
(C) 자동차 정비소
(D) 폐기물 처리 회사

해설 **전체 내용 관련 - 화자의 근무지**
화자가 도입부에 쓰레기 수거 트럭에서 긴 하루를 보냈기 때문에 여러분 모두 피곤하다는 점을 알고 있다(I know you're all tired from a long day in your collection trucks)고 한 뒤, 내년부터 시 거주민들은 쓰레기를 플라스틱 또는 철제 쓰레기통에 담아 배출하도록 요구될 것(~ from next year, city residents will be required to set their trash out for us in plastic or metal bins)이라고 말한 것으로 보아 화자는 폐기물 처리 회사에서 일하고 있음을 알 수 있다. 따라서 정답은 (D)이다.

어휘 waste 폐기물   disposal 처리

---

75 What problem does the speaker mention?
(A) A cost has increased.
(B) A regulation has changed.
(C) A contract has been canceled.
(D) A vehicle has broken down.

번역 화자는 어떤 문제를 언급하는가?
(A) 비용이 올랐다.
(B) 규정이 변경되었다.
(C) 계약이 취소되었다.
(D) 차량이 고장 났다.

해설 **세부 사항 관련 - 화자가 언급하는 문제점**
화자가 중반부에 내년부터 시 거주민들은 쓰레기를 플라스틱 또는 철제 쓰레기통에 담아 배출하도록 요구될 것(~ from next year, city residents will be required to set their trash out for us in plastic or metal bins)이라고 말하고 있으므로 정답은 (B)이다.

어휘 regulation 규정 break down 고장 나다

---

76 What does the speaker reassure the listeners about?
(A) A difficult task will be temporary.
(B) Extra compensation will be offered.
(C) There will still be work available.
(D) They will be able to vote on a proposal.

번역 화자는 청자들에게 무엇에 대해 안심시키는가?
(A) 어려운 일은 일시적일 것이다.
(B) 추가 보상이 제공될 것이다.
(C) 여전히 일거리가 있을 것이다.
(D) 제안서에 대해 투표할 수 있을 것이다.

해설 **세부 사항 관련 - 화자가 청자들을 안심시키는 것**
화자가 후반부에 이 통들은 익숙한 비닐봉지보다 들기에 무거울 것(The cans will be heavier to lift than the plastic bags you're used to)이지만 걱정하지 말라(But don't worry)면서 몇 달 내로 수거함을 자동으로 비울 수 있는 새 트럭을 구매할 것(within a few months, we're going to get new trucks that can empty the bins automatically)이라고 말하고 있으므로 정답은 (A)이다.

어휘 reassure 안심시키다 temporary 일시적인 extra 추가의 compensation 보상 vote 투표하다 proposal 제안

77-79 뉴스 보도

M-Cn In local news, **77 the town council will meet tonight to discuss the plan to build an apartment complex on Stiltner Road**. The developer has proposed a four-story building containing thirty-two apartments and surrounded by a parking lot. **78 The plan has been criticized because of the proposed building site, which borders the woods at the base of Bluft Mountain.** **79 Citizens who live on the opposite side of Stiltner Road are concerned that the complex will lower the value of their homes by blocking this attractive view.**

지역 뉴스입니다. **시 의회는 오늘 밤에 스틸트너 로에 아파트 단지를 짓는 계획에 대해 논의할 예정입니다.** 개발업자는 아파트 32세대를 포함

하며 주차장으로 둘러싸인 4층짜리 건물을 제안했습니다. **이 계획은 제안된 건축 부지가 블루프트 산 기슭의 숲을 접하고 있다는 점 때문에 비판을 받아왔습니다.** 스틸트너 로의 반대편에 거주하는 시민들은 이 단지가 이 매력적인 전망을 가로막음으로써 그들의 주택 가치를 떨어뜨릴 것이라고 우려하고 있습니다.

어휘 town council 시 의회 apartment complex 아파트 단지 developer 개발업자 four-story 4층짜리 contain 들어 있다 be surrounded by ~에 둘러싸이다 criticize 비판하다 border 접하다 lower 낮추다 value 가치 block 막다. 차단하다 attractive 매력적인 view 전망

---

77 What kind of building is being planned?
(A) A hospital
(B) A train station
(C) A manufacturing plant
(D) An apartment complex

번역 어떤 종류의 건물이 계획되고 있는가?
(A) 병원
(B) 기차역
(C) 제조 공장
(D) 아파트 단지

해설 **세부 사항 관련 - 계획 중인 건물**
화자가 도입부에서 시 의회는 오늘 밤에 스틸트너 로에 아파트 단지를 짓는 계획에 대해 논의할 예정(the town council will meet tonight to discuss the plan to build an apartment complex on Stiltner Road)이라고 했으므로 정답은 (D)이다.

---

78 According to the speaker, what is near the proposed building site?
(A) A retail district
(B) A nature area
(C) A primary school
(D) A major highway

번역 화사에 따르면, 제안된 건축 부지 근처에는 무엇이 있는기?
(A) 소매 점포 지구
(B) 자연 지역
(C) 초등학교
(D) 주요 고속도로

해설 **세부 사항 관련 - 제안된 건축 부지 근처에 있는 것**
화자가 중반부에서 이 계획은 제안된 건축 부지가 블루프트 산 기슭의 숲을 접하고 있다는 점 때문에 비판을 받아왔다(The plan has been criticized because of the proposed building site, which borders the woods at the base of Bluft Mountain)고 했으므로 정답은 (B)이다.

어휘 retail 소매 district 지구

> **Paraphrasing**
> 담화의 the woods at the base of Bluft Mountain
> → 정답의 A nature area

79 What does the speaker say some citizens are concerned about?
(A) Effects on wildlife
(B) An increase in noise
(C) A decline in property values
(D) Worsening of road traffic

번역 화자는 일부 시민들이 무엇에 대해 우려하고 있다고 말하는가?
(A) 야생동물에 미치는 영향
(B) 소음 증가
(C) 부동산 가치의 하락
(D) 도로 교통 상황의 악화

해설 **세부 사항 관련 - 일부 시민들의 우려 사항**
화자가 마지막에 스틸트너 로의 반대편에 거주하는 시민들은 이 단지가 그들의 주택 가치를 떨어뜨릴 것이라고 우려하고 있다(Citizens who live on the opposite side of Stiltner Road are concerned that the complex will lower the value of their homes ~)고 했으므로 정답은 (C)이다.

어휘 effect 영향   decline 감소   property 부동산   worsen 악화시키다

> **Paraphrasing**
> 담화의 lower the value of their homes
> → 정답의 A decline in property values

80-82 담화

M-Au **80 The quarterly meeting of our board of directors is coming up next month.** As the last one of the fiscal year, a major item on the agenda will be the budget for the upcoming year. **81 Please send me your estimates of your department's annual expenses soon** so that I can start putting our proposal together. **82 I'll e-mail all of you the template later today.** It has some of the most common expense types, plus space to add others as needed.

이사회 분기별 회의가 다음 달로 다가왔네요. 회계연도의 마지막 회의인 만큼 안건의 주요 항목은 내년도 예산이 될 겁니다. **각 부서의 연간 비용 추정치를 빨리 보내주세요.** 그래야 우리 제안서 작성을 시작할 수 있으니까요. **이따가 여러분 모두에게 서식을 이메일로 보내드릴게요.** 가장 일반적인 비용 유형이 몇 가지 나와 있고요. 필요 시 다른 항목을 추가할 수 있는 공간이 있습니다.

어휘 quarterly 분기별의   board of directors 이사회   come up 다가오다   fiscal year 회계연도   agenda 안건   budget 예산   upcoming 다가오는   estimate 추정   department 부서   annual 연례의   expense 비용, 지출   put together (이것저것을 모아) 만들다   proposal 제안   template 서식, 템플릿   common 흔한   add 추가하다

80 What type of event will take place next month?
(A) A board meeting
(B) An office renovation
(C) An industry conference
(D) A branch opening

번역 다음 달에 어떤 종류의 행사가 열리는가?
(A) 이사회
(B) 사무실 보수 공사
(C) 업계 학회
(D) 지점 개점식

해설 **세부 사항 관련 - 다음 달에 열릴 행사**
화자가 도입부에서 이사회 분기별 회의가 다음 달로 다가왔다(The quarterly meeting of our board of directors is coming up next month)고 말하고 있으므로 정답은 (A)이다.

어휘 renovation 보수 공사   industry 산업

> **Paraphrasing**
> 담화의 The quarterly meeting of our board of directors
> → 정답의 A board meeting

81 What does the speaker tell the listeners to do?
(A) Practice giving a presentation
(B) Distribute surveys to their staff
(C) Submit some budget figures
(D) Arrange their own transportation

번역 화자는 청자들에게 무엇을 하라고 말하는가?
(A) 발표 연습하기
(B) 직원들에게 설문지 배포하기
(C) 예산 금액 제출하기
(D) 각자 교통편 준비하기

해설 **세부 사항 관련 - 화자가 청자들에게 하라고 한 일**
화자가 중반부에 각 부서의 연간 비용 추정치를 빨리 보내달라(Please send me your estimates of your department's annual expenses soon)고 요청하고 있으므로 정답은 (C)이다.

어휘 practice 연습하다   give a presentation 발표하다   distribute 배포하다   survey 설문지   submit 제출하다   figure 수치   arrange 준비하다   transportation 교통

> **Paraphrasing**
> 담화의 send me your estimates of your department's annual expenses
> → 정답의 Submit some budget figures

82 What will the speaker send the listeners?
(A) A catalog
(B) A template
(C) An agenda
(D) A floor plan

번역 화자는 청자들에게 무엇을 보낼 것인가?
(A) 카탈로그
(B) 서식
(C) 안건
(D) 평면도

해설 **세부 사항 관련 - 화자가 청자들에게 보낼 것**
화자가 후반부에서 이따가 모두에게 서식을 이메일로 보내주겠다(I'll e-mail all of you the template later today)고 말하고 있으므로 정답은 (B)이다.

83-85 광고

W-Am Are you a jobseeker in the Covington region? **83 Join the team at Covington Reef, the city's first indoor water park!** Before our launch in October, we're looking to fill roles in dozens of areas, from ticket-taking to maintenance and accounting. And **84 this isn't seasonal work like you'd find at other water parks**—the Reef will be open year-round! This is a great opportunity. **85 Come to our hiring fair on September first to learn more.**

당신은 커빙턴 지역의 구직자이신가요? **시 최초 실내 물놀이 공원인 커 빙턴 리프 팀에 합류하세요!** 10월 개장을 앞두고 검표에서부터 유지보 수 및 회계에 이르기까지 많은 분야에서 일할 사람을 찾는 중입니다. 그 리고 **이것은 다른 물놀이 공원에서 찾을 수 있는 것 같은 계절 일자리가 아닙니다.** 커빙턴 리프는 1년 내내 운영됩니다! 이것은 훌륭한 기회입 니다. **더 많은 정보를 얻으려면 9월 1일에 저희 채용 박람회로 오십 시오.**

어휘 jobseeker 구직자 launch 출시, 개시 fill (일자리에 사람을) 채우다 dozens of 수십의 ticket-taking 검표 maintenance 유지보수 accounting 회계 seasonal 계절적인 year-round 연중 계속되는 opportunity 기회 hiring fair 채용 박람회

83 What kind of business is recruiting employees?
(A) An amusement park
(B) A shopping mall
(C) A sports stadium
(D) A convention center

번역 어떤 종류의 사업체에서 직원을 채용하고 있는가?
(A) 놀이공원
(B) 쇼핑몰
(C) 스포츠 경기장
(D) 컨벤션 센터

해설 **전체 내용 관련 - 직원을 채용하고 있는 업체**
화자가 초반부에 시 최초 실내 물놀이 공원인 커빙턴 리프 팀에 합류하 라(Join the team at Covington Reef, the city's first indoor water park!)고 하고 있으므로 정답은 (A)이다.

> **Paraphrasing**
> 담화의 water park → 정답의 An amusement park

84 What does the speaker imply when she says, "the Reef will be open year-round"?
(A) Many workers will be needed.
(B) The jobs are not suitable for students.
(C) Applications will be accepted at any time.
(D) The positions are relatively stable.

번역 화자가 "커빙턴 리프는 1년 내내 운영됩니다"라고 말할 때, 그 의도는 무엇인가?
(A) 많은 직원이 필요할 것이다.
(B) 일자리가 학생들에게는 적합하지 않다.
(C) 지원서는 상시 접수받을 것이다.
(D) 일자리가 비교적 안정적이다.

해설 **화자의 의도 파악 - 커빙턴 리프는 1년 내내 운영된다는 말의 의도**
앞에서 이것은 다른 물놀이 공원에서 찾을 수 있는 것 같은 계절 일자 리가 아니다(this isn't seasonal work like you'd find at other water parks)라고 말한 뒤 인용문을 언급한 것으로 보아, 1년 4계절 내내 일할 수 있는 안정적인 일자리라는 것을 나타내려는 의도로 한 말 임을 알 수 있다. 따라서 정답은 (D)이다.

어휘 suitable 적합한 application 지원서 accept 받아들이다 relatively 비교적 stable 안정적인

---

85 What should interested listeners do?
(A) Fill out a form online
(B) Attend a recruiting event
(C) E-mail some documents
(D) Call an information line

번역 관심 있는 청자들은 무엇을 해야 하는가?
(A) 온라인으로 양식 작성하기
(B) 채용 행사에 참석하기
(C) 이메일로 서류 보내기
(D) 안내 전화로 전화 걸기

해설 **세부 사항 관련 - 관심 있는 청자들이 해야 할 일**
화자가 후반부에 더 많은 정보를 얻으려면 9월 1일에 채용 박람회로 올 것(Come to our hiring fair on September first to learn more)을 요청하고 있으므로 정답은 (B)이다.

어휘 fill out 작성하다 attend 참석하다 information line 안내 전화

> **Paraphrasing**
> 담화의 Come to our hiring fair
> → 정답의 Attend a recruiting event

86-88 연설

M-Au The rapid expansion of our workforce has caused some difficulties for all of us here at Vindall Incorporated. **86 The most serious one has been the lack of space in our office. 87 The workplace consultant we hired suggested allowing remote work a couple of days per week, and that** change has certainly helped. And setting up the technology to make that possible was no easy thing, so thanks to the IT department for that. I also appreciate everyone's willingness to share their desks. **88 Now we're considering converting one of the conference rooms into another block of desks. That may seem risky, but the same consultant recommended it**, and—we don't have a lot of meetings.

직원 수가 급증하면서 여기 빈들 주식회사에서 일하는 우리 모두에게 어려움이 생겼습니다. 가장 심각한 문제는 사무실에 공간이 부족하다는 점이었습니다. 우리가 고용한 직장 컨설턴트는 일주일에 이틀 정도 원격 근무를 허용하자고 제안했고, 그 변화는 확실히 도움이 되었습니다. 그리고 그것을 가능하게 할 기술 장비를 설치하는 일은 쉬운 일이 아니었습니다. 따라서 그 일을 해준 IT 부서에 감사드립니다. 또 책상을 기꺼이 공유해 주신 여러분 모두에게도 감사드립니다. 지금은 회의실 중 하나를 또 다른 책상 공간으로 개조하는 방안을 검토 중입니다. 모험적으로 보일 수 있겠지만, 같은 컨설턴트가 이 방안을 추천했습니다. 그리고, 우리는 회의가 많지 않습니다.

어휘 rapid 급속한 expansion 확장 workforce 모든 직원
difficulty 어려움 serious 심각한 lack 부족 workplace
직장, 업무 현장 allow 허용하다 remote work 원격 근무
willingness 기꺼이 하는 마음 convert 전환시키다, 개조하다
risky 위험한

86 What problem does the speaker's company have?
(A) Declining sales
(B) A staffing shortage
(C) Limited office space
(D) Outdated equipment

번역 화자의 회사는 어떤 문제를 겪고 있는가?
(A) 매출 감소
(B) 직원 부족
(C) 한정된 사무 공간
(D) 오래된 장비

해설 세부 사항 관련 - 화자의 회사가 겪고 있는 문제점
화자가 초반부에 가장 심각한 문제는 사무실에 공간이 부족하다는 점이었다(The most serious one has been the lack of space in our office)고 말하고 있으므로 정답은 (C)이다.

어휘 declining 감소하는 shortage 부족 limited 한정된
outdated 구식이 된 equipment 장비

> **Paraphrasing**
> 담화의 the lack of space in our office
> → 정답의 Limited office space

87 Why does the speaker thank the IT department?
(A) It provided technology for remote work.
(B) It agreed to move to another location.
(C) It recovered some employees' lost data.
(D) It discovered an issue with some software.

번역 화자는 왜 IT 부서에 감사를 표하는가?
(A) 원격 근무를 위한 기술을 제공해 주어서
(B) 다른 장소로 이전하는 것에 동의해 주어서
(C) 일부 직원들의 잃어버린 데이터를 복구해 주어서
(D) 일부 소프트웨어의 문제를 발견해 주어서

해설 세부 사항 관련 - IT 부서에 감사를 표하는 이유
화자가 중반부에 우리가 고용한 직장 컨설턴트가 일주일에 이틀 정도 원격 근무를 허용하자고 제안했고, 그 변화는 확실히 도움이 되었다(The workplace consultant we hired suggested allowing remote work a couple of days per week, and that change has certainly helped)면서, 그것을 가능하게 할 기술 장비를 설치하는 일은 쉬운 일이 아니라서 그 일을 해준 IT 부서에 감사드린다(And setting up the technology to make that possible was no easy thing, so thanks to the IT department for that)고 말하고 있으므로 정답은 (A)이다.

어휘 provide 제공하다 agree 동의하다 recover 복구하다
discover 발견하다

88 Why does the speaker say, "we don't have a lot of meetings"?
(A) To encourage the listeners to speak now
(B) To announce a change in business practices
(C) To express concern about a company's culture
(D) To support an expert's recommendation

번역 화자가 "우리는 회의가 많지 않습니다"라고 말한 이유는?
(A) 청자들이 지금 말하도록 독려하려고
(B) 사업 관행의 변화를 발표하려고
(C) 회사 문화에 대한 우려를 표명하려고
(D) 전문가의 권고 사항을 지지하려고

해설 화자의 의도 파악 - 회의가 많지 않다는 말의 의도
앞에서 지금은 회의실 중 하나를 또 다른 책상 공간으로 개조하는 방안을 검토 중(Now we're considering converting one of the conference rooms into another block of desks)이라며 모험적으로 보일 수 있겠지만, 같은 컨설턴트가 이 방안을 추천했다(That may seem risky, but the same consultant recommended it)고 말한 뒤 인용문을 언급한 것으로 보아, 컨설턴트의 회의실 개조 권고 사항을 지지하려는 의도로 한 말임을 알 수 있다. 따라서 정답은 (D)이다.

어휘 encourage 독려하다 practice 관행 support 지지하다
expert 전문가

89-91 방송

M-Cn **89 Welcome back to *Around Town*, the show where we explore Harsville. Our last segment today will be a treat for viewers who love animals.** I'm going to introduce you to a unique local business called Kitty Corner. It's a café on Blake Street—but that's not all. **90 Kitty Corner is also**

home to more than ten cats that customers are invited to pet and play with. It's the perfect place to spend an afternoon if you're someone who loves cats but can't keep them yourself. Now, in just a moment, we'll have the company's founder join us to share more about Kitty Corner. This segment is live, **91 so visit our Web site right now to send in questions you'd like me to ask her.**

번역 하스빌을 탐방하는 프로그램인 〈동네 한 바퀴〉에 다시 오신 것을 환영합니다. 오늘의 마지막 순서는 동물을 사랑하는 시청자들을 위한 특별한 선물이 되겠습니다. 여러분께 키티 코너라는 독특한 지역 업체를 소개해 드리고자 합니다. 이곳은 블레이크 가에 있는 카페지만, 그게 다가 아닙니다. 키티 코너는 손님들이 만져보고 놀아줄 수 있는 10마리 이상의 고양이들이 사는 보금자리이기도 합니다. 이곳은 고양이를 좋아하지만 키울 수는 없는 분이라면 오후를 보내기에 더없이 완벽한 장소입니다. 이제, 잠시 후에 키티 코너에 대해 더 많은 이야기를 듣기 위해 회사 창립자를 모시겠습니다. 이 순서는 생방송이므로, **지금 웹사이트를 방문하셔서 제가 그녀에게 물었으면 하는 질문을 보내주십시오.**

어휘 explore 탐방하다 segment 부분 treat 특별한 선물 introduce 소개하다 unique 독특한 be invited to ~하도록 초대받다 pet 어루만지다 founder 창립자

89 Who is the speaker?
(A) A town official
(B) A television host
(C) A company spokesperson
(D) A radio producer

번역 화자는 누구인가?
(A) 시 공무원
(B) TV 진행자
(C) 회사 대변인
(D) 라디오 프로듀서

해설 **전체 내용 관련 - 화자의 직업**
화자가 도입부에 하스빌을 탐방하는 프로그램인 〈동네 한 바퀴〉에 다시 오신 것을 환영한다(Welcome back to *Around Town*, the show where we explore Harsville)면서 오늘의 마지막 순서(Our last segment today will be ~)를 소개하고 있으므로 정답은 (B)이다.

어휘 host 진행자 spokesperson 대변인

90 What does the business do for its customers?
(A) It provides short-term care for their cats.
(B) It shares reviews of local veterinary clinics.
(C) It builds custom play structures for their pets.
(D) It gives them an opportunity to interact with animals.

번역 이 업체는 손님들을 위해 무엇을 하는가?
(A) 손님의 고양이를 위한 단기 돌봄 서비스를 제공한다.
(B) 지역 동물병원의 후기를 공유한다.
(C) 손님의 반려동물을 위한 맞춤 놀이 구조물을 제작한다.
(D) 손님들에게 동물과 교감할 수 있는 기회를 제공한다.

해설 **세부 사항 관련 - 이 업체가 손님들을 위해 하는 일**
화자가 중반부에 키티 코너는 손님들이 만져보고 놀아줄 수 있는 10마리 이상의 고양이들이 사는 보금자리이기도 하다(Kitty Corner is also home to more than ten cats that customers are invited to pet and play with)고 말하고 있으므로 정답은 (D)이다.

어휘 short-term 단기적인 care 돌봄 veterinary clinic 동물병원 custom 주문 제작한 structure 구조물 opportunity 기회 interact with ~와 상호작용하다

> **Paraphrasing**
> 담화의 more than ten cats customers are invited to pet and play with
> → 정답의 an opportunity to interact with animals

91 What can the listeners do on a Web site?
(A) Suggest interview questions
(B) Post videos of themselves
(C) Request a service consultation
(D) Submit a job application

번역 청자들은 웹사이트에서 무엇을 할 수 있는가?
(A) 인터뷰 질문 제안하기
(B) 자신들이 나온 영상 게시하기
(C) 서비스 상담 요청하기
(D) 구직 지원서 제출하기

해설 **세부 사항 관련 - 웹사이트에서 할 수 있는 것**
화자가 마지막에 웹사이트를 방문해서 그녀에게 물었으면 하는 질문을 보내줄 것(so visit our Web site right now to send in questions you'd like me to ask her)을 요청하고 있으므로 정답은 (A)이다.

어휘 suggest 제안하다 post 게시하다 request 요청하다 consultation 상담 submit 제출하다 job application 구직 지원서

> **Paraphrasing**
> 담화의 send in questions you'd like me to ask her
> → 정답의 Suggest interview questions

92-94 공지

W-Br Good morning, everyone. **92 I've just set the date for our organization's annual fund-raising dinner and auction**. It will take place on the evening of May fifteenth. Now, **93 I usually have you all reach out to local businesses about donating items for the auction, but I don't think that's necessary anymore.** Last year we actually had to refuse a few businesses. I'll just call up some of our previous donors. However, your help will still be needed for physical tasks like setup and cleanup of the venue. So **94 please don't make any other plans for the days around the event.**

좋은 아침입니다, 여러분. 방금 우리 단체의 연례 모금 만찬 및 경매 행사를 위한 날짜를 정했습니다. 5월 15일 저녁에 열릴 겁니다. 이제, 제가 평소에는 여러분에게 경매를 위한 물품 기부 건으로 지역 사업체들에 연락을 취하게 하지만, 더 이상 그럴 필요가 없을 것 같아요. 실은 작년에 우리는 몇몇 사업체를 거절해야 했어요. 기존 기부자들 몇 명에게만 전화를 걸 겁니다. 하지만 여전히 행사장 설치 및 정리 같은 물리적인 작업에는 여러분의 도움이 필요할 겁니다. 그러니 행사 날짜 근처에는 다른 계획을 잡지 마십시오.

어휘 set a date 날짜를 정하다 organization 단체 annual 연례의 fund-raising 모금 auction 경매 reach out to ~에게 연락을 취하다 donate 기부하다 necessary 필요한 refuse 거절하다 call up 전화를 걸다 previous 이전의 donor 기부자 physical 물리적인 setup 설치 cleanup 대청소 venue 장소

92 What is being announced?
(A) A trade show
(B) A park cleanup
(C) A charity dinner
(D) An outdoor festival

번역 어떤 내용이 발표되고 있는가?
(A) 무역 박람회
(B) 공원 대청소
(C) **자선 만찬**
(D) 야외 축제

해설 **전체 내용 관련 - 발표의 내용**
화자가 초반부에 방금 우리 단체의 연례 모금 만찬 및 경매 행사를 위한 날짜를 정했다(I've just set the date for our organization's annual fund-raising dinner and auction)고 말하고 있으므로 정답은 (C)이다.

어휘 charity 자선

> **Paraphrasing**
> 담화의 fund-raising dinner → 정답의 A charity dinner

93 What does the speaker imply when she says, "Last year we actually had to refuse a few businesses"?
(A) Many organizations want to participate.
(B) A submission deadline must be followed.
(C) Some registration materials were not complete.
(D) The same recruitment strategy should be used again.

번역 화자가 "실은 작년에 우리는 몇몇 사업체를 거절해야 했어요"라고 말할 때, 그 의도는 무엇인가?
(A) **많은 단체가 참가하기를 원한다.**
(B) 제출 마감 시한은 꼭 지켜져야 한다.
(C) 일부 등록 자료들이 완성되지 않았다.
(D) 동일한 채용 전략을 다시 사용해야 한다.

해설 **화자의 의도 파악 - 작년에 몇몇 사업체를 거절해야 했다는 말의 의도**
앞에서 평소에는 여러분에게 경매를 위한 물품 기부 건으로 지역 사업체들에 연락을 취하게 하지만, 더 이상 그럴 필요가 없을 것 같다(I usually have you all reach out to local businesses about donating items for the auction, but I don't think that's necessary anymore)고 말한 뒤 인용문을 언급한 것으로 보아, 참여를 원하는 사업체가 많다는 의도로 한 말임을 알 수 있다. 따라서 정답은 (A)이다.

어휘 participate 참가하다 submission 제출 deadline 마감 시한 follow 지키다 registration 등록 complete 완전한 recruitment 채용, 모집 strategy 전략

94 What are the listeners asked to do?
(A) Keep some messages short
(B) Keep their records organized
(C) Keep some information confidential
(D) Keep their schedules clear

번역 청자들은 무엇을 하라고 요청받았는가?
(A) 메시지를 짧게 하기
(B) 기록을 정리해 두기
(C) 일부 정보를 기밀로 유지하기
(D) **일정을 비워두기**

해설 **세부 사항 관련 - 청자들이 요청받은 일**
화자가 마지막에 행사 날짜 근처에는 다른 계획을 잡지 말 것(please don't make any other plans for the days around the event)을 요청하고 있으므로 정답은 (D)이다.

어휘 record 기록 organize 정리정돈을 하다 confidential 기밀의

> **Paraphrasing**
> 담화의 don't make any other plans for the days around the event
> → 정답의 Keep their schedules clear

95-97 회의 발췌+양식

W-Am Good morning. **95 I'm Lindsey Reed, one of the organizers of the Maresville Cake Bake-Off. 96 I really appreciate you giving your time and effort to help the town put on this competition.** As you know, it's not just a fun event for the community but also a major tourist attraction that brings in a lot of money for local businesses. Now, what your group will be doing first is handling on-site registration of bake-off contestants. Here's the form that you'll give them. Early registration has ended, so don't let anyone check that box. Also, **[97] please draw older contestants' attention to the "Senior" category, which is a new option this year.**

좋은 아침입니다. 저는 마레스빌 케이크 제빵 경진 대회의 주최자 중 한 명인 린지 리드입니다. 우리 시에서 이 대회를 개최하는 데 시간과 노력을 쏟아주신 여러분께 정말 감사드립니다. 아시다시피 이번 행사는 지역 사회를 위한 재미 있는 행사일 뿐만 아니라 지역 상권에 많은 매출을 올려줄 주요 관광 자원이기도 합니다. 이제 여러분 그룹이 첫 번째로 하실 일은 제빵 경진대회 참가자의 현장 등록을 해주는 일입니다. 이건 그들에게 나눠줄 양식입니다. 조기 등록은 이미 마감되었으니 아무도 그 칸에 체크하지 못하도록 해주세요. 또한, **연령대가 높은 참가자들에게 "중장년" 부문을 안내해 주세요. 이것은 올해 새로 생겼습니다.**

어휘 organizer 주최자 bake-off 빵 굽기 콘테스트 effort 노력 competition 경쟁, 대회 tourist attraction 관광 명소, 관광객을 끌어들이는 것 on-site 현장의 registration 등록 contestant 참가자 draw attention 관심을 끌다

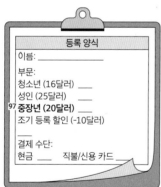

95 What is the speaker organizing?
(A) An art class
(B) A nature hike
(C) A bicycle race
(D) A baking contest

번역 화자는 무엇을 주최하는가?
(A) 미술 수업
(B) 자연 탐사 하이킹
(C) 자전거 경주
(D) 제빵 경연 대회

해설 **세부 사항 관련 - 화자가 주최하는 행사의 종류**
화자가 초반부에 자신이 마레스빌 케이크 제빵 경진대회의 주최자 중 한 명인 린지 리드(I'm Lindsey Reed, one of the organizers of the Maresville Cake Bake-Off)임을 밝히고 있으므로 정답은 (D)이다.

> **Paraphrasing**
> 담화의 Bake-Off → 정답의 A baking contest

96 What does the speaker thank the listeners for?
(A) Being patient during a delay
(B) Volunteering to support the event
(C) Completing registration in advance
(D) Giving feedback on a past event

번역 화자는 청자들에게 무엇에 대해 감사하는가?
(A) 지연되는 동안 인내심을 발휘해 준 것
(B) 행사를 돕기 위해 자원봉사를 해준 것
(C) 미리 등록을 완료해 준 것
(D) 지난 행사에 대해 피드백을 준 것

해설 **세부 사항 관련 - 화자가 청자들에게 감사한 것**
화자가 중반부에 우리 시가 이 대회를 개최하도록 시간과 노력을 쏟아준 여러분에게 정말 감사하다(I really appreciate you giving your time and effort to help the town put on this competition)고 말하고 있으므로 정답은 (B)이다.

어휘 patient 인내심 있는 in advance 미리

> **Paraphrasing**
> 담화의 giving your time and effort
> → 정답의 Volunteering to support

97 Look at the graphic. Which amount has been newly added?
(A) $10
(B) $16
(C) $20
(D) $25

번역 시각 정보에 의하면, 어떤 금액이 새로 추가되었는가?
(A) 10달러
(B) 16달러
(C) 20달러
(D) 25달러

해설 **시각 정보 연계 - 새로 추가된 금액**
화자가 후반부에 연령대가 높은 참가자들에게 "중장년" 부문을 안내해 달라(please draw older contestants' attention to the "Senior" category)며 이것이 올해 새로 생겼다(which is a new option this year)고 했고, 양식에 따르면 중장년 부문의 등록비는 20달러이므로 정답은 (C)이다.

98-100 전화 메시지 + 일정

W-Br Hi, it's Sayuri. Thanks for sending me the schedule for the community center's Italian cooking classes. I agree that it would be fun to take them together. **98 I'm quite interested in learning to make all of these dishes—except meatballs.** You know I'm not a fan of meat! **99 I wonder if I'll still have to pay for that class even though I won't attend it, or if they charge separately for each class.** That information doesn't seem to be on the schedule. **100 I'll call the community center and find out.**

안녕하세요, 사유리예요. 지역 문화 센터의 이탈리아 요리 수업 일정을 보내주셔서 감사합니다. 수업을 함께 들으면 재미있을 것 같아요. **여기 있는 모든 요리를 만드는 법을 배우는 데 매우 관심이 있어요, 미트볼만 빼고요.** 아시다시피 제가 고기를 별로 좋아하지 않잖아요! **제가 참석하지 않더라도 여전히 그 수업에 대한 수업료를 지불해야 하는지, 아니면 수업별로 따로따로 청구하는지 궁금해요.** 그 정보는 일정표에 안 쓰여 있는 것 같아요. **제가 지역 문화 센터에 전화해서 알아볼게요.**

어휘 community center 지역 문화 센터   dish 요리   except ~을 제외하고   attend 참석하다   charge 청구하다   separately 따로따로

Italian Cooking Classes
5 P.M. on Tuesdays

Date	Dish
October 2	Pesto Spaghetti
98October 9	Classic Meatballs
October 16	Eggplant Parmesan
October 23	Cheese Ravioli

이탈리아 요리 수업
화요일 오후 5시

날짜	요리
10월 2일	페스토 스파게티
9810월 9일	클래식 미트볼
10월 16일	가지 파마산
10월 23일	치즈 라비올리

98 Look at the graphic. On which date will the speaker skip a class?
(A) October 2
(B) October 9
(C) October 16
(D) October 23

번역 시각 정보에 의하면, 화자는 어떤 날짜에 수업을 빠지겠는가?
(A) 10월 2일
(B) 10월 9일
(C) 10월 16일
(D) 10월 23일

해설 시각 정보 연계 - 화자가 수업을 빠지는 날짜
화자가 중반부에 여기 있는 모든 요리를 만드는 법을 배우는 데 매우 관심이 있는데 미트볼만 빼고(I'm quite interested in learning to make all of these dishes—except meatballs)라고 말하고 있고, 일정에 따르면 클래식 미트볼(Classic Meatballs)은 10월 9일에 예정되어 있으므로 정답은 (B)이다.

99 What is the speaker unsure about?
(A) Whether some classes are already full
(B) What time the classes will end
(C) Who will teach each class
(D) How the class fees are charged

번역 화자는 무엇에 대해 잘 모르고 있는가?
(A) 일부 수업들이 이미 마감되었는지
(B) 수업들이 몇 시에 끝날지
(C) 수업별로 누가 진행할지
(D) 수업료가 어떻게 청구되는지

해설 세부 사항 관련 - 화자가 잘 모르는 것
화자가 중반부에 자신이 참석하지 않더라도 여전히 그 수업에 대한 수업료를 지불해야 하는지, 아니면 수업별로 따로따로 청구하는지 궁금하다(I wonder if I'll still have to pay for that class even though I won't attend it, or if they charge separately for each class)고 말하고 있으므로 정답은 (D)이다.

어휘 class fee 수업료

100 What will the speaker most likely do next?
(A) Complete a registration form
(B) Wait for a call from the listener
(C) Contact the community center
(D) Read some lists of ingredients

번역 화자는 다음으로 무엇을 하겠는가?
(A) 등록 신청서 작성하기
(B) 청자로부터의 전화 기다리기
(C) 지역 문화 센터에 연락하기
(D) 성분 목록 읽기

해설 세부 사항 관련 - 화자가 다음에 할 일
화자가 마지막에 지역 문화 센터에 전화해서 알아보겠다(I'll call the community center and find out)고 하고 있으므로 정답은 (C)이다.

어휘 complete 작성하다   registration 등록   ingredient 성분

Paraphrasing
담화의 call → 정답의 Contact

TEST 8

TEST 9

1 (D)	2 (D)	3 (B)	4 (B)	5 (C)
6 (A)	7 (A)	8 (B)	9 (A)	10 (A)
11 (C)	12 (C)	13 (B)	14 (C)	15 (A)
16 (B)	17 (A)	18 (C)	19 (B)	20 (C)
21 (A)	22 (B)	23 (A)	24 (C)	25 (B)
26 (C)	27 (C)	28 (B)	29 (B)	30 (A)
31 (A)	32 (A)	33 (C)	34 (D)	35 (C)
36 (A)	37 (D)	38 (C)	39 (B)	40 (A)
41 (C)	42 (B)	43 (D)	44 (A)	45 (C)
46 (A)	47 (A)	48 (D)	49 (B)	50 (C)
51 (A)	52 (C)	53 (B)	54 (A)	55 (D)
56 (D)	57 (D)	58 (A)	59 (D)	60 (B)
61 (A)	62 (C)	63 (B)	64 (C)	65 (D)
66 (D)	67 (C)	68 (B)	69 (C)	70 (C)
71 (C)	72 (D)	73 (A)	74 (D)	75 (D)
76 (C)	77 (A)	78 (C)	79 (B)	80 (D)
81 (A)	82 (B)	83 (D)	84 (B)	85 (C)
86 (B)	87 (C)	88 (A)	89 (B)	90 (D)
91 (C)	92 (A)	93 (B)	94 (D)	95 (D)
96 (B)	97 (C)	98 (B)	99 (B)	100 (B)

PART 1

1

M-Cn

(A) She's getting into a vehicle.
(B) She's clearing snow from a window.
(C) She's bending down to pick up a scarf.
(D) She's shoveling some snow.

번역 (A) 여자가 차에 타는 중이다.
(B) 여자가 창문에 쌓인 눈을 치우고 있다.
(C) 여자가 스카프를 집으려고 허리를 숙이고 있다.
(D) **여자가 삽으로 눈을 치우고 있다.**

해설 **1인 등장 사진**
(A) 동사 오답. 여자가 차에 타는 중인 모습이 아니다.
(B) 위치 오답. 여자가 창문에 쌓인 눈을 치우고 있는 모습이 아니다.
(C) 동사 오답. 여자가 스카프를 집으려고 허리를 숙이고 있는 모습이 아니다.
(D) 정답. 여자가 삽으로 눈을 치우고 있으므로 정답이다.

어휘 get into (차에) 올라타다 bend 굽히다. 숙이다 shovel 삽질하다

2

W-Br

(A) They're carrying furniture into an office.
(B) They're working at computers.
(C) They're using vacuums to clean a carpet.
(D) They're unpacking some cardboard boxes.

번역 (A) 사람들이 가구를 사무실 안으로 나르고 있다.
(B) 사람들이 컴퓨터 앞에서 일하고 있다.
(C) 사람들이 진공청소기로 카펫을 청소하고 있다.
(D) **사람들이 판지 상자들에서 물건을 꺼내고 있다.**

해설 **2인 이상 등장 사진**
(A) 동사 오답. 사람들이 가구를 사무실 안으로 나르고 있는 모습이 아니다.
(B) 위치 오답. 사람들이 컴퓨터 앞에서 일하고 있는 모습이 아니다.
(C) 사진에 없는 명사. 사진에 진공청소기가 보이지 않는다.
(D) 정답. 사람들이 판지 상자들에서 물건을 꺼내고 있는 모습이므로 정답이다.

어휘 carry 나르다 furniture 가구 vacuum 진공청소기 unpack (짐 등을) 꺼내다. 풀다 cardboard box 판지 상자

3

M-Au

(A) He's hanging up a pair of jeans.
(B) He's reaching into a stack of clothing.
(C) He's checking his appearance in a mirror.
(D) He's placing a shopping basket on a shelf.

번역 (A) 남자가 청바지 한 벌을 걸고 있다.
(B) **남자가 옷더미에 손을 넣고 있다.**
(C) 남자가 거울을 보며 자신의 외모를 확인하고 있다.
(D) 남자가 장바구니를 선반에 놓고 있다.

해설 **1인 등장 사진**
(A) 동사 오답. 남자가 청바지 한 벌을 걸고 있는 모습이 아니다.
(B) 정답. 남자가 옷더미에 손을 넣고 있으므로 정답이다.
(C) 사진에 없는 명사. 사진에 거울이 보이지 않는다.
(D) 사진에 없는 명사. 사진에 장바구니가 보이지 않는다.

어휘 hang up 걸다 reach into 손을 뻗어 넣다 a stack of 한 무더기의 appearance 외모, 겉모습 place 놓다. 두다 shopping basket 장바구니

4

W-Br

(A) There are some lights on the wall being repaired.
(B) There are traffic signs attached to the ceiling.
(C) There are metal railings lining both sides of a road.
(D) There is a pedestrian walkway in a tunnel.

번역 (A) 벽에 달린 전등들이 수리되고 있다.
(B) 교통 표지판들이 천장에 붙어 있다.
(C) 도로 양쪽으로 철제 난간들이 세워져 있다.
(D) 터널 안에 보행자용 통행로가 있다.

해설 **사물·풍경 사진**
(A) 동사 오답. 벽에 달린 전등들이 수리되고 있는 모습이 아니다.
(B) 정답. 교통 표지판들이 천장에 붙어 있으므로 정답이다.
(C) 사진에 없는 명사. 사진에 철제 난간들이 보이지 않는다.
(D) 사진에 없는 명사. 사진에 보행자용 통행로가 보이지 않는다.

어휘 repair 수리하다   traffic sign 교통 표지판   attach 붙이다
ceiling 천장   railing 난간   line ~을 따라 늘어서다   pedestrian
보행자   walkway 통행로

5

M-Au

(A) One of the workers is laying some bricks.
(B) One of the workers is pointing toward the roof.
(C) The workers are positioned on ladders.
(D) The workers are unloading some solar panels.

번역 (A) 작업자들 중 한 명이 벽돌을 쌓고 있다.
(B) 작업자들 중 한 명이 지붕을 가리키고 있다.
(C) 작업자들이 사다리 위에 올라가 있다.
(D) 작업자들이 태양 전지판을 내리고 있다.

해설 **2인 이상 등장 사진**
(A) 동사 오답. 벽돌을 쌓고 있는 작업자의 모습이 보이지 않는다.
(B) 동사 오답. 지붕을 가리키고 있는 작업자의 모습이 보이지 않는다.
(C) 정답. 작업자들이 사다리 위에 올라가 있는 모습이므로 정답이다.
(D) 동사 오답. 작업자들이 태양 전지판을 내리고 있는 모습이 아니다.

어휘 lay 깔다   brick 벽돌   be positioned 자리 잡고 있다   ladder
사다리   unload 짐을 내리다   solar panel 태양 전지판

6

W-Am

(A) Cups and glasses have been arranged on a shelf.
(B) A dinner table is set for a meal.
(C) There is an appliance mounted on the wall.
(D) Empty plates have been left on a counter.

번역 **(A) 컵과 유리잔들이 선반 위에 가지런히 놓여 있다.**
(B) 식탁에 식사 준비가 되어 있다.
(C) 가전제품이 벽에 고정되어 있다.
(D) 빈 접시들이 조리대 위에 놓여 있다.

해설 **사물·풍경 사진**
(A) 정답. 컵과 유리잔들이 선반 위에 가지런히 놓여 있으므로 정답이다.
(B) 사진에 없는 명사. 사진에 식탁이 보이지 않는다.
(C) 사진에 없는 명사. 사진에 가전제품이 보이지 않는다.
(D) 사진에 없는 명사. 사진에 조리대가 보이지 않는다.

어휘 arrange 배열하다   be set for a meal 식사 준비가 되어 있다
appliance 가전제품   mount 고정시키다   plate 접시

PART 2

7

W-Am When can we pick up the building permit?
M-Au (A) I just submitted the application.
(B) No more than six months.
(C) His boss gave him permission.

번역 건축 허가증을 언제 받아올 수 있을까요?
(A) 제가 방금 신청서를 제출했어요.
(B) 겨우 6개월이요.
(C) 그의 상사가 그에게 허가해 주었어요.

해설 **When 의문문**
(A) 정답. 건축 허가증을 받아올 수 있는 시기를 묻는 질문에 방금 신청서를 제출했다며 시간이 더 있어야 받아올 수 있다는 것을 간접적으로 알려주고 있으므로 정답이다.
(B) 질문과 상관없는 오답. How long 의문에 대한 응답이므로 오답이다.
(C) 파생어 오답. 질문의 permit과 파생어 관계인 permission을 이용한 오답이다.

어휘 building permit 건축 허가증   submit 제출하다   application
신청서   permission 허가

8

W-Br Do you want anything from the convenience store?

M-Cn (A) That's a great business idea.
(B) A bottle of water would be nice.
(C) Where are they stored?

번역 편의점에서 뭐 필요한 거 있으세요?
(A) 그건 아주 훌륭한 사업안이에요.
(B) 생수 한 병 사다 주시면 감사하죠.
(C) 그것들은 어디에 보관되어 있나요?

해설 **조동사(Do) 의문문**
(A) 질문과 상관없는 오답.
(B) 정답. 편의점에서 필요한 것이 있는지 묻는 질문에 생수 한 병이라고 구체적으로 제시하고 있으므로 정답이다.
(C) 단어 반복 오답. 질문의 store를 반복 이용한 오답이다.

어휘 convenience store 편의점   store 보관하다

9

M-Au Would you like to sign up for our loyalty program?

W-Br (A) I don't shop here very often.
(B) A beautiful design.
(C) I like that TV program, too.

번역 저희 충성 고객 프로그램에 가입하시겠어요?
(A) 저는 여기서 자주 장을 보지 않아요.
(B) 아름다운 디자인이에요.
(C) 저도 그 TV 프로그램 좋아해요.

해설 **요청·제안문**
(A) 정답. 충성 고객 프로그램 가입 제안에 여기서 자주 장을 보지 않는다며 거부의 의사를 간접적으로 표현하고 있으므로 정답이다.
(B) 질문과 상관없는 오답.
(C) 단어 반복 오답. 질문의 program을 반복 이용한 오답이다.

어휘 sign up for ~에 가입하다   loyalty program 충성 고객 프로그램

10

W-Am Thank you for writing a recommendation for me.

M-Cn (A) It was my pleasure.
(B) I ride it to work each morning.
(C) They might have extras.

번역 추천서를 써주셔서 감사합니다.
(A) 제가 좋아서 한 일입니다.
(B) 매일 아침에 그걸 타고 출근해요.
(C) 그들이 여분을 가지고 있을지도 몰라요.

해설 **의견·희망 사항의 평서문**
(A) 정답. 추천서를 써줘서 감사하다는 평서문에 자신이 좋아서 한 일이라며 호응하고 있으므로 정답이다.
(B) 유사 발음 오답. 평서문의 writing과 부분적으로 발음이 유사한 ride it을 이용한 오답이다.
(C) 평서문과 상관없는 오답. 평서문에 3인칭 대명사They로 지칭할 인물들이 언급되지 않았으므로 오답이다.

어휘 recommendation 추천(서)   pleasure 기쁜 일   extra 여분의 것

11

M-Au Is the university library open to the public?

M-Cn (A) They're studying for a test.
(B) The keys are in the director's office.
(C) Only its general collection is.

번역 그 대학교 도서관은 대중에게 개방되어 있나요?
(A) 그들은 시험공부를 하고 있어요.
(B) 열쇠는 관장실에 있어요.
(C) 일반 장서만요.

해설 **Be동사 의문문**
(A) 연상 오답. 질문의 university library에서 연상 가능한 studying을 이용한 오답이다.
(B) 연상 오답. 질문의 open에서 연상 가능한 keys를 이용한 오답이다.
(C) 정답. 도서관이 대중에게 개방되어 있는지를 묻는 질문에 일반 장서만이라며 제한적이지만 개방되어 있음을 알려주고 있으므로 정답이다.

어휘 be open to ~에게 개방되다   public 대중   director 책임자, 관리자   general collection 일반 장서

12

M-Au When is this airport the busiest?

W-Br (A) OK, we'll hire a few more people.
(B) I can't remember her name.
(C) It varies from year to year.

번역 이 공항은 언제 가장 붐비나요?
(A) 알겠습니다, 사람을 몇 명 더 고용할게요.
(B) 그녀의 이름이 기억이 안 나요.
(C) 해마다 달라요.

해설 **When 의문문**
(A) Yes/No 불가 오답. When 의문문에는 Yes/No 응답이 불가능한데, OK도 일종의 Yes 응답이라고 볼 수 있으므로 오답이다.
(B) 질문과 상관없는 오답. 질문에 3인칭 대명사 her로 지칭할 인물이 언급된 적이 없으므로 오답이다.
(C) 정답. 공항이 가장 붐비는 시기를 묻는 질문에 해마다 다르다며 알 수 없음을 우회적으로 알려 주고 있으므로 정답이다.

어휘 hire 고용하다   vary 다르다, 달라지다

13

M-Au Are there any good restaurants near the conference center?

W-Am (A) Just a salad for me, please.
(B) You'd be better off going downtown.
(C) The panel discussions are popular.

번역 그 회의장 근처에 괜찮은 식당들이 있나요?
(A) 저는 샐러드만 주세요.
(B) 시내로 가시는 게 나을 거예요.
(C) 그 공개 토론회는 인기가 많아요.

해설 **Be동사 의문문**
(A) 연상 오답. 질문의 restaurants에서 연상 가능한 salad를 이용한 오답이다.
(B) 정답. 회의장 근처에 괜찮은 식당들이 있는지를 묻는 질문에 시내

로 가는 게 나을 거라며 근처에 괜찮은 식당이 없다는 것을 우회적으로 알려주고 있으므로 정답이다.

(C) 연상 오답. 질문의 conference에서 연상 가능한 panel discussions를 이용한 오답이다.

어휘   be better off -ing ~하는 게 낫다   panel discussion 공개 토론회   popular 인기 있는

14

M-Cn Your company is based in Toronto, right?

W-Am (A) Do you have flowers to put in this vase?
      (B) I'll call a real estate agent today.
      (C) Actually, our headquarters are in Montreal.

번역   당신 회사는 토론토에 본사가 있죠, 맞죠?
     (A) 이 꽃병에 꽂을 꽃이 있으세요?
     (B) 제가 오늘 부동산 중개인에게 전화해 볼게요.
     (C) 실은 저희 본사는 몬트리올에 있어요.

해설   **부가 의문문**
     (A) 유사 발음 오답. 질문의 based와 부분적으로 발음이 유사한 vase를 이용한 오답이다.
     (B) 연상 오답. 질문의 Toronto에서 연상 가능한 real estate를 이용한 오답이다.
     (C) 정답. 토론토에 본사가 있는지 확인하는 질문에 실은 몬트리올에 있다며 아니오(No)를 생략한 부정 답변을 하고 있으므로 정답이다.

어휘   be based in ~에 기반을 두다   vase 꽃병   real estate agent 부동산 중개인   headquarters 본사, 본부

15

M-Cn What should I bring to my first appointment?

W-Br (A) Your insurance card is the most important thing.
      (B) To get a doctor's opinion on my elbow injury.
      (C) As soon as we have an opening.

번역   첫 번째 예약 때 제가 뭘 가져가야 하나요?
     (A) 보험증이 가장 중요한 것입니다.
     (B) 제 팔꿈치 부상에 대한 의사 소견서를 받으려고요.
     (C) 빈자리가 생기자마자요.

해설   **What 의문문**
     (A) 정답. 첫 번째 예약 때 가져가야 할 것을 묻는 질문에 보험증이 가장 중요한 것이라며 관련된 내용으로 응답하고 있으므로 정답이다.
     (B) 연상 오답. 질문의 appointment에서 연상 가능한 doctor를 이용한 오답이다.
     (C) 질문과 상관없는 오답. When 의문문에 대한 응답이므로 오답이다.

어휘   appointment (진료 등의) 예약   insurance card 보험증 doctor's opinion 의사 소견   elbow 팔꿈치   injury 부상 opening 빈자리

16

M-Cn How many items are there on today's agenda?

W-Am (A) A new schedule for our team.
      (B) It should be a quick meeting.
      (C) They were, I think.

번역   오늘 안건에 몇 개의 항목이 있나요?
     (A) 우리 팀의 새 일정이요.
     (B) 분명 짧은 회의일 거예요.
     (C) 그랬을 거예요.

해설   **How+형용사/부사 의문문**
     (A) 연상 오답. 질문의 agenda에서 연상 가능한 schedule을 이용한 오답이다.
     (B) 정답. 오늘 안건에 몇 개의 항목이 있는지 묻는 질문에 분명 짧은 회의일 거라며 항목이 적을 것이라는 것을 간접적으로 알려주고 있으므로 정답이다.
     (C) 질문과 상관없는 오답.

어휘   item 항목   agenda 안건

17

W-Br I've found some job candidates who meet your requirements.

M-Au (A) That's excellent news!
      (B) An interview and a skill test.
      (C) But I like my current job.

번역   당신의 자격 요건을 충족하는 입사 지원자를 몇 명 찾았어요.
     (A) 그거 정말 좋은 소식이네요!
     (B) 면접과 실기 시험이요.
     (C) 하지만 저는 지금 하는 일이 좋아요.

해설   **사실·정보 전달의 평서문**
     (A) 정답. 자격 요건을 충족하는 입사 지원자를 찾았다는 평서문에 정말 좋은 소식이라며 관련된 내용으로 호응하고 있으므로 정답이다.
     (B) 연상 오답. 평서문의 job candidates에서 연상 가능한 interview를 이용한 오답이다.
     (C) 단어 반복 오답. 평서문의 job을 반복 이용한 오답이다.

어휘   candidate 지원자   meet 충족시키다   requirement 자격 요건 skill test 실기 시험   current 현재의

18

W-Am Where's the taxi we ordered?

M-Au (A) I haven't heard any complaints.
      (B) At the bottom of your receipt.
      (C) This is the middle of rush hour.

번역   우리가 부른 택시는 어디에 있나요?
     (A) 저는 불만을 들어본 적이 없어요.
     (B) 영수증 하단에요.
     (C) 지금은 한창 혼잡한 시간이에요.

해설   **Where 의문문**
     (A) 질문과 상관없는 오답.
     (B) 연상 오답. 질문의 ordered에서 연상 가능한 receipt를 이용한 오답이다.
     (C) 정답. 택시의 위치를 묻는 질문에 지금은 한창 혼잡한 시간이라며

아직 택시가 도착하지 않았다는 것을 간접적으로 알려 주고 있으므로 정답이다.

어휘   complaint 불평, 불만   receipt 영수증   rush hour 혼잡 시간대

19

W-Am Isn't this year's workshop a little longer than usual?
W-Br (A) Usually new employees.
    (B) Yes, the instructor has added some content.
    (C) I had to visit a few different stores.

번역   올해 워크숍이 평소보다 조금 더 길지 않나요?
    (A) 보통 신입사원들이요.
    (B) 길어요, 강사가 내용을 추가했거든요.
    (C) 가게를 몇 군데 돌아다녀야 했어요.

해설   **부정 의문문**
    (A) 파생어 오답. 질문의 usual과 파생어 관계인 Usually를 이용한 오답이다.
    (B) 정답. 올해 워크숍이 평소보다 조금 더 긴지를 확인하는 질문에 길다(Yes)고 대답한 뒤, 강사가 내용을 추가했다며 긍정 답변과 일관된 내용을 덧붙였으므로 정답이다.
    (C) 연상 오답. 질문의 workshop을 shop으로만 잘못 들었을 때 연상 가능한 stores를 이용한 오답이다.

어휘   instructor 강사   add 추가하다   content 내용

20

M-Cn Would you rather take a tour or just explore the museum on our own?
W-Br (A) No, I live in the area.
    (B) I'd love to take a few home.
    (C) Let's look around by ourselves first.

번역   투어를 이용하시겠어요, 아니면 우리끼리 그냥 박물관을 돌아볼까요?
    (A) 아니요, 저는 이 동네에 살아요.
    (B) 몇 개를 집으로 가져가고 싶어요.
    (C) 우선은 우리끼리 구경해 봅시다.

해설   **선택 의문문**
    (A) Yes/No 불가 오답. 문장과 문장을 연결하는 경우를 제외하고는 선택 의문문에는 Yes/No 응답이 불가능하므로 오답이다.
    (B) 단어 반복 오답. 질문의 take를 반복 이용한 오답이다.
    (C) 정답. 박물관 투어를 이용할지 우리끼리 돌아볼지 묻는 선택 의문문에 우선은 우리끼리 구경해 보자며 둘 중 하나를 선택해 응답하고 있으므로 정답이다.

어휘   explore 탐방하다   on one's own 스스로, 혼자서   look around 구경하다   by oneself 스스로, 혼자서

21

M-Au You're announcing the price increase to our clients, aren't you?
W-Br (A) Oh, was that decision finalized?
    (B) Our hiring announcement has a lot of views.
    (C) I'll look for a good place to display our prize.

번역   당신이 고객들에게 가격 인상에 대해 공지하죠, 그렇지 않나요?
    (A) 아, 그 결정이 확정되었나요?
    (B) 우리 채용 공고는 조회수가 높아요.
    (C) 제가 우리 상을 전시할 좋은 장소를 찾아볼게요.

해설   **부가 의문문**
    (A) 정답. 고객들에게 가격 인상에 대해 공지하는지 여부를 확인하는 질문에 그 결정이 확정되었는지 관련 내용을 되묻고 있으므로 정답이다.
    (B) 파생어 오답. 질문의 announcing과 파생어 관계인 announcement를 이용한 오답이다.
    (C) 유사 발음 오답. 질문의 price와 부분적으로 발음이 유사한 prize를 이용한 오답이다.

어휘   increase 인상   decision 결정   finalize 마무리 짓다   hiring announcement 채용 공고   display 전시하다

22

W-Am Why are all my photographs out of focus?
M-Cn (A) If we can find the time for it.
    (B) I'm good with cameras.
    (C) Coffee helps me focus.

번역   제 사진은 왜 전부 초점이 안 맞을까요?
    (A) 우리에게 시간이 있다면요.
    (B) 저는 카메라를 잘 다뤄요.
    (C) 커피는 집중하는 데 도움을 줘요.

해설   **Why 의문문**
    (A) 질문과 상관없는 오답.
    (B) 정답. 사진이 전부 초점이 맞지 않는 이유를 묻는 질문에 자신이 카메라를 잘 다룰 줄 안다며 이유를 알려줄 수 있음을 간접적으로 제시하고 있으므로 정답이다.
    (C) 단어 반복 오답. 질문의 focus를 반복 이용한 오답이다.

어휘   be out of focus 초점이 맞지 않다   be good with ~을 잘 다루다   focus 집중하다

23

W-Br Where did you get your travel mug?
M-Au (A) A client sent our team some thank-you gifts.
    (B) Thanks for reminding me!
    (C) No, not much—I don't like to fly.

번역   휴대용 머그컵을 어디서 구하셨어요?
    (A) 한 고객이 우리 팀에 감사의 선물로 보냈어요.
    (B) 상기시켜 줘서 고마워요!
    (C) 아니요, 별로요. 저는 비행기 타는 걸 좋아하지 않아요.

해설   **Where 의문문**
    (A) 정답. 휴대용 머그컵의 출처를 묻는 질문에 한 고객이 감사의 선물로 보냈다고 응답하고 있으므로 정답이다.
    (B) 질문과 상관없는 오답.
    (C) Yes/No 불가 오답. Where 의문문에는 Yes/No 응답이 불가능하므로 오답이다.

어휘   travel mug 휴대용 보온보냉컵   thank-you gift 감사의 선물

24

M-Cn Why aren't you inviting local businesses to sponsor the festival?

W-Am (A) Tickets are available online.
(B) Six months in advance.
(C) Medrano Fashions is a local company.

번역 왜 지역 업체들에 축제 후원을 요청하지 않나요?
(A) 입장권은 온라인에서 구입하실 수 있습니다.
(B) 6개월 전에요.
(C) 메드라노 패션스는 지역 기업이에요.

해설 Why 의문문
(A) 연상 오답. 질문의 festival에서 연상 가능한 Tickets를 이용한 오답이다.
(B) 질문과 상관없는 오답.
(C) 정답. 지역 업체들에 축제 후원을 요청하지 않는 이유를 묻는 질문에 메드라노 패션스는 지역 기업이라며 이미 요청을 한 업체가 있음을 알려주고 있으므로 정답이다.

어휘 invite 요청하다, 초대하다   sponsor 후원하다   in advance 미리

25

M-Au The floor tile shipment has arrived.

W-Br (A) It has twelve floors.
(B) OK, send the forklifts over.
(C) The lobby renovation.

번역 바닥 타일 배송품이 도착했어요.
(A) 12층까지 있어요.
(B) 알겠습니다, 지게차를 그쪽으로 보내세요.
(C) 로비 보수 공사요.

해설 사실·정보 전달의 평서문
(A) 단어 반복 오답. 평서문의 floor를 반복 이용한 오답이다.
(B) 정답. 바닥 타일 배송품이 도착했다는 평서문에 알겠다(OK)고 대답한 뒤, 지게차를 그쪽으로 보내라며 긍정 답변과 일관된 내용을 덧붙이고 있으므로 정답이다.
(C) 연상 오답. 평서문의 floor tile에서 연상 가능한 lobby renovation을 이용한 오답이다.

어휘 floor tile 바닥 타일   shipment 배송품   forklift 지게차
renovation 보수 공사

26

W-Am What are the main ingredients of this dish?

M-Au (A) No, the maintenance work is finished now.
(B) It was canceled yesterday.
(C) The menu only lists names and prices.

번역 이 요리의 주재료는 무엇인가요?
(A) 아니요, 유지보수 공사는 이제 끝났어요.
(B) 그건 어제 취소되었어요.
(C) 메뉴판에는 이름과 가격만 적혀 있어요.

해설 What 의문문
(A) Yes/No 불가 오답. What 의문문에는 Yes/No 응답이 불가능하므로 오답이다.
(B) 질문과 상관없는 오답.
(C) 정답. 요리의 주재료를 묻는 질문에 메뉴판에는 이름과 가격만 적혀 있다며 본인도 알지 못함을 우회적으로 알려 주고 있으므로 정답이다.

어휘 ingredient 재료, 성분   dish 요리   maintenance 유지보수
cancel 취소하다   list 목록에 언급하다

27

W-Br Who from our department volunteered to help with the holiday party?

M-Au (A) Yes, the decorations have been ordered.
(B) An all-day parking pass.
(C) I'd already booked my vacation for that week.

번역 우리 부서에서 누가 휴일 파티를 돕겠다고 자원했나요?
(A) 네, 장식품은 주문되었어요.
(B) 일일 주차권이요.
(C) 저는 그 주에 이미 휴가를 예약했어요.

해설 Who 의문문
(A) Yes/No 불가 오답. Who 의문문에는 Yes/No 응답이 불가능하므로 오답이다.
(B) 질문과 상관없는 오답.
(C) 정답. 휴일 파티를 돕겠다고 자원한 사람이 누구인지 묻는 질문에 그 주에 이미 휴가를 예약했다며 본인은 아니라는 것을 우회적으로 알려 주고 있으므로 정답이다.

어휘 volunteer 자원하다   decoration 장식품   all-day parking pass 일일 주차권

28

M-Cn Shouldn't we schedule a time to practice our presentation?

W-Br (A) A successful medical practice.
(B) I'll grab my calendar.
(C) The large conference room is nice.

번역 우리 발표 연습할 시간을 잡아야 하지 않을까요?
(A) 성공적인 의료 행위요.
(B) 제 달력 좀 가져올게요.
(C) 그 대회의실 좋아요.

해설 부정 의문문
(A) 단어 반복 오답. 질문의 practice를 반복 이용한 오답이다.
(B) 정답. 발표 연습할 시간을 잡아야 하는지 확인하는 질문에 달력 좀 가져오겠다며 일정을 확인하려고 하므로 정답이다.
(C) 연상 오답. 질문의 presentation에서 연상 가능한 conference를 이용한 오답이다.

어휘 practice 연습하다   presentation 발표   successful 성공적인
medical practice 의료 행위   grab 붙잡다

29

M-Au Where can I find the outdoor swimming pool?

W-Am (A) Yes, I watched the championship on TV.
(B) Our seasonal facilities aren't open yet.
(C) Mostly families with young children.

번역   야외 수영장은 어디서 찾을 수 있을까요?
     (A) 네, 저는 TV에서 그 선수권 대회를 봤어요.
     (B) 저희 계절별 시설은 아직 개장하지 않았어요.
     (C) 주로 어린 자녀가 있는 가족들이요.

해설   **Where 의문문**
     (A) Yes/No 불가 오답. Where 의문문에는 Yes/No 응답이 불가능하므로 오답이다.
     (B) 정답. 야외 수영장의 위치를 묻는 질문에 계절별 시설은 아직 개장하지 않았다며 야외 수영장을 사용할 수 없음을 알려 주고 있으므로 정답이다.
     (C) 연상 오답. 질문의 swimming pool에서 연상 가능한 families와 young children을 이용한 오답이다.

어휘   championship 선수권 대회   seasonal 계절적인   facility 시설

30

M-Cn Don't you usually work weekend shifts?
W-Am (A) Samantha called in sick today.
     (B) On the counter next to the register.
     (C) I have a monthly membership.

번역   당신은 보통 주말에 근무하지 않나요?
     (A) 사만다가 오늘 병가를 냈어요.
     (B) 금전 등록기 옆 카운터 위에요.
     (C) 저는 월간 회원권을 가지고 있어요.

해설   **부정 의문문**
     (A) 정답. 주말에 보통 근무하지 않냐는 질문에 사만다가 오늘 병가를 냈다며 오늘은 사만다 대신 근무하고 있음을 우회적으로 말하고 있으므로 정답이다.
     (B) 질문과 상관없는 오답. Where 의문문에 대한 응답이므로 오답이다.
     (C) 질문과 상관없는 오답.

어휘   shift 교대 근무조   call in sick 병가를 내다   register 금전 등록기
     monthly membership 월간 회원권

31

W-Br Who can I talk to about a problem with my company laptop?
M-Cn (A) Tech help requests must be made electronically.
     (B) No, I haven't downloaded it yet.
     (C) In the top drawer of the filing cabinet.

번역   제 회사 노트북 관련 문제는 누구에게 말하면 될까요?
     (A) 기술 지원 요청은 반드시 전자 문서로 하셔야 해요.
     (B) 아니요, 저는 아직 내려받지 않았어요.
     (C) 서류 수납함의 맨 위 서랍이요.

해설   **Who 의문문**
     (A) 정답. 회사 노트북 관련 문제에 대해 말할 수 있는 대상을 묻는 질문에 기술 지원 요청은 전자 문서로 해야 한다며 문제에 대한 도움을 받을 수 있는 방법을 우회적으로 알려 주고 있으므로 정답이다.
     (B) Yes/No 불가 오답. Who 의문문에는 Yes/No 응답이 불가능하므로 오답이다.
     (C) 유사 발음 오답. 질문의 laptop과 부분적으로 발음이 유사한 top을 이용한 오답이다.

어휘   tech help 기술 지원   electronically 전자적으로   drawer 서랍   filing cabinet 서류 수납함

PART 3

32-34

W-Br Hi, I'm Paula Gutierrez, and **³² I'm here to pick up a custom cake order**. It's vanilla-flavored and should be decorated with frosting in the shape of roses.

M-Cn Yes, here's your order. Let me remove the lid of the box so you can confirm that the message is correct.

W-Br It's perfect, as always. **³³ I appreciate that I can count on the staff here to do a great job.**

M-Cn Thank you. Now, it sounds like you're a regular customer—**³⁴ would you still like one of these cards with transport and storage instructions for the cake?**

W-Br **³⁴ Sure, just in case.**

여: 안녕하세요, 폴라 구티에레즈인데요. **주문 제작한 케이크를 찾으러 왔습니다.** 바닐라 맛이고요. 장미꽃 모양의 아이싱으로 장식되어야 하고요.

남: 네, 여기 주문하신 케이크입니다. 상자 뚜껑을 열어서 메시지가 정확하게 되었는지 확인할 수 있게 해드리겠습니다.

여: 늘 그렇듯이 완벽하네요. 여기 직원분들이 일을 잘해주실 거라고 믿을 수 있어서 감사하게 생각해요.

남: 감사합니다. 자, 단골손님이신 것 같은데, 그래도 케이크 운반과 보관 요령이 적힌 이 카드를 한 장 드릴까요?

여: 물론이죠, 혹시 필요할지 모르니까요.

어휘   custom 주문 제작한   vanilla-flavored 바닐라 맛의   decorate 장식하다   frosting 케이크 위에 장식하는 달콤한 크림, 아이싱   remove 제거하다   lid 뚜껑   confirm 확인하다   correct 정확한   count on 의존하다   regular customer 단골손님   transport 운송   storage 보관   instruction 설명, 지시   just in case 만약을 대비해

32 Where does the man most likely work?
    (A) At a bakery
    (B) At a florist shop
    (C) At a jewelry store
    (D) At a tailor shop

번역 남자는 어디서 일하겠는가?
(A) 제과점
(B) 꽃 가게
(C) 보석상
(D) 맞춤 양복점

해설 **전체 내용 관련 - 남자의 근무지**
여자가 첫 대사에서 주문 제작한 케이크를 찾으러 왔다(I'm here to pick up a custom cake order)고 말하는 것으로 보아 남자는 제과점에서 근무하고 있다는 것을 알 수 있다. 따라서 정답은 (A)이다.

어휘 jewelry 보석

---

33 What does the woman like about the business?
(A) Its fast service
(B) Its friendly staff
(C) Its high-quality work
(D) Its reasonable pricing

번역 여자는 이 사업체에 대해 어떤 점을 마음에 들어 하는가?
(A) 빠른 서비스
(B) 친절한 직원
(C) 높은 품질
(D) 합리적인 가격

해설 **세부 사항 관련 - 여자가 사업체에 대해 마음에 들어 하는 점**
여자가 두 번째 대사에서 여기 직원들이 일을 잘해줄 거라고 믿을 수 있어서 감사하게 생각한다(I appreciate that I can count on the staff here to do a great job)고 말하고 있으므로 정답은 (C)이다.

어휘 friendly 우호적인 high-quality 고품질의 reasonable 합리적인

> **Paraphrasing**
> 대화의 do a great job → 정답의 high-quality work

---

34 What does the woman accept from the man?
(A) A receipt
(B) Some samples
(C) A discount coupon
(D) Some instructions

번역 여자는 남자에게 무엇을 받는가?
(A) 영수증
(B) 견본
(C) 할인 쿠폰
(D) 설명서

해설 **세부 사항 관련 - 여자가 남자에게서 받는 것**
남자가 마지막 대사에서 케이크 운반과 보관 요령이 적힌 카드가 필요한지(would you still like one of these cards with transport and storage instructions for the cake?) 묻자 여자가 물론(Sure)이라고 긍정 답변으로 응답하고 있으므로 정답은 (D)이다.

어휘 accept 받다, 받아들이다

> **Paraphrasing**
> 대화의 transport and storage instructions
> → 정답의 Some instructions

35-37

M-Au Excuse me, I've made my decision. **³⁵I'll take this tablet computer**—the one that comes with the free carrying case.

W-Am OK, I'll ring you up… Oh, **³⁶I'm so sorry, but we've just given out the last carrying case we had in stock.** You can still get one, but you'll have to wait a few days.

M-Au I don't live nearby. Will I have to come back here?

W-Am No—if you give me your address, **³⁷I can have it shipped to you at no charge.**

M-Au Thanks, that'd be great.

남: 실례합니다만, 저 결정했어요. **이 태블릿 컴퓨터로 할게요.** 무료 휴대용 가방이 딸려 나오는 제품이요.

여: 알겠습니다, 계산해 드리겠습니다… 어머, **정말 죄송합니다만, 저희가 재고를 보유하고 있던 마지막 휴대용 가방이 방금 나갔네요.** 여전히 받을 수는 있지만 며칠 기다리셔야 합니다.

남: 제가 이 동네에 살지 않아요. 제가 다시 여기로 와야 하나요?

여: 아니요, 주소를 알려주시면 **무료로 배송해 드릴 수 있습니다.**

남: 감사합니다, 좋습니다.

어휘 make a decision 결정하다 come with ~이 딸려 나오다 carrying case 휴대용 가방 ring up 계산해 주다 give out 동이 나다 in stock 재고가 있는 nearby 근처에 ship 배송하다 at no charge 무료로

---

35 Where does the conversation most likely take place?
(A) At a print shop
(B) At a repair shop
(C) At an electronics store
(D) At a sporting goods store

번역 대화는 어디서 이루어지겠는가?
(A) 인쇄소
(B) 정비소
(C) 전자 제품 매장
(D) 스포츠 용품 매장

해설 **전체 내용 관련 - 대화의 장소**
남자가 첫 대사에서 이 태블릿 컴퓨터로 하겠다(I'll take this tablet computer)고 말하고 있으므로 대화 장소는 전자 제품 매장임을 알 수 있다. 따라서 정답은 (C)이다.

36 Why does the woman apologize?
(A) A product is out of stock.
(B) A computer is not working.
(C) An employee is absent.
(D) A sales promotion has ended.

번역 여자는 왜 사과하는가?
(A) 제품의 재고가 떨어져서
(B) 컴퓨터가 작동하지 않아서
(C) 한 직원이 부재 중이어서
(D) 판촉 행사가 끝나서

해설 **세부 사항 관련 - 여자가 사과하는 이유**
여자가 첫 대사에서 재고를 보유하고 있던 마지막 휴대용 가방이 방금 나갔다(I'm so sorry, but we've just given out the last carrying case we had in stock)며 사과하고 있으므로 정답은 (A)이다.

어휘 out of stock 재고가 없는 absent 결근한 sales promotion 판촉 행사

37 What does the woman offer to do for the man?
(A) Take a message
(B) Restart a device
(C) Check a storage room
(D) Ship an item to him

번역 여자는 남자를 위해 무엇을 하겠다고 제안하는가?
(A) 메시지 받아 적기
(B) 기기 재부팅하기
(C) 창고 확인하기
(D) 물건을 남자에게 배송하기

해설 **세부 사항 관련 - 여자의 제안 사항**
여자가 마지막 대사에서 무료로 배송해줄 수 있다(I can have it shipped to you at no charge)고 말하고 있으므로 정답은 (D)이다.

어휘 restart 재부팅하다 device 기기 storage room 창고

38-40

W-Br OK, Mr. Crane, **38 I'll turn my computer screen around so you can see this online listing. 39 I think this property would be a great location for your café.**

M-Au Oh, that is a nice place. What charming architecture.

W-Br Yes, that's what I thought. It's nine hundred square feet, and **39 the location is... fifteen hundred Fogle Bay Road.**

M-Au Oh... that's pretty far outside of town.

W-Br Sure, that's true. Alright, then there's another promising option on Grant Street. Let me take a moment to find it.

M-Au Grant Street? **40 Is that neighborhood within my budget?**

W-Br It's not as expensive as you might think.

여: 알겠습니다, 크레인 씨. 이 온라인 매물 목록을 보실 수 있게 컴퓨터 화면을 돌려드릴게요. 이 매물이 귀하의 카페에 잘 맞는 장소일 것 같습니다.

남: 아, 멋진 곳이네요. 매력적인 건축 양식이에요.

여: 네, 저도 그렇게 생각했어요. 900제곱 피트이고, 위치는… 포글 베이 로 1500번지예요.

남: 아… 시내에서 꽤 멀리 떨어져 있네요.

여: 물론, 그렇습니다. 그러시면 그랜트 가에 또 다른 괜찮은 후보지가 있습니다. 잠깐 찾아볼게요.

남: 그랜트 가요? 그 동네가 제 예산 범위 내에 있나요?

여: 생각하시는 것만큼 비싸지 않습니다.

어휘 turn around 방향을 바꾸다 listing 목록 property 부동산, 건물 charming 매력적인 architecture 건축, 건축 양식 promising 유망한 neighborhood 동네 budget 예산 expensive 비싼

38 What does the woman show the man?
(A) A city map
(B) A business card
(C) A Web page
(D) A brochure

번역 여자는 남자에게 무엇을 보여주는가?
(A) 도시 지도
(B) 명함
(C) 웹페이지
(D) 안내 책자

해설 **세부 사항 관련 - 여자가 남자에게 보여주는 것**
여자가 첫 대사에서 온라인 매물 목록을 볼 수 있게 컴퓨터 화면을 돌려주겠다(I'll turn my computer screen around so you can see this online listing)고 말하고 있으므로 정답은 (C)이다.

39 Why does the man say, "that's pretty far outside of town"?
(A) To ask for help with a move
(B) To reject a suggested property
(C) To point out misinformation in a listing
(D) To express concern about an appointment time

번역 남자가 "시내에서 꽤 멀리 떨어져 있네요"라고 말한 이유는?
(A) 이사하는 데 도움을 요청하려고
(B) 제안된 매물을 거절하려고
(C) 목록에서 잘못된 정보를 지적하려고
(D) 예약 시간에 대한 우려를 표명하려고

해설 화자의 의도 파악 - 시내에서 꽤 멀리 떨어져 있다는 말의 의도
앞서 여자가 이 매물이 귀하의 카페에 잘 맞는 장소일 것 같다(I think this property would be a great location for your café)며 위치는 포글 베이 로 1500번지(the location is... fifteen hundred Fogle Bay Road)라고 한 뒤, 남자가 인용문을 언급한 것으로 보아 위치 때문에 제안된 매물을 거절하려는 의도로 한 말임을 알 수 있다. 따라서 정답은 (B)이다.

어휘 reject 거절하다 suggested 제안된 point out 가리키다, 지적하다 misinformation 잘못된 정보 appointment (진료 등의) 예약

40 What does the man ask about?
(A) An area's affordability
(B) A parking facility
(C) A building's condition
(D) A person's availability

번역 남자는 무엇에 대해 문의하는가?
(A) 지역의 가격 적정성
(B) 주차 시설
(C) 건물의 상태
(D) 사람의 가능한 시간

해설 세부 사항 관련 - 남자의 문의 사항
남자가 마지막 대사에서 그 동네가 예산 범위 내에 있는지(Is that neighborhood within my budget?) 묻고 있으므로 정답은 (A)이다.

어휘 affordability 가격 적정성 condition 상태 availability 일정 가능 여부

41-43

> M-Cn Mayumi, do you think that the city mayor's proposal to ban disposable coffee cups would be a good discussion topic for **41 my advanced English classes?**

> W-Br Yes, but— **42 keep in mind that most people have misunderstood that proposal.** They don't realize that it's only non-recyclable cups that would be banned.
>
> M-Cn Oh, I didn't actually realize that. **43 I'd better research the details of the proposal** before I start my lesson planning.

남: 마유미, 일회용 커피 컵을 금지하자는 시장의 제안이 **제 상급반 영어 수업에 좋은 토론 주제가 될 거라고 생각해요?**
여: 네, 하지만 **대부분의 사람들은 그 제안을 제대로 이해하지 못하고 있다는 사실을 명심하세요.** 사람들은 금지되는 것이 재활용할 수 없는 컵만이라는 사실을 몰라요.
남: 아, 그 점은 미처 몰랐네요. 수업을 준비하기 전에 **그 제안의 세부 내용부터 조사해 보는 게 좋겠네요.**

어휘 mayor 시장 proposal 제안 ban 금지하다 disposable 일회용의 discussion 토론 advanced 상급의 misunderstand 제대로 이해하지 못하다 non-recyclable 재활용할 수 없는

41 Who most likely is the man?
(A) A city official
(B) A café owner
(C) A language teacher
(D) A newspaper reporter

번역 남자는 누구이겠는가?
(A) 시 공무원
(B) 카페 주인
(C) 어학 교사
(D) 신문 기자

해설 전체 내용 관련 - 남자의 직업
남자가 첫 대사에서 자신의 상급반 영어 수업(my advanced English classes)이라고 말하는 것으로 보아 남자는 어학 교사임을 알 수 있다. 따라서 정답은 (C)이다.

> **Paraphrasing**
> 대화의 English → 정답의 language

42 What does the woman say about a proposal?
(A) It will go into effect next year.
(B) It is misunderstood by the public.
(C) It will be expensive to implement.
(D) It was inspired by laws in other cities.

번역 여자는 제안에 대해 뭐라고 말하는가?
(A) 내년에 발효될 것이다.
(B) 대중들이 제대로 이해하지 못하고 있다.
(C) 시행하는 데 비용이 많이 들 것이다.
(D) 다른 도시의 법에서 영감을 받았다.

세부 사항 관련 - 여자가 제안에 대해 하는 말

여자가 첫 대사에서 대부분의 사람들은 그 제안을 제대로 이해하지 못하고 있다는 사실을 명심하라(keep in mind that most people have misunderstood that proposal)고 하므로 정답은 (B)이다.

어휘 go into effect 효력이 발생되다 implement 시행하다
be inspired by ~에서 영감을 받다

> **Paraphrasing**
> 대화의 most people have misunderstood that
> proposal → 정답의 It is misunderstood by the public.

---

43 What does the man decide to do?
(A) Join a volunteer group
(B) Revise a timeline
(C) Post on social media
(D) Conduct some research

번역 남자는 무엇을 하기로 결정하는가?
(A) 자원봉사 단체에 가입하기
(B) 일정표 수정하기
(C) 소셜 미디어에 글 올리기
(D) 조사 실시하기

해설 **세부 사항 관련 - 남자가 하기로 결정한 것**

남자가 마지막 대사에서 그 제안의 세부 내용부터 조사해 보는 게 좋겠다(I'd better research the details of the proposal ~)고 말하고 있으므로 정답은 (D)이다.

어휘 revise 수정하다 timeline 일정표 post 게시하다 conduct 실시하다

> **Paraphrasing**
> 대화의 research the details
> → 정답의 Conduct some research

44-46

W-Br Mr. Gordon, **44 there's something wrong with one of the washing machines. Water started leaking from it after I put in a load of bedsheets from Craddock Hotel.**

M-Au Which machine is it?

W-Br This one. I turned it off.

M-Au Oh, **45 it's probably because of the supply hose. I unscrewed the hoses on this row of machines last night to clear out their intake filters. I must not have reconnected this one tightly enough.** I'll fix it.

W-Br Oh, OK. **46 Would you like me to mop up this water? It's making the floor slippery.**

여: 고든 씨, **세탁기 중 한 대에 문제가 생겼어요. 크래덕 호텔에서 온 침대 시트를 한 가득 넣은 후부터 세탁기에서 물이 새기 시작했어요.**

남: 어떤 세탁기죠?

여: 이거요. 제가 전원을 껐어요.

남: 아, **아마도 급수 호스 때문일 거예요. 흡입 필터를 청소하려고 간밤에 이 줄에 있는 세탁기들에서 호스를 풀었거든요. 제가 이걸 충분히 단단하게 다시 연결하지 않았나 보네요.** 제가 고쳐 놓을게요.

여: 아, 알겠습니다. **제가 여기 물을 걸레로 닦을까요? 물 때문에 바닥이 미끄러워서요.**

어휘 a load of 많은, 한 가득의 leak 물이 새다 turn off 전원을 끄다 unscrew 나사를 풀다 intake filter 흡입 필터 reconnect 다시 연결하다 tightly 단단하게 fix 고치다 mop up (물 등을) 닦다 slippery 미끄러운

---

44 Where do the speakers most likely work?
(A) In a laundry facility
(B) In an appliance store
(C) In a medical center
(D) In a hotel kitchen

번역 화자들은 어디서 일하겠는가?
(A) 세탁 시설
(B) 가전제품 매장
(C) 의료 기관
(D) 호텔 주방

해설 **전체 내용 관련 - 화자들의 근무지**

여자가 첫 대사에서 세탁기 중 한 대에 문제가 생겼다(there's something wrong with one of the washing machines)며 크래덕 호텔에서 온 시트를 넣은 후부터 물이 새기 시작했다(Water started leaking ~ from Craddock Hotel)고 말하고 있으므로 화자들은 세탁 시설에서 근무하고 있음을 알 수 있다. 따라서 정답은 (A)이다.

어휘 laundry 세탁 appliance 가전제품

---

45 According to the man, what probably caused a problem?
(A) A setting was not adjusted.
(B) A material is not water-resistant.
(C) A part was not connected properly.
(D) A power outage occurred last night.

번역 남자에 따르면, 무엇이 문제를 일으켰겠는가?
(A) 설정이 잘못되어 있었다.
(B) 재료가 내수성이 강하지 않다.
(C) 부품이 제대로 연결되지 않았었다.
(D) 간밤에 정전이 일어났었다.

해설 **세부 사항 관련 - 문제를 야기시킨 것**

남자가 마지막 대사에서 아마도 급수 호스 때문일 것(it's probably

because of the supply hose)이라면서 간밤에 이 줄에 있는 세탁기들에서 호스를 풀었는데(I unscrewed the hoses on this row of machines last night ~) 충분히 단단하게 다시 연결하지 않은 것 같다(I must not have reconnected this one tightly enough)고 말하고 있으므로 정답은 (C)이다.

어휘 adjust 조정하다　water-resistant 내수성이 있는　properly 제대로　power outage 정전　occur 발생하다

> **Paraphrasing**
> 대화의 the supply hose → 정답의 A part

46 What does the woman offer to do?
(A) Clean up a hazard
(B) Schedule a training
(C) Locate a warranty
(D) Call a repair person

번역 여자는 무엇을 하겠다고 제안하는가?
(A) 위험 요소 치우기
(B) 교육 일정 잡기
(C) 품질 보증서 찾기
(D) 수리 기사 부르기

해설 **세부 사항 관련 - 여자의 제안 사항**
여자가 마지막 대사에서 물을 걸레로 닦을지(Would you like me to mop up this water?) 제안하면서 물 때문에 바닥이 미끄럽다(It's making the floor slippery)고 말하고 있으므로 정답은 (A)이다.

어휘 hazard 위험 요소　locate ~의 정확한 위치를 찾아내다　warranty 품질 보증서

47-49 3인 대화

W-Am **47 Can you believe we've been leading this book club for a year now?** How do the two of you feel about the way it's going?

M-Au Actually, Dan and I were talking the other day, and—we're a little frustrated. It seems like we can't have an in-depth discussion because the majority of people don't finish the book. **48 We'd like to make it a rule that members have to read the whole book in order to participate in the meeting.**

M-Cn Right. But **49 we're also worried that if we did that, some meetings would only have three or four participants.**

W-Am Yes, we don't want to lose members. Hmm… what about dividing the books into multiple sections? People would be more likely to finish the reading if it were just a few chapters.

여: 우리가 1년째 이 독서 모임을 이끌어가고 있다는 사실이 믿어지시나요? 두 분은 이 모임이 진행되는 방식에 대해 어떻게 생각하세요?

남1: 실은, 댄과 저는 며칠 전에 이야기를 했는데요, 다소 좌절감을 느껴요. 다수가 책을 다 읽지 않기 때문에 깊이 있는 토론을 할 수 없는 것 같아요. 모임에 참가하기 위해서는 회원들이 책을 끝까지 다 읽어야 한다는 규칙을 만들면 좋겠어요.

남2: 맞아요. 하지만 그렇게 하면 모임에 서너 명의 참가자만 올 때도 있을까 봐 염려되기도 해요.

여: 그래요, 회원을 잃고 싶지는 않아요. 음… 책을 여러 부분으로 나누는 건 어떨까요? 몇 챕터만이라면 사람들이 다 읽을 가능성이 높아질 거예요.

어휘 lead 이끌다　book club 독서 모임　frustrated 좌절감을 느끼는　in-depth 깊이 있는　discussion 토론　majority 다수　participate in ~에 참가하다　participant 참가자　lose 잃다　divide into ~으로 나누다　multiple 다수의　section 부분

47 What do members of the speakers' club do together?
(A) Discuss books
(B) Play a sport
(C) Take photographs
(D) Make handicrafts

번역 화자들의 모임 회원들은 모여서 무엇을 하는가?
(A) 책 토론하기
(B) 스포츠 경기하기
(C) 사진 찍기
(D) 수공예품 만들기

해설 **세부 사항 관련 - 모임 회원들이 모여서 하는 것**
여자가 첫 대사에서 1년째 이 독서 모임을 이끌어가고 있다(we've been leading this book club for a year now)고 말하고 있으므로 정답은 (A)이다.

어휘 handicraft 수공예품

48 What is the conversation mainly about?
(A) A learning opportunity
(B) A change in leadership
(C) A promotional campaign
(D) A requirement for members

번역 대화는 주로 무엇에 관한 것인가?
(A) 학습 기회
(B) 리더십의 변화
(C) 홍보 캠페인
(D) 회원들의 자격 요건

해설 **전체 내용 관련 - 대화의 주제**
첫 번째 남자가 모임에 참가하기 위해서는 회원들이 책을 끝까지 다 읽어야 한다는 규칙을 만들면 좋겠다(We'd like to make it a rule that members have to read the whole book in order to

participate in the meeting)고 회원들이 갖추어야 할 자격 요건에 대한 대화를 이어 가고 있으므로 정답은 (D)이다.

49 What are the men concerned about?
(A) Covering an additional expense
(B) Having too few participants
(C) Transporting some supplies
(D) Giving incorrect time estimates

번역 남자들은 무엇에 대해 우려하는가?
(A) 추가 비용을 부담하는 것
(B) 너무 적은 참가자가 오는 것
(C) 용품들을 운송하는 것
(D) 부정확한 예상 시간을 말하는 것

해설 세부 사항 관련 - 남자들이 걱정하는 것
두 번째 남자가 그렇게 하면 모임에 서너 명의 참가자만 올 때도 있을까 봐 염려되기도 한다(we're also worried that if we did that, some meetings would only have three or four participants)고 말하고 있으므로 정답은 (B)이다.

50-52

W-Br Hello, Mr. Joo? This is Shannon Nichols from Nason Professionals. **50 We're a staffing agency based in Flintwood.**

M-Au Hi, Ms. Nichols. What can I do for you today?

W-Br Well, I see that you're the head of human resources for VNX Technology. **51 I'd like to tell you about the benefits of hiring Nason to fill vacancies at your company.**

M-Au Oh, I might be interested, but I don't have time to talk now.

W-Br I understand. **52 May I have your e-mail address, so that I can send you a list of our service rates?** You could look over it when you're free.

여: 안녕하세요, 주 씨? 저는 네이슨 프로페셔널스의 섀넌 니콜스입니다. 저희는 플린트우드에 본사를 둔 채용 대행사입니다.

남: 안녕하세요, 니콜스 씨. 오늘 제가 무엇을 도와드리면 될까요?

여: 음, 주 씨께서 VNX 테크놀로지의 인사부장이신 걸로 압니다. 귀사의 공석을 채우기 위해 네이슨 사를 고용하는 것에 대한 이점을 설명해 드리고 싶습니다.

남: 아, 관심이 있지만, 지금은 제가 이야기할 시간이 없어요.

여: 알겠습니다. 저희 서비스 요금표를 보내드릴 수 있도록 이메일 주소를 알려주시겠어요? 시간이 있을 때 살펴보시면 됩니다.

50 What type of business does the woman work for?
(A) A department store
(B) An insurance company
(C) An employment agency
(D) A landscaping firm

번역 여자는 어떤 유형의 사업체에서 일하는가?
(A) 백화점
(B) 보험 회사
(C) 채용 대행사
(D) 조경 회사

해설 전체 내용 관련 - 여자의 근무 업종
여자가 첫 대사에서 저희는 플린트우드에 본사를 둔 채용 대행사(We're a staffing agency based in Flintwood)라고 했으므로 채용 대행사에서 근무하고 있다는 것을 알 수 있다. 따라서 정답은 (C)이다.

> **Paraphrasing**
> 대화의 a staffing agency
> → 정답의 An employment agency

51 Why is the woman calling the man?
(A) To advertise a business
(B) To arrange a workshop
(C) To offer him a job
(D) To inquire about a loan

번역 여자는 왜 남자에게 전화를 걸고 있는가?
(A) 사업체를 광고하려고
(B) 워크숍을 준비하려고
(C) 일자리를 제안하려고
(D) 대출에 대해 문의하려고

해설 전체 내용 관련 - 여자가 전화한 이유
여자가 두 번째 대사에서 귀사의 공석을 채우기 위해 네이슨 사를 고용하는 것에 대한 이점을 설명해 드리고 싶다(I'd like to tell you about the benefits of hiring Nason to fill vacancies at your company)고 하므로 정답은 (A)이다.

52 What document does the woman mention?
(A) An agreement
(B) A résumé
(C) A rates sheet
(D) A client testimonial

번역   여자는 어떤 서류를 언급하는가?
(A) 계약서
(B) 이력서
(C) 요금표
(D) 고객 추천 후기

해설   **세부 사항 관련 - 여자가 언급하는 서류**
여자가 마지막 대사에서 서비스 요금표를 보낼 이메일 주소를 알려
줄 것(May I have your e-mail address, so that I can send
you a list of our service rates?)을 요청하고 있으므로 정답은
(C)이다.

어휘   testimonial 추천서, 추천의 글

> **Paraphrasing**
> 대화의 a list of our service rates
> → 정답의 A rates sheet

53-55

W-Am	Cedric, do you know much about our travel reimbursement system? **53 I submitted the receipts for my visit to the Guangdong factory last month, and the company still hasn't paid me back.**
M-Cn	Oh, **54 I haven't been on a work trip in years, so I've forgotten how everything works. But you know**… the employee handbook is very detailed.
W-Am	Oh, right! Thanks, I'll take a look.
M-Cn	No problem. And that reminds me—**55 I'm sorry, but I seem to have lost my copy of your report on that factory**. Could you e-mail me a digital version?

여:	세드릭, 우리 출장비 환급 시스템에 대해 잘 아시나요? **지난달 광둥 공장 방문에 대한 영수증을 제출했는데, 회사에서 아직 지급해주지 않았어요.**
남:	아, **저는 몇 년간 출장을 간 적이 없어서 어떻게 돌아가는 건지 잊어버렸어요. 하지만 아시다시피**… 직원 안내서는 매우 상세해요.
여:	아, 맞네요! 감사합니다, 찾아볼게요.
남:	별말씀을요. 그 말을 들으니 생각났는데, **죄송하지만, 그 공장에 대한 당신의 보고서 사본을 잃어버린 것 같아요.** 디지털 버전을 저에게 이메일로 보내주실 수 있나요?

어휘   reimbursement 환급   submit 제출하다   receipt 영수증
factory 공장   pay back 상환하다   handbook 안내서
detailed 상세한   report 보고서

53 What problem does the woman describe?
(A) A receipt is missing some information.
(B) A reimbursement has not been issued.
(C) Some travel plans have not been completed.
(D) The budget for a trip is very limited.

번역   여자는 어떤 문제를 설명하는가?
(A) 영수증에 일부 정보가 빠져 있다.
(B) 환급이 처리되지 않았다.
(C) 일부 여행 계획이 완료되지 않았다.
(D) 여행 예산이 매우 한정적이다.

해설   **세부 사항 관련 - 여자가 언급하는 문제점**
여자가 첫 대사에서 지난달에 광둥 공장에 방문했던 거 영수증을 제출
했는데, 회사에서 아직 지급하지 않았다(I submitted the receipts
for my visit to the Guangdong factory last month, and
the company still hasn't paid me back)고 말하고 있으므로
정답은 (B)이다.

어휘   miss 놓치다, 빠지다   complete 완료하다   budget 예산
limited 한정적인

54 Why does the man say, "the employee handbook
is very detailed"?
(A) To give a recommendation
(B) To decline an offer
(C) To indicate frustration
(D) To praise an accomplishment

번역   남자가 "직원 안내서는 매우 상세해요"라고 말한 이유는?
(A) 추천해 주려고
(B) 제안을 거절하려고
(C) 좌절감을 나타내려고
(D) 업적을 칭찬하려고

해설   **화자의 의도 파악 - 직원 안내서는 매우 상세하다는 말의 의도**
앞에서 남자가 몇 년간 출장을 간 적이 없어서 어떻게 돌아가는 건지
잊어버렸다(I haven't been on a work trip in years, so I've
forgotten how everything works)고 한 뒤 인용문을 언급하고
있는 것으로 보아, 직원 안내서를 참고할 것을 추천하려는 의도로 한
말임을 알 수 있다. 따라서 정답은 (A)이다.

어휘   recommendation 추천   decline 거절하다   indicate 나타내다
frustration 좌절감   praise 칭찬하다   accomplishment 업적

55 Why does the man apologize?
(A) He forgot to process a request.
(B) He did not read an e-mail carefully.
(C) He is not allowed to discuss an issue.
(D) He has misplaced a report.

번역   남자는 왜 사과하는가?
(A) 요청을 처리하는 일을 잊어버렸기 때문에
(B) 이메일을 주의 깊게 읽지 않았기 때문에
(C) 문제에 대해 논의할 수 없기 때문에
(D) 보고서를 잃어버렸기 때문에

TEST 9

남자가 마지막 대사에서 죄송하지만, 그 공장에 대한 당신의 보고서 사본을 잃어버린 것 같다(I'm sorry, but I seem to have lost my copy of your report on that factory)고 사과하고 있으므로 정답은 (D)이다.

어휘 process 처리하다 carefully 주의 깊게 allow 허락하다
misplace 잃어버리다

> **Paraphrasing**
> 대화의 lost my copy of your report
> → 정답의 misplaced a report

56-58 3인 대화

M-Au Julie, **⁵⁶ the representative from Quigley Movers came by this morning to discuss using the windows for our move, right?** What did he say?

W-Am Unfortunately, **⁵⁷ the space next to our side of the building is too narrow for their equipment.** So we won't be able to get our metalworking machinery out through the windows.

W-Br That's disappointing. Then we'll have to postpone our move to the new studio, right?

M-Au We shouldn't have to do that just because the freight elevator is out of order. **⁵⁸ I think we should check our lease agreement.** There may be a clause in there that requires the landlord to fix the elevators promptly.

남: 줄리, 오늘 아침에 퀴글리 무버스 담당자가 우리 이사 때 창문 사용하는 것에 대해 논의하러 왔었죠? 그가 뭐라고 했나요?

여1: 안타깝게도, 우리 건물 옆 공간이 그들의 장비가 들어오기에는 너무 좁대요. 그래서 우리 금속세공 기계를 창문으로 꺼내기는 어려울 기예요.

여2: 실망스럽군요. 그럼 새 작업실로의 이사를 미뤄야 하는 거죠?

남: 화물 승강기가 고장 났다는 이유만으로 그렇게 할 필요는 없어요. 우리 임대 계약서를 확인해 봐야 되겠어요. 건물주가 승강기를 신속히 고쳐야 한다는 조항이 있을지도 몰라요.

어휘 representative 담당자, 대표 narrow 좁은 equipment 장비 metalworking machinery 금속세공 기계 disappointing 실망스러운 postpone 미루다 freight 화물 out of order 고장이 난 lease agreement 임대 계약서 clause 조항 landlord 건물주 fix 고치다 promptly 신속히

---

56 Who visited the speakers' workplace this morning?
(A) A property appraiser
(B) A safety inspector
(C) A building contractor
(D) A moving company agent

번역 오늘 아침에 누가 화자들의 일터에 방문했는가?
(A) 부동산 감정평가사
(B) 안전 감독관
(C) 건축 도급업자
(D) 이사업체 직원

해설 **세부 사항 관련 - 오늘 아침에 화자들의 일터에 방문한 사람**
남자가 첫 대사에서 오늘 아침에 퀴글리 무버스 담당자가 우리 이사 때 창문 사용하는 것에 대해 논의하러 왔었는지(the representative from Quigley Movers came by this morning to discuss using the windows for our move, right?) 묻고 있으므로 정답은 (D)이다.

어휘 property 부동산, 재산 appraiser 감정평가사 safety 안전 inspector 감독관 contractor 도급업자

---

57 What problem does Julie mention?
(A) A window was installed incorrectly.
(B) A permit has not been approved.
(C) Some machinery has been disassembled.
(D) A space is not wide enough for some equipment.

번역 줄리는 어떤 문제를 언급하는가?
(A) 창문이 잘못 설치되었다.
(B) 허가가 승인되지 않았다.
(C) 일부 기계가 분해되었다.
(D) 공간이 장비가 들어갈 만큼 폭이 넓지 못하다.

해설 **세부 사항 관련 - 줄리가 언급하는 문제**
남자가 첫 대사에서 줄리(Julie)의 이름을 부르며 질문을 했고, 첫 번째 여자가 첫 대사에서 우리 건물 옆 공간이 그들의 장비가 들어오기에는 너무 좁다(the space next to our side of the building is too narrow for their equipment)고 답하고 있으므로 정답은 (D)이다.

어휘 install 설치하다 incorrectly 부정확하게 permit 허가 approve 승인하다 disassemble 분해하다

> **Paraphrasing**
> 대화의 too narrow → 정답의 not wide enough

---

58 What does the man suggest doing?
(A) Reviewing a contract
(B) Postponing a start date
(C) Taking some measurements
(D) Seeking another opinion

번역   남자는 무엇을 제안하는가?
(A) 계약서 검토하기
(B) 시작일 미루기
(C) 측정하기
(D) 다른 의견 구하기

해설   **세부 사항 관련 - 남자의 제안 사항**
남자가 마지막 대사에서 임대 계약서를 확인해 봐야 되겠다(I think we should check our lease agreement)며 계약서를 검토할 것을 제안하고 있으므로 정답은 (A)이다.

어휘   review 검토하다   measurement 측정   seek 구하다   opinion 의견

> **Paraphrasing**
> 대화의 check our lease agreement
> → 정답의 Reviewing a contract

59-61

M-Cn   Hi, Hyo-Min. Do you have a moment? The finance department just got the payment request from Jenkins Mining.

W-Am   And **59 you're wondering why I decided to place an order with a second iron supplier?**

M-Cn   Yes—**60 has there been a problem with the supplier you usually purchase our iron from?**

W-Am   No, but these days it's wise to have more than one source for important materials. That way, a shortage at one supplier won't cause a critical disruption to our business. It's part of a practice called "supply-chain diversification."

M-Cn   Oh, that makes sense. Where did you hear about it? I'd like to learn more.

W-Am   **61 My favorite business Web site has published articles about it. I'll send you the links.**

남: 안녕하세요, 효민. 시간 있으세요? 경리부에서 방금 젠킨스 광업으로부터 결제 요청을 받았어요.

여: 그리고 제가 왜 2순위의 철 공급업체에 주문하기로 결정했는지 궁금하신 거겠죠?

남: 네, 평소에 철을 구입하던 공급업체에 무슨 문제라도 있었나요?

여: 아니요, 하지만 요즘에는 중요한 자재를 위해 하나 이상의 공급원을 가지는 것이 현명하죠. 그래야 한 공급업체에서 수급이 부족하더라도 우리 사업에 중대한 지장을 초래하지 않을 테니까요. "공급망 다각화"라고 부르는 관행의 일부분이에요.

남: 아, 일리가 있네요. 그것에 대해 어디서 들으셨어요? 좀 더 배우고 싶어요.

여: 제가 좋아하는 비즈니스 웹사이트에서 그것에 관한 글을 발표했어요. 링크를 보내드릴게요.

어휘   payment 지불   place an order 주문하다   iron 철   supplier 공급업체   purchase 구매하다   material 자재   shortage 부족   critical 중대한   disruption 지장, 혼란   practice 관행   supply-chain 공급망   diversification 다각화   article 글, 기사

59   What is the purpose of the man's visit?
(A) To complete a process
(B) To thank a colleague
(C) To announce a visitor
(D) To ask about a decision

번역   남자의 방문 목적은 무엇인가?
(A) 절차를 완료하려고
(B) 동료에게 감사 인사를 하려고
(C) 방문자가 왔음을 알려주려고
(D) 결정에 대해 문의하려고

해설   **전체 내용 관련 - 남자의 방문 목적**
여자가 첫 대사에서 왜 2순위의 철 공급업체에 주문하기로 결정했는지가 궁금하냐고(you're wondering why I decided to place an order with a second iron supplier?) 묻고 있으므로 정답은 (D)이다.

어휘   complete 완료하다   colleague 동료   visitor 방문자

60   What department does the woman most likely work in?
(A) Human Resources
(B) Purchasing
(C) Marketing
(D) Technical Support

번역   여자는 어떤 부서에서 일하겠는가?
(A) 인사부
(B) 구매부
(C) 마케팅부
(D) 기술지원부

해설   **전체 내용 관련 - 여자의 근무 부서**
남자가 두 번째 대사에서 평소에 철을 구입하던 공급업체에 문제가 있었는지(has there been a problem with the supplier you usually purchase our iron from?) 묻고 있으므로 여자는 구매부에서 근무하고 있다는 것을 알 수 있다. 따라서 정답은 (B)이다.

61   What does the woman say she will do?
(A) Share some Web site links
(B) Cancel a supply order
(C) Practice a presentation
(D) Dispose of some documents

번역   여자는 무엇을 하겠다고 말하는가?
(A) 웹사이트 링크를 공유한다.
(B) 공급 주문을 취소한다.
(C) 발표를 연습한다.
(D) 일부 서류를 폐기한다.

TEST 9

여자가 마지막 대사에서 자신이 좋아하는 비즈니스 웹사이트에서 그것에 관한 글을 발표했다(My favorite business Web site has published articles about it)면서 링크를 보내주겠다(I'll send you the links)고 말하고 있으므로 정답은 (A)이다.

어휘 cancel 취소하다 practice 연습하다 dispose of ~을 폐기하다

> **Paraphrasing**
> 대화의 send you the links
> → 정답의 share some Web site links

62-64 대화 + 명부

M-Cn Good morning, ⁶²**Sanford Tower Facilities Office**. How can I help you?

W-Am Hi, this is Teresa Strauss from Fairview Logistics.

M-Cn Ah, yes. I've just ordered your nameplate for the business directory. I hope you're getting settled in well.

W-Am We are, thanks, except that the heating system isn't working.

M-Cn I can send a technician right now. ⁶³**It's Suite 102, right?**

W-Am ⁶³**That's right.** And ⁶⁴**we still need our passes for the underground parking area. I plan to collect those after lunch.**

M-Cn That's fine. They'll be ready by then.

. . . .

남: 좋은 아침입니다. **샌퍼드 타워 관리실입니다.** 무엇을 도와드릴까요?

여: 안녕하세요. 저는 페어뷰 물류의 테레사 슈트라우스입니다.

남: 아, 네 업체 안내 명부에 올릴 귀시의 명핀을 방금 주문했어요. 잘 적응하고 계신다면 좋겠네요.

여: 그러고 있어요. 감사합니다. 난방이 작동이 안 되는 것만 빼고요.

남: 제가 기술자를 바로 보내드릴 수 있습니다. **102호 맞으시죠?**

여: **맞아요. 또 필요한 게 있는데, 지하 주차장 출입증이에요. 점심시간 후에 가지러 가려고요.**

남: 좋습니다. 그때까지 준비될 거예요.

어휘 logistics 물류 nameplate 명판 directory 명부, 목록 settle in well 잘 적응하다 technician 기술자 pass 출입증 collect 모으다, 가지러 가다

Sanford Tower	
101	Tabor Sales
⁶³102	Ace Publishing
201	Norris Inc.
202	EG Interior Designs

샌퍼드 타워	
101호	테이버 영업
⁶³102호	에이스 출판
201호	노리스 주식회사
202호	EG 실내 디자인

62 Who most likely is the man?
(A) A construction worker
(B) A safety inspector
(C) A facilities manager
(D) A computer technician

번역 남자는 누구이겠는가?
(A) 건설 노동자
(B) 안전 감독관
(C) 시설 관리자
(D) 컴퓨터 기술자

해설 **전체 내용 관련 - 남자의 직업**
남자가 첫 대사에서 샌퍼드 타워 관리실(Sanford Tower Facilities Office)이라고 소개하는 것으로 보아 남자는 관리실에서 근무하는 직원임을 알 수 있다. 따라서 정답은 (C)이다.

어휘 construction 건설, 공사 safety 안전 inspector 감독관

63 Look at the graphic. Which business name will be changed?
(A) Tabor Sales
(B) Ace Publishing
(C) Norris Inc.
(D) EG Interior Designs

번역 시각 정보에 의하면, 어떤 업체명이 바뀌겠는가?
(A) 테이버 영업
(B) 에이스 출판
(C) 노리스 주식회사
(D) EG 실내 디자인

해설 **시각 정보 연계 - 바뀌게 될 업체명**
남자가 세 번째 대사에서 102호가 맞는지(It's Suite 102, right?)를 물었고, 여자가 맞다(That's right)고 답변했다. 명부를 보면 102호는 에이스 출판(Ace Publishing)이므로 정답은 (B)이다.

64 What does the woman say she will do this afternoon?
(A) Wait to greet a visitor
(B) Move in some furniture
(C) Pick up some parking passes
(D) Order some business cards

번역 여자는 오늘 오후에 무엇을 하겠다고 말하는가?
(A) 손님을 맞이하기 위해 기다리기
(B) 가구 옮기기
(C) 주차 출입증 가지러 가기
(D) 명함 주문하기

해설　**세부 사항 관련 - 여자가 오늘 오후에 할 일**
　　여자가 마지막 대사에서 또 필요한 게 있는데, 지하 주차장 출입증(we still need our passes for the underground parking area)이라면서 점심시간 후에 가지러 갈 것(I plan to collect those after lunch)이라고 말하고 있으므로 정답은 (C)이다.

어휘　greet 환영하다　visitor 방문자　furniture 가구

> **Paraphrasing**
> 대화의 passes for the underground parking area
> → 정답의 parking passes
> 대화의 collect → 정답의 Pick up

65-67 대화 + 가격표

M-Au	Welcome to Sandia Beauty Salon. How can I help you?
W-Am	Hi, I'm Janice Simms. **65 I have an appointment for a manicure at eleven**. I booked it yesterday over the phone.
M-Au	Ah, Ms. Simms! I'm the person you spoke with.
W-Am	Oh, I see! Well, thank you again for fitting me in. Like I said yesterday, **66 I've been suddenly scheduled to interview for a bank teller position this afternoon,** and it's important to have well-manicured hands in that kind of work.
M-Au	Yes, good luck. Now, **67 can I get you a cup of tea while you wait?**
W-Am	**67 I'd like that, thank you.**

남:　샌디아 미용실에 오신 것을 환영합니다. 무엇을 도와드릴까요?

여:　안녕하세요, 저는 재니스 심스입니다. **11시에 손톱 관리를 예약했는데요.** 어제 전화로 예약했고요.

남:　아, 심스 씨! 제가 전화 받았던 사람입니다.

여:　오, 그렇군요! 음, 저를 위해 시간을 잡아주셔서 다시 한번 감사 드려요. 제가 어제 말씀드렸던 것처럼 **오늘 오후에 갑자기 은행 창구 직원 면접이 잡혔어요.** 그런 종류의 일에는 손톱이 잘 다듬 어진 손이 중요하거든요.

남:　그렇죠, 행운을 빕니다. 자, 그럼 **기다리시는 동안 차 한 잔 드릴 까요?**

여:　**좋죠, 감사합니다.**

어휘　appointment (진료 등의) 예약　manicure 손톱 관리
　　fit in 일정상에 끼워 넣다　bank teller 은행원　position
　　일자리　well-manicured 손톱이 잘 손질된

Service Prices

Haircut and styling	$60
Facial treatment	$50
Pedicure	$40
65Manicure	$30

서비스 요금

커트와 스타일링	60달러
얼굴 관리	50달러
발톱 관리	40달러
65손톱 관리	30달러

65 Look at the graphic. How much will the woman pay for her service?
(A) $60
(B) $50
(C) $40
(D) $30

번역　시각 정보에 의하면, 여자는 서비스에 얼마를 지불하겠는가?
(A) 60달러
(B) 50달러
(C) 40달러
(D) 30달러

해설　**시각 정보 연계 - 여자가 서비스에 지불할 금액**
　　여자가 첫 대사에서 11시에 손톱 관리를 예약했다(I have an appointment for a manicure at eleven)고 말하고 있고, 가격 표에 따르면 손톱 관리 서비스 요금은 30달러이므로 정답은 (D)이다.

66 What event is the woman going to participate in later?
(A) A photo shoot
(B) An award ceremony
(C) A press conference
(D) A job interview

번역　여자는 잠시 후에 어떤 행사에 참가할 예정인가?
(A) 사진 촬영
(B) 시상식
(C) 기자 회견
(D) 취업 면접

해설　**세부 사항 관련 - 여자가 잠시 후에 참가할 행사**
　　여자가 두 번째 대사에서 오늘 오후에 갑자기 은행 창구 직원 면접이 잡혔다(I've been suddenly scheduled to interview for a bank teller position this afternoon)고 말하고 있으므로 정답은 (D)이다.

TEST 9

67 What will the man most likely do next?
(A) Look for a colleague
(B) Put out some magazines
(C) Prepare a beverage
(D) Accept a payment

번역 남자는 다음으로 무엇을 하겠는가?
(A) 동료 찾기
(B) 잡지 꺼내기
(C) 음료 준비하기
(D) 결제 받기

해설 **세부 사항 관련 - 남자가 다음에 할 일**
남자가 마지막 대사에서 기다리는 동안 차 한 잔을 제안(can I get you a cup of tea while you wait?)하자 여자가 좋다며 감사하다 (I'd like that, thank you)고 수락하고 있으므로 정답은 (C)이다.

어휘 colleague 동료   put out 내놓다   prepare 준비하다
beverage 음료   accept 받다. 받아들이다   payment 지불

> **Paraphrasing**
> 대화의 a cup of tea → 정답의 a beverage

68-70 대화+서랍장

W-Am Hi Nasir, it's Elizabeth. **68 I'm on my way to Springtown Hotel to meet with some potential clients,** and I just realized that I forgot the USB stick with my presentation on it. Could you drive it over here?

M-Cn Right now? Oh... uh, OK.

W-Am Thank you so much. I'm really sorry for the inconvenience. I should have checked my bag more carefully before I left the office this morning.

M-Cn It's alright. **69 I've left important stuff at the office before, too.** So, **70 where's your USB stick?**

W-Am **70 If you go to my workstation, you'll see two drawer units under the desk. The USB's in the top drawer of the one on the right.** It's bright green.

여: 안녕하세요 나시르, 저 엘리자베스인데요. **잠재 고객들을 만나러 스프링타운 호텔로 가는 중인데,** 방금 발표 자료가 담긴 USB를 놓고 왔다는 사실을 깨달았어요. 여기로 좀 갖다 줄 수 있나요?
남: 지금요? 아… 어, 그러죠.
여: 정말 감사합니다. 불편을 끼쳐 정말 죄송해요. 오늘 아침에 사무실에서 나오기 전에 제 가방을 좀 더 꼼꼼히 확인했어야 했는데.
남: 괜찮습니다. 저도 전에 사무실에 중요한 물건을 놓고 온 적이 있어요. 그런데 USB는 어디에 있나요?

여: 제 자리에 가시면 책상 아래에 두 개의 서랍장이 보이실 거예요. USB는 오른쪽에 있는 것의 맨 위 서랍에 있어요. 밝은 녹색이에요.

어휘 potential 잠재적인   presentation 발표 (자료)
inconvenience 불편   carefully 주의 깊게   workstation
사무 공간   drawer 서랍

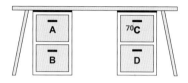

68 Why is the woman away from the office?
(A) For an industry conference
(B) For a client meeting
(C) For a property inspection
(D) For a doctor's appointment

번역 여자는 왜 사무실을 비웠는가?
(A) 업계 컨퍼런스 때문에
(B) 고객과의 회의 때문에
(C) 부동산 점검 때문에
(D) 진료 예약 때문에

해설 **세부 사항 관련 - 여자가 사무실을 비운 이유**
여자가 첫 대사에서 잠재 고객들을 만나러 스프링타운 호텔로 가는 중 (I'm on my way to Springtown Hotel to meet with some potential clients)이라고 말하고 있으므로 정답은 (B)이다.

어휘 property 부동산, 건물   inspection 점검   appointment (진료 등의) 예약

> **Paraphrasing**
> 대화의 to meet with some potential clients
> → 정답의 For a client meeting

69 What does the man say to reassure the woman?
(A) He is not very busy today.
(B) He knows a project is important.
(C) He has made similar mistakes.
(D) He is familiar with a location.

번역 남자는 여자를 안심시키기 위해 뭐라고 말하는가?
(A) 자신은 오늘 별로 바쁘지 않다.
(B) 자신은 프로젝트가 중요하다는 사실을 안다.
(C) 자신도 비슷한 실수를 한 적이 있다.
(D) 자신은 위치를 잘 안다.

해설 **세부 사항 관련 - 남자가 여자를 안심시키기 위해 한 말**
남자가 두 번째 대사에서 자신도 사무실에 중요한 물건을 놓고 온 적이 있다(I've left important stuff at the office before, too)고 말하고 있으므로 정답은 (C)이다.

어휘 reassure 안심시키다   similar 비슷한   be familiar with ~에 대해 잘 알다

70 Look at the graphic. Where should the man look for an item?
(A) In drawer A
(B) In drawer B
(C) In drawer C
(D) In drawer D

번역 시각 정보에 의하면, 남자는 어디서 물건을 찾아야 하는가?
(A) A 서랍에서
(B) B 서랍에서
(C) C 서랍에서
(D) D 서랍에서

해설 **시각 정보 연계 - 남자가 물건을 찾아야 할 장소**
남자가 두 번째 대사에서 USB가 어디에 있는지(where's your USB stick?) 묻자 여자가 자신의 자리에 가면 책상 아래에 두 개의 서랍장이 보일 것(If you go to my workstation, you'll see two drawer units under the desk)이라면서 USB는 오른쪽에 있는 것의 맨 위 서랍에 있다(The USB's in the top drawer of the one on the right)고 말하고 있고, 시각 자료를 보면 오른쪽 맨 위 서랍은 C서랍이므로 정답은 (C)이다.

PART 4

71-73 전화 메시지

M-Cn Hello, Ms. Young, this is Frank Davis with FS London. **71 I'm calling to let you know that you're a finalist for our organization's Rising Star Award.** Your supervisor nominated you. Our judges were quite impressed by her description of the savings that **72 your accounting work** has created for your company. If you're interested, **73 the next step is a meeting with the judges' committee to discuss your accomplishments. I'm sending you an invitation by e-mail right now.**

안녕하세요, 영 씨. 저는 FS 런던의 프랭크 데이비스입니다. **귀하께서 저희 단체의 유망주 상 최종 후보에 오르셨다는 사실을 알려드리려고 전화드립니다.** 귀하의 관리자가 귀하를 지명했습니다. 저희 심사위원들은 **귀하의 회계 업무**가 회사의 비용을 얼마나 절약했는지에 대한 그녀의 설명에 깊은 인상을 받았습니다. 관심이 있으시다면, **다음 단계는 귀하의 업적에 대해 논의하기 위한 심사위원회와의 회의입니다. 제가 지금 바로 이메일로 초대장을 보내드리겠습니다.**

어휘 finalist 결승 진출자 supervisor 감독관, 관리자 nominate 지명하다 judge 심사위원 be impressed by ~에 깊은 인상을 받다 description 설명 saving 절약 accounting 회계 committee 위원회 accomplishment 업적 invitation 초대장

71 What is the main purpose of the call?
(A) To suggest applying for a promotion
(B) To confirm a biographical detail for an article
(C) To tell the listener that she is an award candidate
(D) To thank the listener for joining a committee

번역 전화의 주된 목적은 무엇인가?
(A) 승진 신청을 제안하려고
(B) 기사를 위해 신상 정보를 확인하려고
(C) 청자에게 그녀가 수상 후보자임을 말해주려고
(D) 청자에게 위원회 가입에 대해 감사 인사를 하려고

해설 **전체 내용 관련 - 전화의 목적**
화자가 초반부에 단체의 유망주 상 최종 후보에 올랐다는 사실을 알려주려고 전화한다(I'm calling to let you know that you're a finalist for our organization's Rising Star Award)고 했으므로 정답은 (C)이다.

어휘 apply for ~을 신청하다 promotion 승진 biographical 신상에 관한 article 글, 기사 award candidate 수상 후보자

> **Paraphrasing**
> 담화의 a finalist for our organization's Rising Star Award → 정답의 an award candidate

72 What field does the listener work in?
(A) Shipping
(B) Education
(C) Advertising
(D) Finance

번역 청자는 어떤 분야에 종사하는가?
(A) 운송
(B) 교육
(C) 광고
(D) 금융

해설 **전체 내용 관련 - 청자의 근무 업종**
화자가 중반부에 귀하의 회계 업무(your accounting work)라고 말하고 있으므로 청자는 금융 업종에서 종사하고 있음을 알 수 있다. 따라서 정답은 (D)이다.

> **Paraphrasing**
> 담화의 accounting → 정답의 Finance

73 What is the listener invited to do?
(A) Attend a meeting
(B) Browse a Web site
(C) Submit a work sample
(D) Refer a coworker

번역 청자는 무엇을 하도록 권유받았는가?
(A) 회의에 참석하기
(B) 웹사이트 둘러보기
(C) 작업 견본 제출하기
(D) 동료 추천하기

해설　세부 사항 관련 - 청자가 권유받은 일

화자가 마지막에 다음 단계는 심사위원회와의 회의(the next step is a meeting with the judges' committee ~)라면서 지금 바로 이메일로 초대장을 보내주겠다(I'm sending you an invitation by e-mail right now)고 말하고 있으므로 정답은 (A)이다.

어휘　attend 참석하다　browse 검색하다, 둘러보다　submit 제출하다 refer 추천하다

74-76 광고

W-Am All residents of Holton are invited to Tillsby Park this Saturday for "Tacos for Tillsby," **74 a benefit to raise money for updates to the park.** The Holton Parks Foundation will be selling delicious taco lunches from eleven until supplies run out. **75 Attendees can also enjoy performances from several local bands. 76 Visit the foundation's Web site for event details and to see computer-generated images of what the park will look like after the improvements.**

홀턴의 모든 주민을 이번 주 토요일 <타코 포 틸스비>가 열리는 틸스비 공원으로 초대합니다. **이 행사는 공원 개선을 위한 기금을 모금하는 자선 행사입니다.** 홀턴 공원 재단은 11시부터 물량이 모두 소진될 때까지 맛있는 타코 점심을 판매할 예정입니다. **참석자들은 여러 지역 밴드의 공연도 즐기실 수 있습니다. 행사 세부 내용과 개조 공사 후 공원의 모습을 보여주는 컴퓨터 생성 이미지를 보시려면 재단의 웹사이트를 방문해 주십시오.**

어휘　resident 거주민　benefit 자선 행사　raise money 모금하다　update 개선　foundation 재단　run out 다 떨어지다 attendee 참석자　performance 공연　computer-generated 컴퓨터로 생성한　improvement 개조, 개선

74 What is being advertised?
(A) A store opening
(B) A park cleanup
(C) A sports competition
(D) A community fund-raiser

번역　무엇이 광고되고 있는가?
(A) 매장 개업
(B) 공원 대청소
(C) 스포츠 대회
(D) 지역 모금 행사

해설　전체 내용 관련 - 광고되고 있는 것

화자가 도입부에 이 행사는 공원 개선을 위한 기금을 모금하는 자선 행사(a benefit to raise money for updates to the park)라고 광고하고 있으므로 정답은 (D)이다.

어휘　cleanup 대청소　competition 경쟁, 대회　community 지역사회, 공동체　fund-raiser 모금 행사

Paraphrasing
담화의 a benefit to raise money for updates to the park → 정답의 A community fund-raiser

75 What will happen during the event?
(A) A street will be closed to vehicles.
(B) A government official will give a speech.
(C) Some of the attendees will win prizes.
(D) Musical performances will take place.

번역　행사 기간에 어떤 일이 일어나겠는가?
(A) 거리에 차량이 통제될 것이다.
(B) 정부 공무원이 연설을 할 것이다.
(C) 참석자들 중 일부가 상을 탈 것이다.
(D) 음악 공연이 열릴 것이다.

해설　세부 사항 관련 - 행사 기간에 있을 일

화자가 중반부에서 참석자들은 여러 지역 밴드의 공연도 즐기실 수 있다(Attendees can also enjoy performances from several local bands)고 말하고 있으므로 정답은 (D)이다.

어휘　government official 정부 공무원

Paraphrasing
담화의 performances from several local bands → 정답의 Musical performances

76 What does the speaker say the listeners can do on a Web site?
(A) Make a donation
(B) Complete a registration
(C) View some images
(D) Cast some votes

번역　화자는 청자들이 웹사이트에서 무엇을 할 수 있다고 말하는가?
(A) 기부하기
(B) 등록 완료하기
(C) 이미지 보기
(D) 투표하기

해설　세부 사항 관련 - 청자들이 웹사이트에서 할 수 있는 것

화자가 마지막에 행사 세부 내용과 개조 공사 후 공원의 모습을 보여주는 컴퓨터 생성 이미지를 보려면 재단의 웹사이트를 방문해 줄 것(Visit the foundation's Web site for event details and to see computer-generated images of what the park will look like after the improvements)을 요청하고 있으므로 정답은 (C)이다.

어휘　registration 등록　cast a vote 투표하다

Paraphrasing
담화의 see computer-generated images → 정답의 View some images

77-79 담화

W-Br **77 Welcome back to the new and improved Womack Theater!** It's wonderful that so many of you have returned to work here. And I apologize, again, for the wait. **78 I know that some of you expected that the renovations wouldn't take so long.** But you have to remember—this building was built over seventy years ago. We couldn't have predicted all of the issues that came up. Anyway, now we're back and ready to put on some great shows! Let's start this re-training session with a tour. **79 Leave your coats and bags on the table here**, and follow me.

새롭게 개선된 워맥 극장에 돌아오신 것을 환영합니다! 이렇게 많이 분들이 여기서 일하기 위해 돌아와 주셔서 기쁩니다. 그리고 다시 한번 기다리시게 해서 죄송합니다. 여러분 중 몇몇은 보수 공사가 그렇게 오래 걸리지는 않을 거라고 생각하셨다는 것을 압니다. 하지만 기억하셔야 합니다. 이 건물은 지어진 지 70년이 넘었습니다. 발생한 모든 문제들을 예상할 수는 없었습니다. 아무튼 이제 돌아왔고 멋진 공연을 상연할 준비가 되었습니다! 견학으로 이 재교육 시간을 시작해 봅시다. 외투와 가방은 여기 테이블 위에 두고 저를 따라오세요.

어휘 improved 개선된, 향상된 theater 극장 apologize 사과하다 renovation 보수 공사 predict 예측하다 come up 발생하다 put on 상연하다 retraining 재교육

77 Where do the listeners work?
(A) At a theater
(B) At a television studio
(C) At a university library
(D) At a bank

번역 청자들은 어디서 일하는가?
(A) 극장
(B) 텔레비전 방송국
(C) 대학교 도서관
(D) 은행

해설 전체 내용 관련 - 청자들의 근무지
화자가 도입부에 새롭게 개선된 워맥 극장에 돌아온 것을 환영한다(Welcome back to the new and improved Womack Theater!)고 말하는 것으로 보아 청자들은 극장에서 근무한다는 것을 알 수 있다. 따라서 정답은 (A)이다.

78 What does the speaker imply when she says, "this building was built over 70 years ago"?
(A) The facility lacks some amenities.
(B) The building is a local landmark.
(C) A renovation project was difficult.
(D) An organization should relocate soon.

번역 화자가 "이 건물은 지어진 지 70년이 넘었습니다"라고 말할 때, 그 의도는 무엇인가?
(A) 시설에 편의 시설이 부족하다.
(B) 이 건물이 지역의 랜드마크이다.
(C) 보수 공사가 어려웠다.
(D) 단체가 곧 이전해야 한다.

해설 화자의 의도 파악 - 이 건물은 지어진 지 70년이 넘었다는 말의 의도
앞에서 화자가 여러분 중 몇몇은 보수 공사가 그렇게 오래 걸리지는 않을 거라고 생각하셨다는 것을 안다(I know that some of you expected that the renovations wouldn't take so long)고 말한 뒤 인용문을 언급하고 있으므로, 오래된 건물이라 보수공사가 쉽지 않았다는 의도로 한 말임을 알 수 있다. 따라서 정답은 (C)이다.

어휘 facility 시설 lack 부족하다 amenity 편의 시설 landmark 랜드마크 relocate 이전하다

79 What does the speaker ask the listeners to do?
(A) Rearrange some furniture
(B) Put down their belongings
(C) Take copies of a handout
(D) Silence their mobile phones

번역 화자는 청자들에게 무엇을 하라고 요청하는가?
(A) 가구 재배치하기
(B) 소지품 내려놓기
(C) 유인물 가져가기
(D) 휴대전화 무음으로 하기

해설 세부 사항 관련 - 화자의 요청 사항
화자가 마지막에 외투와 가방은 여기 테이블 위에 둘 것(Leave your coats and bags on the table here ~)을 요청하고 있으므로 정답은 (B)이다.

어휘 rearrange 재배치하다 furniture 가구 put down 내려놓다 belongings 소지품 silence ~의 소리를 없애다

> **Paraphrasing**
> 담화의 Leave your coats and bags on the table
> → 정답의 Put down their belongings

80-82 전화 메시지

M-Au Hi, Emily. It's Daoming. I'm calling about the video that we're making for the company Web site. **80 I'm reviewing the audio file now.** As you requested, I used a speech generating computer program to create the voiceover narration, and for the most part, it sounds pretty good. Except—**81 the program has a hard time pronouncing names correctly.** I can fix the mispronounced names with my sound editing software, but it'll take all day. **82 For our next project, we should probably just hire a professional voice actor again.**

안녕하세요, 에밀리. 다오밍이에요. 회사 웹사이트를 위해 우리가 만들고 있는 영상 때문에 전화드려요. **제가 지금 오디오 파일을 검토하는 중인데요.** 요청하신 대로 음성 생성 프로그램을 사용해 화면 해설 내레이션을 만들었는데, 대부분은 음질이 꽤 좋아요. 다만, **그 프로그램은 이름을 정확하게 발음하는 걸 어려워해요.** 잘못 발음된 이름을 음향 편집 소프트웨어로 수정할 수 있지만, 하루 종일 걸릴 거예요. **다음 프로젝트 때는 아무래도 다시 전문 성우를 고용해야 할 것 같아요.**

어휘 voiceover 화면 해설 have a hard time 고생하다. 어려움을 겪다 pronounce 발음하다 correctly 정확하게 fix 고치다 mispronounced 잘못 발음된 hire 고용하다 voice actor 성우

80 What is the speaker reviewing?
(A) A video script
(B) A research paper
(C) A slide presentation
(D) An audio file

번역 화자는 무엇을 검토하는 중인가?
(A) 영상 대본
(B) 연구 보고서
(C) 슬라이드 발표 자료
(D) 오디오 파일

해설 **세부 사항 관련 - 화자가 검토 중인 것**
화자가 지금 오디오 파일을 검토하는 중(I'm reviewing the audio file now)이라고 말하고 있으므로 정답은 (D)이다.

어휘 script 대본

81 According to the speaker, what caused a problem?
(A) Some names
(B) Some visual aids
(C) A password requirement
(D) A formatting choice

번역 화자에 따르면, 무엇이 문제를 일으켰는가?
(A) 이름들
(B) 시각 보조 자료들
(C) 암호 요구 조건
(D) 서식 선택

해설 **세부 사항 관련 - 문제를 야기한 것**
화자가 중반부에 그 프로그램은 이름을 정확하게 발음하는 걸 어려워한다(the program has a hard time pronouncing names correctly)고 말하고 있으므로 정답은 (A)이다.

어휘 requirement 필요조건

82 What does the speaker recommend doing in the future?
(A) Reading a manual
(B) Hiring a specialist
(C) Marking any changes
(D) Upgrading some equipment

번역 화자는 미래에 무엇을 하기를 추천하는가?
(A) 사용 설명서 읽기
(B) 전문가 고용하기
(C) 변경 사항 표시하기
(D) 장비 업그레이드하기

해설 **세부 사항 관련 - 화자의 미래 추천 사항**
화자가 마지막에 다음 프로젝트 때는 아무래도 다시 전문 성우를 고용해야 할 것 같다(For our next project, we should probably just hire a professional voice actor again)고 말하고 있으므로 정답은 (B)이다.

어휘 manual 사용 설명서 specialist 전문가 mark 표시하다 equipment 장비

> **Paraphrasing**
> 담화의 a professional voice actor → 정답의 a specialist

83-85 공지

W-Am Can I have your attention? I'm Marianne Cross, the manager here at Hudson Fitness Center. **83, 84 I'm sorry to tell you that the eight P.M. cycling class has been canceled due to a dangling light fixture in the studio.** An electrician is coming tomorrow to put it back into place. As for tonight— there is an aerobics class at 8:15. **84 It's in Room Two, for those who are interested.** Also, as a token of apology, you will all receive a coupon for a free smoothie through the Hudson Fitness Center app. **85 Check your smartphone in a few minutes to make sure it has come through.**

주목해 주시겠습니까? 저는 이곳 허드슨 피트니스 센터의 점장인 메리앤 크로스입니다. **죄송하지만 저녁 8시 사이클 수업이 스튜디오의 조명 기구가 떨어져 매달려 있는 관계로 취소되었습니다.** 전기 기술자가 내일 와서 제자리에 맞춰 넣을 겁니다. 오늘 밤에는, **8시 15분에 에어로빅 수업이 있습니다. 관심이 있는 분들을 위해 알려드리자면 2호실에서 해요.** 또한 사과의 뜻으로 여러분은 모두 허드슨 피트니스 센터 앱을 통해 무료 스무디 쿠폰을 받게 되실 거예요. **몇 분 후에 스마트폰을 확인하시고 쿠폰이 들어왔는지 확인해 보세요.**

어휘 cancel 취소하다 dangling 매달린 light fixture 조명 기구 electrician 전기 기술자 put back into place 제자리에 돌려놓다 as a token of apology 사과의 뜻으로 come through (메시지 등이) 들어오다

83 Why is the cycling class canceled?
(A) A staffing issue
(B) A lack of participants
(C) A scheduling conflict
(D) A maintenance problem

번역 사이클 수업은 왜 취소되었는가?
(A) 직원 채용 문제
(B) 참가자 부족
(C) 일정 충돌
(D) 유지보수 문제

해설 **세부 사항 관련 - 사이클 수업이 취소된 이유**
화자가 초반부에 저녁 8시 사이클 수업이 스튜디오의 조명기구가 떨어져 매달려 있는 관계로 취소되었다(I'm sorry to tell you that the eight P.M. cycling class has been canceled due to a dangling light fixture in the studio)고 말하고 있으므로 정답은 (D)이다.

어휘 participant 참가자 conflict 충돌 maintenance 유지보수

---

84 Why does the speaker say, "there is an aerobics class at 8:15"?
(A) To explain a refusal
(B) To propose an alternative
(C) To complain about a timetable
(D) To request some assistance

번역 화자가 "8시 15분에 에어로빅 수업이 있습니다"라고 말한 이유는?
(A) 거절 의사를 설명하려고
(B) 대안을 제안하려고
(C) 시간표에 대해 불평하려고
(D) 도움을 요청하려고

해설 **화자의 의도 파악 - 8시 15분에 에어로빅 수업이 있다는 말의 의도**
앞에서 화자가 저녁 8시 사이클 수업이 취소되었다(I'm sorry to tell you that the eight P.M. cycling class has been canceled ~)고 말한 뒤 인용문을 언급했고, 이어서 관심이 있는 분들을 위해 알려드리자면 2호실에서 한다(It's in Room Two, for those who are interested)고 했으므로 취소된 사이클 수업에 대한 대안으로 에어로빅 수업을 청자들에게 제안하려는 의도로 한 말임을 알 수 있다. 따라서 정답은 (B)이다.

어휘 refusal 거절 propose 제안하다 alternative 대안 assistance 도움

---

85 What are the listeners asked to check?
(A) A list of rules
(B) A membership card
(C) An electronic device
(D) A floor plan

번역 청자들은 무엇을 확인하라고 요청받았는가?
(A) 규칙 목록
(B) 회원증
(C) 전자 기기
(D) 평면도

해설 **세부 사항 관련 - 청자들이 확인하라고 요청받는 일**
화자가 마지막에 몇 분 후에 스마트폰을 확인하고 쿠폰이 들어왔는지 확인해 볼 것(Check your smartphone in a few minutes to

make sure it has come through)을 요청하고 있으므로 정답은 (C)이다.

> **Paraphrasing**
> 담화의 your smartphone
> → 정답의 An electronic device

86-88 연설

M-Au Good morning. **86 I'd like to start by thanking the distinguished members of the Nayona news media for joining me to hear this important announcement.** **87 Our hospital** has just secured thirty-two million dollars in funding to spend on a major expansion. We will be extending the south wing of the building by one thousand square meters and equipping this space with state-of-the-art medical imaging technology. **88 Once it's finished sometime next year, patients will be able to receive imaging services right here in Nayona instead of traveling hours away.**

좋은 아침입니다. **우선 이 중요한 발표를 듣기 위해 함께해 주신 나요나 뉴스 미디어의 저명한 기자 여러분께 감사 인사를 전하고 싶습니다. 저희 병원은** 대규모 확장에 쓸 자금으로 3,200만 달러를 확보했습니다. 건물의 남관을 1,000제곱미터만큼 확장하고 이 공간을 최첨단 의료 영상 기술 장비로 채울 예정입니다. 내년 중에 이 공사가 끝나면 환자들은 몇 시간 떨어진 곳으로 이동하는 대신 바로 이곳 나요나에서 영상 서비스를 받을 수 있을 겁니다.

어휘 distinguished 저명한 secure 확보하다 expansion 확장 extend 확장하다 equip 장비를 갖추다 state-of-the-art 최첨단의 medical imaging technology 의료 영상 기술 patient 환자

---

86 Where is the speech most likely being given?
(A) At a trade show
(B) At a press conference
(C) At a shareholder meeting
(D) At a welcome reception

번역 이 연설은 어디서 진행되고 있겠는가?
(A) 무역 박람회에서
(B) 기자 회견에서
(C) 주주 총회에서
(D) 환영회에서

해설 **전체 내용 관련 - 연설의 진행 장소**
화자가 초반부에서 이 중요한 발표를 듣기 위해 함께해 주신 나요나 뉴스 미디어의 저명한 기자 여러분께 감사 인사를 전하고 싶다(I'd like to start by thanking the distinguished members of the Nayona news media for joining me to hear this important announcement)고 말하는 것으로 보아 연설의 장소는 기자 회견임을 알 수 있다. 따라서 정답은 (B)이다.

87 What industry does the speaker most likely work in?
(A) Law
(B) Energy
(C) Health care
(D) Technology

번역 화자는 어떤 업계에 종사하겠는가?
(A) 법률
(B) 에너지
(C) 의료 서비스
(D) 기술

해설 **전체 내용 관련 - 화자의 근무 업계**
화자가 중반부에서 저희 병원(Our hospital)이라고 했으므로 화자는 의료 업계에 종사하고 있다는 것을 알 수 있다. 따라서 정답은 (C)이다.

> **Paraphrasing**
> 담화의 hospital → 정답의 Health care

88 What will the speaker's business do next year?
(A) Begin offering new services
(B) Acquire one of its competitors
(C) Conduct some market research
(D) Discontinue an employee program

번역 화자의 사업체는 내년에 무엇을 할 것인가?
(A) 신규 서비스 제공을 시작할 것이다.
(B) 경쟁업체 중 하나를 인수할 것이다.
(C) 시장 조사를 실시할 것이다.
(D) 직원 프로그램을 중단할 것이다.

해설 **세부 사항 관련 - 화자의 사업체가 내년에 할 일**
화자가 마지막에 내년 중에 이 공사가 끝나면 환자들은 몇 시간 떨어진 곳으로 이동하는 대신 바로 이곳 나요나에서 영상 서비스를 받을 수 있을 것(Once it's finished sometime next year, patients will be able to receive imaging services right here in Nayona instead of traveling hours away)이라고 말하고 있으므로 정답은 (A)이다.

어휘 acquire 획득하다 competitor 경쟁업체 conduct 실시하다 discontinue 중단하다

89-91 공지

M-Cn **89 Management has decided that our performance review process this year will include peer evaluations.** So instead of just receiving a review from your manager, you'll also exchange evaluations with several coworkers. We hope this will give everyone a fuller understanding of their strengths and areas for improvement. However, the effectiveness of the system does depend on the quality of the feedback given, **90 so please be**

honest in your reviews. Uh, each employee will be allowed to choose their peer reviewers. **91 We'll be issuing the selection guidelines soon** so that you can start thinking about your choices.

경영진은 올해 업무 평가 절차에 동료 평가를 포함하기로 결정했습니다. 따라서 관리자에게만 평가를 받는 것이 아니라 여러 명의 동료와 평가를 교환하게 될 겁니다. 이것이 모두에게 각자의 강점과 개선이 필요한 영역을 더 잘 이해하도록 해주리라 기대합니다. 하지만 이 시스템의 효과는 주어지는 피드백의 질에 달려 있는 만큼 **평가에 솔직해 주시기 바랍니다.** 음, 모든 직원은 동료 평가자를 선택할 수 있을 겁니다. 여러분이 선택에 대한 고민을 시작할 수 있도록 **선택 관련 지침을 곧 발표할 예정입니다.**

어휘 management 경영진 decide 결정하다 performance review 업무 평가 include 포함하다 peer 동료 evaluation 평가 exchange 교환하다 coworker 동료 strength 강점 improvement 향상 effectiveness 효과 depend on ~에 달려 있다 quality 품질 honest 정직한 selection 선택

89 What is the announcement about?
(A) The arrival of new workers
(B) A change in a company practice
(C) The customer reviews for a product
(D) A decision about the yearly budget

번역 공지는 무엇에 관한 것인가?
(A) 신입 직원들의 도착
(B) 회사 관행의 변화
(C) 제품에 대한 고객 평가
(D) 연간 예산에 관한 결정

해설 **전체 내용 관련 - 공지의 주제**
화자가 초반부에 경영진은 올해 업무 평가 절차에 동료 평가를 포함하기로 결정했다(Management has decided that our performance review process this year will include peer evaluations)며 회사의 업무 평가 절차에 변화가 생겼다는 것을 알려주고 있으므로 정답은 (B)이다.

어휘 practice 관행 decision 결정 yearly 연간의 budget 예산

90 What does the speaker encourage the listeners to do?
(A) Take detailed notes
(B) Volunteer for an event
(C) Speak to their managers
(D) Give honest feedback

번역 화자는 청자들에게 무엇을 하라고 장려하는가?
(A) 상세히 기록하기
(B) 행사에 자원하기
(C) 관리자들에게 말하기
(D) 솔직한 피드백 주기

해설 **세부 사항 관련 - 화자가 권장하는 것**
화자가 중반부에 평가에 솔직해 주기 바란다(Please be honest in

your reviews)며 솔직한 평가를 권장하고 있으므로 정답은 (D)이다.

어휘 volunteer 자원하다

> **Paraphrasing**
> 담화의 be honest in your reviews
> → 정답의 Give honest feedback

91 What does the company plan to do soon?
(A) Reorganize a space
(B) Conduct some testing
(C) Send out some guidelines
(D) Finalize a schedule

번역 회사는 곧 무엇을 할 계획인가?
(A) 공간 재구성하기
(B) 테스트 실시하기
(C) 지침 보내기
(D) 일정 확정하기

해설 **세부 사항 관련 - 회사가 계획하는 일**
화자가 마지막에 선택 관련 지침을 곧 발표할 예정(We'll be issuing the selection guidelines soon)이라고 했으므로 정답은 (C)이다.

어휘 reorganize 재편성하다　send out 보내다　finalize 마무리 짓다

> **Paraphrasing**
> 담화의 issuing the selection guidelines
> → 정답의 Send out some guidelines

92-94 회의 발췌

> W-Br　At last week's meeting we determined that our second store will have the same layout as our first. Since then, **92 I've secured supply contracts for most of the merchandise it will stock, including the plants, gardening tools, and soil.** I've also been looking into display racks and similar items, but an issue has come up there. For branding purposes, it would be good for the product category signs to look the same as those at our first store. **93 However, we've received complaints that those signs are hard to read. 94 I think we should have our new print shop draw up some alternatives.** Don't worry—I'll make sure they know that the new location is supposed to open next month.

지난주 회의 때 우리는 2호점을 1호점과 똑같은 배치로 하기로 결정했습니다. 그 후로 저는 **2호점에서 보유할 식물, 원예용 도구, 흙을 비롯한 대부분의 상품을 위한 공급 계약을 확보했습니다.** 또한 진열대와 비슷한 물건들도 찾는 중입니다만, 거기서 문제가 생겼습니다. 브랜딩 목적에서는 제품 카테고리 표지판이 1호점에 있는 것과 동일해 보이면 좋을 것 같습니다. **하지만 그동안 그 표지판이 읽기 어렵다는 불평을 받아왔어요. 아무래도 새 인쇄소에서 대체할 것을 제작하도록 해야 할 것 같아요.** 걱정 마세요. 꼭 전달할게요. 새 지점이 다음 달에 개업할 예정이라고요.

어휘 determine 결정하다　layout 배치　secure 확보하다　supply 공급　contract 계약서　merchandise 상품　stock 재고를 갖추다　gardening tool 원예용 도구　soil 흙　display rack 진열대　come up 발생하다　purpose 목적　sign 표지판　complaint 불평, 불만　draw up 만들다　alternative 대안

92 Where do the listeners most likely work?
(A) At a garden center
(B) At a real estate firm
(C) At a car-rental company
(D) At a grocery store

번역 청자들은 어디서 일하겠는가?
(A) 원예용품점
(B) 부동산 회사
(C) 렌터카 회사
(D) 식료품점

해설 **전체 내용 관련 - 청자들의 근무지**
화자가 초반부에 2호점에서 보유할 식물, 원예용 도구, 흙을 비롯한 대부분의 상품을 위한 공급 계약을 확보했다(I've secured supply contracts for most of the merchandise it will stock, including the plants, gardening tools, and soil)고 말하고 있는 것으로 보아 청자들의 근무 장소는 원예용품점임을 알 수 있다. 따라서 정답은 (A)이다.

어휘 real estate 부동산　grocery 식료품

93 What has the business received complaints about?
(A) The availability of its inventory
(B) The design of its signage
(C) The length of its operating hours
(D) The restrictions of its loyalty program

번역 이 사업체는 무엇에 대해 불평을 받아왔는가?
(A) 재고의 가용성
(B) 표지판의 디자인
(C) 운영 시간의 길이
(D) 충성 고객 프로그램의 제한

해설 **세부 사항 관련 - 사업체가 받은 불평 사항**
화자가 중반부에 그동안 그 표지판이 읽기 어렵다는 불평을 받아왔다(we've received complaints that those signs are hard to read)고 했으므로 정답은 (B)이다.

어휘 availability 가용성　inventory 재고　signage 간판　operating hour 운영 시간　restriction 제한　loyalty program 충성 고객 프로그램

> **Paraphrasing**
> 담화의 signs → 정답의 signage

94 What does the speaker mean when she says, "the new location is supposed to open next month"?
(A) A business is doing well.
(B) Some staff members will be busy.
(C) An announcement should be made later.
(D) Some work should be completed quickly.

번역 화자가 "새 지점이 다음 달에 개업할 예정이라고요"라고 말할 때, 그 의도는 무엇인가?
(A) 사업이 잘되고 있다.
(B) 일부 직원이 바쁠 것이다.
(C) 공지를 나중에 해야 한다.
(D) 일이 빨리 완료되어야 한다.

해설 **화자의 의도 파악 - 새 지점이 다음 달에 개업할 예정이라는 말의 의도**
앞에서 아무래도 새 인쇄소에서 대체할 것을 제작하도록 해야 할 것 같다(I think we should have our new print shop draw up some alternatives)고 하면서 걱정 말라(Don't worry)고 한 뒤 인용문을 언급한 것으로 보아, 새 지점이 다음 달에 개업하기 전에 표지판 제작을 빨리 완료해야 한다는 의도로 한 말임을 알 수 있다. 따라서 정답은 (D)이다.

어휘 complete 완료하다 quickly 빨리

95-97 회의 발췌 + 막대 그래프

M-Cn At today's staff meeting, **95 I'd like to inform you about a few changes we'll be making here at the Worley Theater**. First, **96 we will be renovating a section of the north wing in October.** That will make space for a small coffee shop. Second, please check out this chart of our sales in the gift shop last month. Now, we've just started selling T-shirts, and those are doing well. But take a look at this item—**97 we only sold fifteen last month. So, 97 I'd like to take some time now to discuss it further**, as we either need to improve its sales or possibly replace it with something else.

오늘 직원회의에서는 이곳 월리 극장에서 우리가 시행할 몇 가지 변경 사항에 대해 알려드리고자 합니다. 먼저, 10월에는 북관의 일부를 개조할 겁니다. 그러면 작은 커피숍을 위한 공간이 생길 겁니다. 두 번째로, 지난달 기념품점의 매출 차트를 확인해 보세요. 자, 우리는 이제 막 티셔츠를 팔기 시작했는데, 판매가 잘되고 있습니다. 하지만 이 물품을 보세요. 지난달에 15개밖에 팔지 못했습니다. 그래서, 지금 시간을 내어 이 문제를 좀 더 논의하고 싶습니다. 판매량을 늘리든지, 아니면 다른 것으로 대체해야 하니까요.

어휘 inform 알리다 renovate 개조하다 wing 부속 건물 chart 도표, 그래프 gift shop 기념품점 improve 향상시키다 replace 교체하다

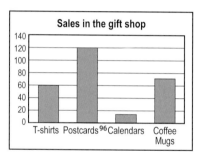

Sales in the gift shop

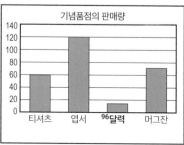

기념품점의 판매량

95 Who most likely is the speaker?
(A) An interior designer
(B) A coffee shop owner
(C) A graphic artist
(D) A theater manager

번역 화자는 누구이겠는가?
(A) 실내 디자이너
(B) 커피숍 주인
(C) 그래픽 디자이너
(D) 극장 관리자

해설 **전체 내용 관련 - 화자의 직업**
화자가 도입부에 오늘 직원회의에서는 이곳 월리 극장에서 우리가 시행할 몇 가지 변경 사항에 대해 알리고자 한다(I'd like to inform you about a few changes we'll be making here at the Worley Theater)고 말하는 것으로 보아 화자는 극장 관리자일 가능성이 높다. 따라서 정답은 (D)이다.

96 What will take place in October?
(A) An annual community festival
(B) A building renovation project
(C) An official press conference
(D) An employee sales contest

번역 10월에는 무슨 일이 일어나겠는가?
(A) 연례 지역 축제
(B) 건축 보수 공사
(C) 공식 기자 회견
(D) 직원 판매 경연 대회

해설 **세부 사항 관련 - 10월에 일어날 일**
화자가 초반부에서 10월에는 북관의 일부를 개조할 것(we will be renovating a section of the north wing in October)이라고 말하고 있으므로 정답은 (B)이다.

어휘 annual 연례의 renovation 보수 공사 official 공식적인
press conference 기자 회견

> **Paraphrasing**
> 담화의 renovating a section of the north wing
> → 정답의 A building renovation project

97 Look at the graphic. Which type of item does the
speaker want to discuss further?
(A) T-shirts
(B) Postcards
(C) Calendars
(D) Coffee mugs

번역 시각 정보에 의하면, 화자는 어떤 유형의 물품에 대해 좀 더 논의하기
를 원하는가?
(A) 티셔츠
(B) 엽서
(C) 달력
(D) 머그잔

해설 **시각 정보 연계 - 화자가 더 논의하기를 원하는 물품**
화자가 후반부에 지난달에 15개밖에 팔지 못했다(we only sold
fifteen last month)면서 지금 시간을 내어 이 문제를 좀 더 논
의하고 싶다(I'd like to take some time now to discuss it
further)고 했고, 그래프에 따르면 달력(Calendars)이 15개이므로
정답은 (C)이다.

98-100 담화+지도

> W-Br Hi, everyone. I'm Joyce McGuire, and **98 I'm
> so excited to be leading today's excursion for
> Whiterose Travel.** Blakely is a charming town, and
> we'll see some incredible views of the coast on the
> train ride over. Now, I have your tickets, so you can
> just look around the train station until it's time to
> board. At 8:50, **99 let's meet in that corner between
> the platforms entrance and the café.** Oh, and there
> might be a slight change to our itinerary if this
> rain doesn't stop. **100 I'll pull up the forecast on my
> mobile phone now,** so that I can let you know when
> we meet up again.

> 안녕하세요, 여러분. 저는 조이스 맥과이어입니다. **화이트로즈 여행사
> 의 오늘 관광을 인솔하게 되어 매우 설렙니다.** 블레이클리는 매력적인
> 도시이며 우리는 기차를 타고 가면서 해안의 멋진 풍경을 보시게 될 겁
> 니다. 자, 이제 여러분의 표는 제가 가지고 있으니 탑승 시각이 될 때까
> 지 기차역을 구경하시면 됩니다. 8시 50분에 **승강장 입구와 카페 사이
> 에 있는 저 모퉁이에서 모일게요.** 아, 그리고 비가 그치지 않는다면 일
> 정에 약간의 변화가 있을 수 있습니다. **지금 제 휴대전화에서 일기예보
> 를 열어볼게요.** 다시 만날 때 알려드릴 수 있도록요.

어휘 lead 이끌다 excursion 짧은 여행 charming 매력적인
incredible 놀라운, 멋진 coast 해안 look around 구경하다
board 탑승하다 platform 승강장 entrance 입구 slight
약간의 itinerary 여정 pull up 화면에 띄우다 forecast 예보

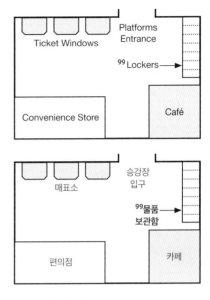

98 Who most likely is the speaker?
(A) A ticket agent
(B) A tour guide
(C) A train conductor
(D) A maintenance supervisor

번역 화자는 누구이겠는가?
(A) 매표원
(B) 여행 가이드
(C) 열차 승무원
(D) 유지보수 관리자

해설 **전체 내용 관련 - 화자의 직업**
화자가 초반부에서 화이트로즈 여행사의 오늘 관광을 인솔하게 되어
매우 설렌다(I'm so excited to be leading today's excursion
for Whiterose Travel)고 말하는 것으로 보아 화자는 여행 가이드
라는 것을 알 수 있다. 따라서 정답은 (B)이다.

어휘 conductor (버스나 기차의) 승무원 maintenance 유지보수
supervisor 감독관, 관리자

---

99 Look at the graphic. What will the listeners meet
in front of?
(A) The ticket windows
(B) The lockers
(C) The convenience store
(D) The café

번역 시각 정보에 의하면, 청자들은 어느 곳 앞에서 만날 것인가?
(A) 매표소
(B) 물품 보관함
(C) 편의점
(D) 카페

해설 **시각 정보 연계 - 청자들이 만날 장소**
화자가 중반부에 승강장 입구와 카페 사이에 있는 저 모퉁이에서 모일 것(let's meet in that corner between the platforms entrance and the café)을 제안하고 있으며, 지도를 보면 승강장 입구와 카페 사이에는 물품 보관함(locker)이 위치해 있으므로 정답은 (B)이다.

---

100 What will the speaker do next?
(A) Post a written notice
(B) Check a weather forecast
(C) Distribute an itinerary
(D) Make a phone call

번역 화자는 다음으로 무엇을 할 것인가?
(A) 서면 공지문 게시하기
(B) 일기예보 확인하기
(C) 여행일정표 나눠주기
(D) 전화 걸기

해설 **세부 사항 관련 - 화자가 다음에 할 일**
화자가 마지막에 지금 제 휴대전화에서 일기예보를 열어보겠다(I'll pull up the forecast on my mobile phone now)고 말하고 있으므로 정답은 (B)이다.

어휘 post 게시하다   distribute 나눠주다

> **Paraphrasing**
> 담화의 pull up the forecast on my mobile
> → 정답의 Check a weather forecast

TEST 10

1 (C)	2 (D)	3 (B)	4 (A)	5 (C)
6 (A)	7 (A)	8 (C)	9 (B)	10 (C)
11 (A)	12 (A)	13 (B)	14 (A)	15 (C)
16 (B)	17 (A)	18 (B)	19 (A)	20 (B)
21 (C)	22 (C)	23 (B)	24 (A)	25 (C)
26 (B)	27 (B)	28 (C)	29 (B)	30 (A)
31 (C)	32 (D)	33 (C)	34 (B)	35 (C)
36 (B)	37 (A)	38 (C)	39 (C)	40 (A)
41 (B)	42 (D)	43 (C)	44 (C)	45 (B)
46 (A)	47 (A)	48 (D)	49 (D)	50 (C)
51 (A)	52 (B)	53 (A)	54 (D)	55 (A)
56 (B)	57 (A)	58 (D)	59 (C)	60 (A)
61 (B)	62 (D)	63 (B)	64 (B)	65 (A)
66 (A)	67 (B)	68 (A)	69 (B)	70 (B)
71 (C)	72 (B)	73 (A)	74 (D)	75 (B)
76 (C)	77 (D)	78 (B)	79 (C)	80 (C)
81 (D)	82 (A)	83 (C)	84 (D)	85 (A)
86 (D)	87 (C)	88 (D)	89 (A)	90 (A)
91 (D)	92 (D)	93 (A)	94 (B)	95 (B)
96 (B)	97 (C)	98 (C)	99 (B)	100 (B)

PART 1

1

M-Cn

(A) One of the men is sawing some boards.
(B) One of the men is putting the lid on a bucket.
(C) The men are laying a piece of flooring.
(D) Some window glass is leaning against a wall.

번역 (A) 남자들 중 한 명이 판자를 톱으로 자르고 있다.
(B) 남자들 중 한 명이 양동이 뚜껑을 닫고 있다.
(C) 남자들이 바닥재를 깔고 있다.
(D) 창유리가 벽에 세워져 있다.

해설 **2인 이상 등장 사진**
(A) 동사 오답. 판자를 톱으로 자르고 있는 남자의 모습이 보이지 않는다.
(B) 동사 오답. 양동이 뚜껑을 닫고 있는 남자의 모습이 보이지 않는다.
(C) 정답. 남자들이 바닥재를 깔고 있는 모습이므로 정답이다.
(D) 동사 오답. 창유리가 벽에 세워져 있는 모습이 아니다.

어휘 saw 톱질하다   put the lid on ~의 뚜껑을 닫다   lay 깔다
flooring 바닥재   lean 기대 놓다

2

W-Br

(A) She's switching off a machine.
(B) She's cutting some fabric with scissors.
(C) She's measuring a table.
(D) She's making clothing in a workroom.

번역 (A) 여자가 기계의 전원을 끄고 있다.
(B) 여자가 가위로 직물을 자르고 있다.
(C) 여자가 탁자의 치수를 재고 있다.
(D) 여자가 작업실에서 옷을 만들고 있다.

해설 **1인 등장 사진**
(A) 동사 오답. 여자가 기계의 전원을 끄고 있는 모습이 아니다.
(B) 동사 오답. 여자가 가위로 직물을 자르고 있는 모습이 아니다.
(C) 동사 오답. 여자가 탁자가 아니라 직물의 치수를 재고 있는 모습이다.
(D) 정답. 여자가 작업실에서 옷을 만들고 있으므로 정답이다.

어휘 switch off 전원을 끄다   fabric 직물, 천   measure 측정하다
workroom 작업실

3

M-Au

(A) One of the women is using some medical equipment.
(B) The women are across the desk from each other.
(C) One of the women is taking a clipboard from a shelf.
(D) The women are shaking hands.

번역 (A) 여자들 중 한 명이 의료 장비를 사용하고 있다.
(B) 여자들이 책상을 사이에 두고 마주 앉아 있다.
(C) 여자들 중 한 명이 선반에서 클립보드를 꺼내고 있다.
(D) 여자들이 악수를 하고 있다.

해설 **2인 이상 등장 사진**
(A) 동사 오답. 의료 장비를 사용하고 있는 여자의 모습이 보이지 않는다.
(B) 정답. 여자들이 책상을 사이에 두고 마주 앉아 있는 모습이므로 정답이다.
(C) 동사 오답. 선반에서 클립보드를 꺼내고 있는 여자의 모습이 보이지 않는다.
(D) 동사 오답. 여자들이 악수를 하고 있는 모습이 아니다.

어휘 medical equipment 의료 장비   clipboard 클립보드   shake
hands 악수하다

4

W-Am

(A) Some loose papers are covering part of a keyboard.
(B) A phone cord is being connected.
(C) Some computer monitors are being repositioned.
(D) A partition is set up next to a workstation.

번역 **(A) 낱장으로 된 종이들이 키보드의 일부분을 덮고 있다.**
(B) 전화선이 연결되는 중이다.
(C) 컴퓨터 모니터들이 옮겨지는 중이다.
(D) 사무 공간 옆에 칸막이가 설치되어 있다.

해설 **사람/사물·풍경 혼합 사진**
(A) 정답. 낱장으로 된 종이들이 키보드의 일부분을 덮고 있는 모습이 므로 정답이다.
(B) 동사 오답. 전화선이 연결되고 있는 모습이 아니다.
(C) 동사 오답. 컴퓨터 모니터들이 옮겨지고 있는 모습이 아니다.
(D) 사진에 없는 명사. 사진에 칸막이가 보이지 않는다.

어휘 loose 묶여 있지 않은 cover 덮다 connect 연결하다
reposition 위치를 바꾸다 partition 칸막이 workstation
사무 공간

5

W-Br

(A) The man is photographing a city skyline.
(B) The woman is unfolding a tourist map.
(C) The woman is gesturing toward some buildings.
(D) The man is grasping the straps of his backpack.

번역 (A) 남자가 도시 스카이라인을 사진 찍고 있다.
(B) 여자가 관광 지도를 펼치고 있다.
(C) 여자가 손짓으로 어떤 건물들을 가리키고 있다.
(D) 남자가 배낭의 끈을 움켜잡고 있다.

해설 **2인 이상 등장 사진**
(A) 동사 오답. 남자가 도시 스카이라인을 사진 찍고 있는 모습이 아니다.
(B) 동사 오답. 여자가 관광 지도를 펼치고 있는 모습이 아니다.
(C) 정답. 여자가 손짓으로 어떤 건물들을 가리키고 있는 모습이므로 정답이다.
(D) 동사 오답. 남자가 배낭의 끈을 움켜잡고 있는 모습이 아니다.

어휘 unfold 펼치다 gesture 손짓[몸짓]으로 가리키다 grasp
움켜잡다 strap 끈

6

M-Cn

(A) Some statues have been placed in a park.
(B) A stone staircase has been built by a bridge.
(C) A trash bin is being emptied.
(D) Some decorations have been hung from trees.

번역 **(A) 공원에 조각상들이 놓여 있다.**
(B) 다리 옆에 돌계단이 지어져 있다.
(C) 쓰레기통이 비워지고 있다.
(D) 나무에 장식품들이 매달려 있다.

해설 **사물·풍경 사진**
(A) 정답. 공원에 조각상들이 놓여 있으므로 정답이다.
(B) 사진에 없는 명사. 사진에 다리가 보이지 않는다.
(C) 동사 오답. 쓰레기통이 비워지고 있는 모습이 아니다.
(D) 사진에 없는 명사. 나무에 매달려 있는 장식품들이 보이지 않는다.

어휘 statue 조각상 staircase 계단 empty 비우다 decoration
장식품

PART 2

7

W-Am When does your flight leave?
M-Au (A) About four hours from now.
(B) From the international terminal.
(C) On a direct flight.

번역 당신의 비행기는 언제 출발하나요?
(A) 약 4시간 후예요.
(B) 국제선 터미널에서요.
(C) 직항편으로요.

해설 **When 의문문**
(A) 정답. 비행기 출발 시간을 묻는 질문에 약 4시간 후라고 응답하고 있으므로 정답이다.
(B) 연상 오답. 질문의 flight에서 연상 가능한 international terminal 을 이용한 오답이다.
(C) 단어 반복 오답. 질문의 flight을 반복 이용한 오답이다.

어휘 leave 떠나다, 출발하다 direct flight 직항편

8

M-Cn How much do you charge for carpet cleaning?
W-Am (A) At least twice a year.
(B) There are mud stains near the entrance.
(C) It depends on the size of the space.

번역　카펫 청소 비용으로 얼마를 청구하시나요?
(A) 적어도 일 년에 두 번이요.
(B) 입구 근처에 진흙 얼룩들이 있어요.
(C) 공간의 크기에 따라 달라요.

해설　**How+형용사/부사 의문문**
(A) 질문과 상관없는 오답. How often 의문문에 대한 응답이므로 오답이다.
(B) 연상 오답. 질문의 cleaning에서 연상 가능한 stains를 이용한 오답이다.
(C) 정답. 카펫 청소 청구 비용을 묻는 질문에 공간의 크기에 따라 다르다며 바로 대답해줄 수 없음을 우회적으로 알려 주고 있으므로 정답이다.

어휘　charge for ~에 대한 요금을 청구하다　mud 진흙　stain 얼룩
depend on ~에 달려 있다, ~에 따라 다르다

9

M-Au　Do you want to try those shoes on?
W-Br　(A) An upcoming hike.
(B) No, I'm just looking.
(C) I'll have the lunch special.

번역　저 신발을 신어보시겠습니까?
(A) 곧 있을 등산이요.
(B) 아니요, 그냥 보는 중이에요.
(C) 저는 점심 특선으로 할게요.

해설　**조동사(Do) 의문문**
(A) 연상 오답. 질문의 shoes에서 연상 가능한 hike를 이용한 오답이다.
(B) 정답. 신발을 신어볼지 묻는 질문에 아니요(No)라고 대답한 뒤, 그냥 보는 중이라며 부정 답변과 일관된 내용을 덧붙이고 있으므로 정답이다.
(C) 질문과 상관없는 오답.

어휘　upcoming 다가오는

10

M-Cn　Who can I talk to about home financing?
W-Br　(A) No, I don't have a finance degree.
(B) Very competitive interest rates.
(C) One of our loan officers.

번역　주택 금융에 대해서는 누구와 이야기할 수 있을까요?
(A) 아니요, 저는 재무학 학위가 없습니다.
(B) 매우 경쟁력 있는 이자율이요.
(C) 저희 대출 담당 직원 중 한 명이요.

해설　**Who 의문문**
(A) Yes/No 불가 오답. Who 의문문에는 Yes/No 응답이 불가능하므로 오답이다.
(B) 연상 오답. 질문의 home financing에서 연상 가능한 interest rates를 이용한 오답이다.
(C) 정답. 주택 금융에 대해서 이야기할 대상을 묻는 질문에 대출 담당 직원 중 한 명이라고 구체적으로 알려 주고 있으므로 정답이다.

어휘　home financing 주택 금융　finance 재무학　degree 학위
competitive 경쟁력 있는　interest rate 이자율　loan 대출

11

W-Am　What should I do with these bottles of water?
M-Cn　(A) Put one in front of each chair.
(B) A decorative water fountain.
(C) That's OK—these plants are fake.

번역　이 물병들을 어떻게 해야 할까요?
(A) 모든 의자 앞에 하나씩 놓으세요.
(B) 장식용 분수요.
(C) 괜찮아요. 이 식물들은 모조품이에요.

해설　**What 의문문**
(A) 정답. 물병들을 어떻게 해야 하는지 묻는 질문에 모든 의자 앞에 하나씩 놓으라고 구체적으로 알려 주고 있으므로 정답이다.
(B) 단어 반복 오답. 질문의 water를 반복 이용한 오답이다.
(C) 단어 반복 오답. 질문의 these를 반복 이용한 오답이다.

어휘　decorative 장식용의　fountain 분수　fake 가짜의

12

W-Br　How was the basketball game?
M-Cn　(A) I see why it's such a popular sport.
(B) The outdoor courts at Campbell Park.
(C) That sounds fun, thanks.

번역　농구 경기는 어땠어요?
(A) 그게 왜 그렇게 인기가 많은 스포츠인지 알겠더라고요.
(B) 캠벨 공원에 있는 야외 코트요.
(C) 재미있겠네요, 감사합니다.

해설　**How 의문문**
(A) 정답. 농구 경기가 어땠는지 묻는 질문에 그게 왜 그렇게 인기가 많은 스포츠인지 알겠더라며 긍정적인 반응을 간접적으로 제시하고 있으므로 정답이다.
(B) 연상 오답. 질문의 basketball game에서 연상 가능한 outdoor courts를 이용한 오답이다.
(C) 연상 오답. 질문의 game에서 연상 가능한 fun을 이용한 오답이다.

어휘　popular 인기 있는　court (테니스 등을 하는) 코트

13

W-Br　The conference runs through Sunday, doesn't it?
W-Am　(A) The organizing committee.
(B) No, it ends on Saturday.
(C) I prefer cycling to running.

번역　그 컨퍼런스는 일요일까지 계속 열리죠, 그렇지 않나요?
(A) 조직 위원회요.
(B) 아니요, 토요일에 끝나요.
(C) 저는 달리기보다 자전거 타기가 더 좋아요.

해설　**부가 의문문**
(A) 연상 오답. 질문의 conference에서 연상 가능한 organizing committee를 이용한 오답이다.
(B) 정답. 회의가 일요일까지 계속 열리는지 확인하는 질문에 아니요(No)라고 대답한 뒤, 토요일에 끝난다며 부정 답변과 일관된 내용을 덧붙이고 있으므로 정답이다.
(C) 유사 발음 오답. 질문의 runs와 부분적으로 발음이 유사한 running을 이용한 오답이다.

어휘 organizing committee 조직 위원회 prefer A to B B보다 A를
선호하다

14

W-Br Why is the elevator blocked off?
M-Cn (A) For some maintenance work.
(B) On the eleventh floor.
(C) Sorry, it's farther than I thought.

번역 승강기가 왜 막혀 있나요?
(A) 유지보수 작업 때문에요.
(B) 11층에요.
(C) 죄송합니다, 제가 생각했던 것보다 머네요.

해설 Why 의문문
(A) 정답. 승강기가 막혀 있는 이유를 묻는 질문에 유지보수 작업 때문
이라고 구체적인 이유를 제시하고 있으므로 정답이다.
(B) 연상 오답. 질문의 elevator에서 연상 가능한 eleventh floor를
이용한 오답이다.
(C) 질문과 상관없는 오답.

어휘 block off 막다, 차단하다 maintenance 유지보수 farther
(공간·시간상으로) 더 먼

15

W-Am Where can I buy a pair of wireless headphones?
M-Au (A) I get my produce at the farmers market.
(B) She usually calls my mobile phone.
(C) Jameson Electronics sells them.

번역 어디서 무선 헤드폰을 살 수 있나요?
(A) 저는 농산물 직판장에서 농산물을 사요.
(B) 그녀는 보통 제 휴대전화로 전화를 걸어요.
(C) 제임슨 전자에서 판매해요.

해설 Where 의문문
(A) 연상 오답. 질문의 buy에서 연상 가능한 market을 이용한 오답
이다.
(B) 유사 발음 오답. 질문의 headphones와 부분적으로 발음이 유
사한 mobile phone을 이용한 오답이다.
(C) 정답. 무선 헤드폰을 살 수 있는 곳을 묻는 질문에 제임슨 전자에
서 판매한다며 구체적인 장소를 알려 주고 있으므로 정답이다.

어휘 wireless 무선의 produce 농산물 farmer 농부

16

M-Cn I can just submit my expense report next week,
right?
W-Am (A) I can save a couple for you.
(B) Yes, but your reimbursement will take longer.
(C) No, it's going to be on your left.

번역 지출 보고서 다음 주에 제출해도 되죠, 맞죠?
(A) 제가 당신을 위해 두어 개 챙겨둘 수 있어요.
(B) 네, 하지만 환급에 시간이 더 걸릴 거예요.
(C) 아니요, 당신의 왼쪽에 있을 거예요.

해설 부가 의문문
(A) 연상 오답. 질문의 expense에서 연상 가능한 save를 이용한 오
답이다.
(B) 정답. 지출 보고서를 다음 주에 제출해도 되는지 확인하는 질문에
네(Yes)라고 대답한 뒤, 하지만 환급에 시간이 더 걸릴 거라며 긍
정 답변과 일관된 내용을 덧붙였으므로 정답이다.
(C) 연상 오답. 질문의 right에서 연상 가능한 left를 이용한 오답이다.

어휘 submit 제출하다 expense 비용, 지출 reimbursement 환급

17

M-Au Are you looking for a part-time or full-time
position?
W-Br (A) I can only work twenty hours per week.
(B) Right, a new physician.
(C) There's a clock on the back wall.

번역 시간제 일자리를 찾고 계세요, 아니면 전일제 일자리를 찾고 계세요?
(A) 저는 주당 20시간만 일할 수 있어요.
(B) 맞아요, 새로 온 내과의사요.
(C) 뒷벽에 시계가 있어요.

해설 선택 의문문
(A) 정답. 시간제와 전일제 중 찾고 있는 일자리를 묻는 질문에 주당
20시간만 일할 수 있다며 우회적으로 시간제를 선택해 응답하고
있으므로 정답이다.
(B) Yes/No 불가 오답. 문장과 문장을 연결하는 경우를 제외하고는
선택 의문문에는 Yes/No 응답이 불가능한데, Right도 일종의
Yes 응답이라고 볼 수 있으므로 오답이다.
(C) 연상 오답. 질문의 time에서 연상 가능한 clock을 이용한 오답이다.

어휘 position 일자리, 직위 physician 내과의사

18

M-Cn Can you help me change my log-on password?
M-Au (A) The corporate account.
(B) Sorry, I have to call a client back.
(C) Don't worry—I'm sure you passed.

번역 제가 접속 암호를 변경하는 걸 도와주실 수 있나요?
(A) 기업 계정이요.
(B) 죄송하지만, 고객에게 회신 전화를 해야 해요.
(C) 걱정하지 마세요. 분명 합격하셨을 거예요.

해설 요청·제안문
(A) 연상 오답. 질문의 password에서 연상 가능한 account를 이
용한 오답이다.
(B) 정답. 접속 암호를 변경하는 걸 도와달라는 요청에 죄송하다
(Sorry)고 사과한 뒤 고객에게 회신 전화를 해야 한다면서 거절
의 이유를 밝히고 있으므로 정답이다.
(C) 유사 발음 오답. 질문의 password와 부분적으로 발음이 유사한
passed를 이용한 오답이다.

어휘 corporate 기업의 pass 합격하다

19

W-Am Why are we being required to use new scheduling software?

M-Au (A) Management hasn't explained the decision yet.
(B) OK, I'll make sure I have the updated version.
(C) The activation code is on the receipt.

번역 우리가 왜 새 일정 소프트웨어를 사용해야 하나요?
(A) 경영진이 아직 그 결정을 설명하지 않았어요.
(B) 알겠습니다, 꼭 최신 버전을 갖고 있을게요.
(C) 활성화 코드는 영수증에 쓰여 있어요.

해설 **Why 의문문**
(A) 정답. 새 일정 소프트웨어를 사용해야 하는 이유를 묻는 질문에 경영진이 아직 그 결정을 설명하지 않아서 알지 못함을 우회적으로 알려 주고 있으므로 정답이다.
(B) Yes/No 불가 오답. Why 의문문에는 Yes/No 응답이 불가능한데, OK도 일종의 Yes 응답이라고 볼 수 있으므로 오답이다.
(C) 연상 오답. 질문의 software에서 연상 가능한 activation code를 이용한 오답이다.

어휘 management 경영진   decision 결정   activation 활성화
receipt 영수증

20

W-Am Which brand makes the best washing machines?

M-Cn (A) No, they're manufactured abroad.
(B) Yeh-Joon is the appliance expert.
(C) The hotel offers laundry services.

번역 어느 브랜드가 가장 좋은 세탁기를 만드나요?
(A) 아니요, 그것들은 해외에서 제조됩니다.
(B) 예준 씨가 가전제품 전문가예요.
(C) 그 호텔은 세탁 서비스를 제공해요.

해설 **Which+명사 의문문**
(A) Yes/No 불가 오답. Which 의문문에는 Yes/No 응답이 불가능하므로 오답이다.
(B) 정답. 가장 좋은 세탁기를 만드는 브랜드를 묻는 질문에 예준 씨가 가전제품 전문가라며 대답해 줄 수 있는 사람을 알려 주고 있으므로 정답이다.
(C) 연상 오답. 질문의 washing machines에서 연상 가능한 laundry를 이용한 오답이다.

어휘 manufacture 제조하다   abroad 해외에서   appliance
가전제품   expert 전문가

21

M-Au Don't you have any apartments available in the next month?

W-Br (A) Yes, she's taking some time off.
(B) On a shelf in the storage room.
(C) No, none of our current leases end that soon.

번역 다음 달에 입주 가능한 아파트 매물은 없으신가요?
(A) 네, 그녀는 휴가 중이에요.
(B) 창고 선반에요.
(C) 없어요, 현재 임대차 계약 중에 그렇게 빨리 끝나는 건 없습니다.

해설 부정 의문문

(A) 질문과 상관없는 오답. 질문에 3인칭 대명사 She로 지칭할 인물이 언급된 적이 없으므로 오답이다.
(B) 질문과 상관없는 오답. Where 의문문에 대한 응답이므로 오답이다.
(C) 정답. 다음 달에 입주 가능한 아파트 매물이 있는지 여부를 묻는 질문에 아니요(No)라고 대답한 뒤, 현재 임대차 계약 중에 그렇게 빨리 끝나는 건 없다며 부정 답변과 일관된 내용을 덧붙이고 있으므로 정답이다.

어휘 take time off 휴가를 내다   storage room 창고   current
현재의   lease 임대차 계약

22

M-Cn I left my umbrella in the taxi!

W-Br (A) The tax isn't included.
(B) He's planning to rent a car.
(C) We have extras at the office.

번역 택시에 우산을 놓고 내렸어요!
(A) 세금은 포함되어 있지 않아요.
(B) 그는 자동차를 대여할 계획이에요.
(C) 사무실에 여분이 있어요.

해설 **사실·정보 전달의 평서문**
(A) 유사 발음 오답. 평서문의 taxi와 부분적으로 발음이 유사한 tax를 이용한 오답이다.
(B) 평서문과 상관없는 오답. 평서문에 3인칭 대명사 He로 지칭할 인물이 언급된 적이 없으므로 오답이다.
(C) 정답. 택시에 우산을 놓고 내렸다는 평서문에 사무실에 여분이 있다며 해결책을 제시하고 있으므로 정답이다.

어휘 umbrella 우산   tax 세금   include 포함하다   extra 여분의 것

23

M-Cn When can we expect the contest winners to be announced?

W-Am (A) A professional announcer.
(B) The judging is in its final stages.
(C) I always bring my own.

번역 경연 대회 수상자는 언제 발표될까요?
(A) 전문 아나운서요.
(B) 심사가 마지막 단계예요.
(C) 저는 언제나 제 것을 가지고 다녀요.

해설 **When 의문문**
(A) 파생어 오답. 질문의 announced와 파생어 관계인 announcer를 이용한 오답이다.
(B) 정답. 경연 대회 수상자의 발표 시점을 묻는 질문에 심사가 마지막 단계라며, 발표까지 시간이 얼마 남지 않았다는 것을 우회적으로 응답하고 있으므로 정답이다.
(C) 질문과 상관없는 오답.

어휘 winner 수상자   professional 전문가의   announcer 아나운서
judging 심사   stage 단계

24

W-Br Where do we put old ink cartridges?

M-Au (A) Tom just left for the recycling center.
       (B) Every three months.
       (C) Sure, you can put in a request.

번역 다 쓴 잉크 카트리지는 어디에 놓아야 하나요?
      (A) 톰이 방금 재활용 센터로 가던데요.
      (B) 3개월마다요.
      (C) 물론이죠, 신청하시면 돼요.

해설 Where 의문문
      (A) 정답. 다 쓴 잉크 카트리지를 버릴 장소를 묻는 질문에 톰이 방금 재활용 센터로 가더라며 재활용 센터에 가서 버려야 함을 간접적으로 알려 주고 있으므로 정답이다.
      (B) 질문과 상관없는 오답. How often 의문문에 대한 응답이므로 오답이다.
      (C) Yes/No 불가 오답. Where 의문문에는 Yes/No 응답이 불가능한데, Sure도 일종의 Yes 응답이라고 볼 수 있으므로 오답이다.

어휘 cartridge 카트리지   recycling 재활용

25

W-Am We should consider replacing our packaging machine.

M-Cn (A) I already printed the welcome packets.
       (B) All of our recyclable waste.
       (C) The repairs are getting more expensive.

번역 우리는 포장 기계 교체를 고려해야 해요.
      (A) 저는 이미 환영 꾸러미를 인쇄했어요.
      (B) 재활용 가능한 쓰레기 전부요.
      (C) 수리 비용이 점점 비싸지고 있어요.

해설 의견·희망 사항의 평서문
      (A) 유사 발음 오답. 평서문의 packaging과 부분적으로 발음이 유사한 packets를 이용한 오답이다.
      (B) 평서문과 상관없는 오답.
      (C) 정답. 포장 기계 교체를 고려해야 한다는 평서문에 수리 비용이 점점 비싸지고 있다며 교체해야 하는 이유를 뒷받침하고 있으므로 정답이다.

어휘 replace 교체하다   packaging machine 포장 기계   welcome packet 환영 꾸러미(신입사원 등에게 제공하는 여러 가지가 담긴 것)   recyclable 재활용 가능한   repair 수리

26

W-Am Will my account be suspended if I use my credit card abroad?

M-Au (A) Have you reactivated your phone service?
       (B) Not if you let us know about your trip in advance.
       (C) You can view your credit card bill on our Web site.

번역 신용카드를 해외에서 사용하면 제 계정이 일시 정지되나요?
      (A) 당신의 전화 서비스를 재개하셨나요?
      (B) 당신의 여행을 미리 알려주신다면 그렇지 않습니다.
      (C) 저희 웹사이트에서 당신의 신용카드 청구서를 조회하실 수 있습니다.

해설 조동사(Will) 의문문
      (A) 연상 오답. 질문의 suspended에서 연상 가능한 reactivated를 이용한 오답이다.
      (B) 정답. 신용카드를 해외에서 사용하면 계정이 일시 정지되는지를 묻는 질문에 여행을 미리 알려준다면 그렇지 않다고 우회적으로 답변하고 있으므로 정답이다.
      (C) 단어 반복 오답. 질문의 credit card를 반복 이용한 오답이다.

어휘 suspend 중단하다   abroad 해외에서   reactivate 재개하다   in advance 미리

27

W-Br Aren't you going to attend the database training?

M-Au (A) The database administrator.
       (B) I missed the registration deadline.
       (C) I thought you didn't like taking the train.

번역 당신은 데이터베이스 교육에 참석 안 하실 건가요?
      (A) 데이터베이스 관리자요.
      (B) 저는 등록 마감 시한을 놓쳤어요.
      (C) 저는 당신이 기차 타는 걸 싫어하는 줄 알았어요.

해설 부정 의문문
      (A) 단어 반복 오답. 질문의 database를 반복 이용한 오답이다.
      (B) 정답. 데이터베이스 교육의 참석 여부를 묻는 질문에 등록 마감 시한을 놓쳤다며 참석할 수 없다는 대답을 우회적으로 표현하고 있으므로 정답이다.
      (C) 유사 발음 오답. 질문의 training과 부분적으로 발음이 유사한 train을 이용한 오답이다.

어휘 attend 참석하다   administrator 관리자   miss 놓치다   registration 등록   deadline 마감 시한

28

W-Br Can you send me the budget proposal for the relocation?

M-Cn (A) The disposable cups cost much less.
       (B) Are there other locations?
       (C) It should be in your inbox.

번역 이전을 위한 예산안을 저에게 보내주실 수 있나요?
      (A) 일회용 컵이 훨씬 저렴해요.
      (B) 다른 장소들이 있나요?
      (C) 당신의 수신함에 있을 거예요.

해설 요청·제안문
      (A) 유사 발음 오답. 질문의 proposal과 부분적으로 발음이 유사한 disposable을 이용한 오답이다.
      (B) 유사 발음 오답. 질문의 relocation과 부분적으로 발음이 유사한 locations를 이용한 오답이다.
      (C) 정답. 이전을 위한 예산안을 보내달라는 요청에 당신의 수신함에 있을 거라며 이미 보냈음을 간접적으로 알려 주고 있으므로 정답이다.

어휘 budget proposal 예산안   relocation 이전   disposable 일회용의   inbox 수신함

29

M-Au Do you want to hold the focus group meetings this week or next week?

W-Am (A) Samples of each product.
(B) There's no reason to wait.
(C) The third-floor conference room.

번역 포커스 그룹 회의를 이번 주에 열까요, 아니면 다음 주에 열까요?
(A) 각 제품의 견본들이요.
(B) 기다릴 이유가 없죠.
(C) 3층 회의실이요.

해설 **선택 의문문**
(A) 연상 오답. 질문의 focus group에서 연상 가능한 Samples를 이용한 오답이다.
(B) 정답. 포커스 그룹 회의를 열 시기를 묻는 질문에 기다릴 이유가 없다며 둘 중 빠른 시일인 이번 주에 여는 것이 낫다는 것을 우회적으로 알려 주고 있으므로 정답이다.
(C) 연상 오답. 질문의 meetings에서 연상 가능한 conference room을 이용한 오답이다.

어휘 focus group 포커스 그룹(시장 조사나 여론 조사를 위해 각 계층을 대표하도록 뽑은 소수의 사람들로 이뤄진 그룹)

30

M-Au Who was the graphic designer for the event T-shirts?

W-Br (A) For the staff or attendees?
(B) We signed the agreement.
(C) That's a lot of exhibitors.

번역 행사 티셔츠를 만든 그래픽 디자이너가 누구였나요?
(A) 직원용이요, 아니면 참석자용이요?
(B) 우리는 계약서에 서명했어요.
(C) 출품자가 정말 많네요.

해설 **Who 의문문**
(A) 정답. 행사 티셔츠를 만든 그래픽 디자이너가 누구인지 묻는 질문에 직원용인지 아니면 참석자용인지 관련된 내용으로 되묻는 응답이므로 정답이다.
(B) 질문과 상관없는 오답.
(C) 연상 오답. 질문의 event에서 연상 가능한 exhibitors를 이용한 오답이다.

어휘 attendee 참석자 agreement 계약서 exhibitor 출품자

31

M-Au It's a long drive to the convention center from here.

W-Am (A) No, it's hosting an award ceremony.
(B) I prefer to save my files to a hard drive.
(C) We can use the time to discuss our presentation.

번역 여기서 컨벤션 센터까지는 차로 한참 가야 하는 거리예요.
(A) 아니요, 시상식이 열리고 있어요.
(B) 저는 파일을 하드디스크 드라이브에 저장하는 걸 선호해요.
(C) 그 시간에 발표에 대해 상의하면 되죠.

해설 **사실·정보 전달의 평서문**
(A) 연상 오답. 평서문의 convention center에서 연상할 수 있는 an award ceremony를 이용한 오답이다.
(B) 단어 반복 오답. 평서문의 drive를 반복 이용한 오답이다.
(C) 정답. 여기서 컨벤션 센터까지는 차로 한참 가야 하는 거리라는 평서문에 그 시간에 발표에 대해 상의하면 된다며 긴 시간을 잘 활용할 수 있는 방법을 제시하고 있으므로 정답이다.

어휘 host 주최하다 award ceremony 시상식 save 저장하다 presentation 발표

PART 3

32-34

M-Cn Hi, there! **[32] I see you're looking at our selection of paints. Would you like some help choosing a product?**

W-Br Yes, thank you. I'm wondering what would be best for the walls in my entryway.

M-Cn I'd recommend semi-gloss paint for that. **[33] It's a good choice for areas with a lot of foot traffic.**

W-Br OK. And roughly how much should I buy?

M-Cn Well, **[34] what would you guess the height and width of your walls are?**

남: 안녕하세요! 저희가 엄선해 놓은 페인트를 보고 계시는군요. 제품 선택에 도움이 필요하신가요?

여: 네, 고맙습니다. 저희 집 현관 벽에 어떤 제품이 가장 좋을지 고민 중이에요.

남: 거기에는 반광택 페인트를 추천해 드립니다. 이 제품은 유동 인구가 많은 구역에 적합한 선택입니다.

여: 알겠습니다. 대략 얼마나 구매해야 할까요?

남: 음, 벽의 높이와 너비를 어느 정도로 짐작하시나요?

어휘 selection 선택된 것들 entryway 현관 semi gloss 반광택 foot traffic 유동 인구 roughly 대략 height 높이 width 너비

32 What most likely is the man's job?
(A) House painter
(B) Interior designer
(C) Real estate agent
(D) Hardware store employee

번역 남자의 직업은 무엇이겠는가?
(A) 주택 페인트공
(B) 실내 디자이너
(C) 부동산 중개인
(D) 철물점 직원

전체 내용 관련 - 남자의 직업

남자가 첫 대사에서 저희가 엄선해 놓은 페인트(our selection of paints)라고 했고 제품 선택에 도움이 필요한지(Would you like some help choosing a product?) 묻는 것을 보아 남자는 철물점 직원이라는 것을 알 수 있다. 따라서 정답은 (D)이다.

어휘 hardware store 철물점

---

33 What does the man say about a type of paint?
(A) It is easy to apply evenly.
(B) It can be used to hide flaws.
(C) It is suitable for busy spaces.
(D) It dries relatively quickly.

번역 남자는 페인트의 한 종류에 대해 뭐라고 말하는가?
(A) 고르게 펴 바르기가 쉽다.
(B) 흠집을 가리는 데 사용될 수 있다.
(C) 혼잡한 공간에 적합하다.
(D) 비교적 빨리 마른다.

해설 세부 사항 관련 - 남자가 페인트의 한 종류에 대해 하는 말

남자가 두 번째 대사에서 이 제품은 유동 인구가 많은 구역에 적합한 선택(It's a good choice for areas with a lot of foot traffic)이라고 말하고 있으므로 정답은 (C)이다.

어휘 apply 바르다 evenly 고르게 hide 숨기다 flaw 흠집
suitable 적합한 relatively 비교적

> **Paraphrasing**
> 대화의 a good choice → 정답의 suitable
> 대화의 areas with a lot of foot traffic
> → 정답의 busy spaces

---

34 What does the man ask the woman to do?
(A) Select a color theme
(B) Estimate some dimensions
(C) Remove furniture from a room
(D) Sign an agreement

번역 남자는 여자에게 무엇을 하라고 요청하는가?
(A) 색상 테마 고르기
(B) 치수 추정하기
(C) 방에서 가구 치우기
(D) 계약서에 서명하기

해설 세부 사항 관련 - 남자의 요청 사항

남자가 마지막 대사에서 벽의 높이와 너비를 어느 정도로 짐작하는지(what would you guess the height and width of your walls are?) 묻고 있으므로 정답은 (B)이다.

어휘 estimate 추정하다 dimension (높이·너비·길이의) 치수
remove 제거하다 furniture 가구 agreement 계약서

> **Paraphrasing**
> 대화의 guess the height and width
> → 정답의 Estimate some dimensions

35-37

M-Au Hi, **35 thank you for visiting Oakley Cinema.** Are you here for the showing of *The Lonely Country*?

W-Br Yes, one ticket, please. I'm a big fan of classic films. **36 It was very exciting to see that article in the *Oakley News* yesterday** about your plan to show them all summer.

M-Au Oh, then **37 you might be interested in our membership program.** For a yearly fee, you can get discounts on tickets and invitations to special screenings.

남: 안녕하세요, **오클리 시네마에 방문해 주셔서 감사합니다.** 〈더 론리 컨트리〉를 보러 오셨나요?

여: 네, 한 장 부탁드립니다. 저는 고전 영화의 열렬한 팬이에요. **어제 <오클리 뉴스>에서** 여름 내내 이 극장에서 고전 영화를 상영할 계획이라는 기사를 보고 너무 반가웠어요.

남: 아, 그럼 **저희 멤버십 프로그램에 관심이 있으실 것 같아요.** 연회비를 내면, 영화표 할인을 받으실 수 있고 특별 상영회 초대권도 받으실 수 있어요.

어휘 showing 영화 상영 a big fan 열렬한 팬 classic film
고전 영화 article 글, 기사 yearly 연간의 invitation
초대, 초대장 screening 상영

---

35 Where are the speakers?
(A) At a radio station
(B) At an art museum
(C) At a movie theater
(D) At a community center

번역 화자들은 어디에 있는가?
(A) 라디오 방송국
(B) 미술관
(C) 영화관
(D) 지역 문화 센터

해설 전체 내용 관련 - 대화의 장소

남자가 첫 대사에서 오클리 시네마에 방문해 주셔서 감사하다(thank you for visiting Oakley Cinema)고 말하고 있으므로 정답은 (C)이다.

> **Paraphrasing**
> 대화의 Cinema → 정답의 a movie theater

---

36 What did the woman do yesterday?
(A) She won a contest.
(B) She read a news article.
(C) She made a reservation.
(D) She requested time off.

번역 여자는 어제 무엇을 했는가?
(A) 경연 대회에서 수상했다.
(B) 뉴스 기사를 읽었다.
(C) 예약을 했다.
(D) 휴가를 신청했다.

해설 **세부 사항 관련 - 여자가 어제 한 일**
여자가 첫 대사에서 어제 <오클리 뉴스>에서 기사를 보고 너무 반가웠다(It was very exciting to see that article in the *Oakley News* yesterday ~)고 말하고 있으므로 정답은 (B)이다.

어휘 make a reservation 예약하다   time off 휴가

> **Paraphrasing**
> 대화의 see that article in the *Oakley News*
> → 정답의 read a news article

---

37 What does the man tell the woman about?
(A) A membership program
(B) A job opening
(C) A building renovation
(D) An anniversary celebration

번역 남자는 여자에게 무엇에 대해 말하는가?
(A) 멤버십 프로그램
(B) 일자리
(C) 건물 보수공사
(D) 기념일 축하 행사

해설 **세부 사항 관련 - 남자가 여자에게 말하는 것**
남자가 마지막 대사에서 저희 멤버십 프로그램에 관심이 있으실 것 같다(you might be interested in our membership program)고 말하고 있으므로 정답은 (A)이다.

어휘 renovation 보수공사

38-40

M-Cn Hello. Would you like to buy a train ticket?

W-Br Actually, I arrived here by train a half hour ago. **38, 39 But now I can't find a taxi to take me across town**. None have come by the station.

M-Cn Yes, that often happens when it rains. **39 Well, there is Wheelo, the ridesharing service.** You just have to download an app.

W-Br Right! OK, it's downloading now.

M-Cn Oh, and you should know that rideshare cars aren't allowed to use the taxi stand.

W-Br **40 Then where should I have the driver meet me?**

M-Cn **40 There's a general drop-off and pickup area in front of the station entrance.**

W-Br I see. Thank you!

남: 안녕하세요. 기차표 구매를 원하십니까?

여: 실은 30분 전에 기차를 타고 여기 도착했는데요. **근데 지금 저를 시내 반대편으로 데려다 줄 택시를 못 찾겠어요.** 역으로 들어오는 택시가 한 대도 없네요.

남: 네, 비가 오면 종종 그래요. **음, 휠로라는 승차 공유 서비스가 있어요. 앱을 내려받기만 하시면 돼요.**

여: 그렇군요! 알겠습니다, 지금 받는 중이에요.

남: 아, 그리고 승차 공유 차량은 택시 승차장을 사용할 수 없다는 점을 알아두세요.

여: **그럼 운전사가 어디서 저랑 만나게 해야 하나요?**

남: **역 입구 앞에 일반 승하차 구역이 있어요.**

여: 그렇군요. 감사합니다!

어휘 station 기차역   ridesharing 승차 공유   taxi stand 택시 승차장   general 일반적인   drop-off and pickup area 승하차 구역   entrance 입구

---

38 What problem does the woman have?
(A) She is unable to contact a friend.
(B) She left an item on a train.
(C) She cannot catch a taxi.
(D) She got off at the wrong station.

번역 여자는 어떤 문제를 가지고 있는가?
(A) 친구에게 연락할 수가 없다.
(B) 기차에 물건을 놓고 내렸다.
(C) 택시를 잡을 수가 없다.
(D) 기차역을 잘못 내렸다.

해설 **세부 사항 관련 - 여자가 가지고 있는 문제**
여자가 첫 대사에서 자신을 시내 반대편으로 데려다 줄 택시를 못 찾겠다(But now I can't find a taxi to take me across town)고 말하고 있으므로 정답은 (C)이다.

어휘 catch a taxi 택시를 잡다   get off (차에서) 내리다

---

39 Why does the man say, "You just have to download an app"?
(A) To request some feedback
(B) To express surprise
(C) To support a suggestion
(D) To disagree with an opinion

번역 남자가 "앱을 내려받기만 하시면 돼요"라고 말한 이유는?
(A) 피드백을 요청하려고
(B) 놀람을 표현하려고
(C) 제안을 뒷받침하려고
(D) 의견에 반대하려고

해설 **화자의 의도 파악 - 앱을 내려받기만 하면 된다는 말의 의도**
앞에서 여자가 자신을 시내 반대편으로 데려다 줄 택시를 못 찾겠다(But now I can't find a taxi to take me across town)고 하자, 남자가 휠로라는 승차 공유 서비스가 있다(there is Wheelo, the ridesharing service)고 말한 뒤 인용문을 언급한 것으로 보아, 승

TEST 10

TEST 10 271

차 공유 서비스에 대한 제안을 뒷받침하려는 의도로 한 말임을 알 수 있다. 따라서 정답은 (C)이다.

어휘 express 표현하다   support 지지하다   suggestion 제안
disagree 동의하지 않다

---

40 What will the woman most likely do soon?
(A) Wait near an entrance
(B) Complete some paperwork
(C) Talk to an official
(D) Check a departure board

번역 여자는 곧 무엇을 하겠는가?
(A) 입구 근처에서 기다리기
(B) 서류 작성하기
(C) 공무원에게 말하기
(D) 출발 안내 전광판 확인하기

해설 **세부 사항 관련 - 여자가 곧 할 일**
여자가 마지막 대사에서 운전사를 어디서 자신과 만나게 해야 하는지(Then where should I have the driver meet me?) 묻자, 남자가 역 입구 앞에 일반 승하차 구역이 있다(There's a general drop-off and pickup area in front of the station entrance)고 했으므로 정답은 (A)이다.

어휘 complete 작성하다   official 공무원   departure board 출발 안내 전광판

> **Paraphrasing**
> 대화의 in front of the station entrance
> → 정답의 near an entrance

41-43

> W-Am **41 This is the front desk.** How can I help you?
>
> M-Au Hi, **41 this is Rodney Burns in Room 214.** I checked in this afternoon but didn't get a chance to settle into my room until now. I looked all over the place and—**42 I don't see the toiletries anywhere.**
>
> W-Am Oh, we only provide toiletries upon request now. It's part of our initiative to become more environmentally friendly. What items do you need?
>
> M-Au Uh... shampoo and body wash.
>
> W-Am Alright, **43 I'll have a staff member bring those to you right away.**
>
> M-Au Thank you. Have a good evening.
>
> 여: **프론트 데스크입니다.** 무엇을 도와드릴까요?

남: 안녕하세요. **214호에 머무는 로드니 번스입니다.** 오늘 오후에 체크인했는데 지금까지도 방에 적응을 못 하고 있어요. 살살이 둘러보았지만, **목욕용품이 어디에도 안 보여요.**

여: 아, 저희가 지금은 요청하실 때만 목욕용품을 제공하고 있습니다. 더 환경친화적인 호텔이 되기 위한 저희 계획의 일환이에요. 어떤 용품이 필요하십니까?

남: 어… 샴푸와 바디 워시요.

여: 알겠습니다. **직원을 통해 바로 가져다 드리도록 하겠습니다.**

남: 감사합니다. 좋은 저녁 보내세요.

어휘 settle into ~에 적응하다   toiletries (샴푸·비누·칫솔 등) 목욕용품   provide 제공하다   upon request 요청에 따라   initiative 계획   environmentally friendly 환경친화적인

---

41 Who most likely is the woman?
(A) An office manager
(B) A hotel receptionist
(C) A laboratory assistant
(D) A construction supervisor

번역 여자는 누구이겠는가?
(A) 사무 관리자
(B) 호텔 접수원
(C) 연구실 조수
(D) 공사 감독관

해설 **전체 내용 관련 - 여자의 직업**
여자가 첫 대사에서 프론트 데스크(This is the front desk)라고 했고 남자가 자신은 214호에 머무는 로드니 번스(this is Rodney Burns in Room 214)라고 했으므로 여자는 호텔 접수원임을 알 수 있다. 따라서 정답은 (B)이다.

어휘 receptionist 접수원

---

42 What problem is the man reporting?
(A) A room is inaccessible.
(B) He will arrive late.
(C) Some work is very noisy.
(D) He cannot find some supplies.

번역 남자는 어떤 문제를 보고하는가?
(A) 방에 들어갈 수가 없다.
(B) 자신이 늦게 도착할 것이다.
(C) 어떤 작업이 매우 시끄럽다.
(D) 어떤 용품을 찾을 수가 없다.

해설 **세부 사항 관련 - 남자가 말하는 문제점**
남자가 첫 대사에서 목욕용품이 어디에도 안 보인다(I don't see the toiletries anywhere)고 말하고 있으므로 정답은 (D)이다.

어휘 inaccessible 접근할 수 없는   noisy 시끄러운

> **Paraphrasing**
> 대화의 the toiletries
> → 정답의 some supplies

43 What does the woman say she will do next?
(A) Research some alternatives
(B) Authorize a discount
(C) Arrange a delivery
(D) Update a schedule

번역 여자는 다음으로 무엇을 하겠다고 말하는가?
(A) 대안 조사하기
(B) 할인 승인하기
(C) 배달 준비하기
(D) 일정 갱신하기

해설 세부 사항 관련 - 여자가 다음에 할 일
여자가 마지막 대사에서 직원을 통해 바로 가져다주겠다('ll have a staff member bring those to you right away)고 말하고 있으므로 정답은 (C)이다.

어휘 alternative 대안 authorize 재가하다, 권한을 부여하다 arrange 준비하다 delivery 배달

44-46 3인 대화

W-Am Carl and Isaiah, **⁴⁴I'd like to start carrying out our own safety inspections. At the business seminar I went to yesterday, they said that routine safety checks help reduce a company's medical and insurance costs.**

M-Cn That seems like a good idea to me. Let's see… **⁴⁵we should probably form an inspection team to carry them out.**

M-Au Yes, and **⁴⁵it could include both managers and employees as members.**

W-Am Sounds ideal. OK, **⁴⁶I'm going to write up an announcement about this initiative.** We can meet to discuss it when I'm done.

여: 칼, 이사야, 우리 회사 자체 안전 점검을 시작하고 싶어요. 제가 어제 갔던 경영 세미나에서 말하기를 정기적인 안전 점검이 회사의 의료 및 보험 비용을 줄이는 데 도움이 된대요.
남1: 좋은 생각인 것 같네요. 어디 보자… 아마도 그걸 수행할 점검 팀을 구성해야겠네요.
남2: 네, 그리고 관리자와 직원을 모두 팀원으로 받도록 하고요.
여: 이상적이네요. 알겠습니다, 제가 이 계획에 대한 공지를 작성할게요. 작성이 끝나면 만나서 논의합시다.

어휘 carry out 수행하다 safety inspection 안전 점검 routine 정기적인 reduce 줄이다 insurance 보험 form 구성하다 ideal 이상적인 announcement 공지 initiative 계획

---

44 What are the speakers mainly discussing?
(A) Investing in some new machinery
(B) Reorganizing a work space
(C) Conducting regular safety inspections
(D) Starting a performance review program

번역 화자들은 주로 무엇에 관해 이야기하는가?
(A) 새 기계에 대한 투자
(B) 작업 공간의 재정비
(C) 주기적인 안전 점검 실시
(D) 업무 평가 프로그램의 개시

해설 전체 내용 관련 - 대화의 주제
여자가 첫 대사에서 우리 회사 자체 안전 점검을 시작하고 싶다('d like to start carrying out our own safety inspections)면서 어제 갔던 경영 세미나에서 말하기를 정기적인 안전 점검이 회사의 의료 및 보험 비용을 줄이는 데 도움이 된다(~ they said that routine safety checks help reduce a company's medical and insurance costs)고 정기적인 안전 점검에 대해 말하고 있으므로 정답은 (C)이다.

어휘 invest in ~에 투자하다 machinery 기계 reorganize 재조직하다 conduct 실시하다 regular 주기적인 performance 성과

> **Paraphrasing**
> 대화의 carrying out → 정답의 Conducting
> 대화의 routine safety checks
> → 정답의 regular safety inspections

45 What do the men suggest doing?
(A) Determining a timeline
(B) Assembling a team
(C) Consulting an expert
(D) Looking for some studies

번역 남자들은 무엇을 제안하는가?
(A) 일정 정하기
(B) 팀 구성하기
(C) 전문가와 상담하기
(D) 연구 결과 찾아보기

해설 세부 사항 관련 - 남자들의 제안 사항
첫 번째 남자가 그걸 수행할 점검 팀을 구성해야겠다(we should probably form an inspection team to carry them out)고 하자 두 번째 남자가 관리자와 직원을 모두 팀원으로 받아야 한다(it could include both managers and employees as members)고 점검 팀을 구성하는 것에 대해 제안하고 있으므로 정답은 (B)이다.

어휘 determine 결정하다 assemble 모으다 consult 상담하다 expert 전문가

> **Paraphrasing**
> 대화의 form an inspection team
> → 정답의 Assembling a team

46 What does the woman decide to do?
(A) Draft an announcement
(B) Reevaluate a budget
(C) Reassign some tasks
(D) Attend an industry event

번역 여자는 무엇을 하기로 결정하는가?
(A) 공지 초안 작성하기
(B) 예산 재평가하기
(C) 업무 이관하기
(D) 산업 행사 참석하기

해설 세부 사항 관련 - 여자가 결정한 일
여자가 마지막 대사에서 이 계획에 대한 공지를 작성하겠다(I'm going to write up an announcement about this initiative)고 했으므로 정답은 (A)이다.

어휘 draft 초안을 작성하다   reevaluate 재평가하다   budget 예산
reassign 이관하다   attend 참석하다   industry 산업

> **Paraphrasing**
> 대화의 write up → 정답의 Draft

47-49

> M-Au Good morning. Tensland Utility Services. How may I help you?
>
> W-Br Hi, my name is Alice Drake. I moved to Tensland last month, and my landlord said that he transferred the utilities to me. But ⁴⁷**I haven't gotten a bill yet.**
>
> M-Au That's a problem on our end. ⁴⁸**We recently upgraded the computer equipment our department uses**, and unfortunately we temporarily lost some financial system data in the process.
>
> W-Br Oh, I see. But the data has been recovered?
>
> M-Au Yes, so you should get something from us soon. And if you'd like to know more about the whole situation, ⁴⁹**there's going to be a public information session at city hall tomorrow.**

남: 좋은 아침입니다. 텐슬랜드 유틸리티 서비스입니다. 무엇을 도와드릴까요?

여: 안녕하세요, 제 이름은 앨리스 드레이크입니다. 지난달에 텐슬랜드로 이사왔는데요, 집주인이 공과금을 제 명의로 변경했다고 말했었는데, **아직 청구서를 받지 못했어요.**

남: 그건 저희 쪽 문제입니다. **저희가 최근에 저희 부서에서 사용하는 컴퓨터 장비를 업그레이드했는데,** 안타깝게도 그 과정에서 일부 재무 시스템 데이터가 일시적으로 날아갔어요.

여: 아, 그렇군요. 그러면 데이터가 복구되었나요?

남: 네, 조만간 저희한테서 연락을 받으실 거예요. 그리고 전체 상황에 대해 더 알고 싶으시면, **내일 시청에서 공개 설명회가 있을 예정입니다.**

어휘 utility (전기·가스 등) 공공 서비스, 공과금   landlord 집주인
transfer 양도하다   bill 청구서   equipment 장비
department 부서   temporarily 일시적으로   financial
재무의   recover 복구하다   situation 상황   public 공공의
information session 설명회

47 What problem does the woman report?
(A) She has not received a bill.
(B) A utility is not working properly.
(C) She needs to update her address.
(D) A charge is higher than usual.

번역 여자는 어떤 문제를 보고하는가?
(A) 청구서를 받지 못했다.
(B) 공공 서비스가 제대로 작동하지 않는다.
(C) 자신의 주소를 갱신해야 한다.
(D) 청구 요금이 평소보다 높다.

해설 세부 사항 관련 - 여자가 언급하는 문제
여자가 첫 대사에서 아직 청구서를 받지 못했다(I haven't gotten a bill yet)고 말하고 있으므로 정답은 (A)이다.

어휘 utility 공공 서비스   properly 적절하게   charge 청구 요금

48 What did the man's department recently do?
(A) It hired additional employees.
(B) It transferred tasks to a new department.
(C) It increased the rates for a service.
(D) It upgraded some equipment.

번역 남자의 부서는 최근에 무엇을 했는가?
(A) 추가 직원을 고용했다.
(B) 업무를 새 부서로 이관했다.
(C) 서비스 요금을 인상했다.
(D) 장비를 업그레이드했다.

해설 세부 사항 관련 - 남자의 부서가 최근에 한 일
남자가 두 번째 대사에서 최근에 부서에서 사용하는 컴퓨터 장비를 업그레이드했다(We recently upgraded the computer equipment our department uses)고 말하고 있으므로 정답은 (D)이다.

어휘 additional 추가의   increase 증가시키다   rate 요금

49 What will take place tomorrow?
(A) A city council meeting
(B) An office closure
(C) Some repair work
(D) An information session

번역 내일 어떤 일이 일어나겠는가?
(A) 시 의회 회의
(B) 사무실 휴업
(C) 수리 공사
(D) 설명회

해설 **세부 사항 관련 - 내일 일어날 일**
남자가 마지막 대사에서 내일 시청에서 공개 설명회가 있을 예정 (there's going to be a public information session at city hall tomorrow)이라고 말하고 있으므로 정답은 (D)이다.

어휘 city council 시 의회   closure (일시적 또는 영구적) 폐쇄

50-52

W-Am Well, Mr. Sasaki, ⁵⁰**it's a good thing that you brought your dog in for a checkup**—you're correct that he's having dental issues. It's very common in older pets.

M-Cn I see. I already brush his teeth every day. Is there anything else I can do?

W-Am Yes—looking over the patient information form you filled out, I do see one area for improvement. ⁵¹**You should switch his dog food to one that's formulated for dental health.**

M-Cn OK, I'll order some today.

W-Am Good. Please bring him back for another checkup next month. Oh, but we'll be in a new facility then. ⁵²**There are flyers at the reception desk with a map of the location. Make sure to take one on your way out.**

M-Cn ⁵²**Will do.**

여: 음, 사사키 씨. **건강검진을 위해 반려견을 데려오길 잘하셨어요.** 치아에 문제가 있는 게 맞네요. 노령인 반려동물들에게는 매우 흔한 일이죠.

남: 그렇군요. 이미 양치질은 매일 해주고 있어요. 할 수 있는 다른 일이 더 있나요?

여: 네, 작성해 주신 문진표를 살펴보니 한 가지 개선해야 할 영역이 보이네요. **사료를 치아 건강을 위해 특별히 배합된 것으로 바꿔 주셔야 해요.**

남: 알겠습니다, 오늘 주문할게요.

여: 좋습니다. 다음 달에 다시 한 번 검진을 받으러 데려와 주세요. 아, 근데 그때는 저희가 새 시설에 있을 거예요. **접수 데스크에 약도가 그려진 전단이 있어요. 나가실 때 꼭 한 장 챙겨가세요.**

남: **그러겠습니다.**

어휘 checkup 건강검진   dental 치과의   common 흔한   patient 환자   fill out 작성하다   improvement 개선   switch 바꾸다   formulate 만들어내다   facility 시설   flyer 전단   location 장소

---

50 Where most likely are the speakers?
(A) At a pet supply store
(B) At a community park
(C) At a veterinary clinic
(D) At an apartment building

번역 화자들은 어디에 있겠는가?
(A) 반려동물용품점
(B) 근린공원
(C) 동물병원
(D) 아파트 건물

해설 **전체 내용 관련 - 대화의 장소**
여자가 첫 대사에서 건강검진을 위해 반려견을 데려오길 잘했다(it's a good thing that you brought your dog in for a checkup)고 말하는 것으로 보아 화자들은 동물병원에서 대화 중임을 알 수 있다. 따라서 정답은 (C)이다.

---

51 How does the woman suggest addressing a problem?
(A) By changing an animal's feed
(B) By spending more time outdoors
(C) By filling out a complaint form
(D) By taking a training course

번역 여자는 어떻게 문제를 해결할 것을 제안하는가?
(A) 동물의 사료를 바꿈으로써
(B) 외부 활동 시간을 늘림으로써
(C) 불만 신고 양식을 작성함으로써
(D) 교육 과정을 이수함으로써

해설 **세부 사항 관련 - 여자가 제안하는 문제 해결 방법**
여자가 두 번째 대사에서 사료를 치아 건강을 위해 특별히 배합된 것으로 바꿔줄 것(You should switch his dog food to one that's formulated for dental health)을 제안하고 있으므로 정답은 (A)이다.

어휘 feed 먹이, 사료   complaint 불평, 불만

> **Paraphrasing**
> 대화의 switch his dog food to one that's formulated for dental health
> → 정답의 changing an animal's feed

---

52 What will the man do next?
(A) Photograph an item
(B) Pick up a flyer
(C) Go for a walk
(D) Check a calendar

번역 남자는 다음으로 무엇을 하겠는가?
(A) 물건 사진 찍기
(B) 전단 가져오기
(C) 산책하러 나가기
(D) 달력 확인하기

TEST 10

해설 **세부 사항 관련 - 남자가 다음에 할 일**
여자가 마지막 대사에서 접수 데스크에 약도가 그려진 전단이 있다 (There are flyers at the reception desk with a map of the location)면서 나갈 때 한 장 챙겨갈 것(Make sure to take one on your way out)을 요청하자, 남자가 그러겠다(Will do)고 수락하고 있으므로 정답은 (B)이다.

해설 **세부 사항 관련 - 남자가 의논하고자 하는 것**
남자가 첫 대사에서 신제품인 42리터짜리 여행용 배낭에 대한 고객들의 후기에 대해 말해달라(tell me about the reviews that customers have been posting for our new forty-two-liter travel backpack)고 요청하고 있으므로 정답은 (A)이다.

어휘 arrangement 준비 manufacturing 제조 procedure 절차 proposed 제안된

53-55 3인 대화

M-Cn Sabrina and Latifah, **53 tell me about the reviews that customers have been posting for our new forty-two-liter travel backpack.**

W-Br Well, most customers seem satisfied with it. They like the large number of pockets and compartments of different sizes.

W-Am Yes, people say it's easy to keep their stuff organized. However, **54 there are some complaints that the backpack puts too much pressure on the wearer's shoulders when it's full.**

M-Cn Hmm, sounds like the hip belt needs to take on more of the weight. **55 Can you two make some sketches for a prototype with a wider hip belt?**

남: 사브리나, 라티파, 우리 신제품인 42리터짜리 여행용 배낭에 대한 고객들의 후기에 대해 말씀해 주세요.

여1: 음, 대부분의 고객들은 만족하는 것 같아요. 주머니가 많다는 점과 다양한 크기의 수납공간을 마음에 들어 하세요.

여2: 맞아요, 사람들이 물건을 정리하기가 쉽다고 말해요. 하지만, 배낭이 가득 차면 착용자의 어깨에 너무 많은 부담을 준다는 불만이 있어요.

남: 음, 허리띠에 좀 더 많은 무게가 실려야 할 것 같네요. 두 분이 허리띠의 폭을 넓힌 시제품을 위한 스케치를 그려주실 수 있나요?

어휘 review 후기, 평가 travel backpack 여행용 배낭 satisfied with ~에 만족한 compartment (물건을 보관하는) 칸 stuff 물건 organize 정리하다 complaint 불평, 불만 pressure 압력, 부담 wearer 착용자 prototype 시제품

---

53 What does the man want to discuss?
(A) Some customer reviews
(B) Some travel arrangements
(C) A manufacturing procedure
(D) A proposed sales event

번역 남자는 무엇에 대해 의논하기를 원하는가?
(A) 고객 후기
(B) 여행 준비
(C) 제조 공정
(D) 제안된 할인 행사

54 What problem is mentioned?
(A) A delivery has been delayed.
(B) An entranceway may be too narrow.
(C) A material has become more expensive.
(D) An item can be uncomfortable to wear.

번역 어떤 문제가 언급되는가?
(A) 배송이 지연되었다.
(B) 진입로가 너무 좁을 수도 있다.
(C) 자재가 더 비싸졌다.
(D) 물품이 착용하기에 불편할 수 있다.

해설 **세부 사항 관련 - 언급된 문제**
두 번째 여자가 배낭이 가득 차면 착용자의 어깨에 너무 많은 부담을 준다는 불평이 있다(there are some complaints that the backpack puts too much pressure on the wearer's shoulders when it's full)고 했으므로 정답은 (D)이다.

어휘 delivery 배송 delay 지연시키다 entranceway 진입로 material 자재 uncomfortable 불편한

> **Paraphrasing**
> 대화의 the backpack puts too much pressure on the wearer's shoulders
> → 정답의 An item can be uncomfortable to wear

55 What does the man ask the women to do?
(A) Make some drawings
(B) Purchase some luggage
(C) Revise an advertisement
(D) Contact a business partner

번역 남자는 여자들에게 무엇을 하라고 요청하는가?
(A) 그림 그리기
(B) 여행 가방 구매하기
(C) 광고 수정하기
(D) 사업 파트너에게 연락하기

해설 **세부 사항 관련 - 남자의 요청 사항**
남자가 마지막 대사에서 시제품을 위한 스케치를 그려줄 것(Can you two make some sketches for a prototype ~?)을 요청하고 있으므로 정답은 (A)이다.

어휘 drawing 그림 purchase 구매하다 luggage 여행 가방, 짐 revise 수정하다 advertisement 광고

> **Paraphrasing**
> 대화의 make some sketches
> → 정답의 Make some drawings

56-58

W-Am Daniel, ⁵⁶**have you had any luck with hiring another project manager?**

M-Au No, we're still not getting suitable applicants.

W-Am Well, ⁵⁷**I have an idea—why don't you lower the educational requirement?** A bachelor's degree isn't really necessary, in my opinion.

M-Au Hmm, I don't know...

W-Am You have to widen the candidate pool somehow.

M-Au That's true. OK, ⁵⁸**go ahead and schedule a meeting with me and the director of operations to talk it over.**

여: 대니얼, 또 다른 프로젝트 관리자를 고용하는 일은 잘되고 있나요?

남: 아니요, 아직 적합한 지원자가 없어요.

여: 음, 저한테 의견이 하나 있는데, 학력 요구조건을 좀 낮추는 건 어때요? 제 생각에는 학사 학위는 굳이 필요하지 않아요.

남: 음, 모르겠어요…

여: 어떻게든 지원자 범위를 넓혀야 해요.

남: 맞아요. 알겠습니다. 그렇게 하시고 그 문제를 상의할 수 있도록 저와 운영 책임자가 참석할 회의 일정을 잡아 주세요.

어휘 suitable 적합한 applicant 지원자 lower 낮추다 educational 교육의 requirement 요구조건 bachelor's degree 학사 학위 widen 넓히다 candidate 지원자, 후보자 pool 이용 가능 인력

---

56 What does the woman ask the man about?
(A) Workshop participants
(B) A hiring process
(C) A project deadline
(D) Remote work policies

번역 여자는 남자에게 무엇에 대해 문의하는가?
(A) 워크숍 참가자
(B) 고용 과정
(C) 프로젝트 마감 시한
(D) 원격 근무 정책

해설 **세부 사항 관련 - 여자의 문의 사항**
여자가 첫 대사에서 또 다른 프로젝트 관리자를 고용하는 일은 잘되고 있는지(have you had any luck with hiring another project manager?) 묻고 있으므로 정답은 (B)이다.

어휘 participant 참가자 deadline 마감 시한 remote work 원격 근무 policy 정책

---

57 What idea does the woman have?
(A) Adjusting a requirement
(B) Advertising on a special Web site
(C) Offering reimbursement for an expense
(D) Gathering opinions from others

번역 여자는 어떤 의견을 가지고 있는가?
(A) 요구조건 조정하기
(B) 특별한 웹사이트에 광고하기
(C) 비용 환급 제공하기
(D) 다른 사람들의 의견 모으기

해설 **세부 사항 관련 - 여자의 의견**
여자가 두 번째 대사에서 자신에게 의견이 하나 있는데 학력 요구조건을 좀 낮추는 건 어떤지(I have an idea—why don't you lower the educational requirement?) 묻고 있으므로 정답은 (A)이다.

어휘 adjust 조정하다 reimbursement 환급 expense 지출, 비용 gather 모으다

> **Paraphrasing**
> 대화의 lower the educational requirement
> → 정답의 Adjusting a requirement

---

58 What does the man tell the woman to do?
(A) Calculate a cost
(B) Forward some résumés
(C) Postpone the release of a report
(D) Organize a meeting

번역 남자는 여자에게 무엇을 하라고 말하는가?
(A) 비용 계산하기
(B) 이력서 전송하기
(C) 보고서 발표 미루기
(D) 회의 준비하기

해설 **세부 사항 관련 - 남자가 여자에게 하라고 한 일**
남자가 마지막 대사에서 자신과 운영 책임자가 참석할 회의 일정을 잡아 줄 것(~ schedule a meeting with me and the director of operations)을 요청하고 있으므로 정답은 (D)이다.

어휘 calculate 계산하다 forward 전송하다 résumé 이력서 postpone 미루다 release 발표 organize 준비하다

> **Paraphrasing**
> 대화의 schedule a meeting
> → 정답의 Organize a meeting

59-61

M-Cn Yun-Hee, ⁵⁹**I heard that we won an award for the patio your team created for Linfair Library.** You must be very proud!

W-Am Yes, I am! ⁵⁹**We put a lot of effort into choosing the right plants for that space.**

M-Cn Well, it paid off. And I think we should all do something to celebrate.

W-Am Actually, **60 the president just told me that he's going to host a barbecue next Saturday.**

M-Cn **60 But the Spring Festival is next Saturday, and...** most of the company is planning to go.

W-Am Ah, I forgot about that. **61 I'd better remind the president too before he sends out the announcement.**

남: 윤희, 당신의 팀이 린페어 도서관을 위해 만든 테라스로 우리가 수상했다고 들었어요. 정말 뿌듯하시겠어요!

여: 네, 정말 그래요! 그 공간에 어울릴 식물을 고르느라 많은 노력을 기울였거든요.

남: 음, 고생한 보람이 있네요. 그리고 우리 기념할 만한 뭔가를 해야 할 것 같아요.

여: 실은, 회장님이 방금 다음 주 토요일에 바비큐 파티를 열 거라고 말씀하셨어요.

남: 하지만 봄 축제가 다음 주 토요일이잖아요, 그래서… 직원들 대부분이 갈 텐데요.

여: 아, 그걸 잊고 있었어요. 회장님이 공지를 보내기 전에 알려드리는 게 좋겠어요.

어휘 win an award 수상하다 put a lot of effort into ~에 많은 노력을 기울이다 pay off 결실을 맺다 celebrate 축하하다 remind 상기시키다 send out 보내다 announcement 공지

59 Where do the speakers most likely work?
(A) At a publishing company
(B) At a catering service
(C) At a landscaping firm
(D) At a television network

번역 화자들은 어디서 일하겠는가?
(A) 출판사
(B) 출장 요리 업체
(C) 조경 회사
(D) 텔레비전 방송국

해설 **전체 내용 관련 - 화자들의 근무지**
남자가 첫 대사에서 당신의 팀이 린페어 도서관을 위해 만든 테라스로 우리가 수상했다고 들었다(I heard that we won an award for the patio your team created for Linfair Library)고 말하자, 여자가 그 공간에 어울릴 식물을 고르느라 많은 노력을 기울였다(We put a lot of effort into choosing the right plants for that space)고 했으므로 화자들은 조경 회사에서 근무하고 있음을 알 수 있다. 따라서 정답은 (C)이다.

어휘 catering 출장 요리 landscaping 조경

---

60 What does the man imply when he says, "most of the company is planning to go"?
(A) An event should be moved to a different date.
(B) Staff members are excited about an award.
(C) They will need to prepare additional food.
(D) It will be difficult to find workers for a shift.

번역 남자가 "직원들 대부분이 갈 텐데요"라고 말할 때, 그 의도는 무엇인가?
(A) 행사를 다른 날짜로 옮겨야 한다.
(B) 직원들이 상에 대해 기뻐하고 있다.
(C) 추가 음식을 준비해야 할 것이다.
(D) 교대 근무자를 찾기 어려울 것이다.

해설 **화자의 의도 파악 - 직원들 대부분이 갈 텐데라는 말의 의도**
앞에서 여자가 회장님이 방금 다음 주 토요일에 바비큐 파티를 열 거라고 말씀하셨다(the president just told me that he's going to host a barbecue next Saturday)고 하자, 남자가 봄 축제가 다음 주 토요일(But the Spring Festival is next Saturday)이라고 말한 뒤 인용문을 언급한 것으로 보아 토요일은 봄 축제와의 일정 겹침으로 바비큐 파티를 다른 날짜로 옮겨야 한다는 의도로 한 말임을 알 수 있다. 따라서 정답은 (A)이다.

어휘 prepare 준비하다 additional 추가의 shift 교대 근무 (시간)

---

61 What does the woman say she will do?
(A) Send out an e-mail
(B) Speak to an executive
(C) Make changes to a menu
(D) Rent some transportation

번역 여자는 무엇을 하겠다고 말하는가?
(A) 이메일 보내기
(B) 임원에게 말하기
(C) 메뉴 변경하기
(D) 교통편 대여하기

해설 **세부 사항 관련 - 여자가 할 일**
여자가 마지막 대사에서 회장님이 공지를 보내기 전에 알려드리는 게 좋겠다(I'd better remind the president too before he sends out the announcement)고 말하고 있으므로 정답은 (B)이다.

어휘 executive 임원, 중역 transportation 교통편

> **Paraphrasing**
> 대화의 remind the president
> → 정답의 Speak to an executive

62-64 대화+웹페이지

W-Br Carey Auto Repair Shop.

M-Cn Hi, I'm having some trouble with the appointment scheduling service on your Web site. **62, 63 It's showing me that your branch**

has an opening at six P.M. today, but when I try to select it, I can't.

W-Br Let me look into that for you... OK, I see the problem. **⁶³Another customer just took that appointment. If you refresh the page, it will disappear. I'm sorry about that.**

M-Cn That's disappointing. That's the only time that works for me.

W-Br Can I ask why you hope to bring your car in?

M-Cn **⁶⁴I need you to fix a crack in one of the windows.**

W-Br Hmm... if it's a minor one, we may be able to fit you in today. Could you send me a picture of the window?

여: 캐리 자동차 정비소입니다.

남: 안녕하세요, 귀사의 웹사이트에 있는 정비 예약 서비스를 이용하려는 데 문제가 있어요. 그 지점에 오늘 저녁 6시에 예약 가능한 자리가 있는 것으로 나오는데, 그 시간을 고르려고 하면 선택이 안 돼요.

여: 제가 확인해 보겠습니다… 아, 문제가 뭔지 알겠네요. 다른 고객이 방금 그 시간대를 예약하셨어요. 페이지를 새로고침해 보시면, 없어질 거예요. 죄송합니다.

남: 실망스럽네요. 그 시간이 제가 유일하게 가능한 시간이거든요.

여: 왜 차를 입고시키려고 하시는지 여쭤봐도 될까요?

남: 창문 중 하나에 금이 간 데를 고쳐주셨으면 해요.

여: 음… 그게 간단한 거라면, 아마도 오늘 해드릴 수 있을 거예요. 창문 사진을 보내주시겠어요?

어휘 appointment (진료 등의) 예약 opening 빈자리 select 고르다 look into ~을 조사하다 refresh 새로고침하다 disappear 사라지다 disappointing 실망스러운 fix 고치다 crack (갈라져 생긴) 금 minor 작은, 중요하지 않은 fit in 시간을 내어 만나다

Carey Auto Repair
Thursday, October 9

Branch	Available Appointments		
Dixon Street	10 A.M.	2 P.M.	5 P.M.
City Center	11 A.M.	3 P.M.	
Rogers Park	9 A.M.	12 P.M.	4 P.M.
Brantfield	1 P.M.	⁶²6 P.M.	

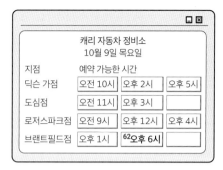

캐리 자동차 정비소
10월 9일 목요일

지점	예약 가능한 시간		
딕슨 가점	오전 10시	오후 2시	오후 5시
도심점	오전 11시	오후 3시	
로저스파크점	오전 9시	오후 12시	오후 4시
브랜트필드점	오후 1시	⁶²오후 6시	

62 Look at the graphic. Which branch does the woman work at?
(A) Dixon Street
(B) City Center
(C) Rogers Park
(D) Brantfield

번역 시각 정보에 의하면, 여자는 어떤 지점에서 일하는가?
(A) 딕슨 가점
(B) 도심점
(C) 로저스파크점
(D) 브랜트필드점

해설 **시각 정보 연계 - 여자의 근무 지점**
남자가 첫 대사에서 여자가 근무하는 지점에 오늘 저녁 6시에 예약 가능한 자리가 있는 것으로 나온다(It's showing me that your branch has an opening at six P.M. today)고 했고, 웹페이지에 따르면 오후 6시에 예약이 가능한 지점은 브랜트필드점이므로 정답은 (D)이다.

63 Why does the woman apologize?
(A) Some instructions are confusing.
(B) A time slot is no longer available.
(C) Appointments cannot be made by phone.
(D) A business is understaffed today.

번역 여자는 왜 사과하는가?
(A) 일부 설명이 헷갈려서
(B) 한 시간대가 더 이상 이용 가능하지 않아서
(C) 전화로 예약할 수 없어서
(D) 사업체가 오늘 일손이 부족해서

해설 **세부 사항 관련 - 여자가 사과하는 이유**
남자가 첫 대사에서 그 지점에 오늘 저녁 6시에 예약 가능한 자리가 있는 것으로 나온다(It's showing me that your branch has an opening at six P.M. today)고 하자 여자가 다른 고객이 방금 그 시간대를 예약했다(Another customer just took that appointment)면서 페이지를 새로고침해 보면, 없어질 것(If you refresh the page, it will disappear)이라고 말한 뒤, 죄송하다(I'm sorry about that)고 사과하고 있으므로 오늘 저녁 6시 시간대는 이용할 수 없음을 알 수 있다. 따라서 정답은 (B)이다.

어휘 instruction 설명, 지시 confusing 혼란스러운 time slot 시간대 be understaffed 일손이 부족하다

64 What service does the man require for his car?
(A) A tire rotation
(B) A window repair
(C) An oil change
(D) A brake replacement

번역 남자는 자동차에 어떤 서비스가 필요한가?
(A) 타이어 위치 교환
(B) 창문 수리
(C) 오일 교환
(D) 브레이크 교체

해설 **세부 사항 관련 - 남자의 자동차에 필요한 서비스**
남자가 마지막 대사에서 창문 중 하나에 금이 간 데를 고쳐주었으면 한다(I need you to fix a crack in one of the windows)고 말하고 있으므로 정답은 (B)이다.

어휘 repair 수리 replacement 교체

> **Paraphrasing**
> 대화의 fix a crack in one of the windows
> → 정답의 A window repair

65-67 대화+쿠폰

M-Au Hi. I got this pack of coupons recently, and I'm hoping to use this one today.

W-Br Yes, that'll be fine. **⁶⁵ Which of the salon's services are you interested in?**

M-Au A haircut—nothing fancy, just a trim.

W-Br **⁶⁶ Let me look over our stylists' schedules...** Bernardo can take you once he's done with his current client. It'll be about ten minutes. Is that all right?

M-Au Sure, I'm not in a hurry.

W-Br OK, then **⁶⁷ you can have a seat over there until it's your turn.** There are magazines and a phone charging station for your convenience.

M-Au Great. Thank you.

남: 안녕하세요. 제가 최근에 이 쿠폰 팩을 받았는데요. 오늘 이걸 사용하고 싶어요.
여: 네, 가능하세요. **저희 미용실의 어떤 서비스에 관심이 있으신가요?**
남: 커트요. 멋을 낼 필요는 없고 그냥 다듬어주세요.
여: **저희 미용사들의 일정을 좀 살펴보겠습니다···** 베르나르도가 현재 손님을 마치면 손님을 해드릴 수 있습니다. 약 10분쯤 걸릴 텐데요. 괜찮으실까요?
남: 그럼요, 급하지 않습니다.
여: 알겠습니다, 그럼 **차례가 될 때까지 저쪽에 있는 의자에 앉아 계세요.** 편의를 위해 잡지와 전화기 충전대도 마련되어 있습니다.
남: 좋네요. 감사합니다.

어휘 recently 최근에 fancy 화려한, 복잡한 trim (머리를) 다듬기 stylist 미용사 current 현재의 in a hurry 바쁜 charging station 충전소 convenience 편의, 편리

Critchfield Plaza
Coupon Pack

⁶⁵**①** 20% off any service
at Vayla Salon

② Free cookie
at Sugaree Bakery

③ Free drink with ticket purchase
at Thacker Cinema

④ 10% off any item
at Ochoa Shoes

크리치필드 플라자
쿠폰 팩

⁶⁵**①** 바일라 미용실의 모든 서비스 20% 할인

② 슈거리 제과점의 무료 쿠키

③ 태커 영화관에서 관람권 구매 시 무료 음료

④ 오초아 제화의 모든 상품 10% 할인

65 Look at the graphic. Which coupon will the man use?
(A) Coupon 1
(B) Coupon 2
(C) Coupon 3
(D) Coupon 4

번역 시각 정보에 의하면, 남자는 어떤 쿠폰을 사용하겠는가?
(A) 쿠폰 1
(B) 쿠폰 2
(C) 쿠폰 3
(D) 쿠폰 4

해설 **시각 정보 연계 - 남자가 사용할 쿠폰**
여자가 첫 대사에서 미용실의 어떤 서비스에 관심이 있는지(Which of the salon's services are you interested in?) 묻고 있고, 쿠폰에 따르면 미용실은 쿠폰 1이므로 정답은 (A)이다.

66 What does the woman check?
(A) Her coworkers' schedules
(B) A purchase receipt
(C) A price list
(D) Some stock levels

번역 여자는 무엇을 확인하는가?
(A) 동료들의 일정
(B) 구매 영수증
(C) 가격표
(D) 재고 수준

해설 **세부 사항 관련 - 여자의 확인 사항**
여자가 두 번째 대사에서 미용사들의 일정을 좀 살펴보겠다(Let me look over our stylists' schedules)고 말하고 있으므로 정답은 (A)이다.

어휘 coworker 동료   receipt 영수증   stock 재고

> **Paraphrasing**
> 대화의 our stylists
> → 정답의 coworkers

67 What will the man most likely do next?
(A) Look at a menu board
(B) Sit in a waiting area
(C) Provide his phone number
(D) Speak with a manager

번역 남자는 다음으로 무엇을 하겠는가?
(A) 메뉴판 보기
(B) 대기 구역에 앉기
(C) 전화번호 알려주기
(D) 관리자와 이야기하기

해설 **세부 사항 관련 - 남자가 다음에 할 일**
여자가 마지막 대사에서 차례가 될 때까지 의자에 앉아 있을 것이(you can have a seat over there until it's your turn)을 제안하고 있으므로 정답은 (B) 이다.

어휘 menu board 메뉴판   provide 제공하다

> **Paraphrasing**
> 대화의 have a seat over there until it's your turn
> → 정답의 Sit in a waiting area

68-70 대화 + 선반 배치도

> M-Au Julia, have you run into any problems with the used computer accessories in the storage room? **⁶⁸ This headset I just got from there can't play sound anymore.**
>
> W-Am Yes, I had the same issue with one of the mouses. **⁶⁹ I'm actually planning on testing all of the mouses this afternoon. Once I've finished with that, I'll check the other accessories too.**
>
> M-Au That would be great. And after you're done, **⁷⁰ why don't you wipe down the accessories that we're going to keep?** Some of them are quite dusty.

남: 줄리아, 창고에 있는 중고 컴퓨터 주변 기기에서 문제를 겪은 적 있나요? **방금 거기에서 가져온 이 헤드셋은 더 이상 소리가 안 나오네요.**

여: 네, 마우스 중에 하나도 같은 문제가 있었어요. **실은 오늘 오후에 모든 마우스를 검사해 볼 계획이에요. 일단 다 마치면 다른 주변 기기들도 확인해 볼게요.**

남: 좋은 생각이에요. 그럼 다 마치면 **우리가 보관할 주변 기기들을 닦아주시겠어요?** 일부 기기들에 먼지가 많이 쌓였더라고요.

어휘 run into (곤경 등을) 우연히 겪다   computer accessories 컴퓨터 주변 기기   storage room 창고   wipe down (물걸레 등으로) 닦다   dusty 먼지가 쌓인

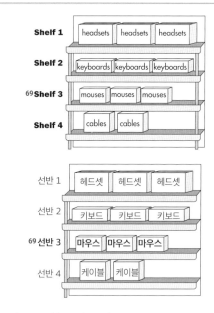

68 What problem does the man report?
(A) A device no longer works.
(B) A storage space is becoming too full.
(C) Some boxes are unorganized.
(D) Employees do not have necessary items.

번역 남자는 어떤 문제를 말하는가?
(A) 장치가 더 이상 작동하지 않는다.
(B) 창고 공간이 너무 꽉 차고 있다.
(C) 상자들이 어지럽게 놓여 있다.
(D) 직원들이 필요한 물건을 갖고 있지 않다.

해설 **세부 사항 관련 - 남자가 말하는 문제**
남자가 첫 번째 대사에서 방금 거기에서 가져온 이 헤드셋이 소리가 안 나온다(This headset I just got from there can't play sound anymore)고 말하고 있으므로 정답은 (A)이다.

어휘 device 장치   unorganized 정돈되지 않은

> **Paraphrasing**
> 대화의 This headset ~ can't play sound anymore
> → 정답의 A device no longer works

69 Look at the graphic. Which shelf's boxes will the woman work on first?
(A) Shelf 1
(B) Shelf 2
(C) Shelf 3
(D) Shelf 4

번역 시각 정보에 의하면, 여자는 어느 선반의 상자를 가장 먼저 작업할 것인가?
(A) 상자 1
(B) 상자 2
(C) 상자 3
(D) 상자 4

해설 **시각 정보 연계 - 여자가 가장 먼저 작업할 선반의 상자**
여자가 첫 번째 대사에서 실은 오늘 오후에 모든 마우스를 검사해 볼 계획(I'm actually planning on testing all of the mouses this afternoon)이라며 일단 다 마치면 다른 주변 기기들도 확인해 보겠다(Once I've finished with that, I'll check the other accessories too)고 덧붙였는데, 선반 배치도에 따르면 마우스는 선반 3에 있으므로 정답은 (C)이다.

---

70 What is the woman asked to do?
(A) Keep an inventory list updated
(B) Clean some of the accessories
(C) Call a specialty recycling service
(D) Implement a new labeling system

번역 여자는 무엇을 하라고 요청받았는가?
(A) 재고 목록 갱신하기
(B) 주변 기기 청소하기
(C) 재활용 서비스 전문 업체에 전화하기
(D) 새로운 라벨링 시스템 시행하기

해설 **세부 사항 관련 - 여자가 요청받은 일**
남자가 마지막 대사에서 보관할 주변 기기들을 닦아줄 것(why don't you wipe down the accessories that we're going to keep?)을 부탁하고 있으므로 정답은 (B)이다.

어휘 inventory 재고 specialty 전문 implement 시행하다

> **Paraphrasing**
> 대화의 wipe down → 정답의 Clean

PART 4

71-73 전화 메시지

> W-Am Hello, my name is Anna Miles, and I'm trying to reach the organizers of the Russell Hills Street Fair. I go to the fair every year, and it's always really fun. **71 I like how there's so much to do—not just eating and shopping, but playing games and making crafts.** Uh, when I was looking for information about this year's event, though, I found only a page on a local events site. **72 I think your fair should have its own Web site.** I have experience in Web design, and **73 I'd be happy to make a simple site for you as a volunteer.** Please call me back at 555-0134 if you're interested. Thanks.

안녕하세요, 제 이름은 애나 마일스인데요. 러셀 힐스 거리 축제의 주최자들과 통화를 하고 싶어요. 저는 매년 그 축제에 가는데, 항상 정말 즐거워요. **할 게 많아서 참 좋아요. 단지 먹고 쇼핑하는 것뿐만 아니라 게임도 하고 공예품도 만들 수 있으니까요.** 어, 그런데 올해 행사에 대한 정보를 찾아보고 있었는데, 지역 행사 사이트에서 달랑 한 페이지만 찾을 수 있었어요. **저는 이 축제만의 웹사이트가 따로 있어야 한다고 생각해요.** 저는 웹 디자인 경험이 있어요. **기꺼이 자원봉사자로서 간단한 사이트를 만들어드리고 싶어요.** 관심이 있으시다면 555-0134로 회신 전화 주세요. 감사합니다.

어휘 reach (전화로) 연락하다 organizer 주최자 street fair 거리 축제 craft 공예품 volunteer 자원봉사자

---

71 What does the speaker like about an event?
(A) It is held in a special location.
(B) It has a long history.
(C) It features various activities.
(D) Its proceeds go toward a good cause.

번역 화자는 행사에 대해 어떤 점을 마음에 들어 하는가?
(A) 특별한 장소에서 열린다.
(B) 오랜 역사를 가지고 있다.
(C) 다양한 활동이 이루어진다.
(D) 수익금이 좋은 일에 사용된다.

해설 **세부 사항 관련 - 화자가 행사에 대해 마음에 들어 하는 점**
화자가 초반부에 할 게 많아서 좋다면서 먹고 쇼핑하는 것뿐만 아니라 게임도 하고 공예품도 만들 수 있다(I like how there's so much to do—not just eating and shopping, but playing games and making crafts)고 말하고 있으므로 정답은 (C)이다.

어휘 feature 특별히 포함하다 various 다양한 activity 활동 proceeds 수익금 cause 대의명분

> **Paraphrasing**
> 담화의 so much to do
> → 정답의 various activities

---

72 According to the speaker, what should the event have?
(A) More food options
(B) A dedicated Web site
(C) Official merchandise
(D) A prize raffle

번역 화자에 따르면, 행사는 무엇을 가지고 있어야 하는가?
(A) 더 많은 음식 종류
(B) 전용 웹사이트
(C) 공식 상품
(D) 경품 추첨

해설 **세부 사항 관련 - 행사에 있어야 할 것**
화자가 중반부에 저는 이 축제만의 웹사이트가 따로 있어야 한다고 생각한다(I think your fair should have its own Web site)고 말하고 있으므로 정답은 (B)이다.

어휘   dedicated 전용의   official 공식적인   merchandise 상품
raffle 추첨

> **Paraphrasing**
> 담화의 its own Web site
> → 정답의 A dedicated Web site

73 What does the speaker offer to do?
(A) Perform volunteer work
(B) Inquire about a regulation
(C) Recommend potential sponsors
(D) Lend the listener some equipment

번역   화자는 무엇을 하겠다고 제안하는가?
(A) 자원봉사 활동 수행하기
(B) 규정에 대해 문의하기
(C) 잠재적 후원자 추천하기
(D) 청자에게 장비 빌려주기

해설   세부 사항 관련 - 화자의 제안 사항
화자가 후반부에 기꺼이 자원봉사자로서 간단한 사이트를 만들어주고 싶다(I'd be happy to make a simple site for you as a volunteer)고 말하고 있으므로 정답은 (A)이다.

어휘   perform 수행하다   inquire 문의하다   regulation 규정
potential 잠재적인   sponsor 후원자   lend 빌려주다
equipment 장비

> **Paraphrasing**
> 담화의 make a simple site for you as a volunteer
> → 정답의 Perform volunteer work

74-76 방송

> M-Au   Thank you for tuning in to *Keltford at Work*, the show about the local business community. **74 On today's program, we're going to talk about pop-up stores.** These temporary retail operations are appearing all over our city, and they often draw large crowds. **75 Consumers love the fact that they stock goods that aren't available elsewhere.** They are also a smart option for retailers. **76 I've invited Patty Tyner to talk to us about this. She's the manager of Keltford Shopping Mall**, which has several spaces it rents out for pop-up stores.

우리 지역의 비즈니스 커뮤니티에 관한 프로그램인 〈켈트포드 앳 워크〉를 청취해 주셔서 감사합니다. **오늘 프로그램에서는 팝업 스토어에 대해 이야기할 예정입니다.** 이 임시 소매업체들은 우리 시 곳곳에 등장하고 있는데, 종종 많은 사람을 끌어모으고 있습니다. **소비자들은 팝업 스토어가 다른 곳에서는 구매할 수 없는 상품을 보유하고 있다는 사실을 좋아합니다.** 팝업 스토어는 소매업자들에게 현명한 대안이기도 합니다. **이 점에 대해 이야기해 줄 패티 타이너를 초대했습니다. 그녀는 켈트포드 쇼핑몰의 관리자입니다.** 이 쇼핑몰은 팝업 스토어용으로 여러 공간을 임대해 주고 있죠.

어휘   tune in 청취하다, 시청하다   pop-up store 팝업 스토어
(단기간 운영하는 상점)   temporary 일시적인   retail 소매
appear 나타나다   draw 끌어모으다   consumer 소비자   stock
재고를 갖추다   retailer 소매업자

74 What is the topic of today's program?
(A) Trends in online shopping
(B) The opening of a retail complex
(C) A custom clothing maker
(D) Pop-up stores

번역   오늘 프로그램의 주제는 무엇인가?
(A) 온라인 쇼핑 동향
(B) 복합 상업 시설의 개장
(C) 맞춤 의상 제작자
(D) 팝업 스토어

해설   전체 내용 관련 - 프로그램의 주제
화자가 초반부에 오늘 프로그램에서는 팝업 스토어에 대해 이야기할 예정(On today's program, we're going to talk about pop-up stores)이라고 말하고 있으므로 정답은 (D)이다.

어휘   trend 동향   opening 개장, 개업   custom 주문 제작한

75 According to the speaker, why is a type of business popular with consumers?
(A) It is convenient to use.
(B) It has unique products.
(C) Its prices are reasonable.
(D) It offers an enjoyable experience.

번역   화자에 따르면, 한 종류의 사업체가 왜 소비자들에게 인기가 있는가?
(A) 이용하기가 편리해서
(B) 독특한 제품을 보유해서
(C) 가격이 합리적이어서
(D) 즐거운 경험을 제공해서

해설   세부 사항 관련 - 한 종류의 사업체가 소비자들에게 인기 있는 이유
화자가 중반부에 소비자들은 팝업 스토어가 다른 곳에서는 구매할 수 없는 상품을 보유하고 있다는 사실을 좋아한다(Consumers love the fact that they stock goods that aren't available elsewhere)고 말하고 있으므로 정답은 (B)이다.

어휘   convenient 편리한   unique 독특한   reasonable 합리적인
enjoyable 즐거운

> **Paraphrasing**
> 담화의 goods that aren't available elsewhere
> → 정답의 unique products

76 Who is Patty Tyner?
(A) A tailor
(B) An entrepreneur
(C) A property manager
(D) An economic researcher

번역 패티 타이너는 누구인가?
(A) 재단사
(B) 기업가
(C) 건물 관리인
(D) 경제 연구원

해설 **전체 내용 관련 - 패티 타이너의 직업**
화자가 후반부에 패티 타이너를 초대했다(I've invited Patty Tyner ~)면서 그녀는 켈트포드 쇼핑몰의 관리자(She's the manager of Keltford Shopping Mall)라고 소개하고 있으므로 정답은 (C)이다.

어휘 property 부동산, 자산 economic 경제의

> **Paraphrasing**
> 담화의 the manager of Keltford Shopping Mall
> → 정답의 A property manager

77-79 연설

> W-Am Hello everyone. I'm Caitlyn Spence, the director of the Benitez Foundation. [77] **I'm glad to be taking part in this conference on bringing fast, reliable Internet access to communities around the world.** Today, I'm going to tell you about our efforts in this area. [78] **Last year we conducted a research study on barriers to Internet access in rural Argentina.** We found that, even after connections are built, network maintenance and repairs can be major issues. [79] **That's why our organization is now funding a program to train technicians who can perform these tasks.**

> 안녕하세요 여러분. 저는 베니테즈 재단의 이사 케이틀린 스펜스입니다. 전 세계 곳곳에 있는 공동체에 빠르고 신뢰할 수 있는 인터넷 접근성을 제공하려는 이 컨퍼런스에 참여하게 되어 기쁩니다. 오늘 저는 이 분야에서 저희가 하고 있는 노력에 대해 말씀드리고자 합니다. 작년에 저희는 아르헨티나의 시골 지역에서 인터넷 접근을 막는 장애물에 대한 연구 조사를 실시했습니다. 저희는 인터넷이 연결된 후에도 네트워크 유지보수와 수리가 주요 문제점이 될 수 있음을 알게 되었습니다. 그것이 바로 현재 저희 재단에서 이 업무를 수행할 수 있는 기술자를 교육하는 프로그램에 자금을 지원하고 있는 이유입니다.

> 어휘 foundation 재단 take part in ~에 참여하다 conference 회의 reliable 신뢰할 만한 access 접속, 접근 effort 노력 conduct 실시하다 barrier 장애물 rural 시골의 connection 연결 maintenance 유지보수 repair 수리 organization 단체 fund 자금을 대다 technician 기술자 perform 수행하다

77 What is the topic of the conference?
(A) Increasing agricultural productivity
(B) Promoting trade between countries
(C) Using an educational technology
(D) Improving access to the Internet

번역 컨퍼런스의 주제는 무엇인가?
(A) 농업 생산성 향상
(B) 국가 간 무역 촉진
(C) 교육 기술 사용
(D) 인터넷 접근성 개선

해설 **전체 내용 관련 - 컨퍼런스의 주제**
화자가 초반부에 전 세계 곳곳에 있는 공동체에 빠르고 신뢰할 수 있는 인터넷 접근성을 제공하려는 이 컨퍼런스에 참여하게 되어 기쁘다(I'm glad to be taking part in this conference on bringing fast, reliable Internet access to communities around the world)고 했으므로 정답은 (D)이다.

어휘 increase 증가시키다 agricultural 농업의 productivity 생산성 promote 촉진하다 trade 무역 educational 교육의 improve 향상시키다

> **Paraphrasing**
> 담화의 bringing fast, reliable Internet access to communities
> → 정답의 Improving access to the Internet

78 What does the speaker say happened in the last year?
(A) A law was enacted.
(B) A study was conducted.
(C) A fund-raising campaign took place.
(D) A product was released.

번역 화자는 작년에 어떤 일이 있었다고 말하는가?
(A) 한 법률이 제정되었다.
(B) 한 연구가 실시되었다.
(C) 한 모금 캠페인이 실시되었다.
(D) 한 제품이 출시되었다.

해설 **세부 사항 관련 - 작년에 있었던 일**
화자가 중반부에 작년에 아르헨티나의 시골 지역에서 인터넷 접근을 막는 상애물에 대한 연구 조사를 실시했다(Last year we conducted a research study on barriers to Internet access in rural Argentina)고 말하고 있으므로 정답은 (B)이다.

어휘 enact 법을 제정하다 fund-raising 모금 release 출시하다

79 What will the speaker's organization provide funding for?
(A) Filming a documentary
(B) Building some facilities
(C) Training some workers
(D) Publicizing a service

번역 화자의 단체는 무엇을 위한 자금을 지원하겠는가?
(A) 다큐멘터리 촬영
(B) 시설 건축
(C) 근로자 교육
(D) 서비스 홍보

해설 **세부 사항 관련 - 화자의 단체가 자금을 지원하는 곳**
화자가 마지막에 그것이 바로 현재 저희 재단에서 이 업무를 수행할
수 있는 기술자를 교육하는 프로그램에 자금을 지원하고 있는 이유
(That's why our organization is now funding a program
to train technicians who can perform these tasks)라고 말
하고 있으므로 정답은 (C)이다.

어휘 film 촬영하다 facility 시설 publicize 홍보하다

> **Paraphrasing**
> 담화의 technicians
> → 정답의 some workers

80-82 전화 메시지

M-Au Hello, **80 this is Sang-Hoon Choi from Weiss
Software**. I came across a post on your legal
blog mentioning that you find it difficult to hold
meetings virtually with your law clients. Well, **81 my
company is considering creating a specialized
version of our videoconferencing software for
the legal field.** However, none of us is a lawyer.
So I was wondering if you'd consider sitting down
with us to discuss your experiences and the
unique needs of your industry. **82 We'd be happy to
compensate you for the service.** Call me back at
555-0192 if you're interested.

안녕하세요, 저는 바이스 소프트웨어의 **최상훈입니다.** 우연히 귀하의
법률 블로그에서 법률 고객들과 온라인으로 회의를 진행하는 것이 어
렵다고 언급하신 게시물을 보았습니다. 음, **저희 회사는 법률 분야에 특
화된 화상회의 소프트웨어 버전을 만들려고 검토 중입니다.** 하지만, **저
희 중에는 변호사가 없습니다.** 그래서 저희와 직접 만나서 귀하의 경험
과 업계만의 독특한 요구 사항에 대해 이야기해 주실 수 있는지 궁금
합니다. **그에 대한 보상은 기꺼이 해드리겠습니다.** 관심이 있으시다면
555-0192로 회신 전화 주세요.

어휘 come across 우연히 만나다 legal 법률과 관련된
virtually 가상으로 specialized 전문화된 videoconferencing
화상 회의 lawyer 변호사 unique 독특한 need 요구 industry
산업 compensate 보상하다

80 Where does the speaker work?
(A) At a law school
(B) At a construction firm
(C) At a software company
(D) At an advertising agency

번역 화자는 어디서 일하는가?
(A) 법학전문대학원
(B) 건설 회사
(C) 소프트웨어 회사
(D) 광고 대행사

해설 **전체 내용 관련 - 화자의 근무지**
화자가 도입부에서 자신을 바이스 소프트웨어의 최상훈(this is
Sang-Hoon Choi from Weiss Software)이라고 소개하고 있
으므로 화자는 소프트웨어 회사에서 근무하고 있음을 알 수 있다. 따라
서 정답은 (C)이다.

어휘 construction 건설 advertising 광고 agency 대행사

81 Why does the speaker say, "none of us is a
lawyer"?
(A) To offer an apology for a mistake
(B) To turn down the listener's request
(C) To complain about a legal requirement
(D) To explain why he needs the listener's help

번역 화자가 "저희 중에는 변호사가 없습니다"라고 말한 이유는?
(A) 실수에 대해 사과하려고
(B) 청자의 요청을 거절하려고
(C) 법적 요구조건에 대해 불평하려고
(D) 왜 청자의 도움이 필요한지 설명하려고

해설 **화자의 의도 파악 - 저희 중에는 변호사가 없다는 말의 의도**
앞에서 저희 회사는 법률 분야에 특화된 화상회의 소프트웨어 버전
을 만들려고 검토 중(my company is considering creating a
specialized version of our videoconferencing software
for the legal field)이라고 말한 뒤 인용문을 언급한 것으로 보아, 법
률 분야에 있는 청자의 도움이 필요한 이유를 설명하려는 의도로 한 말
임을 알 수 있다. 따라서 정답은 (D)이다.

어휘 apology 사과 turn down 거절하다 complain 불평하다
requirement 요구조건

82 What does the speaker offer to do for the
listener?
(A) Pay for a service
(B) Provide a referral
(C) Review a contract
(D) Contribute to a blog

번역 화자는 청자를 위해 무엇을 하겠다고 제안하는가?
(A) 서비스에 대한 비용 지불하기
(B) 추천하기
(C) 계약서 검토하기
(D) 블로그에 기고하기

해설 **세부 사항 관련 - 화자의 제안 사항**
화자가 마지막에 그에 대한 보상은 기꺼이 해드리겠다(We'd be
happy to compensate you for the service)고 말하고 있으므
로 정답은 (A)이다.

어휘 pay for ~의 비용을 지불하다 referral 추천 contract 계약서
contribute to ~에 기고하다

> **Paraphrasing**
> 담화의 compensate you for the service
> → 정답의 Pay for a service

W-Br **83 Welcome to this seminar on designing corporate dress codes.** By the end, you will understand this topic well enough to create and enforce effective clothing policies for your own company. **84 This is an essential practice, because well-dressed employees give others a positive impression of your business.** This is true no matter what field you're in. Now, **85 let me start by passing out copies of a sample policy that I wrote based on my twenty years of human resources experience.**

기업 복장 규정 설계에 대한 본 세미나에 오신 것을 환영합니다. 세미나가 끝날 무렵에는 이 주제를 충분히 이해하여 여러분의 회사에 효과적인 복장 정책을 수립하고 시행하게 될 것입니다. **이것은 매우 중요한 관행입니다. 옷을 잘 입은 직원은 다른 사람들에게 여러분의 사업체에 대한 긍정적인 인상을 심어주니까요.** 여러분이 어떤 분야에 종사하든 이것은 사실입니다. 자, 우선 제가 인사부에서 20년간 일한 경험을 바탕으로 작성한 이 견본 정책을 나눠드리면서 세미나를 시작하겠습니다.

어휘 corporate 기업의 dress code 복장 규정 enforce 시행하다 effective 효과적인 policy 정책 essential 매우 중요한 practice 관행 well-dressed 잘 차려입은 positive 긍정적인 impression 인상 field 분야 pass out 나눠주다 based on ~에 근거하여 human resources 인사부

83 What is the talk mainly about?
(A) Designs for brand logos
(B) Promotional contests for customers
(C) Company policies on staff attire
(D) Online profiles of executives

번역 담화는 주로 무엇에 관한 것인가?
(A) 브랜드 로고 디자인
(B) 고객을 위한 홍보 콘테스트
(C) 직원 복상에 대한 회사 정책
(D) 임원들의 온라인 프로필

해설 전체 내용 관련 - 담화의 주제
화자가 도입부에 기업 복장 규정 설계에 대한 본 세미나에 오신 것을 환영한다(Welcome to this seminar on designing corporate dress codes)고 했으므로 정답은 (C)이다.

어휘 promotional 홍보의 attire 복장 profile 인물 소개 executive 임원, 중역

> **Paraphrasing**
> 담화의 corporate dress codes
> → 정답의 Company policies on staff attire

84 According to the speaker, what is the benefit of a practice?
(A) It can improve employee satisfaction.
(B) It makes a manager's job easier.
(C) It reduces operating costs.
(D) It is good for a business's image.

번역 화자에 따르면, 관행의 이점은 무엇인가?
(A) 직원 만족도를 높일 수 있다.
(B) 관리자의 일을 더 쉽게 해준다.
(C) 운영 비용을 줄여준다.
(D) 사업체의 이미지에 도움이 된다.

해설 세부 사항 관련 - 관행의 이점
화자가 중반부에 이것이 매우 중요한 관행인 이유는 옷을 잘 입은 직원은 다른 사람들에게 사업체에 대한 긍정적인 인상을 심어주기 때문(This is an essential practice, because well-dressed employees give others a positive impression of your business)이라고 말하고 있으므로 정답은 (D)이다.

어휘 improve 향상시키다 satisfaction 만족 reduce 줄이다 operating cost 운영 비용

> **Paraphrasing**
> 담화의 a positive impression of your business
> → 정답의 good for a business's image

85 How did the speaker develop content for a handout?
(A) By drawing on her work experience
(B) By visiting several Web pages
(C) By studying some reference books
(D) By surveying the listeners beforehand

번역 화자는 유인물의 내용을 어떻게 개발했는가?
(A) 자신의 직무 경험을 활용함으로써
(B) 여러 웹페이지를 방문함으로써
(C) 참고 도서를 연구함으로써
(D) 미리 청자들에게 설문조사를 함으로써

해설 세부 사항 관련 - 화자가 유인물의 내용을 개발한 방법
화자가 마지막에 자신이 인사부에서 20년간 일한 경험을 바탕으로 작성한 견본 정책을 나눠주면서 세미나를 시작하겠다(let me start by passing out copies of a sample policy that I wrote based on my twenty years of human resources experience)고 말하고 있으므로 정답은 (A)이다.

어휘 draw on ~을 이용하다, 활용하다 reference book 참고 도서 survey 설문조사를 하다 beforehand 미리

> **Paraphrasing**
> 담화의 twenty years of human resources experience
> → 정답의 work experience

86-88 관광 정보

M-Cn Thank you for joining today's tour of Watkins Stadium despite the heat. **86 There's a water fountain to my left here;** please take a drink if you need to. Now, as you probably know, **87 our stadium's famous for being the home field of the beloved Kanely football club**. I'm sure the fans among you are eager to see the team's changing room—where their uniforms are hung—and the tunnel they use to get to the field. **88 These are all off-limits when the players are here,** but of course there are no matches today!

더운 날씨에도 불구하고 오늘의 왓킨스 경기장 견학에 참여해 주셔서 감사드립니다. 여기 제 왼쪽으로 음수대가 있습니다. 필요하시면 한 모금 드세요. 자, 아마도 잘 아시겠지만, 이 경기장은 인기가 많은 케인리 축구팀의 홈구장으로 유명합니다. 분명 여러분 중 팬들은 이 팀의 유니폼이 걸려 있는 곳인 탈의실과 선수들이 축구장으로 나갈 때 사용하는 터널을 몹시 보고 싶으실 겁니다. 이 장소들은 선수들이 있을 때는 모두 출입금지구역이지만, 물론 오늘은 경기가 없습니다!

어휘 stadium 경기장 heat 더위 fountain 분수 be famous for ~으로 유명하다 home field 홈구장 beloved 인기 많은 be eager to 간절히 바라다 changing room 탈의실 off-limit 출입금지구역 match 경기

86 What does the speaker point out to the listeners?
(A) Some seating
(B) Cooling fans
(C) A venue map
(D) A drinking fountain

번역 화자는 청자들에게 무엇을 가리키는가?
(A) 일부 좌석
(B) 냉각 팬
(C) 장소의 지도
(D) 음수대

해설 **세부 사항 관련 - 화자가 청자들에게 가리키는 것**
화자가 초반부에 여기 제 왼쪽으로 음수대가 있다(There's a water fountain to my left here)고 말하고 있으므로 정답은 (D)이다.

어휘 point out 가리키다 seating 좌석 venue 장소

> **Paraphrasing**
> 담화의 a water fountain
> → 정답의 A drinking fountain

87 According to the speaker, what is Watkins Stadium known for?
(A) Hosting major competitions
(B) Having an unusual architectural style
(C) Being the home field of a popular team
(D) Providing a view of a city skyline

번역 화자에 따르면, 왓킨스 경기장은 무엇으로 유명한가?
(A) 주요 대회를 개최하는 것
(B) 특이한 건축 양식
(C) 인기 있는 팀의 홈구장인 것
(D) 도시 스카이라인을 조망할 수 있는 것

해설 **세부 사항 관련 - 왓킨스 경기장이 유명한 것**
화자가 중반부에 이 경기장은 인기가 많은 케인리 축구팀의 홈구장으로 유명하다(our stadium's famous for being the home field of the beloved Kanely football club)고 말하고 있으므로 정답은 (C)이다.

어휘 competition 경쟁, 대회 unusual 특이한 architectural 건축의 popular 인기 있는

> **Paraphrasing**
> 담화의 famous for → 질문의 known for
> 담화의 the beloved Kanely football club
> → 정답의 a popular team

88 What does the speaker imply when he says, "there are no matches today"?
(A) Most on-site businesses are closed.
(B) There is not much traffic around the stadium.
(C) The listeners should not expect to see athletes.
(D) The listeners will be able to visit special areas.

번역 화자가 "오늘은 경기가 없습니다"라고 말할 때, 그 의도는 무엇인가?
(A) 대부분의 현장 사업체들이 문을 닫았다.
(B) 경기장 주변에 교통량이 많지 않다.
(C) 청자들은 운동선수를 볼 수 있다고 기대하지 말아야 한다.
(D) 청자들은 특별한 구역을 방문할 수 있을 것이다.

해설 **화자의 의도 파악 - 오늘은 경기가 없다는 말의 의도**
앞에서 이 장소들은 선수들이 있을 때는 모두 출입금지구역이지만(These are all off-limits when the players are here, but of course)이라고 말한 뒤 인용문을 언급하고 있으므로, 청자들이 출입이 금지되었던 특별한 구역을 오늘은 방문할 수 있다는 의도로 한 말임을 알 수 있다. 따라서 정답은 (D)이다

어휘 traffic 교통량 athlete 운동선수

89-91 회의 발췌

W-Br Thanks for coming in early for this meeting. As you may have already heard, **89 the restaurant's owner has decided to adopt pay-at-the-table technology. 90 So each table will have a touch-screen machine on it, like this one here, that customers will use to order and pay for their food.** But we'll still need you all to bring the dishes out, clean up the table after customers leave, and of course answer any questions they have. I expect you'll get some questions about the machine, in fact. **⁹¹Let me demonstrate how it works, so you can help customers with it if needed.**

본 회의를 위해 일찍 와주셔서 감사합니다. 아마도 이미 들으셨겠지만, 식당 소유주가 테이블 결제 시스템을 채택하기로 결정했습니다. 따라서 각 테이블에는 손님들이 음식을 주문하고 결제하는 데 사용할 수 있는, 여기 이것과 같은 터치스크린 단말기가 설치될 겁니다. 하지만 여러분은 여전히 음식을 서빙하고, 손님들이 떠난 뒤에 테이블을 치워야 하며, 손님들이 묻는 질문에도 물론 대답해 주셔야 합니다. 사실, 기계에 대한 질문도 받게 될 겁니다. 필요하면 손님들이 사용할 때 도움을 주실 수 있도록 제가 어떻게 작동하는지 시연을 해드리겠습니다.

어휘   decide 결정하다   adopt 채택하다   pay-at-the-table technology 테이블 결제 시스템   bring out (음식 등을) 내오다   demonstrate 시연하다

89 Who most likely are the listeners?
   (A) Restaurant staff
   (B) Security guards
   (C) Factory workers
   (D) Laboratory technicians

번역   청자들은 누구이겠는가?
   (A) 식당 직원
   (B) 경비원
   (C) 공장 근로자
   (D) 실험실 기술자

해설   **전체 내용 관련 - 청자들의 직업**
   화자가 회의 초반부에 식당 소유주가 테이블 결제 시스템을 채택하기로 결정했다(the restaurant's owner has decided to adopt pay-at-the-table technology)고 말하고 있으므로 청자들은 식당 직원임을 알 수 있다. 따라서 정답은 (A)이다.

어휘   factory 공장   laboratory 실험실   technician 기술자

90 What is the purpose of a machine?
   (A) To process orders
   (B) To transmit speech
   (C) To track working hours
   (D) To package some goods

번역   기계의 목적은 무엇인가?
   (A) 주문을 처리하는 것
   (B) 음성을 전달하는 것
   (C) 근무 시간을 추적하는 것
   (D) 상품을 포장하는 것

해설   **세부 사항 관련 - 기계의 목적**
   화자가 중반부에 각 테이블에는 손님들이 음식을 주문하고 결제하는 데 사용할 수 있는, 여기 이것과 같은 터치스크린 단말기가 설치될 것(So each table will have a touch-screen machine on it, like this one here, that customers will use to order and pay for their food)이라고 말하고 있으므로 정답은 (A)이다.

어휘   process 처리하다   transmit 전송하다   track 추적하다   working hour 근무 시간   package 포장하다   goods 상품

Paraphrasing
담화의 order and pay for their food
→ 정답의 process orders

91 How will the listeners learn more about the machine?
   (A) By trying it themselves
   (B) By reading an explanation
   (C) By examining some diagrams
   (D) By watching a demonstration

번역   청자들은 기계에 대해서 어떻게 더 많은 것을 배우겠는가?
   (A) 스스로 이용해 봄으로써
   (B) 설명서를 읽음으로써
   (C) 도표를 자세히 봄으로써
   (D) 시연을 봄으로써

해설   **세부 사항 관련 - 청자들이 기계에 대해 더 많은 것을 배울 방법**
   화자가 마지막에 필요하면 손님들이 사용할 때 도움을 주실 수 있도록 어떻게 작동하는지 시연을 해드리겠다(Let me demonstrate how it works, so you can help customers with it if needed)고 말하고 있으므로 정답은 (D)이다.

어휘   explanation 설명   examine 검토하다   diagram 도표

92-94 회의 발췌

M-Au   **⁹²As the leader of the *Hero's Journey* development team, I'm very proud of the work you've been doing. ⁹³Today, I want to talk to you about the underwater stage that we initially hoped to include in the video game.** It was supposed to feature incredible graphics and an exciting challenge for players, but we had to cut it at the planning stage because of budget concerns. **⁹⁴Today I'm excited to announce that management has allocated funding to add the underwater stage back in! I can see that this move is indeed a big surprise to you all.** Well, the company earned more revenue than expected this year.

〈히어로스 저니〉 개발팀의 팀장으로서 저는 여러분이 해오고 계신 일에 대해 너무나도 자랑스럽습니다. 오늘 저는 우리가 처음에 이 비디오게임에 포함시키기를 원했던 수중 스테이지에 대해 말씀드리고자 합니다. 이 스테이지는 놀라운 그래픽과 플레이어를 위한 신나는 도전을 보여줄 예정이었지만 예산 문제 때문에 기획 단계에서 잘라내야 했습니다. 오늘 저는 경영진이 수중 스테이지를 다시 넣기 위한 자금을 할당했음을 기쁜 마음으로 알려드립니다! 이 조치가 여러분 모두에게 참으로 놀라운 선물일 겁니다. 음, 회사가 올해 예상보다 더 많은 수익을 냈거든요.

어휘   development 개발   underwater 수중의   initially 처음에   include 포함하다   feature 특별히 포함하다   incredible 믿기 힘든   challenge 도전   planning stage 기획 단계   budget 예산   concern 우려, 걱정   management 경영진   allocate 할당하다   funding 자금   move 조치, 행동   earn 벌다   revenue 수익

92 Who is the speaker?
(A) A board member
(B) A financial analyst
(C) A graphic designer
(D) A team leader

번역 화자는 누구인가?
(A) 이사
(B) 재무 분석가
(C) 그래픽 디자이너
(D) 팀장

해설 **전체 내용 관련 - 화자의 직업**
화자가 도입부에 〈히어로스 저니〉 개발팀의 팀장으로서 여러분이 해오고 있는 일에 대해 너무나도 자랑스럽다(As the leader of the *Hero's Journey* development team, I'm very proud of the work you've been doing)고 말하고 있으므로 정답은 (D)이다.

> **Paraphrasing**
> 담화의 the leader of the *Hero's Journey* development team → 정답의 A team leader

93 What project does the speaker mention?
(A) A video game
(B) A Web site redesign
(C) A theme park attraction
(D) A television commercial

번역 화자는 어떤 프로젝트를 언급하는가?
(A) 비디오게임
(B) 웹사이트 개편
(C) 놀이공원의 놀이기구
(D) 텔레비전 광고

해설 **세부 사항 관련 - 화자가 언급한 프로젝트**
화자가 초반부에 우리가 처음에 이 비디오게임에 포함시키기를 원했던 수중 스테이지에 대해 말하고자 한다(Today, I want to talk to you about the underwater stage that we initially hoped to include in the video game)고 했으므로 정답은 (A)이다.

어휘 theme park 놀이공원 attraction 놀이기구 commercial 광고

94 Why does the speaker say, "the company earned more revenue than expected this year"?
(A) To encourage the listeners to make suggestions
(B) To give a reason for a spending decision
(C) To recommend raising some estimates
(D) To congratulate the listeners on an achievement

번역 화자가 "회사가 올해 예상보다 더 많은 수익을 냈거든요"라고 말한 이유는?
(A) 청자들에게 제안하라고 독려하려고
(B) 지출 결정의 이유를 제시하려고
(C) 견적 비용을 올리라고 권고하려고
(D) 청자들에게 업적에 대해 축하하려고

해설 **화자의 의도 파악 - 회사가 올해 예상보다 더 많은 수익을 냈다는 말의 의도**
화자가 후반부에서 경영진이 수중 스테이지를 다시 넣기 위한 자금을 할당했음을 기쁜 마음으로 알려드린다(Today I'm excited to announce that management has allocated funding to add the underwater stage back in!)면서 이 조치가 여러분 모두에게 참으로 놀라운 선물일 것(I can see that this move is indeed a big surprise to you all)이라고 말한 뒤 인용문을 언급한 것으로 보아, 자금 투자를 결정하게 된 이유를 설명하기 위한 의도로 한 말임을 알 수 있다. 따라서 정답은 (B)이다.

어휘 suggestion 제안 spending 지출 raise 올리다 estimate 추정, 견적 congratulate 축하하다 achievement 업적

95-97 담화+점검표

W-Br OK, let's continue our training. **95 Another one of the duties you all will have is helping the pharmacists to manage our inventory of medications.** Each time you receive a shipment of new stock, you'll need to go through this checklist. **96 I'd like to highlight an item on it that's especially important: confirming that the packing slip is accurate.** The product quantities on the slip are entered into our inventory software, which our pharmacists check before recommending medications. If a shipment contains a lot of products, **97 I suggest clearing away the packaging waste to ensure you can see them all easily before starting your count.**

좋습니다, 교육을 계속 진행하겠습니다. **여러분 모두가 맡게 될 또 다른 업무는 약사들이 약품 재고를 관리하는 일을 돕는 것입니다.** 새로운 재고 배송품을 받을 때마다 여러분은 이 점검표를 확인해야 합니다. **점검표에서 특히 중요한 항목을 강조하고 싶어요. 바로 운송 전표가 정확한지 확인하는 것입니다.** 전표에 있는 제품 수량은 재고 소프트웨어에 입력됩니다. 약사들은 약품을 추천하기 전에 이 소프트웨어를 확인하죠. 배송품에 많은 제품이 들어 있다면, **개수를 세기 전에 제품을 전부 한눈에 볼 수 있도록 포장 쓰레기를 모두 치우기를 권해요.**

어휘 duty 업무, 임무 pharmacist 약사 manage 관리하다 inventory 재고 medication 약품 shipment 배송품 go through ~을 살펴보다 checklist 점검표 highlight 강조하다 packing slip 운송 전표 accurate 정확한 quantity 수량 enter 입력하다 contain 들어 있다 clear away ~을 치우다 packaging 포장 waste 쓰레기

TEST 10

```
1. ____ The shipping box is sealed.
96 2. ____ The packing slip is correct.
3. ____ All products' packaging is
           intact.
4. ____ No products are expired.
```

```
1. __ 배송 상자가 봉인된 상태이다.
96 2. __ 운송 전표가 정확하다.
3. __ 모든 제품의 포장이 손상되지
        않았다.
4. __ 제품들의 유효 기간이 만료되
        지 않았다.
```

어휘 seal 봉인하다   intact 손상되지 않은   expire 만료되다

95 What job are the listeners being trained for?
(A) Safety inspector
(B) Pharmacy assistant
(C) Grocery store stocker
(D) Warehouse shipping clerk

번역 청자들은 어떤 직업을 위해 교육받고 있는가?
(A) 안전 감독관
(B) 약국 보조원
(C) 식료품점 진열원
(D) 창고 선적 사무원

해설 **세부 사항 관련 - 청자들이 교육받고 있는 직업**
화자가 초반부에서 여러분 모두가 맡게 될 또 다른 업무는 약사들이 약품 재고를 관리하는 일을 돕는 것(Another one of the duties you all will have is helping the pharmacists to manage our inventory of medications)이라고 하므로 정답은 (B)이다.

어휘 safety inspector 안전 감독관   assistant 보조원   stocker 진열원   warehouse 창고   shipping clerk 선적 사무원

> **Paraphrasing**
> 담화의 helping the pharmacists to manage our inventory of medications
> → 정답의 Pharmacy assistant

96 Look at the graphic. Which item does the speaker highlight?
(A) Item 1
(B) Item 2
(C) Item 3
(D) Item 4

번역 시각 정보에 의하면, 화자는 어떤 항목을 강조하는가?
(A) 1번 항목
(B) 2번 항목
(C) 3번 항목
(D) 4번 항목

해설 **시각 정보 연계 - 화자가 강조하는 항목**
화자가 중반부에서 점검표에서 특히 중요한 항목을 강조하고 싶은데 바로 운송 전표가 정확한지 확인하는 것(I'd like to highlight an item on it that's especially important: confirming that the packing slip is accurate)이라고 했고, 점검표에 따르면 운송 전표가 정확한지(The packing slip is correct) 확인하는 것은 2번 항목이므로 정답은 (B)이다.

97 What does the speaker recommend?
(A) Wearing protective gloves
(B) Writing down some figures
(C) Removing some trash
(D) Learning some special terms

번역 화자는 무엇을 추천하는가?
(A) 보호 장갑 착용하기
(B) 수치 적어두기
(C) 쓰레기 치우기
(D) 특별한 용어 배우기

해설 **세부 사항 관련 - 화자의 추천 사항**
화자가 마지막에 포장 쓰레기를 모두 치울 것(I suggest clearing away the packaging waste ~)을 제안하고 있으므로 정답은 (C)이다.

어휘 protective 보호용의   figure 수치   remove 제거하다   trash 쓰레기   term 용어

> **Paraphrasing**
> 담화의 clearing away the packaging waste
> → 정답의 Removing some trash

98-100 전화 메시지 + 매장 진열

M-Cn Hi, it's Devin calling from the regional office. Our merchandising team has made some changes to the display plans that were e-mailed to you earlier this week. **98 They want to move the watches to the counter so that customers can see them more easily. That will leave an empty display case, which should be filled with our discounted necklaces.** Also, **99 please put the rack of handbags by the fitting rooms**. Since these are popular gifts, it's great to have them where people are waiting around while their friends are changing. Finally, **100 the new posters for our Autumn Sale have been printed. A courier will drop those off this afternoon.**

안녕하세요. 지사의 데빈입니다. 우리 상품 기획팀이 이번 주 초에 당신에게 이메일로 보내드린 진열 계획을 일부 변경했어요. **고객들이 좀 더 쉽게 볼 수 있도록 시계를 카운터로 옮기고 싶어 해요. 그러면 진열장에 빈 곳이 생기는데, 그곳은 할인된 목걸이로 가득 채워야 해요.** 또 핸드백 진열대는 탈의실 옆에 놓아주세요. 이것들은 인기 있는 선물이니까 친구들이 옷을 갈아입는 동안 사람들이 기다리는 곳에 두는 게 좋겠어요. 마지막으로 가을 세일용 새 포스터가 인쇄되었어요. 택배 기사가 오늘 오후에 가지고 올 거예요.

어휘 regional office 지사 merchandising 상품 기획 display case 진열장 be filled with ~으로 가득 차다 rack 받침대 fitting room 탈의실 popular 인기 있는 courier 택배 기사 drop off 배달해 주다

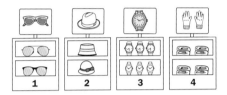

98 Look at the graphic. Where will the discounted necklaces be displayed?
(A) In Display Case 1
(B) In Display Case 2
(C) In Display Case 3
(D) In Display Case 4

번역 시각 정보에 의하면, 할인된 목걸이는 어디에 진열되겠는가?
(A) 1번 진열장
(B) 2번 진열장
(C) 3번 진열장
(D) 4번 진열장

해설 **시각 정보 연계 - 할인된 목걸이가 진열될 곳**
화자가 중반부에서 상품 기획팀에서 고객들이 좀 더 쉽게 볼 수 있도록 시계를 카운터로 옮기고 싶어 한다(They want to move the watches to the counter so that customers can see them more easily)면서 그러면 진열장에 빈 곳이 생기는데, 그곳은 할인된 목걸이로 가득 채워야 한다(That will leave an empty display case, which should be filled with our discounted necklaces)고 했다. 시각 자료를 보면 시계가 있는 곳은 3번 진열장이므로 정답은 (C)이다.

99 What should be placed near the fitting room?
(A) Chairs
(B) Handbags
(C) Gift certificates
(D) Rings

번역 탈의실 근처에는 무엇이 놓여야 하는가?
(A) 의자
(B) 핸드백
(C) 상품권
(D) 반지

해설 **세부 사항 관련 - 탈의실 근처에 놓여야 할 것**
화자가 중반부에서 핸드백 진열대는 탈의실 옆에 놓아줄 것(please put the rack of handbags by the fitting rooms)을 요청하고 있으므로 정답은 (B)이다.

100 What should the listener expect to receive by courier?
(A) Some printer cartridges
(B) Some promotional posters
(C) Some display stands
(D) Some product samples

번역 청자는 택배로 무엇을 받을 것인가?
(A) 프린터 카트리지
(B) 홍보용 포스터
(C) 진열대
(D) 제품 견본

해설 **세부 사항 관련 - 청자가 택배로 받게 될 것**
화자가 마지막 부분에서 가을 세일용 새 포스터가 인쇄되었다(the new posters for our Autumn Sale have been printed)면서 택배 기사가 오늘 오후에 가지고 올 것(A courier will drop those off this afternoon)이라고 말하고 있으므로 정답은 (B)이다.

어휘 promotional 홍보의 display stand 진열대

> **Paraphrasing**
> 담화의 the new posters for our Autumn Sale
> → 정답의 Some promotional posters

TEST 10